THE MIDDLE EAST IN TURMOIL

THE MIDDLE EAST IN TURMOIL

VOLUME 3

THE MIDDLE EAST IN TURMOIL

Additional books in this series can be found on Nova's website
under the Series tab.

Additional E-books in this series can be found on Nova's website
under the E-books tab.

THE MIDDLE EAST IN TURMOIL

THE MIDDLE EAST IN TURMOIL

VOLUME 3

ANGELA N. CASTILLO
EDITOR

Nova Science Publishers, Inc.
New York

Copyright © 2011 by Nova Science Publishers, Inc.

All rights reserved. No part of this book may be reproduced, stored in a retrieval system or transmitted in any form or by any means: electronic, electrostatic, magnetic, tape, mechanical photocopying, recording or otherwise without the written permission of the Publisher.

For permission to use material from this book please contact us:
Telephone 631-231-7269; Fax 631-231-8175
Web Site: http://www.novapublishers.com

NOTICE TO THE READER

The Publisher has taken reasonable care in the preparation of this book, but makes no expressed or implied warranty of any kind and assumes no responsibility for any errors or omissions. No liability is assumed for incidental or consequential damages in connection with or arising out of information contained in this book. The Publisher shall not be liable for any special, consequential, or exemplary damages resulting, in whole or in part, from the readers' use of, or reliance upon, this material. Any parts of this book based on government reports are so indicated and copyright is claimed for those parts to the extent applicable to compilations of such works.

Independent verification should be sought for any data, advice or recommendations contained in this book. In addition, no responsibility is assumed by the publisher for any injury and/or damage to persons or property arising from any methods, products, instructions, ideas or otherwise contained in this publication.

This publication is designed to provide accurate and authoritative information with regard to the subject matter covered herein. It is sold with the clear understanding that the Publisher is not engaged in rendering legal or any other professional services. If legal or any other expert assistance is required, the services of a competent person should be sought. FROM A DECLARATION OF PARTICIPANTS JOINTLY ADOPTED BY A COMMITTEE OF THE AMERICAN BAR ASSOCIATION AND A COMMITTEE OF PUBLISHERS.

Additional color graphics may be available in the e-book version of this book.

Library of Congress Cataloging-in-Publication Data

ISSN: 2161-9492

ISBN 978-1-61324-241-4

Published by Nova Science Publishers, Inc. † New York

CONTENTS

Preface		**7**
Chapter 1	Hamas: Background and Issues for Congress *Jim Zanotti*	**11**
Chapter 2	The United Arab Emirates (UAE): Issues for U.S. Policy *Kenneth Katzman*	**73**
Chapter 3	Afghanistan Casualties: Military Forces and Civilians *Susan G. Chesser*	**89**
Chapter 4	The United Arab Emirates Nuclear Program and Proposed U.S. Nuclear Cooperation *Christopher M. Blanchard and Paul K. Kerr*	**95**
Chapter 5	Syria: Issues for the 112th Congress and Background on U.S. Sanctions *Jeremy M. Sharp*	**115**
Chapter 6	Iraq: Politics, Elections, and Benchmarks *Kenneth Katzman*	**137**
Chapter 7	Iran: U.S. Concerns and Policy Responses *Kenneth Katzman*	**167**
Chapter 8	United Nations Assistance Mission in Afghanistan: Background and Policy Issues *Rhoda Margesson*	**237**
Chapter 9	Afghanistan: Post-Taliban Governance, Security, and U.S. Policy *Kenneth Katzman*	**269**
Chapter 10	Afghanistan: Politics, Elections, and Government Performance *Kenneth Katzman*	**363**
Index		**411**

PREFACE

This book includes the entire spectrum of contemporary politics and economics of the Middle East. The coverage is intended to deal with the Middle East political dynamics, economic policies and institutions. Topics discussed include background information on Hamas and issues for Congress; governance, human rights and reform in the United Arab Emirates; Afghanistan casualties; the United Arab Emirates nuclear program and proposed U.S. nuclear cooperation; bilateral issues affecting U.S.-Syria relations; the politics, elections and benchmarks of Iraq; U.S. concerns and policy responses towards Iran; the United Nations Assistance Mission in Afghanistan and Afghanistan's post-Taliban governance, politics, elections, security and U.S. policy.

Chapter 1- This report and its appendixes provide background information on Hamas, or the Islamic Resistance Movement, and U.S. policy towards it. It also includes information and analysis on (1) the threats Hamas currently poses to U.S. interests, (2) how Hamas compares with other Middle East terrorist groups, (3) Hamas's ideology and policies (both generally and on discrete issues), (4) its leadership and organization, and (5) its sources of assistance. Finally, the report raises and discusses various legislative and oversight options related to foreign aid strategies, financial sanctions, and regional and international political approaches. In evaluating these options, Congress can assess how Hamas has emerged and adapted over time, and also scrutinize the track record of U.S., Israeli, and international policy to counter Hamas.

Chapter 2- The UAE's relatively open borders, economy, and society have won praise from advocates of expanded freedoms in the Middle East while producing financial excesses, social ills such as prostitution and human trafficking, and relatively lax controls on sensitive technologies acquired from the West. These concerns—as well as concerns about the UAE oversight and management of a complex and technically advanced initiative such as a nuclear power program—underscored dissatisfaction among some members of Congress with a U.S.-UAE civilian nuclear cooperation agreement. The agreement was signed on May 21, 2009, and submitted to Congress that day. It entered into force on December 17, 2009. However, U.S. concerns about potential leakage of U.S. and other advanced technologies through the UAE to Iran, in particular, are far from alleviated.

Chapter 3- This report collects statistics from a variety of sources on casualties sustained during Operation Enduring Freedom (OEF), which began on October 7, 2001, and is ongoing. OEF actions take place primarily in Afghanistan; however, OEF casualties also includes American casualties in Pakistan, Uzbekistan, Guantanamo Bay (Cuba), Djibouti, Eritrea,

Ethiopia, Jordan, Kenya, Kyrgyzstan, the Philippines, Seychelles, Sudan, Tajikistan, Turkey, and Yemen.

Chapter 4- The United Arab Emirates (UAE) has embarked on a program to build civilian nuclear power plants and is seeking cooperation and technical assistance from the United States and others. The 111th Congress approved a U.S.-UAE bilateral agreement on peaceful nuclear cooperation pursuant to Section 123 of the Atomic Energy Act (AEA) of 1954. Then-U.S. Secretary of State Condoleezza Rice signed the proposed agreement on peaceful nuclear cooperation with the UAE January 15, 2009. Deputy Secretary of State James Steinberg signed a new version of the agreement May 21, 2009; the Obama Administration submitted the proposed agreement to Congress the same day.

Chapter 5- This report analyzes an array of bilateral issues that continue to affect relations between the United States and Syria.

Despite its weak military and lackluster economy, Syria remains relevant in Middle Eastern geopolitics. Syria plays a key role in the Middle East peace process, acting at times as a "spoiler" by sponsoring Palestinian militants and facilitating the rearmament of Hezbollah. At other times, it has participated in substantive negotiations with Israel. Syria's long-standing relationship with the Iranian clerical regime is of great concern to U.S. strategists. As Syria grew more estranged from the United States over the last ten years, Syrian-Iranian relations improved, and some analysts have called on U.S. policymakers to woo Syrian leaders away from Iran. Others believe that the Administration should go even further in pressuring the Syrian government and consider implementing harsher economic sanctions against it.

Chapter 6- Iraq's political system, the result of a U.S.-supported election process, has been increasingly characterized by peaceful competition, as well as by attempts to form cross-sectarian alliances. Ethnic and factional infighting continues, sometimes involving the questionable use of key levers of power and legal institutions. This infighting—and the belief that holding political power may mean the difference between life and death for the various political communities—significantly delayed agreement on a new government that was to be selected following the March 7, 2010, national elections for the Council of Representatives (COR, parliament). With U.S. intervention, on November 10, 2010, major ethnic and sectarian factions agreed on a framework for a new government, breaking the long deadlock. Iraqi leaders say agreement on a new cabinet is close, and Prime Minister Nuri al-Maliki, tapped to continue in that role, is expected to present his choices to the COR for approval on/about December 23, in advance of a December 25 constitutional deadline.

Chapter 7- The Obama Administration views Iran as a major threat to U.S. national security interests, a perception generated not only by Iran's nuclear program but also by its military assistance to armed groups in Iraq and Afghanistan, to the Palestinian group Hamas, and to Lebanese Hezbollah. Particularly in its first year, the Obama Administration altered the previous U.S. approach by offering Iran's leaders consistent and sustained engagement with the potential for closer integration with and acceptance by the West. To try to convince Iranian leaders of peaceful U.S. intent and respect for Iran's history and stature in the region, the Obama Administration downplayed discussion of potential U.S. military action against Iranian nuclear facilities and repeatedly insisted that it did not seek to change Iran's regime. It held to this position even at the height of the protests by the domestic opposition "Green movement" that emerged following Iran's June 12, 2009, presidential election.

Chapter 8- The United Nations (UN) has had an active presence in Afghanistan since 1988, and it is highly regarded by many Afghans for playing a brokering role in ending the Soviet occupation of Afghanistan. As a result of the Bonn Agreement of December 2001, coordinating international donor activity and assistance have been tasked to a United Nations Assistance Mission in Afghanistan (UNAMA). However, there are other coordinating institutions tied to the Afghan government, and UNAMA has struggled to exercise its full mandate. The international recovery and reconstruction effort in Afghanistan is immense and complicated and, in coordination with the Afghan government, involves U.N. agencies, bilateral donors, international organizations, and local and international non-governmental organizations (NGOs). The coordinated aid programs of the United States and its European allies focus on a wide range of activities, from strengthening the central and local governments of Afghanistan and its security forces to promoting civilian reconstruction, reducing corruption, and assisting with elections.

Chapter 9- Following two high-level policy reviews on Afghanistan in 2009, and another completed in December 2010, the Obama Administration asserts that it is pursuing a well resourced and integrated military-civilian strategy intended to pave the way for a gradual transition to Afghan security leadership to begin in July 2011 and be completed by the end of 2014. The pace of that transition is to be determined by conditions on the ground. The policy is intended to ensure that Afghanistan will not again become a base for terrorist attacks against the United States. At the same time, there appears to be a debate within the Administration and between the United States and Pakistan over whether the war effort should be widened somewhat to include stepped up attacks on Afghan militants inside Pakistan. That debate raises the question of the degree to which Pakistan envisions Afghanistan as part of its strategy to avoid encirclement by or pressure from Pakistan's historic rival, India. At the same time, Afghanistan is achieving ever higher degrees of economic and political integration with its neighbors in Central Asia and the Middle East.

Chapter 10- The limited capacity and widespread corruption of all levels of Afghan governance are growing factors in debate over the effectiveness of U.S. strategy in Afghanistan, as expressed in an Administration assessment of policy released December 16, 2010. A competent, respected, and effective Afghan government is considered a major prerequisite for a transition to Afghan lead that is to take place by 2014, a timeframe agreed by the United States, its international partners, and the Afghan government. Afghan governing capacity has increased significantly since the Taliban regime fell in late 2001, but there is a broad view the Afghan government is ineffective, with many positions unfilled or filled by weak leaders, and that President Hamid Karzai has not moved decisively to reduce corruption. Karzai has agreed to cooperate with U.S.-led efforts to build the capacity of several emerging anti-corruption institutions, but these same institutions have sometimes caused a Karzai backlash when they have targeted his allies or relatives. Some of the effects of corruption burst into public view in August 2010 when major losses were announced by the large Kabul Bank, in part due to large loans to major shareholders, many of whom are close to Karzai. Some in Congress have sought to link further U.S. aid to clearer progress on the corruption issue.

In: The Middle East in Turmoil, Volume 3
Editor: Angela N. Castillo

ISBN: 978-1-61324-241-4
© 2011 Nova Science Publishers, Inc.

Chapter 1

HAMAS: BACKGROUND AND ISSUES FOR CONGRESS[*]

Jim Zanotti

SUMMARY

This report and its appendixes provide background information on Hamas, or the Islamic Resistance Movement, and U.S. policy towards it. It also includes information and analysis on (1) the threats Hamas currently poses to U.S. interests, (2) how Hamas compares with other Middle East terrorist groups, (3) Hamas's ideology and policies (both generally and on discrete issues), (4) its leadership and organization, and (5) its sources of assistance. Finally, the report raises and discusses various legislative and oversight options related to foreign aid strategies, financial sanctions, and regional and international political approaches. In evaluating these options, Congress can assess how Hamas has emerged and adapted over time, and also scrutinize the track record of U.S., Israeli, and international policy to counter Hamas.

Hamas is a Palestinian Islamist military and sociopolitical movement that grew out of the Muslim Brotherhood. The United States, Israel, the European Union, and Canada consider Hamas a terrorist organization because of (1) its violent resistance to what it deems Israeli occupation of historic Palestine (constituting present-day Israel, West Bank, and Gaza Strip), and (2) its rejection of the off-and-on peace process involving Israel and the Palestine Liberation Organization (PLO) since the early 1990s. Since Hamas's inception in 1987, it has maintained its primary base of political support and its military command in the Gaza Strip—a territory it has controlled since June 2007—while also having a significant presence in the West Bank. The movement's political leadership is currently headquartered in exile in Damascus, Syria. Hamas receives assistance and training from Iran, Syria, and the Lebanese Shiite militant group Hezbollah. Hamas is often discussed alongside other groups in the region that engage in militant and terrorist activities to achieve their ends, yet Hamas has confined its militancy to Israel and the Palestinian territories—distinguishing it from the broader aspirations expressed by Al Qaeda and its affiliates.

---

[*] This is an edited, reformatted and augmented version of a Congressional Research Services publication, dated December 2, 2010.

The overarching U.S. goal regarding Hamas is to deter, transform, marginalize, or neutralize it so that it no longer presents a threat to Israel's security, to a peaceful and lasting resolution of the Israeli-Palestinian conflict, or to other U.S. interests—either in its own right or as a proxy of Iran or other actors. Various legislative and policy initiatives designed to accomplish this goal have at most achieved temporary or partial success. It is possible to conclude that U.S. and other international support for Israel and the Palestinian Authority/PLO dominated by Fatah (Hamas's main rival faction) has been counterproductive to some extent when comparing Hamas's domestic, regional, and international strength in the early 1990s—measured by factors such as popularity, military force, and leverage with other actors (including Israel and Fatah)—to its current strength. The Israeli-Egyptian closure regime in Gaza and various U.S. and international initiatives constrain and isolate Hamas to a point and may exacerbate its internal organizational tensions and tactical disagreements. Yet, the threats Hamas continues to pose to Israel, to prospects for a two-state solution and to the future of Palestinian democracy presents considerable risks and difficult trade-offs for any U.S. policy decisions going forward.

The following CRS reports contain additional information on Hamas: CRS Report RL34074, *The Palestinians: Background and U.S. Relations*, by Jim Zanotti; CRS Report R40101, *Israel and Hamas: Conflict in Gaza (2008-2009)* , coordinated by Jim Zanotti; CRS Report R40092, *Israel and the Palestinians: Prospects for a Two-State Solution*, by Jim Zanotti; CRS Report R40664, *U.S. Security Assistance to the Palestinian Authority*, by Jim Zanotti; and CRS Report RS22967, *U.S. Foreign Aid to the Palestinians*, by Jim Zanotti.

INTRODUCTION: ISSUES FOR CONGRESS

Hamas,[1] or the Islamic Resistance Movement, is a Palestinian Islamist military and sociopolitical movement that grew out of the Muslim Brotherhood, a Sunni religious and political organization founded in Egypt in 1928 that has branches throughout the world. The United States, Israel, the European Union, and Canada consider Hamas a terrorist organization because of (1) its violent resistance to what it deems Israeli occupation of historic Palestine (constituting present-day Israel, West Bank, and Gaza Strip), and (2) its rejection of the off-and-on peace process involving Israel and the Palestine Liberation Organization (PLO) since the early 1990s. Hamas seeks assistance and training from other Arab, Islamic, and international actors and organizations, and receives it from Iran, Syria, and the Lebanese Shiite militant group Hezbollah (see "Iran, Syria, and Hezbollah" below).[2]

The overarching U.S. goal regarding Hamas is to deter, transform, marginalize, or neutralize it so that it no longer presents a threat to Israel's security, to a peaceful and lasting resolution of the Israeli-Palestinian conflict, or to other U.S. interests—either in its own right or as a proxy of Iran or other actors. Various legislative and policy initiatives designed to accomplish this goal have at most achieved temporary or partial success. Hamas's activities present challenges for U.S. policymakers and Members of Congress, including

- countering Hamas's military and terrorist threats to Israel, its financial and smuggling networks, and its political influence;

- determining under what circumstances and the manner in which the United States might accept the participation of Hamas or Hamas representatives in a Palestinian Authority (PA) government and/or in Israeli-Palestinian peace negotiations;
- de-linking Hamas from its connections with Iran and Syria; and
- encouraging humanitarian relief efforts and economic development in Gaza without bolstering Hamas.

U.S. efforts and policy debates on these issues, which include foreign aid strategies, financial sanctions, and bilateral, regional, and international political approaches, are discussed further below (see "Possible Options for Congress").

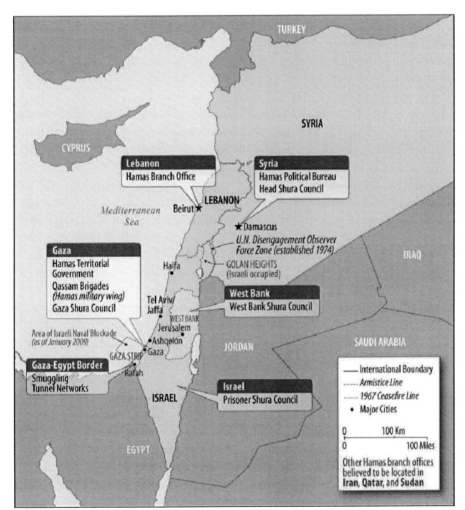

Sources: Congressional Research Service; State of Israel, Ministry of Transport, Notice to Mariners, No. 1/2009 Blockade of Gaza Strip, January 2009; ESRI Community Data, 2008.

Notes: All boundaries and depictions are approximate. The designations employed and the presentation of material on this map do not imply the expression of any opinion whatsoever on the part of CRS concerning the legal status of any country, territory, city or area or of its authorities, or concerning the delimitation of its frontiers of boundaries.

Figure 1. Map of Key Hamas Leadership Nodes.

OVERVIEW

Since Hamas's inception in 1987, it has maintained its primary base of political support and its military command in the Gaza Strip—a territory it has controlled since June 2007—while also having a significant presence in the West Bank. The movement's political leadership is currently headquartered in exile in Damascus, Syria.

Hamas's military wing, the Izz al Din al Qassam Brigades,[3] has killed more than 400 Israelis,[4] and at least 25 U.S. citizens (including some dual U.S.-Israeli citizens)[5] in attacks since 1993. As the Qassam Brigades developed from a small band of guerrillas into a more sophisticated organization with access to greater resources and territorial control, its methods of attack evolved from small-scale kidnappings and killings of Israeli military personnel to suicide bombings and rocket attacks against Israeli civilians. Hamas also has frequently attacked or repressed Palestinian political and factional opponents, particularly in its struggle with Fatah and other groups for control in the Gaza Strip since Israel's military disengagement in 2005. For further information on these points, see "Threats Hamas Poses," Appendix A, and Appendix B below.

Hamas emerged as the main domestic opposition force to Palestinian nationalist leader Yasser Arafat and his secular nationalist Fatah movement in the West Bank and Gaza Strip in the 1980s and 1990s—largely by using violence against Israeli civilian and military targets just as Arafat's PLO began negotiating with Israel. In 2006, a little more than a year after Arafat's death and the election of Fatah's Mahmoud Abbas to replace him as PA president, Hamas became—by most analysts' reckoning—the first Islamist group in the Arab world to gain power democratically after a stunning electoral upset of Fatah gave it control of the Palestinian Legislative Council (PLC) and of Palestinian Authority government ministries.[6]

Subsequent efforts by Israel, the United States, and the international community to neutralize or marginalize Hamas by military, political, and economic means may have changed the outward nature of its influence, but have failed to squelch it. In 2007, Hamas seized control of the Gaza Strip through decisive armed victories over PA and Fatah forces loyal to Abbas (causing Abbas to dismiss Hamas's PA government in the West Bank and appoint a "caretaker" non-Hamas government in its stead). Hamas has since consolidated its power in Gaza despite considerable damage visited on Gaza's people and infrastructure by an Israeli invasion in December 2008-January 2009 (also known as Operation Cast Lead, which was launched by Israel in response to repeated rocket attacks by Hamas and other Palestinian militants) and despite ongoing restrictions (often termed the "blockade" or "closure regime") by Israel and Egypt on the flow of people and goods into and out of the territory.

By consolidating its control over Gaza and pursuing popular support through resistance to Israel, Hamas seeks to establish its indispensability to any Arab-Israeli political arrangement. Many analysts believe that Hamas hopes to leverage this indispensability into sole or shared leadership of the PA in both the West Bank and Gaza—either through a power-sharing arrangement with Abbas and his Fatah movement, or through presidential and legislative elections (which were supposed to take place in January 2010 under PA law, but have been postponed pending factional agreement on conditions for holding them)—and to gain membership in or somehow supplant the Fatah-dominated PLO, which remains internationally recognized as the legitimate representative of the Palestinian people. Fatah's political hegemony inside the occupied territories has been undermined by the inability of the

Fatah-dominated PLO to co-opt or incorporate Hamas, which has proved more resistant than secular Palestinian factions to the PLO's inducements. Egyptian-mediated efforts to forge a PA power-sharing arrangement in the West Bank and Gaza between Hamas and its traditionally dominant rival faction, the secular nationalist Fatah movement, have stalled repeatedly.[7]

Hamas also has gained popularity among many Palestinians at Fatah's expense because of its reputation as a less corrupt provider of social services (funded by donations from Palestinians, other Arabs, and international charitable front groups) and because of the image it cultivates of unflinching resistance to Israeli occupation. Some Palestinians perceive that Hamas is more rooted in the experiences and attitudes of West Bankers and Gazans than Fatah. Most leaders from Fatah's historic core, including current PA President/PLO Chairman Mahmoud Abbas, spent decades in exile with Yasser Arafat's PLO in various Arab states. Although many from Hamas's top leadership, including political bureau chief Khaled Meshaal, also have lived in exile for 30- plus years, Hamas has maintained a strong presence within the Palestinian territories since its inception.

For additional information on Hamas's historical background and on U.S. policy regarding Hamas, see Appendix A.

Threats Hamas Poses

Many Israelis fear the potential long-term threat Hamas could pose to Israel's physical and psychological security if its rocket capabilities expand, if it gains an unchallenged foothold in the West Bank, and/or if it otherwise finds a way to regularly target civilians inside Israel again. Although damage from Palestinian suicide bombings in 1994-1997 and 2000-2008 is difficult to measure qualitatively, the bombings constituted a fearsome means of attack. In the aggregate, suicide bombing attacks by Palestinian militants killed approximately 700 Israelis (mostly civilians within Israel proper),[8] with Hamas directly responsible for more than 400 of these deaths.[9] Israel also fears that Iran, Syria, and possibly other actors in the region might use Hamas's proximity to Israel either to facilitate a coordinated multi-front military attack or to mobilize regional and international political pressure against Israel through the precipitation of crises and *causes clbres*.[10]

The ability of Palestinians from the West Bank and Gaza to target civilians inside Israel (e.g., through suicide bombings) has been drastically reduced in the post-second intifada environment through heightened Israeli security measures. A system of tightly patrolled barriers and crossings limits access to Israel from both territories—in Gaza's case, almost completely. The system also includes the West Bank separation barrier[11] that some Israelis envision as demarcating a border between Israel and a future Palestinian state, even though it strays from the 1948-1967 armistice line, known as the "Green Line," in several places. Israeli military and intelligence operations within the West Bank—including various obstacles to and restrictions on Palestinians' freedom of movement (some of which are designed to protect Israeli settlers and settlements)—buttress the barrier system there.

Rockets and Smuggling Tunnels

In reaction to constraints on access to Israel, Hamas and other Palestinian militant groups in Gaza have increased their strategic reliance on firing rockets and mortars indiscriminately at Israeli targets.[12] Rocket fire and the threat of future rocket fire with greater geographical range precipitated Israel's Operation Cast Lead against targets in Gaza in December 2008.[13] The approximately 8,350 rockets and mortars fired by Palestinians since 2001[14] have killed at least 28 Israelis and wounded dozens,[15] while the persistent threat of rocket fire has had a broader negative psychological effect on Israelis living in targeted communities.[16]

Since the end of Operation Cast Lead, Hamas has permitted far fewer rockets to be fired from Gaza by its military wing and other Palestinian militant groups, perhaps because of a desire to avoid another large-scale Israeli attack. Nevertheless, analysts and Israeli officials say that Hamas continues to manufacture and stockpile hundreds, if not thousands, of "Qassam" rockets.[17] These rockets have limited ranges, and are generally made from household ingredients such as fertilizer, sugar, alcohol, fuel oil, pipes, and scrap metal. The raw materials are generally smuggled into Gaza—thus circumventing the Israeli-Egyptian closure regime—via tunnels under the Egyptian border.

Since Israel's disengagement from Gaza in 2005, Hamas has promoted a dramatic expansion of the network of smuggling tunnels connecting Gaza with Egypt's Sinai Peninsula. Under the closure regime aimed at undermining Hamas's control over the territory, the tunneling network has become Gaza's primary economic engine and mode of rearmament for militants. In addition to raw materials for Qassam rockets and other explosive devices, press and trade reports and Israeli officials allege that thousands of mortars and hundreds of longer-range rockets in Hamas's arsenal[18] (some of which may have been manufactured in Iran or China) have been smuggled into Gaza through the tunnels. As of the summer of 2010, one report said that these longer-range rockets could include dozens of 122-mm Grad or Grad-style rockets (sometimes known as Katyushas) and 230-mm Oghabs, and possibly some 50 modified 240-mm Fajr-3 rockets that could conceivably reach Tel Aviv or Israel's nuclear facilities in the Negev Desert near Dimona.[19] Hamas and other Palestinian militants also have reportedly received small arms and anti-aircraft and anti-tank weapons through the tunnels.[20]

Estimates say that approximately 7,000 people work on over 1,000 tunnels. The tunnels are reportedly of a generally high quality of engineering and construction—with some including electricity, ventilation, intercoms, and a rail system. The openings to many tunnels are found within buildings in or around Gaza's southernmost city of Rafah. Although Israeli airstrikes rendered over 100 tunnels inoperative during Operation Cast Lead, many of them were restored within a few weeks because the main damage was sustained at the openings, not in the middle sections.[21] Israel, Egypt, the United States, and other North Atlantic Treaty Organization (NATO) countries have pledged to stop or slow smuggling to Gaza by land and sea, and some measures such as Egypt's construction of an underground fence along its side of the Gaza-Egypt border (see "Countering Financial and Smuggling Networks") have been taken. Nevertheless, anti-smuggling capabilities remain limited and/or constrained.[22]

It also is possible that Hamas may have the capability to fire rockets from outside of Gaza. In August 2010, rockets fired from Egypt's Sinai Peninsula hit the neighboring cities of Eilat, Israel and Aqaba, Jordan on the Red Sea coast. Israeli and Egyptian officials, along with Palestinian Authority officials from the West Bank, claimed that Hamas was responsible.[23]

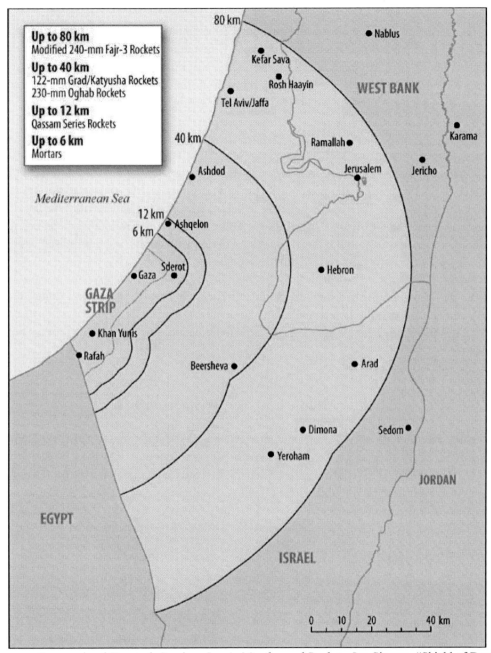

Sources: Congressional Research Service; *Jane's Missiles and Rockets*; Ian Siperco, "Shield of David: The Promise of Israeli National Missile Defense," *Middle East Policy*, Vol. 17, Issue 2, Summer 2010.

Notes: All boundaries, distances, and other depictions are approximate. The designations employed and the presentation of material on this map do not imply the expression of any opinion whatsoever on the part of CRS concerning the presence in Gaza of the rockets described herein. There is no evidence that rockets with a range farther than about 40 km have been fired at Israeli targets, though there have been reports that Hamas has successfully tested longer-range rockets.

Figure 2. Map of Approximate Rocket Ranges from Gaza. (for rockets possibly possessed by Hamas and other Palestinian militant groups).

Gaza Militias and Security Forces

The leadership and most of the manpower—estimated at about 2,500—of Hamas's military wing, the Qassam Brigades, are in Gaza. [24] In addition, the Hamas-led government in Gaza maintains a robust contingent of approximately 13,000-14,000 police, security, and intelligence personnel, many of whom are drawn from the Executive Force that assisted the Qassam Brigades in defeating Fatah-led forces in Gaza in June 2007 (see **Table 3** and "In Gaza" below).[25]

It seems unlikely that the Qassam Brigades and Hamas-commanded Gaza security forces, even working in concert with other Gaza-based militants, could present a significant conventional threat to an Israeli military superior in manpower, equipment, and technology. Perhaps the main threat is the possibility that Hamas might kill or abduct additional Israeli soldiers to add to the leverage it believes it has gained against Israel with current Hamas captive Sergeant Gilad Shalit.[26] The Qassam Brigades and other militant groups engage in periodic border skirmishes with Israeli forces involving small arms and improvised explosive devices, partly to continually refresh their resistance credentials.

Hamas has portrayed its survival of Operation Cast Lead as a victory, but many analysts believe that Israel established some level of deterrence. These analysts say that Hamas did not expect the intensity of the Israeli operation and genuinely feared for the survival of its rule in Gaza. As a result, they suggest the group is now more cautious about possible provocations of Israel.[27]

Comparison with Other Middle East Terrorist Groups

Hamas is often discussed alongside other groups in the region that engage in militant and terrorist activities to achieve their ends. Israeli officials routinely compare Hamas with Al Qaeda. Yet Hamas has confined its militancy to Israel and the Palestinian territories—distinguishing it from the broader violent jihadist[28] aspirations expressed by Al Qaeda and its affiliates. This narrower focus was reflected by the following statement from Hamas political bureau (or politburo) chief Khaled Meshaal in a May 2010 interview with PBS's Charlie Rose:

> Hamas is a national resistance movement. Yet we adopt the Islamic intellectual approach because we are part of the Muslim and Arab region. We have a battle only with the Israeli occupation. We do not have any military act anywhere else in the world. We do not consider any country in the world other than Israel as our enemy. We might say that the American policies are wrong, but we do not have any conflict whatsoever except with the Israeli politics. In other words, we do not practice resistance as an open choice anywhere else in the world but in our occupied territories and against Israel. And we do not launch a religious war. We are not against the Jews nor the Christians. And we do not pass any statements about their religions. We only resist those who occupy our territories and attack us.[29]

Indeed, Al Qaeda voiced intense criticism of Hamas when it opted to engage in the Palestinian political process in 2005-2007 because its leaders believed Hamas was fatally compromising Al Qaeda's ideal of pan-Islamic revolution. Al Qaeda's number-two leader, Ayman al Zawahiri, said in 2006 that "Those trying to liberate the land of Islam through elections based on secular constitutions or on decisions to surrender Palestine to the Jews will not liberate a grain of sand of Palestine."[30]

Furthermore, hundreds of disaffected Palestinians in Gaza who apparently share Al Qaeda's misgivings that Hamas engages in unacceptable compromise have joined violent jihadist groups with Salafist[31] leanings or postures in opposition to Hamas. Nevertheless, Hamas has been willing to tolerate these smaller extremist groups to the extent they refrain from public challenges to Hamas's rule.[32] Hamas also coordinates action with others that reject peace with Israel—both Islamist and secular—under some circumstances.

Comparisons between Hamas and groups that blend political Islam with national or ethnic loyalties and grievances may be more apt. Hezbollah shares many characteristics with Hamas. It participates in electoral politics; it has a distinct geographical base of support; its main foreign backing comes from Iran. Perhaps most importantly, opposition to Israeli occupation or alleged occupation is a key animating factor for its supporters. Yet, significant differences exist between the two organizations, many of them following from Hezbollah's Shiite identity and greater freedom to traverse national borders. Shiites (Hezbollah's core demographic support base) constitute a significantly lower percentage of the population in Lebanon than the percentage Sunnis constitute in the Palestinian territories. Hezbollah's ties with Shiite Iran also are closer and more ideological than Hamas's. Hezbollah operatives actively train other militants (including from Hamas—see "Iran, Syria, and Hezbollah" below). Also, Hezbollah's rockets, other weapons, and militias are believed to present a significantly greater conventional military threat to Israel than Hamas's.[33]

Table 1. Hamas and Hezbollah: A Comparison

	Hamas	Hezbollah
Established	1987	1982
National Identity	Palestinian	Lebanese
Sectarian Identity	Sunni Muslim	Shiite Muslim
Estimated Percentage of National Population That Shares Sectarian Identity	99%	28-49%a
Named Foreign Terrorist Organization by State Department	1997	1997
Major Sources of Assistance	Iran, Syria, Hezbollah, private individuals and organizations	Iran, Syria, private individuals and organizations
Members of National Legislature	74 of 132b	10 of 128
Ministers in National Government	All ministers in de facto Gaza government; no ministers in PA government in West Bank	2 of 30 (Agriculture and Administrative Reform); part of "March 8" coalition that has 10 ministers total

Table 1. (Continued).

	Hamas	Hezbollah
Estimated Troop Strength	2,500 in Qassam Brigades (military wing) 13,000-14,000 (some non-Hamas) in Gaza security forces	A few hundred terrorist operatives and potentially thousands more volunteers for defensive operations
Approximate Maximum Rocket/Missile Range	80 km	Over 100 km (and possibly over 200 km)
Territorial Control	Gaza Strip (using de facto control of national institutions and mechanisms)	Areas of southern and eastern Lebanon
Probable Main Weapon Supply Route	Tunnels under patrolled and fenced Gaza-Egypt border (14 km)	Loosely patrolled and unfenced Lebanon-Syria border (260 km)
Trains Militants of Other Nationalities	No evidence	Yes
Has Intentionally Struck at U.S. Targets in Middle East	Says noc	Yes

Sources: CRS Report R41446, *Hezbollah: Background and Issues for Congress*, by Casey L. Addis and Christopher M. Blanchard; Central Intelligence Agency; State Department; Council on Foreign Relations; Yezid Sayigh; International Foundation for Electoral Systems.

Notes: This comparison is not meant to be exhaustive.

a U.S. State Department, International Religious Freedom Report 2009, available at http://www.state.gov/g/drl/rls/irf/2009/127352.htm; Pew Forum for Religion & Public Life, *Mapping the Global Muslim Population*, October 2009, available at http://pewforum.org/uploadedfiles/Orphan_Migrated_Content/Muslimpopulation.pdf. Because parity among confessional groups in Lebanon remains a sensitive issue, a national census has not been conducted since 1932.

b Hamas won this legislative majority in 2006, but the Palestinian Legislative Council (PLC) has not been functional since Hamas's takeover of Gaza in June 2007 due to a lack of a quorum caused by the territorial political divide between Gaza and the West Bank. Furthermore, the PLC's four-year term expired in January 2010 under PA law, although the PLO Central Council extended its term in December 2009 (along with the PA presidential term of Mahmoud Abbas, which also expired in January 2010 under PA law) until new elections can be held. The legality of this extension has been questioned. For further information, see CRS Report RL34074, *The Palestinians: Background and U.S. Relations*, by Jim Zanotti.

c Hamas has not claimed responsibility for any attacks targeting Americans, and insists that it targets only Israelis, but has killed at least 14 U.S. citizens (some of whom were dual U.S.-Israelis) in attacks aimed at Israelis.

Hamas retains its claim to an electoral mandate because the majority it won in the Palestinian Legislative Council (PLC) in 2006 elections has not been displaced through subsequent elections (some say mainly due to reluctance by both Hamas and Fatah to risk their respective spheres of control in Gaza and the West Bank because of uncertainty regarding Palestinians' political preferences and factional advantages). As a result, many Hamas leaders, followers, and sympathizers identify the movement with other Sunni-led,

Islamist-influenced groups and parties in the region that participate non-violently in their respective political arenas. These include Turkey's ruling Justice and Development Party (AKP) and non-militant branches and affiliates of the Muslim Brotherhood. Hamas's model of having a foot in both political and military realms serves as inspiration for other regional Islamist groups. This leads to concerns among regional states and the broader international community that Islamist groups elsewhere that participate or seek to participate non-violently in the political arena could turn to violence.

Ideology and Policies

Hamas combines Palestinian nationalism with Islamic fundamentalism, although opinions differ about how these two driving forces interact in Hamas's ideology and policies.[34] Its leaders strive to connect Hamas to the longer narrative of Palestinian national struggle—dating to the time of the British Mandate—and to past leaders such as the anti-colonialist Izz al Din al Qassam (see footnote 3), Mohammed Amin al Husseini (the Grand Mufti of Jerusalem during the British Mandate), and Abd al Qader al Husseini (a political and military leader who died in the 1948 war with Israel).

Some analysts insist that Hamas's actions show that it remains best defined by reference to its 1988 founding charter or "covenant," which sets forth a particularly militant, uncompromising, and anti-Semitic agenda.[35] These observers maintain this view despite and perhaps because of statements and documents issued over subsequent years by Hamas leaders purporting to redefine the movement's agenda or distance it from the charter, but failing formally to disavow it.[36]

Other analysts see Hamas as a pragmatic, evolving movement.[37] They argue that Hamas has already moderated its positions by participating in 2006 elections for the Palestinian Legislative Council, agreeing to short-term cease-fires with Israel through indirect negotiation, and expressing willingness to enter into a long-term cease-fire (or *hudna*) with Israel. Also, these observers say, Hamas signed the Mecca Accord in February 2007, pursuant to which it agreed to share power with Fatah, "respect" previous agreements signed by the PLO, and allow the PLO to negotiate with Israel and submit any agreement reached to the Palestinian people for their approval. Finally, these observers liken Hamas to the PLO from earlier times. The PLO, also once a terrorist group, altered some of its tenets in the late 1980s and early 1990s—agreeing to eschew violence, enter into negotiations with Israel (under the "land-for-peace" rubric of U.N. Security Council Resolutions 242 and 338), and recognize its right to exist.[38]

Still other analysts do not assume that Hamas remains committed to every word of its charter, but maintain that a decisive majority of Hamas members are unwilling to deviate from core principles of the movement—namely, its ability to resort to violence and its unwillingness to agree to a permanent peace or territorial compromise with Israel.[39] These analysts readily say that Hamas is not monolithic. Yet, they assert that in the instances in which Hamas conveys an impression of its pragmatism or potential moderation, consensus exists among its various political and military leadership bodies and councils that such actions are tactical, confined within the limits its core principles allow, and only bind Hamas as long as circumstances favor a diplomatic approach over a more confrontational one. Under this interpretation, statements from Hamas leaders hinting at permanent compromise of its core principles would either be deceptive or represent a marginalized view. For example, these analysts claim, Hamas's stated willingness to contemplate a long-term cease-fire in the event of the establishment of a Palestinian state in the West Bank (including East Jerusalem) and Gaza would allow Hamas to consolidate its position and await a more propitious moment to assault Israeli targets.[40]

Overall Goals

Hamas's primary goal is to achieve the "liberation" of all of historic Palestine (comprising present-day Israel, West Bank, and Gaza Strip) for Palestinian Arabs in the name of Islam. There is vigorous debate among analysts and perhaps within Hamas regarding the essential aspects of this goal. Hamas's charter is explicit about the struggle for Palestine being a religious obligation. It describes the land as a *waqf*, or religious endowment, saying that no one can "abandon it or part of it."

Those who believe that Hamas is pragmatic are less likely to believe that it considers itself bound by its charter or by rhetoric intended to rally domestic support. Those, on the other hand, who contend that consensus exists within Hamas not to compromise on core principles believe that Hamas sees events from a different perspective than U.S. and other international analysts. They assert that Hamas has a much different concept of time, borne out by a gradual but consistent rise in the movement's fortunes over the course of generations (within its greater Muslim Brotherhood context) in the face of significant internal challenges and external opposition.

On Israel's Existence and the Jews

The 1988 charter commits Hamas to the destruction of Israel and the establishment of an Islamic state in all of historic Palestine.[41] It calls for the elimination of Israel and Jews from Islamic holy land and portrays Jews in decidedly negative terms, citing anti-Semitic texts and conspiracies.

Many observers claim that subsequent statements from Hamas have refrained from or deemphasized blanket negative references to Jews and supposed global Zionist conspiracies. Some might say, however, that this is belied by numerous anti-Semitic statements and references to pejorative stereotypes in media controlled by Hamas, including programming for both children and adults on Hamas's Al Aqsa satellite television channel.[42]

On a Two-State Solution

Although Hamas's charter is uncompromising in its call for the liberation of all of historic Palestine, those observers who contend that Hamas is essentially pragmatic point to past statements in which leaders pledged hypothetically to respect actions taken through a potential Palestinian referendum or PA power-sharing government (that includes Hamas) to accept a two-state solution.[43] Hamas politburo chief Khaled Meshaal, however, in an August 2010 interview, said:

> Hamas does accept a Palestinian state on the lines of 1967—and does not accept the two-state solution. There is [a] big difference between these two. I am a Palestinian. I am a Palestinian leader. I am concerned with accomplishing what the Palestinian people are

looking for—which is to get rid of the occupation, attain liberation and freedom, and establish the Palestinian state on the lines of 1967. Talking about Israel is not relevant to me—I am not concerned about it. It is an occupying state, and I am the victim. I am the victim of the occupation; I am not concerned with giving legitimacy to this occupying country. The international community can deal with this (Israeli) state; I am concerned with the Palestinian people. I am as a Palestinian concerned with establishing the Palestinian state only.[44]

In a May 2010 interview with PBS's Charlie Rose, Meshaal clarified the circumstances under which Hamas would respect the outcome of a Palestinian referendum on the relationship with Israel held *after*, not before or concurrently with, the establishment of a Palestinian state:

> If Israel withdraws to the borders of 1967, and from East Jerusalem, that will become the capital of the Palestinian state with the right of self—with the right of return for the refugees and with a Palestinian state with real sovereignty on the land and on the borders and on the checkpoints. Then we—the Palestinian state will decide the future of the relationship with Israel. And we will respect the decision that will reflect the viewpoint of the majority of the Palestinian people.... Don't request the Palestinian people to have a certain stance from Israel while living under the Israeli occupation. Give the Palestinian people the opportunity to live in a normal situation in a Palestinian state, and then the Palestinian people with complete freedom will decide.[45]

On the Use of Violence

Hamas's 1988 charter says, "There is no solution for the Palestinian question except through Jihad. Initiatives, proposals and international conferences are all a waste of time and vain endeavors."[46]

In the years since, the movement's willingness to halt violence and emphasize political over military methods in some circumstances, most notably the decision to participate in the 2006 PLC elections, has prompted some analysts to express hope that it might contemplate demilitarizing. Nevertheless, Hamas's leadership and many other analysts insist that no matter what other means Hamas may tactically employ from time to time, armed resistance remains its ultimate trump card.

In a July 2010 interview with the Jordanian newspaper *Al Sabeel*, Meshaal discussed how having the option to use violence enhances Hamas's ability to negotiate, in contrast to the lack of leverage he said the PLO has had since renouncing violence:

> The [PLO] negotiators say: "Negotiation is the option, the course and the only plan." They coordinate security with the enemy and implement the "Road Map" and its security requirements freely, with Israel offering nothing in return. What is there to force Olmert or Netanyahu to grant the Palestinians anything?
>
> Negotiation in the [PLO] case is out of its objective context; it is, merely from the perspective of political logic, lacking resistance and not based on the necessary power balance. The Vietnamese—for instance—negotiated with the Americans as the latter were retreating; thus negotiations were useful for turning the last page on American occupation and aggression. You are successful in negotiation and in imposing your conditions on the enemy depending on the number of power cards you have on the ground.[47]

On Its Model for an Islamic State

Hamas's charter envisions that Palestine will become an Islamic society that allows for coexistence of all religions "under its wing":

> The Islamic Resistance Movement is a distinguished Palestinian movement, whose allegiance is to Allah, and whose way of life is Islam. It strives to raise the banner of Allah over every inch of Palestine, for under the wing of Islam followers of all religions can coexist in security and safety where their lives, possessions and rights are concerned. In the absence of Islam, strife will be rife, oppression spreads, evil prevails and schisms and wars will break out.[48]

However, by reshaping PA institutions, laws, and norms to fit its ends—instead of fully overhauling them—and by allowing the U.N. Relief and Works Agency for Palestine Refugees in the Near East (UNRWA) and other international and non-governmental organizations to operate in Gaza, Hamas has opted—for the time being at least—for stability over a comprehensive societal transformation. Hamas interior minister Fathi Hamad has insisted:

> Claims that we are trying to establish an Islamic state are false. Hamas is not the Taliban. It is not al-Qaeda. It is an enlightened, moderate Islamic movement.[49]

Some ideologues who believed that Hamas would or should have implemented *sharia* law and formally and fully Islamized public and private life soon after taking power have been disappointed. This disappointment has resulted in some Islamists joining more extremist groups, though it does not appear to present a near-term challenge to Hamas's rule and it is unclear how pronounced or significant this trend will be long term.

Yet, there has been some movement toward a greater Islamization of society through the broader Hamas community network of mosques, reconciliation committees, government ministries and courts, security forces, religious scholars, and schools. Islamic *fatwas* (legal opinions) have been offered as an alternative to secular justice for some police detainees. "Morality police," judges, and school principals advocate for and enforce Islamic dress codes—especially for women—in publicly conspicuous places, although resistance to these measures has slowed or reversed their implementation in some instances.[50] How this has affected the minority of Palestinian Christians in Gaza is unclear. In February 2010, interior minister Fathi Hamad (in a statement that some could interpret as contradicting his above-quoted statement regarding Hamas's supposed moderation) "called for '*Da'wa* efforts to reach all institutions, not just mosques,' signaling an intent to systematically Islamize government agencies, starting with his own."[51]

Use of Media

Hamas has used its control over Gaza's media and a robust Internet presence[52] to cast Islamist, anti-Israel, and anti-Semitic teachings within a narrative portraying "martyrdom" and violence against Israel and Jews as heroic. Public dissent is suppressed, and Hamas uses its Al Aqsa television and radio channels and summer camps[53] to indoctrinate children and youth with its hybrid Islamist/Palestinian nationalist views. In 2009, Hamas even produced its first feature-length film celebrating the life and death of a Qassam Brigades militant from the first intifada.[54] It encourages support and often recruits from "mosque youth" who assist neighborhood imams and sometimes act as informants for Hamas-controlled Gaza intelligence organizations.[55]

Hamas leaders also skillfully use regional and international media outlets to craft messages to its various audiences: including Arabs and Muslims, Americans, Europeans, and Israelis. Israeli officials insist that Hamas delivers the same message to Arab and Western audiences with a different tone and emphasis for each,[56] creating what some might call purposeful and convenient ambiguity over questions such as Hamas's possible pragmatism.

Leadership and Organization

In General

Hamas has a variety of movement-wide and regional leadership organs, along with branches that conduct its political, military, and social welfare activities with varying levels of formal association to the group. In addition, the de facto Hamas government in Gaza has its own leadership structures and public stature. Who controls overall strategy, policy, and financial decisions, and how control is exercised, remain open questions with opaque answers. The State Department and some analysts believe that Hamas generally follows a hierarchical model in which ultimate control resides with the 15-member political bureau (or politburo) and the movement-wide consultative council (known as the *shura* council) headquartered in Damascus.[57] According to Matthew Levitt of the Washington Institute for Near East Policy, "Under this Shura council are committees responsible for supervising a wide array of activities, from media relations to military operations. At the grassroots level in the West Bank and Gaza, local Shura committees answer to the overarching Shura council and carry out its decisions on the ground."[58] One reason to believe that substantial authority resides with the movement-wide and regional *shura* councils is that Hamas closely guards the secrecy of these councils' membership. Hamas also maintains branch offices in areas where it enjoys support, such as Lebanon, Sudan, the Gulf, and possibly Iran.[59]

Some analysts, however, believe that Hamas's formal hierarchical structures remain subject to a dispersion of control given that the geographical division of the organization's core activities among Damascus and Gaza—maintained out of necessity for the organization's security and survival—creates a system of mutual leverage. This system is based on how the actions and funding streams of Hamas's political, military, and social welfare branches affect their interactions, as these interactions both shape and are shaped by events.

Hamas seeks to mitigate the tension inherent between its activities as (1) a militant organization uncompromisingly opposed to Israel in defiance of international opprobrium and countermeasures; and (2) the de facto government in Gaza accountable to its people for managing security, economic, and other basic societal issues that largely depend upon Israeli and international actions. Some might express this as Hamas's desire to maximize its power while minimizing its accountability. Hamas claims it draws a bright line bifurcating the organization's leadership from its members in the Gaza government, which, if true, helps it deflect accountability. This could discourage the United States and other international actors from including Hamas in political discussions tied to Palestinian governance or negotiations with Israel.

Internal Tensions?

Various U.S. and international policymakers, including Secretary of State Hillary Rodham Clinton, have said or implied that organizational fissures may exist within Hamas.[60] These possible fissures are somewhat overlapping. One supposedly runs between Gaza-based leaders accountable to local public opinion and Damascus-based leaders seen as closer to Iran. Another supposedly runs between so-called pragmatists and more hardline elements in the Gaza leadership (often Qassam Brigades militants and their sympathizers). Yet another is said to exist between two groups of Damascus exiles: (1) native Gazans with personal links to Hamas's Gaza founders (such as Musa Abu Marzouk), and (2) displaced West Bankers used to operating outside of the Palestinian territories who forged links with the Gaza founders mostly through Islamist organizations in Kuwait (known as *Kuwaitiyya*, this group includes Khaled Meshaal).

Within the Qassam Brigades, some analysts speculate that internal struggles may partly explain the rise of Jaljalat (an Arabic word for "thunder"), an "amorphous network of armed militants numbering some 2,500-3,000" that reportedly includes many disaffected Brigades members. Yezid Sayigh of King's College London, a longtime analyst of Palestinian security and politics and a former PLO advisor, claimed in a March 2010 report that Jaljalat fears that, "by taking on the mundane tasks of government and public service delivery, Hamas has jeopardized its nationalist and Islamic purity and its commitment to armed resistance against Israel." Sayigh's report also said that Jaljalat is suspected of several attacks on Hamas vehicles and security offices, as well as on Internet cafés. Additionally, the report said that Qassam Brigades commander Ahmed al Jaabari may be concerned that some Hamas leaders in Gaza may be building alternative power bases that could threaten the internal unity of Hamas and the Brigades.[61]

Hamas could be more united than it seems, although it benefits from the portrayal of its leadership as divided because this perception provides Hamas with greater flexibility in dealing with both Western actors who hold out hope of its moderation and its Syrian and Iranian benefactors who are reminded not to take its rejectionist stance for granted. Presenting a divided front also may serve Hamas by providing it with a rationale to explain policy inconsistencies or changes of direction to the Palestinian people.

In Gaza

Hamas directs the Gaza government and security forces through a self-appointed cabinet of Hamas ministers led by Ismail Haniyeh, who served as PA prime minister prior to Hamas's dismissal from government after the June 2007 Gaza takeover. The process by which decisions are taken is opaque, but analysts believe that it involves the movement-wide and Gaza regional *shura* councils, the Damascus politburo, and Qassam Brigades leadership.[62] Along with an unknown amount it may receive from Hamas's organization and external benefactors, the Hamasled government may receive revenue from Gaza's *zakat* committees (which collect Muslims' obligatory donations of 2.5% of their surplus wealth) and from licensing fees and taxes. Although Hamas is believed to make tens of millions of dollars annually from operating Gaza's smuggling tunnels (the estimate for 2009, according to Yezid Sayigh, was $150-200 million), most of its profit reportedly goes to the organization (the Qassam Brigades, in particular), and not the Gaza regime.[63] The people of Gaza still rely on Israel, Egypt, the PA in the West Bank, UNRWA, and other international and non-governmental organizations for access to and resources from the outside world (including banking, water, and fuel for electricity).

Reference to the government in Gaza as the "Hamas regime" does not mean that all or even most of the people employed in ministries, civil service positions, and even security forces are necessarily members of Hamas or even Hamas sympathizers. Hamas partisans are, however, intermingled throughout. *The Jerusalem Report*, an Israeli weekly, states that since the June 2007 takeover, the PA in the West Bank has continued paying salaries to tens of thousands of public sector employees in Gaza—mostly in education- and health-related positions—while paying salaries to thousands more (including from the security forces) on the condition that they *not* perform their duties.[64] Although this policy might allow the PA to maintain the loyalties of its workers, it also has relieved the regime of the economic burden of supporting those paid by the PA. It also has given the regime the opportunity to create a critical mass of Hamas loyalists within the government by filling vacated positions in the security forces and other key public institutions. Additionally, the Hamas-led regime has created its own ad hoc judicial framework and hired its own judges,[65] many of them from *sharia* courts.[66]

Table 2. Public Budget Comparisons: Gaza and West Bank

	Gaza Hamas-led Regime	West Bank Palestinian Authority
Palestinian Population in Territory	1.55 mil	2.04 mil
Public Employees	32,000	145,000
Overall Annual Budget Estimates (2010)	$320-540 mila	$2.78 bil
Annual Internal Revenue (2010)	$60 mil	$1.54 bil
External Support Requirements (2010)	$260-480 mil	$1.24 bil

Sources: Central Intelligence Agency, State Department, Yezid Sayigh. Notes: All figures are as of March 2010 and are approximate.

a. The Hamas-led regime in Gaza states that its 2010 budget is $540 million, but it is possible that the actual budget is closer to the actual budget for 2009, which was $320 million. CRS correspondence with Yezid Sayigh, October 2010.

Although much international attention has focused on the improved professionalization of PA security forces in the West Bank, analysts say that Hamas-led security forces in Gaza also exhibit impressive levels of discipline and efficiency that have succeeded in keeping order. There are, however, widespread reports of mistreatment and torture of Hamas political opponents (particularly Fatah members) and other prisoners at the same time similar reports circulate about PA treatment of Hamas members and sympathizers in the West Bank.[67]

Table 3. Major Hamas-commanded Security Forces in Gaza

Branch	Role	Estimated Manpower
Internal Security Service	Counterintelligence and infiltration of rivals (possibly including external intelligence arm)	500
VIP Protection Force	Bodyguards for Hamas leadership and key facilities	2,000
National Security Force	Border guard with early warning function	930
Police	Routine civil and criminal policing functions (largely derived from former "Executive Force")	10,000

Source: Mohammed Najib, "Hamas creates external intelligence arm," *Jane's Islamic Affairs Analyst*, January 29, 2010.

Many analysts believe that Hamas rule remains stable and effective in some areas despite the miserable post-Operation Cast Lead situation and Gaza's dilapidated infrastructure.[68] Some see the beginnings of a patronage system, citing, among other evidence, the $60 million in handouts Hamas is reported to have distributed in $1,500-6,000 increments to families whose homes were lost or damaged in the conflict.[69] According to Yezid Sayigh, Hamas benefits from "unbroken territorial control over the entirety of the Gaza Strip." This stands in contrast to the difficulties faced by the Palestinian Authority in the West Bank, whose jurisdiction and operations are "fundamentally circumscribed by the 'Swiss cheese' model of intermeshed Palestinian autonomy areas and Israeli-controlled settlements and military zones..."[70]

Popular Support

Although Hamas's rule in Gaza is authoritarian, it did win PLC elections in 2006 and some believe that the future possibility of elections makes it responsive to public opinion. Polls taken in the West Bank (including East Jerusalem) and Gaza Strip between August-October 2010 indicated that Palestinians favored Fatah over Hamas by nearly two-to-one to over three-to-one margins in each territory.[71] Large groupings of Palestinians (ranging in the various polls from 15% to nearly 40%), however, did not identify a factional preference,[72] possibly indicating popular malaise or cynicism regarding political developments and processes, or potential for volatility.

However, according to a September-October 2010 poll by the Palestinian Center for Policy and Survey Research, over 60% of Gazans (contrasted with just over 40% of West Bankers) supported both Hamas's August-September 2010 shooting attacks on Israeli settlers in the West Bank[73] and the idea of attacking civilians inside Israel.[74] Might the possible resumption by Hamas of regular attacks or other active opposition to Israeli-PLO negotiations gain it support from this demographic? In the same poll, Palestinians were almost evenly divided (those agreeing came out slightly ahead, by a 49%-48% margin) on the following question related to a possible two-state solution:

There is a proposal that after the establishment of an independent Palestinian state and the settlement of all issues in dispute, including the refugees and Jerusalem issues, there will be a mutual recognition of Israel as the state of the Jewish people and Palestine as the state of the Palestinians people. Do you agree or disagree to this proposal?[75]

Some reports indicate that Hamas is building its support base among Palestinian refugees outside of the West Bank and Gaza Strip, particularly in Lebanon.[76] Gaining the loyalty of refugee camp populations could give Hamas additional leverage with Fatah, Israel, and other regional actors.

Sources of Assistance

Iran, Syria, and Hezbollah

According to the State Department, Iran provides financial and military assistance to Hamas and other Palestinian militant groups.[77] During a December 2009 visit to Tehran, Hamas politburo chief Khaled Meshaal said, "Other Arab and Islamic states also support us ... but the Iranian backing is in the lead, and therefore we highly appreciate and thank Iran for this."[78] Meshaal and his politburo colleagues, along with Hamas's movement-wide *shura* council, have safe haven in Damascus, Syria. From Damascus, Hamas's leadership-in-exile can direct the group's operations through financial transactions and unrestrained access to travel and communications. The Iran-backed Hezbollah movement in Lebanon provides military training as well as financial and moral support and has acted in some ways as a mentor or role model for Hamas,[79] which has sought to emulate the Lebanese group's political and media success. Some Palestinians who are skeptical of the Arab-Israeli peace process believe that Iranian support for Palestinian militants and Hezbollah provides needed leverage with Israel that the United States and Europe are unlikely to deliver to PA President/PLO Chairman Mahmoud Abbas.

Some reports say that contributions to Hamas's political and military wings from Iran range from $20-30 million annually.[80] Yet, even though Hamas welcomes direct and indirect Iranian assistance and Iran's reputation among Arab populations has arguably been bolstered in recent years by its anti-Western and anti-Israel positions and rhetoric, Hamas and Iran may intentionally maintain a measure of distance from one another. An alternate interpretation is that they merely understate the extent of their ties.[81] They appear to understand the importance of Hamas maintaining an image among its domestic constituents as an authentic Palestinian offshoot of the Muslim Brotherhood, instead of as an Iranian proxy—owing to the ethnic, sectarian, and linguistic differences between Palestinians (who are predominantly Arab, Sunni, and Arabic-speaking) and Iranians (who are mostly non-Arab, Shiite, and Persian-speaking).

Iran's future influence over the Palestinian political scene seems tied to Hamas's fortunes, which have been on the rise since Hamas's political emergence in the late-1980s, and bolstered by its victory in Palestinian Legislative Council elections in 2006 and takeover of Gaza in 2007. Possible Iranian-supported smuggling of weapons, cash, and other contraband into the Gaza Strip,[82] along with Iranian training for Gaza-based Hamas militants (who are able to travel to and from Iran and Lebanon after using the Gaza-Sinai tunnels),[83] is believed to reinforce both Hamas's ability to maintain order and control over Gaza and its population, and Palestinian militants' ability to fire mortars and rockets into Israel.[84]

Charities and Individuals

U.S. officials and many analysts have concluded that, drawing upon its historical roots in and continuing ties to the Palestinian *dawa* (social welfare) community, Hamas receives much of its support from private individuals and organizations in the Palestinian diaspora and greater Arab and Muslim worlds (particularly in Saudi Arabia and other Gulf states).[85] Since 1995, the United States has taken active measures—in concert with Israel, the PA, and other international actors—to disrupt Hamas's use of charities as front organizations (see **Table 4** below and **Appendix A** for additional details).

Table 4. U.S. Terrorist Designations and Financial Sanctions Against Hamas and Affiliates

Hamas Designation	Statutory Basis	Financial Sanctions	Subject to Civil and/or Criminal Liability[a]
Specially Designated Terrorist (SDT) January 1995 Executive Order 12947	International Emergency Economic Powers Act (P.L. 95-223, 50 U.S.C. §1701, et seq.)	Blocks all U.S. property of SDT (or of party controlled by SDT or acting on its behalf)	Any transaction or dealing by a U.S. person or within the United States with SDT or SDT property
Foreign Terrorist Organization (FTO) October 1997 State Department	Antiterrorism and Effective Death Penalty Act of 1996 (P.L. 104-132, 110 Stat. 1214-1319)	Requires financial institutions to block all funds in which FTOs or their agents have an interest	U.S. persons providing material support or resources to FTOs; failure of financial institutions to block funds
Specially Designated Global Terrorist (SDGT) October 2001 Treasury Department (Under Executive Order 13224)	International Emergency Economic Powers Act (P.L. 95-223, 50 U.S.C. §1701, et seq.)	Blocks all U.S. property of SDGT (or of party controlled by SDGT or acting on its behalf) and of those who provide material support to SDGT Directs executive branch to work with other countries to prevent acts of terrorism, deny financing to terrorists, and share intelligence about terrorist funding activities	Any transaction or dealing by a U.S. person or within the United States with SDGT or SDGT property

Source: U.S. Treasury Department, Office of Foreign Assets Control, "What You Need to Know About U.S. Sanctions," available at http://www.ustreas.gov/offices/enforcement/ofac/programs/terror/terror.pdf.

a. See footnote 87 and footnote 88, respectively, for discussion of the statutory bases for U.S. criminal and civil liability for material support of terrorism (18 U.S.C. §2333, §2339A, §2339B).

Yet, it appears that, either through the international banking system or the Gaza-Sinai smuggling tunnels (or both), Hamas's political and military wings both still receive funding from their own networks of affiliated Islamic charities,[86] including some that have operated and may still operate in the United States, Canada, and Europe. The most illustrative case was that of the Texas-based Holy Land Foundation for Relief and Development (HLF), once the largest Islamic charity in the United States. After U.S. investigators determined that HLF was funneling money to Hamas and had close ties with Hamas leader Musa Abu Marzouk when he lived in the United States in the early 1990s, the Treasury Department named HLF a specially designated global terrorist (SDGT) in 2001 and froze its assets. In 2008, five HLF leaders (four of whom are U.S. citizens) were found guilty on criminal charges of providing more than $12 million in material support to Hamas (through contributions to Hamas-linked charities) after President Bill Clinton had named Hamas a specially designated terrorist (SDT) by executive order in 1995.[87] For providing financing, HLF and two affiliated organizations also were found liable in 2004 in federal civil court for the 1996 Hamas shooting death of an Israeli-American dual citizen in Jerusalem, although the verdict against HLF was reversed on appeal in 2007 on procedural grounds.[88]

The December 2004 findings of the Intelligence and Terrorism Information Center (an Israeli non-governmental organization), as paraphrased in a November 2008 Washington Institute for Near East Policy report, claimed that there were two separate categories of Hamas-linked charitable fronts:

> The first category includes those fronts directly tied to Hamas. These typically employ Hamas activists, are established with the assistance of the Hamas political leadership, and see the vast majority of their funds dispensed to Hamas charities in the West Bank and Gaza. Such charities bring in an estimated $15–$20 million a year and include the Palestinian Relief and Development Fund (Interpal) and the al-Aqsa International Foundation, among others. The second category includes fronts that support radical Islamist elements generally but are not Hamas specific. A majority of these fronts are based in Persian Gulf states and most of the funds they send to the West Bank and Gaza are also channeled through Hamas organizations there.[89]

In November 2008, the Treasury Department identified one of these alleged front organizations, a Saudi Arabia-based charity known as the Union of Good, as an SDGT, claiming that the organization had been responsible for the transfer of tens of millions of dollars to Hamasmanaged associations in the Palestinian territories. The Union of Good is reportedly chaired by Yusuf al Qaradawi,[90] a renowned Egyptian scholar of Islam and Hamas supporter based in Qatar whose popular religious program on the Al Jazeera satellite television channel attracts approximately 40 million viewers. At the time of the Union's SDGT designation, the Treasury Department stated:

> The leadership of Hamas created the Union of Good in late-2000, shortly after the start of the second Intifada, in order to facilitate the transfer of funds to Hamas. The Union of Good acts as a broker for Hamas by facilitating financial transfers between a web of charitable organizations—including several organizations previously designated under E.O. 13224 for providing support to Hamas—and Hamas-controlled organizations in the West Bank and Gaza. The primary purpose of this activity is to strengthen Hamas' political and military position in the West Bank and Gaza, including by: (i) diverting charitable donations to support Hamas members and the families of terrorist operatives;

and (ii) dispensing social welfare and other charitable services on behalf of Hamas....
[S]ome of the funds transferred by the Union of Good have compensated Hamas
terrorists by providing payments to the families of suicide bombers.[91]

According to the Israel Security Agency (also known as the Shin Bet), several Islamic
charitable organizations withdrew their funding from the Union of Good shortly after its
SDGT designation.[92]

Some analysts believe that Hamas and other Palestinian militant groups may benefit from
trade-based money laundering.[93] Charities, companies, and individuals purchase high-
demand commodities like sugar, tea, coffee, and cooking oil to be sold in Palestinian areas
because of the scarcity of these items under the Israeli-Egyptian closure regime. Orders can
be worth hundreds of thousands of dollars.[94] Some groups, such as the Anti-Defamation
League, have raised concerns over the participation of U.S. citizens and use of U.S. funds in
protest convoys (including the May 2010 *Mavi Marmara* flotilla discussed below—see
"International Dimensions") directed at the Israeli-Egyptian closure regime that have raised
money and donated supplies to Palestinians in Gaza, partly because of the difficulty in
confirming that the recipients are not linked with Hamas. In July 2009, approximately 200
U.S. activists participated in a convoy organized by the British organization Viva Palestina
(led by then British parliamentarian George Galloway) that entered Gaza from Egypt and
donated approximately $500,000 worth of medical supplies (purchased from funds raised in
the United States earlier in 2009) to Palestinian groups.[95]

POSSIBLE OPTIONS FOR CONGRESS

In considering legislative and oversight options, Congress can assess how Hamas has
emerged and adapted over time, and also scrutinize the track record of U.S., Israeli, and
international policy to counter Hamas. There have been multiple attempts to marginalize
Hamas through a variety of measures—political and foreign aid strategies, financial
sanctions, arrests and deportations, physical blockades and border closures, and Israeli
military operations and assassinations. Some of these measures have achieved temporary or
partial success, but none has yet prevented Hamas from playing a major role in Israeli-
Palestinian politics or prevented assistance to Hamas from states and other non-state actors in
its region. Some might contend that U.S. policy with respect to Hamas since its initial U.S.
terrorist designation in 1995 has strengthened instead of weakened the organization given its
increased regional and international profile. Perhaps U.S. policy also has increased Hamas's
reliance on the type of grassroots support that is not easily countered by governmental means.
Others might say that the proper goal is to further strengthen the measures that have achieved
temporary or partial success.

The following questions could be useful in evaluating legislative or oversight options.

- Is Hamas stronger than it was five years ago? 15 years ago? Why or why not? Have
  its rivals become stronger or weaker over that same period of time? (Strength could
  be measured by one of more of the following factors: popularity, military force,
  leverage with Israel, regional and global influence.)

- What are the U.S.'s ultimate goals for Israel, the Palestinians, and the broader region? How do particular options regarding Hamas fit into these goals?
- What are Hamas's ultimate goals and how might Hamas act proactively to achieve these goals? How might it react to particular U.S. options that it perceives could serve or frustrate these goals?
- Once implemented, when are various options likely to produce results? What are U.S. capacities and political will for implementing and monitoring various options over time? What are intervening variables (i.e., other relevant actors, other issues that might distract from those addressed by various options, political timelines) and how might their potential negative impact on different options be minimized?
- How would the success of various options be measured?

U.S. Aid to Palestinians

Aid to Strengthen Non-Hamas Groups and Individuals

The current U.S. aid program for the West Bank-based PA led by President Mahmoud Abbas and Prime Minister Salam Fayyad dates back to June 2007. Since that time, U.S. bilateral assistance to the West Bank and Gaza Strip has amounted to approximately $2 billion, and assistance to UNRWA for Palestinian refugees (including in Gaza) has totaled over $700 million.[96]

This assistance includes $395.4 million (including $100 million in FY2010 funding) that have been appropriated or reprogrammed for use in the West Bank since 2007 to train, reform, advise, house, and provide non-lethal equipment for PA civil security forces in the West Bank loyal to President Abbas. A small amount of training assistance also has been provided to strengthen and reform the PA criminal justice sector. The Obama Administration has requested an additional $150 million in FY2011 funding for the security assistance program, which U.S. officials insist is only designed for West Bank security, and not for a prospective PA invasion of Hamas's stronghold in Gaza.

The current U.S. aid program appears to reflect a threefold strategy with respect to Hamas:

- First, humanitarian aid is provided to Gaza to provide the people with basic needs and to prevent destabilization.
- Second, assistance (budgetary, development, security) provided for the West Bank is intended to create a virtuous cycle of prosperity for Palestinians under Abbas's rule to contrast with the relative indigence of Gaza under Hamas, with the idea that Palestinians will reject the Hamas model and embrace the West Bank model.
- Third, the West Bank security assistance is largely intended to combat, neutralize, and prevent terrorism from Hamas and other militant organizations.

Reevaluations might focus on the prospects for these three strategies to achieve their purposes. Some analysts argue that improvements in Palestinians' material well-being brought about by the current aid program might be necessary, but are unlikely to be sufficient in achieving lasting support for non-Hamas political elements without more direct progress on (1) Hamas-Fatah power-sharing, (2) Palestinian political reform (including presidential and legislative elections), and/or (3) Israeli-Palestinian negotiations.[97] Nathan Brown of the Carnegie Endowment for International Peace, a longtime U.S. analyst of Palestinian politics, warned in June 2010 that the problem with "soldiering on" with the current strategy is that U.S. and Israeli policy inertia cedes the initiative to other actors:

> As has been shown time and again in recent years (most recently with the Gaza blockade), both Israel and the United States have unfortunately but unmistakably (and quite consistently) maintained policies until a crisis forces them to reevaluate....
> .... A political misstep by the West Bank government, an eruption of violence against Israeli targets originating either in the West Bank or Gaza, an upsurge in the conflict in Jerusalem, an extensive Israeli military campaign in Gaza, or the loss of one of the two indispensible men of the moment (Fayyad and Abbas) would likely leave both countries once more desperately rather than deliberately adjusting their policies toward internal Palestinian politics, and doing so most likely on unfavorable terms.[98]

Some analysts present U.S. involvement with Palestinian politics and institutions over the past 15 years as a cautionary tale,[99] stating or implying that the continuation of U.S. policies intended to present the West Bank as a model for Gazans to emulate might backfire—due either to negative outcomes or negative perceptions (or both).[100]

Some Members of Congress advocate expanding the level and type of humanitarian and development assistance to Gaza—often at the same time they advocate easing, ending, or even challenging the Israeli-Egyptian closure regime—because Gazans are seen as needing more support to improve their economic, physical, and psychological situations.[101] Senator John Kerry, Chairman of the Senate Foreign Relations Committee, and Representatives Brian Baird and Keith Ellison visited U.N. officials in Gaza in February 2009 (in the first official U.S. government visits to Gaza since 2003) to highlight Gazans' needs immediately following Operation Cast Lead. Representative Baird has since returned to Gaza twice, once in May 2009 with Representatives Donna Edwards and Peter Welch, and once in February 2010. In January 2010, 54 Representatives signed a letter to President Obama that requested a substantive lifting of the closure regime.[102]

U.S. Security Assistance in the West Bank[103]

As mentioned above, the Bush and Obama Administrations have given non-lethal aid for PA civil security forces in the West Bank loyal to President Abbas in an effort both to counter militants from Hamas and other militants, and to establish the rule of law for an expected Palestinian state. This U.S. assistance program exists alongside other assistance and training programs reportedly provided to Palestinian security forces and intelligence organizations by the European Union and various countries, including probable covert U.S. assistance programs.[104] By most accounts, the PA forces receiving training have shown increased professionalism and have helped substantially improve law and order and lower the profile of terrorist organizations in West Bank cities.

However, the aspiration to coordinate international security assistance efforts and to consolidate the various PA security forces under unified civilian control that is accountable to rule of law and to human rights norms remains largely unfulfilled. PA forces have come under criticism for the political targeting of Hamas—in collaboration with Israel and the

United States—through massive shutdowns and forced leadership changes to West Bank charities with alleged ties to Hamas members and through reportedly arbitrary detentions of Hamas members and supporters.[105] A September-October 2010 Palestinian Center for Policy and Survey Research poll indicated that 76% of Palestinians (with opinions nearly uniform between Gazans and West Bankers) opposed or strongly opposed the PA's mass arrests of Hamas members and sympathizers following Hamas's August-September 2010 shooting attacks against Israeli settlers in the West Bank.[106] Some Palestinians and outside observers also assert that the effectiveness and credibility of PA operations are undermined by Israeli restrictions—including curfews, checkpoints, no-go zones, and limitations on international arms and equipment transfers—as well as by Israel's own security operations in the West Bank[107] and the Gaza closure regime.

United Nations Relief and Works Agency for Palestine Refugees in the Near East (UNRWA) in Gaza

The United States is the largest single-state donor to UNRWA, which provides food, shelter, medical care, and education for many of the original refugees from the 1948 Arab-Israeli war and their descendants—now comprising approximately 4.8 million Palestinians in Jordan, Syria, Lebanon, the West Bank, and Gaza.[108] Most observers acknowledge that the role of UNRWA in providing basic services (i.e., food, health care, education) in Gaza takes much of the governing burden off Hamas. As a result, some complain that this amounts to UNRWA's enabling of Hamas and is an argument militating for discontinuing or scaling back UNRWA's activities. However, many others, U.S. and Israeli officials included, believe that UNRWA plays a valuable role by providing stability and serving as the eyes and ears of the international community in Gaza. They generally prefer UNRWA to the uncertain alternative that might emerge if UNRWA were removed from the picture.[109]

Restrictions on Aid to Hamas or PA Government Including Hamas

Under current appropriations legislation, the United States cannot provide financial assistance to Hamas under any conditions. This law also prohibits U.S. assistance to a PA government with Hamas ministers unless all the government's ministers accept the "Section 620K principles": (1) recognition of "the Jewish state of Israel's right to exist" and (2) acceptance of previous Israeli-Palestinian agreements—named after the section in the Palestinian Anti-Terrorism Act of 2006 (P.L. 109-446) that sets them forth. These principles have some similarity to the principles the so-called international Quartet (United States, European Union, United Nations, and Russia) has required Hamas to meet before accepting dealings with it: (1) recognizing Israel's right to exist, (2) renouncing violence, and (3) accepting previous Israeli-Palestinian agreements. Hamas has alleged that the United States has used its leverage with Abbas to "veto" any serious attempt to broker a power-sharing compromise (by threatening an aid cutoff if Hamas rejoins the PA without accepting the Section 620K principles and/or Quartet principles), and some analysts understand the situation similarly.[110]

Future debates might focus on the following issues.

- Whether to relax or tighten U.S. restrictions on which Palestinian party/ies should be answerable for accepting and complying with the Section 620K principles.

- Whether to grant the U.S. President discretion—under certain conditions and/or for specific purposes—to waive aid restrictions relating to a power-sharing government that includes Hamas and does not meet the Section 620K principles.

Secretary of State Hillary Rodham Clinton gave testimony at an April 2009 congressional hearing regarding the possibility of Hamas members serving in a PA government that would accept the Quartet principles and/or the Section 620K principles. She stated that "we are currently funding the Lebanese government, which has Hezbollah in it" because of a U.S. interest in supporting a government working to prevent the "further incursion of extremism."[111]

U.S. Assistance to Israel to Counter Rocket Threat

The Obama Administration and both houses of Congress have proposed funding to support Israel's development of a short-range missile defense system known as Iron Dome that is designed to counter the rocket threat from Hamas. The United States and Israel also are co-developing a missile defense system known as David's Sling that could potentially be deployed against Hamas's longer-range rockets.[112] For fuller detail on this subject, see CRS Report RL33222, *U.S. Foreign Aid to Israel* , by Jeremy M. Sharp; and CRS Report RL33476, *Israel: Background and Relations with the United States*, by Carol Migdalovitz.

Countering Financial and Smuggling Networks

Terrorist Designations and Legal Action

As discussed elsewhere in this report (see "Charities and Individuals" and **Appendix A**), U.S. executive orders and designations dating from 1995 that identify Hamas, affiliated organizations, and some of its leaders as terrorists (see **Table 4**) have authorized efforts, including those in concert with other international actors, to target Hamas funding sources. As also discussed elsewhere, existing anti-terrorism legislation has been used by U.S. courts to find U.S. citizens and/or organizations civilly and criminally liable for their material support of Hamas. Congress could evaluate how it might

- support the Administration's anti-terrorism financial and legal actions;
- mandate or advocate complementary or alternative actions; and
- provide greater oversight.

Some analysts believe that the effectiveness of U.S. cooperation with Israel, the PA, and other international actors in freezing Hamas's assets and global financial transfers has hindered Hamas's capacity to carry out terrorist attacks and significantly influenced its political decisions over the past decade—including its attempt to seek popular legitimacy in 2005-2006 Palestinian elections and its allegedly increased reliance on Iranian support.[113] Even though Hamas physically controls Gaza, the legal banking system there remains answerable to the PA in the West Bank and still applies controls in deference to U.S. policy.[114] Most analysts believe, therefore, that smuggling cash and valuable goods (trade-based money laundering) through the Gaza-Sinai tunnels remains a preferred option for Hamas.[115] Increasing scrutiny of charities and perhaps the specter of legal liability have reduced the effectiveness of Hamas financing networks in North America and Europe. Yet, political sensitivity to Hamas's popularity among Arab populations and an inclination to hedge bets on the outcome of the Fatah-Hamas rivalry may make Arab governments less likely to crack down on their own charities, even under U.S. pressure.

Sanctions on Iran and Syria

U.S. and international sanctions against Iran and Syria appear not to have had a significant effect on the two regimes' support for Hamas.[116] However, supporters of the sanctions may believe that even if the sanctions do not compel Iran and Syria to curtail or cease support for Hamas, they might make the two regimes' future support for Hamas less robust and effective. If sanctions weaken Iran and Syria in general terms, one could argue, resources and efforts allocated to helping Hamas and other potential proxies could be redirected to core internal matters related to regime survival. One, however, also might argue the reverse—that weaker Iranian and Syrian regimes could be *more* rather than *less* likely to sponsor potential proxies in order to draw domestic attention away from internal problems and focus it on common external adversaries and issues of regional or international concern.

Anti-Smuggling Efforts in Egypt and Elsewhere

The ongoing Israeli-Egyptian closure regime—consisting of an Israeli naval blockade plus heavy restrictions on the passage of people and goods through land crossings—places most of the focus of other anti-smuggling efforts on the Gaza-Sinai tunnels. Targeting these tunnels, however, remains problematic. The State Department's Country Reports on Terrorism 2009 said that "Israeli officials asserted that Egypt took steps to prevent arms smuggling from the Sinai into Gaza, but can do much more in terms of arresting, prosecuting, and incarcerating smugglers, destroying tunnel infrastructure, and providing socio-economic alternatives for Bedouin involved in smuggling activities."[117]

Egypt, with U.S. support, is nearing completion of an underground fence at its border with Gaza:

> United States army engineers are helping Egypt build the 6-8 km long steel wall, which is scheduled for completion in 2011. It was designed in the US and reportedly fits together like a jigsaw. The border is approximately 14 km long in total, but it is impossible to tunnel under the 5 km stretch approaching the sea, meaning that the wall is designed to cover all potential areas of tunnel construction. It has been bomb proofed and the 40 cm thick steel is super-strength, although these factors, if Abu Murrad [a Qassam Brigades commander] is to be believed, have not proved impervious. The wall is designed to run as deep as 25 m, representing a major construction project.[118]

Many observers, however, remain skeptical because of the ineffectiveness of past anti-smuggling efforts. According to some, smugglers have already penetrated the Egyptian underground border fence and Hamas remains able to count on tunnels for money and weapons.[119] Egypt's inability or unwillingness to fully shut down tunnel traffic shows that external influence on its actions may have distinct limits. Egypt's motivations with regard to the Gaza-Sinai border are unique and complex—influenced by factors such as Hamas's potential to fan Islamist sentiment in Egyptian politics, fear that Israel might seek to transfer responsibility for Gaza to Egypt, Egypt's historical relationship to Gaza, a desire to accommodate traditional economic and cultural practices in Sinai, and comfort with the status quo.[120]

For additional information on U.S. support for Egyptian anti-smuggling measures, see CRS Report RL33003, *Egypt: Background and U.S. Relations*, by Jeremy M. Sharp; and CRS Report RL34346, *The Egypt-Gaza Border and its Effect on Israeli-Egyptian Relations*, by Jeremy M. Sharp.

Some analysts argue that easing or ending the Israeli-Egyptian closure regime, and hence facilitating normalized trade in everyday goods, would facilitate a narrower and potentially more effective military, intelligence, and law enforcement focus on keeping money and weapons out.[121] Although restrictions on non-dual-use goods entering Gaza from Israel were loosened in June 2010, the continued Israeli restriction on exports largely limits the goods legally entering Gaza to those provided through humanitarian aid.

Near the end of Operation Cast Lead in January 2009, the Bush Administration signed a Memorandum of Understanding with the Israeli government pledging additional U.S. support to counter weapons smuggling through a "multi-dimensional, results-oriented effort with a regional focus and international components working in parallel," including efforts to counter societal incentives for smuggling.[122] In March 2009, eight NATO member states agreed with the United States on a Gaza anti-smuggling program that "provides a comprehensive platform for enhanced cooperation and coordination in the areas of information and intelligence sharing; diplomatic engagement; and military and law enforcement activities."[123] Actions ascribed by most reports to Israel have occasionally occurred, including the January 2009 bombing of an apparent arms-smuggling convoy in Sudan moving in the direction of the Egypt-Gaza border[124] and the February 2010 assassination of Qassam Brigades leader Mahmoud al Mahbouh during his trip to allegedly purchase weapons from Iranian sources in Dubai.[125] It is not known whether those or similar actions involved intelligence sharing.

Countering Hamas Media

In March 2010, the Treasury Department named Hamas's Al Aqsa Television as a specially designated global terrorist (SDGT), thus allowing the United States to target Al Aqsa's finances. Three months later, in June 2010, France's official broadcast regulator ordered the French satellite operator Eutelsat to cease broadcast of Al Aqsa (which was carried through one of its satellites by Bahrain-based Noorsat).[126] This occurred following repeated urgings from the European Commission that Al Aqsa's programming violated European anti-incitement laws. It is unclear whether the U.S. designation of Al Aqsa also might have influenced the regulator's decision.

The 111th Congress considered legislation to counter Hamas incitement. H.R. 2278, which passed the House of Representatives on December 8, 2009 (by a vote of 395-3) and was referred to the Senate Foreign Relations Committee, would seek to make it U.S. policy to urge all parties with influence over satellite transmissions to halt broadcasts of Hamas-run Al Aqsa TV and similar channels (including Hezbollah's Al Manar TV) and to consider implementing punitive measures against satellite providers that do not halt such broadcasts. H.R. 2278 also would require an annual presidential report to Congress on "anti-American incitement to violence" that would include a country-by-country breakdown of (1) all media outlets that engage in such incitement and (2) all satellite providers that carry programming classified as such incitement.[127]

Addressing Hamas in a Regional Context

Another possible way to approach Hamas is by seeking to persuade other regional actors to cease support for Hamas or to influence Hamas to act more in accordance with U.S. interests. Although the United States and much of the Western world regards Hamas as a terrorist organization, it is regarded differently in many Middle Eastern states. As discussed above, Hamas is actively supported by Iran and Syria. Most others, including not only Qatar and Turkey, but also those considered to be the United States's closest Arab allies (such as Egypt, Jordan, and Saudi Arabia) acknowledge that Hamas is an integral part of Palestinian society and needs to be involved in both an internal Palestinian political solution and an Israeli-Palestinian peace. They maintain contact with Hamas to varying degrees and are sensitive to the strong support for Hamas believed to exist among their populations.

Oversight

Inclusion of Hamas in Negotiations?[128]

A major open question regarding congressional oversight of Administration policy is whether Hamas, with which U.S. government representatives are currently prohibited from having contact, could be included (either directly or indirectly) in U.S.-facilitated final-status negotiations between Israel and the Palestinians—in the event it wanted to be included. Acquiescing to the inclusion of Hamas in the peace process in some manner could involve its integration or reintegration into existing Palestinian leadership structures such as the PA and the PLO.

The Obama Administration has not departed from the Bush Administration's stance on Hamas. It has conditioned Hamas's participation in the peace process on its meeting the Quartet principles. The U.S. Special Envoy for Middle East Peace, former Senator George Mitchell, routinely cites distinguishing factors between the inclusion of the Irish Republican Army-affiliated Sinn Fein in the talks he brokered over Northern Ireland in the 1990s and the exclusion of Hamas in Israeli-Palestinian negotiations—the main one being Hamas's unwillingness to renounce violence as a means to redress its grievances. A number of meetings by former U.S. officials with senior Hamas leaders since 2009, however, has led some to wonder if the Administration might be open to indirect or secret talks with Hamas even in the absence of its acceptance of the Quartet principles.[129] In an October 2010 *Newsweek* interview, Khaled Meshaal said that one day U.S. officials "will not have any other alternative except to hear from Hamas and listen to Hamas."[130]

Any possibility of U.S. policy shifts regarding Hamas's role, however, could trigger heated debate. Those opposing policy shifts say dealing with Hamas would likely strengthen its political hand at the expense of Abbas and other more moderate Palestinians, allowing the movement to argue that its hardline tactics with Israel are more effective than Abbas's approach. They also might say that any move toward legitimizing Hamas and integrating it into Palestinian organs of governance such as the PLO or the PA could embolden it and other

Palestinian militants to use these organs of governance to mount attacks on Israel—either before or after the establishment of a Palestinian state.[131] Those favoring policy shifts might say that Hamas is less likely to attack Israel if it is made a stakeholder that is accountable to revived Palestinian hopes of a Palestinian state.[132]

The U.S. military perceives the ongoing Israeli-Palestinian conflict as a growing threat to other U.S. interests in the region. In testimony before the Senate Armed Services Committee in March 2010, then U.S. Central Command (CENTCOM) commander (and current commander of the International Security Assistance Force in Afghanistan) General David Petraeus stated:

> The enduring hostilities between Israel and some of its neighbors present distinct challenges to our ability to advance our interests in the AOR [CENTCOM's area of responsibility]. Israeli-Palestinian tensions often flare into violence and large-scale armed confrontations. The conflict foments anti-American sentiment, due to a perception of U.S. favoritism for Israel. Arab anger over the Palestinian question limits the strength and depth of U.S. partnerships with governments and peoples in the AOR and weakens the legitimacy of moderate regimes in the Arab world. Meanwhile, al-Qaeda and other militant groups exploit that anger to mobilize support. The conflict also gives Iran influence in the Arab world through its clients, Lebanese Hizballah and Hamas.[133]

If the military's perception of Israeli-Palestinian tensions as a challenge to its objectives holds or expands, pressure could build for greater efforts to counteract these tensions. Such pressure may in turn lead to more urgent discussion of alternatives to prevent the expansion of Hamas's influence.[134] Some analysts who remain skeptical of Hamas's ultimate capacity for moderation nevertheless believe that the United States could gain some marginal or temporary advantages through some form of direct or indirect engagement of Hamas leaders (or some of them). Such efforts could be part of either a broad "carrots and sticks" strategy or a narrower focus on issues such as improving the economic and humanitarian situation in Gaza.[135] This is partly because these analysts do not see better alternatives for addressing the reality of Hamas and the leverage it holds. They sometimes cite U.S. willingness to engage or to consider engaging Sunni insurgents in Iraq and Taliban elements in Afghanistan as possible precedents.[136] Some high-ranking former Israeli officials, such as Ephraim Halevy (former Mossad director) and Giora Eiland (former head of Israel's National Security Council) also have advocated negotiating with Hamas.[137]

International Dimensions

Future debates might take place over whether the United States should actively dissuade others in the international community—particularly European actors—from engagement with and contributions to Hamas.[138] Although the other Quartet members formally espouse the Quartet principles, Russia has regular dealings with Hamas, legislators from various EU countries have met publicly with Khaled Meshaal and other Hamas leaders, and Hamas representatives claim that high-ranking European officials—including ambassadors—are talking to them regularly.[139] Some analysts believe that Khaled Meshaal's media overtures following President Obama's 2009 Cairo speech were largely aimed at gaining EU (if not U.S.) acceptance of a Hamas role in Palestinian affairs and/or the peace process without having to commit to the Quartet principles. Some might argue that European governments could be useful as go-betweens for Hamas and the United States, while others might counter that the go-between role may have limited utility— using Bush Administration-era European diplomacy with Iran as a case in point.

Activism and discourse on the international stage present additional challenges for U.S. policy regarding Hamas. The *Mavi Marmara* Gaza flotilla incident in May 2010 drew international attention—encouraged by Turkey—to the Gaza closure regime, leading the Obama Administration to persuade Israel to loosen restrictions on the importation of non-dual-use items such as food and medical supplies, and to greater relaxations by Egypt of the Rafah border crossing. This highlighted that even though the United States might be wary of pressing hard to change the status quo in Gaza, lest Hamas is boosted as a result, outside actors and events could in some cases force a response. Additional attempts to break the naval blockade are expected. For further details, see CRS Report R41275, *Israel's Blockade of Gaza, the Mavi Marmara Incident, and Its Aftermath*, by Carol Migdalovitz. The example established by the Turkey-based Islamist non-governmental organization IHH (Foundation for Human Rights and Freedoms and Humanitarian Relief), the lead sponsor of the flotilla, could inspire organizations that sympathize with Hamas, but seek to avoid sanctions for materially supporting it, to find creative ways to provide moral and political support.

Additionally, international investigations of both the May 2010 flotilla incident and Operation Cast Lead, as well as the publicity surrounding these investigations, have demonstrated that the United States has limited capacity to influence the direction of the debate. Attempts by the United States, Israel, and several European states to draw attention to Hamas's alleged culpability for recklessly endangering civilians during Operation Cast Lead, unjust and inhumane treatment of political opponents, and the difficult conditions faced by Gaza's population have generally been countered by representatives of other governments at various U.N. bodies who focus their criticism on Israel for alleged violations of international law.

For example, the *Report of the U.N. Fact Finding Mission on the Gaza Conflict* (commonly known as the "Goldstone Report," after South African judge Richard Goldstone, the mission's leader), which was endorsed by the U.N. Human Rights Council and the U.N. General Assembly in the fall of 2009, has generated controversy because of what many U.S. officials and analysts have deemed its disproportionate and hyperbolic condemnation of Israeli strategy and actions during the conflict.[140] Most critics of the report believe that it did not sufficiently investigate or criticize Hamas for endangering Gaza's civilian population (including its allegedly intentional use of hospitals, schools, mosques, and residential neighborhoods as command and operations centers or as weapons caches, and of its civilians as "human shields"[141]). On November 3, 2009, the House of Representatives passed H.Res. 867 ("Calling on the President and the Secretary of State to oppose unequivocally any endorsement or further consideration of the 'Report of the United Nations Fact Finding Mission on the Gaza Conflict' in multilateral fora") by a vote of 344-36 (with 22 voting "present").

CONCLUSION

Hamas's integral role in Palestinian society and politics is seen by many as problematic because it is devoted to violent opposition to Israel. U.S. efforts to deter, transform, marginalize, or neutralize Hamas have at most achieved temporary or partial success. It is possible to conclude that U.S. and other international support for Israel and the PA/PLO/Fatah has been counterproductive to some extent when comparing Hamas's domestic, regional, and international strength in the early 1990s—measured by factors such as popularity, military force, and leverage with other actors (including Israel and Fatah)—to its current strength. Hamas routinely portrays U.S. efforts to counter its influence as part of an agenda to weaken Palestinians at the expense of Israel, hoping to convince Palestinians of Israel's implacability and of the futility of peace negotiations aimed at Palestinian statehood. Factional and geographical divisions—reflected in Hamas's control of Gaza and the Abbas-led PA's control of the West Bank—present fundamental dilemmas both for prospects for a two-state solution and for the future of Palestinian democracy.

U.S. policy and law reject dealings with and aid to Hamas or any PA government that includes Hamas without the acceptance of conditions that appear antithetical to Hamas's core principles. This could limit the Administration's ability to offer incentives even if regional conditions present possible advantages to doing so for U.S., Israeli, and/or Palestinian interests.

The Israeli-Egyptian closure regime in Gaza and various U.S. and international initiatives constrain and isolate Hamas to a point and may exacerbate internal organizational tensions and tactical disagreements. Overall, however, Hamas maintains a unified public stance on its core principle of violent opposition to Israel. It continues to threaten Israel through its rockets and the possibility of other attacks and to receive assistance from Iran, Syria, Hezbollah, and private individuals and organizations. Additionally, Gaza's poor humanitarian conditions and morale contributes to an image of Hamas-as-victim and to local and international hostility toward Israel. In this context, any U.S. policy decision going forward will likely present considerable risks and difficult trade-offs.

APPENDIX A. HISTORICAL BACKGROUND AND U.S. POLICY

Pre-1987: Hamas's Emergence

Hamas's politicization and militarization can be traced to the first Palestinian intifada ("uprising") that began in the Gaza Strip in 1987 in resistance to the Israeli occupation. Its precursor, Al Mujamma al Islami (known simply as Mujamma, or "The Islamic Center"), was established in Israeli-occupied Gaza in the 1970s under the auspices of the Palestinian Muslim Brotherhood, which had links to Muslim Brotherhood chapters in Egypt and Jordan and later developed links to branches elsewhere—most notably among Palestinian refugees and expatriates living in Kuwait. Sheikh Ahmed Yassin, the group's leader, concentrated the Mujamma's activities on religious and social services, following some models provided by the Egyptian and Jordanian Muslim Brotherhood branches, whose open political activism was repressed by state authorities. Yassin's and his associates' activities—which led to Hamas's founding—were countenanced and sometimes supported by Israel, which believed the Islamists to be a convenient foil for the secular nationalist factions such as Fatah that Israel then perceived to be greater threats.[142]

Motivation to become more politically active grew within Mujamma and the Palestinian Muslim Brotherhood after the 1979 Iranian Revolution led many in the Middle East to imagine the possibilities of political Islam, and in light of increased Palestinian concern for the status of the West Bank, Gaza, and Palestinian refugees following the deferral of the Palestinian question by the Israel-Egypt peace treaty of 1979 and Israel's 1982 invasion of Lebanon that forced the Palestine Liberation Organization (PLO) into exile in Tunisia. The formation in Gaza of other armed resistance groups such as Palestinian Islamic Jihad (PIJ) created pressure for the Palestinian Brotherhood to arm. Yassin's efforts to help the organization stockpile weapons led to his arrest by Israel in 1984, but the Brotherhood's gradual transformation into a militant organization regained momentum following Yassin's release in a 1985 prisoner swap. Yassin and his associates, who proceeded with outside support from their colleagues in Kuwait and elsewhere, officially established Hamas in 1987 when the first Palestinian intifada (or uprising) provided widespread Palestinian support for resistance against Israel.

1987-1995: Gaining Attention

In Hamas's early years during the first intifada, international political attention remained focused on Yasser Arafat's Fatah movement and the PLO, under the rationale that other Palestinian groups had marginal political legitimacy or would take cues from Arafat. When Israel deported several top Hamas leaders to southern Lebanon in December 1992 (along with several other Palestinian Islamists—more than 400 total) in response to a number of Hamas kidnappings and killings of Israeli soldiers, the United States joined human rights organizations in pressuring Israel to repatriate the leaders to the West Bank and Gaza, which it did in late 1993.[143]

Following the signing of the Israel-PLO Declaration of Principles (or Oslo Accord) in September 1993, Hamas joined with other Islamist and some leftist Palestinian factions in rejecting Oslo framework limiting Palestinian national aspirations to the West Bank and Gaza (and thus giving up the national dream for all of "Palestine" as it existed under the British Mandate) and creating multi-tiered zones of Palestinian self-rule circumscribed by a continuing Israeli occupation whose future remained subject to negotiation. Hamas also refused to participate in elections for the new Palestinian Authority (until subsequent developments led to a change of strategy in 2005-2006).

Hamas and other rejectionist groups engaged in sporadic attacks on Israeli targets inside the Palestinian territories. However, following a February 1994 shooting and grenade attack by an Israeli settler that killed 29 and injured several more Palestinians worshiping at the historic Mosque of Abraham in the West Bank city of Hebron, Hamas significantly shifted its strategy. It began a spate of attacks aimed at civilians in Israel, including its first use of suicide bombings in crowded public places.

Meanwhile U.S. Federal Bureau of Investigation investigations, Israeli investigations, and media reporting revealed that Hamas had apparently been recruiting and fundraising on U.S. soil since its inception. As mentioned in the main body of the report (see "Charities and Individuals"), an alleged hub of Hamas financing was the Holy Land Foundation for Relief and Development headquartered near Dallas, Texas, and which had offices in California, New Jersey, and Illinois. As this information became public and Hamas and other Palestinian groups continued attacks on Israeli targets (sometimes killing or injuring U.S. citizens), pressure mounted for the Clinton Administration to act.

1995-2004: Violence and International Opposition

In January 1995, then President Bill Clinton signed Executive Order 12947, which blocked the assets of and prohibited U.S. transactions with Hamas and 11 other specially designated terrorist organizations (SDTs) deemed threats to the Middle East peace process, including the Israeli extremist groups Kach and Kahane Chai.[144]

Meanwhile, Israel was vigorously pursuing operatives from Hamas and pressuring the newly formed Palestinian Authority (PA) led by Yasser Arafat to crack down as well. Israel had allowed the PA to establish internal security forces in Gaza and the West Bank from former PLO and Fatah militias. Arafat encouraged the formation of additional paramilitary and intelligence organizations populated with many close Arafat associates that Israel tolerated (despite their not being sanctioned under the Oslo agreements) with the hope that they would help neutralize Hamas and other terrorist organizations. In addition to targeting Hamas militants, the PA forces periodically suppressed the activities of Hamas-affiliated charities and social organizations.

In early 1996, following another round of Hamas suicide bombings, the United States became actively involved in fostering Israeli-Palestinian security cooperation in combating terrorism. Likely determining that the paramilitary and intelligence organizations with personal ties to Arafat and patronage networks were more relevant than the official police, the Clinton Administration reportedly began providing these organizations with tens of millions of dollars in covert assistance through the Central Intelligence Agency (CIA), according to the *New York Times*.[145] The European Union also reportedly began a counterterrorism program.[146] Additionally, in October 1997, the State Department listed Hamas as a Foreign Terrorist Organization (FTO), shortly after a major September suicide bombing in a Jerusalem pedestrian shopping area that left one U.S. citizen among the dead and several others among the injured.

The fruits of U.S. counterterrorism assistance to the PA continue to be debated. Although Hamas suicide and other attacks did not immediately cease, they abated from the end of 1998 until the second Palestinian intifada (also known as the Al Aqsa intifada) began in September 2000. The effects of U.S. assistance are unclear partly because of its covert nature, and because of several other intervening factors—including Israeli counterterrorism actions and ongoing Israeli-Palestinian negotiations. Some observers point to the drop-off in attacks as evidence that U.S. assistance helped the PA prevent and deter terrorist attacks until the collapse of peace process negotiations in 2000. Others believe that although PA capacities were enhanced, Arafat's on-again, off-again crackdowns on Hamas and other militants were of little lasting value. Suspects detained to placate U.S. and Israeli pressure were often released shortly thereafter due to internal political pressure on Arafat and the PA not to appear to be "collaborating" with the Israelis or because of insufficient evidence owing to the political nature of the arrests.

Upon the outbreak of the second intifada in September 2000, Hamas demonstrated that it still had the capacity to carry out attacks inside Israel. Following Al Qaeda's attacks against multiple U.S. targets on September 11, 2001, then President George W. Bush issued

Executive Order 13224 authorizing his Administration to take action domestically and in concert with international actors to suppress the activities and block the financing of a list of specially designated global terrorist individuals and organizations (SDGTs). Hamas was added to the list in October 2001, and the Holy Land Foundation for Relief and Development was added in December 2001. Six Hamas leaders (including Khaled Meshaal, Musa Abu Marzouk, and Osama Hamdan—see **Appendix C**), along with five Hamas-affiliated charities (four based in Europe, one based in Lebanon) were later added in August 2003.[147] Al Aqsa Television and Hamas's Islamic National Bank were added in March 2010.[148] As discussed in the main body of the report (see "Charities and Individuals"), a Hamas-related, Saudi Arabia-based organization known as the Union of Good was added to the list in November 2008.

Although some U.S. counterterrorism assistance to the Arafat-led PA continued during the second intifada, such assistance was complicated by the fact that offshoots (known as Tanzim and the Al Aqsa Martyrs' Brigades) from Arafat's own Fatah faction that included former PA security force commanders were participating in attacks on Israeli military and civilian targets—possibly with Arafat's tacit approval. Following the deadliest attack of the intifada in March 2002, a Hamas suicide bombing of the Park Hotel in Netanya during a Passover seder that killed 22 Israelis and injured over 100 more, Israel mounted Operation Defensive Shield. During March and April of 2002, the Israel Defense Forces (IDF) moved into major West Bank cities, established martial law, destroyed much of the PA's security and civilian infrastructure, and besieged Arafat's compound in Ramallah. In the post-September 11 environment, the Bush Administration acquiesced to Israel's characterization of Operation Defensive Shield as a necessary counterterrorism operation. In June 2002, President Bush indicated that Arafat was no longer a trusted part of the peace process, and that future U.S. support for the PA would need to come through another leader.[149]

Hamas did not escape Israeli countermeasures. Israel embarked on a targeted assassination campaign, killing many top Hamas leaders in Gaza between 2002-2004, including co-founders Sheikh Ahmed Yassin and Abdel Aziz al Rantissi. As a natural consequence, the geographical locus of Hamas's leadership shifted to Khaled Meshaal and the political bureau in Damascus, where it is less vulnerable to Israeli assassination operations than in Gaza. Even though Hamas had to absorb the shock of losing much of its founding core, its reputation and institutions were strengthened relative to Fatah and the PA owing to the damage done to PA infrastructure and security institutions and to public confidence in Palestinian leadership. Additionally, Hamas was able to elevate its cause in the eyes of many Palestinians by portraying its assassinated leaders as lionized martyrs.

2005-2006: Israel's Gaza Disengagement and the Palestinian Legislative Council Election Campaign

During the second intifada, the popularity of Hamas began to increase as Fatah's fell. At the same time, the Israel Defense Forces (IDF) effectively dismantled the security organizations and infrastructure of the Fatah-dominated PA, which had the unintended consequence of leaving Fatah more vulnerable to domestic security threats. Cognizant of its increasing strength and popularity relative to Fatah, Hamas's leaders made the momentous decision in the spring of 2005 to participate in Palestinian Authority elections even as they maintained Hamas's rejection of the principle of Israeli-Palestinian agreement that had established the PA. Hamas made a strong showing in a series of municipal elections held in 2005. Still, many observers were surprised when Hamas won a controlling majority in the PLC in its first-ever national election campaign in January 2006, leading to its heightened international profile and current situation.

After Yasser Arafat's death in November 2004, the United States encouraged the emergence of a successor committed to the peace process. With the central figure of Palestinian nationalism gone, Hamas saw an opportunity. Mahmoud Abbas was elected to succeed Arafat as PA President in January 2005, an election that Hamas did not contest. Hamas had not participated in the initial Palestinian Legislative Council (PLC) elections of 1996 because of its opposition to the Oslo framework that created the PA and PLC. Yet, by late 2004, the situation was different. Hamas may have been feeling pressure to transform its international image from that of a militant group operating in the shadows to that of a political movement with domestic legitimacy. U.S. and international efforts to curb Hamas's activities and financing, combined with Israeli opposition, also may have played a part in Hamas's thinking, which one Palestinian analyst in Gaza explained as follows in 2006:

> For two years now Hamas has been feeling that the jihadi approach was reaching a dead end.... It was classified as a terrorist movement by the US and some other countries. From this point it decided to log into the Palestinian political system. It felt besieged by the outside world. They froze all their money and stopped all its institutions. So they started seeking new legitimacy through the ballot box.... Not, I think, because they believe in democracy, but because they want legitimacy, to say to the world that they are a party or a movement that represents the Palestinian people through democratic elections.[150]

The 2006 PLC election (the first PLC election in 10 years) took place at a time when the Bush Administration was advocating for democratic elections throughout the Arab world, including in post-invasion Iraq, Lebanon, Egypt, and the Gulf. Abbas wanted to include Hamas in order to erase all doubt that Fatah remained the Palestinian people's clear choice to succeed Arafat, and Hamas agreed to participate as the "Change and Reform" party. The United States, the international community, and Israel acceded to this plan without preconditions for Hamas's involvement, partly because of the plan's popularity among Palestinians and the outside actors' desire to avoid interfering in internal Palestinian politics, and partly because the outside actors underestimated Hamas's prospects. Most pollsters and observers also underestimated Hamas's prospects, even if some had misgivings and forecast a close election.[151] Many analysts believe that Hamas received a boost from Israel's August 2005 disengagement from Gaza because it was amenable to the interpretation that Hamas precipitated it through resistance.[152]

The Bush Administration provided direct financial assistance to the PA to boost its public profile during the run-up to the elections, knowing that Palestinians closely identified the PA with Fatah given their overlapping leadership cadres. The U.S. Agency for International Development (USAID) allocated $2 million—purportedly at least double Hamas's entire campaign budget—for this media, public outreach, and public services initiative. It was coordinated by a U.S. contractor and Palestinian subcontractors through Abbas's office. According to the *Washington Post*, some involved in the project debated its wisdom, and the *Post* itself expressed concerns:

The program highlights the central challenge facing the Bush administration as it promotes democracy in the Middle East. Free elections in the Arab world, where most countries have been run for years by unelected autocracies or unchallenged parties like Fatah, often result in strong showings by radical Islamic movements opposed to the policies of the United States and to its chief regional ally, Israel. But in attempting to manage the results, the administration risks undermining the democratic goals it is promoting.[153]

When elections took place in January 2006, Hamas only outpolled Fatah in the party-list vote 44% to 41%. Yet, Hamas deployed a superior campaign strategy that took advantage of division and complacency among Fatah and its candidates to win individual geographical districts in greater proportion to Hamas's overall share of the vote and secure a majority of seats in the PLC. It is unclear whether U.S. involvement made a difference, but the perception that Hamas lunged ahead at campaign's end in the face of significant U.S. backing for its opponent fed claims that the U.S. strategy had backfired with the Palestinian public, negatively impacting views of U.S. competence in the region.[154]

2006-2010: Confronting an Empowered Hamas

Once Hamas's electoral victory was clear, Israel insisted that it would not cooperate with a PA that included a hostile Hamas, even discontinuing transfer of customs revenues it collected for the PA. The United States and other members of the international Quartet (European Union, Russia, United Nations) announced that Hamas would have to meet three conditions in order for a PA under its control to receive aid and political support: (1) recognize Israel's right to exist, (2) renounce violence, and (3) accept prior Israeli-Palestinian agreements.

Hamas and its incoming government ministers—led by Prime Minister Ismail Haniyeh—rejected the Quartet principles, and therefore began their term leading the PA government without access to U.S. and European aid. They turned to Gulf states, Iran, and Russia (despite Russia's status as a member of the Quartet), all of which were willing to provide funding under the rationale that Hamas had entered power legitimately through the established political process. The United States's and European Union's unwillingness to provide financial assistance to the elected government, on the heels of their support for the elections, was seen by many analysts as inconsistent with the principle of democracy both claimed to advocate for the region.[155]

Not wanting to contribute to possible destabilization of the West Bank and Gaza through an aid cutoff, Congress and the Bush Administration devised a way to bypass the Hamas-led PA ministries in delivering aid to Palestinians.[156] They continued humanitarian and development assistance through UNRWA and other international and non-governmental organizations that were subjected to increasing levels of U.S. government scrutiny to guard against enriching Hamas or its supporters.

Factional tensions worsened considerably following Fatah's defeat at the hands of Hamas. Although Abbas and Fatah formally accepted the PLC election results, Fatah loyalists with key roles in the PA civil service and security forces refused to accede to Hamas's control and actively sought to undermine it. The rivalry played out dramatically in Gaza, where Hamas was more strongly rooted than in the West Bank, and where the recent Israeli disengagement had left an uncertain security situation amid widespread political corruption and clan-dominated lawlessness.

Congress and the Administration addressed this situation by enacting the Palestinian Anti-Terrorism Act of 2006 (P.L. 109-446), which approved funding PA offices and security forces under the control of President Abbas, as contrasted with those controlled by Hamas-led government ministries. Lines of command and control over existing PA forces remained blurred, a legacy from Yasser Arafat's rule, so Fatah played on the loyalties of personnel to align most of the security forces with Abbas, and Hamas organized its own shadow "Executive Force" from its loyalists in Gaza. Instead of containing the situation, these developments appear to have escalated it.

Tensions did not abate significantly after the Mecca Accord of February 2007, a Saudi Arabia-brokered power-sharing deal that brought some Fatah members and independents into the Hamasled government. This may have been the case in part because the United States and European Union did not believe the agreement changed the nature of the PA government sufficiently to justify the resumption of direct budgetary assistance to the PA.

The story of Hamas's takeover of the Gaza Strip and subsequent dismissal from power in the West Bank by Abbas in June 2007 is told in different ways from different perspectives. Some have cited U.S. deliberations with Abbas to support the idea that an offensive move against Hamas's government and security forces in Gaza was imminent.[157] Others say that Hamas was judiciously biding its time for the right moment to strike, but debate whether it intended to seize power in Gaza or simply weaken the PA forces targeting it.[158] Most can agree on certain basic facts. U.S., Canadian, and European training and consulting was provided to strengthen PA forces—headed by Fatah strongman Muhammad Dahlan—loyal to Abbas in Gaza. These forces, still systematically weakened from the second intifada, were less-than-optimally equipped, organized, and disciplined. When directly engaged by the Qassam Brigades and other Hamas-led forces, the PA forces loyal to Abbas gave way within a week, with many personnel fleeing to the West Bank or abstaining from the fight (including some who later chose to stay with the security forces after Hamas assumed their command). Hamas then seized the opportunity to secure full control over Gaza.[159]

The subsequent bifurcation of Palestinian leadership in the West Bank and Gaza resulted in U.S. and international support for the "caretaker" West Bank PA government led by Prime Minister Salam Fayyad that Abbas appointed, and even in renewed Israeli ties with the PA and PLO. Support for the PA remains a strategy the international community, with some exceptions, generally pursues in tandem with isolation of Hamas. Many Palestinians fear that the longer the West Bank and Gaza remain under divided leadership, the less likely restoration of unitary government over both territories will be, and the easier it could be for the societies to drift apart economically and culturally as well. As presidential, legislative, and even local elections continue to be postponed, some analysts warn of growing authoritarianism in both territories.[160]

Facing international isolation and the Israeli-Egyptian border closure regime, Hamas focused its energies on consolidating its control within Gaza. To preserve its status as an organization committed to resistance against an Israel that it cannot confront easily in a conventional warfare setting, Hamas has relied on smuggling rockets and mortars through the tunnels and firing them in concert with other militant groups. When these attacks led to Operation Cast Lead in 2008- 2009, Hamas's forces were shown to be little match operationally for the IDF, but relatively few of its personnel were killed and the IDF did not attempt to eliminate its presence in Gaza or seize control of the territory. Hamas has portrayed its survival as victory, but many believe that Hamas did not expect the intensity of the Israeli operation and genuinely feared for the survival of its rule in Gaza, and, as a result, has since been more cautious about possible provocations.

U.S. humanitarian assistance to Gaza and comprehensive assistance to the West Bank continues, as does U.S. political support and assistance for anti-smuggling efforts on land and at sea. Under the various terrorist designations it has attached to Hamas, the United States collaborates with Israel and other governments to thwart Hamas financing and attack capabilities. Attempts at forwarding Israel-PLO peace negotiations are being facilitated by the United States, with Hamas conspicuously uninvited. Nevertheless, events such as the May 2010 *Mavi Marmara* flotilla incident and the reaction it provoked complicate U.S. policy towards Hamas because they demonstrate divisions in international approaches toward Gaza.

APPENDIX B. KEY DATES IN HAMAS'S HISTORY

	Chronology
1946	Establishment of Palestinian Muslim Brotherhood
1948	Arab-Israeli war (Israeli war of independence/Palestinian nakba, or "catastrophe") leaves West Bank under Jordanian administration and Gaza Strip under Egyptian administration
1967	Six-Day Arab-Israeli war; Israel occupies West Bank (including East Jerusalem), Gaza Strip, Sinai Peninsula, and Golan Heights
1970-1971	Jordan evicts PLO through "Black September" military operations; PLO leadership relocates to Lebanon
1973	Yom Kippur War between Israel and Egypt Al Mujamma al Islami (the Islamic Center) established by Sheikh Ahmed Yassin and Muslim Brotherhood associates in Gaza Strip
1978	Muslim Brotherhood helps establish Islamic University in Gaza
1979	Israel-Egypt peace treaty; Palestinian question deferred Iranian Revolution
Early 1980s	Muslim Brotherhood branches in Gaza and West Bank develop ties with each other and with branches outside of the Palestinian territories— especially those with heavy representation from the Palestinian diaspora (such as in Kuwait)
1981	Palestinian Islamic Jihad established in Gaza Strip
1982	Israel invades Lebanon; PLO leadership forced to relocate to Tunisia
1984	Yassin imprisoned by Israel
1985	Yassin released in prisoner exchange
1987	Outbreak of first Palestinian intifada Establishment of Hamas as political and military resistance organization in Palestinian territories
1988	Hamas publishes its founding charter

Appendix B. (Continued).

	Chronology
1989	Yassin and several other Hamas leaders imprisoned by Israel in response to Hamas attacks on Israeli military targets (first of many waves of detentions and subsequent releases of Hamas leaders in Gaza and West Bank); Hamas outside leadership becomes more prominent
1990	Yassin sentenced to life in prison
1990-1991	Saddam Hussein's Iraq invades and occupies Kuwait and is expelled by a U.S.-led coalition in Operation Desert Storm; Hamas's outside leadership relocates from Kuwait to Jordan
1992-1993	Over 400 Hamas leaders and other Palestinian Islamists deported to southern Lebanon by Israel after the abduction and killing of an Israeli policeman; repatriated as a result of pressure from the United States and human rights organizations; consequently Hamas's leadership outside the Palestinian territories is elevated to a more important role within the movement
1993	Signing of Israel-PLO Declaration of Principles (Oslo Accord); Hamas and other Palestinian factions reject the agreement
1994	Israeli settler Baruch Goldstein kills 29 Palestinians at Mosque of Abraham in Hebron, West Bank Hamas retaliates with first suicide bombings in Israel; similar attacks will continue periodically before abating in 1997 Establishment of Palestinian Authority with Yasser Arafat's arrival in Gaza Israel-Jordan peace treaty complicates Hamas's ongoing presence in Jordan
1995	United States designates Hamas and 11 other organizations obstructing the Middle East peace process as specially designated terrorists (SDTs) Musa Abu Marzouk, then Hamas politburo chief, arrested at New York's Kennedy Airport and remains in U.S. custody for nearly two years; Khaled Meshaal eventually succeeds him Assassination of Israeli prime minister Yitzhak Rabin by Israeli law student Yigal Amir
1996	Hamas kills 59 Israelis in Jerusalem, Tel Aviv, and Ashqelon in four suicide bombings (one in collaboration with Palestinian Islamic Jihad) within a two-week period in February and March
1997	Failed Israeli Mossad assassination attempt of Meshaal in Amman, Jordan following two Hamas street-side suicide bombings (21 killed) that summer in Jerusalem; Yassin released in exchange for release of Mossad agents in Jordanian custody State Department designates Hamas a Foreign Terrorist Organization (FTO)
1999	Hamas's politburo leaders imprisoned in Jordan and ultimately expelled to Doha, Qatar
2000	Failure to reach Israel-PLO final-status agreement at Camp David summit Second Palestinian intifada (Al Aqsa intifada) begins

	Chronology
2001	Hamas reinstitutes suicide bombings and other attacks on Israel; first rockets fired on Israeli targets from Gaza Hamas's politburo leaders relocate to Damascus, Syria, where Hamas's head shura council is located September 11 attacks in the United States by Al Qaeda United States designates Hamas a specially designated global terrorist (SDGT) in October (will add various Hamas leaders and affiliated organizations to SDGT in subsequent months and years)
2002	Hamas and Palestinian Islamic Jihad carry out suicide bombing at Park Hotel in Netanya during Passover seder, killing 30
2003	Council of the European Union adds Hamas to its consolidated list of terrorist organizations
2004	Hamas co-founders Yassin and Abdel Aziz al Rantissi are assassinated within less than a month of each other by Israeli airstrikes in Gaza Death of Yasser Arafat
2005	Hamas decides to participate in Palestinian elections; makes strong showing in municipal elections Israel withdraws its troops and settlers from Gaza Strip; resulting Palestinian rivalry for security primacy in Gaza begins
2006	Hamas wins majority in Palestinian Legislative Council election Hamas forms PA government under Prime Minister Ismail Haniyeh; United States and European Union cease aid to PA ministries, instead funneling aid through PA President Mahmoud Abbas or alternative mechanisms and organizations Palestinian militants abduct Israeli corporal Gilad Shalit near Gaza border and deliver him into Hamas's custody, helping spark limited conflict in Gaza Strip between Israel and Palestinian militants (including Hamas) Israel engages in conflict with Hezbollah in southern Lebanon (at the same time the conflict in Gaza continued) following Hezbollah's abduction and killing of Israeli soldiers near the Lebanese border
2007	Hamas and Fatah reach Mecca Accord for power-sharing PA government; United States and European Union refuse to resume aid to PA ministries After armed clash with PA/Fatah forces, Hamas gains control of Gaza Strip; Abbas dismisses Hamas ministers from PA government and appoints non-Hamas government headed by Prime Minister Salam Fayyad; PLC loses quorum to do business; Palestinian rocket attacks from Gaza on Israel and Israeli-Egyptian closure regime both intensify Israel declares Gaza a "hostile entity"
2008	Hamas breaks open Gaza-Egypt border crossing at Rafah; tens of thousands of Gazans pour into Egypt temporarily Hamas and Israel agree to informal cease-fire (brokered by Egypt) Cease-fire ends; Hamas resumes major rocket fire into Israel
2008-2009	Operation Cast Lead (Gaza conflict with Israel)

Appendix B. (Continued).

	Chronology
2009	Senator John Kerry and Representatives Brian Baird and Keith Ellison visit Gaza to assess humanitarian needs and to meet with U.N. officials (not Hamas officials); first congressional visits to Gaza since October 2003 roadside bombing of U.S. convoy by non-Hamas militants Goldstone Report released PA elections scheduled for president and for the Palestinian Legislative Council in January 2010 are canceled after Hamas announces it will not permit balloting in Gaza; PLO Central Council indefinitely extends terms of Mahmoud Abbas as PA President and of Palestinian Legislative Council
2010	Qassam Brigades operative Mahmoud al Mahbouh is murdered in a Dubai hotel room, an action ascribed by most reports to Israel MV Mavi Marmara flotilla incident and aftermath; Israel and Egypt ease Gaza closure regime (Israel allows greater importation of non-dual-use items) Coinciding with relaunch of direct Israel-PLO negotiations, Hamas militants stage two shooting attacks against Israeli settlers in the West Bank, killing four and injuring two

APPENDIX C. MAJOR HAMAS LEADERS

Political Leaders

Outside of Gaza

Khaled Meshaal[161]

Khaled Meshaal, based in Damascus, is the chief of Hamas's politburo. He was named a specially designated global terrorist (SDGT) by the Treasury Department in August 2003.

Born in 1956 near Ramallah, Meshaal (alternate spellings: Mishal, Mashal) moved with his family to Jordan in 1967 following Israel's occupation of the West Bank in the Six-Day War. As a student and schoolteacher in Kuwait, he became a leader in the Palestinian Islamist movement. After the founding of Hamas in 1987, Meshaal led the Kuwaiti branch of the organization, then moved to Jordan in 1991 after Iraq's invasion of Kuwait. He took over as Hamas politburo chief following the 1995 U.S. arrest of then chief Musa Abu Marzouk.

In September 1997, Meshaal was targeted in Amman by the Mossad (Israel's foreign intelligence service) in an assassination attempt that became a major international incident—culminating in King Hussein of Jordan threatening to abrogate the 1994 Israel-Jordan peace treaty in order to get Binyamin Netanyahu (in his first stint as Israeli prime minister) to supply an antidote to the nerve toxin to which Meshaal had been exposed.[162] After the Hamas leadership was expelled from Jordan in November 1999, Meshaal first moved to Doha, Qatar, then settled two years later in Damascus, Syria. He became acknowledged as Hamas's overall leader in 2004, following the assassination of Abdel Aziz al Rantissi by Israel. Meshaal also serves as Hamas's top diplomat, traveling and meeting with various governments and political leaders (including his political rival Mahmoud Abbas, Iran, Turkey, Arab countries, Russia, European legislators, and former U.S. President Jimmy Carter).

Musa Abu Marzouk

Musa Abu Marzouk, born in 1951 in the Rafah refugee camp in Gaza, and now based in Damascus, is a deputy chief of Hamas's politburo. He was named an SDT in August 1995 and an SDGT in August 2003 by the Treasury Department.

Marzouk, a legal U.S. resident for 15 years during the 1980s and early 1990s, also played a key role in defining the relationship between Hamas's Gaza organization and its outside political leadership following the mass arrests of Hamas leaders in Gaza during the first intifada. Marzouk himself headed the outside leadership until 1995. He is credited as the mastermind behind the construction of Hamas's financial networks in the United States, including involvement with the Holy Land Foundation for Relief and Development. Marzouk was detained in New York's Kennedy Airport in July 1995 (after arriving on a flight from Jordan) following the naming of Hamas as an SDT in January 1995. Israel sought his extradition, but later dropped its request due to retaliation concerns and Marzouk rejoined Hamas's political bureau in Jordan in 1997, becoming deputy chief to Khaled Meshaal.

Osama Hamdan

Osama Hamdan, a member of Hamas's politburo, has led Hamas's branch office in Beirut, Lebanon since 1998, and has been a SDGT since August 2003. He was born in 1965 in the Bureij refugee camp in Gaza, but became active in Islamist movements while a student and young professional in Jordan and Kuwait. He relocated to Beirut after having spent six years during the 1990s based in Iran.

Hamdan often represents Hamas in Palestinian factional talks with Fatah and in discussions with Western officials. He and Mahmoud al Zahar have reportedly met periodically with former U.S. officials since 2009.

In Gaza

Ismail Haniyeh

Ismail Haniyeh is Hamas's "prime minister" in Gaza.

Haniyeh was born in or around 1955 in the Shati refugee camp in the Gaza Strip. In 1989, he was imprisoned for three years by Israeli authorities for participation in the first intifada. Following his release in 1992, he was deported to Lebanon along with approximately 400 other Hamas activists, but was eventually allowed to return to Gaza in 1993.[163] Upon his return, he was appointed dean of the Islamic University, and became the leader of Hamas's student movement. He was closely associated with Hamas co-founder and spiritual leader Sheikh Ahmed Yassin, and, following the assassination of Yassin and much of the Hamas leadership in 2004, became a prominent Hamas leader in Gaza.

Haniyeh favored Hamas's participation in the 2006 PLC elections, and headed the Hamas list of candidates. Following Hamas's victory, he served as PA prime minister from March 2006 until June 2007. Following Hamas's takeover of Gaza and its dismissal from the PA government in the West Bank, Hamas has continued to insist that Haniyeh is the PA prime minister, and he is treated as such in Gaza. Some observers believe that Haniyeh is more responsive to political realities than Hamas's leadership-in-exile, and use this rationale to argue that Haniyeh and/or other Gaza-based Hamas leaders might be persuaded to moderate their goals and tactics, even though he continues to advocate violent resistance against Israel. In Palestinian opinion polls for hypothetical presidential elections, Haniyeh consistently gets the most support among Hamas leaders, and sometimes runs close to Mahmoud Abbas in head-to-head pairings.

Mahmoud al Zahar

Mahmoud al Zahar, is a medical doctor born in 1945 and based in Gaza, and also was one of the 400-plus deportees to Lebanon in 1992. Thought to have close ties with the politburo in Damascus, Zahar appears to have played a key role in the decision for Hamas to participate in the 2006 PLC elections. After being elected to the PLC, he served as foreign minister from 2006- 2007 in the Hamas-led PA government, and continues to serve in that capacity for the Hamas-led regime in Gaza. He is one of the most outspoken members of Hamas's Gaza leadership with international media.

Ahmed Yousef

Ahmed Yousef (born 1950 in Gaza) is deputy foreign minister and a prominent media spokesman for the Hamas-led regime. Yousef lived in the United States from the 1980s until his return to Gaza around 2005. While a U.S. resident, Yousef earned multiple graduate degrees, and then served as director of the allegedly Hamas-linked United Association for Studies and Research in northern Virginia and as editor-in-chief of the *Middle East Affairs Journal*. One journalist has described Yousef's role in Hamas as follows:

> On the one hand, some people regard him as the representative of the moderate face of the movement capable of interacting with the world, while others believe his proposals are different to those held by the rest of the movement's leadership.... In any case, we are confronted by a talented man who bears the ideology of Hamas and deals with the media in an 'American' manner.[164]

Fathi Hamad

Fathi Hamad (born 1961 in Gaza) is the Hamas-led regime's interior minister, with charge over the regime's security forces. He became interior minister in 2009 after his predecessor Said Siyam was killed in an Israeli airstrike during Operation Cast Lead. Previously, he was the director of Hamas's public affairs department, which includes Hamas's Al Aqsa satellite television channel. He was elected to the PLC in 2006.

Hamad is thought by many to be a proponent of using both media and the security forces to effect greater Islamization of Gaza, although he has issued contradictory statements on the subject. A statement he made in 2008 has fueled allegations by Israel and others that Hamas uses civilians in Gaza as "human shields" to enable its militancy.[165]

Military Leaders in Gaza

Ahmed al Jaabari

Ahmed al Jaabari is thought to be the Gaza-based commander of the Izz Al Din al Qassam Brigades, Hamas's military wing. Jaabari, who has reportedly escaped multiple assassination attempts, does not make public appearances. Muhammad Deif, Jaabari's predecessor (and possibly still his equal or superior), has kept an even lower profile in recent years, possibly as the result of injury from a 2006 Israeli airstrike.[166]

Raed al Atar

Raed al Atar is the commander of the Rafah company of the Qassam Brigades. His command is important due to Rafah being the destination point for the smuggling tunnels from Egypt. Reports claim that Atar authorized the August 2010 firing of Grad-style rockets from the Sinai Peninsula at Eilat, Israel and Aqaba, Jordan, possibly raising questions about Atar's accountability and leverage within the Qassam Brigades chain of command and Hamas political-military structure.

APPENDIX D. CONGRESSIONAL ACTIONS PERTAINING TO HAMAS

Table D-1. Current Legislation Pertaining to Hamas

Item	Brief Description	Disposition
Consolidated Appropriations Act, 2010 (P.L. 111-117)	Prohibits U.S. aid to Hamas and its affiliates and to any PA government with Hamas ministers unless all government ministers accept the Section 620K (from P.L. 109-446) principles: (1) recognition of the "Jewish state of Israel's right to exist," (2) acceptance of previous Israeli-Palestinian agreements.	Enacted December 16, 2009 Extended through December 3, 2010 by Continuing Appropriations Act, 2011 (P.L. 111-242)
Palestinian Anti-Terrorism Act of 2006 (P.L. 109-446)	Places various conditions and restrictions on U.S. aid intended for a "Hamas-controlled Palestinian Authority," including the Section 620K principles. Permits U.S. aid to be provided to non-Hamas-controlled branches of the PA under certain conditions.	Enacted December 21, 2006
Syria Accountability and Lebanese Sovereignty Restoration Act of 2003 (P.L. 108-175)	Requires President to levy sanctions against Syria unless he/she certifies that Syria has met certain conditions, with an end to support and safe haven for Hamas being one of them.	Enacted December 12, 2003

Table D-1. (Continued).

Item	Brief Description	Disposition
Iran Sanctions Act (originally titled the Iran and Libya Sanctions Act of 1996) (P.L. 104-172, as amended, including by P.L. 107-24, P.L. 109-293, and P.L. 111-195)	Requires President to levy sanctions against Iran and entities that engage in certain transactions unless he/she certifies that Iran has met certain conditions, with Iran's removal from the U.S. list of state sponsors of terrorism being one of them.	Enacted August 5, 1996 Most recently amended July 1, 2010 by Comprehensive Iran Sanctions, Divestment, and Accountability Act of 2010 (P.L. 111-195)

Table D-2. Selected Bills and Resolutions Pertaining to Hamas

Item	Brief Description	Disposition
S.Res. 571	Calls for the immediate and unconditional release of Israeli soldier Gilad Shalit held captive by Hamas, and for other purposes.	Passed Senate June 28, 2010 (Unanimous consent)
H.Res. 1359	Calls for the immediate and unconditional release of Israeli soldier Gilad Shalit, who is held captive by Hamas, and for other purposes.	Passed House June 24, 2010 (Voice vote)
UNRWA Humanitarian Accountability Act H.R. 5065	Would withhold U.S. contributions to UNRWA unless Secretary of State certifies every 180 days that (1) no UNRWA official or employee belongs to a terrorist organization, engages in incitement, or uses his/her position for political purposes; (2) no UNRWA recipient of funds or loans belongs to a terrorist organization; (3) UNRWA facilities and educational materials are not used by terrorist organizations or for purposes of incitement; (4) UNRWA implements vetting and oversight mechanisms and submits to regular independent third-party audits; and (5) UNRWA is not affiliated with financial institutions believed to be engaged or complicit in terrorist financing or money laundering. Would limit U.S. annual contributions to UNRWA to the lesser of (1) 22% of UNRWA's budget, (2) the largest annual contribution made by an Arab League member state, (3) a contribution that makes the U.S. percentage contribution to UNRWA's budget equal to the U.S. percentage contribution to the U.N. High Commissioner for Refugees' budget.	Referred to House Foreign Affairs Committee April 20, 2010

Item	Brief Description	Disposition
H.R. 2278	Would seek to make it U.S. policy to urge all parties with influence over satellite transmissions to halt broadcasts of Hamas-run Al Aqsa TV and similar channels (including Hezbollah's Al Manar TV) and to name as SDGTs satellite providers that do not halt such broadcasts. Would also require an annual presidential report to Congress on "anti-American incitement to violence" that would include a country-by-country breakdown of (1) all media outlets that engage in such incitement and (2) all satellite providers that carry programming classified as such incitement.	Passed House December 8, 2009 (395-3) Referred to Senate Foreign Relations Committee
H.Res. 867	Calls on the President and the Secretary of State to oppose unequivocally any endorsement or further consideration of the Report of the United Nations Fact Finding Mission on the Gaza Conflict (also known as the Goldstone Report) in multilateral fora.	Passed House November 3, 2009 (344-36)
H.Con.Res. 29	Expresses the sense of Congress that the United Nations should take immediate steps to improve the transparency and accountability of UNRWA to ensure that it is not providing funding, employment, or other support to terrorists.	Referred to House Foreign Affairs Committee January 28, 2009
H.Res. 34	Recognizes Israel's right to defend itself against attacks from Gaza, reaffirming the United States' strong support for Israel, and supporting the Israeli-Palestinian peace process	Passed House January 9, 2009 (390-5)
S.Res. 10	Recognizes the right of Israel to defend itself against attacks from Gaza, reaffirming the United States's strong support for Israel in its battle with Hamas, and supporting the Israeli-Palestinian peace process.	Passed Senate January 8, 2009 (Unanimous consent)
H.Res. 1069	Condemns Hamas's Al Aqsa TV (among other Middle East TV channels, including Hezbollah's Al Manar) for anti-Israel, anti-Semitic, and anti-U.S. incitement; calling upon satellite TV providers Arabsat (Arab League-owned, Saudi-based) and Eutelsat (privately owned, France-based) to cease transmitting Al Aqsa programming.	Passed House September 9, 2008 (409-1)
H.Res. 951	Condemns the ongoing Palestinian rocket attacks on Israeli civilians by Hamas and other Palestinian terrorist organizations, and for other purposes.	Passed House March 5, 2008 (404-1)

Table D-2. (Continued).

Item	Brief Description	Disposition
S.Res. 92	Calls for the immediate and unconditional release of soldiers of Israel held captive by Hamas and Hezbollah.	Passed Senate April 12, 2007 (Unanimous consent)
H.Res. 107	Calls for the immediate and unconditional release of Israeli soldiers held captive by Hamas and Hezbollah, and for other purposes	Passed House March 13, 2007 (Voice vote)
H.Res. 921	Condemns the recent attacks against the State of Israel, holding terrorists and their state sponsors accountable for such attacks, supporting Israel's right to defend itself, and for other purposes.	Passed House July 20, 2006 (410-8)
S.Res. 534	Condemns Hezbollah and Hamas and their state sponsors and supporting Israel's exercise of its right to self-	Passed Senate July 18, 2006 (Voice vote)
H.Con.Res. 338	Expresses the sense of Congress regarding the activities of Islamist terrorist organizations in the Western Hemisphere.	Passed House June 12, 2006 (364-0) Referred to Senate Foreign Relations Committee
S.Con.Res. 79	Expresses the sense of Congress that no United States assistance should be provided directly to the Palestinian Authority if any representative political party holding a majority of parliamentary seats within the Palestinian Authority maintains a position calling for the destruction of Israel.	Passed Senate February 1, 2006 (Unanimous consent) Passed House February 15, 2006 (418-1)
H.Res. 575	Asserts that Hamas and other terrorist organizations should not participate in elections held by the Palestinian Authority, and for other purposes.	Passed House December 16, 2005 (397-17)
S.Res. 82	Urges the European Union to add Hezbollah to the European Union's wide-ranging list of terrorist organizations (partly because of Hezbollah's support for Hamas)	Passed Senate April 29, 2005 (Unanimous consent)
H.Res. 101	Urges the European Union to add Hezbollah to the European Union's wide-ranging list of terrorist organizations (partly because of Hezbollah's support for Hamas)	Passed House March 14, 2005 (380-3)

Item	Brief Description	Disposition
S.Res. 393	Endorses progress toward realizing the vision of two states living side by side in peace and security, as a real contribution toward peace, and as important steps under the Road Map; supports efforts to continue working with others in the international community, to build the capacity and will of Palestinian institutions to fight terrorism, dismantle terrorist organizations, and prevent the areas from which Israel has withdrawn from posing a threat to the security of Israel; and for other purposes.	Passed Senate June 24, 2004 (95-3)
H.Con.Res. 460	Supports continuing efforts with others in the international community to build the capacity and will of Palestinian institutions to fight terrorism, dismantle terrorist organizations, and prevent the areas from which Israel has withdrawn from posing a threat to the security of Israel; and for other purposes.	Passed House June 23, 2004 (407-9)
H.Res. 294	Recognizes and respects Israel's right to fight terrorism and acknowledges Israel's fight against terrorism as part of the global war against terrorism; calls on all states to cease recognition of and political and material support for any Palestinian and other terrorist groups; calls on all states immediately to establish effective mechanisms to ensure that funding from private citizens cannot be directed to terrorist groups for any purpose whatsoever, including ostensible humanitarian purposes; calls on all states to provide support to the Palestinian Authority in its effort to confront and fight terror; and for other purposes.	Passed House June 25, 2003 (399-5)
H.Res. 61	Urges the Palestinian leadership to abide by its commitments made to the United States and to Israel and urges the Palestinian people to act on President Bush's call of June 24, 2002, to dismantle the terrorist infrastructure, end incitement to violence in official media, elect new leaders not compromised by terror, and embrace democracy; and for other purposes.	Passed House February 11, 2003 (411-2)
H.Res. 392	Expresses solidarity with Israel as it takes necessary steps to provide security to its people by dismantling the terrorist infrastructure in the Palestinian areas; condemns the recent wave of Palestinian suicide bombings; demands that the Palestinian Authority at last fulfill its commitment to dismantle the terrorist infrastructure in the Palestinian areas, including any such infrastructure associated with PLO and Palestinian Authority entities tied directly to Yasir Arafat; urges all Arab states to declare their unqualified opposition to all forms of terrorism, including suicide bombing; and for other purposes.	Passed House May 2, 2002 (352-21)

Item	Brief Description	Disposition
H.Con.Res. 280	Expresses solidarity with Israel in the fight against terrorism; expresses outrage at the ongoing Palestinian terrorist campaign (especially the attacks of December 1-2, 2001 that killed 26 and injured at least 175) and insists that the Palestinian Authority take all steps necessary to end it; urges the President to insist that all countries harboring, materially supporting, or acquiescing in the private support of Palestinian terrorist groups end all such support, dismantle the infrastructure of such groups, and bring all terrorists within their borders to justice; and for other purposes.	Passed House December 5, 2001 (384-11)
S.Con.Res. 88	Essentially similar to H.Con.Res. 280.	Passed Senate December 5, 2001 (Unanimous consent)
S.Amdt. 3528 (to Foreign Operations, Export Financing, and Related Programs Appropriations Act, 1999 (S. 2334))	Expresses the finding of the Senate that according to the Department of State, Iran continues to support international terrorism, providing training, financing and weapons to such terrorist groups as Hezbollah, Islamic Jihad, and Hamas.	Passed Senate September 2, 1998 (Voice vote) S. 2334 passed Senate September 2, 1998 (90-3)
S.Res. 228	Condemns terror attacks in Israel.	Passed Senate February 29, 1996 (Voice vote)
H.Con.Res. 149	Condemns terror attacks in Israel; urging PA President/PLO Chairman Yasser Arafat to (1) apprehend and punish the perpetrators of terror attacks; (2) eliminate the terrorist structure and terrorist activities of Hamas.	Passed House March 12, 1996 (406-0) Referred to Senate Foreign Relations Committee

APPENDIX E. SELECTED BIBLIOGRAPHY ON HAMAS

Biersteker, Thomas J. and Sue E. Eckert (eds.), *Countering the Financing of Terrorism*, Routledge, New York, 2008.

Brown, Nathan J. and Amr Hamzawy, "Hamas: Battling to Blend Religion, Politics, Resistance, and Governance," *Between Religion and Politics*, Carnegie Endowment for International Peace, Washington, DC, 2010.

Chehab, Zaki, *Inside Hamas: The Untold Story of the Militant Islamic Movement*, Nation Books, New York, 2007.

Cohen, Yoram and Matthew Levitt (with Becca Wasser), *Deterred but Determined: Salafi-Jihadi Groups in the Palestinian Arena*, Washington Institute for Near East Policy PolicyFocus #99, January 2010, available at http://www.washingtoninstitute.org/pubPDFs/PolicyFocus%2099.pdf.

Cohen, Yoram and Jeffrey White, *Hamas in Combat: The Military Performance of the Palestinian Islamic Resistance Movement*, Washington Institute for Near East Policy, Policy Focus #97, October 2009, available at http://www.washingtoninstitute.org/pubPDFs/PolicyFocus97.pdf.

Gold, Dore, et al. (eds.), *Iran, Hizbullah, Hamas and the Global Jihad : A New Conflict Paradigm for the West*, Jerusalem Center for Public Affairs, Jerusalem, 2007.

Gunning, Jeroen, *Hamas in Politics: Democracy, Religion, Violence*, Columbia University Press, New York, 2008.

Hroub, Khaled, *Hamas: A Beginner's Guide*, Pluto Press, Ann Arbor, Michigan, 2006.

Human Rights Watch, *Internal Fight: Palestinian Abuses in Gaza and the West Bank*, July 29, 2008, available at http://www.hrw.org/en/reports/2008/07/29/internal-fight-0.

Human Rights Watch, *Rockets from Gaza: Harm to Civilians from Palestinian Armed Groups' Rocket Attacks*, August 6, 2009, available at http://www.hrw.org/en/reports/2009/08/06/rockets-gaza-0.

Human Rights Watch, *Under Cover of War: Hamas Political Violence in Gaza*, April 20, 2009, available at http://www.hrw.org/node/82366.

Jensen, Michael Irving, *Political Ideology of Hamas: A Grassroots Perspective*, Palgrave Macmillan, New York, 2009.

Kepel, Gilles, *Jihad: The Trail of Political Islam*, Harvard University Press (Belknap Press), Cambridge, Massachusetts, 2003.

Levitt, Matthew, *Hamas: Politics, Charity, and Terrorism in the Service of Jihad*, Yale University Press, New Haven, Connecticut, 2006.

Levitt, Matthew and Michael Jacobson, *The Money Trail: Finding, Following, and Freezing Terrorist Finances*, Washington Institute for Near East Policy, Policy Focus #89, November 2008, available at http://www.washingtoninstitute.org/pubPDFs/PolicyFocus89.pdf.

Levy, Gideon, *The Punishment of Gaza*, Verso Books, New York, 2010.

Lia, Brynjar, *Building Arafat's Police: The Politics of International Police Assistance in the Palestinian Territories after the Oslo Agreement*, Ithaca Press, Reading, UK, 2007.

Lia, Brynjar, *A Police Force Without a State: A History of the Palestinian Security Forces in the West Bank and Gaza*, Ithaca Press, Reading, UK, 2006.

Milton-Edwards, Beverley and Stephen Farrell, *Hamas: The Islamic Resistance Movement*, Polity Press, Malden, Massachusetts, 2010.

Mishal, Shaul and Avraham Sela, *The Palestinian Hamas: Vision, Violence, and Coexistence*, Columbia University Press, New York, 2006.

McGeough, Paul, *Kill Khalid: The Failed Mossad Assassination and the Rise of Hamas*, The New Press, New York, 2009.

Nüsse, Andrea, *Muslim Palestine: The Ideology of Hamas*, Harwood Academic Publishers, Amsterdam, 1998.

Perry, Mark, *Talking to Terrorists: Why America Must Engage with Its Enemies*, Basic Books, New York, 2010.

Rubin, Barry (ed.), *The Muslim Brotherhood: The Organization and Policies of a Global Islamist Movement*, Palgrave Macmillan, New York, 2010.

Schanzer, Jonathan, *Hamas vs. Fatah: The Struggle for Palestine*, Palgrave Macmillan, New York, 2008.

Shachar, Nathan, *The Gaza Strip: Its History and Politics: From the Pharoahs to the Israeli Invasion of 2009*, Sussex Academic Press, Eastbourne, UK, 2010.

Shamir, Jacob and Khalil Shikaki, *Palestinian and Israeli Public Opinion: The Public Imperative in the Second Intifada*, Indiana University Press, Bloomington, Indiana, 2010.

Tamimi, Azzam, *Hamas: A History from Within*, Olive Branch Press, Northampton, Massachusetts, 2007.

United Nations, *Report of the U.N. Fact Finding Mission on the Gaza Conflict* (the "Goldstone Report"), September 25, 2009, available at http://www2.ohchr.org/english/bodies/hrcouncil/specialsession/9/FactFindingMission.htm.

Yousef, Mosab Hassan with Ron Brackin, *Son of Hamas*, Salt River, Carol Stream, Illinois, 2010.

Zuhur, Sherifa, *Hamas and Israel: Conflicting Strategies of Group-Based Politics*, U.S. Army War College Strategic Studies Institute, Carlisle, Pennsylvania, December 2008.

ACKNOWLEDGMENTS

Brent Cottrell contributed significant research and writing assistance to this report during his internship at CRS in the summer of 2010.

End Notes

[1] Hamas is the transliterated acronym for the group's Arabic name, "Harakat al Muqawama al Islamiyya," or the "Islamic Resistance Movement." The acronym "Hamas" itself is an Arabic word meaning "zeal."

[2] See U.S. State Department, "Country Reports on Terrorism 2009," Chapter 6. Terrorist Organizations, available at http://www.state.gov/s/ct/rls/crt/2009/140900.htm: "HAMAS receives some funding, weapons, and training from Iran. In addition, fundraising takes place in the Persian Gulf countries, but the group also receives donations from Palestinian expatriates around the world. Some fundraising and propaganda activity takes place in Western Europe and North America. Syria provides safe haven for its leadership." See also Anna Fitfield, "Hizbollah Confirms Broad Aid for Hamas," *Financial Times*, May 12, 2009.

[3] Izz Al Din al Qassam was a Muslim Brotherhood member, preacher, and leader of an anti-Zionist and anti-colonialist resistance movement in historic Palestine during the British Mandate period. He was killed by British forces on November 19, 1935.

[4] Figures culled from Israel Ministry of Foreign Affairs website at http://www.mfa.gov.il/MFA/Terrorism-+Obstacle+to+Peace/Palestinian+terror+before+2000/Suicide%20and%20Other%20Bombing%20Attacks%20in%20Israel%20Since and http://www.mfa.gov.il/MFA/Terrorism-+Obstacle+to+Peace/Palestinian+terror+since+2000/Victims+of+Palestinian+Violence+and+Terrorism+sinc.htm; and from Jewish Virtual Library website at http://www.jewishvirtuallibrary.org/jsource/Terrorism/TerrorAttacks.html. In the aggregate, other Palestinian militant groups (such as Palestinian Islamic Jihad, the Fatah-affiliated Al Aqsa Martyrs' Brigades, and the Popular Front for the Liberation of Palestine) also have killed scores, if not hundreds, of Israelis since 1993.

[5] Figures culled from Jewish Virtual Library website at http://www.jewishvirtuallibrary.org/jsource/Terrorism/usvictims.html.

Hamas: Background and Issues for Congress 63

[6] Detailed descriptions of Palestinian organizations, governance organs, and political factions are contained in CRS Report RL34074, *The Palestinians: Background and U.S. Relations*, by Jim Zanotti.

[7] The only previous power-sharing arrangement between Hamas and Fatah, the Saudi Arabia-brokered Mecca Accord of February 2007, quickly deteriorated into factional fighting that led to Hamas's takeover of Gaza in June 2007 (see Appendix A and Appendix B).

[8] Suicide bombing figures culled from Israel Ministry of Foreign Affairs website at http://www.mfa.gov.il/MFA/Terrorism-+Obstacle+to+Peace/Palestinian+terror+before+2000/Suicide%20and%20Other%20Bombing%20Attacks%20in%20Israel%20Since.

[9] See footnote 4.

[10] Examples of international pressure on Israel are the various convoys and flotillas, including the so-called "Gaza Freedom Flotilla" in May 2010, seeking to thwart the Israeli-Egyptian closure regime and to raise awareness of the humanitarian and economic situation in Gaza. For more information, see CRS Report R41275, *Israel's Blockade of Gaza, the Mavi Marmara Incident, and Its Aftermath*, by Carol Migdalovitz.

[11] The barrier is referred to in different ways by different groups and individuals that are often reflective of various political or national ideologies. Commonly used alternative names are the "security fence" (often used by Israeli sources) and the "apartheid wall" (favored by Palestinians), although neither appellation describes the barrier's physical nature completely accurately. In some places, the barrier is mainly concrete; in others, mainly chain-link and/or wire.

[12] Since 2001, Hamas and several other Palestinian terrorist groups based in the Gaza Strip have attacked communities in southern and coastal areas of Israel with thousands of indiscriminately fired rockets and mortars. During the second Palestinian intifada in 2001, Hamas militia members and others fired homemade mortars at Israeli settlements in the Gaza Strip and launched the first locally produced "Qassam" rockets, named after the early-20th Century militant leader Sheikh Izz al Din al Qassam. Teams of engineers, chemists, and machinists have improved the range and payload of the Qassam series rockets over time, and Israeli military raids have targeted several individuals and facilities associated with rocket research and production operations.

[13] Over the years, rockets have expanded in range beyond relatively small Israeli communities near the Gaza border, such as the town of Sderot (population est. 24,000), to the larger coastal cities of Ashqelon (population est.120,000) and Ashdod (population est. 200,000) and to the Negev city of Beersheva (population est. 185,000). Mid-range Grad-style rockets (thought to be smuggled into Gaza) that travel farther than Qassam rockets have been fired from Gaza by Hamas, Palestinian Islamic Jihad (Al Quds series) and the Popular Resistance Committees (Nasser series).

[14] Information provided by Israeli government to CRS, November 2010.

[15] "Q&A: Gaza conflict," *BBC News*, January 18, 2009, available at http://news.bbc.co.uk/2/hi/middle_east/7818022.stm.

[16] For a comprehensive treatment of this subject, see Human Rights Watch, *Rockets from Gaza: Harm to Civilians from Palestinian Armed Groups' Rocket Attacks*, August 6, 2009, available at http://www.hrw.org/en/reports/2009/08/06/rockets-gaza-0.

[17] Information provided to CRS by Israeli government, November 2010.

[18] Ibid.

[19] Ian Siperco, "Shield of David: The Promise of Israeli National Missile Defense," *Middle East Policy*, Vol. 17, Issue 2, Summer 2010.

[20] See "Report: Egypt seizes anti-aircraft weapons bound for Gaza," *haaretz.com*, September 7, 2010.

[21] Much of the information from this paragraph came from a CRS meeting with an Israeli official in August 2009. For a description of past smuggling activities related to Gaza, see CRS Report R40849, *Iran: Regional Perspectives and U.S. Policy*, coordinated by Casey L. Addis.

[22] See CRS Report RL33003, *Egypt: Background and U.S. Relations*, by Jeremy M. Sharp; and CRS Report RL34346, *The Egypt-Gaza Border and its Effect on Israeli-Egyptian Relations*, by Jeremy M. Sharp.

[23] "Netanyahu: Hamas responsible for rockets on Eilat; we will retaliate," *haaretz.com*, August 4, 2010; Anshel Pfeffer and Avi Issacharoff, "PA: Hamas military chief in Rafah ordered rocket attacks on Eilat, Aqaba," *haaretz.com*, August 6, 2010.

[24] Yezid Sayigh, *"We serve the people": Hamas policing in Gaza*, Crown Paper, Crown Center for Middle East Studies, Brandeis University, 2011 (forthcoming). This same source says that some of the security forces' personnel were holdovers from before the Hamas takeover. Some come from Fatah and other non-Hamas backgrounds.

[25] Mohammed Najib, "Hamas creates external intelligence arm," *Jane's Islamic Affairs Analyst*, January 29, 2010.

[26] Shalit, then a corporal, was taken captive in a June 2006 raid of an Israeli army post just outside Gaza. Two of Shalit's comrades were killed in the raid. The raid was organized jointly by the Popular Resistance Committees, Hamas, and an extremist jihadist group calling itself the Army of Islam. Shalit has remained in Hamas's custody since then, and his status figures prominently in speculation about negotiations with Hamas associated with a possible prisoner swap, cease-fire, or breakthrough in Palestinian power-sharing or Israeli-Palestinian negotiations. His wellbeing is a matter of major Israeli national concern.

[27] Yoram Cohen and Jeffrey White, *Hamas in Combat: The Military Performance of the Palestinian Islamic Resistance Movement*, Washington Institute for Near East Policy, Policy Focus #97, October 2009, available at http://www.washingtoninstitute.org/pubPDFs/PolicyFocus97.pdf.

[28] Jihadism is a concept with many different levels of meaning in Islam, from internal striving to external conflict between Muslims and non-Muslims (or sometimes between Muslims and other Muslims deemed to be insufficiently faithful). For more information, see CRS Report RS21695, *The Islamic Traditions of Wahhabism and Salafiyya*, by Christopher M. Blanchard.

[29] Transcript of remarks by Khaled Meshaal, "Charlie Rose," *PBS*, May 28, 2010, available at http://www.charlierose.com/view/interview/11032#frame_top. For additional information both supporting and countering Meshaal's statement above on Hamas's general stance toward Jews and Judaism, see "On Israel's Existence and the Jews" in the main body of the report.

[30] Beverley Milton-Edwards and Stephen Farrell, *Hamas: The Islamic Resistance Movement*, Polity Press, Malden, Massachusetts, 2010, p. 268. After Hamas agreed to a Saudi-brokered power-sharing arrangement with Fatah in February 2007 known as the Mecca Accord, Zawahiri claimed that "The leadership of Hamas government has committed an aggression against the rights of the Islamic nation by accepting what it called ... respecting international agreements. I am sorry to have to offer the Islamic nation my condolences for the [virtual demise] of the Hamas leadership as it has fallen in the quagmire of surrender." "Hamas rejects al-Zawahiri's claims," *aljazeera.net*, March 12, 2007.

[31] Salafism refers to a broad subset of Sunni revivalist movements that seek to purify contemporary Islamic religious practices and societies by encouraging the application of practices and views associated with the earliest days of the Islamic faith. The world's Salafist movements hold a range of positions on political, social, and theological questions and include both politically quietist and violent extremist groups. Salafists generally eschew accommodation of "unIslamic" political mechanisms such as Western-style democracy. For more information, see CRS Report RS21695, *The Islamic Traditions of Wahhabism and Salafiyya*, by Christopher M. Blanchard.

[32] Hamas took swift and brutal retributive action against the Army of Islam in September 2008 (in Gaza City) and Jund Ansar Allah in August 2009 (in Rafah) when confronted with challenges to its authority. Nicolas Pelham and Max Rodenbeck, "Which Way for Hamas?", *New York Review of Books*, November 5, 2009, available at http://www.nybooks.com/articles/archives/2009/nov/05/which-way-for-hamas/.

[33] For more information on Hezbollah and the threats it potentially poses, see CRS Report R41446, *Hezbollah: Background and Issues for Congress*, by Casey L. Addis and Christopher M. Blanchard.

[34] See Matthew Levitt, "Political Hardball Within Hamas: Hardline Militants Calling Shots in Gaza," Washington Institute for Near East Policy, PolicyWatch #1450, January 6, 2009, available at http://www.washingtoninstitute.org/templateC05.php?CID=2982. This article contends that debate is most contentious within Hamas over which of these two driving forces to prioritize.

[35] See, e.g., Michael Herzog, "Can Hamas Be Tamed?", *Foreign Affairs*, March/April 2006; Charles Krauthammer, "Moral Clarity in Gaza," *Washington Post*, January 2, 2009.

[36] Many of these documents written subsequent to the Hamas charter can be found in Azzam Tamimi, *Hamas: A History from Within*, Olive Branch Press, Northampton, Massachusetts, 2007, Appendices. However, Fatah, whose leaders populate the main leadership positions of the PA and the PLO (which have dealings with Israel and the West), has not purged its 1960s charter of its clauses calling for the destruction of the Zionist state and its economic, political, military, and cultural supports (even though the PLO has recognized Israel's right to exist).

[37] See Henry Siegman, "US Hamas policy blocks Middle East peace," Norwegian Peacebuilding Centre, September 2010, available at http://www.usmep.us/usmep/wp-content/uploads/NorefReport_Siegman_Hamas-Israel_Sep10.pdf; Michael Bröning, "Hamas 2.0," *foreignaffairs.com*, August 5, 2009.

[38] See footnote 131.

[39] CRS interview in September 2010 with U.S. analyst covering Middle East terrorism at major Washington, DC think tank.

[40] See Matthew Levitt, "Score One for 'Hamaswood,'" Middle East Strategy at Harvard, August 11, 2009, available at http://blogs.law.harvard.edu/mesh/2009/08/score-one-for-hamaswood/.

[41] For a translation of the 1988 Hamas charter (from the original Arabic), see http://avalon.law.yale.edu/20th_century/hamas.asp.

[42] Matthew Levitt, "Hamas's Ideological Crisis," *Current Trends in Islamist Ideology Vol. 9*, Hudson Institute Center of Islam, Democracy, and the Future of the Muslim World, November 6, 2009, available at http://www.currenttrends.org/research/detail/hamass-ideological-crisis.

[43] Steven Erlanger, "Academics View Differences Within Hamas," *New York Times*, January 29, 2006.

[44] Sharmine Narwani, "Khaled Meshaal Interview: Hamas Chief Weighs In on Eve of Peace Talks," *The Huffington Post*, August 31, 2010.

[45] Transcript of remarks by Khaled Meshaal, "Charlie Rose," op. cit.

[46] 1988 Hamas charter, op. cit.

[47] Translation (from the original Arabic) of *Al Sabeel* (Jordan) newspaper interview with Khaled Meshaal, available at http://www.middleeastmonitor.org.uk/articles/middle-east/1491-khaled-meshal-lays-out-new-hamas-policy-direction.

[48] 1988 Hamas charter, op. cit.

[49] Pelham and Rodenbeck, op. cit..

[50] Ibid.

[51] Yezid Sayigh, "Hamas Rule in Gaza: Three Years On," Crown Center of Middle East Studies, Brandeis University, March 2010, available at http://www.brandeis.edu/crown/publications/meb/MEB41.pdf.

[52] Sayigh, *"We serve the people"...*, op. cit. For example, the Qassam Brigades (www.qassam.ps) and Al Aqsa TV (www.aqsatv.ps/ar/) maintain their own websites, and most (if not all) of the Hamas-run Gaza ministries, including the Ministry of Interior (http://www.moi.gov.ps), also maintain websites. Some of these websites have English and other foreign-language versions as well as Arabic.

[53] In May and June 2010, two separate incidents of arson were reported against Gaza summer camps run by UNRWA (that served approximately 250,000 Gaza youth in Summer 2010). Some analysts in Israel and the West believe that the incidents may have taken place with the tacit or express approval of Hamas in an attempt to promote its model for influencing youth over UNRWA's (Hamas's camps reportedly served approximately 100,000 Gaza youth in Summer 2010), given the criticism Hamas has reportedly leveled at the UNRWA camps for their focus on entertainment and potentially "corrupting" influences. See "This year Hamas' summer camps in the Gaza Strip...," Meir Amit Intelligence and Terrorism Information Center, September 14, 2010, available at http://www.terrorisminfo.org.il/malam_multimedia/English/eng_n/html/hamas_e128.htm; Sarah A. Topol, "Hamas's Summer Camp War," *Slate.com*, July 27, 2010.

[54] Levitt, "Hamas's Ideological Crisis," op. cit.

[55] Sayigh, *"We serve the people"...*, op. cit.

[56] Israel Defense Forces Intelligence, "The forked tongue of Hamas: How it speaks differently to Western and Arab media," April 11, 2006, available at http://www.mfa.gov.il/MFA/Terrorism+Obstacle+to+Peace/Terror+Groups/The%20forked%20tongue%20of%20Hamas%2011-Apr-2006

[57] See U.S. State Department, "Country Reports on Terrorism 2009," Chapter 6, op. cit.

[58] Levitt, "Political Hardball Within Hamas...," op. cit.

[59] See Cohen and White, op. cit.

[60] In testimony before the House Appropriations Subcommittee on State, Foreign Operations and Related Programs, Secretary of State Hillary Rodham Clinton said, "In fact, we think there is [sic] some divisions between the Hamas leadership in Gaza and in Damascus. There's no doubt that those in Damascus take orders directly from Tehran." Transcript of Subcommittee hearing: "Supplemental Request," April 23, 2009.

[61] The source for this paragraph is Sayigh, "Hamas Rule in Gaza: Three Years On," op. cit.

[62] In a conversation with CRS in August 2009, an Israeli official claimed that the Damascus politburo, headed by Khaled Meshaal, exercises more strategic control over Hamas's activities than Hamas's other leadership organs because (the Israeli official claimed) the politburo is responsible for arranging the transport of cash, weapons, and other supplies to the Gaza Strip.

[63] CRS correspondence with Yezid Sayigh, October 2010.

[64] Danny Rubenstein, "Planet Gaza," *The Jerusalem Report*, June 7, 2010. U.S. appropriations legislation (including the Consolidated Appropriations Act, 2010 (P.L. 111-117)) prohibits U.S. aid to be "obligated for salaries of personnel of the Palestinian Authority located in Gaza." The U.S. Agency for International Development (USAID) says that direct U.S. budgetary assistance to the PA is used "to service debt to commercial suppliers and commercial banks." USAID FY2011 Congressional Notification #1, October 7, 2010.

[65] Nathan J. Brown, "Palestine: The Schism Deepens," Carnegie Endowment for International Peace, August 20, 2009, available at http://carnegieendowment.org/publications/index.cfm?fa=view&id=23668

[66] Sayigh, "Hamas Rule in Gaza: Three Years On," op. cit. *Sharia* courts seek the direct application of Islamic legal principles to society without reference to secular legal principles as possible supplements or alternatives.

[67] See, e.g., Human Rights Watch, *Internal Fight: Palestinian Abuses in Gaza and the West Bank*, July 29, 2008, available at http://www.hrw.org/en/reports/2008/07/29/internal-fight-0.

[68] See, e.g., Daniel Byman, "How to Handle Hamas," *Foreign Affairs*, September/October 2010; Thanassis Cambanis, "Letter from Gaza," *foreignaffairs.com*, June 18, 2010.

[69] "Country Report: Palestinian Territories," *Economist Intelligence Unit*, October 2009. Yet, some observers note that Hamas leaders have mostly avoided the type of conspicuous consumption in which many Fatah leaders have engaged since the 1990s, and which feeds widespread perceptions of corruption.

[70] Sayigh, "Hamas Rule in Gaza: Three Years On," op. cit.

[71] Palestinian Center for Policy and Survey Research, Palestinian Public Opinion Poll No. 37 (September 30-October 2, 2010), available at http://www.pcpsr.org/survey/polls/2010/p37e.html#table; Arab World for Research and Development, "Middle East Peace Process: Silver Linings Remain," August 8-14, 2010, available at http://www.awrad.org/pdfs/Oversample%20Results%20-%20Analysis%20%28final%29.pdf; Jerusalem Media and Communications Centre, Poll No. 71 (September 11-15, 2010), available at http://www.jmcc.org/documentsandmaps.aspx?id=808.

[72] Ibid.

[73] The shooting attacks, which coincided with the relaunch of Israel-PLO negotiations, killed four Israelis (including a pregnant mother) and injured two more.

[74] Palestinian Center for Policy and Survey Research, Palestinian Public Opinion Poll No. 37 (September 30-October 2, 2010), op. cit.

[75] Ibid.

[76] See U.S. State Department, "Country Reports on Terrorism 2009," Chapter 6, op. cit.; International Crisis Group, *Nurturing Instability: Lebanon's Palestinian Refugee Camps*, Middle East Report No. 84, February 19, 2009, available at http://www.crisisgroup.org/~/media/Files/Middle%20East%20North%20Africa/Israel%20Palestine/84%20nurturing%2 0instability%20lebanons%20palestinian%20refugee%20camps.ashx.

[77] See U.S. Department of State, "Country Reports on Terrorism 2009," Chapter 3. State Sponsors of Terrorism, available at http://www.state.gov/s/ct/rls/crt/2009/140889.htm.

[78] Transcript of remarks by Khaled Meshaal, *Al Jazeera TV*, December 15, 2009, Open Source Document GMP20091215648001 (translated from Arabic).

[79] Fitfield, op. cit; Thanassis Cambanis, *A Privilege to Die: Inside Hezbollah's Legions and Their Endless War Against Israel*, Free Press, New York, 2010, pp. 17, 267-272.

[80] See Council on Foreign Relations Backgrounder, "Hamas," updated August 27, 2009, available at http://www.cfr.org/publication/8968/#p8; Matthew Levitt, "The Real Connection Between Iran and Hamas," *Counterterrorism Blog*, January 12, 2009, available at http://counterterrorismblog.org/2009/01/the_real_connection_between_ir.php.

[81] See, e.g., Ehud Yaari, "Sunni Hamas and Shiite Iran Share a Common Political Theology," Washington Institute of Near East Policy, PolicyWatch #1716, November 9, 2010.

[82] Uzi Mahnaimi, "US navy seeks arms bound for Hamas," *The Sunday Times* (UK), January 25, 2009.

[83] Byman, op. cit.

[84] According to the State Department, in 2009, "Iran remained the principal supporter of groups that are implacably opposed to the Middle East Peace Process. The Qods Force, the external operations branch of the Islamic Revolutionary Guard Corps (IRGC), is the regime's primary mechanism for cultivating and supporting terrorists abroad. Iran provided weapons, training, and funding to HAMAS and other Palestinian terrorist groups, including Palestine Islamic Jihad (PIJ) and the Popular Front for the Liberation of Palestine-General Command (PFLP-GC)." U.S. Department of State, "Country Reports on Terrorism 2009," Chapter 3, op. cit. See also Marie Colvin, "Hamas Wages Iran's Proxy War on Israel," *The Sunday Times* (UK), March 9, 2008.

[85] See U.S. Treasury Department press release: "U.S. Designates Five Charities Funding Hamas and Six Senior Hamas Leaders as Terrorist Entities," August 22, 2003, available at http://www.ustreas.gov/press/releases/js672.htm; U.S. Treasury Department press release: "Treasury Designates Al-Salah Society Key Support Node for Hamas," August 7, 2007, available at http://www.treas.gov/press/releases/hp531.htm. See also Don Van Natta, Jr., with Timothy L. O'Brien, "Flow of Saudi Cash to Hamas Is Under Scrutiny by U.S.," *New York Times*, September 17, 2003.

[86] Matthew Levitt and Michael Jacobson, *The Money Trail: Finding, Following, and Freezing Terrorist Finances*, Washington Institute for Near East Policy, Policy Focus #89, November 2008, available at http://www.washingtoninstitute.org/pubPDFs/PolicyFocus89.pdf.

[87] See U.S. Department of Justice press release, Holy Land Foundation, Leaders, Accused of Providing Material Support to Hamas Terrorist Organization, July 27, 2004, available at http://www.justice.gov/opa/pr/2004/July/04_crm_514.htm. Criminal liability for material support of terrorism is authorized under 18 U.S.C. §2339A and §2339B. For further information, see CRS Report R41333, *Terrorist Material Support: An Overview of 18 U.S.C. 2339A and 2339B*, by Charles Doyle.

[88] Laura B. Rowe, "Ending Terrorism with Civil Remedies: Boim v. Holy Land Foundation and the Proper Framework of Liability," 4 Seventh Circuit Review 372 (2009), available at http://www.kentlaw.edu/7cr/v4-2/rowe.pdf. In addition to other civil penalties that may accrue, civil liability for damages caused by a party's support of terrorism is authorized under 18 U.S.C. §2333, which states: "Any national of the United States injured in his or her person, property, or business by reason of an act of international terrorism ... may sue therefor ... and shall recover threefold the damages he or she sustains..."

[89] Levitt and Jacobson, op. cit., citing the Intelligence and Terrorism Information Center.

[90] Israel Security Agency (also known as the Shin Bet), "The Union of Good – Analysis and Mapping of Terror Funds Network," available at http://www.shabak.gov.il/SiteCollectionImages/english/ TerrorInfo/coalition_en.pdf.

[91] U.S. Treasury Department press release HP-1267, "Treasury Designates the Union of Good," November 12, 2008, available at http://www.ustreas.gov/press/releases/hp1267.htm.

[92] Israel Security Agency, op. cit.

[93] Glenn R. Simpson and Benoit Faucon, "A Trail of Sugar to Gaza," *Wall Street Journal*, July 2, 2007.

[94] For example, an allegedly suspicious 2005 food shipment to Gaza by the *Comit de Bienfaisance et de Secours aux Palestiniens*, a French organization the United States considers to be a Specially Designated Terrorist Organization due to its ties to Hamas, was worth $521,130. Simpson and Faucon, op. cit.

[95] Anti-Defamation League, "Viva Palestina: Supporting Hamas Under the Guise of Humanitarianism," July 22, 2009, available at http://www.adl.org/main_Anti_Israel/galloway_ us_tour_09.htm?Multi_page_sections=sHeading_4. Concerns about possible links to Hamas may have been fueled by Galloway's actions during a previous European convoy's trip to Gaza in March 2009, when he gave approximately $1.5 million in cash and 110 vehicles directly to the Hamas-led regime.

[96] For further information, see CRS Report RS22967, *U.S. Foreign Aid to the Palestinians*, by Jim Zanotti.

[97] See, e.g., Nathan J. Brown, "Fayyad Is Not the Problem, but Fayyadism Is Not the Solution to Palestine's Political Crisis," op. cit.; Michele Dunne, "A Two-State Solution Requires Palestinian Politics," Carnegie Endowment for International Peace, June 2010, available at http://www.carnegieendowment.org/files/palestine_politics.pdf.

[98] Nathan J. Brown, "Are Palestinians Building a State?", Carnegie Endowment for International Peace Commentary, June 2010, available at http://www.carnegieendowment.org/files/palestinian_state1.pdf.

[99] See Dunne, op. cit.

100 See, e.g., Mohammed Najib, "Struggling on – Khaled Mashal, political chief of Hamas," *Jane's Intelligence Weekly*, August 20, 2010.

[101] For further information on conditions in Gaza, see, e.g., Amnesty International UK, et al., "Dashed Hopes: Continuation of the Gaza Blockade," November 30, 2010, available at http://www.oxfam.org/sites/www.oxfam.org/files/dashed-hopes-continuation-gaza-blockade-301110-en.pdf; Sarah A. Topol, "'Gaza Is Not Darfur!'", *Slate.com*, August 5, 2010.

[102] Text of Letter to the President, January 20, 2010, available at http://docs.google.com/viewer?url=http%3A%2F%2Fellison.house.gov%2Fimages%2Fstories%2FDocuments%2F2010%2FGaza_letter_to_Obama.pdf.

[103] For more information on this subject, see CRS Report R40664, *U.S. Security Assistance to the Palestinian Authority*, by Jim Zanotti; Government Accountability Office, Palestinian Authority: U.S. Assistance Is Training and Equipping Security Forces, but the Program Needs to Measure Progress and Is Facing Logistical Constraints, May 2010, available at http://www.gao.gov/new.items/d10505.pdf.

[104] See, e.g., Ian Cobain, "CIA working with Palestinian security agents," *guardian.co.uk*, December 17, 2009; Yezid Sayigh, "'Fixing Broken Windows': Security Sector Reform in Palestine, Lebanon and Yemen," Carnegie Endowment for International Peace, October 2009, available at http://www.carnegieendowment.org/files/security_sector_reform.pdf.

[105] See, e.g., Nathan Thrall, "Our Man in Palestine," *New York Review of Books*, October 14, 2010, available at http://www.nybooks.com/articles/archives/2010/oct/14/our-man-palestine/. For further discussion of human rights concerns surrounding PA security forces in the West Bank and Hamas in Gaza, see CRS Report R40664, *U.S. Security Assistance to the Palestinian Authority*, by Jim Zanotti; Human Rights Watch, *Internal Fight: Palestinian Abuses in Gaza and the West Bank*, op. cit.

[106] Palestinian Center for Policy and Survey Research, Palestinian Public Opinion Poll No. 37 (September 30-October 2, 2010), available at http://www.pcpsr.org/survey/polls/2010/p37e.html#table.

[107] See International Crisis Group, *Squaring the Circle: Palestinian Security Reform Under Occupation*, Middle East Report No. 98, September 7, 2010, available at http://www.crisisgroup.org/~/media/ Files/Middle% 20East%20North%20Africa/Israel%20Palestine/98%20Squaring%2 0the%20Circle%20--%20Palestinian% 20Security%20Reform%20under%20Occupation.ashx; International Crisis Group, *Ruling Palestine II: The West Bank Model?* Middle East Report No. 79, July 17, 2008, available at http://www.crisisgroup. org/library/documents/middle_east___north_africa/arab_israeli_conflict/79_ruling_palestine_ii ___the_west_bank_model.pdf. These operations underscore the fact that the Israeli-Palestinian agreements that authorized the creation of Palestinian security forces in the 1990s in areas of limited Palestinian self-rule contained clauses that preserved Israel's prerogative to conduct operations in those areas for purposes of its own security.

[108] For further information on UNRWA, see CRS Report RS22967, *U.S. Foreign Aid to the Palestinians*, by Jim Zanotti; and CRS Report RS21668, *United Nations Relief and Works Agency for Palestine Refugees in the Near East (UNRWA)*, by Rhoda Margesson.

[109] See FY2011 Congressional Budget Justification for Foreign Operations, Department of State (Volume 2), p. 86, available at http://www.state.gov/documents/organization/137936.pdf: "U.S. government support for UNRWA directly contributes to the U.S. strategic interest of meeting the humanitarian needs of Palestinians, while promoting their self-sufficiency. UNRWA plays a stabilizing role in the Middle East through its assistance programs, serving as an important counterweight to extremist elements."

[110] See Dunne, op. cit.

[111] Transcript of House Appropriations Subcommittee on State, Foreign Operations and Related Programs hearing: "Supplemental Request," April 23, 2009.

[112] U.S.-Israel cooperation also takes place on a missile defense system known as "Arrow" that targets rockets of a longer range that what Hamas may currently possess.

[113] See, e.g., Milton-Edwards and Farrell, op. cit.

[114] Sayigh, *"We serve the people"...*, op. cit.

[115] See, e.g., Omar Karmi, "Going underground – Egypt's new wall may destabilize Gaza," *Jane's Intelligence Review*, March 12, 2010.

[116] For general information on sanctions against Iran and Syria, see CRS Report RS20871, *Iran Sanctions*, by Kenneth Katzman; and CRS Report RL33487, *Syria: Background and U.S. Relations*, by Jeremy M. Sharp.

[117] U.S. State Department, "Country Reports on Terrorism 2009," Chapter 2. Country Reports: Middle East and North Africa Overview, available at http://www.state.gov/s/ct/rls/crt/2009/140886.htm.

[118] Karmi, op. cit.

[119] See Ben Knight, "New Israeli-Egyptian border barrier has more than one purpose," *Deutsche Welle*, November 14, 2010. This article claimed that a new Israeli project to build a fence along the Israel-Egypt border might also target the Gaza-Egypt smuggling tunnels, although Egyptian officials have denied this. Ibid.

[120] See Karmi, op. cit.

[121] Colloquium attended by CRS at major U.S. think tank, October 2010.

[122] "Text of U.S.-Israel Agreement to End Gaza Arms Smuggling," *Ha'aretz*, January 17, 2009. Shortly afterward, the United States interdicted the Cypriot-flagged ship *Monchegorsk* in the Red Sea after it reportedly left Iran with weapons-related equipment.

[123] U.S. Department of State, "U.S. Welcomes Agreement on Gaza Weapons Smuggling," March 16, 2009, available at http://www.state.gov/r/pa/prs/ps/2009/03/120436.htm. The eight NATO member-states are Canada, Denmark, France, Germany, Italy, the Netherlands, Norway, and the United Kingdom.

[124] "How Israel Foiled an Arms Convoy Bound for Hamas," *Time*, March 30, 2009.

[125] The Mahbouh killing, ascribed by most reports to the Israeli Mossad, caused a diplomatic backlash against Israel because the purported assassins used falsified or fraudulently obtained European and Australian passports to gain entry to Dubai. For a detailed account, see Alon Ben-David, "Spy games – Mossad returns to form," *Jane's Intelligence Review*, June 23, 2010.

[126] An Israeli organization has reported, however, that Hamas later agreed to a new Al Aqsa broadcast deal with Kuwait-based Gulfsat, which also broadcasts using a Eutelsat satellite. Intelligence and Terrorism Information Center, "Hamas' Al-Aqsa TV has circumvented the French media regulator's ban," July 12, 2010, available at http://www.terrorism-info.org.il/malam_multimedia/English/eng_n/html/hamas_e120.htm. Al Aqsa is also broadcast through Arab League-owned, Saudi Arabia-based Arabsat.

[127] It is unclear whether the executive branch would consider such legislation binding on its formulation of U.S. policy. On September 9, 2008 (during the 110th Congress), the House of Representatives passed H.Res. 1069 (by a 409-1 vote), which condemned Hamas's Al Aqsa TV (among other Middle East TV channels, including Al Manar) for anti-Israel, anti-Semitic, and anti-U.S. incitement and called upon satellite TV providers Arabsat (Arab League-owned, Saudi-based) and Eutelsat (privately owned, France-based) to cease transmitting Al Aqsa programming.

[128] For more on this subject, see "The Role of Hamas" in CRS Report R40092, *Israel and the Palestinians: Prospects for a Two-State Solution*, by Jim Zanotti.

[129] Charles Levinson, "U.S. Ex-Officials Engage with Hamas," *Wall Street Journal*, April 2, 2010. Several former U.S. officials signed the 2009 U.S./Middle East Project report submitted to the Obama Administration that advocated taking a more "pragmatic approach" toward Hamas. The report acknowledged that direct U.S. engagement with Hamas might not now be practical, but recommended that the United States "offer [Hamas] inducements that will enable its more moderate elements to prevail, and cease discouraging third parties from engaging with Hamas in ways that might help clarify the movement's views and test its behavior." Zbigniew Brzezinksi, Chuck Hagel, et al., "A Last Chance for a Two-State Israel-Palestine Agreement: A Bipartisan Statement on U.S. Middle East Peacemaking," 2009 U.S./Middle East Project, available at http://www.usmep.us/bipartisan_recommendations/A_Last_Chance_for_a_Two-State_Israel-Palestine_Agreement.pdf.

[130] Babak Dehghanpisheh and Ranya Kadri, "Hamas Sticks to the Hard Line," *Newsweek*, October 14, 2010.

[131] These opponents might assert that Hamas should be dealt with only after it is marginalized. Israel did not agree to formal negotiations with Yasser Arafat of the PLO or with other historical Arab adversaries of Israel—such as former Egyptian President Anwar Sadat and King Hussein of Jordan—until it had established a position of strength relative to each of them. Some might say that doing this helped lead to diplomatic breakthroughs in each case. However, at a February 2009 hearing of the House Foreign Affairs Subcommittee on the Middle East and South Asia, Carnegie Endowment for International Peace analyst Michele Dunne provided an explanation for why the analogy may not apply to Hamas: "Regarding Hamas, I think that our problem as the United States is we want Hamas to walk the road that the PLO walked 20 years ago. And Hamas sees very well that the PLO walked that road, and it failed." See Transcript of Hearing, "Gaza After the War: What Can Be Built on the Wreckage," House Foreign Affairs Subcommittee on the Middle East and South Asia, February 12, 2009, available at http://foreignaffairs.house.gov/111/47420.pdf.

[132] See Joshua Mitnick, "As Peace Talks Sputter, Israelis and Palestinians Eye Plan B," *Christian Science Monitor*, September 15, 2008.

[133] Prepared statement of General David Petraeus, Senate Armed Services Committee Hearing, March 16, 2010, available at http://armed-services.senate.gov/statemnt/2010/03%20March/Petraeus%2003-16-10.pdf.

[134] See Mark Perry, "Red Team," *foreignpolicy.com*, June 30, 2010; Bilal Y. Saab, "What Do Red Teams Really Do?", *foreignpolicy.com*, September 3, 2010.

[135] See, e.g., Byman, op. cit.; Cambanis, "Letter from Gaza," op. cit.; Peter Beinart, "Hamas: U.S. Diplomacy's Final Frontier," *Time*, May 1, 2009; Muriel Asseburg, "Ending the Gaza Blockade – But How?", German Institute for International and Security Affairs (SWP), July 2010, available at http://www.swp-berlin.org/common/get_document.php?asset_id=7274.

[136] Beinart, op. cit.

[137] Byman, op. cit.

[138] On the previous occasions in which Hamas participated in the PA government from 2006-2007, the European Union joined the United States in refusing to provide direct assistance to the PA. There are indications, however, that Europeans might be less willing to follow the U.S. lead in the event that another PA government including Hamas is formed. See Muriel Asseburg and Paul Salem, "No Euro-Mediterranean Community without peace," EU Institute for Security Studies and European Institute of the Mediterranean, September 2009, available at http://www.iss.europa.eu/uploads/media/10Papers-01.pdf.

[139] Andrew Rettman, "EU Countries Practice 'Secret' Diplomacy, Hamas Says," *euobserver.com*, September 14, 2009.

[140] The Goldstone Report, dated September 25, 2009, is available at http://www2.ohchr.org/english/bodies/hrcouncil/specialsession/9/FactFindingMission.htm.

[141] The Goldstone Report found that Israel used Palestinian civilians as human shields during Operation Cast Lead, while stating that Israel had not provided sufficient evidence for a finding that Hamas had done the same. Ibid. In October 2010, an Israeli military court convicted two IDF soldiers of reckless endangerment and conduct unbecoming for using a nine-year-old Gaza boy to check suspected booby-traps. "Two Israeli soldiers guilty of using human shield in Gaza," *BBC News*, October 3, 2010, available at http://www.bbc.co.uk/news/world-middle-east-11462635.

[142] Andrew Higgins, "How Israel Helped to Spawn Hamas," *Wall Street Journal*, January 25, 2009.

[143] Some believe this Israeli measure strengthened, rather than weakened, Hamas. Not only did its deported leaders persevere and bond through the hardships of a year in exile, but they also cultivated relations with and received mentorship from the Iran-backed Hezbollah movement before being repatriated to the West Bank and Gaza in 1993 as a result of pressure on Israel from human rights organizations and the United States. See Paul McGeough, *Kill Khalid: The Failed Mossad Assassination and the Rise of Hamas*, The New Press, New York, 2009, p. 68.

[144] Executive Order 12947 of January 23, 1995, "Prohibiting Transactions with Terrorists Who Threaten to Disrupt the Middle East Peace Process," available at http://www.treas.gov/offices/enforcement/ofac/legal/eo/12947.pdf.

[145] Elaine Sciolino, "Violence Thwarts C.I.A. Director's Unusual Diplomatic Role in Middle Eastern Peacemaking," *New York Times*, November 13, 2000. See also Vernon Loeb, "CIA Emerges to Resolve Mideast Disputes; Out of Shadows, Agency Is Directly Involved in Israeli-Palestinian Security Talks," *Washington Post*, September 30, 1998.

[146] See Brynjar Lia, *Building Arafat's Police*, Ithaca Press, Reading, UK, 2007, p. 300, et seq.

[147] U.S. Treasury Department, Office of Foreign Assets Control, "What You Need to Know About U.S. Sanctions," available at http://www.ustreas.gov/offices/enforcement/ofac/programs/terror/terror.pdf

[148] U.S. Treasury Department press release TG-594, "Treasury Designates Gaza-Based Business, Television Station for Hamas Ties," March 18, 2010, available at http://www.ustreas.gov/press/releases/tg594.htm.

[149] The first attempt at cultivating an Arafat alternative under the rubric of the international Quartet's "Roadmap for Peace" effort in 2003 was to transfer several of Arafat's powers to Mahmoud Abbas as PA Prime Minister. Although an Arafat associate, Abbas had a reputation as an advocate for a negotiated peace with Israel, and was critical of the Palestinian turn to violence during the second intifada. The U.S. and international attempt to empower Abbas, however, proved abortive, as Arafat would not relinquish control over key PA security and financial power centers, and Abbas resigned in frustration in October 2003 after only six months in office.

[150] Interview with Ibrahim Ibrach, as quoted in Milton-Edwards and Farrell, op. cit., pp. 246-247.

[151] See Palestinian Center for Policy and Survey Research, Special Public Opinion Poll on the Upcoming Palestinian Elections (January 17-19, 2006), available at http://www.pcpsr.org/survey/polls/2006/preelectionsjan06.html (forecasting a 7% margin of victory for Fatah, with a 2% margin of error); Jerusalem Media and Communications Centre, Poll No. 56, January 2006, available at http://www.jmcc.org/documentsandmaps.aspx?id=444 (forecasting a 2% margin of victory for Fatah).

[152] A Hamas banner flown in Gaza shortly after the August 2005 disengagement read, in English, "Jerusalem and West Bank after Gaza HAMAS." Milton-Edwards and Farrell, op. cit., p. 246. See also Palestinian Center for Policy and Survey Research, Palestinian Public Opinion Poll #17 (September 7-9, 2005), available at http://www.pcpsr.org/survey/polls/2005/p17a.html: "On The Eve Of The Israeli Withdrawal From The Gaza Strip, 84% See It As Victory For Armed Resistance And 40% Give Hamas Most Of The Credit For It".

[153] Scott Wilson and Glenn Kessler, "U.S. Funds Enter Fray in Palestinian Elections," *Washington Post*, January 22, 2006.

[154] See, e.g., Glenn Kessler, "Bush Is Conciliatory in Accepting Victory of Hamas," *Washington Post*, January 27, 2006. In their 2010 book on Hamas, Beverley Milton-Edwards and Stephen Farrell wrote the following about the 2006 elections: "The foreign interventions proved pointless, even counterproductive. To neutralize them Hamas held back its closing message until the final days of the campaign—huge banners across the main streets of Palestinian cities which proclaimed: 'Israel and America say no to Hamas. What do you say?'" Milton-Edwards and Farrell, op. cit., p. 256.

[155] See, e.g., Rami G. Khouri, "On Democracy, Arabs Mistrust the American Messenger," *Daily Star* (Lebanon), February 4, 2006.

[156] The European Union also provided aid directly to Palestinians in the West Bank and Gaza for humanitarian and development purposes (including support for Gaza's power plant) through its Temporary International Mechanism (TIM).

[157] See David Rose, "The Gaza Bombshell," *Vanity Fair*, April 2008.

[158] See, e.g., Sayigh, *"We serve the people"...*, op. cit.

[159] A detailed account is found in Milton-Edwards and Farrell, op. cit., pp. 282-292.

[160] Nathan J. Brown, "Are Palestinians Building a State?", op. cit.

[161] See also "Khaled Mishal, external leader, Hamas Political Bureau," *Jane's Intelligence Weekly*, December 16, 2009.

[162] For a detailed account of the failed assassination attempt and Meshaal's rise to power within Hamas, see McGeough, op. cit.

[163] See footnote 143.

[164] Osama Al-Essa, "The Smiling Face of Hamas," *Asharq Alawsat* (English edition), July 14, 2007, available at http://aawsat.com/english/news.asp?section=3&id=9575.

[165] Israel Ministry of Foreign Affairs, "Video: Hamas uses civilians as a means to achieving military goals," January 11, 2009, available at http://www.mfa.gov.il/MFA/Terrorism+Obstacle+to+Peace/Hamas+war+against +Israel/Video_civilians_military_goals_Jan+2009.htm

[166] Yaakov Katz, "Meet the Hamas military leadership," *jpost.com*, December 22, 2008.

In: The Middle East in Turmoil, Volume 3
Editor: Angela N. Castillo

ISBN: 978-1-61324-241-4
© 2011 Nova Science Publishers, Inc.

Chapter 2

THE UNITED ARAB EMIRATES (UAE): ISSUES FOR U.S. POLICY*

Kenneth Katzman

SUMMARY

The UAE's relatively open borders, economy, and society have won praise from advocates of expanded freedoms in the Middle East while producing financial excesses, social ills such as prostitution and human trafficking, and relatively lax controls on sensitive technologies acquired from the West. These concerns—as well as concerns about the UAE oversight and management of a complex and technically advanced initiative such as a nuclear power program—underscored dissatisfaction among some members of Congress with a U.S.-UAE civilian nuclear cooperation agreement. The agreement was signed on May 21, 2009, and submitted to Congress that day. It entered into force on December 17, 2009. However, U.S. concerns about potential leakage of U.S. and other advanced technologies through the UAE to Iran, in particular, are far from alleviated.

Despite its social tolerance and economic freedom, the UAE government is authoritarian, although with substantial informal citizen participation and consensus-building. Assessments by a wide range of observers say that members of the elite (the ruling families of the seven emirates and clans allied with them) routinely obtain favored treatment in court cases, obtain access to lucrative business opportunities, and exert preponderant influence on national decisions. The UAE federation president, Shaykh Khalifa bin Zayid al-Nuhayyan, technically serves a five-year term, renewable by the Federal Supreme Council (composed of the seven heads of the individual emirates), although in practice leadership changes have generally taken place only after the death of a leader. After several years of resisting electoral processes similar to those instituted by other Gulf states, and despite an absence of popular pressure for elections, the UAE undertook its first electoral process in December 2006. The process was criticized as far

---

* This is an edited, reformatted and augmented version of a Congressional Research Services publication, dated December 7, 2010.

from instituting Western-style democratic processes, because the electorate was limited and selected by the government, and it voted for only half of the membership of a body with limited powers. The other half of the body continues to be appointed.

Partly because of substantial UAE federal government financial intervention and ample financial reserves, the political and social climate remained calm through the 2008-2009 global financial crisis and recession. The downturn hit Dubai emirate particularly hard and called into question its strategy of rapid, investment-fueled development, especially of luxury projects. Many expatriate workers left UAE after widespread layoffs, particularly in the financial and real estate sectors, and the decline affected property investors and the economies of several neighboring countries, including Afghanistan.

For details and analysis of the U.S.-UAE nuclear agreement and legislation concerning that agreement, see CRS Report R40344, *The United Arab Emirates Nuclear Program and Proposed U.S. Nuclear Cooperation*, by Christopher M. Blanchard and Paul K. Kerr.

GOVERNANCE, HUMAN RIGHTS, AND REFORM[1]

The United Arab Emirates (UAE) is a federation of seven emirates (principalities): Abu Dhabi, the oil-rich capital of the federation; Dubai, its free-trading commercial hub; and the five smaller and less wealthy emirates of Sharjah, Ajman, Fujayrah, Umm al-Qaywayn, and Ras al-Khaymah. After Britain announced in 1968 that it would no longer ensure security in the Gulf, six "Trucial States" decided to form the UAE federation in December 1971; Ras al-Khaymah joined in 1972. The UAE federation has completed a major leadership transition since the death of its key founder, Shaykh Zayid bin Sultan Al Nuhayyan, long-time ruler of Abu Dhabi and UAE president, on November 2, 2004.

His son, Crown Prince Shaykh Khalifa bin Zayid al-Nuhayyan, born in 1948, was named ruler of Abu Dhabi and, keeping with tradition, was subsequently selected by all seven emirates (Federal Supreme Council) as UAE president. The third son of Zayid, Shaykh Mohammad bin Zayid alNuhayyan, is Abu Dhabi crown prince and heir apparent. The ruler of Dubai traditionally serves concurrently as vice president and prime minister of the UAE; that position has been held by Mohammad bin Rashid Al Maktum, architect of Dubai's modernization drive, since the death of his elder brother Maktum bin Rashid Al Maktum on January 5, 2006. Shaykh Mohammad bin Rashid also continued as defense minister. The crown prince of Dubai is his son, Hamdan bin Mohammad Al Maktum, who heads the "Dubai Executive Committee," the equivalent of a cabinet for Dubai emirate. Under a Dubai-level reorganization announced in January 2010, five committees were set up to help the Executive Committee on various major issues.

The federation president and vice president serve five-year terms, but they technically owe their positions to the UAE's highest body, the Federal Supreme Council, which is composed of the leaders of each of the seven emirates of the UAE. Two emirates, Sharjah and Ras al-Khaymah, have a common ruling family: the Al Qawasim tribe. The Federal Supreme Council meets four times per year to establish general policy guidelines, although the leaders of the seven emirates consult frequently with each other. It met on November 3, 2009, to decide whether Shaykh Khalifa and Shaykh Mohammad would continue in their posts and, as expected, no major changes were made. In practice, posts at that level of UAE leadership change only in the event of death of an incumbent.

A UAE cabinet reshuffle in May 2009 resulted in a change in two new deputy prime ministers, one of whom serves concurrently as interior minister (the lead agency on internal security). The shift was viewed by observers as strengthening the hand of Crown Prince Mohammad bin Zayid because the new deputy prime ministers are close to him, although there are no evident rifts between him and his brother, the UAE president.

Some Basic Facts About UAE

Population	4.8 million, of which about 900,000 are citizens. Expatriates are 85% of the work force.
Religions	96% Muslim, of which 16% are Shiite; 4% Christian and Hindu
Ethnic Groups	19% Emirati (citizenry); 23% other Arab and Iranian; 50% South Asian; 8% western and other Asian expatriate
Size of Armed Forces	About 50,000
Gross Domestic Product (purchasing power parity)	$201 billion; per capita is $42,000 per year
Inflation Rate	About 14.5%
Oil Exports	About 2.7 million barrels per day
Foreign Exchange and Gold Reserves	About $67 billion
U.S. Exports to the UAE (2009)	$12.2 billion, making UAE the largest U.S. export market in the Arab world (2008). Goods sold to UAE are mostly machinery, aircraft, industrial materials, and other high value items.
Imports from UAE by the United States (2009)	$1.5 billion. About half of the total was crude oil. Other major categories include clothing and diamonds.
U.S. citizens resident in UAE	About 30,000
Major Projects	Dubai inaugurated 2,000+ foot "Burj Khalifa," world's tallest building, on January 4, 2010. Dubai metro has begun operations and is expanding service. Burj al Arab hotel in Dubai bills itself as "world's only 7-star hotel." UAE participating in Gulf country-wide railroad network to become operational by 2017. Abu Dhabi building local branches of Guggenheim and Louvre museums.

Sources: CIA World Factbook.

The leaders of the other individual emirates are Dr. Sultan bin Muhammad Al Qassimi (Sharjah); Saud bin Saqr Al Qassimi, (Ras al-Khaymah, see below); Humaid bin Rashid Al Nuaimi (Ajman); Hamad bin Muhammad Al Sharqi (Fujayrah); and Saud bin Rashid Al-Mu'alla (Umm al-Qaywayn). Shaykh Saud of Umm al-Qaywayn, who is about 57 years old, was named leader of that emirate in January 2009 upon the death of his father, Shaykh Rashid Al-Mu'alla. In Ras alKhaymah, there was a brief leadership struggle upon the October 27, 2010, death of the ailing longtime ruler, Shaykh Saqr bin Mohammad Al Qassim. He was succeeded by Shaykh Saud bin Saqr, who was the crown prince since 2003 when the ruler replaced Saud's elder brother, Shaykh Khalid bin Saqr, as crown prince. During 2003-2010, often using public relations campaigns in the United States and elsewhere, Shaykh Khalid had claimed to remain as crown prince even though the UAE federal government had repeatedly stated that his removal was legitimate and that he held no official position in the UAE. Shaykh Khalid's home in Ras al-Khaymah was surrounded by security forces the night his father died, enforcing the rulership rights of Shaykh Saud.

In part because of its small size, the UAE is one of the wealthiest of the Gulf states, as shown in the table above, and there is little unrest. Islamist movements in UAE, including those linked to the Muslim Brotherhood, are generally non-violent and perform social and relief work. UAE residents of Iranian origin tend to oppose governmental criticism of Iran, but this community does not constitute an organized opposition to the UAE government.

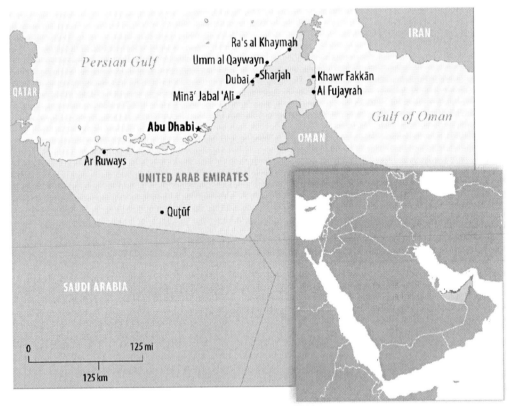

Source: CRS graphics.

Figure 1. Map of United Arab Emirates.

Status of Political Reform

Despite or perhaps because of the lack of significant opposition, the UAE has lagged on political reform. UAE leaders long delayed instituting any electoral processes, even as such elections began to expand in the other Gulf states, arguing that elections would inevitably aggravate long dormant schisms among tribes and clans, and potentially cause Islamist factions to become more radical. (Formal political parties are not permitted.) UAE leaders say

The United Arab Emirates (UAE): Issues for U.S. Policy

that UAE citizens are able to express their concerns directly to the leadership through traditional consultative mechanisms, such as the open *majlis* (councils) held by many UAE leaders, including Shaykh Khalifa.

The UAE leadership decided it had fallen too far behind its Gulf neighbors, and, in December 2006, it instituted a limited and controlled electoral process for half of the 40-seat Federal National Council (FNC). The other 20 seats would continue to be appointed. Previously, all 40 members of the FNC were appointed by all seven emirates. The seat distribution of the FNC remains weighted in favor of Abu Dhabi and Dubai (eight seats each). Sharjah and Ras alKhaymah have six each, and the others have four seats each.

The electorate was to be limited to a "local council," convened by the rulers of each emirate, numbering 100 persons per FNC seat. So, for example, the Abu Dhabi electoral council would be 100 x 8 = 800 electors, and the total UAE-wide electorate would be 4,000 persons. However, the Election Commission approved a slightly larger 6,595-person electorate, or about 160 persons per FNC seat. Of this total, 1,162 electors were women. Out of the total of 452 candidates for the 20 FNC elected seats, there were 65 female candidates. Only one woman was elected (from Abu Dhabi), but another seven women were appointed to the remaining 20 seats. The "election" process was spread over three different days— December 16, 18, and 20, 2006.

UAE plans are to gradually expand the size of the FNC and to broaden its powers, according to the Minister of State for FNC Affairs (also Minister of State for Foreign Affairs) Anwar Gargash. However, no specific expansion of powers or time frames for such expansions have been announced. The FNC can review, but not enact or veto, federal legislation, and it can question, but not impeach, federal cabinet ministers. It has questioned government ministers mostly on economic and social issues. Its sessions are open to the public. According to the State Department, in 2008 the government accepted 80% of the FNC's recommendations on legislation. Each emirate also has its own consultative council. On the other hand, the State Department human rights report on UAE for 2009 says that in April 2009, the government prohibited the FNC from discussing the economic ramifications for the UAE of the global financial downturn.

Human Rights-Related Issues

The human rights record of the UAE is relatively positive on some issues, but relatively poor on others, according to U.S. and outside assessments. The State Department human rights report for 2009 was somewhat more critical of the UAE than previous years' reports, asserting that there are unverified reports of torture, government restrictions of freedoms of speech, and lack of judicial independence. Some human rights problems in UAE, such as human trafficking, are caused in part because the government is relatively lax in some cases, not because it is too strict. Political rights and democratization are discussed above; among other specific measures, freedom of assembly is forbidden by law, but in practice small demonstrations on working conditions and some other issues have been tolerated.

The United States has sought to promote democracy, rule of law, and civil society in the Persian Gulf region, including in UAE. Some State Department programs to promote student and women's political participation, entrepreneurship, legal reform, civil society, independent media, and international trade law compliance are funded by the State Department's Middle

East Partnership Initiative (MEPI). The U.S. Embassy in Abu Dhabi houses a MEPI office/staff that runs the MEPI programs throughout the Gulf region.

Press Freedoms

Some ministerial rank officials are committed to reform, including Foreign Minister Shaykh Abdullah bin Zayid al-Nuhayyan and Minister of State Anwar Gargash, mentioned above. Shaykh Abdullah's former post of information minister was abolished in 2006 to allow media independence. On the other hand, in April 2009, a new media law drew opposition from some human rights groups who said it allows for penalties against journalists who personally criticize UAE leaders. Provisions governing media licensing do not clearly articulate the standards the government will apply in approving or denying licenses for media organs to operate. The UAE government says the law does not apply to the "Free Zones" in UAE in which major foreign media organizations operate.

Justice/Rule of Law

Many observers note that justice in UAE is selective. For example, on January 10, 2010, a UAE court acquitted the UAE president's brother, Shaykh Issa bin Zayid Al Nuhayyan, on charges of torturing an Afghan merchant. He was acquitted even though there was a video available of Shaykh Issa beating the Afghan and driving over his legs with a sport vehicle, and even though three others involved in the incident, all non-royals, were convicted. The UAE court ruled that Shaykh Issa was not liable because he was taking prescription drugs that may have prompted his actions. Others say that arrests of expatriates and non-citizens have increased along with the continuing economic downturn, possibly out of citizen frustration that globalization and dramatic economic expansion have led to bursting of the economic "bubble" in UAE. In 2007, human rights groups criticized the conservative-dominated justice system for threatening to prosecute a 15-year-old French expatriate for homosexuality, a crime in UAE, when he was raped by two UAE men; the UAE men were later sentenced for sexual assault and kidnapping.

Women's Rights

Progress on women's political rights has been steady and observers say the UAE is perhaps the only country in the Middle East where expatriate women are fully accepted working in high-paying professions such as finance and banking. There are now four women in the cabinet: Shayha Lubna al-Qassimi, minister of foreign trade and planning; Mariam al-Roumi, minister of social affairs; and two ministers without portfolio—Reem al-Hashimi and Maitha al-Shamsi. Nine women are in the Federal National Council, and seven women serve on the 40-seat consultative council in Sharjah emirate. About 10% of the UAE diplomatic corps is now female; none served prior to 2001. In November 2008, Dubai emirate appointed 10 female public prosecutors. The UAE Air Force has four women fighter pilots.

Religious Freedom

The November 17, 2010, State Department report on international religious freedom repeated the previous year's assessment that there was "no change" in the status of respect for religious freedom by the government during the reporting period." The constitution provides for freedom of religion but also declares Islam as the official religion of the country. In practice, non-Muslims in UAE are free to practice their religion; there are 34 Christian churches built on land donated by the ruling families of the various emirates, but there are no Jewish synagogues or Buddhist temples. The Shiite Muslim minority is free to worship and maintain its own mosques, but Shiite mosques receive no government funds and there are no Shiites in top federal posts.

Labor Rights

On several occasions, foreign laborers working on the large, ambitious construction projects in Dubai have conducted strikes to protest poor working conditions and non-payment of wages.

Some of these concerns have been addressed by the Labor Ministry's penalizing of employers, and a process, formulated in June 2008, to have workers' salaries deposited directly in banks.

Human Trafficking

Other social problems might be a result of the relatively open economy of the UAE, particularly in Dubai. The UAE is still considered a "destination country" for women trafficked from Asia and the former Soviet Union. The Trafficking in Persons report for 2010 placed the UAE in "Tier 2"—an upgrade from the "Tier 2: Watch List" placement in 2009. The 2010 upgrade was made on the grounds that the UAE is taking steps to eliminate trafficking in persons, particularly against sex trafficking offenders. The UAE has made progress in curbing trafficking of young boys as camel jockeys; it has repatriated at least 1,050 children out of a suspected 5,000 trafficked for camel racing, provided $3 million for their care and repatriation, and it now uses robot jockeys at camel races.

COOPERATION AGAINST TERRORISM AND PROLIFERATION

These issues are of particular concern to the United States because of a pattern of lax UAE enforcement of export and border controls, with respect particularly to the leakage of U.S. or other technology to Iran. The relatively small sums of U.S. aid to UAE are generally for programs to improve UAE performance on enforcing export control laws.

The UAE was one of only three countries (Pakistan and Saudi Arabia were the others) to have recognized the Taliban during 1996-2001 as the government of Afghanistan, even though the Taliban was harboring Osama bin Laden and other Al Qaeda leaders during that time. During Taliban rule, the UAE allowed Ariana Afghan airlines to operate direct service, and Al Qaeda activists reportedly spent time there.[2] Two of the September 11 hijackers were UAE nationals, and they reportedly used UAE-based financial networks in the plot.

Since then, the UAE has been credited in State Department "Country Reports on Terrorism" with assisting in the arrests of senior Al Qaeda operatives;[3] denouncing terror attacks; improving border security; prescribing guidance for Friday prayer leaders; investigating suspect financial transactions; criminalizing use of the Internet by terrorist groups, and strengthening its bureaucracy and legal framework to combat terrorism. The UAE Central Bank is credited in the State Department terrorism report for 2008 and 2009 with providing training programs to UAE financial institutions on money laundering and terrorism financing, although actions against informal financial transmittals (*hawala*) require "further vigilance." It was reported in September 2009 that earlier in 2009, UAE security officials had broken up an Al Qaeda plot to blow up targets in Dubai emirate.[4] In November 2010, the UAE's National Committee to Combat Terrorism announced that the UAE was reviewing a 2004 counterterrorism law to better fight evolving threats and money laundering.

The UAE has signed on to several U.S. efforts to prevent proliferation and terrorism. These include the Container Security Initiative Statement of Principles, aimed at screening U.S.-bound containerized cargo transiting Dubai ports. Under it, three U.S. Customs and Border Protection officers are co-located with the Dubai Customs Intelligence Unit at Port Rashid in Dubai. The program results in about 20 ship inspections per week of U.S.-bound containers, many of them apparently originating in Iran, according to the State Department terrorism report for 2008 (published April 30, 2009). The UAE is a signator to the proliferation Security Initiative, the Megaports Initiative designed to prevent terrorist from using major ports to ship illicit material, and the Customs-Trade Partnership Against Terrorism.

Record on Proliferation Cooperation

The UAE record on preventing the re-export of advanced technology, particularly to Iran, is mixed, although said to be improving as of mid-2010. Taking advantage of geographic proximity and the high volume of Iran-Dubai trade ($10 billion per year), numerous Iranian entities involved in Iran's energy sector and its WMD programs have offices in the UAE that are used to try to procure needed technology and equipment. However, the UAE has enhanced its cooperation at times when U.S. officials or outside experts have questioned its performance. In connection with revelations of illicit sales of nuclear technology to Iran, Libya, and North Korea by Pakistan's nuclear scientist A.Q. Khan, Dubai was named as a key transfer point for Khan's shipments of nuclear components. Two Dubai-based companies were apparently involved in transshipping components: SMB Computers and Gulf Technical Industries.[5] On April 7, 2004, the Administration sanctioned a UAE firm, Elmstone Service and Trading FZE, for allegedly selling weapons of mass destruction-related technology to Iran, under the Iran-Syria Non-Proliferation Act (P.L. 106-178). In June 2006, the Bureau of Industry and Security (BIS) released a general order imposing a license requirement on Mayrow General Trading Company and related enterprises in the UAE. This was done after Mayrow was implicated in the transhipment of electronic components and devices capable of being used to construct improvised explosive devices (IED) used in Iraq and Afghanistan.[6] In February 2007 the Administration threatened to form a new category of control called "Destinations of Diversion Control" with UAE as the intended designee country, and P.L. 111-195 sets up a provision for a category of countries similar to that, which would be sanctioned (restrictions on dual use U.S. exports) for a determination of non-cooperation. Earlier, in September 2007, the FNC headed off U.S. penalties by adopting a law strengthening export controls (April 2007). In September 2007, the UAE used the new law to shut down 40 foreign and UAE firms allegedly involved in dual use exports to Iran and other countries. However, UAE officials publicly acknowledged that the UAE's application of this law is still evolving. On July 22, 2010, Deputy Assistant Secretary of State for International Security and Nonproliferation Vann Van Diepen testified before the House Foreign Affairs Committee (Subcommittee on Terrorism, Nonproliferation and Trade) that the UAE is augmenting the staff of the office that implements the 2007 law. He added that the UAE's enforcement bodies— customs, law enforcement, and intelligence services—are functioning to that end.[7]

Still, allegations recur periodically. In January 2009, the Institute for Science and International Security issued a report entitled "Iranian Entities' Illicit Military Procurement Networks," published January 12, 2009. The report asserts that Iran has used UAE companies to obtain technology from U.S. suppliers, and that the components obtained have been used to construct improvised explosive devices (IEDs) shipped by Iran to militants in Iraq and Afghanistan. Other UAE companies the report alleges were involved in this network included not only Mayrow but also Majidco Micro Electronics, Micatic General Trading, and Talinx Electronics.

The issue of leakage of technology has sometimes caused U.S. criticism or questioning of UAE investment deals. In December 2008 some members of Congress called for a review by the interagency "Committee on Foreign Investment in the United States" (CFIUS) of a proposed joint venture between Advanced Micro Devices and Advanced Technology Investment Co. of Abu Dhabi for the potential for technology transfers. In February 2006, CFIUS approved the takeover by the Dubai-owned "Dubai Ports World" company of a British firm that manages six U.S. port facilities. Members, concerned that the takeover might weaken U.S. port security, opposed it in P.L. 109-234, causing the company to divest assets involved in U.S. port operations (divestment completed in late 2006 to AIG Global Investments). Little opposition was expressed to a September 2007 Borse Dubai plan to take a 20% stake in the NASDAQ stock market, or to a November 2007 investment of $7.5 billion in Citigroup by the Abu Dhabi Investment Authority (ADIA), which manages excess oil revenues estimated at over $500 billion.

Nuclear Agreement

It is the concern about the leakage of technology to Iran, via the UAE, that underpins much of the concern about a U.S.-UAE agreement, signed January 15, 2009, to help the UAE develop a nuclear power program. The agreement, which was revised slightly and signed again by the Obama Administration on May 21, 2009 (and submitted to Congress that day), would be subject to conditions specified in Section 123 of the Atomic Energy Act of 1954 [42 U.S.C. 2153(b)], and was subject to congressional approval (in the form of passage of a joint resolution of approval or non-passage of a joint resolution of disapproval within 90 days of continuous legislative session following the May 21 submission). In the 111th Congress, concerns were encapsulated in H.R. 364, which would require the President to certify that the UAE has taken a number of steps to stop illicit trade with Iran before any agreement would take effect. However, several congressional resolutions of approval of the agreement (S.J.Res. 18 and H.J.Res. 60) have been introduced, whereas one resolution of disapproval (H.J.Res. 55) was introduced. No measure blocking the agreement was enacted, and the "1-2-3 Agreement" entered into force on December 17, 2009. See CRS Report R40344, The United Arab Emirates Nuclear Program and Proposed U.S. Nuclear Cooperation, by Christopher M. Blanchard and Paul K. Kerr

FOREIGN POLICY AND DEFENSE COOPERATION WITH THE UNITED STATES

Following the 1991 Gulf War to oust Iraqi forces from Kuwait, the UAE determined that it needed a closer security relationship with the United States. The UAE did not fear a direct threat from Saddam Hussein's Iraq, which is at the north end of the Persian Gulf, but it primarily sought to deter and balance out Iranian power, which remains the primary UAE concern.

Security Cooperation with the United States

The UAE may be emerging as a lynchpin of U.S. strategy to defend the Gulf, despite the small size of the UAE armed forces (about 50,000). The Iraqi invasion of Kuwait in August 1990 prompted the UAE to enter into substantial defense cooperation with the United States. The framework for U.S.-UAE defense cooperation is a July 25, 1994, bilateral defense pact, the text of which is classified, including a "status of forces agreement" (SOFA). Under the pact, during the years of U.S. "containment" of Iraq (1991-2003), the UAE allowed U.S. equipment pre-positioning and U.S. warship visits at its large Jebel Ali port, capable of handling aircraft carriers, and it permitted the upgrading of airfields in the UAE that were used for U.S. combat support flights during Operation Enduring Freedom in Afghanistan and Operation Iraqi Freedom (OIF).[8] About 1,800 U.S. forces, mostly Air Force, are in UAE, up from 800 before OIF; they use Al Dhafra air base (mostly KC-10 refueling) and naval facilities at Fujairah to support U.S. operations in Iraq and Afghanistan, even though UAE officials say that OIF benefitted Iran strategically.

Suggesting it wants to broaden its defense relations, in January 2008 the UAE signed an agreement with French President Nicolas Sarkozy to allow a French military presence. The facilities were inaugurated during a visit by Sarkozy to UAE on May 27, 2009, and include (1) a 900-foot section of the Zayid Port for use by the French navy; (2) an installation at Dhafra Air Base to be used by France's air force; and (3) a barracks at an Abu Dhabi military camp that will house about 400 French military personnel. On the other hand, in October 2010, the UAE reportedly threatened to ask Canada to evacuate a UAE base, Camp Mirage, used by Canada as a staging point for its forces to deploy to Afghanistan, when Canada refused additional landing slots in Canada for Emirates Air.[9] The two countries reportedly agreed to try to negotiate a solution to the mutual concerns.

Relations with Iran

The UAE remains highly wary of Iran's ambitions and powers, but it has sought to reach out to Iran's government and deny Iran any justification for aggression or adverse action against the UAE. Commercial ties between the two are extensive and relatively free of complaints by either side and, as discussed above, these Iran-UAE ties have caused U.S. concerns about leakage of key dual-use technology to Iran and to U.S.-UAE measures to limit such leakage.

Aside from trying to limit technology leakage to Iran via UAE, the United States has enlisted the UAE in a multilateral effort to stiffen international sanctions on Iran, in part by alleviating the concerns of China (a permanent U.N. Security Council member) about its oil supplies. The Obama Administration has encouraged the UAE and other oil exporters to offer to boost oil supplies to China to compensate for any loss of imports from Iran that may result from China's cooperation against Iran.[10] In early October 2010, the UAE government directed its banks to fully comply with the restrictions on dealing with Iranian banks outlined in U.N. Security Council Resolution 1929, adopted June 9, 2010. The move caused a 15% drop in the value of Iran's currency, the rial. The UAE is also a key participant in U.S. efforts to build a missile defense shield for the Gulf, in order to deter or contain Iran, as noted below. In October 2009, Foreign Minister Abdullah bin Zayid was uncharacteristically public in expressing support for "political and diplomatic pressure on Iran to stop it from acquiring nuclear technology." The statements were made at a joint news conference with visiting NATO Secretary General Anders Fogh Rasmussen. The 2010 GCC summit, held in Abu Dhabi and concluded December 7, 2010, called for a peaceful resolution of the Iran nuclear issue, although expressing "utmost concern" about Iran's program. This latter comment appears to support press reports and UAE statements in 2010 that reflect GCC backing for more aggressive U.S. action to set back Iran's program.

Some Iranian actions may account for the UAE's strategic closeness to the United States and other Western powers. UAE fears of Iran have been elevated since April 1992, when Iran asserted complete control of the largely uninhabited Persian Gulf island of Abu Musa, which it and the UAE shared under a 1971 bilateral agreement. (In 1971, Iran, then ruled by the U.S.-backed Shah, seized two other islands, Greater and Lesser Tunb, from the emirate of Ras al-Khaymah, as well as part of Abu Musa from the emirate of Sharjah.) In October 2008, the UAE and Iran signed an agreement to establish a joint commission to resolve the dispute; that agreement came two months after the UAE protested Iran's opening in August 2008 of administrative and maritime security offices on Abu Musa. Iran has allowed Sharjah to open power and water desalination facilities on the island. The 2010 GCC summit in Abu Dhabi, referenced above, nodded to UAE concerns by demanding Iran return the UAE islands. The United States is concerned about Iran's physical control over the islands, but takes no position on the legal sovereignty of the islands.

The UAE, particularly Abu Dhabi, has long feared that the large Iranian-origin community in Dubai emirate (estimated at 400,000 persons) could pose a "fifth column" threat to UAE stability. Illustrating the UAE's attempts to avoid antagonizing Iran, in May 2007, Iranian President Mahmoud Ahmadinejad was permitted to hold a rally for Iranian expatriates in Dubai when he made the first high-level visit to UAE since UAE independence in 1971. Still, reflecting the underlying tensions and volatility of UAE-Iran relations, the two countries issued mutual recriminations in January 2009 over the UAE decision in late 2008 to begin fingerprinting Iranian visitors to UAE.

Cooperation on Iraq

Aside from allowing U.S. use of UAE military facilities, the UAE has undertaken several initiatives to support U.S. efforts to stabilize Iraq since the fall of Saddam Hussein. The UAE has provided facilities for Germany to train Iraqi police. It pledged $215 million for Iraq reconstruction but has provided the funds not in cash but in the form of humanitarian contributions. Some of the funds were used to rebuild hospitals in Iraq and to provide medical treatment to Iraqi children in the UAE. Agreeing with the U.S. view that Sunni Arab states need to engage the Shiite-dominated government in Baghdad, in June 2008, the UAE appointed an Ambassador to Iraq, the first Arab country to do so. The following month it wrote off $7 billion (including interest) in Iraqi debt. Abu Dhabi Crown Prince Shaykh Mohammad bin Zayid visited Iraq in October 2008. The UAE has tended to defer to Saudi Arabia in its efforts to encourage inclusion of high profile Sunni Arabs in new Iraqi government being formed in late 2010.

Cooperation on Afghanistan and Pakistan

In addition to placing some of its military facilities at U.S. and allied disposal for use in Afghanistan (and Iraq), the UAE is assisting the U.S. and international mission to stabilize Afghanistan. Despite the small size of its military force, a 250-person contingent of UAE troops has been serving in Afghanistan since 2004. The UAE forces, the only Arab combat forces in Afghanistan, are operating in the restive southern part of Afghanistan, particularly Uruzgan Province, where they appear to be welcomed by the Muslim population there.

The UAE has pledged a total of $323 million in economic aid for Afghanistan since the fall of the Taliban. Among the projects funded with UAE aid include "Zayed University," a college serving over 6,000 Afghan students per year; six medical clinics; a major hospital with a capacity of 7,000 patients; the building of "Zayed City" that houses 200 Afghan families displaced by violence; 160 drinking wells; and 38 mosques.[11]

In related aid for U.S. regional policy, Abu Dhabi hosted the November 2008 meeting of the "Friends of Pakistan" donors group that is attempting to help Pakistan through its financial difficulties. The UAE provided about $100 million to aid victims of a major earthquake in Pakistan in October 2005. The UAE also has appointed a direct counterpart to the Obama Administration's Special Representative for Afghanistan and Pakistan, Ambassador Richard Holbrooke.

U.S. and Other Arms Sales

The UAE views arms purchases from the United States as enhancing the U.S. commitment to UAE security. The United States views these sales as a means to enhance the U.S.-led security architecture for the Gulf in which the Gulf partners take on increased responsibilities. In 2009, the UAE bought about $18 billion worth of U.S. military equipment, according to June 16, 2010, testimony by CENTCOM Commander General David Petraeus. Until 2008, the most significant buy was the March 2000 purchase of 80 U.S. F-16 aircraft, equipped with the Advanced Medium Range Air to Air Missile (AMRAAM) and the HARM (High Speed Anti-Radiation Missile), a deal exceeding $8 billion. Congress did not try to block the aircraft sale, but some members questioned the AMRAAM as an introduction of the weapon into the Gulf. Among other sales with the potential to enhance the UAE's offensive capability, a sale of High Mobility Artillery Rocket Systems (HIMARS) and Army Tactical Missile Systems (ATACMs), valued at about $750 million, notified on September 21, 2006.

More recent sales to UAE, some with offensive potential, have been in concert with the U.S.-led "Gulf Security Dialogue," intended to help the Gulf states contain Iran. The most significant is the Terminal High Altitude Air Defense System (THAAD), the first sale ever of that sophisticated missile defense system (notified September 9, 2008, valued at about $7 billion). The main manufacturer, Lockheed Martin, said in June 2010 that a firm agreement might be signed in the next few months. Among the most significant other recent sales are the advanced Patriot antimissile systems (PAC-3, up to $9 billion value, notified December 4, 2007) and kits for the Joint Direct Attack Munition (JDAM) kits ($326 million value, notified

January 3, 2008). Also notified on September 9, 2008, were sales to UAE of a surface launched AMRAAM ($445 million value) and vehicle mounted "Stinger" anti-aircraft systems ($737 million value). In conjunction with the international defense exhibit in Abu Dhabi in March 2009, the UAE signed agreements with Boeing Co. and Lockheed Martin Corp. to buy $3 billion worth of military transport aircraft (C17 and C-130, respectively). On November 4, 2010, the Defense Security Cooperation Agency notified Congress of two potential sales: $140 million worth of ATACMs (see above) and associated support; and a possible $5 billion worth of AH-64 Apache helicopters (30 helicopters, remanufactured to Block III configuration).[12]

The United States is in competition with France for further aircraft sales. France is hoping that, as part of the facilities basing agreement discussed above, the UAE will buy about 60 Rafale combat aircraft, which could be valued at about $8 billion. The UAE has already bought 380 French-made Leclerc tanks and 60 Mirage 2000 warplanes. However, the United States is hoping to sell the UAE additional F-16's, according to press reports.

UAE Provision of Foreign Aid

The UAE asserts that it has provided billions of dollars in international aid through its government and through funds controlled by royal family members and other elites. Among the foreign aid activities reported are $100 million to aid victims of the December 2004 tsunami in the Indian Ocean and $100 million to help victims of Hurricane Katrina in the United States.

Other Regional Issues

On most regional issues, including the Arab-Israeli dispute, the UAE does not follow U.S. policy strictly or uncritically, but it does generally agree with most U.S. assessments of regional threats, and it supports U.S. diplomatic efforts to resolve regional issues. On the Arab-Israeli issue, the UAE wants to ensure that any settlement between Israel and the Palestinians is "just," and it sometimes criticizes the United States as excessively supportive of Israel. However, the UAE has not advanced its own far-reaching proposals to resolve the Israeli-Palestinian dispute, as has King Abdullah of Saudi Arabia. It also tends to defer to Saudi Arabia rather than try to emerge as a major direct mediator between Palestinian factions, as have Saudi Arabia, Qatar, and Egypt.

The UAE's steps to support U.S. policy on the Middle East peace process have tended to come in concert with other Gulf states. In 1994 the UAE joined with the other Gulf monarchies in ending enforcement of the Arab League's boycott of companies doing business with Israel and on companies that deal with companies that do business with Israel. The UAE formally bans direct trade with Israel, although UAE companies reportedly do business with Israeli firms and some Israeli diplomats have attended multilateral meetings in the UAE. Unlike Qatar and Oman, the UAE did not host multilateral Arab-Israeli working groups on regional issues when those talks took place during 1994-1998. In 2007, the UAE joined a "quartet" of Arab states (the others are Saudi Arabia, Egypt, and Jordan) to assist U.S. diplomacy on Israeli-Palestinian issues. In December 2008 and January 2009, the UAE government permitted street demonstrations in support of Hamas during its war with Israel. In

February 2009, the UAE denied a visa to an Israeli tennis player who was to participate in a Dubai tennis tournament, earning the UAE some international criticism.

The UAE has expressed concerns about the plight of the Palestinians, and has put its considerable financial resources to work on their behalf. One major UAE action has been to fund a housing project in Rafah, in the Gaza Strip, called "Shaykh Khalifa City." It also has given economic aid to Lebanon, perhaps in part to counter Iranian and Syrian influence there—an objective that UAE shares with Saudi Arabia and the other GCC states.

The UAE cooperates with virtually all GCC-wide development and economic initiatives, although some past border disputes and other disagreements with Saudi Arabia occasionally flare. A 1974 "Treaty of Jeddah" with Saudi Arabia formalized Saudi access to the Persian Gulf via a corridor running through UAE, in return for UAE gaining formal control of villages in the Buraymi oasis area.

ECONOMIC ISSUES

The UAE, a member of the World Trade Organization (WTO), has developed a free market economy. Partly as a result, the UAE, particularly Dubai emirate, whose strategy was built on attracting investment to construct large numbers of opulent and futuristic projects, built up a "bubble" in real estate prices and other assets. The UAE, particularly Dubai, has therefore been hurt significantly by the global economic downturn. Abu Dhabi has 80% of the federation's proven oil reserves of about 100 billion barrels, enough for over 100 years of exports at the current export rate of about 2.7 million barrels per day (mbd). Small amounts go to the United States. Abu Dhabi has been hurt by the fall in oil prices, but its reliance on oil has given it a certain financial cushion, relative to Dubai, which relies almost entirely on trade, financial products, investment in big projects such as the "Atlantis Hotel Dubai," and tourism.

The federal government has used some of the country's purported $700 billion "sovereign wealth fund" to inject into Dubai banks to help them ride out the downturn. In December 2009, Abu Dhabi pledged about $5 billion in additional funds (beyond $5 billion committed in November 2009) to help Dubai World (major real estate developer) avert outright default on about $26 billion in debt repayment. The severe recession has resulted in widespread layoffs in UAE and the departure of thousands of foreign workers, who often have abandoned cars and properties that were financed, leaving UAE banks with additional non-performing loans.[13] During 2008-2009, real estate prices fell about 40%-50% from the 2007 levels. The downturn in real estate prices has also affected regional investors, such as those in Afghanistan, who bought into high-end housing such as on the Palm Islands. The fall in value nearly caused a collapse of a major Afghan bank, Kabul Bank, in September 2010; the bank had made large loans to prominent Afghan power brokers and officials to buy property there.

On November 15, 2004, the Administration notified Congress it had begun negotiating a free trade agreement (FTA) with the UAE. Several rounds of talks were held prior to the June 2007 expiration of Administration "trade promotion authority," but progress was been halting.

The United Arab Emirates (UAE): Issues for U.S. Policy

The UAE is seeking to diversify its energy production and consumption to plan for the day when the developed world is no longer reliant on oil imports. While well endowed with oil, the UAE lacks non-associated natural gas. It has entered into a deal with neighboring gas exporter Qatar to construct pipeline that will bring Qatari gas to UAE (Dolphin project). The nuclear power program, discussed above, is also intended to address the country's fast growing energy consumption, although the global economic downturn has also served that purpose, at least temporarily.

The UAE, which is considered wealthy, receives small amounts of U.S. assistance. The primary purpose of the aid is to make the UAE eligible for advice and programming to improve its border security and export controls, as shown below.

Table 1. Recent U.S. Aid to UAE

	FY2007	FY2008	FY2009	FY2010 (est)	FY2011 (request)
NADR (Nonproliferation, Anti-Terrorism, Demining, and Related) - Counterterrorism Programs (ATA)	$1.409 million		$725,000		
NADR-Combating WMD	$172,000	$300,000	$200,000	$230,000	$230,000
International Military Education and Training (IMET)				$10,000	$10,000
Totals	$1.581 million	$300,000	$925,000	$240,000	$240,000

End Notes

[1] Information in this section is from the following State Department reports: Country Reports on Human Rights Practices-2009 (March 11, 2010); Trafficking in Persons Report for 2010 (June 14, 2010); and International Religious Freedom report: 2009 (October 26, 2009).

[2] Department of State. Office of the Coordinator for Counterterrorism. Country Reports on Terrorism 2009. August 5, 2010. CRS conversations with executive branch officials, 1997-2000.

[3] "U.S. Embassy to Reopen on Saturday After UAE Threat." *Reuters*, March 26, 2004.

[4] Lake, Eli and Sarah Carter. "UAE Kept Tight Lid on Disrupted Terror Plot." *Washington Times*, September 17, 2009.

[5] Milhollin, Gary and Kelly Motz. "Nukes 'R' US." *New York Times* op.ed. March 4, 2004.

[6] BIS, "General Order Concerning Mayrow General Trading and Related Enterprises," 71 *Federal Register* 107, June 5, 2006.

[7] Testimony of Mr. Vann Van Diepen before the House Foreign Affairs Committee. July 22, 2010.

[8] Jaffe, Greg. "U.S. Rushes to Upgrade Base for Attack Aircraft." *Wall Street Journal*, March 14, 2003.

[9] Chase, Steven and Brent Jang. "UAE Threatens to Kick Canada Out of Covert Military Base Camp Mirage." Toronto Globe and Mail, October 8, 2010.

[10] Solomon, Jay. "U.S. Enlists Oil to Sway Beijing's Stance on Tehran." *Wall Street Journal*, October 20, 2009.

[11] Information provided to CRS by the UAE Embassy in Washington, D.C. December 2009. [12] DSCA transmittal number 10-52. http://www.dsca.mil

[13] Worth, Robert. "Laid Off Foreigners Flee as Once Booming Dubai Spirals Down." *New York Times*, February 12, 2008.

In: The Middle East in Turmoil, Volume 3
Editor: Angela N. Castillo

ISBN: 978-1-61324-241-4
© 2011 Nova Science Publishers, Inc.

Chapter 3

AFGHANISTAN CASUALTIES: MILITARY FORCES AND CIVILIANS[*]

Susan G. Chesser

SUMMARY

This report collects statistics from a variety of sources on casualties sustained during Operation Enduring Freedom (OEF), which began on October 7, 2001, and is ongoing. OEF actions take place primarily in Afghanistan; however, OEF casualties also includes American casualties in Pakistan, Uzbekistan, Guantanamo Bay (Cuba), Djibouti, Eritrea, Ethiopia, Jordan, Kenya, Kyrgyzstan, the Philippines, Seychelles, Sudan, Tajikistan, Turkey, and Yemen.

Casualty data of U.S. military forces are compiled by the U.S. Department of Defense (DOD), as tallied from the agency's press releases. Also included are statistics on those wounded but not killed. Statistics may be revised as circumstances are investigated and as records are processed through the U.S. military's casualty system. More frequent updates are available at DOD's website at http://www.defenselink.mil/news/ under "Casualty Update."

A detailed casualty summary of U.S. military forces that includes data on deaths by cause, as well as statistics on soldiers wounded in action, is available at the following DOD website: http://siadapp.dmdc.osd.mil/personnel/CASUALTY/castop.htm.

NATO's International Security Assistance Force (ISAF) does not post casualty statistics of the military forces of partner countries on the ISAF website at http://www.isaf.nato.int/. ISAF press releases state that it is ISAF policy to defer to the relevant national authorities to provide notice of any fatality. For this reason, this report uses fatality data of coalition forces as compiled by CNN.com and posted online at http://www.cnn.com/SPECIALS/2004/oef.casualties/index.html.

The United Nations Assistance Mission to Afghanistan (UNAMA) reports casualty data of Afghan civilians semiannually, and the U.S. Department of Defense occasionally includes civilian casualty figures within its reports on Afghanistan. From July 2009 through April 2010, the Special Inspector General for Afghanistan Reconstruction (SIGAR) included statistics of casualties of members of the Afghan National Army and

---

[*] This is an edited, reformatted and augmented version of a Congressional Research Services publication, dated December 8, 2010.

Afghan National Police in its quarterly reports to Congress. SIGAR has ceased this practice, and there is no other published compilation of these statistics. This report now derives casualty figures of Afghan soldiers and police from the press accounts of the Reuters "Factbox: Security Developments in Afghanistan" series and the Pajhwok Afghan News agency. Both services attribute their reported information to officials of the NATO-led ISAF or local Afghan officials. Pajhwok Afghan News frequently concludes its accounts with statements from representatives of the Taliban, however, these figures are not included in this report.

Because the estimates of Afghan casualties contained in this report are based on varying time periods and have been created using different methodologies, readers should exercise caution when using them and should look to them as guideposts rather than as statements of fact.

This report will be updated as needed.

The following tables present data on U.S. military casualties in Operation Enduring Freedom, deaths of coalition partners in Afghanistan, and Afghan casualties, respectively.

Table 1. Operation Enduring Freedom, U.S. Fatalities and Wounded.
(as of December 6, 2010, 10 a.m. EST from October 7, 2001)

	Fatalities In and Around Afghanistan[a]	Fatalities in Other Locations[b]	Total Fatalities[c]		Wounded in Action
Hostiled	1,079	11	1,090		
Non-Hostile[e]	234	83	317		
Total	1,313	94	1,407	Total	9,583

Source: U.S. Department of Defense, http://www.defense.gov/news/casualty.pdf.

a "Fatalities in and around Afghanistan" includes casualties that occurred in Afghanistan, Pakistan, and Uzbekistan.

b "Other locations" includes casualties that occurred in Guantanamo Bay (Cuba), Djibouti, Eritrea, Ethiopia, Jordan, Kenya, Kyrgyzstan, the Philippines, Seychelles, Sudan, Tajikistan, Turkey, and Yemen.

c Fatalities include two Department of Defense civilian personnel.

d According to the Department of Defense *Dictionary of Military and Associated Terms*, as amended through 31 August 2005, a "hostile casualty" is a victim of a terrorist activity or a casualty as the result of combat or attack by any force against U.S. forces, available at http://handle.dtic.mil/100.2/ADA43918.

e The above-named reference defines a "nonhostile casualty" as a casualty that is not directly attributable to hostile action or terrorist activity, such as casualties due to the elements, self-inflicted wounds, or combat fatigue.

Afghanistan Casualties: Military Forces and Civilians

Table 2. American Casualties by Year through December 6, 2010

Year	Total Deaths	Total Wounded in Action
2001	11	33
2002	49	74
2003	45	99
2004	52	214
2005	98	267
2006	98	401
2007	117	752
2008	155	793
2009	311	2,139
2010 through December 6	471	4,811

Source: U.S. Department of Defense, Statistical Information Analysis Division, http://siadapp.dmdc. osd.mil/personnel/CASUALTY/oefmonth.pdf.

Table 3. Deaths of Coalition Partners in Afghanistan

Country	# of Deaths	Country	# of Deaths
Australia	21	Lithuania	1
Belgium	1	Netherlands	24
Canada	154	New Zealand	2
Czech Republic	3	Norway	9
Denmark	39	Poland	23
Estonia	8	Portugal	2
Finland	1	Romania	17
France	49	South Korea	1
Georgia	5	Spain	30
Germany	44	Sweden	4
Hungary	4	Turkey	2
Italy	31	United Kingdom	345
Latvia	4		
Total Non-U.S. Coalition Fatalities			824

Sources: CNN Casualties in Afghanistan, http://www.cnn.com/SPECIALS/war.casualties/ table.afghanistan.html; Canada's Department of National Defence, http://www.forces.gc.ca/ site/news-nouvelles/fallen-disparus/indexeng.asp; United Kingdom Ministry of Defense, http://www.mod.uk/DefenceInternet/FactSheets/OperationsFactsheets/OperationsInAfghanistanBri tishFatalities.htm; Australia's Department of Defence, http://www.defence.gov.au/op/afghanistan/ info/personnel.htm; "Factbox: Military Deaths in Afghanistan," Reuters News, September 28, 2010.

Table 4. Afghan Casualties

Group	Period	# of Casualties	Note
Afghan Civilians	January 1, 2010- September 30, 2010a	1,634 killed 2,809 injured	In the third quarter of 2010, 90% of civilian deaths and injuries were caused by anti-Government elements, which includes the Taliban as well as other individuals or groups who engage in armed conflict with the Government of Afghanistan or members of the International Military Forces.
	2009b	2,412 killed 3,566 injured	67% of civilian deaths were attributed to actions of anti-Government elements (78% of these deaths were caused by improvised explosive devices and suicide attacks).
			25% of civilian deaths were attributed to pro-Government forces.
			8% of civilian deaths were the result of cross-fire or improperly detonated ordnance.
	2008c	2,118 killed	
	2007c	1,523 killed	
Afghan National Army	January 1 - November 30,	314 killed	
	2010d	737 wounded	
	2009e	292 killed	
		859 wounded	
	2008f	259 killed	
		875 wounded	
	2007f	278 killed	
		750 wounded	
Afghan National Police	January 1 – November 30,	401 killed	
	2010g	728 wounded	
	2009h	639 killed	
		1,145 wounded	
	2008i	724 killed	
		1,209 wounded	
	2007i	688 killed	
		1,036 wounded	

Sources: Compiled by the Congressional Research Service from noted sources.

a United Nations Assistance Mission to Afghanistan, Human Rights Unit, *Afghanistan: Mid-Year Report on Protection of Civilians in Armed Conflict, 2010*, August 10, 2010, p. i, http://unama.unmissions.org/Portals/ UNAMA/Publication/August102010_MIDYEAR%20 REPORT%202010_Protection%20of%20Civilians%20in%20Armed%20Conflict.pdf; U.S. Department of Defense, *Report on Progress Toward Security and Stability in Afghanistan*, November 2010, p. 56, http://www.defense.gov/pubs/November_1230_Report_FINAL.pdf.

b United Nations Assistance Mission to Afghanistan, Human Rights Unit, *Afghanistan: Annual Report on Protection of Civilians in Armed Conflict, 2009*, January 2010, p. I, http://unama.unmissions.org/Portals/ UNAMA/human%20rights/Protection%20of%20Civilian%202009%20report%20English.pdf.

c United Nations Assistance Mission to Afghanistan, Human Rights Unit, *Afghanistan: Annual Report on Protection of Civilians in Armed Conflict, 2008*, January 2009, p. 12, http://unama.unmissions.org/Portals/UNAMA/human%20rights/UNAMA_09february-Annual%20Report_PoC%202008_FINAL_11Feb09.pdf.

d Special Inspector General for Afghanistan Reconstruction, *Quarterly Report to the United States Congress*, April 30, 2010, p. 58, http://www.sigar.mil/pdf/quarterly reports/Apr2010/SIGARapril_Lores.pdf; response via e-mail from the staff of the Special Inspector General for Afghanistan Reconstruction, August 9, 2010; and press reports from Reuters and the Pajhwok Afghan News agency.

e Special Inspector General for Afghanistan Reconstruction, *Quarterly Report to the United States Congress*, July 30, 2009, p. 55. http://www.sigar.mil/pdf/quarterlyreports/Jul09/pdf/Report_-_July_2009.pdf; *Quarterly Report to the United States Congress*, October 30, 2009, p. 62, http://www.sigar.mil/pdf/quarterlyreports/ Oct09/pdf/SIGAROct2009Web.pdf; and Special Inspector General for Afghanistan Reconstruction, *Quarterly Report to the United States Congress*, January 30, 2010, p. 64, http://www.sigar.mil/pdf/quarterlyreports/jan2010/pdf/ SIGAR_Jan2010.pdf.

f Special Inspector General for Afghanistan Reconstruction, *Quarterly Report to the United States Congress*, July 30, 2009, p. 55, http://www.sigar.mil/pdf/quarterlyreports/Jul09/pdf/Report_-_July_2009.pdf.

g Special Inspector General for Afghanistan Reconstruction, *Quarterly Report to the United States Congress*, April 30, 2010, p. 64, http://www.sigar.mil/pdf/quarterlyreports/Apr 2010/ SIGARapril_Lores.pdf; response via e-mail from the staff of the Special Inspector General for Afghanistan Reconstruction, August 9, 2010; and press reports from Reuters and the Pajhwok Afghan News agency.

h Special Inspector General for Afghanistan Reconstruction, *Quarterly Report to the United States Congress*, July 30, 2009, p. 60, http://www.sigar.mil/pdf/quarterlyreports/Jul09/pdf/Report_-_July_2009.pdf; *Quarterly Report to the United States Congress*, October 30, 2009, p. 66, http://www.sigar.mil/pdf/quarterlyreports/ Oct09/pdf/SIGAROct2009Web.pdf; and Special Inspector General for Afghanistan Reconstruction, *Quarterly Report to the United States Congress*, January 30, 2010, p. 69, http://www.sigar.mil/pdf/ quarterlyreports/jan2010/pdf/ SIGAR_Jan2010.pdf.

i Special Inspector General for Afghanistan Reconstruction, *Quarterly Report to the United States Congress*, July 30, 2009, p. 60, http://www.sigar.mil/pdf/quarterlyreports/Jul09/pdf/Report_-_July_2009.pdf.

In: The Middle East in Turmoil, Volume 3
Editor: Angela N. Castillo

ISBN: 978-1-61324-241-4
© 2011 Nova Science Publishers, Inc.

Chapter 4

THE UNITED ARAB EMIRATES NUCLEAR PROGRAM AND PROPOSED U.S. NUCLEAR COOPERATION[*]

Christopher M. Blanchard and Paul K. Kerr

SUMMARY

The United Arab Emirates (UAE) has embarked on a program to build civilian nuclear power plants and is seeking cooperation and technical assistance from the United States and others. The 111th Congress approved a U.S.-UAE bilateral agreement on peaceful nuclear cooperation pursuant to Section 123 of the Atomic Energy Act (AEA) of 1954. Then-U.S. Secretary of State Condoleezza Rice signed the proposed agreement on peaceful nuclear cooperation with the UAE January 15, 2009. Deputy Secretary of State James Steinberg signed a new version of the agreement May 21, 2009; the Obama Administration submitted the proposed agreement to Congress the same day.

Congress had the opportunity to review the proposed agreement for 90 days of continuous session, a period which ended on October 17, 2009. The UAE cabinet approved the agreement on October 26. The agreement entered into force after the two governments exchanged diplomatic notes on December 17, 2009. The agreement text states the intent of both governments to cooperate in a number of areas including, but not limited to, the development of the UAE's "civilian nuclear energy use in a manner that contributes to global efforts to prevent nuclear proliferation" and, "the establishment of reliable sources of nuclear fuel for future civilian light water reactors deployed" in the UAE. In January 2010, the UAE announced that it had chosen the Korea Electric Power Corporation (KEPCO of South Korea) to construct four APR1400 reactors. During 2010, the UAE's administrative preparations have continued apace, including site selection, environmental surveys, and security planning. All four plants are scheduled to be online by 2020. The UAE brought into force the Additional Protocol to its IAEA Safeguards agreement on December 20, 2010.

Some members of Congress welcomed the UAE government's stated commitments not to pursue proliferation-sensitive nuclear capabilities, such as uranium enrichment or spent fuel reprocessing. Other members signaled their intention to weigh the proposed bilateral agreement in light of parallel and specific concerns about the UAE's cooperation

---

[*] This is an edited, reformatted and augmented version of a Congressional Research Services publication, dated December 20, 2010.

with international efforts (such as sanctions) to prevent Iran from developing nuclear weapons and ballistic missiles, as well as the potential proliferation or safety risks inherent to exporting U.S. nuclear technology.

In the 111th Congress, legislation was introduced that would have required President Obama to certify that the UAE had taken a number of steps to strengthen its export controls and stem illicit trade with Iran before any agreement could come into effect or related U.S. exports of nuclear technology to the UAE could be approved. In 2007, the UAE adopted a stronger export control law, but as of mid-2010 had not issued implementing regulations for the law or fully staffed a national export control body to enforce it. In the interim, export control enforcement functions remain the responsibility of authorities in the UAE's individual emirates, in coordination with a new national interagency Committee on Commodities Subject to Import and Export Control established in April 2009. According to UAE officials, cooperation with the United States has resulted in a number of joint interdiction operations.

This report provides background information on the UAE nuclear program, reviews developments to date, analyzes proposed nuclear cooperation with the United States, and discusses relevant legislative proposals and options. See also CRS Report RS21852, *The United Arab Emirates (UAE): Issues for U.S. Policy*, by Kenneth Katzman, and CRS Report RS22937, *Nuclear Cooperation with Other Countries: A Primer*, by Paul K. Kerr and Mary Beth Nikitin.

THE UNITED ARAB EMIRATES: BACKGROUND AND U.S. RELATIONS[1]

The United Arab Emirates (UAE) is a federation of seven emirates (principalities): Abu Dhabi, Dubai, Sharjah, Ajman, Fujayrah, Umm Al Qawayn, and Ras Al Khaymah. National authority rests in the hands of a Federal Supreme Council, which is composed of the hereditary rulers of the country's constituent emirates and elects the national president from among its members. Sheikh Khalifa bin Zayed Al Nahyan, the ruler of Abu Dhabi, was elected UAE president in 2004 following the death of his father Sheikh Zayed bin Sultan Al Nahyan, who had ruled Abu Dhabi since 1966 and served as UAE president since 1971. Sheikh Khalifa was reelected for a second five-year term in November 2009. In practice, the wealthier and more powerful emirates of Abu Dhabi and Dubai exercise the strongest influence over the country's affairs; under current convention, the ruler of oil-rich Abu Dhabi serves as the UAE president, and the ruler of the UAE's commercial hub, Dubai, serves as vice president. The Supreme Council appoints the Prime Minister and the Council of Ministers (cabinet), which initiates legislation for ratification by the Supreme Council and the president.

The United States and the UAE have enjoyed close and cooperative relations in recent years, in spite of periodic differences with regard to political reform, the Israel-Palestinian conflict, counterterrorism, and U.S. policies regarding Iraq and Iran. Military cooperation and arms sales form a key pillar of U.S.-UAE relations. The UAE hosts frequent port calls and shore visits for U.S. naval vessels and allows the U.S. military to use Al Dhafra air base in support of a variety of missions in the U.S. Central Command (CENTCOM) area of operations. In 2007 and 2008, the Bush Administration notified Congress of over $19.4 billion in potential arms sales to the UAE, including what would be the first overseas sale of the Terminal High Altitude Air Defense system. In 2009 and 2010, the Obama

Administration notified Congress of a further $8.8 billion in potential sales, including the potential sale of 60 remanufactured and new AH-64D Block III APACHE helicopters.

Bilateral trade has increased in recent years, with 2009 U.S. exports valued at over $12.2 billion, making the UAE the largest U.S. export market in the Middle East. The Bush Administration began negotiating a free trade agreement with the UAE in 2004, but did not conclude the negotiations. The United States does not import a significant amount of oil from the UAE. However, the UAE exports over 2 million barrels of oil per day, making it a key global energy producer.

THE UNITED ARAB EMIRATES NUCLEAR PROGRAM

The government of the United Arab Emirates (UAE), like others in the Middle East, has announced plans to acquire nuclear energy production technology as a means of meeting projected national energy consumption needs.[2] Renewed global interest in nuclear power has led some experts and observers to express concern that the projected spread of nuclear technology in coming years could contribute to nuclear proliferation. In the Middle East, added scrutiny is often applied to the motives and choices of regional actors regarding nuclear technology because of concern that Iran's nuclear program and Israel's presumed nuclear weapons may motivate other regional governments to seek nuclear technology for strategic or military purposes. Other concerns about nuclear safety relate to potential terrorist attacks or political instability, both of which have threatened some regional countries in recent years. UAE officials report that they have considered these potential risks carefully, and have announced plans and measures intended to address proliferation and security concerns. Most prominently, the UAE has based its nuclear program on a decision to forgo domestic uranium enrichment or fuel reprocessing and to rely on international market sources for its nuclear fuel services. This decision has significantly reduced proliferation concerns among many observers, including some members of Congress.[3]

Policymakers and advisers in the government of Abu Dhabi, in consultation with representatives from the other six emirates, have set out an ambitious agenda for the program and are guiding its implementation. In April 2008, the UAE government issued a policy statement[4] that provides a rationale for the country's perceived need for nuclear energy and states guiding principles for the nuclear energy program. Operating and regulatory bodies have been formed and have begun their formal work. The end goal of the program, according to officials and related documents, is to build and operate a "fleet" of nuclear power plants to generate electricity for the UAE, supported by advanced, indigenously managed safety, regulatory, and security agencies.

In January 2010, the UAE announced that it had chosen the Korea Electric Power Corporation (KEPCO of South Korea) to construct the first of four APR1400 nuclear reactors that would sell electricity to the Abu Dhabi Water and Electricity Authority. During 2010, the UAE's administrative preparations have continued apace, including site selection, environmental surveys, and security planning. The plant construction is to take place at Baraka, near Abu Dhabi's western border with Saudi Arabia (see **Figure 1** below). All four plants are scheduled to be online by 2020. South Korea's export financing bank Kexim has agreed to supply $10 billion in financing to support the KEPCO project in Abu Dhabi.[5] In

November 2010, KEPCO was invited to purchase shares in the Emirates Nuclear Energy Corporation (ENEC) that is to operate the plants.[6]

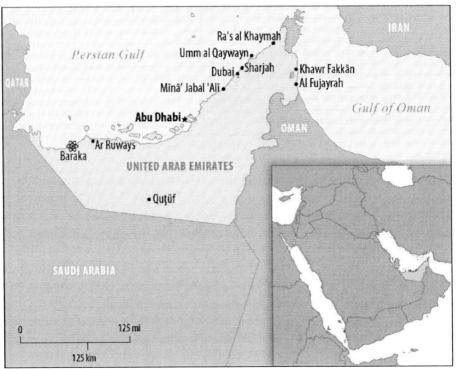

Source: CRS Graphics.

Figure 1. Map of United Arab Emirates.

Rationale

UAE officials estimate that their country must expand its power generation and transmission capacity from the current level of 16 gigawatts to 40 gigawatts by 2020 in order to meet projected demand increases, which they estimate will continue growing at a 9% annual rate. In spite of the recent slowdown in global and domestic economic activity, representatives of the UAE nuclear program believe that the energy demand projections they are using to justify and plan the acquisition of nuclear plants remain accurate, particularly in light of planned industrial and commercial projects in energy-intensive sectors in the emirate of Abu Dhabi.[7] To date, UAE officials and representatives have not publicly shared economic cost and energy use data referred to in briefings on their nuclear program.

In arguing for nuclear energy as a solution to the country's projected energy needs, the UAE government policy statement concludes that "known volumes of natural gas that could be made available to the nation's electricity sector would be insufficient to meet future demand."[8] The UAE currently exports roughly 600 million standard cubic feet per day of natural gas to Japan under long-term supply arrangements and imports roughly 2 billion cubic feet of natural gas from Qatar via the underwater Dolphin pipeline system.[9] Similarly, UAE officials believe that crude oil and diesel could be "logistically viable" sources of energy, but would impose high economic opportunity costs (as a result of lost export revenue) and environmental costs. Officials determined that coal could be a more economical solution, but would have even greater environmental costs and, as an import, also would raise concerns for the UAE about the security of supply. UAE officials believe that solar and wind energy sources could supply "only 6-7% of peak electricity demand by 2020," even after "aggressive development."

Development Plans

The end goal of the program, according to officials and related documents, is to build and operate a "fleet"[10] of nuclear power plants to generate electricity for the UAE, supported by advanced, indigenously managed safety, regulatory, and security agencies that will be developed over time and with outside assistance. The UAE government is seeking to bring its first nuclear power plant online by 2017 along with required facilities and equipment for safety, storage, and system management. Under current plans, capacity would expand thereafter to three further nuclear power plants. A contract bidding and award process concluded in late 2009, and UAE officials chose South Korea's Korea Electric Power Corporation (KEPCO) as the primary engineering, procurement, and construction contractor. A number of U.S. and European firms have secured administrative and financial advisory contracts with the program. No specific decisions have been made regarding the source of nuclear fuel for the planned nuclear reactor or on handling spent reactor fuel.

Current Infrastructure and Regulatory Regime

The UAE currently has no nuclear material under IAEA safeguards. It signed the NPT in 1995 and completed a Small Quantities Protocol in 2003. Non-nuclear weapons states without significant nuclear programs or nuclear material are permitted to conclude such Protocols. The UAE also has undertaken Technical Cooperation projects with the Agency, some of which are directly related to nuclear electricity generation. For example, a project begun in 1977 advised the government "on the establishment of a nuclear energy administration." A 1984 project focused on uranium exploration. More recently, a Technical Cooperation project approved in 2005 was designed to assess the "technical and economic feasibility" of a nuclear power and desalination plant. Active IAEA Technical Cooperation projects with the UAE focus on human resources development for atomic energy, feasibility studies for waste management, environmental monitoring, and nuclear accident early warning preparedness and response.[11]

A national law authorizing the program was adopted by the Federal Supreme Council in early October 2009. According to the State Department, the law, Federal Law 6 of 2009, "prohibits uranium enrichment and spent fuel reprocessing, creates a Federal Authority for Nuclear Regulation (FANR), and develops a nuclear material licensing and control system."[12] UAE government representatives report that the UAE sought and received input on its draft nuclear law from the United States, United Kingdom, Japan, Korea, and France.[13] In conjunction with the issuance of the law, a Board of Management for the FANR was announced, and the board named former U.S. Nuclear Regulatory Commission Executive

Director for Operations Dr. William Travers as the FANR's first Director General. A nuclear energy policy advisory board reportedly has been formed, and UAE officials report that its members, though unnamed, include leading international nuclear energy industry officials.[14] The UAE has also adopted a law governing export controls, but has not yet issued implementing regulations (see section on "Export Control Concerns"). The UAE has also stated that it intends to establish a "separate nuclear liability regime for third-party compensation modeled on the four as-yet un-ratified IAEA instruments on nuclear liability."[15]

Consulting and contracting between U.S. firms and the UAE related to the UAE's nuclear program has already taken place. In August 2008, Virginia's Thorium Power Ltd. signed two consulting and advisory services contracts related to the establishment of the Abu Dhabi-based Emirates Nuclear Energy Corporation (ENEC)[16] and the FANR. In October 2008, ENEC announced that Colorado's CH2M Hill, Inc. was selected for a 10-year contract as the managing agent for the evaluation and design stage of the nuclear energy program. Pennsylvania-based Rizzo and Associates Inc., has been hired to survey potential nuclear plant sites in the UAE. The contracts were signed with the government of Abu Dhabi.

U.S.-UAE NUCLEAR COOPERATION

During 2008 and early 2009, the Bush Administration and the UAE government negotiated and signed a Memorandum of Understanding (MOU) (see below) and a proposed bilateral agreement on peaceful nuclear cooperation pursuant to Section 123 of the Atomic Energy Act (AEA) of 1954. The nuclear cooperation agreement entered into force after the two governments exchanged the relevant diplomatic notes on December 17, 2009.

Memorandum of Understanding

On April 21, 2008, the United States and the UAE signed a MOU "Concerning Cooperation in Peaceful Uses of Nuclear Energy." The MOU states that the two countries "intend to cooperate, subject to their respective national laws," in a variety of nuclear activities. The MOU is a statement of intent regarding future cooperation, but is not legally binding. Although such memoranda are not prerequisites for concluding future nuclear cooperation agreements, the State Department has argued that they are useful tools for cooperating with countries which are interested in the responsible use of nuclear energy because they create opportunities to solicit specific commitments with regard to safeguards and technology choices. An April 21, 2008, State Department press release described the U.S.-UAE MOU as a "tangible expression of the United States' desire to cooperate with states in the Middle East, and elsewhere, that want to develop peaceful nuclear power in a manner consistent with the highest standards of safety, security and nonproliferation." The United States has concluded similar MOUs with Bahrain, Jordan, and Saudi Arabia in May 2008.

Proposed Bilateral Agreement Pursuant to Section 123 of the Atomic Energy Act of 1954

On May 21, 2009, Deputy Secretary of State James Steinberg and UAE Ambassador to the United States Yousef Al Otaiba signed the text of a bilateral agreement on peaceful nuclear cooperation. Although then-Secretary of State Condoleezza Rice and UAE Foreign Minister Abdullah bin Zayed Al Nahyan signed a similar agreement in January 2009, the two governments reopened the text for negotiation after the Obama Administration took office.

Under the Atomic Energy Act of 1954 (AEA), all significant nuclear cooperation with other countries requires a peaceful nuclear cooperation agreement. Such agreements, which require congressional approval, are "framework" agreements which set the terms of reference and provide authorization for cooperation. The AEA includes requirements for an agreement's content, presidential determinations, and other supporting information to be submitted to Congress, conditions affecting the implementation of an agreement once it takes effect, as well as procedures for Congress to consider and approve the agreement (see "Nuclear Cooperation Agreements, Approval Process, and Proposed Changes" below). The agreement would enter into force on the date when the two governments "exchange diplomatic notes informing each other that they have completed all applicable requirements." As noted, the two governments exchanged these notes December 17, 2009.

According to the proposed U.S.-UAE agreement,[17] the two countries "intend to cooperate" on a variety of nuclear activities, including

- Developing "requirements for grid-appropriate power reactors and fuel service arrangements;"
- Promoting the "establishment of a reliable source of nuclear fuel for future civil light water nuclear reactors;"
- "Civil nuclear energy training, human resource and infrastructure development;"
- Cooperating on nuclear security and nonproliferation, "including physical protection, export control and border security;"
- Developing the UAE's "civil nuclear energy use in a manner that supports global efforts to prevent nuclear proliferation, including, for example, the Global Nuclear Energy Partnership;"[18]
- Applying "radioisotopes and radiation in industry, agriculture, medicine and the environment;"
- Managing "radioactive waste and spent fuel;" and
- Identifying "uranium mining and milling resources."

According to the agreement, cooperation could include

- "Exchange of scientific and technical information and documentation;"
- "Exchange and training of personnel;"
- "Organization of symposia and seminars;"
- "Provision of relevant technical assistance and services;"
- Transfers of "material, equipment and components."

The agreement contains a variety of provisions which are required by the AEA and are designed to ensure that the UAE's nuclear program remains exclusively for peaceful purposes. It also includes two provisions which are not found in any other U.S. nuclear cooperation agreement. First, the agreement provides that the UAE bring into force its Additional Protocol to its IAEA safeguards agreement before the United States licenses "exports of nuclear material, equipment, components, or technology" pursuant to the agreement. The IAEA Board of Governors approved the Protocol March 3, 2009. The UAE signed it April 8, 2009, and brought it into force on December 20, 2010.[19] Such protocols give IAEA officials greater access to an NPT state's nuclear-related facilities and information.

Second, the agreement states that the UAE

> shall not possess sensitive nuclear facilities within its territory or otherwise engage in activities within its territory for, or relating to, the enrichment or reprocessing of material, or for the alternation in form or content (except by irradiation or further irradiation or, if agreed by the Parties, post-irradiation examination) of plutonium, uranium 233, high enriched uranium, or irradiated source or special fissionable material.

A May 21, 2009, letter to Congress, which President Obama submitted along with the agreement, described this provision as a "legally binding obligation." According to the Nuclear Proliferation Assessment Statement submitted with the agreement, this provision "survives any termination of the Agreement so long as nuclear items subject to the Agreement remain in the territory of the UAE or under its jurisdiction or control anywhere." Furthermore, the agreement provides the United States with the right to terminate nuclear cooperation and to require the return of any nuclear "material, equipment or components ... and any special fissionable material produced through their use" if, after the agreement's entry into force, the UAE "possesses sensitive nuclear facilities within its territory or otherwise engages in activities within its territory relating to enrichment of uranium or reprocessing of nuclear fuel."[20]

Another provision, which is not typically included in nuclear cooperation agreements, requires both parties to give "due consideration ... to non-proliferation and physical protection aspects" when selecting a storage facility for special fissionable material.[21]

According to the agreement, the United States may also require that any special fissionable material that has been transferred to the UAE or "used in or produced through the use of any material or equipment" transferred pursuant to the agreement be transferred to either the United States or an unspecified "third country" if Washington "considers that exceptional circumstances of concern from a nonproliferation standpoint so require." A 1981 U.S. nuclear cooperation agreement with Egypt contains a similar restriction.

It is worth noting that an Agreed Minute to the U.S.-UAE agreement includes a provision which establishes its conditions as minimum standards for future such U.S. agreements in the Middle East. Stating that "the fields of cooperation, terms and conditions" accorded by the U.S.-UAE agreement "shall be no less favorable in scope and effect than those which may be accorded, from time to time, to any other non-nuclear-weapon State in the Middle East in a peaceful nuclear cooperation agreement," the Minute explains that, in the event that Washington concludes a more-favorable agreement with another regional government, the

United States will, at the UAE's request, consult with the UAE "regarding the possibility of amending" the agreement in order to make its terms equally favorable to the new agreement.

A similar provision in the U.S.-Egypt agreement meant that the United States had to ensure that the agreement with the UAE would be at least as stringent. Since the latter agreement is more stringent, it has established a higher standard for future such U.S. agreements in the region.[22] (See the **Appendix**.)

Additionally, the U.S.-UAE agreement provides a potential way for the UAE to transfer spent nuclear fuel to other countries. The Agreed Minute states that the UAE may transfer spent nuclear fuel to France or the United Kingdom for storage or reprocessing. In the past, such advance U.S. consent has been given only to Japan, Switzerland, and Norway.[23] The transferred material is to be held within EURATOM, and any separated plutonium cannot be returned to the UAE without additional U.S. consent.24 [25] According to the agreement, approval for such UAE spent fuel transfers would be subject to several conditions, including the UAE's adherence to its declared policy of refraining from enrichment and reprocessing. The UAE may also not engage in fabricating nuclear fuel containing plutonium. Additionally, the United States can terminate an agreement regarding spent fuel transfers if Washington decides that the UAE has not met one of the relevant conditions or if the United States "considers that exceptional circumstances of concern from a non-proliferation or security standpoint so require." The agreement explains that "[s]uch circumstances include, but are not limited to, a determination ... that the approval cannot be continued without a significant increase of the risk of proliferation or without jeopardizing its national security."

Nuclear Cooperation Agreements, Approval Process, and Proposed Changes

As noted, all significant nuclear cooperation[26] with other countries requires a peaceful nuclear cooperation agreement.[27] Section 123 of the Atomic Energy Act (AEA) specifies that proposed nuclear cooperation agreements are to include the terms, conditions, duration, nature, and scope of cooperation. It also requires that any such agreement meet a series of nonproliferation criteria and that the President submit any such agreement to the House Committee on Foreign Affairs and the Senate Committee on Foreign Relations. The Department of State is required to provide the President an unclassified Nuclear Proliferation Assessment Statement (NPAS), which the President is to submit to the committees of referral along with the agreement. The State Department also is required to provide a classified annex to the NPAS, prepared in consultation with the Director of National Intelligence. The NPAS is meant to explain how a proposed agreement would meet the aforementioned nonproliferation criteria. The President also must make a written determination "that the performance of the proposed agreement will promote and will not constitute an unreasonable risk to, the common defense and security." President Bush issued such a determination November 14, 2008.[28] President Obama issued an identical determination May 19, 2009, and submitted the agreement, along with the unclassified NPAS, May 21. President Obama also submitted the classified NPAS.

Under the AEA, Congress has the opportunity to review a 123 agreement for two time periods totaling 90 days of continuous session.[29] The President must submit the text of the proposed nuclear cooperation agreement, along with required supporting documents (including the unclassified NPAS) to the House Foreign Affairs Committee and the Senate

Foreign Relations Committee. The President is to consult with the committees "for a period of not less than 30 days of continuous session." After this period of consultation, the President is to submit the agreement to Congress, along with the classified annex to the NPAS and a statement of his approval of the agreement and determination that it will not damage the national security interests of the United States. This action begins the second period, which spans 60 days of continuous session. In practice, the President has submitted the agreement to Congress, along with the unclassified NPAS, its classified annex, and his approval and determination, at the beginning of the full 90- day period. The 60-day period has been considered as following immediately upon the expiration of the 30-day period. If the President has not exempted the agreement from any requirements of Section 123(a), it becomes effective at the end of the 60-day period unless, during that time, Congress adopts a joint resolution disapproving the agreement and the resolution becomes law.[30] The agreement with the UAE was not an exempt agreement.

In the 110th Congress, some members of Congress proposed several amendments to the AEA that would have changed the AEA's procedures for the negotiation and approval of peaceful nuclear cooperation agreements.[31] For example, H.R. 7316, which Representative Ileana Ros-Lehtinen introduced in December 2008, would have required Congress to enact a joint resolution of approval before any peaceful nuclear cooperation agreement could become effective. As noted above, such agreements currently become effective unless Congress enacts a joint resolution of disapproval. The bill also proposed adding a section to the AEA which would have required the President to keep the House Foreign Affairs Committee and the Senate Foreign Relations Committee "fully and currently informed of any initiative or negotiations relating to a new or amended agreement for peaceful nuclear cooperation ... prior to the President's announcement of such initiative or negotiations." The proposed section also would have mandated periodic presidential consultation with the committees about the progress of negotiations concerning such agreements. In the 111th Congress, H.R. 547, which Representative Ros-Lehtinen introduced January 15, 2009, contains the same language.

ISSUES FOR CONGRESS

Although the final text of the proposed U.S.-UAE nuclear agreement was agreed in early November 2008, the Bush Administration, reportedly at the UAE's request, did not submit the agreement to the 110th Congress.[32] After the Obama Administration took office, the UAE agreed to reopen the text for negotiation. On May 21, 2009, the Administration submitted the agreement to Congress to begin the consultation periods required under the AEA. Some members of Congress welcomed the UAE government's stated commitments to foreswear proliferation-sensitive nuclear capabilities, such as uranium enrichment or spent fuel reprocessing. Other members signaled their intention to evaluate the proposed bilateral agreement in light of parallel and specific concerns about the UAE's cooperation with international efforts to prevent Iran from developing nuclear weapons and the potential proliferation or safety risks inherent to exporting U.S. nuclear technology.[33] Broader diplomatic implications of the proposed agreement also were being weighed by concerned parties on all sides. The agreement, however, entered into force following the December 17, 2009 exchange of diplomatic notes because the 90 days of continuous session expired on

October 17, 2009. State Department spokesperson Ian Kelly told reporters October 22 that the United States has "completed all ... internal procedures" for the agreement to enter into force. The UAE cabinet approved the agreement October 26.[34]

Congressional Concerns

Export Control Concerns

Since 2001, the UAE has been under increased U.S. scrutiny as an alleged transshipment point for military and dual-use exports to Iran, as an alleged hub of operations for weapons proliferators,[35] and as an alleged transit zone and financial conduit for terrorists and money launderers. At present, particular attention remains focused on U.S. concerns about the UAE government's willingness and ability to halt transfers of militarily sensitive technology to Iran. Some members of Congress have claimed that the UAE has not acted sufficiently to halt transfers of militarily sensitive technology to Iran and argued that the UAE should not have been able to conclude a nuclear cooperation agreement with the United States until the UAE government had taken additional measures against Iranian procurement activities of concern.

The United States government has stated publicly that some UAE-based entities have been involved in Iranian weapons procurement, nuclear, and ballistic missile program activities.[36] The Department of the Treasury designated two such entities under Executive Order 13382, which freezes assets under U.S. jurisdiction belonging to designated foreign entities engaged in activities related to the proliferation of Weapons of Mass Destruction (WMD).[37] The Treasury Department has also designated other UAE-based entities under the same executive order because of their ties to Iranian banks which, according to the United States, are involved in proliferation activities.[38] The UAE has not been the only conduit for suspicious goods destined for Iran; Tehran has also used a network based in Malaysia for procuring dual-use items.

Administration and UAE officials have highlighted steps taken by the UAE in recent years to strengthen export controls and to take action against entities suspected of illicit proliferation activities, including targets associated with Iran. Concerns about suspicious transfers to Iran prompted U.S. action in 2007 to encourage the UAE to improve its national export control system. In February 2007, the U.S. Department of Commerce released an advanced notice of proposed rule-making that would have created a new export control designation known as "Country Group C" that would have established license requirements on exports and re-exports to countries that represent a diversion or transshipment risk for goods subject to the Export Administration Regulations.[39] Although no countries were mentioned in the notice, the proposal was widely considered to be directed at the UAE.[40]

In August 2007, the UAE adopted a stronger national export control law, but, as of July 2010, the government had yet to issue implementing regulations for the law or to fully staff a national export control body to enforce it. In the interim, export control enforcement functions remain the responsibility of authorities in the UAE's individual emirates, and are being carried out in coordination with a national interagency Committee on Commodities Subject to Import and Export Control.[41] UAE Minister of State for Foreign Affairs Dr. Anwar Mohammed Gargash said in a statement released in conjunction with the April 2009 inaugural meeting of the committee that, "We will not compromise on issues of security and our export control reflects our intention to ensure tough safeguards over the movement of sensitive materials." UAE Ambassador to the United States Yousef Al Otaiba described the law as a "work in progress" during a June 3, 2009, briefing. On July 22, 2010, Acting Assistant Secretary of State for International Security and Nonproliferation Vann Van Diepen stated in testimony before the House Foreign Affairs Subcommittee on Terrorism, Nonproliferation and Trade:

> they're continuing to staff up the implementation office that would oversee implementation of the law. Now, it's not the enforcement arm. That already exists. It's being enforced by the existing customs and law enforcement services, intelligence services and so on and so forth. But the people who would oversee the implementation of the law, that office is still being staffed up.[42]

U.S. cooperation with national and emirate level officials on proliferation issues appears to be strong. A bilateral nonproliferation working group meets annually to review and discuss nonproliferation issues of shared concern. In a September 2008 letter to then-U.S. Secretary of Commerce Carlos Gutierrez, Ambassador Otaiba detailed six joint and unilateral interdictions on Iran-bound ships completed since June 2008.[43] In 2009, the UAE seized "arms and related materials" from a ship en route to Iran, according to Australian officials. The UAE conducted the seizure, which reportedly took place in late July or early August 2009, pursuant to U.N. Security Council resolution 1874.[44] According to U.S. Permanent Representative to the United Nations Ambassador Susan Rice, the U.N. committee charged with monitoring implementation of the sanctions is investigating the matter.

Otaiba's letter further stated that "the UAE fully supports and has vigorously enforced United Nations resolutions barring the shipment of sensitive materials and technologies to Iran." The UAE also has "closed dozens of international and local companies involved in the transshipment of dual-use and controlled materials," according to the letter, which also highlighted the government's participation in several U.S. security initiatives, including the Container Security Initiative, the Proliferation Security Initiative, and the Department of Energy Megaports Initiative. UAE officials report they remain committed to fully implementing the 2007 law at the national level, including clarifying roles and responsibilities for export control enforcement. Acting Assistant Secretary Van Diepen confirmed the Administration's shared view of the UAE's commitment to export control enforcement in July 2010, stating:

> it's very clear to us that the UAE government at the highest levels and also broadly throughout their interagency, you know, has internalized and understands the importance of nonproliferation and of dealing with the proliferation problems through effective action. And the UAE has taken a lot of very important steps, not just passing legislation but in terms of stopping specific shipments, shutting down companies, dealing with specific individuals. So a lot of concrete real world activities have been engaged in by the UAE to really do things in the real world that matter.

Nonproliferation Concerns

The most proliferation-sensitive part of a nuclear power program is the capability to produce fuel for nuclear reactors, either by enriching uranium or reprocessing spent nuclear fuel to obtain plutonium. Low-enriched uranium is used as fuel for nuclear reactors. Both highly enriched uranium and plutonium can be used as fuel in some types of nuclear reactors but are also used as fissile material in nuclear weapons. The dual-use nature of nuclear fuel facilities frequently generates concern that ostensibly peaceful facilities may aid nuclear weapons programs.

The 2008 MOU states that the UAE has agreed to the policy commitments described earlier in its April 2008 policy statement, which are designed to boost confidence that the state's nuclear program is exclusively for peaceful purposes. For example, the statement indicates that the UAE will forgo "domestic enrichment and reprocessing capabilities in favor of long-term commitments of the secure external supply of nuclear fuel." Moreover, as noted above, the nuclear cooperation agreement's text states that the United States can end nuclear cooperation with the UAE if it acquires enrichment or reprocessing facilities. Without such capabilities, a nuclear program poses little proliferation risk. IAEA Director-General Mohamed ElBaradei explained in an August 2007 interview:

> One nuclear reactor by itself means nothing, you are still far from having an atom bomb. I am more worried when a country has a plant for industrial-scale uranium enrichment... In this case it can make a nuclear bomb within a few months. [45]

As noted above, the U.S. State Department reports that the UAE's new nuclear regulatory law (Federal Law 6 of 2009) prohibits domestic enrichment and reprocessing.[46]

As a party to the nuclear Nonproliferation Treaty (NPT), any future UAE nuclear facilities would be subject to IAEA safeguards.[47] Additionally, the UAE agreed to conclude an Additional Protocol to its safeguards agreement. As noted, such protocols give IAEA officials greater access to an NPT state's nuclear-related facilities and information. The UAE currently has a Small Quantities Protocol to its safeguards agreement, but, according to the nuclear cooperation agreement, will terminate that Protocol before the United States issues export licenses for the export of "nuclear material, equipment, components, or technology" pursuant to the cooperation agreement.[48]

It is also worth noting that the UAE's 2008 policy statement on its nuclear program states that the government plans to rely on light-water reactors, which are considered among the most proliferation-resistant, partly because of the difficultly in producing and obtaining weapons-grade plutonium without detection. Moreover, a May 2008 International Institute for Strategic Studies report points out that "no successful nuclear-weapons program has ever relied on commercial reactors."[49] Although a civilian nuclear power program could provide cover for a country's procurement of dual-use items that could aid a nuclear weapons program, such a program would need to include some covert facilities.

Human Rights Concerns

A video depicting the torture of an Afghan grain merchant named Muhammad Shah Poor by Abu Dhabi ruling family member Sheikh Issa bin Zayed al Nahayan and uniformed security officers has drawn widespread condemnation following its publication by ABC News in April 2009.[50] In response, some members of Congress and congressional staff raised questions about the appropriateness of moving forward with the proposed U.S.-UAE nuclear cooperation agreement, pending UAE action on the case.[51] The U.S. State Department has indicated that the Obama Administration's review of the proposed nuclear cooperation agreement and concerns the Administration may have about the torture depicted on the video "are two separate issues."[52] Abu Dhabi authorities announced on May 11, 2009, that "the

Public Prosecution Office has officially launched a criminal investigation into the events depicted on video, and detained Sheikh Issa bin Zayed Al Nahyan pending the outcome of this investigation."[53]

In January 2010, Sheikh Issa was acquitted following trial in which the court heard testimony that he had been drugged by Lebanese business associates who sought to use the video to blackmail him. The business partners were convicted in absentia and, along with others depicted in the tape, sentenced to serve terms ranging from one to five years. The victim reportedly settled out of court. In the wake of the acquittal, H.R. 5378 (introduced May 25, 2010) sought to make members of the royal families of the UAE and employees of the UAE government ineligible for non-immigrant visas to enter the United States until the Secretary of State "has determined that Sheikh Issa bin Zayed al Nahyan has been tried, in accordance with what the Secretary determines to be appropriate international legal norms and human rights standards." The bill would provide national interest waiver authority for the Secretary of State.

Possible Diplomatic Implications

Shaping Nonproliferation Standards and Best Practices

The Bush Administration argued that nuclear cooperation with the UAE could set a useful precedent for mitigating the dangers of nuclear proliferation as an increasing number of countries consider developing nuclear power. The State Department stated in April 2008 that the UAE's choice to forgo enrichment and reprocessing "serves as a model for the economical and responsible pursuit of nuclear power." Similarly, President Obama's May 21, 2009, letter of transmittal argued that the agreement "has the potential to serve as a model for other countries in the region that wish to pursue responsible nuclear energy development." As noted, the proposed U.S.-UAE agreement includes a provision which apparently intends to establish the agreement's conditions as minimum standards for future such agreements in the Middle East. On July 8, 2009, Under Secretary of State for Arms Control and International Security Ellen Tauscher testified before the House Foreign Affairs Committee on the proposed agreement and argued that

> In addition to being indicative of our strong partnership with the UAE, the proposed Agreement is a tangible expression of the United States' desire to cooperate with states in the Middle East, and elsewhere, that want to develop peaceful nuclear power in a manner consistent with the highest nonproliferation, safety, and security standards.... U.S. cooperation with the UAE will also serve as a distinct counterpoint to those countries that have chosen a different path, in particular Iran.[54]

However, the standard set by the UAE may not be preferred by other governments in the region seeking to develop nuclear energy programs of their own. Negotiations over a U.S.-Jordanian nuclear cooperation agreement were delayed during 2009 and 2010 as Jordanian officials debated the relative merits of adopting the UAE model or preserving their ability to pursue domestic uranium enrichment at some point in the future.[55] In July 2010, Representative Howard Berman stated in a letter to the New York Times about Jordan that "the more states that forswear enrichment, the safer the whole region."[56]

Commercial Opportunities

Licensed nuclear technology contracts with the UAE provide commercial benefits to the U.S. nuclear industry or its international competitors. While Emirati officials have stated their strong desire for nuclear cooperation with the United States and have incorporated former U.S. government officials and U.S. contractors into their early plans and activities, the UAE has similar cooperation from other international sources and awarded the main engineering and construction contracts (worth tens of billions of dollars) to South Korea's KEPCO. The UAE and France signed a nuclear cooperation agreement in with France in January 2008 and a similar agreement with South Korea June 22, 2009. The UAE signed a nuclear cooperation agreement with Japan in January 2009 and approved a nuclear cooperation agreement with the United Kingdom in December 2010.

UAE officials explained during a June 3, 2009, briefing that the government's nuclear cooperation agreement with France contains preambulary language describing the UAE's commitment to refrain from enrichment and reprocessing. However, the agreement does not explicitly refer to that commitment. Transferring such technologies is not within the agreement's scope, the officials said, adding that all future UAE nuclear cooperation agreements with other countries will reflect the government's policy regarding enrichment and reprocessing.

Bilateral Relations and UAE Cooperation in Nonproliferation Activities

As noted above, the United States and the UAE have enjoyed close and cooperative relations in recent years, in spite of periodic differences over some issues. Prior to the approval of the 123 agreement, some observers speculated that a failure to conclude the proposed nuclear cooperation agreement would have been viewed by officials and influential figures in the UAE as an indication of a lack of faith and commitment by the United States government in the UAE, which could have had negative implications for other aspects of the bilateral relationship. These fears appear to have been based largely on the perceived repercussions of Dubai Ports World's failed 2006 bid to acquire and operate U.S. port terminals. However, others believed that while the Dubai Ports World incident had undermined feelings of mutual trust and had set back some planned commercial ties, the failed initiative did not otherwise damage U.S.-Emirati political or military relations in any tangible, lasting way.

Emirati authorities continue to move forward with the implementation of their nuclear development plans and, while they appear to strongly desire U.S. technical assistance and advice, they have not chosen the United States as their main contracting partner for the program. To date, the U.S. government has not signaled that there has been any negative change in their view of the bilateral relationship because of the UAE government's decision to partner with South Korea. As noted above, other international parties are providing technical assistance on a commercial basis and others continue to seek contracts to support the implementation of the program. Some observers have argued that without U.S. involvement, the UAE program could adopt technology or systems more vulnerable to proliferation or security concerns. UAE representatives state that their commitment to forgo domestic enrichment or reprocessing is fundamental and applies under cooperative arrangements with non-U.S. suppliers.

Legislative Developments in the 110th and 111th Congress

In the 110th Congress, Representative Ros-Lehtinen introduced H.R. 7316, the "Limitation on Nuclear Cooperation with the United Arab Emirates Act of 2008." The bill would have prohibited the proposed U.S.-UAE agreement from coming into effect without presidential certification that the UAE had taken specific steps to improve its export controls and to limit the transfer of certain items to Iran. As noted above, H.R. 7316 also sought to change the procedures for the negotiation and approval of peaceful nuclear cooperation agreements by amending the Atomic Energy Act. (See "Nuclear Cooperation Agreements, Approval Process, and Proposed Changes" above.)

In the 111th Congress, Representative Markey introduced a joint resolution of disapproval on May 21, 2009 (H.J.Res. 55). House and Senate joint resolutions of approval were introduced on July 13, 2009 (S.J.Res. 18 and H.J.Res. 60). Representative Ros-Lehtinen is an original co-sponsor of H.J.Res. 60, although she had previously introduced two pieces of legislation to establish conditions on U.S.-UAE nuclear cooperation and to change negotiation and approval procedures for nuclear cooperation agreements:

- H.R. 364, the "Limitation on Nuclear Cooperation with the United Arab Emirates Act of 2009" was introduced and referred to the House Foreign Affairs Committee on January 9, 2009. The bill states that a U.S. civil nuclear cooperation agreement with the UAE may not enter into force "unless not less than 30 legislative days prior to such entry into force the President certifies" to the House Foreign Affairs Committee and the Senate Foreign Relations Committee that the UAE has improved its export control system and halted UAE-based entities' transfers of technology relating to Weapons of Mass Destruction programs, particularly to Iran. The bill also requires the UAE to stop the transfer of certain conventional weapons and related components to Iran. H.R. 364 also states that, if the United States and the UAE do conclude a nuclear cooperation agreement, the United States may not grant an export license for "nuclear material, equipment, or technology" to the UAE unless the President certifies within 30 legislative days that the UAE has met the above requirements.
- H.R. 547, was introduced and referred to the House Foreign Affairs Committee January 15, 2009. It contains the language from H.R. 7316 relating to procedural changes for nuclear cooperation agreements pursuant to the Atomic Energy Act.

APPENDIX. PROVISIONS IN U.S. NUCLEAR COOPERATION AGREEMENTS WITH THE UAE AND EGYPT RELEVANT TO ESTABLISHING STANDARDS FOR OTHER SUCH AGREEMENTS

UAE[57]

The Government of the United States of America confirms that the fields of cooperation, terms and conditions accorded by the United States of America to the United Arab Emirates for cooperation in the peaceful uses of nuclear energy shall be no less favorable in scope and effect than those which may be accorded, from time to time, to any other non-nuclear-weapon State in the Middle East in a peaceful nuclear cooperation agreement. If this is, at any time, not the case, at the request of the Government of the United Arab Emirates the Government of the United States of America will provide full details of the improved terms agreed with another nonnuclear-weapon State in the Middle East, to the extent consistent with its national legislation and regulations and any relevant agreements with such other non-nuclear weapon State, and if requested by the Government of the United Arab Emirates, will consult with the Government of the United Arab Emirates regarding the possibility of amending this Agreement so that the position described above is restored.

EGYPT[58]

The Government of the United States confirms that fields of cooperation, terms and conditions accorded by the United States to the Arab Republic of Egypt for cooperation in the peaceful uses of nuclear energy shall be no less favorable in scope and effect than those which may be accorded by the United States to any other non-nuclear weapon state in the Middle East in a peaceful nuclear cooperation agreement. In this connection it is understood that the safeguards required by this agreement shall be no more restrictive than those which may be required in any peaceful nuclear cooperation agreement between the United States and any other state in the region. By entering into this agreement the United States confirms its recognition of the importance of the Arab Republic of Egypt's adherence to the NPT, and its longstanding support of international non-proliferation measures, including establishment of a nuclear weapon free zone in the Middle East. If any situation arises which could increase the risk of proliferation of nuclear weapons, the United States and the Arab Republic of Egypt, at the request of either, shall enter into consultations with respect thereto with a view to maintaining the objectives of the NPT.

End Notes

[1] For more information, see CRS Report RS21852, *The United Arab Emirates (UAE): Issues for U.S. Policy* by Kenneth Katzman.

[2] The governments of Turkey, Egypt, Jordan, Saudi Arabia, and Algeria have announced their intent to acquire nuclear energy production capabilities; their respective programs have moved forward in recent years with varying degrees of specificity and commitment. To date, Turkey, Jordan, and Egypt appear to have made the most progress toward their stated goals of constructing and operating domestic nuclear power plants. Like the UAE, their plans do not envision operational plants before 2015. Turkey and Egypt have active peaceful nuclear cooperation agreements with the United States pursuant to Section 123 of the Atomic Energy Act (AEA) of 1954.

[3] The UAE government also pledged $10 million in August 2008 toward an international nuclear fuel bank proposed by the Nuclear Threat Initiative, a non-governmental organization. The bank, which the International Atomic Energy Agency Board of Governors approved December 3, 2010, is to be administered by the agency .,. Mr. Hamad Al Kaabi, UAE Special Representative for International Nuclear Cooperation, explained August 7, 2008 that the contribution is part of the UAE's policy to support multilateral fuel supply efforts—a policy consistent with the country's decision to rely on foreign fuel suppliers and forgo domestic uranium enrichment or fuel reprocessing.

[4] Policy of the United Arab Emirates on the Evaluation and Potential Development of Peaceful Nuclear Energy, released April 20, 2008. Available at https://pcs.enec.gov.ae/Content/Home.aspx.

[5] Emily Meredith and Song Yen Ling, "Cash-Rich Abu Dhabi Seeks Nuclear Financing," *Uranium Intelligence Weekly*, October 18, 2010.

[6] Samji Chung, "ENEC Asks KEPCO to Buy Shares for UAE Nuclear Power Plant," *Maeil Business Newspaper*, November 14, 2010.

[7] CRS meeting with Abu Dhabi Executive Authority and Emirates Nuclear Energy Corporation representatives, Abu Dhabi, December 14, 2008. Large scale petrochemicals and aluminum production projects are already underway in Abu Dhabi's Kalifa Industrial Zone. See Chris Stanton, "Taweelah to host chemical city," *The National* (Abu Dhabi), May 4, 2008; and, Chris Stanton and Ivan Gale, "EMAL smelter remains on schedule," *The National* (Abu Dhabi), January 13, 2009.

[8] "Policy of the United Arab Emirates on the Evaluation and Potential Development of Peaceful Nuclear Energy," released April 20, 2008. Available at https://pcs.enec.gov.ae/Content/Home.aspx.

[9] One economic press report suggested that the UAE may be paying as little as $1.25/million BTU of natural gas. *Middle East Economic Digest*, "UAE purchases gas from Dolphin pipeline at reduced rate," May 16, 2008. For more information on the pipeline, see http://www.oxy.com/Our_Businesses/ oil_and_gas/ Pages/og_mena_dolphin.aspx.

[10] Correspondence between CH2M Hill and U.S. Department of Energy, National Nuclear Security Administration, June 2008.

[11] See IAEA-Technical Cooperation, National and Regional Asia and the Pacific Projects query page at http://www-tc.iaea.org/tcweb/tcprogramme/recipients/eastasiapacific/query/default.asp.

[12] Statement of Vann H. Van Diepen, Acting Assistant Secretary, State Department Bureau of International Security and Nonproliferation before the Senate Foreign Relations Subcommittee on Near Eastern and South and Central Asian Affairs, October 7, 2009.

[13] CRS analyst interview with UAE official, Washington, DC, March 6, 2009.

[14] UAE Minister of Foreign Affairs Shaykh Abdullah bin Zayed Al Nahyan, "Why Go Nuclear?" *Bulletin of the Atomic Scientists*, September/October 2008; and, CRS meeting with Abu Dhabi Executive Authority and Emirates Nuclear Energy Corporation representatives, Abu Dhabi, December 14, 2008.

[15] "Policy of the United Arab Emirates." The four instruments are: the Vienna Convention on Civil Liability for Nuclear Damage, the Protocol to Amend the Vienna Convention on Civil Liability, the Joint Protocol on the Application of the Vienna and Paris Conventions, and the Convention on Supplementary Compensation for Nuclear Damage.

[16] See ENEC homepage at https://pcs.enec.gov.ae/Content/Home.aspx.

[17] The full text of the agreement is available in House Document 111-43, Agreement for Cooperation Between the Government of the United States and the Government of the United Arab Emirates, May 21, 2009.

[18] For more information on the Partnership, see CRS Report RL34234, *Managing the Nuclear Fuel Cycle: Policy Implications of Expanding Global Access to Nuclear Power*, coordinated by Mary Beth Nikitin.

[19] "UAE Brings into Force Additional Protocol to Safeguards Agreement with the IAEA," Emirates News Agency (WAM), December 20, 2010.

[20] Uranium enrichment and reprocessing spent nuclear fuel are the dual-use nuclear activities of greatest proliferation concern. Uranium enrichment can produce low-enriched uranium for nuclear reactor fuel or highly enriched uranium, which can be used as fissile material in nuclear weapons. Reprocessing spent nuclear fuel separates plutonium from that fuel. Plutonium can also be used as fissile material in nuclear weapons.

[21] According to the agreement text, "special fissionable material means (1) plutonium, uranium 233, or uranium enriched in the isotope 235, or (2) any other material so designated by agreement of the Parties." A similar provision is contained in a 1981 U.S. nuclear cooperation agreement with Egypt.

[22] CRS Analyst interview with State Department official March 9, 2009.

[23] U.S. agreements with Finland and Sweden also granted such consent rights, but those agreements have been replaced by the 1996 U.S.-EURATOM agreement.

[24] Japan and Switzerland have received advance consent to take back recovered plutonium for use in their civil nuclear programs.

[25] CRS Analyst interviews with State Department official March 12, 2009 and former State Department official Fred McGoldrick March 10, 2009.

[26] Significant nuclear cooperation includes the transfer of U.S.-origin special nuclear material subject to licensing for commercial, medical, and industrial purposes. The term "special nuclear material," as well as other terms used in the statute, is defined in 42 U.S.C. §2014. "Special nuclear material" means (1) plutonium, uranium enriched in the isotopes 233 or 235, and any other material that is determined to be special nuclear material,

but does not include source material, or (2) any material artificially enriched by any of the foregoing, but does not include source material.

[27] For a primer on such agreements, which are frequently referred to as "123 agreements," see CRS Report RS22937, *Nuclear Cooperation with Other Countries: A Primer*, by Paul K. Kerr and Mary Beth Nikitin.

[28] Presidential Determination No. 2009–7, November 14, 2008.

[29] When calculating periods of "continuous session" under the AEA, every calendar day is counted, including Saturdays and Sundays. Only days on which either chamber has adjourned for more than three days pursuant to the adoption of a concurrent resolution authorizing the adjournment do not count toward the total. If Congress adjourns its final session *sine die*, continuity of session is broken, and the count must start anew when it reconvenes.

[30] The AEA allows the President to exempt a proposed nuclear cooperation agreement from the nonproliferation criteria specified in Section 123. Such agreements have different procedures for Congressional review. Since the proposed agreement with the UAE is apparently a non-exempt agreement, those procedures are not discussed here.

[31] For additional details on these proposals, see CRS Report RS22937, *Nuclear Cooperation with Other Countries: A Primer*, by Paul K. Kerr and Mary Beth Nikitin.

[32] "UAE, USA Complete Negotiations on Peaceful Nuclear Energy Agreement," Emirates News Agency, December 15, 2008; and, Mark Hibbs, "US-UAE Cooperation Pact Initialed; Approval Left to Obama, New Congress," Nucleonics Week, November 20, 2008.

[33] See, for example, a November 24, 2008, statement from Representative Brad Sherman, a January 15, 2009, letter from Representative Edward Markey, and an April 6, 2009, letter from Markey, Sherman, and Representative Ileana Ros-Lehtinen.

[34] "Cabinet Approves UAE-U.S. Agreement on Peaceful Nuclear Cooperation," *Emirates News Agency*, October 26, 2009.

[35] In connection with revelations of illicit sales of nuclear technology to Iran, Libya, and North Korea by Pakistan's nuclear scientist A.Q. Khan, Dubai was named as a key transfer point for Khan's shipments of nuclear components. For more detail, see CRS Report RL32745, *Pakistan's Nuclear Proliferation Activities and the Recommendations of the 9/11 Commission: U.S. Policy Constraints and Options*.

[36] For example, an October 2008 Department of Justice fact sheet states that eight companies, five of which are based in the UAE, were charged the previous month with crimes related to their participation in exporting dual-use items to Iran. Additionally, two men were indicted in July 2008 for "participation in a conspiracy to export U.S.-made military aircraft parts to Iran" via a company based in the UAE, according to the fact sheet. "Fact Sheet: Major U.S. Export Enforcement Prosecutions During Past Two Years," U.S. Department of Justice, October 28, 2008.

[37] Specifically, the Treasury Department designated Oriental Oil Kish in October 2007 for unspecified "proliferation activities." Oriental Oil Kish is an entity affiliated with Iran's Islamic Revolutionary Guard Corps (IRGC), a department press release said, adding that the IRGC develops and tests ballistic missiles. In September 2008, the Treasury Department similarly designated Oasis Freight Agencies as a company affiliated with the Islamic Republic of Iran Shipping Lines (IRISL). Adam Szubin, director of the department's Office of Foreign Assets Control, indicated during a September 10, 2008, press conference that IRISL has procured items for Iran's ballistic missile programs.

[38] For example, the Department designated Melli Investment Holding International and BMIIC International General Trading Ltd. in March 2009 because of their ties to Iran's Bank Melli, which, according to a March 3 Treasury Department statement, has been involved in procurement activities and other forms of support for Iran's nuclear and missile programs. More recently, the Treasury Department announced May 12, 2009, that it had specifically designated several UAE-based branches of that bank. Previously, all worldwide offices of Bank Melli had been designated, but they were not named specifically. Additionally, the Department the same day designated the UAE office of Persia International Bank, a subsidiary of Bank Mellat. The Department stated in October 2007 that Bank Mellat has provided "banking services in support of Iran's nuclear entities."

[39] "Country Group C: Destinations of Diversion Control," Advanced Notice of Proposed Rulemaking, 72 Federal Register 8315, February 26, 2007.

[40] *Inside U.S. Trade*, "UAE Drafts New Export Control Law With U.S. Help," Vol. 25, No. 11, March 16, 2007.

[41] The Committee was authorized in April 2009. The Foreign Ministry serves as the chair, and other members include the Interior Ministry, the Armed Forces, the Ministry of Economy, and the Federal Customs Authority. The Committee met in May 2009 and reportedly discussed "creating a mechanism to implement the law." Mahmoud Habboush, "Arms export control committee meets," *The National* (Abu Dhabi), May 10, 2009.

[42] Vann Van Diepen, Acting Assistant Secretary Of State For The Bureau Of International Security And Nonproliferation before the Terrorism, Nonproliferation and Trade Subcommittee of the House Foreign Affairs Committee, July 22, 2010.

[43] Letter from UAE Ambassador to the United States Yousef Al Otaiba to U.S. Secretary of Commerce Carlos Gutierrez, September 17, 2008.

[44] Brendan Nicholson, "Australian Ship in Arms Row," *The Age*, August 31, 2009; Rod Mcguirk, "Australia Probes North Korean Weapons Shipment," The Associated Press, August 30, 2009. For additional information on the Security Council resolution, see CRS Report R40684, *North Korea's Second Nuclear Test: Implications of U.N. Security Council Resolution 1874*, coordinated by Mary Beth Nikitin and Mark E. Manyin.

[45] "We're approaching the brink: PROFIL Interview with Mohamed El Baradei." *Profil*, August 8, 2007. Available at http://www.iaea.org/NewsCenter/Transcripts/2007/PROFIL3507.html.

[46] Statement of Vann H. Van Diepen, Acting Assistant Secretary, State Department Bureau of International Security and Nonproliferation before the Senate Foreign Relations Subcommittee on Near Eastern and South and Central Asian Affairs, October 7, 2009.

[47] For more information about IAEA safeguards, see CRS Report RL33865, *Arms Control and Nonproliferation: A Catalog of Treaties and Agreements*, by Amy F. Woolf, Mary Beth Nikitin, and Paul K. Kerr. The UAE has had an IAEA safeguards agreement in force since 2003. The text is available at http://www.iaea.org/Publications/Documents/ Infcircs/2003/infcirc622.pdf.

[48] Some NPT state-parties with small quantities of fissionable materials have concluded a Small Quantities Protocol to their IAEA safeguards agreements. Certain IAEA verification requirements are suspended for such states.

[49] International Institute for Strategic Studies, *Nuclear Programmes in the Middle East: In the Shadow of Iran*, May 2008.

[50] Vic Walter, Rehab El-Buri, Angela Hill, and Brian Ross, "Torture Tape Implicates UAE Royal Sheikh," *ABC News: Nightline*, April 22, 2009. Available at http://abcnews.go.com/Blotter/Story?id=7402099&page=1.

[51] For example, Congressman James McGovern, the co-chairman of the House Human Rights Commission has asked, "How can we move forward with such a delicate agreement in the face of such an atrocious human rights violation?" adding, "If it [the proposed 123 agreement] were brought to Congress now I would certainly ask that it be rejected." Robert F. Worth, "Abu Dhabi Torture Video Raises Doubts in U.S. About Nuclear Pact," *New York Times*, May 2, 2009.

[52] Robert Wood, Acting State Department Spokesman, Daily Press Briefing, Washington, DC, April 30, 2009.

[53] "Video matter referred to the Abu Dhabi Public Prosecution Office," Emirates News Agency (WAM), May 11, 2009.

[54] Testimony of Under Secretary Ellen Tauscher Before the House Foreign Affairs Committee, July 8, 2009.

[55] See Rana al Sabbagh, "Will Amman and Washington Sign Long-Awaited Peaceful Nuclear Cooperation Agreement?" *Al Arab Al Yawm*, July 25, 2010; and, Emily Meredith, "Jordan Hopes to Finalize Nuclear Accord Despite Enrichment Stance," *The Oil Daily*, September 29, 2010.

[56] Hon. Howard Berman, "Jordan's Nuclear Power: A View From Capitol Hill," *New York Times*, July 10, 2010.

[57] House Document 111-43, Agreement for Cooperation Between the Government of the United States and the Government of the United Arab Emirates, May 21, 2009, p. 36.

[58] "Agreement for Cooperation Between the Government of the United States of America and the Government of the Arab Republic of Egypt Concerning Peaceful Uses of Nuclear Energy," Treaties and Other International Acts Series (TIAS) 10208, December 29, 1981.

In: The Middle East in Turmoil, Volume 3
Editor: Angela N. Castillo

ISBN: 978-1-61324-241-4
© 2011 Nova Science Publishers, Inc.

Chapter 5

SYRIA: ISSUES FOR THE 112TH CONGRESS AND BACKGROUND ON U.S. SANCTIONS[*]

Jeremy M. Sharp

SUMMARY

This report analyzes an array of bilateral issues that continue to affect relations between the United States and Syria.

Despite its weak military and lackluster economy, Syria remains relevant in Middle Eastern geopolitics. Syria plays a key role in the Middle East peace process, acting at times as a "spoiler" by sponsoring Palestinian militants and facilitating the rearmament of Hezbollah. At other times, it has participated in substantive negotiations with Israel. Syria's long-standing relationship with the Iranian clerical regime is of great concern to U.S. strategists. As Syria grew more estranged from the United States over the last ten years, Syrian-Iranian relations improved, and some analysts have called on U.S. policymakers to woo Syrian leaders away from Iran. Others believe that the Administration should go even further in pressuring the Syrian government and consider implementing harsher economic sanctions against it.

A variety of U.S. legislative provisions and executive directives prohibit direct aid to Syria and restrict bilateral trade relations, largely because of the U.S. State Department's designation of Syria as a sponsor of international terrorism. On December 12, 2003, President Bush signed the Syria Accountability Act, H.R. 1828, as P.L. 108-175, which imposed additional economic sanctions against Syria. In recent years, the Administration has designated several Syrian entities as weapons proliferators and sanctioned several Russian companies for alleged weapons of mass destruction or advanced weapons sales to Syria.

For two years, the Obama Administration attempted to promote some U.S. engagement with Syria. However, the Administration now appears to be somewhat shifting its tactics by applying more pressure on the Syrian government to play a more constructive role in stabilizing Lebanon and advancing the Arab-Israeli peace process. With U.S.-Syrian relations possibly headed toward more tense footing, some in Congress may choose to impose new sanctions against the Asad regime. Other lawmakers may

---

[*] This is an edited, reformatted and augmented version of a Congressional Research Services publication, dated December 21, 2010.

LATEST DEVELOPMENTS

- **Possible IAEA Special Inspection**. In early November 2010, Director General of the International Atomic Energy Agency (IAEA) Yukiya Amano said in an interview that he was open to the possibility of a special inspection of Syria's alleged nuclear facility that Israel bombed in 2007, stating "We need to think: What will be the future possibilities.... I'm open...I'm open for various options."
- **U.S. Criticism of Syria**. On October 28, 2010, the U.S. Ambassador to the United Nations Susan E. Rice accused Syria of destabilizing Lebanon, saying "We continue to have deep concerns about Hezbollah's destructive and destabilizing influence in the region ... as well as the attempts by other foreign players, including Syria and Iran, to undermine Lebanon's independence and endanger its stability."
- **Iran-Hezbollah-Syria**. In October 2010, President Bashar al Asad traveled to Iran to reinforce Syrian-Iranian ties. During his trip, he remarked that "The [Israeli-Palestinian peace] talks are only aimed at supporting Obama's position inside the U.S." Asad's visit came just weeks after President Mahmoud Ahmadinejad went to Syria. Ahmadinejad then traveled to Lebanon where he expressed Iran's support for Hezbollah.
- **Iraqi-Syrian Relations**. In October 2010, Iraqi Prime Minister Nouri (alt. sp. Nuri) al Maliki traveled to Syria as part of a wider tour of the region in order to gain external support for a second term in office. The visit was the first meeting between Asad and Maliki since Iraq and Syria withdrew their respective envoys from each other's capitals following deadly bombings in Baghdad that Maliki blamed partially on Syria. During the visit, the two leaders signed a pipeline agreement to ship an unspecified amount of Iraqi crude to Syrian ports on the Mediterranean. Reportedly, Maliki was seeking Syria's help in convincing the Iraqi Shiite party known as the Supreme Iraqi Islamic Council, headed by Ammar al Hakim, to support Maliki's bid to form a ruling coalition.
- **Explosives Destined for Syria**. In September 2010, Italian customs police seized six to seven tons of high-grade RDX explosives being shipped from Iran to Syria. The cargo was hidden among packs of powdered milk. In recent years, terrorist groups have used RDX in bomb attacks against civilian targets in Moscow, Mumbai, and Istanbul, among other places.
- **Syrian-Saudi Summit**. In late July 2010, in attempt to stabilize Lebanon in light of rumors that the Special Tribunal for Lebanon may indict members of Hezbollah for the 2005 murder of the Lebanese Prime Minister Rafik Hariri, King Abdullah of Saudi Arabia and President Asad met in Beirut with Lebanese President Michel Suleiman. The visit was intended to project a sense of calm from key external players amidst a tense internal atmosphere stemming from public fear that Hezbollah may use violence to stop both the tribunal's activities and the political support behind it.

ISSUES FOR CONGRESS

Syria-Iran-Hezbollah-Hamas: The "Axis of Resistance"

Syria derives much of its regional importance from being considered a weak link in the so-called Syria-Iran-Hezbollah-Hamas "Axis of Resistance" against Western, moderate Arab, and Israeli interests in the Middle East. For many years, some experts have hoped that a Israeli-Syrian land for peace deal would not only promote Middle East peace, but permanently reorient Syria foreign policy toward the more moderate Sunni Arab regimes, such as Egypt and Jordan, and away from Iran, the primary U.S. adversary in the Middle East. However, with the Arab-Israeli peace process stalled, Syria lacks the incentive to switch "camps" and may continue to behave in ways contrary to U.S. goals in the Middle East. Some experts suggest that even if Syria made peace with Israel, it would not cut its ties entirely to Iran and others.

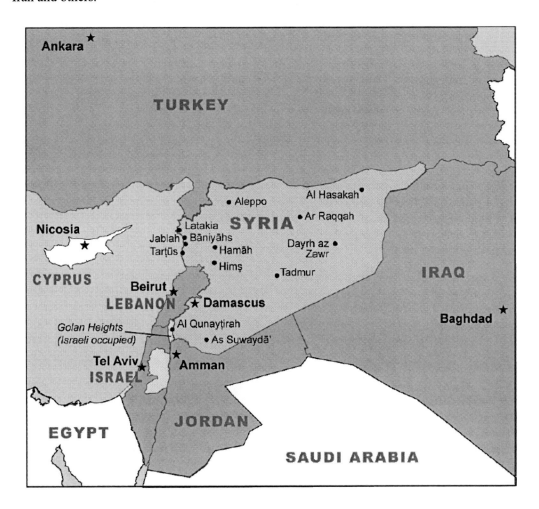

Figure 1. Map of Syria.

Syria and Iran

Syria's historic rivalry with neighboring Iraq[1] created opportunities for improved Syrian relations with Iran, Iraq's main rival until the 2003 U.S. overthrow of the Saddam Hussein regime. The Syrian-Iranian alliance has always been considered a "marriage of convenience," as both countries have placed a higher value on regional strategic interests rather than shared cultural and religious affinities.[2] In recent years, as Syria has grown more estranged from the West, Syrian-Iranian relations have improved, and some analysts have called on U.S. policymakers to "flip" Syria and woo it away from Iran. Others assert that the foundation of the Syrian-Iranian relationship—a shared concern over a resurgent Iraq, support for Hezbollah in Lebanon, and countering Israel—is deeply rooted in the geopolitics of the region and cannot be easily overturned.

Reliable information on the extent of Iranian economic influence in Syria is difficult to quantify. Nevertheless, there have been several reports of increased Iranian investment and trade with Syria. In the financial sector, Iran has stated its intention to establish a joint Iranian-Syrian bank, possibly involving Bank Saderat and the Commercial Bank of Syria – two entities which have been sanctioned by the U.S. Treasury Department.[3] In the manufacturing and industrial sectors, the Iran Khodro Industrial Group has established a car assembly plant in Syria through a joint venture known as the Syrian-Iranian Motor Company (Siamco).[4] Another joint venture, the Syrian-Iranian Vehicle Company (Siveco), assembles Iranian cars in Syria. Its chief stakeholder is the Iranian company Saipa. Iranian companies also have invested in concrete production, power generation, and urban transportation. In the energy sector, Syria, Iran, Venezuela and Malaysia jointly established a petroleum refinery in Homs, Syria. In addition, Iran and Syria reached a natural gas deal that would allow Iran to export gas to Syria via Iraq (Persian Pipeline). Despite increased Iranian investments, the overall volume of Iranian-Syrian trade remains low. According to the *Economist Intelligence Unit*, bilateral trade may total between $160 and $400 million.[5] Ironically, the total volume of U.S. trade with Syria exceeds that of Iran-Syria.

Iran also supplies Syria with weaponry, though Russia and North Korea have traditionally been Syria's two main suppliers. In June 2010, Iran reportedly sent Syria an air defense radar system designed to detect Israeli aircraft or possibly increase the accuracy of Syrian and Hezbollah missile strikes against Israel in the event of a regional war. According to one unnamed U.S. official, "The Iranians have two interests.... They need Hezbollah to be a powerful threat against Israel, and they are interested in knowing what is coming to them from Israel."[6] In response to the alleged transfer, U.S. State Department Spokesman Philip J. Crowley stated that "Well, it's hard for us to determine if such a transfer has taken place. We have concerns about the relationship between Iran and Syria. And as we've said before, we don't believe that Iran's designs for the region are in Syria's best interest."[7]

Syria's Role in Lebanon

Syria still exerts a great deal of influence in Lebanese domestic affairs through its local surrogates and through Hezbollah. Syria has benefitted both internationally (improved relations with France and Saudi Arabia) and inside Lebanon since the 2008 formation of a unity government comprised of pro and anti-Syrian political parties, and led by Sunni politician Saad Hariri, the son of the late Prime Minister Rafiq Hariri who was assassinated in 2005. As prime minister of a unity government that includes Hezbollah, Saad Hariri has had to accommodate his formerly anti-Syrian political positions to new regional realities, even though his father was assassinated in a plot that many observers believe was hatched by Syrian leaders, Hezbollah, or both. Saad Hariri has not only refrained from challenging Syria, but has gone out of his way to accommodate his larger, more powerful neighbor, traveling to Damascus and even publicly absolving Syria of any responsibility for his father's murder. In November 2010, he remarked in an interview that "I do not think that President Assad had anything to do with that.... I'm the Prime Minister. I do not have the luxury of speculating these days."[8] Other Lebanese leaders also have accommodated Syria. In March 2010, Lebanese Druze leader Walid Jumblatt met President Asad, having previously apologized for past criticisms of Syria's role in Lebanon. Jumblatt said that his remarks were "indecent, out of context and go beyond the political manners."

The Special Tribunal *for Lebanon (STL)*

With possible indictments pending from the Special Tribunal for Lebanon (STL) at The Hague, Syria's role in Lebanon has resurfaced as a major issue of concern. Syria is clearly worried that its high level officials could be named as possible suspects in the 2005 Hariri assassination. Syria does not consider the STL a legitimate international legal body, and many observers believe that it has worked behind the scenes to obstruct the STL's investigation while signaling that any move against its leadership could destabilize Lebanon. Government officials have denounced the STL's work, and a Syrian judge issued arrest warrants for a number of officials who were accused of having helped provide false testimony to tribunal investigators. In late October 2010, President Asad remarked that "The political situation in Lebanon is not good—it is even troubling.... Any clash at any given moment ... will destroy Lebanon."[9] Hezbollah has forcefully said that anyone cooperating with the STL will be considered an agent of Israel.

At the same time, Syria has benefitted from almost three years of stability in Lebanon and has therefore approached the issue cautiously. At times, it has tried to portray itself as a disinterested third party. Syria and Saudi Arabia have urged all sides in Lebanon to refrain from sectarian strife and have worked to keep the coalition government led by Saad Hariri together. If Hezbollah members are indicted and a trial takes place (perhaps with Hezbollah members in absentia), Syrian officials may be called as witnesses.

Support for Hezbollah

Syria cannot match Israel's conventional warfare capability and therefore relies on Hezbollah's guerilla tactics, terrorist attacks, and rocket and missile arsenals as a deterrent and source of pressure against Israel. According to one unnamed U.S. official, "The Syrians are doing things in terms of deepening their entanglement with Iran and Hezbollah that truly are mind-boggling. They are integrating their military/defense systems to unprecedented levels. Hafez al-Assad never would have gone so far and it is becoming hard to see how they can possibly extricate themselves."[10]

For years, media reports have revealed Syria's repeated attempts to supply Hezbollah with weapons originating either from its own stocks or from Iran, North Korea, and elsewhere. In November 2009, Israeli forces seized the *Francop*, a freighter allegedly en route from Iran to the Syrian port of Latakia which contained, according to reports, thousands of medium-range 107- and 122-millimeter rockets, armor-piercing artillery, mortar bombs, hand grenades, and ammunition for Kalashnikov rifles possibly destined for Lebanon for Hezbollah.[11] In April 2010, multiple reports surfaced suggesting that Syria may have transferred Scud[12] missiles to Hezbollah in Lebanon or trained Hezbollah members based in Syria on the use of Scud missiles at Syrian missile bases.[13] In the fall of 2010, media reports indicated that rockets resembling Scuds missiles were visible on satellite images using Google Earth at a military encampment north east of Damascus near the town of Adra.[14] In addition, Israel has accused Syria of transferring its own M-600 rockets to Hezbollah. The M-600 is a copy of Iran's Fateh-110 surface-to-surface missile and has a range of 155 miles.

Hamas

Syria's support for Palestinian terrorist groups, such as Hamas, is a major impediment both to improved Israeli-Syrian relations and to Syria's relationship with the United States. For years, U.S. policymakers and some lawmakers have sought Syrian cooperation in moderating Hamas. Syria has indirectly supported a number of U.S. State Department-designated Foreign Terrorist Organizations (FTOs), including Hezbollah in Lebanon and the Palestinian groups Hamas, Palestinian Islamic Jihad (PIJ), the Popular Front for the Liberation of Palestine (PLFP), and the Popular Front for the Liberation of Palestine-General Command (PFLP-GC), all of which have offices in Damascus and operate within Syria's borders. Syria acknowledges its support for Palestinians pursuing armed struggle in Israeli occupied territories and for Hezbollah raids against Israeli forces on the Lebanese border, but insists that these actions represent legitimate resistance activity as distinguished from terrorism.

The Israeli-Syrian Peace Process

Israel and Syria are technically still in a state of war, as direct or indirect peace negotiations during the Clinton Administration and most recently brokered by Turkey in 2008 have failed to resolve their conflict. Syria seeks to regain sovereignty over the Golan Heights, 450 square miles of land along the border that Israel seized in 1967. Israel applied its law and administration to the region in December 1981, an act other governments do not recognize. Approximately 20,000 Israeli settlers reside in 33 settlements on the Golan.

Although the Obama Administration would like to see the Israeli-Syrian peace track revived, both parties continue to differ over the framework for a resumption in either direct or indirect negotiations. Israel insists that any new negotiations with Syria should be conducted without preconditions (such as an Israeli pledge to withdraw fully from the Golan Heights) and has ruled out a return to Turkish-mediated talks. Syria would like Turkey to mediate indirect talks with Israel before moving on to direct talks and wants full withdrawal to be the basis of the talks.

In November 2010, the Israeli *Knesset* (parliament) passed a bill that would require any peace deal involving the ceding of territory annexed by Israel — namely East Jerusalem and the Golan Heights —to be put to a national referendum. This new "Referendum Law" mandates that a public referendum over ceding land under Israeli sovereignty to another country, whether by treaty or unilateral decision, be held if the *Knesset* fails to approve the deal by a two-thirds majority (80 votes). The Palestinians and Syria have condemned the new law, which also was criticized by the Israeli left-wing labor party.

Russian Arms Sales to Syria

Over the past several years, Russia and Syria have concluded several arms deals, and Russia remains Syria's primary arms supplier.[15] In May 2010, Russian President Dmitry Medvedev became the first modern Russian leader to visit Syria, and in 2010 there have been reports of new arms agreements, though Russian-Syrian arms deals are notoriously opaque.[16] Some sources have reported that Russia intends to upgrade Syria's Mig-29 fighters and possibly sell Syria advanced Mig-31(Foxhound) aircraft.[17] In September 2010, Russian news sources indicated that a planned sale of P-800 Yakhont anti-ship supersonic cruise missiles worth $300 million was moving ahead as planned. Israel protested the deal, asserting that Syria would transfer the missiles to Hezbollah. Russian Defense Minister Anatoly Serdyukov responded, saying that "The United States together with Israel ask us not to supply the Yakhont system to Syria. But we see no (grounds) for apprehensions expressed by them that these weapons will get into the hands of terrorists."[18]

In January 2007, under the legal authority set forth in the 2005 Iran and Syria Nonproliferation Act (P.L. 109-112), the Administration imposed sanctions against three Russian companies (Rosoboronexport, Tula Instrument-Making Design Bureau, and Kolomna Machine-Building Design Bureau) for WMD or advanced weapons sales to Syria. The sanctions banned U.S. government business and support to the companies for two years and blocked U.S. firms from selling them items that require export licenses. On October 13, 2006, President Bush signed P.L. 109-353 which further expanded the scope of the original law by adding North Korea to its provisions, thereby renaming the law the Iran, North Korea, and Syria Nonproliferation Act (or INKSNA for short).

Nuclear Proliferation and the IAEA

On September 6, 2007, an Israeli air strike inside Syrian territory destroyed what is now referred to as Al Kibar (or Dair Alzour), a remote desert facility which may have housed a nuclear reactor.

According to reports in the *Washington Post*, Syria and North Korea were suspected of collaborating on a secret nuclear program since 1997.[19] Since then, senior North Korean officials and scientists from North Korea's Yongbyon nuclear complex reportedly visited Syria several times before construction began at Al Kibar, between 2001 and 2003. In the spring of 2007, Israel reportedly provided the Administration with photographs of the interior of the alleged facility still under construction. According to the *Washington Post*, the "pictures depicted a site similar to the one at Yongbyon, which produces plutonium for nuclear weapons."

In June 2008, U.N. inspectors visited some areas surrounding Al Kibar. In late 2008, the U.N. International Atomic Energy Agency (IAEA) concluded that the facility had similarities to a nuclear reactor and chemically processed uranium particles were found at the site, but that a final determination could not be made until Syria provides "the necessary transparency."[20] Syria has barred any additional IAEA access since 2008.

In a follow-up report in early 2009, the IAEA said that enough uranium particles had turned up in soil samples to constitute a "significant" find. In response, Syria claimed that the uranium particles came from depleted uranium used in Israeli munitions. Syria also claimed that the site was a conventional military base, but then disclosed in February 2009 that a new missile facility had been constructed at Al Kibar.[21]

The IAEA reported in February 2010 that uranium particles found at a Syrian desert complex bombed by Israel in 2007 point to possible Syrian covert nuclear activity. Previous IAEA reports said only that the uranium particles raised concern because they did not come from Syria's declared inventory.

In September 2010, Ambassador Glyn Davies, the Permanent Representative of the United States to the International Atomic Energy Agency (IAEA), told the 35-member IAEA board that unless Syria cooperates with the agency's probe of its suspected nuclear site bombed by Israel in 2007, then the IAEA must "consider all available measures and authorities to pursue the verification assurances the international community seeks," in other words, a special inspection.[22] Nevertheless, some suggest that the board is divided over pressuring Syria, and the lack of consensus will lead to continued stalemate. In August, Davies said "Our position is we are not going to postpone this indefinitely, we can't. The agency needs to do its duty and it needs to get answers to these questions. A special inspection is one of the tools that is available, so that's something that needs to be considered."

In November 2010, the IAEA reported that "With the passage of time, some of the information concerning the Dair Alzour site is further deteriorating or has been lost entirely. It is critical, therefore, that Syria actively cooperate with the Agency on these unresolved safeguards implementation issues without further delay."[23] In November and December 2010, a German newspaper revealed three suspected nuclear sites related to the Al Kibar near the cities/towns of Masyaf, the village of Marj as-Sultan near Damascus, and Iskandariyah.[24]

Human Rights and Democracy

The Syrian Arab Republic is a dictatorship in which little opposition is tolerated. The president is not elected, but rather approved by a voter "yes or no" referendum, held most recently in 2007. In the parliament, the ruling Ba'th party controls 134 of 250 seats, with no other party holding more than 8 seats. Since 1963, Syria has been under a State of Emergency which gives the security services free reign in suppressing dissent. According to the U.S. State Department's most recent report on human rights in Syria, "During the year the government and members of the security forces committed numerous serious human rights abuses, and the human rights situation worsened. The government systematically repressed citizens' abilities to change their government. In a climate of impunity, there were instances of arbitrary or unlawful deprivation of life. Members of the security forces tortured and physically abused prisoners and detainees. Security forces arrested and detained individuals—including activists, organizers, and other regime critics—without due process."[25]

Authoritarianism persists in Syria for several reasons. First, before the late Hafez al Asad came to power, Syria suffered repeated coups and counter-coups perpetrated by competing regime elites that left it politically unstable for several decades. Factionalism within the armed forces was a key cause of instability in the past, as military cliques jockeyed for power and secured and toppled governments frequently. This situation changed abruptly after 1970 as the late Hafez al Asad gained a position of unquestioned supremacy over the military and security forces. The power base that he built, an alliance of his immediate and extended

Alawite[26] family, the Alawitecontrolled military intelligence services, the socialist pan-Arab Ba'th Party,[27] and various Sunni business families, has persisted for four decades and shows no sign of weakening.

Second, the Alawites, as a religious minority, fear sectarian conflict and are committed to maintaining the primacy of the their community, and the Asads have sought with some success to coopt support from other sects; many senior positions, including that of prime minister, are held by members of the Sunni Muslim majority. However, most key positions, particularly in the security institutions, remain in Alawite hands, and some observers believe that any weakening of the central regime or an outbreak of political turmoil could precipitate a power struggle between entrenched Alawites and the majority Sunni Muslims, who comprise over 70% of the population. In addition to the Sunni Muslims, Syria has several religious sectarian minorities including three small sects related to Islam (Alawites, Druze, and Ismailis) and several Christian denominations.

Since its independence in 1946, Syria has defined itself as an Arab state, despite the presence of a large, ethnically distinct Kurdish population in Damascus and in several non-contiguous areas along Syria's borders with Turkey and Iraq. Syria's Kurds are the largest distinct ethnic/linguistic minority in Syria (7%-10% of total population). Discrimination against Kurdish citizens is prevalent, and Kurdish political activism is not tolerated.

There is little organized political opposition in Syria. Once considered the most imminent threat to Syrian stability, the Syrian Muslim Brotherhood, formerly the largest Islamist opposition group, has been largely in exile since its crushing defeat at the hands of the Asad regime in 1982, when Syrian forces attacked the Brotherhood's stronghold in the city of Hama and killed approximately 10,000 people. In 2005, a group of 274 civil society activists, reformers, communists, Kurdish rights advocates, Islamists, and intellectuals signed the Damascus Declaration, a document calling for the Syrian government to end the decades-old state of emergency and allow greater freedom of speech. Some signatories were subsequently arrested. Since it is difficult for opposition activists to organize inside Syria, an array of dissident groups and individuals operate abroad, particularly in Western Europe.

In 2010, the Democracy Council of California conducted a public opinion survey inside Syria. The survey, which was not approved by the Syrian government, resulted in many findings. Among these are the following: first, a majority believes that the political and economic condition of Syria is poor, and worse than it was five years ago; second, a majority has little faith in the government's ability to confront the country's problems; third, a substantial majority believes that corruption is widespread; and, fourth, a substantial majority believes that the State of Emergency should be lifted.[28]

U.S.-SYRIAN RELATIONS

After months of attempting to engage Syria diplomatically, the Obama Administration appears to be shifting its tactics somewhat toward applying more pressure on the Syrian government to play a more constructive role in stabilizing Lebanon and advancing the Arab-Israeli peace process.[29] This shift has coincided with renewed international concern over Lebanon. Hezbollah has threatened to destabilize the country should, as anticipated, the Special Tribunal for Lebanon indict Hezbollah members for the murder of former Lebanese

Prime Minister Rafik Hariri. The Administration's shift also comes after nearly two years of unsuccessfully attempting to restart Israeli-Syrian peace talks due to resistance by both Israel and Syria to relaunch either direct or indirect negotiations. Though the Obama Administration has made small gestures toward the Asad government, such as sending several high level delegations to Damascus for discussions[30] and allowing sanctions-exempted materials to be exported to Syria, it has not fundamentally changed the U.S. approach to Syria that was established during the George W. Bush Administration. U.S. sanctions have remained in force since President Obama took office in January 2009. Barring an unforeseen breakthrough in Israeli-Syrian relations, most observers contend that the United States and Syria will remain at odds over a host of issues, such as Iran, Hezbollah, and nuclear proliferation (among others), for the foreseeable future. According to Paul Salem, an expert at the Carnegie Endowment for International Peace, "Syria wants to engage but it is not desperate.... It has no real dependency on the US particularly as the peace process is pretty much dead. Syria is doing well with Turkey, the Gulf, the Saudis, China, some European countries. The US is not the only game in town."[31]

Robert S. Ford's appointment as Ambassador to Syria remains on hold in the Senate, and there is no vote planned on confirmation scheduled.[32] Supporters of sending an ambassador to Syria (there has been no U.S. Ambassador in Damascus since 2005) assert that the lack of a high level U.S. presence there only hurts U.S. interests. According to Ambassador Ryan C. Crocker, Dean and Executive Professor, George Bush School of Government and Public Service at Texas A&M University, "Sending an ambassador is not a concession. It improves our access, expands our understanding, allows us to identify potential weaknesses and differences including between Damascus and Tehran—in short it would be to our advantage, not theirs."[33] Opponents charge that it is a concession to a rogue Syrian regime.

U.S. SANCTIONS

Syria remains a U.S.-designated State Sponsor of Terrorism and is therefore subject to a number of U.S. sanctions. Syria was placed on the State Department's State Sponsors of Terrorism List in 1979. Moreover, between 2003 and 2006 Congress passed legislation and President Bush issued new Executive Orders that expanded U.S. sanctions on Syria. At present, a variety of legislative provisions and executive directives prohibit U.S. aid to Syria and restrict bilateral trade.[34] Principal examples follow.

General Sanctions Applicable to Syria

The International Security Assistance and Arms Export Control Act of 1976 [P.L. 94-329]. Section 303 of this act [90 Stat. 753-754] required termination of foreign assistance to countries that aid or abet international terrorism. This provision was incorporated into the Foreign Assistance Act of 1961 as Section 620A [22 USC 2371]. (Syria was not affected by this ban until 1979, as explained below.)

The International Emergency Economic Powers Act of 1977 [Title II of P.L. 95-223 (codified at 50 U.S.C. § 1701 et seq.)]. Under the International Emergency Economic Powers

Act (IEEPA), the President has broad powers pursuant to a declaration of a national emergency with respect to a threat "which has its source in whole or substantial part outside the United States, to the national security, foreign policy, or economy of the United States." These powers include the ability to seize foreign assets under U.S. jurisdiction, to prohibit any transactions in foreign exchange, to prohibit payments between financial institutions involving foreign currency, and to prohibit the import or export of foreign currency.

The Export Administration Act of 1979 [P.L. 96-72]. Section 6(i) of this act [93 Stat. 515] required the Secretary of Commerce and the Secretary of State to notify Congress before licensing export of goods or technology valued at more than $7 million to countries determined to have supported acts of international terrorism. (Amendments adopted in 1985 and 1986 relettered Section 6(i) as 6(j) and lowered the threshold for notification from $7 million to $1 million.)

A by-product of these two laws was the so-called state sponsors of terrorism list. This list is prepared annually by the State Department in accordance with Section 6(j) of the Export Administration Act. The list identifies those countries that repeatedly have provided support for acts of international terrorism. Syria has appeared on this list ever since it was first prepared in 1979; it appears most recently in the State Department's annual publication Country Reports on Terrorism, 2009, issued on August 5, 2010. Syria's inclusion on this list in 1979 triggered the above-mentioned aid sanctions under P.L. 94-329 and trade restrictions under P.L. 96-72.

Omnibus Diplomatic Security and Antiterrorism Act of 1986 [P.L. 99-399]. Section 509(a) of this act [100 Stat. 853] amended Section 40 of the Arms Export Control Act to prohibit export of items on the munitions list to countries determined to be supportive of international terrorism, thus banning any U.S. military equipment sales to Syria. (This ban was reaffirmed by the Anti-Terrorism and Arms Export Amendments Act of 1989—see below.) Also, 10 U.S.C. 2249a bans obligation of U.S. Defense Department funds for assistance to countries on the terrorism list.

Omnibus Budget Reconciliation Act of 1986 [P.L. 99-509]. Section 8041(a) of this act [100 Stat. 1962] amended the Internal Revenue Code of 1954 to deny foreign tax credits on income or war profits from countries identified by the Secretary of State as supporting international terrorism. [26 USC 901(j)]. The President was given authority to waive this provision under Section 601 of the Trade and Development Act of 2000 (P.L. 106-200, May 18, 2000).

The Anti-Terrorism and Arms Export Control Amendments Act of 1989 [P.L. 101-222]. Section 4 amended Section 6(j) of the Export Administration Act to impose a congressional notification and licensing requirement for export of goods or technology, irrespective of dollar value, to countries on the terrorism list, if such exports could contribute to their military capability or enhance their ability to support terrorism.

Section 4 also prescribes conditions for removing a country from the terrorism list: prior notification by the President to the Speaker of the House of Representatives and the chairmen of two specified committees of the Senate. In conjunction with the requisite notification, the President must certify that the country has met several conditions that clearly indicate it is no longer involved in supporting terrorist activity. (In some cases, certification must be provided 45 days in advance of removal of a country from the terrorist list).

The Anti-Economic Discrimination Act of 1994 [Part C, P.L. 103-236, the Foreign Relations Authorization Act, FY1994-1995]. Section 564(a) bans the sale or lease of U.S.

defense articles and services to any country that questions U.S. firms about their compliance with the Arab boycott of Israel. Section 564(b) contains provisions for a presidential waiver, but no such waiver has been exercised in Syria's case. Again, this provision is moot in Syria's case because of other prohibitions already in effect.

The Antiterrorism and Effective Death Penalty Act of 1996 [P.L. 104-132]. This act requires the President to withhold aid to third countries that provide assistance (Section 325) or lethal military equipment (Section 326) to countries on the terrorism list, but allows the President to waive this provision on grounds of national interest. A similar provision banning aid to third countries that sell lethal equipment to countries on the terrorism list is contained in Section 549 of the Foreign Operations Appropriations Act for FY2001 (H.R. 5526, passed by reference in H.R. 4811, which was signed by President Clinton as P.L. 106-429 on November 6, 2000).

Also, Section 321 of P.L. 104-132 makes it a criminal offense for U.S. persons (citizens or resident aliens) to engage in financial transactions with governments of countries on the terrorism list, except as provided in regulations issued by the Department of the Treasury in consultation with the Secretary of State. In the case of Syria, the implementing regulation prohibits such transactions "with respect to which the United States person knows or has reasonable cause to believe that the financial transaction poses a risk of furthering terrorist acts in the United States." (31 CFR 596, published in the Federal Register August 23, 1996, p. 43462.) In the fall of 1996, the then Chairman of the House International Relations Committee reportedly protested to then President Clinton about the Treasury Department's implementing regulation, which he described as a "special loophole" for Syria.

In addition to the general sanctions listed above, specific provisions in foreign assistance appropriations legislation enacted since 1981 have barred Syria by name from receiving U.S. aid. The most recent ban appears in Section 7007 of P.L. 111-117, the Consolidated Appropriations Act, 2010, which states that "None of the funds appropriated or otherwise made available pursuant to titles III through VI of this Act shall be obligated or expended to finance directly any assistance or reparations for the governments of Cuba, North Korea, Iran, or Syria: Provided, That for purposes of this section, the prohibition on obligations or expenditures shall include direct loans, credits, insurance and guarantees of the Export-Import Bank or its agents."

Section 307 of the Foreign Assistance Act of 1961, amended by Section 431 of the Foreign Relations Authorization Act for FY1994-1995 (P.L. 103-236, April 30, 1994), requires the United States to withhold a proportionate share of contributions to international organizations for programs that benefit eight specified countries or entities, including Syria.

The Iran Nonproliferation Act of 2000, P.L. 106-178, was amended by P.L. 109-112 to make its provisions applicable to Syria as well as Iran. The amended act, known as the Iran and Syria Nonproliferation Act, requires the President to submit semi-annual reports to designated congressional committees, identifying any persons involved in arms transfers to or from Iran or Syria; also, the act authorizes the President to impose various sanctions against such individuals. On October 13, 2006, President Bush signed P.L. 109-353 which expanded the scope of the original law by adding North Korea to its provisions, thereby renaming the law the Iran, North Korea, and Syria Nonproliferation Act (or INKSNA for short). The list of Syrian entities designated under INKSNA include: Army Supply Bureau (2008), Syrian Navy (2009), Syrian Air Force (2009), and Ministry of Defense (2008).[35]

Specific Sanctions Against Syria

Specific U.S. sanctions levied against Syria fall into three main categories: (1) sanctions resulting from the passage of the 2003 Syria Accountability and Lebanese Sovereignty Act (SALSA) that, among other things, prohibit most U.S. exports to Syria; (2) sanctions imposed by Executive Order from the President that specifically deny certain Syrian citizens and entities access to the U.S. financial system due to their participation in proliferation of weapons of mass destruction, association with Al Qaeda, the Taliban or Osama bin Laden; or destabilizing activities in Iraq and Lebanon; and (3) sanctions resulting from the USA Patriot Act levied specifically against the Commercial Bank of Syria in 2006.

The 2003 Syria Accountability Act

On December 12, 2003, President Bush signed H.R. 1828, the Syria Accountability and Lebanese Sovereignty Restoration Act into law, as P.L. 108-175. This law requires the President to impose penalties on Syria unless it ceases support for international terrorist groups, ends its occupation of Lebanon, ceases the development of weapons of mass destruction (WMD), and has ceased supporting or facilitating terrorist activity in Iraq (Section 5(a) and 5(d)). Sanctions include bans on the export of military items (already banned under other legislation, see above[36]) and of dual use items (items with both civil and military applications) to Syria (Section 5(a)(1)). In addition, the President is required to impose two or more sanctions from a menu of six:

- a ban on all exports to Syria except food and medicine;
- a ban on U.S. businesses operating or investing in Syria;
- a ban on landing in or overflight of the United States by Syrian aircraft;
- reduction of diplomatic contacts with Syria;
- restrictions on travel by Syrian diplomats in the United States; and
- blocking of transactions in Syrian property (Section 5(a)(2)).

Implementation

On May 11, 2004, President Bush issued Executive Order 13338, implementing the provisions of P.L. 108-175, including the bans on munitions and dual use items (Section 5(a)(1)) and two sanctions from the menu of six listed in Section 5(a)(2). The two sanctions he chose were the ban on exports to Syria other than food and medicine (Section 5(a)(2)(A) and the ban on Syrian aircraft landing in or overflying the United States (Section 5(a)(2)(D). In issuing his executive order, the President stated that Syria has failed to take significant, concrete steps to address the concerns that led to the enactment of the Syria Accountability Act. The President also imposed two additional sanctions based on other legislation.

- Under Section 311 of the USA PATRIOT Act, he instructed the Treasury Department to prepare a rule requiring U.S. financial institutions to sever correspondent accounts with the Commercial Bank of Syria because of money laundering concerns.
- Under the International Emergency Economic Powers Act (IEEPA), he issued instructions to freeze assets of certain Syrian individuals and government entities involved in supporting policies inimical to the United States.

Waivers

In the executive order and in an accompanying letter to Congress, President Bush cited the waiver authority contained in Section 5(b) of the Syria Accountability Act and stated that he wished to issue the following waivers on grounds of national security:

- Regarding Section 5(a)(1) and 5(a)(2)(A): The following exports are permitted: products in support of activities of the U.S. government; medicines otherwise banned because of potential dual use; aircraft parts necessary for flight safety; informational materials; telecommunications equipment to promote free flow of information; certain software and technology; products in support of U.N. operations; and certain exports of a temporary nature.[37]

Regarding Section 5(a)(2)(D): The following operations are permitted: takeoff/landing of Syrian aircraft chartered to transport Syrian officials on official business to the United States; takeoff/landing for non-traffic and non-scheduled stops; takeoff/landing associated with an emergency; and overflights of U.S. territory.

Targeted Financial Sanctions

Since the initial implementation of the Syria Accountability Act (in Executive Order 13338 dated May 2004), the President has repeatedly taken action to sanction individual members of the Asad regime's inner circle.[38] E.O. 13338 declared a national emergency with respect to Syria and authorized the Secretary of the Treasury to block the property of individual Syrians. Based on section 202(d) of the National Emergencies Act (50 U.S.C. 1622(d)), the President has annually extended his authority to block the property of individual Syrians (latest on May 3, 2010). When issuing each extension, the President has noted that the actions and policies of the government of Syria continued to pose an unusual and extraordinary threat.[39]

The following individuals and entities have been targeted by the U.S. Treasury Department (Office of Foreign Assets Control or OFAC):

- On June 30, 2005, the U.S. Treasury Department designated two senior Syrian officials involved in Lebanon affairs, Syria's then-Interior Minister and its head of military intelligence in Lebanon (respectively, the late General Kanaan and General Ghazali), as Specially Designated Nationals, thereby freezing any assets they may have in the United States and banning any U.S. persons, including U.S. financial institutions outside of the United States, from conducting transactions with them.[40] Kanaan allegedly committed suicide in October 2005, though some have speculated that he may have been murdered.
- On January 18, 2006, U.S. Treasury Department took the same actions against the President's brother-in-law, Assef Shawkat, chief of military intelligence.
- On April 26, 2006, President Bush issued Executive Order 13399 that authorized the secretary of the Treasury to freeze the U.S.-based assets of anyone found to be involved in the February 2005 assassination of former Lebanese Prime Minister Rafiq Hariri. It also affects anyone involved in bombings or assassinations in Lebanon since October 2004, or anyone hindering the international investigation into the Hariri assassination. The order allows the United States to comply with UNSCR

1636, which calls on all states to freeze the assets of those persons designated by the investigating commission or the government of Lebanon to be involved in the Hariri assassination.

- On August 15, 2006, the U.S. Treasury Department froze assets of two other senior Syrian officers: Major General Hisham Ikhtiyar, for allegedly contributing to Syria's support of foreign terrorist organizations including Hezbollah; and Brigadier General Jama'a Jama'a, for allegedly playing a central part in Syria's intelligence operations in Lebanon during the Syrian occupation.[41]
- On January 4, 2007, the U.S. Treasury Department designated three Syrian entities, the Syrian Higher Institute of Applied Science and Technology, the Electronics Institute, and the National Standards and Calibration Laboratory, as weapons proliferators under an executive order (E.O.13382) based on the authority vested to the President under IEEPA. The three state-sponsored institutions are divisions of Syria's Scientific Studies and Research Center, which was designated by President Bush as a weapons proliferator in June 2005 for research on the development of biological and chemical weapons.[42]
- On August 1, 2007, the President issued E.O. 13441[43] blocking the property of persons undermining the sovereignty of Lebanon or its democratic processes and institutions. On November 5, 2007, the U.S. Treasury Department designated four individuals reportedly affiliated with the Syrian regime's efforts to reassert Syrian control over the Lebanese political system, including Assaad Halim Hardan, Wi'am Wahhab and Hafiz Makhluf (under the authority of E.O.13441) and Muhammad Nasif Khayrbik (under the authority of E.O.13338).[44]
- On February 13, 2008, President Bush issued another Order (E.O.13460) blocking the property of senior Syrian officials. According to the U.S. Treasury Department, the order "targets individuals and entities determined to be responsible for or who have benefitted from the public corruption of senior officials of the Syrian regime. The order also revises a provision in Executive Order 13338 to block the property of Syrian officials who have undermined U.S. and international efforts to stabilize Iraq.[45] One week later, under the authority of E.O.13460, the U.S. Treasury Department froze the U.S. assets and restricted the financial transactions of Rami Makhluf, the 38 year-old cousin of President Bashar al Asad. Makhluf is a powerful Syrian businessman who serves as an interlocutor between foreign investors and Syrian companies. According to one report, "Since a military coup in 1969, the Asads have controlled politics while the Makhlufs have been big business players. The tradition continues in the next generation, with Bashar al-Assad (sic) as president and Rami Makhluf as a leading force in business."[46] Makhluf is a major stakeholder in Syriatel, the country's largest mobile phone operator. In 2008, the Turkish company Turkcell was in talks to purchase Syriatel, but, according to *Reuters*, negotiations over the sale were taking longer than expected because some Turkcell executives have U.S. passports.[47] Then, in August 2008, Turkcell said it had frozen its plans for a venture in Syria amid U.S. opposition to the project. Makhluf's holding company, Cham, is involved in several other large deals, including an agreement with Syria's state airline and a Kuwaiti company to set up a new airline. Several months ago, Dubai-based real-estate company Emaar Properties announced it had agreed to set up a $100 million venture with Cham to develop real estate projects

in Syria. Makhluf also is a minority shareholder in Gulfsands Petroleum,[48] a publicly-traded, United Kingdom-incorporated energy company. According to the *Wall Street Journal*, a Gulfsands executive said the Treasury Department's sanctioning of Makhlouf would have no impact on the company pursuing its partnership with Cham.[49]

Sanctions Against the Commercial Bank of Syria

As previously mentioned, under Section 311 of the USA PATRIOT Act, President Bush instructed the Treasury Department in 2004 to prepare a rule requiring U.S. financial institutions to sever correspondent accounts with the Commercial Bank of Syria because of money laundering concerns. In 2006, the Treasury Department issued a final ruling that imposes a special measure against the Commercial Bank of Syria as a financial institution of primary money laundering concern. It bars U.S. banks and their overseas subsidiaries from maintaining a correspondent account with the Commercial Bank of Syria, and it also requires banks to conduct due diligence that ensures the Commercial Bank of Syria is not circumventing sanctions through its business dealings with them.[50]

Effect of U.S. Sanctions on Syria's Economy

U.S. sanctions against Syria have clearly dissuaded some U.S. and some foreign businesses from investing in Syria. With the exception of certain specified goods, most U.S. exports to Syria are prohibited, a policy that has prevented the country's national air carrier, Syrian Air, both from repairing the few Boeing planes in its fleet and from procuring new planes from Europe, since Airbus uses certain American content in its planes. In a possible early good-will gesture, on February 9, 2009, the U.S. Department of Commerce approved an export license for Boeing 747 spare parts[51] to Syrian Air.[52] In July 2009, the Obama Administration pledged to grant more waivers under the Syria Accountability Act to allow for increased U.S. export to Syria of goods related to information technology, telecommunication equipment, and civil aviation components. However, in December 2009, the United States rejected an Airbus request to sell new planes to Syria because the average Airbus plane contains an estimated 40% component parts of U.S. origin – thus making it illegal to export to Syria without an export license under the Department of Commerce's Export Administration Regulations (EAR) implementing provisions in the Syria Accountability and Lebanese Sovereignty Restoration Act (P.L. 108-175).[53] In October 2010, Syria's Transport Minister suggested that due to U.S. sanctions, Syria would consider buying six Russian Tupolev Tu-204 planes for Syrian Air.

According to one report, General Electric, the French power company Alstom, and Japanese-owned Mitsubishi all declined to bid on a Syrian government contract for the construction of power plants.[54] As mentioned above, Turkcell withdrew its bid to purchase Syriatel in August 2008 after the United States sanctioned Syriatel's primary stakeholder, Rami Makluf. U.S. sanctions under the Patriot Act against the Commercial Bank of Syria have deterred private Western banks from opening branches inside Syria. As Syria's energy production levels decline, sanctions have prevented major Western energy companies from making new investments there, though other foreign companies have supplanted U.S. firms. One company, Gulfsands Petroleum, moved its principle office to London in order to circumvent U.S. sanctions against its local partner, Rami Makluf.

Syria is still an importer of U.S. agricultural products such as corn and soybeans. According to the U.S. embassy in Damascus, the United States is Syria's primary corn supplier, and corn sales from the United States to Syria increased from $61 million in 2001 to $102 million in 2005. Soybean exports also increased from approximately $1 million in 2001 to $28 million in 2005. For the last five years, eastern Syria has experienced a severe drought which has wiped out significant portions of the livestock industry and curtailed wheat farming. Syria used to export wheat, and it is now a net importer, mainly from Russia and the Ukraine.

Although U.S. sanctions have deterred American and some foreign investment in Syria, other countries have sought entry into the Syrian market.[55] Foreign investment from the Arab Gulf States and Iran has been substantial in recent years. Syria's largest trading partners within the Middle East are Saudi Arabia ($1.9 billion), Egypt ($1 billion), Lebanon ($600 million) and Jordan ($560 million). Syria's primary non-Arab trading partners are Italy ($3.5 billion total volume), France ($1.2 billion), China ($1.1 billion), and Turkey ($1.1 billion).[56]

Table 1. U.S.-Syrian Trade Statistics 2005-2009
($ in millions)

	2005	2006	2007	2008	2009
U.S. Exports to Syria	$155.0	$224.3	$361.4	$408.8	$300.0
U.S. Imports from Syria	$323.5	$213.7	$110.5	$352.0	$285.9
Totals	**$478.5**	**$438.0**	**$471.9**	**$760.8**	**$585.9**

Source: TradeStats Express – National Trade Data, Presented by the Office of Trade and Industry Information (OTII), Manufacturing and Services, International Trade Administration, U.S. Department of Commerce.

Syria's Need for Economic Growth

Syria is seeking aid, trade, and foreign investment from the international community, particularly the West, to boost its lackluster, mostly state-controlled economy, which is highly dependent on dwindling oil production[57] and foreign remittances.[58] To date, the government has enacted some reforms, such as liberalizing the financial sector, reducing fuel subsidies, opening a stock exchange, and cutting some import tariffs. Nevertheless, President Asad has yet to tackle the most difficult reforms, such as reducing the government payroll, combating elite corruption such as fuel smuggling, liberalizing other sectors of the economy and breaking up family-run business monopolies, halting tax evasion, modernizing the bureaucracy, and increasing overall economic transparency. Some observers believe that the regime cannot act boldly in the economic sphere due to the political backlash and possible unrest it would face from many different parts of Syrian society. Economic reforms may clash with the vested, status quo interests of Syrian business and political elites with ties to the Asad family. Others suggest that the opaque nature of Syria's authoritarian government inhibits the natural development of a transparent market economy that is attractive to foreign capital.

Although Syria has attracted more foreign investment from China, Gulf Arab countries, Iran, and Turkey lately, Syria also is responsible for the lack of strong economic ties to the West. After years of stalled negotiations, the European Union finally ratified its Association Agreement with Syria in 2009, only to see Syria refuse to sign the accord at the last minute. The deal, which would loosen bilateral trade restrictions and increase the flow of European aid to Syria, raised concern among Syrian business elites due to increased European competition in the agricultural and manufacturing sectors.

FUTURE PROSPECTS AND THE ROLE OF CONGRESS

For the foreseeable future, most analysts agree that relations between the United States and Syria will remain static, as neither government has shown interest in fundamentally altering policies opposed by the other side. Though Syria wants the Obama Administration to unilaterally lift sanctions, U.S. policymakers may be holding out for real changes in Syrian regime behavior, such as cutting or downgrading ties to Iran, Hamas, or Hezbollah. Syria feels that it has already acceded to previous U.S. demands by normalizing relations with Lebanon. Syria appears reluctant to make further changes without a clear indication of benefits it would accrue from major shifts in its foreign policy. From the U.S. standpoint, Syria is far down the list of current foreign policy priorities and, with an Israeli government that has appeared generally uneager to take steps viewed as necessary to revive the bilateral peace track, there is little to be gained from additional substantive U.S.-Syrian engagement other than a return to normal diplomatic relations.

With U.S.-Syrian relations possibly headed toward more tense footing, Some members of Congress may choose to impose new sanctions against the Asad regime. Other lawmakers may seek to continue U.S. engagement, as several Congressional delegations visited Syria during the 111th Congress. Also during the 111th Congress, lawmakers introduced H.R. 1206, the Syria Accountability and Liberation Act, which would have placed new sanctions on countries and individuals which help Syria gain access to weapons of mass destruction. It also called for sanctions against those who invest $5 million or more in Syria's energy sector. Appropriators also may choose to fund democracy and governance programs inside Syria for opposition members and human rights activists repressed by the Asad government.

End Notes

[1] For many years, Syria and Iraq had an uneven and often troubled relationship, stemming from political disputes, border tensions, demographic differences, and personal animosity between the two countries' late leaders: Syrian President Hafiz al Asad and Iraqi President Saddam Hussein. Moreover, the two countries were governed by rival wings of the pan-Arab Baath Party. Syria severed diplomatic relations with Iraq in 1982 after it accused Saddam Hussein's regime of inciting and supporting Syrian Muslim Brotherhood-led riots. In the late 1990s bilateral relations improved markedly, primarily in the economic sphere. The two countries formally restored relations in November 2006.

[2] Thousands of Iranian Shiites visit Syria annually on pilgrimages to several famous shrines and mosques.

[3] Iranian state news reported in August 2010 that the bank is to be named Al Aman. Its initial capitalization is estimated at $32 million, and Iran's Saderat Bank, Alghadir Company, and Saipa Company own 25%, 16%, and 8% of the bank's shares respectively. The rest will be offered on Syria's new stock exchange. See, Open Source Center, "Iran, Syria To Establish Private Bank In Damascus," IAP20100801950070, *Tehran Mehr News Agency* in English, August 1, 2010.

[4] In May 2010, an Iranian businessman and shareholder in Siamco, was killed outside his home in Damascus in an apparent assassination. No group has claimed responsibility for the killing

[5] "Syria Economy: Iran Bank Deal?," *Economist Intelligence Unit*, October 14, 2008.

[6] "Iran Arms Syria With Radar," *Wall Street Journal*, June 30, 2010.

[7] "U.S. State Department Press Release," Daily Press Briefing, July 1, 2010.

[8] "Prime Minister Absolves Syria of Blame over Father's Assassination in Bid to end Tension," *The Times* (London), November 1, 2010.

[9] "Syria Working to Prevent Lebanon Violence: Assad," *Agence France Presse*, October 26, 2010.

[10] International Crisis Group, *DRUMS OF WAR: ISRAEL AND THE "AXIS OF RESISTANCE,"* Middle East Report #97, August 2010.

[11] "Israeli Navy Seizes Weapons Believed to Be for Hezbollah," *Wall Street Journal*, November 5, 2009.

[12] According to *Janes*, Syria possesses an indigenously produced 'Scud D' variant of the North Korean Hwasong 7 that can travel up to 430 miles. See, "Israel Claims Syria has Transferred 'Scuds' to Hizbullah," *Jane's Defence Weekly*, April 16, 2010.

[13] Open Source Center, "Syria Sends Scud Missiles to Hizballah, Israel Threatens War," *Kuwait Al-Ra'y Online in Arabic*, April 11, 2010, GMP20100411184001.

[14] "Scud Missiles Spotted from Space may be in the Hands of Hezbollah Militants; Lebanon," *The Times (London)*, October 9, 2010.

[15] The former Soviet Union was a longtime ally of Syria and a main supplier of arms to the Syrian military. Soviet advisors and military personnel were welcomed by the late Syrian President Hafiz al Asad, even as Soviet relations with other Arab governments, such as Egypt, deteriorated after successive Arab defeats at the hands of the Israeli military in 1967 and 1973 respectively. It is estimated that the Soviet Union provided Syria with up to $26 billion worth of arms until 1991. Between 1999 and 2003, Russian-Syrian military relations revived. In 2005, Russia cancelled most of Syria's $13.4 billion debt from previous arms agreements.

[16] According to one Israeli analyst, "Syria has not purchased any significant weapon system from Russia since the fall of the Soviet Union; the only purchases were the Kornet-E anti-tank missiles (some of which ultimately reached Hizbollah), and the Pantsyr-S1 air defense system. In the past year, Syria was offered a number of MiG-31 planes (almost certainly to be used for intelligence missions). Other Syrian requests, such as the S-300 air defense system or the Iskander-E surface-to-surface missiles, were refused." See, Zvi Magen and Yiftah S. Shapir, "Adornment of the Syrian Bride?," *INSS Insight,* No. 209, September 21, 2010.

[17] "Syria: PROCUREMENT," *Jane's Sentinel Security Assessment—Eastern Mediterranean* , November 26, 2010.

[18] "Israel DM Concerned over RF's Yakhont Missile Supply to Syria," *Itar-Tass*, September 21, 2010.

[19] "U.S. Details Reactor in Syria," *Washington Post*, April 25, 2008.

[20] Introductory Statement to the Board of Governors by IAEA Director General Dr. Mohamed ElBaradei, November 27, 2008, Vienna, Austria, IAEA Board of Governors.

[21] "Diplomats: Damascus has Built Missile Facility on Suspected Nuclear Site," *Associated Press*, February 25, 2009.

[22] The IAEA's director general has the authority to call for a special inspection of suspect facilities in any member country suspected of violating its commitment to non-proliferation. If the member country rejects the IAEA's request, the agency can refer the case to the United Nations Security Council as an act of noncompliance, potentially triggering sanctions.

[23] Implementation of the NPT Safeguards Agreement in the Syrian Arab Republic, Report by the Director General, GOV/2010/63, Date: 23 November 2010.

[24] David Albright and Paul Brannan, *Satellite Image Shows Syrian Site Functionally Related to Al Kibar Reactor*, Institute for Science and International Security, December 1, 2010.

[25] "2009 Human Rights Report: Syria," Bureau of Democracy, Human Rights, and Labor, 2009 Country Reports on Human Rights Practices, March 11, 2010.

[26] The Alawite religious sect, which evolved from the Shi'ite sect of Islam, constitutes approximately 12% of the Syrian population. Formerly the most economically deprived and socially disadvantaged group in Syria, the Alawites rose rapidly in the ranks of the military establishment and the ruling Ba'th Party in the 1960s and have dominated political life since then.

[27] The socialist, pan-Arab Ba'th Party, whose rival wing governed Iraq before the collapse of Saddam Hussein's regime, came to power in Syria in 1963. Although the Syrian constitution specifies a leading role for the Ba'th Party and the party provides the regime with political legitimacy, the Ba'th is more an instrument for the execution of policy than an originator of policy. Many Ba'thists are not Alawites, but there is a complex synergistic relationship between the party and the community. Still, barring a major governmental change, a Syrian leader would need to enjoy the support of the Ba'th Party apparatus. The party's top decision-making

body, known as the "Regional Command," sits at the top of the policy-making process, and membership in this body is a stepping stone to top positions in Syria.

[28] Democracy Council Of California, "Survey Findings: Syria 2010 Public Opinion Survey," August 5, 2010.

[29] Administration officials admonished Syria several times in the fall of 2010. On October 26, 2010, U.S. State Department Spokesman Philip Crowley said, "Syria continues to transfer weapons to Hezbollah and recently issued arrest warrants for 33 Lebanese and foreign nationals, including the Lebanese Government state prosecutor and head of the national police. These activities by Syria directly undermine Lebanon's sovereignty and directly undermine Syria's stated commitments to Lebanon's sovereignty and independence." On October 28, U.S. Ambassador to the United Nations Susan E. Rice remarked that "We continue to have deep concerns about Hezbollah's destructive and destabilizing influence in the region...as well as the attempts by other foreign players, including Syria and Iran, to undermine Lebanon's independence and endanger its stability." Then, in a November 1 interview with the *Washington Post*, Jeffrey D. Feltman, Assistant Secretary of State for Near Eastern Affairs, stated that "Syria has said it wants a better bilateral relationship with us. We would like to have a better bilateral relationship with Syria. Syria and the United States have taken some modest steps to see if we can improve the bilateral relationship. But this cannot go very far as long as Syria's friends are undermining stability in Lebanon. We have made that absolutely clear to the Syrians. There is a cost to the potential in our bilateral relationship to what Syria's friends are doing in Lebanon." On November 10, 2010, Secretary of State Hillary Roadham Clinton remarked in an interview that "Syria's behavior has not met our hopes and expectations over the past 20 months – and Syria's actions have not met its international obligations. Syria can still choose another path and we hope that it does."

[30] U.S. Special Envoy for Middle East Peace Senator George Mitchell has made several trips to Syria. His deputy, Fred Hof, also has traveled to Syria to jumpstart Syrian-Israeli peace negotiations. In September 2010, Secretary Clinton met with Syrian Foreign Minister Walid Mouallem on the sidelines of the U.N. General Assembly meeting in New York. In June 2010, State Department officials and a delegation of American senior executives from Microsoft Corp., Dell Inc., Cisco Systems Inc., and Symantec Corp. traveled to Damascus and Aleppo for meetings with President Asad and Syrian businessmen. The visit was intended to encourage the Syrian government to promote free speech over the Internet and pass legislation safeguarding intellectual property. Most analysts believe that at a macro level, the delegation was intended to show Syria what the benefits of a better relationship with the United States could look like if it provided the diplomatic cooperation being sought by the Administration.

[31] "US-Iran Dynamic: Why U.S. Effort to Leverage Syria is Flagging," *Christian Science Monitor*, July 3, 2010.

[32] The Senate Foreign Relations Committee approved the nomination on April 13, 2010.

[33] Statement of Ryan C. Crocker Dean and Executive Professor, George Bush School of Government and Public Service Texas A&M University, Committee on Senate Foreign Relations Subcommittee on Near Eastern and South and Central Asian Affairs, June 8, 2010.

[34] Because of a number of legal restrictions and U.S. sanctions, many resulting from Syria's designation as a country supportive of international terrorism, Syria is no longer eligible to receive U.S. foreign assistance. Between 1950 and 1981, the United States provided a total of $627.4 million in aid to Syria: $34.0 million in development assistance, $438.0 million in economic support, and $155.4 million in food assistance. Most of this aid was provided during a brief warming trend in bilateral relations between 1974 and 1979. Significant projects funded under U.S. aid included water supply, irrigation, rural roads and electrification, and health and agricultural research. No aid has been provided to Syria since 1981, when the last aid programs were closed out.

[35] See, State Department Press Releases And Documents "Near East: Iran, North Korea, and Syria Nonproliferation Act: Imposed Sanctions," July 20, 2010.

[36] Syria's inclusion on the State Sponsors of Terrorism List as well as SALSA requires the President to restrict the export of any items to Syria that appear on the U.S. Munitions List (weapons, ammunition) or Commerce Control List (dual-use items).

[37] According to U.S. regulations, any product that contains more than 10% *de minimis* U.S.-origin content, regardless of where it is made, is not allowed to be exported to Syria. For U.S. commercial licensing prohibitions on exports and reexports to Syria, see 15 C.F.R. pt. 736 Supp No. 1. The Department of Commerce reviews license applications on a case-by-case basis for exports or reexports to Syria under a general policy of denial. For a description of items that do not require export licenses, see, Bureau of Industry and Security (BIS), U.S. Department of Commerce, Implementation of the Syria Accountability Act, available online at http://www.bis.doc.gov/licensing/syriaimplementationmay14_04.htm.

Syria: Issues for the 112th Congress and Background on U.S. Sanctions 135

[38] According to the original text of E.O. 13338, the President's authority to declare a national emergency authorizing the blocking of property of certain persons and prohibiting the exportation or reexportation of certain goods to Syria is based on "The Constitution and the laws of the United States of America, including the International Emergency Economic Powers Act (50 U.S.C. 1701 et seq.) (IEEPA), the National Emergencies Act (50 U.S.C. 1601 et seq.) (NEA), the Syria Accountability and Lebanese Sovereignty Restoration Act of 2003, P.L. 108-175 (SAA), and section 301 of title 3, United States Code." available online at http://www.treas.gov/offices/enforcement/ofac/legal/eo/ 13338.pdf.

[39] The President last extended the State of Emergency on May 3, 2010, stating that "While the Syrian government has made some progress in suppressing foreign fighter networks infiltrating suicide bombers into Iraq, its actions and polices, including continuing support for terrorist organizations and pursuit of weapons of mass destruction and missile programs, pose a continuing unusual and extraordinary threat to the national security, foreign policy, and economy of the United States. For these reasons, I have determined that it is necessary to continue in effect the national emergency declared with respect to this threat and to maintain in force the sanctions to address this national emergency. As we have communicated to the Syrian government directly, Syrian actions will determine whether this national emergency is renewed or terminated in the future." See, Message to the Congress Continuing the National Emergency with Respect to Syria, The White House, Office of the Press Secretary, May 3, 2010.

[40] See, http://www.treas.gov/press/releases/js2617.htm.

[41] See, http://www.treas.gov/press/releases/hp60.htm.

[42] See, http://www.treas.gov/press/releases/hp216.htm.

[43] On July 29, 2010, President Obama extended that National Emergency with respect to Lebanon for another year, stating that "While there have been some recent positive developments in the Syrian-Lebanese relationship, continuing arms transfers to Hizballah that include increasingly sophisticated weapons systems serve to undermine Lebanese sovereignty, contribute to political and economic instability in Lebanon, and continue to pose an unusual and extraordinary threat to the national security and foreign policy of the United States." See, Notice of July 29, 2010-- Continuation of the National Emergency With Respect to the Actions of Certain Persons to Undermine the Sovereignty of Lebanon or Its Democratic Processes and Institutions, Federal Register, Title 3--The President, [Page 45045].

[44] See, http://www.treas.gov/press/releases/hp666.htm.

[45] A previous executive order, E.O. 13315, blocks property of former Iraqi President Saddam Hussein and members of his former regime. On June 9, 2005, the Treasury Department blocked property and interests of a Syrian company, SES International Corp., and two of its officials under the authority of E.O.13315.

[46] "Sanctions on Businessman Target Syria's Inner Sanctum," *Washington Post*, February 22, 2008.

[47] "Turkcell Continues Talks on Syriatel Stake," *Reuters*, April 14, 2008.

[48] Gulfsands' chief executive and largest shareholder, John Dorrier, is an American citizen, and the company has offices in Houston.

[49] "Syrian Tycoon Bristles At US Sanctions Against Him," the *Wall Street Journal*, March 26, 2008.

[50] See, "U.S. Trade and Financial Sanctions Against Syria." Available online at: [http://damascus.usembassy.gov/sanctions-syr.html]

[51] In 2008, Syrian Air and European aerospace manufacturer Airbus tentatively agreed to a sale of up to 54 commercial aircraft; however, the sale was never completed because Airbus planes contain more than 10% U.S. components.

[52] Executive Order 13338, which implements the Syria Accountability Act, states that the Secretary of Commerce shall not permit the exportation or reexportation to Syria of U.S. products "except to the extent provided in regulations, orders, directives, or licenses issued pursuant to the provisions" of the order. U.S. Department of Commerce Bureau of Industry and Security regulations [Code of Federal Regulations, Title 15, Chapter VII, Part 742.9(b)] state U.S. export licensing policy with regard to Syria. According to the BIS regulations, "applications for export and reexport to all end-users in Syria ... will generally be denied," including licenses for aircraft, helicopters, engines, and related spare parts and components, "except that parts and components intended to ensure the safety of civil aviation and the safe operation of commercial passenger aircraft will be reviewed on a case-by-case basis, with a presumption of approval."

[53] "US prohibited Airbus selling planes to Syria: Damascus," *Agence France Presse*, December 29, 2009.

[54] "Tired of Energy Ills, Syrians Doubt the West Is to Blame," *New York Times*, August 15, 2007.

[55] According to one study by the German Marshall Fund, "From 2000 to 2009, the stock of FDI [foreign direct investment] in Syria witnessed a sharp increase from $1.244 billion to $7.334 billion. Specifically, in the 2007-2009 period alone, the stock has increased by more than $4 billion." See, Franco Zallio, "The Future of

Syria's Economic Reforms between Regional Integration and Relations with the West," Mediterranean Policy Program—*Series on the Region and the Economic Crisis*, German Marshall Fund, November 2010.

[56] U.S. Department of Commerce, Doing Business in Syria: 2009 Country Commercial Guide for U.S. Companies.

[57] According to the Department of Energy's Energy Information Administration, "Since peaking at 583,000 barrels per day (bbl/d) in 1996, Syrian crude oil production declined to an estimated 368,000 bbl/d in 2009, down from 390,000 bbl/d in 2008." See, [http://www.eia.doe.gov/emeu/cabs/Syria/Full.html]

[58] Syria needs electric power generation, as its demand is projected to nearly triple by 2025. Already, during the summer months, some Syrians experience lengthy power outages. Companies from Russia, China, India, Qatar, and Iran, among others, have invested in Syria's electricity sector. Syria also receives natural gas from Egypt and Turkey. See, "Damascus Turns to Private Sector," *Middle East Economic Digest*, May 14, 2010.

In: The Middle East in Turmoil, Volume 3
Editor: Angela N. Castillo

ISBN: 978-1-61324-241-4
© 2011 Nova Science Publishers, Inc.

Chapter 6

IRAQ: POLITICS, ELECTIONS, AND BENCHMARKS[*]

Kenneth Katzman

SUMMARY

Iraq's political system, the result of a U.S.-supported election process, has been increasingly characterized by peaceful competition, as well as by attempts to form cross-sectarian alliances. Ethnic and factional infighting continues, sometimes involving the questionable use of key levers of power and legal institutions. This infighting—and the belief that holding political power may mean the difference between life and death for the various political communities—significantly delayed agreement on a new government that was to be selected following the March 7, 2010, national elections for the Council of Representatives (COR, parliament). With U.S. intervention, on November 10, 2010, major ethnic and sectarian factions agreed on a framework for a new government, breaking the long deadlock. Iraqi leaders say agreement on a new cabinet is close, and Prime Minister Nuri al-Maliki, tapped to continue in that role, is expected to present his choices to the COR for approval on/about December 23, in advance of a December 25 constitutional deadline.

The difficulty in reaching agreement had multiple causes that could still cause instability over the long term. Among the causes were the close election results. With the results certified, a mostly Sunni Arab-supported "Iraqiyya" slate of former Prime Minister Iyad al-Allawi unexpectedly gained a plurality of 91 of the 325 COR seats up for election. Maliki's State of Law slate won 89, and a rival Shiite coalition was third with 70, of which about 40 seats are held by those supporting Moqtada Al Sadr. The main Kurdish parties, again allied, won 43 seats, with another 14 seats held by other Kurdish factions. On the basis of his first place showing, Allawi had demanded to be given the first opportunity to put together a majority coalition and form a government. However, his bloc was unable to win the allegiance of the Shiite blocs, and Iraqiyya has reluctantly agreed to join a coalition in which Maliki remains prime minister.

Allawi, who is viewed as even-handed and not amenable to Iranian influence, was considered to be favored by the Obama Administration and by Sunni-dominated regional neighbors such as Saudi Arabia. However, the support of these neighboring countries was

---

[*] This is an edited, reformatted and augmented version of a Congressional Research Services publication, dated December 22, 2010.

insufficient to restructure the post-election government formation process to Allawi's favor. Iran, which exercises major influence over the Shiite factions in Iraq, worked, with some success, to ensure that pro-Iranian Shiites lead the next government. However, the inclusion of Allawi's bloc indicates that Iran did not meet all of its objectives. The participation of all major factions in the new government could complicate efforts to overcome the roadblocks that have thus far prevented passage of key outstanding legislation crucial to attracting foreign investment, such as national hydrocarbon laws. U.S. officials and Iraqi citizens also hope that the new government can resolve the increasingly contentious shortages of electricity that have plagued Iraqi cities during 2010.

The long political vacuum, coupled with the drawdown of U.S. forces to 50,000 and formal end of the U.S. combat mission on August 31, 2010, was perceived as contributing to major high profile attacks in Iraq and a sense of uncertainty and disillusionment on the part of the Iraqi public. The continuing violence has caused some experts to question whether stability will continue after all U.S. forces are to depart at the end of 2011. Some believe that the reduction in U.S. leverage and influence in Iraq will cause the rifts among major ethnic and sectarian communities to widen to the point where Iraq could still become a "failed state" after 2011, unless some U.S. troops remain after that time. See CRS Report RL31339, *Iraq: Post-Saddam Governance and Security*, by Kenneth Katzman.

OVERVIEW OF THE POLITICAL TRANSITION

Iraq has completed a formal political transition from the dictatorship of Saddam Hussein to a plural polity that encompasses varying sects and ideological and political factions. However, disputes continue over the relative claim of each community on power and economic resources. These disputes permeate almost every issue in Iraq, including security, the terms and framework for elections, economic decision making, and foreign policy.

After the fall of Saddam Hussein's regime in April 2003, the United States set up an occupation structure, reportedly based on concerns that immediate sovereignty would favor major factions and not produce democracy. In May 2003, President Bush, reportedly seeking strong leadership in Iraq, named Ambassador L. Paul Bremer to head a "Coalition Provisional Authority" (CPA), which was recognized by the United Nations as an occupation authority. Bremer discontinued a tentative political transition process and instead appointed (July 13, 2003) a non-sovereign Iraqi advisory body, the 25-member "Iraq Governing Council" (IGC). After about one year of occupation, the United States handed sovereignty to an appointed Iraqi interim government on June 28, 2004. It was headed by a prime minister, Iyad al-Allawi, leader of the Iraq National Accord, a secular, non-sectarian faction. Allawi is a Shiite but many INA leaders were Sunnis, and some of them were formerly members of the Baath Party. The president of this interim government was Ghazi al-Yawar, a Sunni tribal figure who spent many years in Saudi Arabia.

January 2005 National Assembly and Provincial Elections

A series of elections in 2005 produced the full-term government that is in power today. In line with a March 8, 2004, "Transitional Administrative Law" (TAL, interim constitution), the first post-Saddam election was held on January 30, 2005, for a 275-seat transitional National Assembly (which formed an executive), four-year term provincial councils in all 18 provinces and a Kurdistan regional assembly (111 seats). According to the "proportional representation/closed list" election system, voters chose among "political entities" (a party, a coalition of parties, or persons); 111 entities were on the national ballot, of which nine were multi-party coalitions. Sunni Arabs (20% of the overall population) boycotted, winning only 17 Assembly seats, and only one seat on the 51-seat Baghdad provincial council. That council was dominated (28 seats) by representatives of the Islamic Supreme Council of Iraq (ISCI), led by Abd al-Aziz al-Hakim. Radical Shiite cleric Moqtada Al Sadr, then at odds with U.S. forces, also boycotted, leaving his faction poorly represented on provincial councils in the Shiite south and in Baghdad. The resulting transitional government placed Shiites and Kurds in the highest positions—Patriotic Union of Kurdistan (PUK) leader Jalal Talabani was president and Da'wa (Shiite party) leader Ibrahim al-Jafari was prime minister. Sunnis were Assembly speaker, deputy president, a deputy prime minister, and six ministers, including defense.

Permanent Constitution

The elected Assembly was to draft a constitution by August 15, 2005, to be put to a referendum by October 15, 2005, subject to veto by a two-thirds majority of voters in any three provinces. On May 10, 2005, a 55-member drafting committee was appointed, but with only two Sunni Arabs (15 Sunnis were later added as full members and 10 as advisors). In August 2005, the talks produced a draft, providing for a December 31, 2007, deadline to hold a referendum on whether Kirkuk (Tamim province) would join the Kurdish region (Article 140); designation of Islam as "a main source" of legislation;[1] a 25% electoral goal for women (Article 47); families choosing which courts to use for family issues (Article 41); making only primary education mandatory (Article 34); and having Islamic law experts and civil law judges on the federal supreme court (Article 89). Many women opposed the two latter provisions as giving too much discretion to male family members. It made all orders of the U.S.-led occupation authority (Coalition Provisional Authority, CPA) applicable until amended (Article 126), and established a "Federation Council" (Article 62), a second chamber with size and powers to be determined in future law (not adopted to date).

The major disputes—still to some extent unresolved—centered on regional versus centralized power. The draft permitted two or more provinces together to form new autonomous "regions"— reaffirmed in passage of an October 2006 law on formation of regions. Article 117 allows "regions" to organize internal security forces, legitimizing the fielding of the Kurds' *peshmerga* militia (allowed by the TAL). Article 109 requires the central government to distribute oil and gas revenues from "current fields" in proportion to population, and gave regions a role in allocating revenues from new energy discoveries. Disputes over these concepts continue to hold up passage of national hydrocarbons legislation. Sunnis dominate areas of Iraq that have few proven oil or gas deposits, and favor centralized control of oil revenues, whereas the Kurds want to maintain maximum control of their own burgeoning energy sector.

With contentious provisions unresolved, Sunnis registered in large numbers (70%-85%) to try to defeat the constitution, prompting a U.S.-mediated agreement (October 11, 2005) providing for a panel to propose amendments within four months after a post-December 15 election government took office (Article 137), to be voted on within another two months (under the same rules as the October 15 referendum). The Sunni provinces of Anbar and Salahuddin had a 97% and 82% "no" vote, respectively, but the constitution was adopted because Nineveh province only voted 55% "no," missing the threshold for a "no" vote by a two-thirds majority in three provinces.

December 15, 2005, Elections

The December 15, 2005, elections were for a full-term (four-year) national government (in line with the schedule laid out in the TAL). Under the voting mechanism used for that election, each province contributed a predetermined number of seats to a "Council of Representatives" (COR)— a formula adopted to attract Sunni participation. Of the 275-seat body, 230 seats were allocated this way, with 45 "compensatory" seats for entities that would have won additional seats had the constituency been the whole nation. There were 361 political "entities," including 19 multi-party coalitions, competing in a "closed list" voting system (in which party leaders choose the persons who will actually sit in the Assembly). As shown in Table 5, voters chose lists representing their sects and regions, and the Shiites and Kurds again emerged dominant. The COR was inaugurated on March 16, 2006, but political infighting caused the Shiite bloc "United Iraqi Alliance" to replace Jafari with another Da'wa figure, Nuri Kamal al-Maliki, as prime minister.

On April 22, 2006, the COR approved Talabani to continue as president. His two deputies are Adel Abd al-Mahdi (incumbent) of the Islamic Supreme Council of Iraq (ISCI) and Tariq alHashimi, leader of the broad Sunni-based coalition called the Accord Front ("Tawafuq"—within which Hashimi leads the Iraqi Islamic Party). Another Accord figure, the hardline Mahmoud Mashhadani (National Dialogue Council party), became COR speaker. Maliki won COR approval of a 37-member cabinet (including two deputy prime ministers) on May 20, 2006. Three key slots (Defense, Interior, and National Security) were not filled permanently until June 2006, due to infighting. Of the 37 posts, there were 19 Shiites; nine Sunnis; eight Kurds; and one Christian. Four were women.

POLITICAL RECONCILIATION AND SUBSEQUENT ELECTIONS

The 2005 elections were considered successful by the Bush Administration but did not resolve the Sunni-Arab grievances over their diminished positions in the power structure. The Sunni-led insurgency accelerated in the two subsequent years, in turn prompting the empowerment of Shiite militia factions to counter the insurgency. The sectarian violence was so serious that many experts said that the U.S. mission in Iraq was failing.

In August 2006, the Administration and Iraq agreed on a series of "benchmarks" that, if adopted and implemented, might achieve political reconciliation. Under Section 1314 of a FY2007 supplemental appropriation (P.L. 110-28), "progress" on 18 political and security benchmarks— as assessed in Administration reports due by July 15, 2007, and then September 15, 2007—was required for the United States to provide $1.5 billion in Economic

Support Funds (ESF) to Iraq. President Bush used the waiver provision. The law also mandated an assessment by the GAO, by September 1, 2007, of the degree to which the benchmarks have been met, as well as an outside assessment of the Iraqi security forces (ISF).

In early 2007, the United States began a "surge" of about 30,000 additional U.S. forces (bringing U.S. troop levels to about 170.000 at the height of the surge) intended to blunt insurgent momentum and take advantage of growing Sunni Arab rejection of extremist groups. As 2008 progressed, citing the achievement of many of the major legislative benchmarks and a dramatic drop in sectarian violence that was attributed to surge—the Bush Administration asserted that political reconciliation was advancing. However, U.S. officials maintained that the extent and durability of reconciliation would depend on the degree of implementation of adopted laws, on further compromises among ethnic groups, and on continued attenuated levels of violence. For Iraq's performance on the benchmarks, see Table 6.

The Strengthening of Maliki and the Iraqi Government: 2008-2009

The passage of key legislation in 2008 (see chart below) and the continued reductions in violence enhanced Maliki's political position. A March 2008 offensive ordered by Maliki against the Sadr faction and other militants in Basra and environs ("Operation Charge of the Knights") succeeded in pacifying the city, and caused many Sunnis and Kurds to see Maliki as even-handed and less sectarian. This contributed to a decision in July 2008 by the Accord Front to end its one-year boycott of the cabinet. Other cabinet vacancies were filled with independents, essentially putting to rest indicators that major blocs might vote Maliki out of the prime ministership. (In 2007 the Accord Front, the Sadr faction, and the bloc of former Prime Minister Iyad al-Allawi pulled out of the cabinet, leaving it with 13 vacant seats, out of 37 cabinet slots.)

Although Maliki's growing strength increased the Bush and then Obama Administration's optimism for continued stability, Maliki's strength caused concern among Maliki's erstwhile political allies. They saw him as increasingly building a following in the security forces and creating new security organs loyal to him and his faction. Through his Office of the Commanderin-Chief, he directly commands the National Counter-Terrorism Force (about 10,000 personnel) as well as the Baghdad Brigade, responsible for security in the capital. In 2008, the Kurds were highly critical of his formation of government-run "tribal support councils" in northern Iraq, which the Kurds see as an effort to prevent them from gaining control of disputed territories that they want to integrate into their Kurdistan Regional Government (KRG). Other support councils were created in southern Iraq. As a later example, in February 2010, Maliki's government reportedly directed the Iraqi Army's Fourth Division to cordon a provincial council building in Tikrit to influence the resolution of a dispute over the Salahuddin provincial council's ousting of the former governor of the province.[2]

January 31, 2009, Provincial Elections and Implications

The political fears of some factions about Maliki's intentions to consolidate power were evident in the January 31, 2009, provincial elections. Under a 2008 law, provincial councils in Iraq choose the governor and provincial governing administrations in each province, making them powerful bodies that provide ample opportunity to distribute patronage and guide provincial politics. ISCI, which had already been distancing itself from its erstwhile ally, Maliki's Da'wa Party, ran under a separate slate in the provincial elections—thus splitting up the formerly powerful UIA. Ideologically, ISCI favors more power for the provinces and less for the central government; Maliki prefers centralization.

The provincial elections had originally been planned for October 1, 2008, but were delayed when Kurdish restiveness over integrating Kirkuk and other disputed territories into the KRG caused a presidential council veto of the July 22, 2008, election law needed to hold these elections. That draft provided for equal division of power in Kirkuk (among Kurds, Arabs, and Turkomans) until its status is finally resolved, a proposal strongly opposed by the Kurds. On September 24, 2008, the COR passed a final election law, providing for the elections by January 31, 2009 and putting off provincial elections in Kirkuk and the three KRG provinces.[3]

In the elections, about 14,500 candidates vied for the 440 provincial council seats in the 14 Arab-dominated provinces of Iraq. About 4,000 of the candidates were women. The average number of council seats per province was about 30,[4] down from a set number of 41 seats per province (except Baghdad) in the 2005-2009 councils. The Baghdad provincial council has 57 seats. This yielded an average of more than 30 candidates per council seat. However, the reduction in number of seats also meant that many incumbents were not reelected.

The provincial elections were conducted on an "open list" basis—voters were able to vote for a party slate, or for an individual candidate (although they also had to vote for that candidate's slate). This procedure encouraged voting for slates and strengthened the ability of political parties to choose who on their slate will occupy seats allotted for that party. This election system was widely assessed to favor larger, well-organized parties, because smaller parties might not meet the vote threshold to obtain any seats on the council in their province.[5] This was seen as likely to set back the hopes of some Iraqis that the elections would weaken the Islamist parties, both Sunni and Shiite, that have dominated post-Saddam politics.

About 17 million Iraqis (any Iraqi 18 years of age or older) were eligible for the vote, which was run by the Iraqi Higher Election Commission (IHEC). Pre-election-related violence was minimal, although five candidates and several election/political workers were killed. There were virtually no major violent incidents on election day. Turnout was about 51%, somewhat lower than some expected. Some voters complained of being turned away at polling places because their names were not on file. Other voters had been displaced by sectarian violence in prior years and were unable to vote in their new areas of habitation.

The vote totals were finalized on February 19, 2009, and were certified on March 29, 2009. Within 15 days of that (by April 13, 2009) the provincial councils began to convene under the auspices of the incumbent provincial governor, and to elect a provincial council chairperson and deputy chairperson. Within another 30 days after that (by May 12, 2009) the provincial councils elected (by absolute majority) a provincial governor and deputy governors. The term of the provincial councils is four years from the date of their first convention.

Outcomes

The fears of Maliki's opponents were realized when his list ("State of Law Coalition") was the clear winner of the provincial elections. His Shiite opponents (his former allies) all ran separate slates and fared generally poorly. With 28 out of the 57 total seats, the Maliki slate gained effective control, by itself, of the Baghdad provincial council (displacing ISCI). Da'wa also emerged very strong in most of the Shiite provinces of the south, including Basra, where it won an outright majority (20 out of 35 seats).

Although Maliki's coalition was the clear winner, the subsequent efforts to form provincial administrations demonstrated that he still needed to strike bargains with rival factions, including Sadr, ISCI, and even the Sunni list of Saleh al-Mutlaq (National Dialogue Front) that contains many ex-Baathists. The provincial administrations that took shape, mostly in line with set deadlines above, are in Table 6. Aside from the victory of Maliki's slate, the unexpected strength of secular parties, such as that of former Prime Minister Iyad al-Allawi, corroborated the view that voters favored slates committed to Iraqi nationalism and strong central government.

The apparent big loser in the elections was ISCI, which had been favored because it is well organized and well funded. ISCI did not win in Najaf province, which it previously dominated and which, because of Najaf's revered status in Shiism, is considered a center of political gravity in southern Iraq. It won seven seats there, the same number that was won by the Maliki slate. ISCI won only 3 seats on the Baghdad province council, down from the 28 it held previously, and only five in Basra. Some observers believe that the poor showing for ISCI was a product not only of its call for devolving power out of Baghdad, but also because of its perceived close ties to Iran, which some Iraqis believe is exercising undue influence on Iraqi politics. Others say ISCI was perceived as corrupt, and interested in political gain primarily to enrich its members and supporters.

The Sadr faction, represented mainly in the "Independent Liberals Trend" list, did not come close to winning outright control of any councils, although it won enough seats in several southern provinces to, through deal-making, gain senior positions in a few southern provinces. The showing of the Sadrists was viewed as reflecting voter disillusionment with parties that continue to field militias—which many Iraqis blame for much of the violence that has plagued Iraq since the fall of Saddam Hussein.

In Diyala Province, hotly contested among Shiite and Sunni Arab and Kurdish slates, the provincial version of the (Sunni Arab) Accord Front edged out the Kurds for first place, and subsequently allied with the Kurds and with ISCI to set up the provincial administration. There continues to be substantial friction between Sunni and Shiite Arabs in that province, in part because Sunni militants drove out many Shiites from the province at the height of the civil conflict during 2005-2007.

Maliki's Position as March 7, 2010, Elections Approached

Because of his slate's strong showing in the 2009 provincial elections, Maliki was deemed throughout 2009 to be well positioned for the March 7, 2010, COR elections. The elected COR chooses the next full-term government, as discussed above. Perceiving Maliki as the likely winner, Maliki was able to include some political competitors in some provinces, including those dominated by Sunni Arabs and Sunni tribalists, into his State of Law coalition which would compete in the March 2010 COR vote. However, Sunnis were not in high positions on his slate and State of Law was perceived as primarily a Shiite slate.

Maliki derived further political benefit from the U.S. implementation of the U.S.-Iraq "Security Agreement" (sometimes referred to as the Status of Forces Agreement, or SOFA), which passed the COR on November 27, 2008, over Sadrist opposition. The pact took effect January 1, 2009, limiting the prerogatives of U.S. troops to operate in Iraq and setting a timetable of December 31, 2011, for a complete U.S. troop withdrawal. President Obama, on February 27, 2009, outlined a U.S. troop drawdown plan that comports with the major provisions of the agreement. The President's plan provided for a drawdown of U.S. combat brigades by the end of August 2010—a benchmark which was met—with a residual force of 50,000 primarily for training the Iraq Security Forces, to remain until the end of 2011.

Another interim benchmark in the winding down of U.S. military involvement was provided by the U.S.-Iraq Security Agreement. It was the June 30, 2009, withdrawal of U.S. combat troops from Iraq's cities. This was strictly implemented by U.S. forces, to the point where U.S. forces pulled out of locations in the restive Mosul area and from Sadr City, where General Raymond Odierno (outgoing top U.S. commander in Iraq) felt U.S. forces should stay. Maliki hailed this interim milestone as a "victory" and declared it a national holiday.

As 2009 progressed, Maliki's image as protector of law and order was tarnished by the several high-profile attacks since June 2009, including several major multiple bombing attacks in central Baghdad. Additional bombings took place in Baghdad, Diyala Province, Anbar Province, and elsewhere as the election approached. Some believe that insurgents conducted these attacks with the intent of weakening Maliki's image as a strong leader. Others saw these incidents as an effort by Al Qaeda in Iraq or other un-reconciled Sunni insurgent groups to reduce Sunni participation in the elections and/or reignite civil war.

Realizing the potential for security lapses to reduce his chances to remain prime minister, Maliki ordered several ISF commanders questioned for lapses in connection with the major bombings in Baghdad on August 20, 2009, in which almost 100 Iraqis were killed and the Ministry of Finance and of Foreign Affairs were heavily damaged. The makeshift new Ministry of Finance buildings were attacked again on December 7, 2009. After this bombing, which also resulted in the parliament's insistence that it hear Maliki's explanation of his responses, Maliki replaced the commander of the Baghdad Brigade. He also attempted to place substantial blame for the lapses on Interior Minister Jawad Bolani, who headed a rival slate in the elections. (See **Table 1** on major slates in the election.)

THE MARCH 7, 2010, ELECTIONS: COALITIONS AND POLITICAL INFIGHTING

Although Maliki began 2009 as a clear favorite to retain his post as prime minister in the March 7, 2010 elections, the disturbances and criticisms during 2009 tarnished his image and created a sense of open competition and an uncertain outcome. Politically, the Shiite factions were divided over who would become the next national leader and could not rebuild their UIA alliance for the March 7 elections, despite urging to do so from Grand Ayatollah Ali al-Sistani, the senior clerical leader in Iraq. A rival Shiite slate emerged as a competitor to Maliki's State of Law—the "Iraqi National Alliance (INA)" was composed of ISCI, Sadr, and other Shiite figures. The INA coalition believed that each of its component factions would draw support from their individual constituencies to produce an election majority or clear

Iraq: Politics, Elections, and Benchmarks

plurality. Sistani remained completely neutral in the election, endorsing no slate, but calling on all Iraqis to participate.

Table 1. Major Coalitions Formed for 2010 National Elections

State of Law Coalition (slate no. 337)	Led by Maliki and his Da'wa Party. Includes Anbar Salvation Front of Shaykh Hatim al-Dulaymi, which is Sunni, and the Independent Arab Movement of Abd al-Mutlaq al-Jabbouri. Appealed to Shiite sectarianism during the campaign by backing the exclusion of candidates with links to outlawed Baath Party. Was widely favored in the 2010 election because of strong showing in January 2009 provincial elections.
Iraqi National Alliance (slate no. 316)	Formed in August 2009, was initially considered the most formidable challenger to Maliki's slate. Consists mainly of his erstwhile Shiite opponents and is perceived as somewhat more Islamist than the other slates. Includes ISCI, the Sadrist movement, the Fadilah Party, the Iraqi National Congress of Ahmad Chalabi, and the National Reform Movement (Da'wa faction) of former Prime Minister Ibrahim al-Jafari. Possible Prime ministerial candidate from this bloc is current deputy President Adel Abd al-Mahdi, a moderate ISCI leader well respected by U.S. officials. However, some observers say Chalabi—the key architect of the effort to exclude candidates with Baathist ties—wanted to replace Maliki as prime minister. This slate is considered close to Ayatollah Sistani, but did not receive his formal endorsement.
Iraqi National Movement ("Iraqiyya"—slate no. 333)	Formed in October 2009. Led by former Prime Minister Iyad al-Allawi (Iraq National Accord) who is Shiite but his faction appeals to Sunnis, and Sunni leader Saleh al-Mutlaq (ex-Baathist who leads Iraq Front for National Dialogue). Backed by Iraqi Islamic Party leader and Deputy President Tariq Al-Hashimi as well as other powerful Sunnis, including Usama al-Nujaifi and Rafi al-Issawi. However, Justice and Accountability Commission (formerly the De-Baathification Commission) disqualified Mutlaq and another senior candidate on this slate, Dhafir al Ani, for supporting the outlawed Baath Party. An appeals court affirmed their disqualification.
Kurdistan Alliance (slate no. 372)	Competed again in 2010 as a joint KDP-PUK Kurdish list. However, Kurdish solidarity was shaken by July 25, 2009, Kurdistan elections in which a breakaway PUK faction called Change (Gorran) did unexpectedly well. Gorran is running its own separate list for the March 2010 elections, and there has been some violence between PUK and Gorran supporters. PUK's ebbing strength in the north not likely to jeopardize Talabani's continuation as president, although Sunnis said to seek that position.
Unity Alliance of Iraq (slate no. 348)	Led by Interior Minister Jawad Bolani, a moderate Shiite who has a reputation for political independence. Bolani has not previously been affiliated with the large Shiite parties such as ISCI and Dawa, and was only briefly affiliated with the Sadrist faction (which has been strong in Bolani's home town of Amarah, in southeastern Iraq). Considered a non-sectarian slate, this list Includes Sunni tribal faction led by Shaykh Ahmad Abu Risha, brother of slain leader of the Sunni Awakening movement in Anbar. The list includes first post-Saddam defense minister Sadun al-Dulaymi.
Iraqi Accordance (slate no. 338)	A coalition of Sunni parties, including breakaway factions of the Iraqi Islamic Party (IIP). Led by Ayad al-Samarrai, speaker of the COR. Viewed as a weak competitor for Sunni votes against Allawi slate.

Sources: Carnegie Endowment for International Peace; various press.

Election Law Dispute and Final Provisions

While coalitions formed to challenge Maliki, disputes emerged over the ground rules for the election. The holding of the elections required passage of an election law setting out the rules and parameters of the election. Under the Iraqi constitution, the elections were to held by January 31, 2010, in order to allow 45 days before the March 15, 2010, expiry of the current COR's term. Iraq's election officials had ideally wanted a 90-day time frame between the election law passage and the election date, in order to facilitate the voter registration process.

Because the provisions of the election law (covering such issues as voter eligibility, whether to allot quota seats to certain constituencies, the size of the next COR) have the potential to shape the election outcome, the major Iraqi communities were divided over the substance of the law. These differences caused the COR to miss almost every self-imposed deadline to pass it. One dispute was over the election system, with many COR members leaning toward a closed list system (which gives the slates the power to determine who occupies actual COR seats after the election), despite a call by Grand Ayatollah Sistani for an open list vote (which allows voters to also vote for candidates as well as coalition slates). Each province served as a single constituency and a fixed number of seats for each province (see **Table 2**, which includes number of COR seats per province).

There was also a dispute over how to apply the election in disputed Kirkuk province, where Kurds feared that the election law drafts would cause Kurds to be underrepresented in the election. The version of the election law passed by the COR on November 8, 2009 (141 out of 195 COR deputies voting), called for using 2009 food ration lists as representative of voter registration. The Kurds had sought this provision, facing down the insistence of many COR deputies to use 2005 voter lists, which presumably would contain fewer Kurds. A compromise in that version of the law allowed for a process to review, for one year, complaints about fraudulent registration, thus easing Sunni and Shiite Arab fears about an excessive Kurdish vote in Kirkuk.

However, this version guaranteed only a small quota of seats for Iraqis living abroad or who are displaced—and Sunnis believed they would therefore be undercounted because it was mainly Sunnis who had fled Iraq. On this basis, one of Iraq's deputy presidents, Tariq al Hashimi, a Sunni Arab, vetoed the law. The veto, on November 18, sent the law back to the COR. A new version was adopted on November 23, but it was viewed as even less favorable to Sunni Arabs than the first version, because it eliminated any reserved seats for Iraqis in exile. Hashimi again threatened a veto, which he was required to exercise within 10 days. As that deadline was about to lapse, the major factions, reportedly at the urging of U.S. and other diplomats, adopted a new law (December 6, 2009).

Election Parameters

The compromise version was not vetoed by any member of the presidency council, and provided for the following:

- Expansion of the size of the COR to 325 total seats. Of these, 310 allocated by province, with the constituency sizes ranging from Baghdad's 68 elected seats to Muthanna's seven seats. The COR size, in the absence of a recent census, was based on taking 2005 population figures and addiing 2.8% per year growth. [6] (A new census was scheduled to begin on October 24, 2010, although on October 2, 2010, Prime Minister Maliki postponed the census until December 2010. The move presumably was intended to allow time for a full term government to be put in place, which would oversee the census.)

- The remaining 15 seats are minority reserved seats (8) and "compensatory seats" (7)—seats allocated from "leftover" votes; votes for parties and slates that did not meet a minimum threshold to achieve any seats outright.
- No separate electoral constituency for Iraqis in exile, so Iraqis in exile had their votes counted in the provinces where these voters originated.
- An open list election system.
- An election date set for March 7, 2010.

Flashpoint: Disqualification of Some Prominent Sunnis

The electoral process since the end of 2005 has, to a large extent, been intended to bring Sunni Arabs ever further into the political structure and to turn them away from violence and insurgency. Sunnis boycotted the January 2005 parliamentary and provincial elections and were, as a result, poorly represented in all governing bodies. Sunni slates, consisting mainly of urban, educated Sunnis, did participate in the December 2005 parliamentary elections. This represented an apparent calculation that it would not serve Sunni interests to remain permanently alienated from the political process.

The 2009 provincial elections furthered the Sunni entry into the political process by attracting the new Sunni groups previously out of the process. These included the Sunni tribal leaders ("Awakening Councils") who had recruited the "Sons of Iraq" fighters and who were widely credited for turning Iraqi Sunnis against Al Qaeda-linked extremists in Iraq. These Sunni tribalists had largely stayed out of the December 2005 elections because their attention was focused primarily on the severe violence and instability in the Sunni provinces, particularly Anbar. These tribal figures were, at the time of the December 2005 election, still intimidated by Al Qaeda in Iraq, which urged Sunnis to stay completely out of the political process.

In the 2009 provincial elections, as the violence ebbed, these Sunni tribalists offered election slates and showed strength at the expense of the established Sunni parties, particularly the Iraqi Islamic Party (IIP). The main "Iraq Awakening" tribal slate came in first in Anbar Province, according to the final results. At the same time, the established, mostly urban Sunni parties, led by the IIP, had been struggling in 2008 as the broader Accord Front (Tawafuq) fragmented. In the provincial elections, one of its component parties—the National Dialogue Council—ran on slates that competed with the IIP in several provinces.

In the March COR elections, the Iraq National Movement ("Iraqiyya") of Iyad al-Allawi had strong appeal among Sunnis. There was an openly Sunni slate, leaning Islamist, called the Accordance slate ("Tawaffuq") led by IIP figures, but it was not expected to fare well compared to Allawi's less sectarian bloc. Some Sunni figures joined the predominantly Shiite slates as part of an effort by the leaders of those blocs to appear non-sectarian.

Disqualification Crisis

The Sunni commitment to the political process appeared in some jeopardy in the context of a major dispute over candidate eligibility for the March 7, 2010, elections. Although a

Sunni boycott of the elections did not materialize, there was a Sunni Arab perception that the election might be unfair because of this dispute.

The acute phase of this political crisis began in January 2010 when the Justice and Accountability Commission (the successor to the "De-Baathification Commission" that worked since the fall of Saddam to purge former Baathists from government) invalidated the candidacies of 499 individuals (out of 6,500 candidates running), spanning many different slates, including some candidates of Maliki's State of Law list. The Justice and Accountability Commission is headed by Ali al-Lami, a Shiite who had been in U.S. military custody during 2005-2006 for alleged assistance to Iranian agents active in Iraq. He is perceived as answerable to or heavily influenced by Ahmad Chalabi, who had headed the De-Baathification Commission. Both are part of the Iraqi National Alliance slate and both are Shiites, leading many to believe that the disqualifications represented an attempt to exclude prominent Sunnis from the vote.

The Justice and Accountability Commission argued that the disqualifications were based on law and careful evaluation of candidate backgrounds and not based on sect, because many of the candidates disqualified were Shiites. The IHEC reviewed and backed the invalidations on January 14, 2010. Disqualified candidates had three days to file an appeal in court. Apparently due in part to entreaties from the U.S. Embassy, Vice President Joseph Biden (during a visit to Iraq on January 22, 2010) and partner embassies in Iraq—all of which fear a return to instability that could result from the disqualifications—the appeals court at first ruled that disqualified candidates could run in the election and clear up questions of Baathist affiliation afterwards.

However, reported pressure by Maliki and other Shiites caused the court to reverse itself on February 12, 2010, and announce that 145 candidates would be ineligible to run. Twenty-six candidates who had been barred were reinstated. The remaining approximately 300 disqualified candidates had already accepted their disqualification and been replaced by other candidates on their respective slates. The slate most affected by the disqualifications is the Iraq National Movement slate, because two of its leading candidates, National Dialogue Front party leader Saleh al-Mutlaq and Dhafir al-Ani, both Sunnis, were barred from running. This caused the slate to suspend its campaign for three days subsequent (Feb. 12-15).

The slate did not, as a whole, call for a broad boycott and Mutlaq himself dropped his own calls for boycotting the election. Mutlaq was replaced as a candidate by his brother. The slate campaigned vigorously, and many Sunnis seemed to react by recommitting to a high turnout among their community, in order to achieve political results through the election process. It did not boycott even though, on the night before the election, the De-Baathification Commission disqualified an additional 55 candidates, mostly from the Allawi slate.

The crisis appeared to prompt the February 16, 2010, comments by outgoing General Ray Odierno, the top U.S. commander in Iraq (who was replaced as of September 1, 2010, by his deputy, General Lloyd Austin), that Iran was working through Chalabi and al-Lami to undermine the legitimacy of the elections. General Odierno specifically asserted that Chalabi is in close contact with a close Iraqi ally of Iranian General Qasem Soleimani, who commands the Qods Force unit of Iran's Islamic Revolutionary Guard Corps (IRGC).[7] The Iraqi, whose name is Jamal al-Ibrahimi, is a member of the COR. Chalabi's successful efforts to turn the election into a campaign centered on excluding ex-Baathists—which Sunnis view as a codeword for their sect— has caused particular alarm among experts.

This crisis added to already growing Sunni resentment because of the slow pace with which the Maliki government has implemented its pledge to fully integrate the "Sons of Iraq" fighters into the Iraqi Security Forces (ISF). About 100,000 (80% are Sunni Arab) of these fighters nationwide cooperated with U.S. forces against Al Qaeda in Iraq and other militants. As of December 2010, about half of them (about 50,000) had been integrated into the ISF or given the civilian government jobs they were promised. Others say they have been dropped from payrolls, harassed, arrested, or sidelined—indications that the Maliki government no longer views the Sons of Iraq program as useful. The disqualifications issue continued after the election, as discussed below, but has been mostly resolved.

Election Unlikely to Resolve KRG-Central Government Disputes

The COR elections, by themselves, were not expected to heal KRG-central government disputes. KRG President Masoud Barzani visited Washington, DC, in January 2010 and, according to participants in his meetings, discussed with senior officials ways in which the Kurds would cooperate with Iraq's Arabs after the election to form a new government. That was widely interpreted as an Administration admonition not to establish territorial-related preconditions to join a governing coalition after the elections. However, KRG Prime Minister Barham Salih said on June 15, 2010, that Kurdish leaders sought guarantees from Iraq's Arab leaders that nineteen specific demands (retaining the presidency for one of their own was one such demand) would be addressed by the next government, as a condition of providing Kurdish votes for any new governing coalition. Although receiving from Maliki only partial or vague guarantees on their key demands, the main Kurdish factions nonetheless threw their weight behind Maliki to continue as prime minister, as discussed below.

KRG-central government differences had been aggravated by the 2009 provincial elections because Sunni Arabs wrested control of the Nineveh (Mosul) provincial council from the Kurds, who won control of that council in the 2005 election because of the broad Sunni Arab boycott of that election. A Sunni list (al-Hadba'a) won a clear plurality of the Nineveh vote and subsequently took control of the provincial administration there. Al-Hadba'a is composed of hardline Sunni Arabs who openly oppose Kurdish encroachment in the province and who are committed to the "Arab and Islamic identity" of the province. A member of the faction, Atheel al-Nufaiji, is the governor (brother of COR speaker Usama al-Nujaifi), and the Kurds have prevented his visitation of areas of Nineveh where the Kurds' *peshmerga* militia operates.

In part to prevent outright violence, General Odierno, in August 2009, developed a plan to partner U.S. forces with *peshmerga* units (a development without precedent) and with ISF units in the province to build confidence between the two forces and reassure Kurdish, Arab, Turkomen, and other residents of the province. Implementation began in January 2010 and U.S. officials said on August 16, 2010, that the joint (ISF-U.S-Kurdish) patrols, maintenance of checkpoints and training would continue until the U.S. pullout at the end of 2011. Fifteen joint checkpoints were established, but, as of October 2010, the United States had ceased participating at four of them, in concert with the U.S. change of mission to a non-combat role (Operation New Dawn) on September 1, 2010. There have been some speculation that a United Nations force could take over this mediating and confidence-building role thereafter, although it is not clear that this idea is supported by the Iraqi factions involved. There is also speculation that some U.S. forces might be asked to remain after 2011 to continue the confidence-building mission.

Additional friction was created in the context of the KRG's parliamentary and presidential elections on July 25, 2009. The KRG leadership had been planning, during that vote, to conduct a referendum on a separate KRG constitution. However, the central government asserted that a KRG constitution would conflict with the publicly adopted national constitution, and that the KRG draft constitution, adopted by the Kurdish parliament on June 23, 2009, claimed Kurdish control over disputed territories and oil resources. The KRG did not hold the referendum.

Intra-Kurdish Divisions

Further complicating the post-COR election landscape were widening divisions within the Kurdish community. The KRG elections also, to some extent, shuffled the political landscape. A breakaway faction of President Talabani's PUK, called "Change" ("Gorran"), won an unexpectedly high 25 seats (out of 111) in the Kurdistan national assembly, embarrassing the PUK and weakening it relative to the KDP. KRG President Masoud Barzani, leader of the KDP, easily won reelection against weak opposition. Gorran ran its own list in the March 2010 elections and constituted a significant challenge to the Kurdistan Alliance in Sulaymaniyah Province, according to election results. As a result, of the 57 total Kurdish seats in the COR, 14 are held by Gorran, the Kurdistan Islamic Union, and other Kurdish groups outside the KDP-PUK alliance.

The Sadr Faction Competes

As noted above, Sadr joined the anti-Maliki Shiite coalition (Iraqi National Alliance) for the March 2010 national elections. On October 17, 2009, the Sadr movement held a "primary" election to determine who would fill the 329 total candidate slots that will be fielded by the Sadr movement in the elections (as part of the broader Iraqi National Alliance bloc discussed above). About 800 total candidates competed for the slots.

As discussed further below, the Sadr faction was extensively involved in bargaining over the next government and, for the first six months after the election, took the stance that Maliki should be replaced by another Shiite. However, the shift by the faction in late September 2010, including public outreach to its followers in Iraq as to what would be the implications of supporting Maliki's re-selection, was decisive in Maliki's success in achieving another term as prime minister. Observers say that Sadrists will hold several seats in the cabinet Maliki will propose on/about December 23, 2010.

Some accounts say that the Sadrists, in return for supporting Maliki, are pressing him to support the naming of a Sadrist as governor of Maysan province, which includes the Sadrist stronghold of Amara. At the same time, there are reports that the Sadrist and offshoot Shiite militias—for now still disarmed—may be planning to reactivate. If these reports are accurate, it could suggest that the Shiite militias sense a power vacuum in top leadership and see militia activity as a means to ensure political influence. In addition, the Sadr faction is said to be using its fundraising ability to develop charity and employment networks that rival or displace those of the central government – employing a political model similar to that of Hizballah in Lebanon.[8]

Election Results

About 85 total coalitions were accredited for the March 7, 2010, election. There were about 6,170 total candidates running on all these slates and, as noted, Iraqis were able to vote for individual candidates as well as overall slates. Aside from that of Maliki, only a few of the coalitions were perceived as having major support, and those coalitions are depicted in **Table 1**. All blocs offered voters gifts and favors at pre-election rallies, and all available press reports indicate that campaigning was vibrant and vigorous. Total turnout was about 62%, according to the IHEC. Turnout was slightly lower in Baghdad because of the multiple insurgent bombings that took place there just as voting was starting.

The final count was announced on March 26, 2010, by the IHEC. As noted in **Table 2** below, the Iraqiyya slate of Iyad al-Allawi won a plurality of seats, winning a narrow two-seat margin over Maliki's State of Law slate. The Iraqi constitution (Article 73) mandates that the COR "bloc with the largest number" of members gets the first opportunity to form a government. On that basis, Allawi had demanded to be given the first opportunity to put together a majority coalition and form a government. However, on March 28, 2010, Iraq's Supreme Court issued a preliminary ruling that any group that forms after the election could be deemed to meet that requirement, laying the groundwork for Allawi to be denied the right to the first opportunity to form a government.

The vote was to have been certified by April 22, 2010, but factional wrangling delayed this certification. On March 21, 2010, before the count was final, Prime Minister Maliki issued a statement, referring to his role as armed forces commander-in-chief, demanding the IHEC respond to requests from various blocs for a manual recount of all votes. The IHEC responded that any recount decisions are under its purview and that such a comprehensive recount would take an extended period of time. Several international observers, including U.N. Special Representative for Iraq Ad Melkert, indicated that there was no cause, at that point, to suggest widespread fraud.

However, in response to an appeal by Maliki's faction, on April 19, an Iraqi court ordered a recount of votes in Baghdad Province. The recount in the province, which has 68 elected seats, was completed on May 15, 2010, and did not result in an alteration of the seat totals. This followed a few days after the major factions agreed to put aside any disqualifications of winning candidates by the Justice and Accountability Commission. With the seat count holding, the way was set for Iraq's Supreme Court to certify the results, with the subsequent steps to form a government to follow.

The final certification came on June 1, 2010. and the following timelines applied:

- Fifteen days after certification (by June 15), the new COR was to be seated and to elect a COR speaker and deputy speaker. (The deadline to convene was met, although, as noted, the COR did not elect a leadership team and did not meet again until November 11, 2010.)
- After electing a speaker, but with no deadline, the COR is to choose a president (by a two-thirds vote). (According to Article 138 of the Iraqi constitution, after this election, Iraq is to have a president and at least one vice president—the "presidency council" concept was an interim measure that expired at the end of the first full term government.)

- Within another 15 days, the largest COR bloc is tapped by the president to form a government. (The selection of a president occurred on November 11, 2010, and Maliki was formally tapped to form a cabinet on November 25, 2010.)
- Within another 30 days, (by December 25), the prime minister-designate (Maliki) is to present a cabinet to the COR for confirmation (by majority vote).

Post-Election Government Formation Efforts

In accordance with timelines established in the Constitution, the newly elected COR did convene on June 15, 2010. However, the session ended after only 18 minutes and, because of the political deadlock among the various factions, it did not elect a COR leadership team. Under Article 52 of the Constitution, the "eldest member" of the COR (Kurdish legislator Fouad Massoum) became acting COR speaker. During the period when no new government was formed, the COR remained inactive, with most COR members in their home provinces, but still collecting their $10,000 per month salaries.

Allawi's chances of successfully forming a government appeared to suffer a substantial setback in late May 2010 when Maliki's slate and the rival Shiite INA bloc agreed to an alliance called the "National Alliance." However, the alliance was not able to agree to a prime minister selectee, with Sadrists and the ISCI faction opposed to Maliki's continuation. With no agreement, the COR aborted its second meeting scheduled for July 27, 2010. On August 3, 2010, the deep disagreements among the Shiite factions broke up this putative alliance.

The various factions made little progress through August, as Maliki insisted he remain prime minister for another term. Some observers believe that bilateral meetings among bloc leaders would not resolve the impasse and that only a broad meeting of the four major COR blocs— Maliki's bloc; the INA, Allawi's Iraqiyya, and the Kurdistan Alliance—and discussing all outstanding issues that face Iraq—would result in an agreement on a government. With the factional disputes unresolved, Maliki remained prime minister in a caretaker role. Some observers assert that he continued to govern beyond a caretaker mandate and had little incentive to see a new government formed.

With the end of the U.S. combat mission on August 31 , 2010, approaching, the United States reportedly stepped up its involvement in political talks. Some discussions were held between Maliki and Allawi's bloc on a U.S.-proposed formulas under which Allawi, in return for supporting Maliki, would head a powerful new council that would have broad powers to rival those of the prime minister. Alternate proposals had Allawi being given the presidency, although the Kurds were said to be insistent on retaining that post for one of their own as a guarantee of movement on their core territorial demands. This insistence was despite the fact that there will not be a "presidency council" with an executive veto in the next government, the transitional provision for that power having expired after the first four year government ended. No agreement on the U.S.-backed proposals was announced, even though there was an expectation that the August 10-September 11, 2010, Ramadan period would give ample time for the blocs to reach an agreement.

On October 1, 2010, Iraq became a country with the distinction of having gone longer than any other country without an agreed government, following an election. Part of the difficulty forming a government was the close result, and the dramatic implications of gaining or retaining power in Iraq, where politics is often seen as a "winner take all" proposition.

Iraq: Politics, Elections, and Benchmarks

Others blamed Allawi for the impasse, claiming that he was insisting on a large, powerful role for himself even though he could not assemble enough COR votes to achieve a majority there.

Political Resolution

On October 1, 2010, Maliki, possibly due to Iranian intervention, received the backing of the 40 COR deputies of Shiite cleric Moqtada Al Sadr, bringing Maliki within striking distance of obtaining the necessary votes to obtain another term as prime minister. The United States reportedly was alarmed at the prospect that Maliki might be able to form a government primarily on the strength of Sadr's backing, but, in early November 2010, the United States, Allawi, and many of the Sunni Arab regional states acquiesced to a second Maliki term. The key question that remained was whether Maliki, and Iraq's Kurds—who held the swing vote that could determine the next government—would agree to form a broad based government that meets the demands of Iraqiyya for substantial Sunni Arab inclusion. Illustrating the degree to which the Kurds reclaimed their former role of "kingmakers," Maliki, Allawi, and other Iraqi leaders met in the capital of the Kurdistan Regional Government-administered region in Irbil on November 8, 2010, to continue to negotiate on a new government. (Sadr did not attend the meeting in Irbil, but Iraq National Alliance leader Ammar Al Hakim did.)

Achieving a broad-based government, rather than one that is narrow and sectarian, has been a key U.S. objective, and U.S. officials, including Vice President Joseph Biden, reportedly were in touch with many Iraqi factions to stress that outcome. Most experts considered the key to such an outcome a formula that satisfies Allawi and his political base (mostly Sunni Arabs, even though he himself is Shiite) that they will wield significant influence in the next government.

On November 10, 2010, with reported direct intervention by President Obama by phone, Allawi agreed to direct his bloc to support another Maliki term, to support another term for Kurdish leader Jalal Talabani as president, and to join the government. In exchange, according to several press accounts, an Iraqiyya figure would become COR Speaker, another (perhaps Allawi himself) would chair the enhanced oversight body discussed above, though renamed the "National Council for Strategic Policies,"[9] and a member of the bloc would be named foreign minister. Despite some unrest within his bloc, Allawi agreed to direct his bloc to support the "deal" at the November 11, 2010 COR session. Some observers praised the agreement as helpful to U.S. policy because an agreement was signed among major factions, in Baghdad, with Masoud Barzani and U.S. Ambassador to Iraq James Jeffries attending. The agreement did not specify concessions to the Sadr faction, which observers viewed as a setback to Iran's policy of supporting Shiite militant factions.

The session was held, and Iraqiyya figure Usama al-Nujaifi was elected COR speaker, as agreed. However, Allawi and his most of his bloc walked out after three hours over the refusal of the other blocs to readmit the three members of the Iraqiyya bloc that had been disqualified from running for the COR by the "Accountability and Justice Commission" (see above on the disqualification crisis). The walkout raised U.S. and other fears that the agreement might immediately unravel, but the remaining COR members were sufficient for a quorum and Talabani was re-elected president after two rounds of voting. Some fears were calmed on November 13, 2010 when most of Allawi's bloc attended the COR session and continued to implement the settlement agreement; Allawi himself did not attend, instead traveling to Britain. On November 25, 2010, Talabani formally tapped Maliki as the prime minister-designate, giving him 30 days (until December 25) to name and achieve majority COR confirmation for a new cabinet.

Implementation of Political Agreements and New Government Taking Shape[10]

On December 21, 2010, in advance of the December 25, 2010 deadline, Maliki presented a cabinet to the COR, receiving broad approval. However, no permanent appointments were named for seven ministries—including the three main security ministries Defense, Interior, and National Security (intelligence). Still, the appointments indicated that the major factions were implementing their political agreements and that the government formed was inclusive of all major factions. Among major outcomes:

- The cabinet selections fell into place after December 19, when Iyad al-Allawi said his bloc would join the government. His faction obtained about 10 out of the 42 seats of the cabinet (which includes the prime minister, three deputy prime ministers, and 38 ministries and minister of state posts). Aside from Maliki, seven posts were assigned to figures associated with Maliki's State of Law coalition.
- Allawi's assurance came the same day that the COR voted (with barely a quorum achieved after a Shiite walkout of the vote) to reinstate to politics the three senior members of his bloc, including Saleh al-Mutlaq, who had been barred from the March 2010 election by the Justice and Accountability Commission (see above section on the disqualification crisis). Mutlaq was subsequently named one of the three deputy prime ministers.
- Hussein Shahristani, previously the oil minister and a member of State of Law, was elevated to a deputy prime ministership, with a focus on the energy sector. His current deputy, Abd al Karim Luaibi, a technocrat but associated with Maliki's State of Law/Da'wa Party, was appointed oil minister.
- The third deputy prime minister is Kurdish figure (PUK faction) Rows Shaways, who has served in various central and KRG positions since the fall of Saddam.
- The current deputy presidents, Tariq al-Hashimi (Iraqiyya) and Adel Abdul Mahdi (INA/ISCI), remain in their posts.
- A major Iraqiyya figure, Rafi al-Issawi (previously a deputy prime minister), was appointed finance minister.
- Kurdish (KDP) stalwart Hoshyar Zebari, who has been foreign minister since the transition governments that followed the fall of Saddam, remains in position. However, there is also a minister of state for foreign affairs. Iraqiyya had been promised the Foreign Ministry in the November 10 agreement but Iraqiyya receives major influence overall and agreed to cede that post.
- Maliki did not name figures for the three security ministries: defense, interior, or national security, and will hold those posts himself until permanent appointments are agreed. Iraqi figures say that Iraqiyya, possibly former Interior Minister Falah al-Naqib, might get the defense minister post. A member of Maliki's State of Law bloc, possibly Adnan al-Assadi, is likely to become interior minister.
- Some were disappointed that only one woman was named, and that to a minister of state without portfolio post. She is Bushra Saleh, a member of the Shiite party Fadila (Virture), which is part of the INA coalition. Another Fadila activist was named minister of justice.

- Sadrist figures have been named to the following ministries: Housing, Labor and Social Affairs, Water Resources, Tourism and Antiquities, and one ministry of state position. These positions are relatively junior within the cabinet and appeared to represent less influence for the Sadrists than was anticipated when Sadr threw his backing to Maliki in October. However, as noted, the Sadr faction may receive some compensatory influence in local appointments such as Maysan Province.
- Another element of continued uncertainty is that the "National Council for Strategic Policies" concept has not specifically been voted on by the COR. Current proposals call for the council to include the prime minister, president, their deputies, and a representative of all major blocs—and for decisions of the council to be binding on Maliki if they achieve support of 80% of the council members. However, because it is unclear that these powers will be accorded the council, it is not certain whether Allawi himself will accept heading the body at the session.

RELATED GOVERNANCE AND REGIONAL ISSUES, AND IMPLICATIONS FOR U.S. POLICY

In terms of immediate Iraqi legislative business, the COR is needed to pass the calendar year 2011 budget. A draft $67 billion budget was submitted to the COR on December 18. U.S. officials are looking to the formation of the new government to overcome longer term roadblocks that have prevented passage of legislation considered crucial to political comity in the future, such as national hydrocarbon laws, which are needed to encourage foreign investment in Iraq's relatively undeveloped energy sector. Some note that efforts to rein in official corruption are failing because no comprehensive anti-corruption law has been passed. Also not passed are laws on the environment, those governing other elections, consumer protections, intellectual property rights, building codes, and a new national flag. Moreover, many Iraqis blamed the long political deadlock, in part, for the government's inability to alleviate severe shortages of electricity during Iraq's characteristically hot summer. Iraqis who cannot afford their own generators, or to share a generator with a few other homes, can count on only two hours of power per day.

General Human Rights Issues

The State Department's report on human rights for 2009 released March 11, 2010, repeated the previous year's characterizations of Iraq's human rights record as "Insurgent and extremist violence, coupled with weak government performance in upholding the rule of law, resulted in widespread and severe human rights abuses."[11] The State Department report cites a wide range of human rights problems committed by Iraqi government security and law enforcement personnel, including: arbitrary or unlawful killings; torture and other cruel punishments; poor conditions in prison facilities; denial of fair public trials; arbitrary arrest; arbitrary interference with privacy and home; limits on freedoms of speech, assembly and association due to sectarianism and extremist threats; lack of protection of stateless persons; widescale governmental corruption; human trafficking; and limited exercise of labor rights.

In regards to human rights, a major concern is the safety and security of Iraq's Christian population, which is concentrated in northern Iraq as well as in Baghdad. In the run-up to the January 2009 provincial elections, about 1,000 Christian families reportedly fled the province in October 2008, although Iraqi officials report that most families returned by December 2008. The issue faded in 2009 but then resurfaced late in the year when about 10,000 Christians in northern Iraq, fearing bombings and intimidation, fled the areas near Kirkuk during October-December 2009. On October 31, 2010, a major attack on Christians occurred when a church in Baghdad was besieged by militants and about 51 worshippers were killed. The siege shook the faith of the Christian community in their security. Other attacks appearing to target Iraqi Christians have taken place since.

Some Iraqi Christians blame the attacks on Al Qaeda in Iraq, which is still somewhat strong in Nineveh Province and associates Christians with the United States. UNAMI coordinated humanitarian assistance to the Christians and others displaced. Previously, some human rights groups alleged Kurdish abuses against Christians and other minorities in the Nineveh Plain, close to the KRG-controlled region. Kurdish leaders deny the allegations. The FY2008 Consolidated Appropriation earmarked $10 million in ESF from previous appropriations to assist the Nineveh plain Christians. A supplemental appropriation for 2008 and 2009 (P.L. 110-252) earmarked another $10 million for this purpose. The Consolidated Appropriations Act of 2010 (P.L. 111-117) made a similar provision for FY2010.

Before the latest rounds of violence against Christians, about 400,000 Christians had left Iraq since the fall of Saddam Hussein—a large proportion of the approximately 1 million Christian population that was there during Saddam's time. Christian priests have been kidnapped and killed; the body of Chaldean Catholic archbishop Faraj Rahho was discovered in Mosul on March 13, 2008, two weeks after his reported kidnapping. However, some Christians in Baghdad have felt safe enough to celebrate Christmas at churches in Baghdad since 2007. An attack on the Yazidis in August 2007, which killed about 500 persons, appeared to reflect the precarious situation for Iraqi minorities. Even at the height of the U.S. military presence in Iraq, U.S. forces did not specifically protect Christian sites at all times, partly because Christian leaders do not want to appear closely allied with the United States.

Regional Dimension

For Iraq's neighbors as well as for the United States, the stakes in the outcome of the political process in Iraq have been high. First and foremost, according to most experts, the United States sought to prevent the emergence of a governing coalition that left Sunni Arabs disillusioned, and which bolstered the influence of pro-Iranian factions that do or could again wield arms for political purposes. The key U.S. objectives appear to have been met, in large part because of the inclusion of senior Iraqiyya figures in high positions and the relative lack of influence of Sadrists in the new cabinet. The relatively junior ministries assigned to Sadrist figures could be interpreted by many as a setback to Iranian influence. However, the sense of ethno-sectarian reconciliation produced by the government that has been formed could be subject to reversal over the longer term. Iran reportedly was a key broker of the decision by the Sadrists to support Maliki, raising the potential for Iran to continue to support Sadrist interests and influence over time.

The United States sought to achieve a government that can integrate with all of Iraq's neighbors, including Saudi Arabia, Jordan, and Turkey. That objective also appears to have been reached, although the degree of acceptance for the new government might depend on how much influence the new National Council for Strategic Policies has as a counterweight to the power of the prime minister. Allawi had been favored for prime minister by the Sunni-dominated regional neighbors such as Saudi Arabia and even by Syria, which is mostly Sunni but allied with Iran. Syria hosted numerous meetings among faction leaders, although no agreement was reached among them under Syrian sponsorship.

Implications for the Wind Down of the U.S. Military Mission

For the U.S. interest in a stable Iraq, the long political vacuum in Iraq, coupled with the drawdown of U.S. forces to 50,000 and the formal end of the U.S. combat mission on August 31, 2010, has contributed to major high profile attacks in Iraq and a sense of uncertainty and disillusionment on the part of the Iraqi public. Although overall levels of violence are 90% lower than they were at the height of the sectarian conflict of 2006-2007, there have been politically motivated assassinations and other violence. For example, a suicide bombing at an Iraqi Army recruiting station in Baghdad in August 2010 killed nearly 60 Iraqis; the Islamic State of Iraq, an umbrella group that includes Al Qaeda in Iraq, claimed responsibility. A wave of approximately 15 bombings across Baghdad on the night of November 2, 2010, killed at least 60 Iraqis and shook confidence in the ability of the government to protect the population. Motives and suspects of most of the continuing violence include not only Al Qaeda in Iraq but also Shiite militia forces seeking to assassinate any Sunnis who have political power. A tactic increasingly in use appears to be adhesive or magnetic bombs attached to officials' vehicles.

Although it did not delay the ending of the U.S. combat mission, the continuing violence has caused some experts to question whether stability will continue after all U.S. forces are to depart at the end of 2011. That is the date set by the 2009 U.S.-Iraq Security Agreement for the complete withdrawal of U.S. forces, although that agreement could be amended. Some believe that the reduction in U.S. leverage and influence in Iraq already under way will allow rifts among major ethnic and sectarian communities to widen to the point where Iraq could still become a "failed state" after 2011, unless some U.S. troops remain after that time. Retaining U.S. troops in Iraq beyond 2011 would require the re-negotiation of the U.S.-Iraq "Security Agreement," which entered into force on January 1, 2009. However, the prolonged delay in the formation of a government has meant that there has been no counterpart Iraqi team in place to begin such negotiations. The Sadrist faction, although not as strong in the new government as was expected, is said to be pushing for a complete U.S. withdrawal by the end of 2011, with no extensions of the Security Agreement or other arrangements for a continued U.S. military presence in Iraq.

On the other hand, the government has been formed with enough time to renegotiate amendments to the Security Agreement before its expiry at the end of 2011, if a mutual decision is reached that substantial numbers of U.S. forces are requested after 2011. It is possible that there will be a decision not to retain large numbers of U.S. forces, but only to establish a large (1,000 person) military liaison office engaged mostly in training and assisting Iraq in the use of U.S. arms sold to Iraq, such as combat aircraft. It is not clear whether such an arrangement would require formal amendment of the security agreement.

As U.S. forces draw down, the State Department will transition to the lead U.S. agency in Iraq, with all attendant responsibilities. There is a vibrant U.S. debate over whether the State Department, using security contractors, will be able to fully secure its personnel in Iraq if all U.S. forces were to depart. Some believe that there will need to be a substantial DOD presence in Iraq after 2011, if only to protect U.S. personnel in Iraq.

Table 2. March 2010 COR Election: Final, Certified Results by Province (100% of the vote counted as of March 26)

Province	Elected Seats in COR	Results
Baghdad	68	Maliki: 26 seats; Iraqiyya: 24 seats; INA: 17 seats; minority reserved: 2 seats
Nineveh (Mosul)	31	Iraqiiya: 20; Kurdistan Alliance: 8; INA: 1; Accordance: 1; Unity (Bolani): 1; minority reserved: 3
Qadisiyah	11	Maliki: 4; INA: 5; Iraqiyya: 2
Muthanna	7	Maliki: 4; INA: 3
Dohuk	10	Kurdistan Alliance: 9; other Kurdish lists: 1; minority reserved: 1
Basra	24	Maliki: 14 ; INA: 7; Iraqiyya: 3
Anbar	14	Iraqiyya: 11; Unity (Bolani): 1; Accordance: 2
Karbala	10	Maliki: 6; INA: 3; Iraqiyya: 1
Wasit	11	Maliki: 5; INA: 4; Iraqiyya: 2
Dhi Qar	18	Maliki: 8; INA: 9; Iraqiyya: 1
Sulaymaniyah	17	Kurdistan Alliance: 8; other Kurds: 9
Kirkuk (Tamim)	12	Iraqiyya: 6; Kurdistan Alliance: 6
Babil	16	Maliki: 8; INA: 5; Iraqiyya: 3
Irbil	14	Kurdistan Alliance: 10; other Kurds: 4
Najaf	12	Maliki: 7; INA: 5
Diyala	13	Iraqiyya: 8; INA: 3; Maliki: 1; Kurdistan Alliance: 1
Salahuddin	12	Iraqiyya: 8; Unity (Bolani): 2; Accordance: 2
Maysan	10	Maliki: 4; INA: 6
Total Seats	325	Iraqiyya: 89 + 2 compensatory = 91
	(310 elected + 8 minority reserved + 7 compensatory)	Maliki: 87 + 2 compensatory = 89 INA: 68 + 2 compensatory = 70 (of which about 40 are Sadrist) Kurdistan Alliance: 42 +1 compensatory = 43
		Unity (Bolani): 4
		Accordance: 6
		other Kurdish: 14
		minority reserved: 8

Source: Iraqi Higher Election Commission, March 26, 2010.

Notes: Seat totals are approximate and their exact allocation may be subject to varying interpretations of Iraqi law. Total seat numbers include likely allocations of compensatory seats. Total seats do not add to 325 total seats in the COR due to some uncertainties in allocations.

No matter the outcome of that debate, State Department officers will continue to promote Iraqi political reconciliation and peaceful dispute resolution. **Table 3** provides information on U.S. assistance to promote Iraqi democracy and peaceful political competition and consensus building. If Iraq's major factions have permanently shifted away from supporting violence and toward peaceful political competition, some might argue that U.S. funding has contributed to that transition. Others might argue that the change was caused by numerous factors, such as the improvement of security and rejection of foreign terrorist influence, and that it is virtually impossible to assess the contribution made by U.S. assistance.

Other Elections Possible

There had been speculation that the March COR elections would be held concurrently with a referendum on the U.S.-Iraq Security Agreement. The referendum was to be held by July 31, 2009, but the United States, which views the referendum as unnecessary, supported a delay. In mid-October 2009, Iraqi parliamentarians quietly shelved the referendum vote by failing to act on legislation to hold the referendum and focusing instead on the broader election law needed for the National Assembly elections.[12]

District and sub-district elections were previously slated for July 31, 2009, as well. However, those are delayed, and the United Nations Secretary General Ban Ki Moon said in a report on U.N. operations in Iraq, released August 3, 2009, that these elections would likely be held later in 2010, after the National Assembly elections. No date for these elections has been announced, suggesting a delay beyond 2010.

Several other possible elections in Iraq are as yet unscheduled. If there is a settlement between the KRG and Baghdad over Kirkuk and other territories, there could be a referendum to ratify any settlement that is reached. Under Article 140 of the Constitution, a referendum was to be held by December 31, 2007, but the Kurds have agreed to repeated delays in order to avoid jeopardizing overall progress in Iraq. Because the three Kurdish-controlled provinces and the disputed province of Kirkuk did not hold provincial elections with the rest of Iraq on January 31, 2009, elections are required in those provinces at some point, presumably subsequent to a settlement of the Kirkuk dispute. Absent such a settlement, observers believe these elections might be held in the fall of 2010. (For more information on Kurd-Baghdad disputes, see CRS Report RS22079, *The Kurds in Post-Saddam Iraq*, by Kenneth Katzman.)

There could also be a vote on amendments to Iraq's 2005 constitution if and when the major factions agree to finalize the recommendations of the constitutional review commission (CRC). There have been no recent major developments reported that would indicate if and when such a referendum might be ready.

Table 3. Recent Democracy Assistance to Iraq
(in millions of current US$)

	FY2009	FY2010 (est.)	FY2011 (req.)
Rule of Law and Human Rights	46.55	73.50	22.50
Good Governance	143.64	117.00	90.33
Political Competition/ConsensusBuilding	41.00	50.50	30.00
National Endowment for Democracy	3.59	0	0
Totals	322.31	326.50	175.33

USAID Foreign Assistance Database, July 26, 2010.

Table 4. January 31, 2009, Provincial Election Results (Major Slates)

Baghdad—55 regular seats, plus one Sabean and one Christian set-aside seat	State of Law (Maliki)—38% (28 seats); Independent Liberals Trend (pro-Sadr)—9% (5 seats); Accord Front (Sunni mainstream)—9% (9 seats); Iraq National (Allawi)— 8.6%; Shahid Mihrab and Independent Forces (ISCI)—5.4% (3 seats) ; National Reform list (of former P.M. Ibrahim al-Jafari)—4.3% (3 seats)
Basra—34 regular seats, plus one Christian seat	State of Law—37% (20); ISCI—11.6% (5); Sadr—5% (2); Fadhila (previously dominant in Basra)—3.2% (0); Allawi—3.2% (0); Jafari list—2.5% (0). New Governor : Shiltagh Abbud (Maliki list); Council chair: Jabbar Amin (Maliki list)
Nineveh—34 regular seats, plus one set aside for Shabaks, Yazidis, and Christians	Hadbaa—48.4%; Fraternal Nineveh—25.5%; IIP—6.7%; Hadbaa has taken control of provincial council and administration, excluding the Kurds. Governor is Atheel al-Nujaifi of Hadbaa.
Najaf—28 seats	State of Law—16.2% (7); ISCI—14.8% (7); Sadr—12.2% (6); Jafari—7% (2); Allawi— 1.8% (0); Fadhila—1.6% (0). Council chairman: Maliki list
Babil—30 seats	State of Law—12.5% (8); ISCI—8.2% (5); Sadr—6.2% (3); Jafari— 4.4% (3); Allawi— 3.4%; Accord Front—2.3% (3); Fadhila—1.3%. New Council chair: Kadim Majid Tuman (Sadrist)
Diyala—29 seats	Accord Front list—21.1%; Kurdistan Alliance—17.2%; Allawi— 9.5%; State of Law— 6 %. New council leans heavily Accord, but allied with Kurds and ISCI.
Muthanna—26 seats	State of Law—10.9% (5); ISCI—9.3% (5); Jafari—6.3% (3); Sadr— 5.5% (2); Fadhila— 3.7%.
Anbar—29 seats	Iraq Awakening (Sahawa-Sunni tribals)—18%; National Iraqi Project Gathering (established Sunni partics, excluding IIP)—17.6%;; Allawi—6.6%; Tribes of Iraq— 4.5%.
Maysan—27 seats	State of Law—17.7% (8); ISCI—14.6% (8); Sadr—7; Jafari—8.7% (4); Fadhila—3.2%; Allawi—2.3%. New Governor: Mohammad al-Sudani (Maliki); Council chair: Hezbollah Iraq
Dhi Qar—31 seats	State of Law—23.1% (13); pro-Sadr—14.1% (7); ISCI—11.1% (5); Jafari—7.6% (4); Fadhila—6.1%; Allawi—2.8%. New governor— Maliki list; Council chair: Sadrist
Karbala—27 seats	List of Maj. Gen. Yusuf al-Habbubi (Saddam-era local official)— 13.3% (1 seat); State of Law—8.5% (9); Sadr—6.8% (4); ISCI—6.4% (4); Jafari—2.5% ; Fadhila—2.5%.
Salah Ad Din—28 seats	IIP-led list—14.5%; Allawi—13.9%; Sunni list without IIP—8.7%; State of Law—3.5%; ISCI—2.9%. New council leans Accord/IIP
Qadissiyah—28 seats	State of Law—23.1% (11); ISCI—11.7% (5); Jafari—8.2% (3); Allawi—8%; Sadr— 6.7% (2); Fadhila—4.1%. New governor: Salim Husayn (Maliki list)
Wasit—28 seats	State of Law—15.3% (13); ISCI—10% (6); Sadr—6% (3); Allawi— 4.6%; Fadhila— 2.7%. New governor: Shiite independent; Council chair: ISCI

Source: UNAMI translation of results issued February 2, 2009, by the Independent Higher Election Commission of Iraq; Vissar, Reidar. The Provincial Elections: The Seat Allocation Is Official and the Coalition-Forming Process Begins. February 19, 2009.

Table 5. Election Results (January and December 2005)

Bloc/Party	Seats (Jan. 05)	Seats (Dec. 05)
United Iraqi Alliance (UIA, Shiite Islamist). 85 seats after departure of Fadilah (15 seats) and Sadr faction (28 seats) in 2007. Islamic Supreme Council of Iraq of Abd al-Aziz al-Hakim has 30; Da'wa Party (25 total: Maliki faction, 12, and Anizi faction, 13); independents (30).	140	128
Kurdistan Alliance—KDP (24); PUK (22); independents (7)	75	53
Iraqis List (secular, Allawi); added Communist and other mostly Sunni parties for Dec. vote.	40	25
Iraq Accord Front. Main Sunni bloc; not in Jan. vote. Consists of Iraqi Islamic Party (IIP, Tariq al-Hashimi, 26 seats); National Dialogue Council of Khalaf Ulayyan (7); General People's Congress of Adnan al-Dulaymi (7); independents (4).	—	44
National Iraqi Dialogue Front (Sunni, led by former Baathist Saleh al-Mutlak) Not in Jan. 2005 vote.	—	11
Kurdistan Islamic Group (Islamist Kurd) (votes with Kurdistan Alliance)	2	5
Iraqi National Congress (Chalabi). Was part of UIA list in Jan. 05 vote	—	0
Iraqis Party (Yawar, Sunni); Part of Allawi list in Dec. vote	5	—
Iraqi Turkomen Front (Turkomen, Kirkuk-based, pro-Turkey)	3	1
National Independent and Elites (Jan)/Risalyun (Message, Dec) pro-Sadr	3	2
People's Union (Communist, non-sectarian); on Allawi list in Dec. vote	2	—
Islamic Action (Shiite Islamist, Karbala)	2	0
National Democratic Alliance (non-sectarian, secular)	1	—
Rafidain National List (Assyrian Christian)	1	1
Liberation and Reconciliation Gathering (Umar al-Jabburi, Sunni, secular)	1	3
Ummah (Nation) Party. (Secular, Mithal al-Alusi, former INC activist)	0	1
Yazidi list (small Kurdish, heterodox religious minority in northern Iraq)	—	1

Notes: Number of polling places: January: 5,200; December: 6,200; Eligible voters: 14 million in January election; 15 million in October referendum and December; Turnout: January: 58% (8.5 million votes)/ October: 66% (10 million)/December: 75% (12 million).

Table 6. Assessments of the Benchmarks

Benchmark	July 12, 2007, Admin. Report	GAO (Sept. 07)	Sept. 14, 2007 Admin. Report	Subsequent Actions and Assessments—May 2008 Administration report, June 2008 GAO report, International Compact with Iraq Review in June 2008, and U.S. Embassy Weekly Status Reports (and various press sources)
1. Forming Constitutional Review Committee (CRC) and completing review	(S) satisfactory	unmet	S	CRC filed final report in August 2008 but major issues remain unresolved and require achievement of consensus among major faction leaders.
2. Enacting and implementing laws on De-Baathification	(U) unsatisfact.	unmet	S	"Justice and Accountability Law" passed Jan. 12, 2008. Allows about 30,000 fourth ranking Baathists to regain their jobs, and 3,500 Baathists in top three party ranks would receive pensions. Could allow for judicial prosecution of all ex-Baathists and bars ex-Saddam security personnel from regaining jobs. As noted, De-Baathification officials used this law to try to harm the prospects of rivals in March 2010 elections.
3. Enacting and implementing oil laws that ensure equitable distribution of resources	U	unmet	U	Framework and three implementing laws stalled over KRG-central government disputes; only framework law has reached COR to date. Revenue being distributed equitably, and 2009 budget maintains 17% revenue for KRG. Kurds also getting that share of oil exported from newly producing fields in KRG area. Some U.S. assessments say factions unlikely to reach agreement on these laws in the near term.
4. Enacting and implementing laws to form semi-autonomous regions	S	partly met	S	Regions law passed October 2006, with relatively low threshold (petition by 33% of provincial council members) to start process to form new regions, but main blocs agreed that law would take effect April 2008. November 2008: petition by 2% of Basra residents submitted to IHEC (another way to start forming a region) to convert Basra province into a single province "region. Signatures of 8% more were required by mid-January 2009; not achieved.

Table 6. (Continued).

5. Enacting and implementing: (a) a law to establish a higher electoral commission, (b) provincial elections law; (c) a law to specify authorities of provincial bodies, and (d) set a date for provincial elections	S on (a) and U on the others	overall unmet; (a) met	S on (a) and (c)	Draft law stipulating powers of provincial governments adopted February 13, 2008, took effect April 2008. Implementing election law adoped September 24, 2008, provided for provincial elections by January 31, 2009. Those elections were held, as discussed above.
6. Enacting and implementing legislation addressing amnesty for former insurgents	no rating	unmet	Same as July	Law to amnesty "non-terrorists" among 25,000 Iraq-held detainees passed February 13, 2008. Of 23,000 granted amnesty, about 6,300 released to date. 19,000 detainees held by U.S. have been transferred to Iraqi control under Security Agreement.
7. Enacting and implementing laws on militia disarmament	no rating	unmet	Same as July	Basra operation, discussed above, viewed as move against militias. On April 9, 2008, Maliki demanded all militias disband as condition for their parties to participate in provincial elections. Law on militia demobilization stalled.
8. Establishing political, media, economic, and services committee to support U.S. "surge"	S	met	met	No longer applicable; U.S. "surge" has ended and U.S. troop total in Iraq now about 50,000, down from about 170,000 at the 2008 height of the surge.
9. Providing three trained and ready brigades to support U.S. surge	S	partly met	S	No longer applicable. Eight brigades were assigned to assist the surge when it was in operation.
10. Providing Iraqi commanders with authorities to make decisions, without political intervention, to pursue all extremists, including Sunni insurgents and Shiite militias	U	unmet	S to pursue extremists U on political interference	No significant change. Still some U.S. concern over the Office of the Commander in Chief (part of Maliki's office) control over appointments to the ISF—favoring Shiites. Ssome politically motivated leaders remain in ISF. But, National Police said to include more Sunnis in command jobs and rank and file than one year ago. Defense and Interior ministers filed candidacies for the March 2010 elections, involving them in national political contest.

11. Ensuring Iraqi Security Forces (ISF) providing even-handed enforcement of law	U	unmet	S on military, U on police	U.S. interpreted Basra operation as effort by Maliki to enforce law even-handedly. Tribal support councils not even-handed, and still widespread Iraqi public complaints of politically-motivated administration of justice.
12. Ensuring that the surge plan in Baghdad will not provide a safe haven for any outlaw, no matter the sect	S	partly met	S	No longer applicable with end of surge. Ethno-sectarian violence has fallen sharply in Baghdad.
13. (a) Reducing sectarian violence and (b) eliminating militia control of local security	Mixed. S on (a); U on (b)	unmet	same as July 12	Sectarian violence has not re-accelerated. Shiite militias weak.
14. Establishing Baghdad joint security stations	S	met	S	Over 50 joint security stations operated in Baghdad at the height of U.S. troop surge. Closed in compliance with June 30, 2009, U.S. pull out from the cities.
15. Increasing ISF units capable of operating independently	U	unmet	U	ISF expected to secure Iraq by the end of 2011 under the Security Agreement, which requires U.S. troops to depart. Obama Administration officials say ISF will meet the challenges. Iraqi Air Force not likely to be able to secure airspace by then and DOD has approved potential sale to Iraq of F-16s and other major equipment.
16. Ensuring protection of minority parties in COR	S	met	S	No change. Rights of minority parties protected by Article 37 of constitution. Minorities given a minimum seat allocated in election law for march vote.
17. Allocating and spending $10 billion in 2007 capital budget for reconstruction.	S	partly met	S	About 63% of the $10 billion 2007 allocation for capital projects was spent.
18. Ensuring that Iraqi authorities not falsely accusing ISF members	U	unmet	U	Some governmental recriminations against some ISF officers still observed.

Source: Compiled by CRS.

End Notes

[1] http://www.washingtonpost.com/wp-dyn/content/article/2005/10/12/AR2005101201450.html.

[2] Myers, Steven Lee and Anthony Shadid. "Maliki Faulted On Using Army in Iraqi Politics." *New York Times*, February 11, 2010.

[3] The election law also stripped out provisions in the vetoed version to allot 13 total reserved seats, spanning six provinces, to minorities. An October 2008 amendment restored six reserved seats for minorities: Christian seats in Baghdad, Nineveh, and Basra; one seat for Yazidis in Nineveh; one seat for Shabaks in Nineveh; and one seat for the Sabean sect in Baghdad

[4] Each provincial council has 25 seats plus one seat per each 200,000 residents over 500,000.

[5] The threshold for winning a seat is the total number of valid votes divided by the number of seats up for election.

[6] Analysis of Iraq expert Reidar Visser. "The Hashemi Veto." http://gulfanalysis.wordpress.com/2009/11/18/the-hashemi-veto/.

[7] Gertz, Bill. "Inside the Ring." *Washington Times*, February 18, 2010.

[8] Healy, Jack. "Cleric's Anti-U.S. Forces Poised for Gains in Iraq." New York Times, December 20, 2010.

[9] Fadel, Leila and Karen DeYoung. "Iraqi Leaders Crack Political Deadlock." *Washington Post*, November 11, 2010.

[10] The following information is taken from Iraqi news accounts presented in: http://www.opensource.gov

[11] Report is at: http://www.state.gov/g/drl/rls/hrrpt/2009/nea/136069.htm

[12] Sly, Liz. "Iraqi Push Fades For Referendum on U.S. Troop Pullout." *Los Angeles Times*, October 16, 2009.

In: The Middle East in Turmoil, Volume 3
Editor: Angela N. Castillo

ISBN: 978-1-61324-241-4
© 2011 Nova Science Publishers, Inc.

Chapter 7

IRAN: U.S. CONCERNS AND POLICY RESPONSES[*]

Kenneth Katzman

SUMMARY

The Obama Administration views Iran as a major threat to U.S. national security interests, a perception generated not only by Iran's nuclear program but also by its military assistance to armed groups in Iraq and Afghanistan, to the Palestinian group Hamas, and to Lebanese Hezbollah. Particularly in its first year, the Obama Administration altered the previous U.S. approach by offering Iran's leaders consistent and sustained engagement with the potential for closer integration with and acceptance by the West. To try to convince Iranian leaders of peaceful U.S. intent and respect for Iran's history and stature in the region, the Obama Administration downplayed discussion of potential U.S. military action against Iranian nuclear facilities and repeatedly insisted that it did not seek to change Iran's regime. It held to this position even at the height of the protests by the domestic opposition "Green movement" that emerged following Iran's June 12, 2009, presidential election.

Iran's refusal to accept the details of an October 1, 2009, tentative agreement on nuclear issues— a framework that was the product of nearly a year of diplomacy with Iran—caused the Administration to shift toward building multilateral support for additional economic sanctions against Iran. The Administration efforts bore fruit throughout the summer of 2010 with the adoption of new sanctions by the U.N. Security Council (Resolution 1929), as well as related "national measures" by the European Union, Japan, South Korea, and other countries. Additional measures designed to compel foreign firms to exit the Iranian market were contained in U.S. legislation passed in June 2010 (the Comprehensive Iran Sanctions, Accountability, and Divestment Act, P.L. 111-195). Still, the Administration and its partners assert that these sanctions are intended to pave the way for successful diplomacy with Iran to limit its nuclear program. Iran accepted December 6-7, 2010, talks in Geneva with the six power contact group negotiating with Iran. No substantive progress was reported but the parties did accept follow-on talks in Turkey for an unspecified date in January 2011. U.S. officials have

---

[*] This is an edited, reformatted and augmented version of a Congressional Research Services publication, dated December 22, 2010.

indicated additional pressure could be forthcoming, although concrete steps might await the outcome of the talks in Turkey.

There is broad agreement that the U.S., U.N., and other sanctions enacted since mid-2010 are pressing Iran economically. However, because the sanctions have not and might not cause Iran to fundamentally alter its commitment to its nuclear program, some are pressing the Administration not to de-emphasize military action as a means of setting Iran's nuclear program back. The Administration has stepped up arms sales and engagement with regional states that might be helpful to contain Iranian power, were Iran's nuclear program to advance dramatically. Some believe that only a victory by the domestic opposition in Iran, which in late 2009 appeared to pose a potentially serious challenge to the regime's grip on power, can permanently reduce the multiplicity of threats posed by Iran's regime. Congressional resolutions and legislation since mid-2009 show growing congressional support for steps to enhance the opposition's prospects, or, at the very least, to sharply increase international criticism of Iran's human rights practices. However, Obama Administration officials say they believe that the opposition's prospects are enhanced by a muting of U.S. public support for the opposition. For further information, see CRS Report RS20871, *Iran Sanctions*; CRS Report R40849, *Iran: Regional Perspectives and U.S. Policy*; and CRS Report RL34544, *Iran's Nuclear Program: Status*.

INTRODUCTION

Much of the debate over U.S. policy toward Iran has centered on the nature of the current regime; some believe that Iran, a country of about 70 million people, is a threat to U.S. interests because hardliners in Iran's regime dominate and set a policy direction intended to challenge U.S. influence and allies in the region. President George W. Bush, in his January 29, 2002, State of the Union message, labeled Iran part of an "axis of evil" along with Iraq and North Korea.

POLITICAL HISTORY

The United States was an ally of the late Shah of Iran, Mohammad Reza Pahlavi ("the Shah"), who ruled from 1941 until his ouster in February 1979. The Shah assumed the throne when Britain and Russia forced his father, Reza Shah Pahlavi (Reza Shah), from power because of his perceived alignment with Germany in World War II. Reza Shah had assumed power in 1921 when, as an officer in Iran's only military force, the Cossack Brigade (reflecting Russian influence in Iran in the early 20th century), he launched a coup against the government of the Qajar Dynasty. Reza Shah was proclaimed Shah in 1925, founding the Pahlavi dynasty. The Qajars had been in decline for many years before Reza Shah's takeover. That dynasty's perceived manipulation by Britain and Russia had been one of the causes of the 1906 constitutionalist movement, which forced the Qajars to form Iran's first Majles (parliament) in August 1906 and promulgate a constitution in December 1906. Prior to the Qajars, what is now Iran was the center of several Persian empires and dynasties, but whose reach shrunk steadily over time. Since the 16th century, Iranian empires lost control of Bahrain (1521), Baghdad (1638), the Caucasus (1828), western Afghanistan (1857), Baluchistan (1872), and what is now Turkmenistan (1894). Iran adopted Shiite Islam under the Safavid Dynasty (1500-1722), which brought Iran out from a series of Turkic and Mongol conquests.

The Shah was anti-Communist, and the United States viewed his government as a bulwark against the expansion of Soviet influence in the Persian Gulf and a counterweight to pro-Soviet Arab regimes and movements. Israel maintained a representative office in Iran during the Shah's time and the Shah supported a peaceful resolution of the Arab-Israeli dispute. In 1951, under pressure from nationalists in the Majles (parliament) who gained strength in the 1949 Majles elections, he appointed a popular nationalist parliamentarian, Dr. Mohammad Mossadeq, as prime minister. Mossadeq was widely considered left-leaning, and the United States was wary of his policies, which included his drive for nationalization of the oil industry. Mossadeq's followers began an uprising in August 1953 when the Shah tried to dismiss Mossadeq, and the Shah fled. The Shah was restored in a successful CIA-supported uprising against Mossadeq.

The Shah tried to modernize Iran and orient it toward the West, but in so doing he also sought to marginalize Iran's Shiite clergy. He exiled Ayatollah Ruhollah Khomeini in 1964 because of Khomeini's active opposition, which was based on the Shah's anti-clerical policies and what Khomeini alleged was the Shah's forfeiture of Iran's sovereignty to the United States. Khomeini fled to and taught in Najaf, Iraq, a major Shiite theological center that contains the Shrine of Imam Ali, Shiism's foremost figure. There, he was a peer of senior Iraqi Shiite clerics and, with them, advocated direct clerical rule or *velayat-e-faqih* (rule by a supreme Islamic jurisprudent). In 1978, three years after the March 6, 1975, Algiers Accords between the Shah and Iraq's Baathist leaders, which settled territorial disputes and required each party to stop assisting each other's oppositionists, Iraq expelled Khomeini to France, from which he stoked the Islamic revolution. Mass demonstrations and guerrilla activity by pro-Khomeini forces, allied with a broad array of anti-Shah activists, caused the Shah's government to collapse in February 1979. Khomeini returned from France and, on February 11, 1979, declared an Islamic Republic of Iran, as enshrined in the constitution that was adopted in a public referendum in December 1979 (and amended in 1989). Khomeini was strongly anti-West and particularly anti-U.S., and relations between the United States and the Islamic Republic turned hostile even before the November 4, 1979, seizure of the U.S. Embassy by pro-Khomeini radicals.

REGIME STRUCTURE, STABILITY, AND OPPOSITION

Iran's regime has always been considered authoritarian, but with a degree of popular input and checks and balances among power centers. The Shiite cleric that led the revolution that founded the Islamic Republic of Iran, Ayatollah Ruhollah Khomeini, died on June 3, 1989, but his regime is enshrined in an Islamic republican constitution adopted in October 1979 and amended in a national referendum of April 1989. It provides for some elected and some appointed positions.

Until the serious popular and intra-regime unrest that followed the June 12, 2009, presidential election, the regime had faced only episodic, relatively low-level unrest from minorities, intellectuals, students, labor groups, and women. Since the elections, the regime has struggled to contain popular dissatisfaction, which some believe will be satisfied only with the outright replacement of the regime. In late 2009, several Iran experts believed this opposition movement—calling itself "The Green Path of Hope" or "Green movement" (*Rah-e-Sabz*)—posed a serious challenge to the current regime. However, the success of the regime in preventing the Green movement from holding a large counter-demonstration on the 2010 anniversary of "Revolution Day" (February 11)—and the movement's subsequent public quiescence—has led some to conclude the Green movement has withered. Others believe that the fundamental popular anger at the government has only grown and that the movement, after reevaluating its strategy, organizing its leadership, and perhaps gaining adherents from other segments of society, will eventually regain outward momentum.

The Supreme Leader, His Powers, and Other Ruling Councils

Upon Khomeini's death, one of his disciples, Ayatollah Ali Khamene'i, was selected Supreme Leader by an elected 86-seat "*Assembly of Experts.*"[1] Although he has never had Khomeini's undisputed authority, Khamene'i has vast formal powers as Supreme Leader that help him maintain his grip on power. Some of his peers criticized his handling of the protest movement, and Secretary of State Clinton said in February 2010 that the Supreme Leader's authority is being progressively usurped by regime security forces, most notably the Islamic Revolutionary Guard Corps (IRGC). However, Khamene'i is said to believe that the virtual disappearance of street protests in 2010 validated his strategy of forceful repression.

Formally, the Supreme Leader is commander in chief of the armed forces, giving him the power to appoint commanders and to be represented on the highest national security body, the Supreme National Security Council, composed of top military and civilian security officials. He appoints half of the 12-member *Council of Guardians*;[2] and the head of Iran's judiciary (currently Ayatollah Sadeq Larijani). Headed by Ayatollah Ahmad Jannati, the conservative-controlled Council of Guardians reviews legislation to ensure it conforms to Islamic law, and it screens election candidates and certifies election results. The Supreme Leader also has the power, under the constitution, to remove the elected president if either the judiciary or the elected *Majles* (parliament) say the president should be removed, with cause. The Supreme Leader appoints members of the 42-member *Expediency Council*, set up in 1988 to resolve legislative disagreements between the *Majles* and the Council of Guardians but its powers were expanded in 2006 to include oversight of the executive branch (cabinet) performance. Expediency Council members serve five-year terms. The Council, appointed most recently in February 2007, is still headed by Rafsanjani; its executive officer is former Revolutionary Guard commander-in-chief Mohsen Reza'i.

The Assembly of Experts is empowered to oversee the work of the Supreme Leader and replace him if necessary, as well as to amend the constitution. The Assembly serves a six-year term; the fourth election for that Assembly was held on December 15, 2006. After that election, Akbar Hashemi-Rafsanjani, still a major figure having served two terms as president himself (1989- 1997), was named deputy leader of the Assembly. After the death of the leader of the Assembly, Rafsanjani was selected its head in September 2007. See Figure 1. for a chart of the Iranian regime.)

Iran: U.S. Concerns and Policy Responses

Table 1. Major Factions, Personalities, and Interest Groups

Conservatives	
Supreme Leader Ali Khamene'i	Born in July 1939 to an Azeri (Turkic) family from Mashhad. Lost use of right arm in assassination attempt in June 1981. Was jailed by the Shah of Iran for supporting Ayatollah Khomeini's revolution. After the regime took power in 1979, helped organize Revolutionary Guard and other security organs. Served as elected president during 1981-1989 and was selected Khomeini's successor in June 1989 upon his death. Upon that selection, Khamene'i religious ranking was advanced in official organs to "Ayatollah" from the lower ranking "Hojjat ol-Islam." Although with Khomeini's undisputed authority, Khamene'I, like Khomeini, generally stays out of day-to-day governmental business and saves his prestige to resolve factional disputes or to quiet popular criticism of regime performance. Took more direct role to calm internal infighting in wake of June 2009 election dispute, but perceived as increasingly reliant on Revolutionary Guard to keep regime grip on power. Considered moderate-conservative on domestic policy but hardline on foreign policy and particularly toward Israel. Seeks to challenge U.S. hegemony and wants Israel defeated but respects U.S. military power and fears military confrontation with United States. Has generally supported the business community (bazaaris), and opposed state control of the economy. Senior aides in his office include second son, Mojtaba, who is said to be acquiring increasing influence and who Khamene'i may want to succeed him. Has made public reference to letters to him from President Obama asking for renewed U.S.-Iran relations.
Expediency Council and Assembly of Experts Chair Ali Akbar Hashemi-Rafsanjani	Long a key strategist of the regime, and longtime advocate of "grand bargain" to resolve all outstanding issues with United States, although on Iran's terms. A mid-ranking cleric, leads both Expediency Council and Assembly of Experts, although now perceived as a tacit ally of the Green movement because of his criticism of Khamene'i and Ahmadinejad's Ahmadinejad's 2009 campaign allegations of Rafsanjani corruption, and purportedly financed much of Musavi's election campaign. Daughter Faizah participated in several 2009 protests. The arrest of five Rafsanjani family members in June 2009 (and another briefly detained in March 2010), and a May 2010 threat to arrest his son, Mehdi, if he returns from exile in Britain—may have reflected pressure on him. Opposition activists say his sister and brother-in-law have relocated to New York. In September 2010, criticized Ahmadinejad for minimizing the effects of growing international sanctions against Iran. In October 2010, Khamene'i blocked Rafsanjani's efforts to convert endowment of Islamic Azad University, which Rafsanjani helped found, to a religious trust. Was Majles speaker during 1981-89 and President 1989-1997. One of Iran's richest men, family owns large share of Iran's total pistachio production.
President Mahmoud Ahmadinejad	Declared reelected on June 12, 2009, and inaugurated August 5, but results still not accepted by most Green movement adherents. Increasingly criticized by Majles opponents and some experts say he is losing the confidence of the Supreme Leader. See box below.

Table 1. (Continued).

Conservatives	
Majles Speaker Ali Larijani	Overwhelming winner for Majles seat from Qom on March 14, 2008, and selected Majles Speaker (237 out of 290 votes). Former state broadcasting head (1994-2004) and minister of culture and Islamic guidance (1993), was head of Supreme National Security Council and chief nuclear negotiator from August 2005 until October 2007 resignation. Sought to avoid U.N. Security Council isolation. Politically close to Khamene'i but criticized election officials for the flawed June 12, 2009, election and subsequent crackdown. Increasingly backed arrests of protesters as Green movement gained strength. Brother of judiciary head.
Tehran Mayor Mohammad Baqer Qalibaf	Former Revolutionary Guard Air Force commander and police chief, but a moderate-conservative and ally of Larijani. Encourages comparisons of himself to Reza Shah, invoking an era of stability and strong leadership. Lost in the 2005 presidential elections, but supporters won nine out of 15 seats on Tehran city council in December 2006 elections, propelling him to current post as mayor of Tehran. Recruited moderate-conservatives for March 2008 Majles election.
Senior Clerics	The most senior clerics, most of whom are in Qom, including several Grand Ayatollahs, are generally "quietist"—they believe that the senior clergy should refrain from direct involvement in politics. These include Grand Ayatollah Nasser Makarem Shirazi, Grand Ayatollah (former judiciary chief) Abdol Karim Musavi-Ardabili, and Grand Ayatollah Yusuf Sanei, all of whom have criticized regime crackdown against oppositionists. Others believe in political involvement, including Ayatollah Mohammad Taqi Mesbah Yazdi. He is founder of the hardline Haqqani school, and spiritual mentor of Ahmadinejad. Yazdi, an assertive defender of the powers of the Supreme Leader and a proponent of an "Islamic state" rather than the current "Islamic republic," fared poorly in December 2006 elections for Assembly of Experts. Another politically active hardline senior cleric is Ayatollah Kazem Haeri, mentor of Iraqi cleric Moqtada Al Sadr.
Judiciary Chief/Ayatollah Sadeq Larijani	Named judiciary head in late August 2009, replacing Ayatollah Mahmoud Shahrudi, who had headed the Judiciary since 1999. Brother is Majles Speaker Ali Larijani; both are close to the Supreme Leader but are conservative political opponents of Ahmadinejad. Both also support hard line against Green movement oppositionists. Another Larijani brother, Mohammad Javad, was deputy foreign minister (1980s.)
Militant Clerics Association	Longtime organization of hardline clerics headed by Ayatollah Mohammad Mahdavi-Kani. Did not back Ahmadinejad in June 12 presidential elections.

Conservatives	
Bazaar Merchants ("Bazaaris")	The core interests of the urban bazaar merchants are their livelihoods, and therefore they have generally supported the regime as a source of political stability and economic stability. Have conducted only a few strikes or other organized action since the 1979 revolution. In July 2010, many Tehran bazaaris—and bazaaris in several other major cities—closed their shops for two weeks to protest a 70% tax increase, ultimately compelling the government to reduce the increase to 15%. Some interpreted the strikes as an indication that the bazaaris may be shifting against the regime which they see as causing the international community to sanction Iran's economy and bringing economic damage. The bazaaris are also not a monolithic group; each city's bazaars are organized by industry (ex. carpets, gold, jewelry, clothing) and bazaari positions tend to be reached by consensus among elders representing each industry represented at the bazaar.

Opposition/"Green Movement" (Rah-e-Sabz)
All of the blocs and personalities below can be considered, to varying degrees, as part of the Green movement. However, overall leadership of the movement and decision-making on protest activities is unclear, with several components competing for preeminence. Some Green supporters have left for Europe, Asia, or the United States.

Titular Green Movement Leaders: Mir Hossein Musavi/ Mohammad Khatemi/Mehdi Karrubi	Khatemi—reformist president during 1997-2005 and declared he would run again for President in June 2009 elections, but withdrew when allied reformist Mir Hossein Musavi entered the race in late March 2009. Khatemi elected May 1997, with 69% of the vote; reelected June 2001 with 77%. Rode wave of sentiment for easing social and political restrictions among students, intellectuals, youths, and women. These groups later became disillusioned with Khatemi's failure to stand up to hardliners on reform issues. Now heads International Center for Dialogue Among Civilizations. Visited U.S. in September 2006 to speak at Harvard and the Washington National Cathedral on "dialogue of civilizations." Has hewed to staunch anti-Israel line of most Iranian officials, but perceived as open to accepting a Palestinian-Israeli compromise. Perceived as open to a political compromise that stops short of replacement of the regime but guarantees social and political freedoms.
	Musavi is a non-cleric. About 68. An architect by training, and a disciple of Ayatollah Khomeini, he served as foreign minister (1980), then prime minister (1981-89), at which time he successfully managed the state rationing program during the privations of the Iran-Iraq war but often feuded with Khamene'i, who was then President. At that time, he was an advocate of state control of the economy. His post was abolished in the 1989 revision of the constitution.

Table 1. (Continued).

Conservatives	
	Musavi later adopted views similar to Khatemi on political and social freedoms and on reducing Iran's international isolation, but supports strong state intervention in the economy to benefit workers, lower classes. Appeared at some 2009 protests, sometimes intercepted or constrained by regime security agents. However, may have lost ground to harder line opposition leaders who criticize his statements indicating reconciliation with the regime is possible. IRGC and about 125 parliamentary hardliners urged his arrest for his continued calls for demonstrations, and his main bodyguard reportedly was arrested on May 15, 2010, suggesting increased regime pressure on him. Wife, Zahra Rahnevard, a major presence during Musavi's presidential campaign, physically attacked as part of regime's blockage of February 11, 2010, protests.
	A founder of the leftwing Association of Combatant Clerics (different organization but with similar name from that above), Mehdi Karrubi was Speaker of the Majles during, 1989-92 and 2000-2004. Formed a separate pro-reform "National Trust" faction after losing 2005 election. Ran again in 2009, but received few votes and subsequently emerged, along with Musavi, as a symbol of the opposition. Indicated in late January 2010 that Ahmadinejad is the chief executive of Iran by virtue of the Supreme Leader's backing, but later reiterated strong criticism of regime's use of force against protesters. Has been physically blocked by regime from attending Green demonstrations during 2010.
Other Green Movement Dissidents	Other leading dissidents have challenged the regime long before the presidential election. For example, journalist Akbar Ganji conducted hunger strikes to protest regime oppression; he was released on schedule on March 18, 2006, after sentencing in 2001 to six years in prison for alleging high-level involvement in 1999 murders of Iranian dissident intellectuals. Another prominent dissident is Abdol Karim Soroush, who challenged the doctrine of clerical rule. Others include former Revolutionary Guard organizer Mohsen Sazegara, former Culture Minister Ataollah Mohajerani, and Mohsen Kadivar. All are said to have substantial followings among Green movement supporters in Iran.

Conservatives	
Student Opposition Leaders/Confederation of Iranian Students/Office of Consolidation of Unity (Daftar Tahkim-e-Vahdat)	Staunch oppositionists and revolutionaries, many now favor replacement of the regime with secular democracy. The well-educated urban youth are the backbone of the Green movement – they want free and open media and contact with the West. Many are women. One key bloc in this group is the Confederation of Iranian Students (CIS), led by Amir Abbas Fakhravar, who was jailed for five years for participating in July 1999 student riots. CIS, committed to non-violent resistance, is an offshoot/competitor of the Office of Consolidation Unity, which led the 1999 riots. At the time of those riots, most students were strong Khatemi supporters, but turned against him for acquiescing to hardliner demands that he crack down on the rioting. The crackdown killed four students. Student leaders currently attempting, with mixed success, to gain support of older generation, labor, clerics, village-dwellers, and other segments. CIS supports total oil sale embargo to deprive the regime of the funds it needs to pay its security forces.
Islamic Iran Participation Front (IIPF)	The most prominent and best organized pro-reform grouping, but has lost political ground to more active and forceful core of the Green movement of which Musavi is the most visible symbol. Its leaders include Khatemi's brother, Mohammad Reza Khatemi (a deputy speaker in the 2000-2004 Majles) and Mohsen Mirdamadi. Backed Musavi in June 12 election; several IIPF leaders, including Mirdamadi, detained and prosecuted in postelection dispute. The grouping was outlawed by the regime in late April, 2010
Mojahedin of the Islamic Revolution Organization (MIR)	Composed mainly of left-leaning Iranian figures who support state control of the economy, but want greater political pluralism and relaxation of rules on social behavior. A major constituency of the reformist camp. Its leader is former Heavy Industries Minister Behzad Nabavi, who supported Musavi in 2009 election and remains jailed for post-election unrest. The organization was outlawed by the regime simultaneously with the outlawing of the IIPF, above.
Labor Unions	Organized labor has suffered from official repression for many years. Organized labor is not a core constituency of the Green Movement, but laborers are viewed as increasingly sympathetic to dramatic political change. Some labor protests took place in Tehran on "May Day" 2010.
Shirin Abadi	A number of dissidents have struggled against regime repression for many years, long before the election dispute. One major longtime dissident and human rights activist is Nobel Peace Prize laureate (2003) and Iran human rights activist lawyer Shirin Abadi. Subsequent to the passage of the U.N. General Assembly resolution above, Iranian authorities raided the Tehran office of the Center for Defenders of Human Rights, which she runs. She has often represented clients persecuted or prosecuted by the regime. She left Iran for Europe, fearing arrest in connection with the postelection dispute. In December 2009, the regime confiscated her Nobel Prize.

Table 1. (Continued).

Conservatives	
Son of the Late Shah of Iran—Reza Pahlavi	Some Iranian exiles, as well as some elites still in Iran, want to replace the regime with a constitutional monarchy led by Reza Pahlavi, the U.S.-based son of the late former Shah and a U.S.-trained combat pilot. In January 2001, the Shah's son, who is about 50 years old, ended a long period of inactivity by giving a speech in Washington, DC, calling for unity in the opposition and the institution of a constitutional monarchy and democracy in Iran. He has since broadcast messages into Iran from Iranian exile-run stations in California,3 and has delivered statements condemning the regime for the post-2009 election crackdown. He does not appear to have largescale support inside Iran, but he may be trying to capitalize on the opposition's growing popularity. In January 2010, he called for international governments to withdraw their representation from Tehran.
Other U..S.-Based Activists	Some organizations, such as The National Iranian American Council (NIAC) and the Public Affairs Alliance of Iranian-Americans (PAAIA), are not necessarily seeking change within Iran. The mission of NIAC, composed largely of Iranian-Americans, is to promote discussion of U.S. policy and the group has advocated engagement with Iran. PAAIA's mission is to discuss issues affecting Iranian-Americans, such as discrimination caused by public perceptions of association with terrorism or radical Islam.
	Numerous Iranians-Americans of differing ideologies in the United States want to see a change of regime in Tehran. Many of them are based in California, where there is a large Iranian-American community, and there are about 25 small-scale radio or television stations that broadcast into Iran. A growing number of U.S.-based Iranian activists appear to be supporting or affiliated with the Green movement. Many of them protested Ahmadinejad's visit to the United Nations in September 2009, and many others sport green bracelets showing support for the Green movement.

The Presidency/Mahmoud Ahmadinejad

Although subordinate to the Supreme Leader, the presidency is a coveted position which provides vast opportunities for the holder of the post to empower his political base and to affect policy. The presidency, a position held since 2005 by Mahmoud Ahmadinejad, appoints and supervises the work of the cabinet. Cabinet appointments are subject to confirmation by the Majles (parliament). The Supreme Leader is believed to have significant input into security-related cabinet appointments, including ministers of defense, interior, and intelligence (Ministry of Information and Security, MOIS).

After suffering several presidential election defeats at the hands of President Mohammad Khatemi and the reformists in the 1997 and 2001 presidential elections, hardliners successfully moved to regain the sway they held when Khomeini was alive. Conservatives won the February 20, 2004, Majles elections (which are always held one year prior to each presidential election), although the conservative win was the result of the Council of Guardians' disqualification of 3,600 reformist candidates, including 87 Majles incumbents. That helped conservatives win 155 out of the 290 seats. The George W. Bush Administration and the Senate (S.Res. 304, adopted by unanimous consent on February 12, 2004) criticized the elections as unfair.

As the reformist faction suffered setbacks, the Council of Guardians narrowed the field of candidates for the June 2005 presidential elections to 8 out of the 1,014 persons who filed. Rafsanjani [4] was considered the favorite against several opponents more hardline than he is—three had ties to the Revolutionary Guard: Ali Larijani; Mohammad Baqer Qalibaf; and Tehran mayor Mahmoud Ahmadinejad. In the June 17, 2005, first round, turnout was about 63% (29.4 million votes out of 46.7 million eligible voters). With 21% and 19.5%, respectively, Rafsanjani and Ahmadinejad, who did unexpectedly well because of tacit backing from Khamene'i and the Basij militia arm of the Revolutionary Guard, moved to a runoff. Reformist candidates (Mehdi Karrubi and Mostafa Moin) fared worse than expected. Ahmadinejad won in the June 24 runoff, receiving 61.8% to Rafsanjani's 35.7%. He first took office on August 6, 2005.

June 12, 2009, Presidential Elections

Prospects for reformists to unseat Ahmadinejad through the established election process seemed to brighten in February 2009, when Khatemi—who is still highly popular among reform-minded Iranians—said that he would run. However, on March 18, 2009, Khatemi withdrew from the race in favor of another reformist, former Prime Minister Mir Hossein Musavi. Musavi was viewed as somewhat less divisive—and therefore more acceptable to the Supreme Leader—because Musavi had served as prime minister during the 1980-1988 Iran-Iraq war. Khatemi endorsed Musavi.

A total of about 500 candidates for the June 12, 2009, presidential elections registered their names during May 5-10, 2009. The Council of Guardians decide on four final candidates on May 20: Ahmadinejad, Musavi, Mehdi Karrubi, and former Commander-in-Chief of the Revolutionary Guard Mohsen Reza'i. The Interior Ministry, which runs the election, also instituted an unprecedented series of one-on-one debates, which including Ahmadinejad's acrimonious accusations of corruption against Rafsanjani and against Musavi's wife. If no candidate received more than 50% of the vote on June 12, there would have been a runoff one week later.

The challengers and their backgrounds and platforms were as follows.

- Mir Hosein Musavi. The main reformist candidate. See box above.
- Mehdi Karrubi. See box above.
- Mohsen Reza'i. As noted above, he was commander in chief of the Revolutionary Guard through the Iran-Iraq war. About 58 years old, he is considered an anti-Ahmadinejad conservative. Reza'i dropped out just prior to the 2005 presidential election. He alleged fraud in the 2009 election but later dropped his formal challenge.

The outcome of the election was always difficult to foresee; polling was inconsistent. Musavi supporters held large rallies in Tehran, but pro-Ahmadinejad rallies were large as well. During the campaign, Khamene'i professed neutrality, but he and Musavi were often at odds during the Iran-Iraq war, when Khamene'i was president and Musavi was prime minister. Turnout was high at about 85%; 39.1 million valid (and invalid) votes were cast. The Interior Ministry announced two hours after the polls closed that Ahmadinejad had won, although in the past results have been announced the day after. The totals were announced on Saturday, June 13, 2009, as follows:

- Ahmadinejad: 24.5 million votes—62.6%
- Musavi: 13.2 million votes—33.75%
- Reza'i: 678,000 votes—1.73%
- Invalid: 409,000 votes—1%
- Karrubi: 333,600 votes—0.85%

Ahmadinejad's Policies and Divisions within the Regime

Even before the 2009 Iranian presidential election campaign, discussed below, major portions of the population, particularly younger, well educated and urban Iranians, were expressing concern that Ahmadinejad's defiance of the international community was isolating Iran. This sentiment was evident in several university student protests against him. Splits have widened over a number of issues, although these schisms do not appear to have rendered Ahmadinejad incapable of governing.

During 2008-2010, splits have widened between Ahmadinejad and other conservative members of his "Principalist" faction. That rift was evident in the March 2008 Majles elections. During 2010, Ahmadinejad's conservative critics have become more vocal in finding fault with his performance. Such figures as Larijani and Qalibaf, discussed above, who may be more amenable to compromise with the international community, are now considered opponents of Ahmadinejad rather than allies. Khamene'i has tended to back Ahmadinejad, if only to prevent the appearance of divisions. However, on September 14, 2010, Khamene'i criticized Ahmadinejad for his appointments of "special envoys" to several world regions as unnecessary duplication of efforts by the Foreign Ministry. The appointments reportedly led the Foreign Minister to threaten to resign, withdrawing that threat only after intervention by the office of the Supreme Leader.

Further disputes between Ahmadinejad and his conservative opponents (primarily Larijani) erupted in September 2010 when Ahmadinejad refused to carry out certain expenditures appropriated by the Majles and approved by the Expediency Council (which is headed by Ahmadinejad rival, Rafsanjani).

That disagreement subsequently widened into a conflict over the powers of the Majles vs. those of the President. In October 2010, the politically powerful Revolutionary Guard, in one of its publications, appeared to side with the Majles. The dispute has reignited a movement by some Majles deputies—shelved in early 2010 at the insistence of the Supreme Leader—to impeach or at least to formally question Ahmadinejad. There are 74 signatures needed to compel Ahmadinejad to appear before the Majles, and deputies reportedly are keeping their signatures secret, meaning it is not known how close to achieving the needed number of signatures are the organizers of this drive. Outright impeachment is unlikely because it would, under Iran's constitution, require certification of the Supreme Leader to be implemented, who reportedly views an impeachment as highly divisive and destabilizing. A further split was exposed in mid-November when the Majles voted to removed the President from the post of Chairman of the governing board of Iran's Central Bank.

On the other hand, the Supreme Leader sided primarily with Ahmadinejad in October 2010 in preventing Rafsanjani from placing the endowment assets of Islamic Azad University, which has branches countrywide, into a religious trust. That move would have permanently blocked Ahmadinejad from a government takeover of that university system. Ahmadinejad also apparently succeeded, after trying for several months, to obtain Khamene'i's backing to dismiss Foreign Minister Mottaki. The firing came on December 13, 2010, while Mottaki was abroad, prompting Majles criticism of Ahmadinejad for the handling of the move. Ahmadinejad replaced him with civilian nuclear chief Ali Akbar Salehi. This follows a previous schism over Ahmadinejad's efforts to appoint special envoys for key issues and regions – a move that was opposed by Foreign Ministry career diplomats and eventually led to the Supreme Leader's intervention to downgrade the appointments to that of "advisers."

Table 2. Factions in the Eighth Majles
(Elected March 14-April 25, 2008)

Pro-Ahmadinejad Conservatives (United Front of Principalists)	117
Anti-Ahmadinejad Conservatives (Coalition of Principalists)	53
Reformists (39 seats in seventh Majles)	46
Independents	71
Seats annulled or voided	3
Total	**290**

Political Divisions Over How to Handle Popular Unrest

The opposition activities since the June 12, 2009, election have also contributed to widening schisms within the regime. The Supreme Leader, appears to believe that its suppressions have placed the Green challenge on the defensive. The success in preventing or limiting the protests in 2010 has circumscribed those in the regime that sought compromise with the opposition. However, some say that the most serious effect of the opposition criticism has been to significantly narrow the base of the regime to hardline purists, backed by the revolutionary security forces (Revolutionary Guard and Basij). This view might have been corroborated by Ahmadinejad's own comments in July 2010 that Iran now has "one party."

Others say that even the most loyal security forces are open to compromise with the opposition if protests and places severe pressure on the regime. A bomb in October 2010 at a Revolutionary Guard base in western Iran, which killed 20 Guard officers, was widely suspected by opposition activists to be the work of saboteurs and could reflect growing schisms within the Guard itself. Most reformists and even some senior clerics in Qom have left the regime fold and many prominent reformists were imprisoned and are still incarcerated. In order to shore up loyalty to the regime, Khamene'i visited Qom in mid-October and demanded that senior clerics, such as Grand Ayatollah Nasser Makarem-Shirazi, cease criticizing Ahmadinejad.

Economy and Sanctions-Driven Schisms

On economic matters, many middle class Iranians have long criticized Ahmadinejad for favoring the lower classes economically by raising some wages and lowering interest rates for poorer borrowers, cancelling some debts of farmers, and increasing some social welfare payments. These moves fed inflation, but poorer Iranians saw Ahmadinejad as attentive to their economic plight. These divisions have increased as Ahmadinejad has won Majles approval to reduce state subsidies on staple goods—which cost Iran about $30 billion per year according to outside estimates (the government puts the cost at about $100 billion per year)—over the subsequent five years. As a temporary measure, direct cash handouts are being given to poorer Iranians. After several delays to plan for anticipated unrest, the subsidy elimination program began on December 19 with the lifting of prices for gasoline. A certain amount is available at a subsidized price but amounts over a threshold have to be purchased at near world prices of about $2.50 per gallon. Poor Iranians were given about $80 for December and January to compensate them. Unrest is said to have been minimal, perhaps because the regime deployed security forces to confront any such unrest. However, Iran's trucking industry may have reacted by striking, which may further increase the cost of bringing goods into the major cities and throughout the country.

Major economic sectors or markets are controlled by the quasi-statal "foundations" (*bonyads*), run by powerful former officials, and there are special trading privileges for them and the bazaar merchants, a key constituency for some conservatives. The same privileges—and more— reportedly apply to businesses run by the Revolutionary Guard, as discussed below, leading to criticism that the Guard is using its political influence to win business contracts.

Since mid-2010, Ahmadinejad has also appeared to be losing support among more traditional segments of society who are feeling the effects of international sanctions. In July 2010, when the government attempted to raise taxes on the bazaar merchant incomes by 70%, several major bazaars shuttered in protest. To end the strike, the government eventually renegotiated a 15% tax increase, although there were reports of security force intimidation of the merchants. Some read the strikes as evidence of growing belief among the bazaaris that youth-led unrest has gone underground and that the government can be challenged successfully.

Others interpreted the bazaari unrest as an indication that international sanctions are starting to pressure the Iranian private sector. On November 16, 2010, Secretary of Defense Gates said there are indications that the Supreme Leader may perceive that Ahmadinejad is not informing him of the true impact of international sanctions on Iran's economy. Senior longtime regime stalwart Rafsanjani, who heads two key regime bodies, upbraided Ahmadinejad publicly in October 2010 for downplaying the effect of international sanctions on Iran's economy. The issue of sanctions and their economic and policy effects are discussed in substantial depth in CRS Report RS20871, *Iran Sanctions*, by Kenneth Katzman.

Mahmoud Ahmadinejad

First non-cleric to be president of the Islamic republic since the assassination of then-president Mohammad Ali Rajai in August 1981. About 57, he asserts he is a "man of the people," the son of a blacksmith who lives in modest circumstances, who would promote the interests of the poor and return government to the original principles of the Islamic revolution. Has burnished that image as president through regular visits to poor areas and through subsidies directed at the lower classes. His official biography says he served with the "special forces" of the Revolutionary Guard, and he served subsequently (late 1980s) as a deputy provincial governor. Has been part of the "Isargaran" faction composed of former Guard and Basij (volunteer popular forces) leaders and other hardliners. U.S. intelligence reportedly determined he was not one of the holders of the 52 American hostages during November 1979-January 1981. Other accounts say Ahmadinejad believes his mission is to prepare for the return of the 12th Imam—Imam Mahdi—whose return from occultation would, according to Twelver Shiite doctrine, be accompanied by the establishment of Islam as the global religion. Earned clerical criticism in May 2008 for again invoking intervention by Imam Mahdi in present day state affairs.

Following limited recount, declared winner of June 12, 2009, election. Well earlier, had been a controversial figure for inflammatory statements. He attracted significant world criticism for an October 26, 2005, Tehran conference entitled "A World Without Zionism" by stating that "Israel should be wiped off the map." In an October 2006 address, Ahmadinejad said, "I have a connection with God." He insisted on holding a December 2006 conference in Tehran questioning the Holocaust, a theme he has returned to several times since, including at a September 2007 speech at Columbia University. A U.N. Security Council statement and Senate and House resolutions (H.Res. 523 and S.Res. 292), passed by their respective chambers, condemned the statement. On June 21, 2007, the House passed H.Con.Res. 21, calling on the U.N. Security Council to charge Ahmadinejad with violating the 1948 Convention on the Prevention and Punishment of the Crime of Genocide; the Convention includes "direct and public incitement" of genocide as a punishable offense. On March 6, 2010, Ahmadinejad called the September 11, 2001, attacks on the United States a "big lie" used to justify intervention in Afghanistan. Was apparent target of an unsuccessful grenade attack on his motorcade in the city of Hamedan on August 4, 2010. Attending U.N. General Assembly in New York again during September 21-24, 2010, and in advance of the trip called Iran a major world power, downplayed the effect of U.S. and international sanctions against Iran, and warned that any U.S. attack against Iran would embroil the United States in a war more expansive than World War II.

The Opposition: 2009 Election Dispute and Emergence of the "Green Movement"

Until 2009, outward opposition to the regime was muted, sporadic, and relatively easy for the regime to suppress. Many experts said opposition was growing for many years, but, until the June 2009, presidential election, frustration had not reached the point where large segments of the public were willing to outwardly express dissent. That has changed since the June 12, 2009, presidential election. Almost immediately after the results of the election were announced on June 2009, Musavi supporters began protesting the results on June 13, as he,

Karrubi, and Reza'i asserted outright fraud and called for a new election, citing the infeasibility of counting 40 million votes so quickly; the barring of candidate observers at many polling stations; regime shut-down of Internet and text services; and repression of postelection protests. Khamene'i declared the results a "divine assessment," appearing to certify the results even though formal procedures require a three day complaint period. Some outside analysts said the results tracked pre-election polls, which showed strong support for Ahmadinejad in rural areas and among the urban poor.[5]

Green Movement Formation

The opposition "Green movement" grew out of the protests, later moving well beyond that issue into an outright challenge to the pillars of the regime. The demonstrations built throughout June 13-19, large in Tehran but also held in other cities. Security forces used varying amounts of force to control them, causing 27 protester deaths (official tally) during that period, with figures from opposition groups running over 100. The protesters' hopes of having Khamene'i annul the election were dashed by his major Friday prayer sermon on June 19 in which he refuted allegations of vast fraud and threatened a crackdown on further protests. Protesters defied Khamene'i the following day, but faced a crackdown that killed at least 10 protesters. On June 29, 2009, the Council of Guardians tried to address the complaints by performing a televised recount of 10% of the votes of Tehran's districts and some provincial ballots and, finding no irregularities, certified the results.

Protests continued, but more sporadically thereafter, including on the July 9 anniversary of the suppression of the 1999 student riots; the August 5, 2009, official inauguration of Ahmadinejad; and September 18, 2009, "Jerusalem Day." The opposition made considerable use of Internet-based sites (Facebook, Twitter) to organize their demonstrations around official holidays when people can gather easily. Several demonstrations—on November 4, 2009, the 30th anniversary of the takeover of the U.S. embassy in Tehran, and the Ashura Shiite holy day (December 27, 2009), which also marked the seventh day since the death of Ayatollah Montazeri, a major regime critic, were marked by the seizure and burning of several police vehicles, the refusal by some anti-riot police to beat protesters, the spreading to smaller cities, and the involvement of some clerics.

The momentum of the Green movement led some experts to predict the potential downfall of the regime, but the movement has not visibly recovered from the setback it suffered when its demonstration planned for the February 11, 2010, anniversary of the founding of the Islamic Republic (in 1979) did not amount to a large "show of force." Musavi and Karrubi both backed the protests. With weeks to prepare, the regime limited opposition communication and made several hundred preemptive arrests, as well as executing some oppositionists in late January. Another protest attempt was made on March 16, 2010, a Zoroastrian holiday (Fire Festival) celebrated by many Iranians, despite an explicit statement from Khamene'i saying the festival has no basis in Islam and should not be celebrated. Many Iranians defied the edict by combining the celebration of the festival with protest in numerous neighborhoods. Other scattered protests, including by some labor groups, were held in major cities on May 1, 2010 (May Day). Students at Seyed Beheshti University held a spontaneous protest against Ahmadinejad's visit there on May 10. Musavi and Karrubi called for a huge demonstration on the June 12, 2010, anniversary of the election, leading to some movement by parliament hardliners to have them arrested. Others viewed the execution of five Kurdish oppositionists in early May as an effort to intimidate the opposition in advance of the June 12 anniversary. Sensing regime preparations for repression, the two publicly "called off" the planned June 12, 2010, protest in order to avoid harm to protesters. Since then, Karrubi's home has been attacked by pro-regime militiamen, the state media have been directed not to discuss Musavi or Karrubi, and Tehran prosecutor Dowlatabadi has stated in September 2010 that he has begun building a prosecution against them. On the other hand, Ahmadinejad, in an interview with *ABC News* on September 19, 2010, said that the time to prosecute them would have been in 2009, at the height of the protest movement. Earlier, the regime prevented Khatemi from attending an international conference in Japan (April 2010).

Since the quieting of the demonstrations, signs have continued of underground Green movement activism. Some experts believe the Green movement is increasingly well organized and popular even though it is not demonstrated publicly in recent months.[6] In September 2010, two high ranking Iranian diplomats, including the number two at Iran's Embassy in Helsinki, Finland, resigned and sought protection as oppositionists to the regime. They and others subsequently formed a commission intended to persuade additional Foreign Ministry colleagues to defect. In October 2010, the regime publicly acknowledged that some of its nuclear program technicians were providing information to the West on Iran's program, and several "nuclear spies" were arrested. Another scientist was killed in a November 28, 2010, bombing by unknown assailants.

Armed Opposition Factions

Some groups have been committed to the replacement of the regime virtually since its inception, and have used, or are still using, violence to achieve their objectives. Their linkages to the Green Path movement are unclear, and some indications are these movements want to dominate any coalition that might topple the regime.

People's Mojahedin Organization of Iran (PMOI)/Camp Ashraf

One of the best-known exiled opposition groups is the People's Mojahedin Organization of Iran (PMOI).[7] Secular and left-leaning, it was formed in the 1960s to try to overthrow the Shah of Iran and has been characterized by U.S. reports as attempting to blend several ideologies, including Marxism, feminism, and Islamism, although the organization denies that it ever advocated Marxism. It allied with pro-Khomeini forces during the Islamic revolution and, according to past State Department reports, supported the November 1979 takeover of the U.S. Embassy in Tehran, although the group claims that it is the regime that alleged this support in order to discredit the group with the West. The group was driven into exile when it rose up against the Khomeini regime in September 1981. Even though it is an opponent of Tehran, since the late 1980s the State Department has refused contact with the PMOI and its umbrella organization, the National Council of Resistance of Iran (NCRI). The State Department designated the PMOI as a foreign terrorist organization (FTO) in October 1997[8] and the NCR was named as an alias of the PMOI in the October 1999 redesignation. In August 14, 2003, the State Department designated the NCR offices in the United States an alias of the PMOI, and NCR and the Justice Department closed down those offices.

The FTO designation is a widely debated issue. The State Department's annual reports on international terrorism, including the report for 2009 issued August 5, 2010, asserts that the organization—and not just a radical element of the organization as the group asserts—was responsible for the alleged killing of seven American military personnel and contract advisers to the former Shah in 1975-1976. The State Dept.'s August 5, 2010, terrorism report also alleges the group responsibility for bombings at U.S. government facilities in Tehran in 1972 as a protest of the visit to Iran of then-President Richard Nixon. The August 5, 2010, State Dept. reports also list as terrorist acts numerous attacks by the group against regime officials, facilities in Iran and abroad, and security officers, all prior to 2001. However, the report does not list any attacks by the group that purposely targets civilians—a key distinction that leads several experts to argue that the group should not be considered "terrorist." The State Dept. report does not state that the group has, as of mid-2001, fulfilled pledges to end all use of violence inside Iran and that there are no reports that it has resumed those activities. The group's alliance with Saddam Hussein's regime in the 1980s and 1990s has contributed to the U.S. criticism of the organization.

The PMOI also asserts that, by retaining the group on the FTO list, the United States is unfairly preventing the PMOI from participating in the growing opposition movement. The regime accuses the group of involvement in the post-June 2009 presidential election violence, and some of those tried for *mohareb* since February 2010 are members of the organization, according to statements issued by the group and by human rights groups such as Amnesty International.

The group is trying to build on recent legal successes in Europe; on January 27, 2009, the European Union (EU) removed the group from its terrorist group list; the group had been so designated by the EU in 2002. In May 2008, a British appeals court determined that the group should no longer be considered a terrorist organization on the grounds that the British government did not provide "any reliable evidence" that the PMOI would "resort to terrorist activities in the future." Currently, the governments that still list the group as a "terrorist organization," include the United States, Canada, and Australia. In June 2003, France arrested about 170 opposition activists, including Maryam Rajavi (wife of PMOI founder Masoud Rajavi, whose whereabouts are unknown), the "President-elect" of the NCRI. She was released and remains based in France, and is frequently received by European parliamentarians and other politicians in Europe.

In regard to the group's contesting its FTO designation by the State Department, in July 2008, the PMOI formally petitioned to the State Department that its designation be revoked, on the grounds that it renounced any use of terrorism in 2001. However, the State department announced in mid-January 2009 that the group would remain listed. The group remained on the FTO list when the list was reviewed and reissued in January 2010. The Department said it would "carefully review" a July 16, 2010, Court of Appeals decision to ask the State Department to review the decision to retain the group on the FTO list; the decision was based on a ruling that the group had not been given proper opportunity to rebut allegations against it. H.Res. 1431, introduced June 10, 2010, "invites the Secretary of State" to remove the PMOI from the FTO list. Some advocate that the United States not only remove the group from the FTO list but also enter an alliance with the group against Iran.

Camp Ashraf Issue

The issue of group members in Iraq is increasingly pressing. U.S. forces attacked PMOI military installations in Iraq during Operation Iraqi Freedom and negotiated a ceasefire with PMOI military elements in Iraq, requiring the approximately 3,400 PMOI fighters to remain confined to their Ashraf camp near the border with Iran. Its weaponry is in storage, guarded by U.S. personnel. Another 200 Ashraf residents have taken advantage of an arrangement between Iran and the ICRC for them to return to Iran if they disavow further PMOI activities; none is known to have been persecuted since returning.

In July 2004, the United States granted the Ashraf detainees "protected persons" status under the 4th Geneva Convention. However, the U.S.-led security mandate in Iraq was replaced on January 1, 2009, by a bilateral U.S.-Iraq agreement that limits U.S. flexibility in Iraq. Iraq now has sovereignty over Ashraf, which the United States recognizes. The residents are not protected persons under the 4th Geneva Convention, according to the Administration, although that it disputed by some scholars of international humanitarian law. Iraq has pledged the residents would not be extradited to Tehran or forcibly expelled as long as U.S. forces have a mandate to help secure Iraq.

The group has long feared that Iraqi control of the camp would lead to the expulsion of the group to Iran. The Iraqi government tried to calm those fears in January 2009 by saying that it would adhere to all international obligations not to do so, but that trust was lost on July 28, 2009, when Iraq used force to overcome resident resistance to setting up a police post in the camp. At least eleven residents of the Camp were killed. In December 2009, Iraq announced the group would be relocated to a detention center near Samawah, in southern Iraq; substantial resistance by the Ashraf residents is expected if and when Iraq attempts to implement that decision. No date has been set for the relocation. Secretary of State Clinton testified before the House Foreign Affairs Committee on February 25, 2010, that it is U.S. understanding that adequate food, fuel, and medical supplies are reaching camp residents. However, the ranking member of the House Foreign Affairs Committee cited reports that dispute that assertion during a November 18, 2010, hearing of the Committee on Iraq. The EU "de-listing," discussed above, might help resolve the issue by causing EU governments to take in those at Ashraf. H.Res. 704 deplores Iraqi government violence against Ashraf residents and calls on the U.S. government to "take all necessary and appropriate steps" to protect Ashraf residents in accordance with international law and U.S. treaty commitments. The Ashraf residents' fears have heightened as of June 10, 2010, when the U.S. military announced that full physical control over Ashraf would pass to the Iraqi Security Forces as of July 1, 2010. That transfer has occurred and the U.S. military post near the Camp has closed.

Pro-Monarchy Radical Groups

One issue that has arisen in 2010 is that a pro-monarchist armed group in Iran, called *Tondar* (Thunder)/Kingdom Assembly of Iran is accused of conducting attacks inside Iran. One attack, a bombing of a mosque in Shiraz that took place in April 2008, killed 14 Iranian worshippers, including some children. There are some allegations that Iranians living in California are directing the group's activities in Iran.

Ethnic or Religiously Based Armed Groups

Some armed groups are operating in Iran's border areas, and are generally composed of ethnic or religious minorities. These groups are not known to be cooperating with the mostly Persian members of the Green movement. One such group is *Jundullah*, composed of Sunni Muslims primarily from the Baluchistan region bordering Pakistan. Since mid-2008, it has conducted several successful attacks on Iranian security personnel, apparently including in May 2009, claiming revenge for the poor treatment of Sunnis in Iran. On October 18, 2009, it claimed responsibility for killing five Revolutionary Guard commanders during a meeting they were holding with local groups in Sistan va Baluchistan Province. The regime claimed a major victory against the group in late February 2010 by announcing the capture of Jundullah's top leader, Abdolmalek Rigi. The regime executed him in June 2010, and the group retaliated in July 2010 with a major bombing in Zahedan, which killed 28 persons, including some Revolutionary Guards. Secretary of State Clinton publicly condemned this bombing. On the grounds that the group has attacked civilians in the course of violent attacks in Iran, Jundallah was formally placed on the U.S. of Foreign Terrorist Organizations on November 3, 2010. Some saw the designation as an overture toward the Iranian government, while others saw it as a sign that the United States does not support ethnic or sectarian opposition groups that use violence, but only groups that are committed to peaceful protest. The group is believed responsible for a December 15, 2010, bombing at a mosque in Chahbahar, also in the Baluchistan region, that killed 38 persons.

An armed Kurdish group operating out of Iraq is the Free Life Party, known by its acronym PJAK. PJAK was designated in early February 2009 as a terrorism supporting entity under Executive Order 13224, although the designation statement indicated the decision was based mainly on PJAK's association with the Turkish Kurdish opposition group Kongra Gel, also known as the PKK. The five Kurds executed in May 2010 were alleged members of PJAK. In June 2010, Iran is reported to have conducted some shelling of reputed PJAK bases inside Iraq, reportedly killing some Kurdish civilians. Another militant group, the *Ahwazi Arabs*, operates in the largely Arab inhabited areas of southwest Iran, bordering Iraq.

OTHER HUMAN RIGHTS PRACTICES

International criticism of Iran's human rights practices predates and transcends the crackdown against the Green movement. **Table 3**, which discusses the regime's record on a number of human rights issues, is based largely on the latest State Department human rights report (for 2009, March 11, 2010) and State Department *International Religious Freedom* report (for 2009, October 26, 2009). These reports cite Iran for a wide range of serious abuses, including unjust executions, politically motivated abductions by security forces, torture, arbitrary arrest and detention, and arrests of women's rights activists. The State Department human rights report said the government's "poor human rights record degenerated during the year, particularly after the disputed June presidential elections." The report cited the regime's arrests, deaths in custody, and other abuses against the protesters. According to the State Department report, in August 2009 Iran's judiciary estimated that 4,000 oppositions had been detained; an unknown but significant number of oppositionists remain incarcerated.

A U.N. General Assembly resolution, finalized on December 18, 2008, by a vote of 69-54, called on Iran to allow visits by U.N. personnel investigating the status of human rights practices in Iran. The post-election crackdown on the Green movement was a focus of the U.N. four-year review of Iran's human rights record that took place in mid-February 2010 in Geneva. Despite the criticism, on April 29, 2010, Iran acceded to the U.N. Commission on the Status of Women, after earlier dropping its attempt to win a seat on the higher-profile U.N. General Assembly Human Rights Council. Still, on June 10, 2010, Iran was formally questioned by the U.N. Human Rights Council about its record. On November 19, 2010, by a vote of 74-48, with 59 countries abstaining, the General Assembly's "Third Committee" expressed "deep concern" about Iran's forms of punishments and other abuses. On September 29, 2010, President Obama, acting in accordance with Section 105 of P.L. 111-195, issued Executive Order 13553 sanctioning Iranian persons determined to have committed serious human right abuses subsequent to the Iranian presidential election.

Table 3. Human Rights Practices

Group/Issue	Regime Practice/Recent Developments
Ethnic and Religious Breakdown	Persians are about 51% of the population, and Azeris (a Turkic people) are about 24%. Kurds are about 7% of the population, and about 3% are Arab. Of religions, Shiite Muslims are about 90% of the Muslim population and Sunnis are about 10%. About 2% of the population is non-Muslim, including Christians, Zoroastrians (an ancient religion in what is now Iran), Jewish, and Baha'i.
Media Freedoms	Even before the election-related unrest, Iran's Ministry of Culture and Islamic Guidance had an active program of blocking pro-reform websites and blogs, and had closed hundreds of reformist newspapers, although many have tended to reopen under new names. In August 2007, the government closed a major reformist daily, Shargh, which had previously been suspended repeatedly. In February 2008, the regime closed the main women's magazine, Zanan ("women" in Farsi) for allegedly highlighting gender inequality in Islamic law. In November 2008, the regime arrested famed Iranian blogger Hossein Derakshan; reports in September 2010 say prosecutors are seeking a death sentence. Canadian journalist (of Iranian origin) Zahra Kazemi was detained in 2003 for filming outside Tehran's Evin prison and allegedly beaten to death in custody. The intelligence agent who conducted the offense was acquitted July 25, 2004.
Labor Restrictions	Independent unions are technically legal but not allowed in practice. The sole authorized national labor organization is a state-controlled "Workers' House" umbrella. However, some activists show independence and, in 2007, the regime arrested labor activists for teachers' associations, bus drivers' unions, and a bakery workers' union. A bus drivers union leader, Mansur Osanloo, has been in jail since July 2007. Some additional crackdown noted in November 2010 because of labor unrest caused by anticipation of the abolition of subsidies for staple goods.
Women	Regime strictly enforces requirement that women cover themselves in public, generally with a garment called a chador, including through detentions. In March 2007, the regime arrested 31 women activists who were protesting the arrest in 2006 of several other women's rights activists; all but 3 of the 31 were released by March 9. In May 2006, the Majles passed a bill calling for increased public awareness of Islamic dress; the bill did not contain a requirement that members of Iran's minority groups wear badges or distinctive clothing. Women can vote and run in parliamentary and municipal elections. Iranian women can drive, and many work outside the home, including owning their own businesses. There are nine women in the 290-seat Majles.

Table 3. (Continued).

Group/Issue	Regime Practice/Recent Developments
Religious Freedom	Each year since 1999, the State Department religious freedom report has named Iran as a "Country of Particular Concern" under the International Religious Freedom Act (IRFA). No sanctions have been added under IRFA, on the grounds that Iran is already subject to extensive U.S. sanctions. Continued deterioration in religious freedom noted in the International Religious Freedom report for 2010 (November 17, 2010), which stated that "Government rhetoric and actions created a threatening atmosphere for nearly all non-Shi'a religious groups.
Baha'is	Iran repeatedly cited for repression of the Baha'i community, which Iran's Shiite Muslim clergy views as a heretical sect. It numbers about 300,000-350,000. At least 30 Baha'is remain imprisoned. Several were sentenced to death in February 2010. Seven Baha'i leaders were sentenced to 20 years in August 2010, but their sentences were reduced in September 2010 to ten years. In the 1990s, several Baha'is were executed for apostasy (Bahman Samandari in 1992; Musa Talibi in 1996; and Ruhollah Ruhani in 1998). Another, Dhabihullah Mahrami, was in custody since 1995 and died of unknown causes in prison in December 2005. Virtually every year, congressional resolutions have condemned Iran's treatment of the Baha'is.
Jews	Along with Christians, a "recognized minority," with one seat in the Majles, the 30,000-member Jewish community (the largest in the Middle East aside from Israel) enjoys somewhat more freedoms than Jewish communities in several other Muslim states. However, in practice the freedom of Iranian Jews to practice their religion is limited, and Iranian Jews remain reluctant to speak out for fear of reprisals. During 1993-1998, Iran executed five Jews allegedly spying for Israel. In June 1999, Iran arrested 13 Jews (mostly teachers, shopkeepers, and butchers) from the Shiraz area that it said were part of an "espionage ring" for Israel. After an April-June 2000 trial, 10 of the Jews and two Muslim accomplices were convicted (July 1, 2000), receiving sentences ranging from 4 to 13 years. An appeals panel reduced the sentences, and all were released by April 2003. On November 17, 2008, Iran hanged businessman Ali Ashtari (a Muslim), who was arrested in 2006, for allegedly providing information on Iran's nuclear program to Israel.
Kurds/Other Sunni Muslims	The cited reports note other discrimination against Sufis and Sunni Muslims, although abuses against Sunnis could reflect that minority ethnicies, including Kurds, are mostly Sunnis. No reserved seats for Sunnis in the Majles but several are usually elected in their own right. Five Kurdish oppositionists executed in May 2010.
Human Trafficking	The June 14, 2010, (latest), State Department "Trafficking in Persons" report continues to place Iran in Tier 3 (worst level) for failing to take significant action to prevent trafficking in persons. Girls are trafficked for sexual exploitation within Iran and from Iran to neighboring countries.
Executions Policy	Human rights groups say executions have increased sharply since the dispute over the June 2009 election. Iran executed six persons under the age of 18 in 2008, the only country to do so. As a party to the International Covenant on Civil and Political Rights and the Convention on the Rights of the Child, Iran is obligated to abolish such executions.

Iran: U.S. Concerns and Policy Responses

Table 3. (Continued).

Group/Issue	Regime Practice/Recent Developments
Stonings	In 2002, the head of Iran's judiciary issued a ban on stoning. However, Iranian officials later called that directive "advisory" and could be ignored by individual judges. On December 2, 2008, Iran confirmed the stoning deaths of two men in Mashhad who were convicted of adultery. A sentence of stoning against a 45-year old woman (Sakineh Ashtiani) convicted of adultery and assisting in the murder of her husband was set aside for further review in July 2010. Brazil has offered her asylum. She reportedly was lashed in August 2010, and she reportedly may face execution by hanging, although perhaps not by stoning.
Azeris	Azeris are one quarter of the population, but they complain of ethnic and linguistic discrimination. In 2008, there were several arrests of Azeri students and cultural activists who were pressing for their right to celebrate their culture and history.
Arrests of Dual Nationals and Foreign Nationals	An Iranian-American journalist, Roxanna Saberi, was arrested in January 2009 allegedly because her press credentials had expired; was charged on April 9, 2009, with espionage for possessing an Iranian military document. Sentenced to eight years in jail, she was released on appeal on May 12, 2009, and left Iran. Another dual national, Esha Momeni, arrested in October 2008, is unable to leave Iran. U.S. national, former FBI agent Robert Levinson, remains missing after a visit in 2005 to Kish Island. Iran was given a U.S. letter on these cases at a March 31, 2009, meeting in the Netherlands on Afghanistan. Three American hikers were arrested in August 2009 after crossing into Iran, possibly mistakenly, from a hike in northern Iraq. Families say two of the hikers having health problems. The mothers visited the hikers during May 20-21, 2010, but left Iran with their children still incarcerated. On September 15, 2010, after Sara Shourd reported possible health issues, she was released on $500,000 bail, and her departure was brokered by Oman. Her fiancé, Shane Bauer, and Josh Fattal, remain incarcerated and were to go on trial beginning November 5, 2010, but now scheduled for February 6, 2011. In response to criticism about the holding of the three hikers, Ahmadinejad has claimed the United States should release eight Iranian nationals held in the United States (for alleged sanctions violations). An ailing 72 year old Iranian-American, Reza Taghavi, was incarcerated since May 2008, but was released in October 2010 when the regime judged him not a threat to Iranian security. While on a visit to Iran, he delivered a small amount of funds from an Iranian-American to this person's relative in Iran who, unbeknownst to Taghavi, was part of the Tondar group, mentioned above.

Sources: Most recent State Department reports on human rights (March 11, 2010), trafficking in persons (June 14, 2010), and on religious freedom (November 17, 2010). httpi/www.state.gov.

IRAN'S STRATEGIC CAPABILITIES AND WEAPONS OF MASS DESTRUCTION PROGRAMS

Many in the Obama Administration view Iran, as the Bush Administration did, as one of the key national security challenges facing the United States.[9] This assessment is based largely on Iran's weapons of mass destruction (WMD) programs and its ability to exert influence in the region counter to U.S. objectives.[10] Many experts agree that Iran's core national security goals are to protect itself from foreign, primarily U.S., interference or attack, and to exert regional influence that Iran believes is commensurate with its size and concept of nationhood. A nuclear armed Iran, in the view of many experts, would be more assertive than it now is in supporting countries and movements that oppose U.S. interests and allies because Iran would likely conclude that the United States would hesitate to take military action against a nuclear power.

Conventional Military/Revolutionary Guard/Qods Force

Iran's armed forces are extensive but they are widely considered relatively combat ineffective in a head-on confrontation against a well-trained, sophisticated military such as that of the United States or even a major regional power such as Turkey. Iran is believed to largely lack the logistical ability to project power much beyond its borders. Still, Iranian forces could cause damage to U.S. forces and allies in the Gulf region, and they are sufficiently effective to deter or fend off conventional threats from Iran's weaker neighbors such as post-war Iraq, Turkmenistan, Azerbaijan, and Afghanistan. Iran's armed forces have few formal relationships with foreign militaries, but Iran and India have a "strategic dialogue" and some Iranian naval officers reportedly have undergone some training in India. Iran and Turkey agreed in principle in April 2008 to jointly fight terrorism along their border. Most of Iran's other military-to-military relationships, such as with Russia, Ukraine, Belarus, North Korea, and a few others, generally center on Iranian arms purchases or upgrades (although such activity is now banned by U.N. Resolution 1929 of June 2010). This assessment was presented in the Defense Department's mandated *Unclassified Report on Military Power of Iran* released in April 2010.[11]

Iran's armed forces are divided organizationally. The Islamic Revolutionary Guard Corps (IRGC, known in Persian as the *Pasdaran*)[12] controls the *Basij* (Mobilization of the Oppressed) volunteer militia that enforces adherence to Islamic customs and has been the main instrument to repress the postelection protests in Iran. The IRGC and the regular military report to a joint headquarters, headed by Dr. Hassan Firuzabadi.

Table 4. Iran's Conventional Military Arsenal

Military Personnel	Tanks	Surface-Air Missiles	Combat Aircraft	Ships	Defense Budget (billions U.S. $)
460,000+. Regular ground force is about 220,000, Revolutionary Guard Corps (IRGC) ground force is about 130,000. Remainder are regular and IRGC navy (18,000 and 20,000 personnel respectively) and Air Forces (52,000 regular Air Force personnel and 5,000 Guard Air Force personnel.) About 12,000 air defense.	1,800+ (incl. 480 T-72)	150+ I-Hawk plus some Stinger	330+ (incl. 25 MiG-29 and 30 Su-24). Still dependent on U.S. F-4's, F-5's and F-14 bought during Shah's era.	100+ (IRGC and regular Navy) (incl. 4 Corvette; 18 IRGC-controlled Chinese-made Hudong, 40 Boghammer) Also has 3 Kilo subs (reg. Navy controlled)	About $10.00 billion (2008-9), about 2.8% of GDP

Table 5. The Revolutionary Guard

The IRGC is generally loyal to Iran's hardliners politically and is clearly more politically influential than is Iran's regular military, which is numerically larger, but was held over from the Shah's era. IRGC influence has grown sharply as the regime has relied on it to suppress dissent to the point where Secretary of State Clinton sees it as wielding preponderant influence. As described in a 2009 Rand Corporation study," Founded by a decree from Ayatollah Khomeini shortly after the victory of the 1978-1979 Islamic Revolution, Iran's Islamic Revolutionary Guards Corps (IRGC) has evolved well beyond its original foundations as an ideological guard for the nascent revolutionary regime. Today the IRGC functions as an expansive socio-political-economic conglomerate whose influence extends into virtually every corner of Iranian political life and society. Bound together by the shared experience of war and the socialization of military service, the Pasdaran have articulated a populist, authoritarian, and assertive vision for the Islamic Republic of Iran that they maintain is a more faithful reflection of the revolution's early ideals. The IRGC's presence is particularly powerful in Iran's highly factionalized political system, in which [many senior figures] hail from the ranks of the IRGC. Outside the political realm, the IRGC oversees a robust apparatus of media resources, training activities, education programs designed to bolster loyalty to the regime, prepare the citizenry for homeland defense, and burnish its own institutional credibility vis-à-vis other factional actors."

Through its Qods (Jerusalem) Force, the IRGC has a foreign policy role in exerting influence throughout the region by supporting pro-Iranian movements, as discussed further below. The Qods Force numbers approximately 10,000- 15,000 personnel who provide advice, support, and arrange weapons deliveries to pro-Iranian factions in Lebanon, Iraq, Persian Gulf states, Gaza/West Bank, Afghanistan, and Central Asia. It also operates a worldwide intelligence network to give Iran possible terrorist option and to assist in procurement of WMD-related technology. The Qods Force commander, Brigadier General Qassem Soleimani, is said to have his own independent channel to Supreme Leader Khamene'i, bypassing the IRGC and Joint Staff command structure. The Qods Force commander during 1988- 1995 was Brigadier General Ahmad Vahidi, confirmed as defense minister on September 3, 2009. He led the Qods Force when it allegedly assisted two bombings of Israeli and Jewish targets in Buenos Aires (he is wanted by Interpol for a role in the 1994 bombing there); recruited Saudi Hezbollah activists later accused of the June 1996 Khobar Towers bombing; and assassinated Iranian dissident leaders in Europe in the early 1990s.

IRGC leadership developments are significant because of the political influence of the IRGC. On September 2, 2007, Khamene'i replaced Rahim Safavi with Mohammad Ali Jafari as commander in chief of the Guard; Jafari is considered a hardliner against political dissent and is reputedly close to the Supreme Leader and less so to Ahmadinejad. The *Basij* reports to the IRGC commander in chief; its leadership was changed in October 2009, to Brigadier General Mohammad Reza Naqdi (replacing Hossein Taeb). It operates from thousands of positions in Iran's institutions. Command reshuffles in July 2008 integrated the Basij more closely with provincially based IRGC units; furthered the view that the Basij is playing a more active role in internal security. In November 2009, the regime gave the IRGC's intelligence units greater authority, perhaps surpassing those of the Ministry of Intelligence, in monitoring dissent, an apparent response to the Green movement. The IRGC Navy now has responsibility to patrol the entire Persian Gulf, and the regular Navy is patrolling the Strait of Hormuz. More information on how the Iranian military might perform against the United States is discussed later.

As noted, the IRGC is also increasingly involved in Iran's economy, acting through a network of contracting businesses it has set up, most notably *Ghorb* (also called *Khatem ol-Anbiya*, Persian for "Seal of the Prophet"). Active duty IRGC senior commanders reportedly serve on Ghorb's board of directors. In September 2009, the Guard bought a 50% stake in Iran Telecommunication Company at a cost of $7.8 billion. In the past five years, Guard affiliated firms have won 750 oil and gas and construction contracts, and the Guard has its own civilian port facilities.

However, questions arose about the IRGC firms' capabilities in July 2010 when *Ghorb* pulled out of a contract to develop part of the large South Pars gas field, citing the impact of expanded U.S. and international sanctions (which might have caused foreign partner firms to refuse to cooperate with *Ghorb*). On October 21, 2007, the Treasury Department designated several IRGC companies as proliferation entities under Executive Order 13382. Also that day, the IRGC as a whole, the Ministry of Defense, several IRGC commanders, and several Iranian banks were sanctioned under that same executive order. Simultaneously, the Qods Force was named as a terrorism supporting entity under Executive Order 13224. These orders freeze the U.S.-based assets and prevent U.S. transactions with the named entities, but these entities are believed to have virtually no U.S.-based assets. **Sources:** Frederic Wehrey et al. "The Rise of the Pasdaran." Rand Corporation. 2009. Katzman, Kenneth. "The Warriors of Islam: Iran's Revolutionary Guard." Westview Press, 1993.

Nuclear Program and Related International Diplomacy

The United States and its partners accept Iran's right to pursue peaceful uses of nuclear energy, but they have sought, without success to date, to induce Iran to verifiably demonstrate that its nuclear program is for only those purposes. According to the February 2, 2010, annual intelligence community threat assessment, Iran "is keeping open the option to develop nuclear weapons in part by developing various nuclear capabilities that bring it closer to being able to produce such weapons, should it choose to do so." This assessment, reportedly reiterated by an intelligence report of March 3, 2010,[13] was foreshadowed on September 25, 2009, when President Obama and French and British leaders publicized long-standing information that Iran is developing a uranium enrichment site on a Revolutionary Guard base at Fordo, near Qom, that appears unsuitable for purely civilian use. This, and other findings contained in International Atomic Energy Agency (IAEA) reports of February 18, 2010, May 31, 2010, September 6, 2010,[14] and November 23, 2010,[15] call into question Iran's assertions that it does not have a nuclear *weapons* program. Several IAEA reports (January 31, 2006; February 27, 2006; May 26, 2008; and September 15, 2008) describe Iranian documents that show a possible involvement of Iran's military in the program.

Estimates differ as to when Iran might achieve a nuclear weapons capability if there were a decision to pursue that course. U.S. officials, possibly basing their comments on a reported new draft National Intelligence Estimate, (NIE), say that this might be achieved in "3-5 years" from April 2010 if there were a decision to acquire a nuclear weapons capability, and with no indications that such a decision has been made in Iran.[16]

Iranian Recent Nuclear Activities

International scrutiny of Iran's nuclear program intensified in late 2002, when Iran confirmed PMOI allegations that Iran was building two facilities that could potentially be used to produce fissile material useful for a nuclear weapon: a uranium enrichment facility at Natanz and a heavy water production plant at Arak,[17] considered ideal for the production of plutonium. It was revealed in 2003 that the founder of Pakistan's nuclear weapons program, A.Q. Khan, sold Iran nuclear technology and designs.[18]

The Obama Administration faces policy choices in light of a judgment based on the September 6, 2010, IAEA reports that Iran has now enriched enough uranium for two nuclear weapons (if enriched to 90%). Most of Iran's enrichment thus far has been primarily to less that 5%, which is a level that would permit only civilian uses, but it has enriched some to the 20% level, which is necessary for medical use but also shows Iran's capability to enrich to ever higher levels. The November 23, 2010, report by the International Atomic Energy Agency (IAEA) said that Iran's program has encountered technical difficulties but that Iran continued to expand its stockpile of low-enriched uranium.[19] There continues to be no evidence that Iran has diverted any nuclear material for a nuclear weapons program, although the September 6, 2010, IAEA report said Iran has impeded access by some of the agency's inspectors and has broken some seals on controlled material. As noted, Iran has arrested some of its technicians for alleged spying for the West, and a computer virus (Stuxnet) in September-October 2010 appeared to target Iranian nuclear facility computers by altering their spin rate. As noted, a nuclear scientist was killed in an unexplained bombing in Tehran on November 28, 2010.

Iran's Arguments

Iranian leaders assert that Iran's nuclear program is for electricity generation, given finite oil and gas resources, and that enrichment is its "right" as a party to the 1968 Nuclear Non-Proliferation Treaty.[20] An analysis was published by the National Academy of Sciences challenging the U.S. view that Iran is petroleum rich and therefore has no need for a nuclear power program. According to the analysis, the relative lack of investment could cause Iran to have negligible exports of oil by 2015.[21] U.S. officials have said that Iran's gas resources make nuclear energy unnecessary. Iran professes that WMD is inconsistent with its ideology and says that its leaders, including the late Ayatollah Khomeini, have issued formal pronouncements (*fatwas*) that nuclear weapons are un-Islamic.

Iran's assertions of a purely peaceful program are met with widespread skepticism, not only because of the activities discussed above but also because Iran's governing factions perceive a nuclear weapons capability as a means of ending Iran's perceived historic vulnerability to invasion and domination by great powers, and as a symbol of Iran as a major nation. Others believe a nuclear weapon represents the instrument with which Iran intends to intimidate its neighbors and dominate the Persian Gulf region. There are also fears Iran might transfer WMD to extremist groups or countries.

On the other hand, some Iranian strategists agree with U.S. assertions that a nuclear weapon will not deliver Iran absolute security, but will instead make Iran less secure. According to this view, moving toward a nuclear weapons capability will bring Iran further sanctions, military containment, U.S. attempted interference in Iran, and efforts by neighbors to develop countervailing capabilities. Some members of the domestic opposition, such as Musavi, have positions on the nuclear issue similar to those of regime leaders, but several

Green movement factions see the nuclear program as an impediment to eventual reintegration with the West and might be willing to significantly limit the program.

U.S. officials have generally been less concerned with Russia's work, under a January 1995 contract, on an $800 million nuclear power plant at Bushehr. Russia insisted that Iran sign an agreement under which Russia would reprocess the plant's spent nuclear material; that agreement was signed on February 28, 2005. The plant was expected to become operational in 2007, but Russia had insisted that Iran first comply with the U.N. resolutions discussed below. In December 2007, Russia began fueling the reactor. Some tests of the plant began in February 2009, but Russia appeared to delay opening it to pressure Iran on the broader nuclear issue. However, the plant was fueled by Russia and inaugurated on August 21, 2010, and fueling was completed by October 25, 2010. It is scheduled to be operational as of January 2011. As part of this work, Russia has trained 1,500 Iranian nuclear engineers.

The International Response
The international response to Iran's nuclear program has evolved into a growing global consensus to apply substantial pressure on Iran—coupled with incentives and diplomacy—to limit its program.

Diplomatic Efforts in 2003 and 2004/Paris Agreement
In 2003, France, Britain, and Germany (the "EU-3") opened a separate diplomatic track to curb Iran's program. On October 21, 2003, Iran pledged, in return for peaceful nuclear technology, to (1) fully disclose its past nuclear activities, (2) to sign and ratify the "Additional Protocol" to the NPT (allowing for enhanced inspections), and (3) to suspend uranium enrichment activities. Iran signed the Additional Protocol on December 18, 2003, although the *Majles* has not ratified it. Iran discontinued abiding by the Protocol after the IAEA reports of November 10, 2003, and February 24, 2004, stated that Iran had violated its NPT reporting obligations over an 18-year period.

In the face of the U.S. threat to push for Security Council action, the EU-3 and Iran reached a more specific November 14, 2004, "Paris Agreement," committing Iran to suspend uranium enrichment (which it did as of November 22, 2004) in exchange for renewed trade talks and other aid.[22] The Bush Administration did not openly support the track until March 11, 2005, when it announced it would drop U.S. objections to Iran applying to join the World Trade Organization (it applied in May 2005) and to selling civilian aircraft parts to Iran. The Bush Administration did not participate directly in the talks.

Reference to the Security Council
The Paris Agreement broke down just after Ahmadinejad's election; Iran rejected as insufficient an EU-3 offer to assist Iran with peaceful uses of nuclear energy and provide limited security guarantees in exchange for Iran's (1) permanently ending uranium enrichment; (2) dismantling the Arak heavy-water reactor;[23] (3) no-notice nuclear inspections; and (4) a pledge not to leave the NPT (it has a legal exit clause). On August 8, 2005, Iran broke the IAEA seals and began uranium "conversion" (one step before enrichment) at its Esfahan facility. On September 24, 2005, the IAEA Board declared Iran in non-compliance with the NPT and decided to refer the issue to the Security Council,[24] but no time frame was set for the referral. After Iran resumed enrichment activities, on February 4, 2006, the IAEA board voted 27-3[25] to refer the case to the Security Council. On March 29, 2006, the Council

agreed on a presidency "statement" setting a 30-day time limit (April 28, 2006) for ceasing enrichment.[26]

Establishment of "P5+1" Contact Group/June 2006 Incentive Package

Taking a multilateral approach, the George W. Bush Administration offered on May 31, 2006, to join the nuclear talks with Iran if Iran first suspends its uranium enrichment. Such talks would center on a package of incentives and possible sanctions—formally agreed on June 1, 2006—by a newly formed group of nations, the so-called "Permanent Five Plus 1" (P5+1: United States, Russia, China, France, Britain, and Germany). EU representative Javier Solana formally presented the P5+1 offer to Iran on June 6, 2006. (The package is Annex I to Resolution 1747.)

Incentives:

- Negotiations on an EU-Iran trade agreements and acceptance of Iran into the World Trade Organization.
- Easing of U.S. sanctions to permit sales to Iran of commercial aircraft/parts.
- Sale to Iran of a light-water nuclear reactor and guarantees of nuclear fuel (including a five-year buffer stock of fuel), and possible sales of light-water research reactors for medicine and agriculture applications.
- An "energy partnership" between Iran and the EU, including help for Iran to modernize its oil and gas sector and to build export pipelines.
- Support for a regional security forum for the Persian Gulf, and support for the objective of a WMD free zone for the Middle East.
- The possibility of eventually allowing Iran to resume uranium enrichment if it complies with all outstanding IAEA requirements.

Sanctions:[27]

- Denial of visas for Iranians involved in Iran's nuclear program and for high-ranking Iranian officials.
- A freeze of assets of Iranian officials and institutions; a freeze of Iran's assets abroad; and a ban on some financial transactions.
- A ban on sales of advanced technology and of arms to Iran; and a ban on sales to Iran of gasoline and other refined oil products.
- An end to support for Iran's application to the WTO.

First Set of U.N. Security Council Resolutions Adopted

Iran did not immediately respond to the offer. In response, the U.N. Security Council began its efforts, still ongoing, to impose sanctions on Iran in an effort to shift Iran's calculations toward compromise.

- *Resolution 1696.* On July 31, 2006, the Security Council voted 14-1 (Qatar voting no) for U.N. Security Council Resolution 1696, giving Iran until August 31, 2006, to fulfill the long-standing IAEA nuclear demands (enrichment suspension, etc.). Purportedly in deference to Russia and China, it was passed under Article 40 of the U.N. Charter, which makes compliance mandatory, but not under Article 41, which refs to economic sanctions, or Article 42, which would authorize military action. It called on U.N. member states not to sell Iran WMD-useful technology. On August 22, 2006, Iran responded, but Iran did not offer enrichment suspension, instead offering vague proposals of engagement with the West.

- *Resolution 1737.* With the backing of the P5+1, chief EU negotiator Javier Solana negotiated with Iran to try arrange a temporary enrichment suspension, but talks ended on September 28, 2006, without agreement. The Security Council adopted U.N. Security Council Resolution 1737 unanimously on December 23, 2006, under Chapter 7, Article 41 of the U.N. Charter. It prohibits sale to Iran— or financing of such sale—of technology that could contribute to Iran's uranium enrichment or heavy-water reprocessing activities. It also required U.N. member states to freeze the financial assets of 10 named Iranian nuclear and missile firms and 12 persons related to those programs. It called on—but did not mandate— member states not to permit travel by these persons. In deference to Russia, the Resolution did not apply to the Bushehr reactor.

- *Resolution 1747.* Resolution 1737 demanded enrichment suspension by February 21, 2007. With no Iranian compliance, on March 24, 2007, after only three weeks of P5+1 negotiations, Resolution 1747 was adopted unanimously, which demanded Iran suspend enrichment by May 24, 2007, and:
  - added 10 military/WMD-related entities, 3 Revolutionary Guard entities, 7 Revolutionary Guard commanders, 8 other persons, and Bank Sepah.
  - banned arms transfers by Iran, a provision targeted at Iran's alleged arms supplies to Lebanese Hezbollah and to Shiite militias in Iraq.
  - required all countries to report to the United Nations when sanctioned Iranian persons travel to their territories.
  - called for (but did not require) countries to avoid selling arms or dual use items to Iran and for countries and international financial institutions to avoid any new lending or grants to Iran. The Resolution specifically exempted loans for humanitarian purposes, thereby not applying to World Bank loans.
  - Iran did not comply with Resolution 1747, but, in August 2007, it agreed to sign with the IAEA an agreement to clear up outstanding questions on past nuclear activities by the end of 2007. On September 28, 2007, the P5+1 grouping—along with the EU itself—agreed to a joint statement pledging to negotiate another sanctions resolution if there is no progress reported by the IAEA in implementing the August 2007 agreement or in negotiations with EU representative Javier Solana. The IAEA and Solana indicated that Iran's responses fell short; Solana described a November 30, 2007, meeting with Iranian negotiator Sayid Jallili as "disappointing."

- *Resolution 1803 and Additional Incentives for Iran.* After several months of negotiations, Resolution 1803 was adopted by a vote of 14-0 (Indonesia abstaining) on March 3, 2008. It:
  - banned virtually all sales of dual use items to Iran, citing equipment listed as dual use in various proliferation conventions and documents;
  - authorized, but did not require, inspections of shipments by Iran Air Cargo and Islamic Republic of Iran Shipping Line, if such shipments are suspected of containing banned WMD-related goods;

- imposed a firm travel ban on five Iranians named in Annex II to the Resolution and requires reports on international travel by 13 individuals named in Annex I;
- called for, but did not impose, a prohibition on financial transactions with Iran's Bank Melli and Bank Saderat;
- added 12 entities to those sanctioned under Resolution 1737;
- stated the willingness of the P5+1 to consider additional incentives to resolve the Iranian nuclear issue through negotiation "beyond those of June 2006.

- The Bush Administration agreed to expand the June 2006 incentive package at a meeting in London on May 2, 2008, offering to add political cooperation and enhanced energy cooperation for Iran. EU envoy Solana presented the package (which included a signature by Secretary of State Rice) on June 14, 2008, but Iran was non-committal. (The text of the enhanced incentive offer to Iran is contained in an Annex to Resolution 1929.)
- Iran did not accept the enhanced package of incentives as a basis of further discussion but, in July 2008, Iran indicated it might be ready to first accept a six week "freeze for freeze:" the P5+1 would freeze further sanctions efforts and Iran would freeze any expansion of uranium enrichment (though not suspend outright). To try to take advantage of this opening, the Bush Administration sent Under Secretary of State for Political Affairs William Burns to join Solana and the other P5+1 representatives at a meeting in Geneva on July 19, 2008. Iran did not accept the "freeze for freeze" by an extended deadline of August 2, 2008.
- *Resolution 1835.* As a result of the lack of progress, the P5+1 began discussing another sanctions resolution. However, the August 2008 crisis between Russia and Georgia contributed to Russia's opposing new U.N. sanctions on Iran. In an effort to demonstrate to Iran continued unity, the Council adopted Resolution 1835 (September 27, 2008), calling on Iran to comply with previous resolutions, but restating a willingness to negotiate and imposing no new sanctions.
- The P5+1 met again in October and in November of 2008, but U.S. partner officials were uncertain about what U.S. policy toward Iran might be under a new U.S. Administration. No consensus on additional sanctions was reached.

The International Response under the Obama Administration

After President Obama was inaugurated, the P5+1 met in Germany (February 4, 2009), reportedly focusing on the new Administration's approach on Iran. The other members of the P5+1 sought to incorporate the Administration's commitment to direct U.S. engagement with Iran into the U.N. sanctions and negotiating framework. The meeting recommitted to the "two track" strategy of incentives and sanctions.[28] At another P5+1 meeting in London on April 8, 2009, Under Secretary Burns told the other members of the group that, henceforth, a U.S. diplomat would attend all of the group's meetings with Iran. Iran put off new meetings until after its Iranian June 12, 2009, election.[29] The P5+1 did not materially alter its approach because of the unrest in Iran that erupted after that election, and a July 9, 2009, G-8 summit statement, which included Russian concurrence, mentioned late September 2009 (G-20 summit on September 24) as a time by which the P5+1 would expect Iran to attend new talks and offer constructive proposals, lest the P5+1 consider imposing "crippling sanctions" on Iran.

Sensing pressure, on September 1, 2009, Iran's senior negotiator, Sayid Jallili, said Iran would come to new talks. On September 9, 2009, Iran distributed its long-anticipated proposals to settle the nuclear issue to P5+1 representatives in Iran (the Swiss ambassador represented the United States).[30] The Iranian proposals were criticized as vague, but the P5+1 considered it a sufficient basis to meet with Iran in Geneva on October 1, 2009.

October 1, 2009, Agreement on Reprocessing Iran's Enriched Uranium
In light of September 25, 2009, revelations about the previously unreported Iranian nuclear site, little progress was expected at the meeting. However, the seven-hour session, in which U.S. Under Secretary of State William Burns, representing the United States, also met privately with Iranian negotiator Sayed Jallili, resulted in tentative agreements to (1) meet again later in October; (2) allow the IAEA to inspect the newly revealed Iranian facility near Qom; and (3) allow Russia and France, subject to technical talks to begin by mid-October, to reprocess 2,600 pounds (about 75% of Iran's low-enriched uranium) for medical use. (The Qom facility was inspected during October 25-29, 2009, as agreed.)

The technical talks were held October 19-21, 2009, at IAEA headquarters in Vienna, Austria, and chaired on the U.S. side by Deputy Energy Secretary Daniel Poneman. A draft agreement was approved by the P5+1 countries and the IAEA. Despite Ahmadinejad's comments in early February 2010 that he "did not have a problem" with the arrangement, Iran did not formally accept the draft, instead floating counter-proposals to ship its enriched uranium to France and Russia in increments, to ship the uranium to Turkey, or to reprocess the uranium in Iran itself.

Iran-Brazil-Turkey Uranium Exchange Deal ("Tehran Declaration")
All of Iran's counter-proposals were deemed insufficiently specific or responsive to meet P5+1 demands. Iran also rebuffed a specific U.S. proposal in January 2010 to allow it to buy on the open market isotopes for its medical reactor. However, as international discussions of new sanctions accelerated in April 2010, Brazil and Turkey negotiated with Iran to revive the October 1, 2009, arrangement. On May 17, 2010, with the president of Brazil and prime minister of Turkey in Tehran, the three signed an arrangement for Iran to send 2,600 pounds of uranium to Turkey, which would be exchanged for medically useful reprocessed uranium along the lines discussed in October 2009.[31] As required by the agreement, Iran forwarded to the IAEA a formal letter accepting the agreement terms. Even though some assert that the Obama Administration quietly supported the Brazil-Turkey initiative, the Obama Administration did not accept the Tehran Declaration, asserting that the amount of enriched uranium to be reprocessed does not therefore preclude enrichment of enough uranium for a nuclear weapon and did not address Iran's enrichment to the 20% level.

Resolution 1929 and EU Follow-Up
On May 18, 2010, one day after the signing of the Tehran Declaration, Secretary of State Clinton announced that the P5+1 had reached agreement on a new sanctions resolution. The resolution reflects a compromise designed to attract support from Russia and China, which believe sanctions might threaten their own interests in Iran, while also giving U.S. allies authority to take substantial new measures against Iran. It largely met the insistence of Russia and China that new sanctions not target Iran's civilian economy or its population, although it does provide authority for those countries that want to limit banking or other corporate

relationships with Iran. During the negotiations, China received U.S. briefings on the likely adverse implications for the oil market if Iran's nuclear program proceeds apace. China was also reportedly reassured that the UAE and Saudi Arabia would compensate for Iran's oil exports to China if Iran cut off supplies to retaliate for China's support for new sanctions.[32] Simultaneously with Russian agreement on the draft, several Russian entities, including the main state arms export agency Rosoboronexport, were removed from U.S. lists of sanctioned entities. (See CRS Report RS20871, *Iran Sanctions* for a table of entities under sanction.)

The main points of the draft, which was adopted on June 9, 2010 (Resolution 1929), by a vote of 12-2 (Turkey and Brazil) with one abstention (Lebanon) are:[33]

- It adds 15 Iranian firms affiliated with the Revolutionary Guard firms to the list of U.N.-sanctioned entities, although some of these firms are alternate names for the *Khatem ol-Anbiya* (Seal of the Prophet) engineering firm under Guard control. Twenty-two other Iranian entities, including the "First East Export Bank," and one individual, AEIO head Javad Rahiqi, were also added to the list.
- It makes mandatory a ban on travel for Iranian persons named in it and in previous resolutions—including those Iranians for whom there was a nonbinding travel ban in previous resolutions.
- It gives countries the authorization to inspect any shipments—and to dispose of their cargo—if the shipments are suspected to carry contraband items. However, inspections on the high seas are subject to concurrence by the country that owns that ship. This provision is modeled after a similar provision imposed on North Korea, which did cause that country to reverse some of its shipments.
- It prohibits countries from allowing Iran to invest in uranium mining and related nuclear technologies, or nuclear-capable ballistic missile technology.
- It bans sales to Iran of most categories of heavy arms and requests restraint in sales of light arms, but does not bar sales of missiles not on the "U.N. Registry of Conventional Arms" (meaning that the delivery of the S-300 system, discussed above, would not be banned).
- It requires countries to insist that their companies refrain from doing business with Iran *if* there is reason to believe that such business could further Iran's WMD programs.
- It requests, but does not mandate, that countries prohibit Iranian banks to open in their countries, or for their banks to open in Iran, *if* doing so could contribute to Iran's WMD activities.
- The resolution sets up a "panel of experts," which the Obama Administration announced on June 10 would be chaired by longtime arms control official Robert Einhorn. The panel is to assess the effect of the resolution and previous Iran resolutions, and suggest ways of more effective implementation.
- The resolution did not require a ban on investment in Iranian bond offerings; insurance for transport contracts for shipments involving Iran; international investment in Iran's energy sector; or the provision of trade credits to Iran.

President Obama, in a statement, said Resolution 1929 "will put in place the toughest sanctions ever faced by the Iranian government,"[34] but he and other senior officials noted that the intent of Resolution 1929 was to bring Iran back to the bargaining table. The annex to the resolution reinforced that point by presenting a modified offer of incentives for Iran to rejoin the international community. The subsequent adoption on July 27, 2010, by the European Union to use many of the authorities of the Resolution and impose major new sanctions against Iran (for example banning export credit and credit guarantees, as well as investment in and supplies to Iran's energy sector) led to new assessments by experts that the sanctions are exerting substantial pressure on Iran that could induce new Iranian flexibility. That assessment was reinforced by similar sanctions announcements in September 2010 by Japan and South Korea. The sanctions by these countries followed the signature by President Obama on U.S. sanctions legislation that primarily seeks to stop sales of gasoline and oil refinery equipment to Iran (Comprehensive Iran Sanctions, Accountability, and Divestment Act of 2010, P.L. 111-195). More detail on sanctions against Iran and the effect of them is in CRS Report RS20871, *Iran Sanctions*, by Kenneth Katzman.

On the other hand, press reports in October 2010 point to some leakage in the sanctions. The Obama Administration reportedly has concluded that Chinese firms, possibly acting without Chinese government knowledge, may still be aiding Iran's nuclear and missile programs.[35] Other reports say Iran is able to use small front companies in many countries to help it illicitly import spare parts for its arsenal.

Most Recent Diplomatic Developments

After the passage of Resolution 1929, EU foreign policy chief Baroness Catherine Ashton issued a letter to Iran inviting it to attend new talks. Iran's chief nuclear negotiator Seyed Jallili responded on July 6, 2010, by letter, saying that Iran might welcome new talks after the Ramadan observance, which would end in mid-September 2010, although his letter indicated Iran might want to raise broader issues beyond just the nuclear question. Iran subsequently took the position that any new talks should take place with the "Vienna Group" (Russia, France, and the United States) that were the pivotal countries that would have implemented the October 1, 2009 agreement to reprocess Iran's enriched uranium. Iran also wanted Brazil and Turkey, the two countries that orchestrated the "Tehran Declaration," to attend any new meetings between Iran and the Vienna Group. Upon his arrival at the U.N. General Assembly in New York on September 20, 2010, Ahmadinejad said on September 24 that Iran might consider ceasing enrichment to the 20% level (although not all enrichment). The P5+1 countries met on September 22 to urge Iran to come back to the bargaining table and EU foreign affairs chief Ashton (on October 14) sent a new invitation to Iran for talks with the P5+1, although the meeting would be between Iran and the P5+1, not the smaller "Vienna Group." Ashton's letter did imply that Iran could raise issues beyond the nuclear issue at the meetings.

Iran did accept talks during December 6-7, 2010, with the P5+1, in Geneva. By all accounts, the meeting made little progress on core issues. The United States and Iran did not, as they did in the October 2009 talks, hold direct bilateral talks during the two days of meetings. Iran reportedly focused on complaints about "unfair" treatment by the international community and the purported "double standard" that allow Israel to go unpunished for its reputed nuclear weapons arsenal.

Still, there was agreement to hold additional talks in Turkey in January 2011, which some say might lead Iran to show more flexibility, in light of Turkey's apparent willingness to take Iran's viewpoints into account. However, as evidence of the lack of progress in the Geneva talks, White House adviser on non-proliferation Gary Samore said at a public forum on

December 10. 2010 that the United States and its allies might discuss further sanctions to compel Iran into more flexibility.

Table 6. Summary of Provisions of U.N. Resolutions on Iran Nuclear Program (1737, 1747, 1803, and 1929)

Requires Iran to suspend uranium enrichment.

Prohibits transfer to Iran of nuclear, missile, and dual use items, except for use in light-water reactors. Prohibits Iran from exporting arms or WMD-useful technology.

Prohibits Iran from investing abroad in uranium mining, related nuclear technologies or nuclear capable ballistic missile technology.

Freezes the assets of over 80 named Iranian persons and entities, including Bank Sepah, and several corporate affiliates of the Revolutionary Guard.

Requires that countries ban the travel of over 40 named Iranians. Mandates that countries not export major combat systems to Iran.

Calls for "vigilance" (a non-binding call to cut off business) with respect to all Iranian banks, particularly Bank Melli and Bank Saderat.

Calls for vigilance (voluntary restraint) with respect to providing international lending to Iran and providing trade credits and other financing and financial interactions.

Calls on countries to inspect cargoes carried by Iran Air Cargo and Islamic Republic of Iran Shipping Lines—or by any ships in national or international waters—if there are indications they carry cargo banned for carriage to Iran. Searches in international waters would require concurrence of the country where the ship is registered.

A Sanctions Committee, composed of the fifteen members of the Security Council, monitors implementation of all Iran sanctions and collects and disseminates information on Iranian violations and other entities involved in banned activities. A "panel of experts" is empowered to make recommendations for improved enforcement.

Possible Additional International and Multilateral Sanctions to Address Iran's Nuclear Program[36]

There are a number of other possible U.N. or multilateral measures to isolate Iran that have received varying amounts of consideration. Some of these possibilities include:

- *Mandating Reductions in Diplomatic Exchanges with Iran or Prohibiting Travel by Iranian Officials.* Some have suggested a worldwide ban on travel to Iranian civilian officials, such as those involved in suppressing democracy activists. Some have called on countries to reduce their diplomatic presence in Iran, or to expel some Iranian diplomats from Iranian embassies in their territories. A further option is to limit sports or cultural exchanges with Iran, such as Iran's participation in the World Cup soccer tournament. However, many experts oppose using sporting events to accomplish political goals.
- *Banning Passenger Flights to and from Iran.* Bans on flights to and from Libya were imposed on that country in response to the finding that its agents were responsible for the December 21, 1988, bombing of Pan Am 103 (now lifted). There are no

indications that a passenger aircraft flight ban is under consideration among the P5+1.

- *A Ban on Exports to Iran of Refined Oil Products and Energy Equipment.* As noted, the EU sanctions formalized July 27, 2010, did not ban sales of gasoline but did ban the sale to Iran of equipment for Iran's energy sector (refineries as well as exploration and drilling). Another possibility would be to make such a general ban on sales of energy equipment universal in a new U.N. resolution. U.N. sanctions against Libya for the Pan Am 103 bombing banned the sale of energy equipment to Libya.

- *Financial and Trade Sanctions, Such as a Freeze on Iran's Financial Assets Abroad.* Existing U.N. resolutions do not freeze all Iranian assets abroad, and such a broad freeze does not appear to be under Security Council consideration. An effort to shut Iran's banks out of the Western banking system, potentially including the Central Bank of Iran (Bank Markazi), reportedly has been under consideration but is opposed by some European companies who fear harm to the civilian Iranian population from currency instability. A call for vigilance dealing with Iran's Central Bank is mentioned in Resolution 1929.

- *Limiting Lending to Iran by International Financial Institutions.* Resolution 1747 calls for restraint on but does not outright ban international lending to Iran. An option is to make a ban on such lending mandatory.

- *Banning Trade Financing or Official Insurance for Trade Financing.* Another option is to mandate a ban on official trade credit guarantees. This was not made mandatory by Resolution 1929, but several countries imposed this sanction (as far as most trade financing) subsequently. In February-March 2010 discussions on a new resolution, a ban on investment in Iranian bonds reportedly was considered but deleted to attract China and Russia's support.

- *Banning Worldwide Investment in Iran's Energy Sector.* This option would represent an "internationalization" of the U.S. "Iran Sanctions Act," which is discussed in CRS Report RS20871, *Iran Sanctions*, by Kenneth Katzman. Such a step is authorized, but not mandated by Resolution 1929, although several countries have used that authority to impose these sanctions on Iran.

- *Restricting Operations of and Insurance for Iranian Shipping.* One option, reportedly long under consideration, has been to ban the provision of insurance, or reinsurance, for any shipping to Iran. A call for restraint is in Resolution 1929, but is not mandatory. The EU and other national measures announced subsequently did include this sanction (IRISL) to operate. (The United States has imposed sanctions on IRISL.)

- *Imposing a Worldwide Ban on Sales of Arms to Iran.* Resolution 1929 imposes a ban on sales of major weapons systems to Iran, but another option is to extend that ban to all lethal equipment.

- *Imposing an International Ban on Purchases of Iranian Oil or Other Trade.* This is widely considered the most sweeping of sanctions that might be imposed, and would be unlikely to be considered in the Security Council unless Iran was found actively developing an actual nuclear weapon. Virtually all U.S. allies conduct extensive trade with Iran, and would oppose sanctions on trade in civilian goods with Iran. A ban on oil purchases from Iran is unlikely to be imposed because of the potential to return world oil prices to the high levels of the summer of 2008.

Chemical Weapons, Biological Weapons, and Missiles

Official U.S. reports and testimony continue to state that Iran is seeking a self-sufficient chemical weapons (CW) infrastructure, and that it "may have already" stockpiled blister, blood, choking, and nerve agents—and the bombs and shells to deliver them. This raises questions about Iran's compliance with its obligations under the Chemical Weapons Convention (CWC), which Iran signed on January 13, 1993, and ratified on June 8, 1997. These officials and reports also say that Iran "probably maintain[s] an offensive [biological weapons] BW program ... and probably has the capability to produce at least small quantities of BW agents."

Ballistic Missiles/Warheads

In his February 2010 Annual Threat Assessment of the Intelligence Community, Director of National Intelligence Dennis Blair testified "Iran's growing inventory of ballistic missiles and its acquisition of indigenous production of anti-ship cruise missiles (ASCMs) provide capabilities to enhance its power projection. Tehran views its conventionally armed missiles as an integral part of its strategy to deter—and if necessary retaliate against—forces in the region, including U.S. forces." However, Iran's technical capabilities are a matter of some debate among experts, and Iran appears to be focusing more on missiles capable of hitting regional targets rather than those of intercontinental range. **Table 7** contains some details on Iran's missile programs. [37]

In August 2008, the George W. Bush Administration reached agreements with Poland and the Czech Republic to establish a missile defense system to counter Iranian ballistic missiles. These agreements were reached over Russia's opposition, which was based on the belief that the missile defense system would be used to neutralize Russian capabilities. However, reportedly based on assessments of Iran's focus on missiles of regional range, on September 17, 2009, the Obama Administration reoriented this missile defense program to focus, at least initially, on ship-based systems, possibly later returning to the idea of Poland and Czech-based systems. Some saw this as an effort to win Russia's support for additional sanctions on Iran. In February 2010, Romania's top defense policy body approved a U.S. plan to base missile interceptors there. Russia is considered less resistant to placement in Romania because Russia's own missiles would not need to overfly that territory if they were ever fired. At the November 19-20, 2010, NATO meeting in Lisbon, NATO adopted the concept of a missile defense system, and to work with Russia to conceive a system that Russia could support, but the Lisbon summit did not specifically name Iran as a threat the system is intended to address.

FOREIGN POLICY AND SUPPORT FOR TERRORIST GROUPS

Iran's foreign policy is a product of the ideology of Iran's Islamic revolution, blended with longstanding national interests and what some describe as a near obsession about U.S. strategic power. Some of Iran's leaders, including Ahmadinejad, increasingly assert that Iran is a major regional power whose interests must be taken into account. Others interpret Iran's objectives as well beyond defensive—as a vision of overturning of the power structure in the

Iran: U.S. Concerns and Policy Responses

Middle East, which Iran believes favors the United States, Israel, and their "collaborators"-Sunni Muslim regimes such as Egypt, Jordan, and Saudi Arabia.

Table 7. Iran's Ballistic Missile Arsenal

Shahab-3 ("Meteor")	800-mile range. The Defense Department report of April 2010, cited earlier, has the missile as "deployed." Still, several of its tests (July 1998, July 2000, and September 2000) reportedly were unsuccessful or partially successful, and U.S. experts say the missile is not completely reliable. Iran tested several of the missiles on September 28, 2009, in advance of the October 1 meeting with the P5+1.
Shahab-3 "Variant" /Sijjil	1,200-1,500-mile range. The April 2010 Defense Department report has the liquid fueled Shahab-3 "variant" as "possibly deployed" The solid fuel version, called the Sijil, is considered "not" deployed by the Defense Department. The Sijil is alternately called the "Ashoura." These missiles potentially put large portions of the Near East and Southeastern Europe in range, including U.S. bases in Turkey.
BM-25	1,500-mile range. On April 27, 2006, Israel's military intelligence chief said that Iran had received a shipment of North Korean-supplied BM-25 missiles. Missile said to be capable of carrying nuclear warheads. The Washington Times appeared to corroborate this reporting in a July 6, 2006, story, which asserted that the North Korean-supplied missile is based on a Soviet-era "SS-N-6" missile. Press accounts in December 2010 indicate that Iran may have received components but not the entire BM-25 missile from North Korea.
ICBM	U.S. officials believe Iran might be capable of developing an intercontinental ballistic missile (3,000 mile range) by 2015, a time frame reiterated by the April 2010 DOD report.
Other Missiles	On September 6, 2002, Iran said it successfully tested a 200 mile range "Fateh 110" missile (solid propellent), and Iran said in late September 2002 that it had begun production. Iran also possesses a few hundred short-range ballistic missiles, including the Shahab-1 (Scud-b), the Shahab-2 (Scud-C), and the Tondar-69 (CSS-8). In January 2009, Iran claimed to have tested a new air-to-air missile. On March 7, 2010, Iran claimed it was now producing short-range cruise missiles that it claimed are highly accurate and can destroy heavy targets.
Space Vehicle	In February 2008 Iran claimed to have launched a probe into space, suggesting its missile technology might be improving to the point where an Iranian ICBM is realistic. Following an August 2008 failure, in early February 2009, Iran successfully launched a small, low-earth satellite on a Safir-2 rocket (range about 155 miles). The Pentagon said the launch was "clearly a concern of ours" because "there are dual-use capabilities here which could be applied toward the development of long-range missiles."
Warheads	Wall Street Journal report of September 14, 2005, said that U.S. intelligence believes Iran is working to adapt the Shahab-3 to deliver a nuclear warhead. Subsequent press reports say that U.S. intelligence captured an Iranian computer in mid-2004 showing plans to construct a nuclear warhead for the Shahab.38 The IAEA is seeking additional information from Iran.

Many U.S. experts see Iran as increasingly isolated by international sanctions and by the blemish on its image from the crackdown against the Green movement. Iran's leaders have sought new allies in Africa and Latin America, as well as Turkey, to try to show that Iran is still accepted globally and to counter the loss of support from big powers such as Russia and China. Other experts say that Iran has been strategically constrained by the installation of pro-U.S. regimes in Iraq and Afghanistan, and by the strong support for the United States in the Persian Gulf. Elections in Lebanon in 2009 that boosted pro-U.S. factions, as well as U.S. engagement with Syria, also have rendered Iran weaker than it has been in recent years, according to this view.

A contrary view is that Iran is ascendant in the region because of the installation of pro-Iranian regimes in Iraq and Afghanistan, and the strength of Hezbollah in Lebanon and Hamas in Gaza. Iran might, according to this view, seek to press its advantage to strengthen regional Shiite movements and possibly drive the United States out of the Gulf. Others say Iran's attendance at a June 8, 2010, regional summit of Turkey, Russia, and Iran—and its hosting on August 5, 2010, of a summit of Persian speaking countries (Iran, Afghanistan, and Tajikistan)—demonstrates that Iran is far from isolated.

The State Department report on international terrorism for 2009 released August 5, 2010, again stated (as it has for more than a decade) that Iran "remained the most active state sponsor of terrorism" in 2009, and it again attributes the terrorist activity primarily to the Qods Force of the Revolutionary Guard. On October 27, 2008, the deputy commander of the Basij became the first top Guard leader to publicly acknowledge that Iran supplies weapons to "liberation armies" in the region, a reference to pro-Iranian movements discussed below. The appointment of Brigadier General Ahmad Vahidi, the former Qods Forces commander, as defense minister in September 2009 (who got the highest number of Majles votes for his confirmation) caused concern in some neighboring states. The April 2010 Defense Department report on Iran, cited earlier, contains substantial discussion of the role of the Qods Force in supporting the movements and factions discussed below.

In the 1990s, Iran allegedly was involved in the assassination of several Iranian dissidents based in Europe. In May 2010, France allowed the return to Iran of Vakili Rad, who had been convicted in the 1991 stabbing of the Shah's last prime minister, Shahpour Bakhtiar. At the same time, in 2010 Iran allowed a French academic, Clotide Reiss, to return to France. She was accused of assisting the Green movement in 2009. Iran has not been accused of dissident assassinations abroad in over a decade.

Relations with the Persian Gulf States

The Persian Gulf monarchy states (Gulf Cooperation Council, GCC: Saudi Arabia, Kuwait, Bahrain, Qatar, Oman, and the United Arab Emirates) are concerned about Iranian strategic influence. They have not openly supported U.S. conflict with Iran that might cause Iran to retaliate against Gulf state targets, although the November 2010 "Wikileaks" presentation of U.S. diplomatic cables purports to show private urgings by several Gulf leaders that the United States move decisively to end Iran's nuclear potential. The Gulf states are, for the most part, cooperating with U.S. containment strategies discussed in the sections, below. That is evident from the large quantities of potential arms sales to the Gulf states—

possibly totaling more than $120 billion over the next several years—that are in varying stages of processing, according to press reports in September 2010.

Outwardly, both diplomatic and commercial relations between the Gulf states and Iran are relatively normal. Several of the Gulf states, particularly Kuwait, Bahrain, and UAE, have excess oil refining capacity and some refiners in the Gulf, particularly UAE, may still be selling gasoline to Iran, while others, such as those in Kuwait, reportedly have cut off such supplies.

Since the mid-1990s, Iran has tried to blunt Gulf state fears of Iran by curtailing activity, conducted during the 1980s and early 1990s, to sponsor Shiite Muslim extremist groups in these states, all of which are run by Sunni governments. Iran found, to its detriment, that such activity caused the Gulf states to ally closely with the United States. Seeking to avoid further tensions with Iran, the GCC leaders invited Ahmadinejad to the December 2007 summit of the GCC leaders in Doha, Qatar, marking the first time an Iranian president had been invited since the GCC was formed in 1981. He has not been invited to subsequent GCC summits, including the December 2010 GCC summit in UAE.

- *Saudi Arabia.* Many observers closely watch the relationship between Iran and Saudi Arabia because of Saudi alarm over the emergence of a pro-Iranian government in Iraq and Iran's nuclear program. Saudi Arabia sees itself as leader of the Sunni Muslim world and views Shiite Muslims as heretical and disloyal internally. However, the Saudis, who do not want a repeat of Iran's sponsorship of disruptive and sometimes violent demonstrations at annual Hajj pilgrimages in Mecca in the 1980s and 1990s—or an increase in Iranian support for Saudi Shiite dissidents—are receptive to easing tensions with Iran. The Saudis continue to blame a pro-Iranian movement in the Kingdom, Saudi Hezbollah, for the June 25, 1996, Khobar Towers housing complex bombing, which killed 19 U.S. airmen.[39] After restoring relations in December 1991 (after a four-year break), Saudi-Iran ties progressed to high-level contacts during Khatemi's presidency, including Khatemi visits in 1999 and 2002. Ahmadinejad has visited on several occasions. Both Saudi Arabia and the UAE reportedly have pledged to increase oil supplies to China in part to help persuade China to sanction Iran.
- *United Arab Emirates* (UAE) concerns about Iran never fully recovered from the April 1992 Iranian expulsion of UAE security forces from the Persian Gulf island of Abu Musa, which it and the UAE shared under a 1971 bilateral agreement. (In 1971, Iran, then ruled by the U.S.-backed Shah, seized two other islands, Greater and Lesser Tunb, from the emirate of Ras al-Khaymah, as well as part of Abu Musa from the emirate of Sharjah.) In general, the UAE (particularly the federation capital, Abu Dhabi, backs U.S. efforts to dissuade Iran from developing its nuclear capability through international sanctions. The UAE reportedly has increased scrutiny of exports to Iran since the passage of Resolution 1929 to ensure no WMD-related technology is being reexported, and it has frozen the assets of 41 Iranians sanctioned subject to asset freezes under the U.N. resolutions. These moves may reduce the estimated $12 billion in trade between the two. UAE enforcement of banking sanctions on Iran in September 2010 reportedly caused a 15% drop in the value of Iran's currency.

Within the UAE, Abu Dhabi generally takes a harder line against Iran than does the emirate of Dubai, which has an Iranian-origin resident community as large as 300,000 and business ties to Iran. This view could explain comments by the UAE Ambassador to the United States on July 6, 2010, when, on a panel at the Aspen Institute, Ambassador Yusuf Otaiba said, when asked about UAE support for military action to try to halt Iran's nuclear program, "We cannot live with a nuclear Iran... I am willing to absorb what takes place at the expense of the security of the UAE." On the islands dispute, the UAE wants to refer the dispute to the International Court of Justice (ICJ). Iran insists on resolving the issue bilaterally. The UAE formally protested Iran's setting up of a maritime and ship registration office on Abu Musa in July 2008. The United States supports UAE proposals but takes no formal position on sovereignty. Still seeking to avoid antagonizing Iran, in May 2007 the UAE received Ahmadinejad (the highest-level Iranian visit since the 1979 revolution) and allowed him to lead an anti-U.S. rally of several hundred Iranian-origin residents of Dubai at a stadium there.

- *Qatar*, like most of the other Gulf states, does not seek confrontation and seeks to accommodate some of its interests, yet Qatar remains wary that Iran might eventually seek to encroach on its large North Field (natural gas). It shares that field with Iran (called South Pars on Iran's side) and Qatar earns large revenues from natural gas exports from it. Qatar's fears were heightened on April 26, 2004, when Iran's deputy oil minister said that Qatar is probably producing more gas than "her right share" from the field and that Iran "will not allow" its wealth to be used by others. Possibly to try to ease such implied threats, Qatar invited Ahmadinejad to the December 2007 GCC summit there.

- *Bahrain* is about 60% Shiite-inhabited, many of whom are of Persian origin, but its government is dominated by the Sunni Muslim Al Khalifa family. In 1981 and again in 1996, Bahrain publicly accused Iran of supporting Bahraini Shiite dissidents (the Islamic Front for the Liberation of Bahrain, Bahrain-Hezbollah, and other Bahraini dissident groups) in efforts to overthrow the ruling Al Khalifa family. Bahraini allegations that Iran would try to interfere in Bahrain's November 25, 2006, and October 23, 2010, parliamentary elections by providing support to Shiite candidates were not substantiated. Tensions have flared several times since July 2007 when Iranian editorialists asserted that Bahrain is part of Iran—that question was the subject of the 1970 U.N.-run referendum in which Bahrainis opted for independence. The issued flared again after a February 20, 2009, statement by Ali Akbar Nateq Nuri, an adviser to Khamene'i, that Bahrain was at one time an Iranian province. The statement contributed to a decision by Morocco to break relations with Iran. Still, Bahrain has sought not to antagonize Iran and has apparently allowed Iran's banks to establish a presence in Bahrain's vibrant banking sector. On March 12, 2008, the Treasury Department sanctioned the Bahrain-based Future Bank under Executive Order 13382 that sanctions proliferation entities. Future Bank purportedly is controlled by Bank Melli, but it remains in operation.

- *Oman*. Of the GCC states, the Sultanate of Oman is closest politically to Iran and has refused to ostracize or even harshly criticize Iranian policies. Some press reports say local Omani officials routinely turn a blind eye to or even cooperate in the smuggling of western goods to Iran. Sultan Qaboos made a state visit to Iran in August 2009, coinciding with the inauguration of Ahmadinejad, and despite the substantial unrest inside Iran over his reelection. As noted, Oman supplied the aircraft to fly U.S. hiker Sara Shourd out of Iran in September 2010, suggesting it played a brokering role in her release. Subsequent Omani diplomacy has not led to movement on the freedom of the other two hikers. Secretary of Defense Gates visited Oman on December 5, 2010, for talks with Sultan Qaboos on Iran and other regional issues.

- *Kuwait* has enjoyed generally good relations with Iran because it saw Iran as the counterweight to Saddam Hussein, who invaded Kuwait in August 1990. Since Saddam's overthrow in 2003, Kuwait has become somewhat more distant from Iran and, in April 2010, Kuwaiti newspapers reported that security officials had broken up a cell of spies for the Qods Force inside Kuwait. About 25% of Kuwaitis are Shiite Muslims, and Iran supported Shiite radical groups in Kuwait in the 1980s as a means to try to pressure Kuwait not to support the Iraqi war effort in the Iran-Iraq war (1980-1988). Kuwaiti refineries also have ceased sales of gasoline to Iran as of mid-2010, according to the State Department.

Iranian Policy in Iraq[40]

The U.S. military ousting of Saddam Hussein benefitted Iran strategically. In an effort by Iran to reap those benefits, during 2004-2008, U.S.-Iran differences in Iraq widened to the point where some were describing the competition as a U.S.-Iran "proxy war" inside Iraq. The acute source of tension was evidence, detailed on several occasions by U.S. commanders in Iraq, that the *Qods* Force was providing arms (including highly lethal "explosively forced projectiles," EFPs, which have killed U.S. soldiers), training, guidance, and financing to pro-Iranian Shiite militias involved in sectarian violence. The State Department report on terrorism for 2009, released August 5, 2010, says much of this activity continues, although U.S. assessments indicate this material support may have fallen off as Shiite militia activity has declined more generally.

However, Iran and the United States both accepted the return of Nuri al-Maliki to a second term as prime minister because he is considered acceptable to both; he was formally tapped on November 25, 2010, to assemble a new government within 30 days. He presented a new, broad-based government on December 21, 2010, and it achieved confirmation by the full Iraqi parliament. The government included senior Sunni Arabs in key positions and appeared to offer less room for Iranian influence than was expected earlier in 2010. The major issues involved in Iran's relationship with Iraq and interference in it are discussed in CRS Report RS22323, *Iran-Iraq Relations*, by Kenneth Katzman.

Supporting Palestinian Militant Groups

Iran's support for Palestinian militant groups has long concerned U.S. Administrations, as part of an apparent effort by Tehran to obstruct an Israeli-Palestinian peace, which Iran believes would strengthen the United States and Israel. Ahmadinejad's various statements on Israel were discussed above, and Supreme Leader Khamene'i has repeatedly called Israel a "cancerous tumor." He used a similar term ("disease") in an August 18, 2010, speech. In

December 2001, Rafsanjani, now considered a moderate, said that it would take only one Iranian nuclear bomb to destroy Israel, whereas a similar strike against Iran by Israel would have far less impact because Iran's population is large.

Iran has hosted numerous conferences to which anti-peace process terrorist organizations were invited (for example: April 24, 2001, and June 2-3, 2002). During his presidency, Khatemi also issued sharp criticisms and recriminations against Israel, but he also conversed with Israel's president at the 2005 funeral of Pope John Paul II. The formal position of the Iranian Foreign Ministry, considered a bastion of moderates, is that Iran would not seek to block an Israeli-Palestinian settlement but that the process is too weighted toward Israel to yield a fair result.

Iran and Hamas

The State Department report on terrorism for 2009 (mentioned above) again accused Iran of providing "extensive" funding, weapons, and training to Hamas, Palestinian Islamic Jihad (PIJ), the Al Aqsa Martyr's Brigades, and the Popular Front for the Liberation of Palestine-General Command (PFLP-GC). All are named as foreign terrorist organizations (FTO) by the State Department for their use of violence to undermine the Arab-Israeli peace process. Some saw Iran's regional policy further strengthened by Hamas's victory in the January 25, 2006, Palestinian legislative elections, and even more so by Hamas's June 2007 armed takeover of the Gaza Strip. Hamas activists downplay Iranian influence on them, asserting that Iran is mostly Shiite, while Hamas members are Sunni Muslims.[41] Hamas was reputed to receive about 10% of its budget in the early 1990s from Iran, although since then Hamas has cultivated funding from wealthy Persian Gulf donors and supporters in Europe and elsewhere.

It was evident from the December 27, 2008-January 17, 2009, Israel-Hamas war in Gaza, that Iran provides material support to Hamas. Joint Chiefs Chairman Admiral Mike Mullen said on January 27, 2009, that the United States boarded but did not seize a ship carrying light arms to Hamas from Iran; the ship (the *Monchegorsk*) later went to Cyprus. On March 11, 2009, a U.N. committee monitoring Iran's compliance with Resolution 1747, which bans Iranian arms exports, said Iran might have violated that resolution with the alleged shipment. Hamas appeared to corroborate allegations of Iranian weapons supplies when its exiled leader, Khaled Meshal, on February 1, 2009, publicly praised Iran for helping Hamas achieve "victory" over Israel in the conflict.[42] On December 29, 2008, Khamene'i said that Muslims worldwide were "duty-bound" to defend Palestinians in the Gaza Strip against the Israeli offensive against the Hamas-run leadership there, but the Iranian leadership did not attempt to send Iranian volunteers to Gaza to fight on Hamas' behalf. Iranian weaponry might also have been the target of a January 2009 strike on a weapons delivery purportedly bound for Gaza in transit via Sudan (presumably via Egypt). Iran joined in regional criticism of Israel for its May 31, 2010, armed inspection of a Turkish ship, carrying humanitarian goods, that attempted to evade Israel's naval blockade of Gaza, and Iran subsequently threatened—but has not implement these threats to date—to provide naval escorts for future such shipments or to organize a blockade-running shipment.

Sunni Arab leaders in Egypt, Jordan, Saudi Arabia, and throughout the region apparently fear Iran's reported attempts to discredit these leaders for what Iran considers insufficient support for Hamas in its recent war with Israel. Some Iranian efforts reportedly involve establishing Hezbollah cells in some of these countries, particularly Egypt, purportedly to stir up opposition to these governments and build public support for Hezbollah and Hamas.[43]

Lebanese Hezbollah and Syria[44]

Iran has maintained a close relationship with Hezbollah since the group was formed in 1982, and then officially unveiled in 1985, by Lebanese Shiite clerics of the pro-Iranian Lebanese Da'wa Party. Hezbollah was responsible for several acts of anti-U.S. and anti-Israel terrorism in the 1980s and 1990s.[45] Hezbollah's attacks on Israeli forces in southern Lebanon contributed to an Israeli withdrawal in May 2000, but Hezbollah maintained military forces along the border. Hezbollah continued to remain armed and outside Lebanese government control, despite U.N. Security Council Resolution 1559 (September 2, 2004) that required its dismantlement. In refusing to disarm, Hezbollah says it was resisting Israeli occupation of some Lebanese territory (Shib'a Farms).

Ahmadinejad advertised Iran's strong commitment to Hezbollah during his October 14-15, 2009 visit to Lebanon, the first by a president of the Islamic Republic of Iran, which included his visiting villages near the border with Israel. Ahmadinejad did not commit any direct acts of provocation, which some feared, such as throwing stones across the Israeli border. Demonstrating Iran's strong influence over Lebanon, Lebanon's Prime Minister Saad Hariri visited Iran on November 27, 2010, for a three-day visit. Hariri represents factions in Lebanon generally opposed to Hezbollah, and his visit suggested a need to try to assuage Iran that he is not a threat to Iran's interests or to Hezbollah.

Although Iran likely did not instigate Lebanese Hezbollah to provoke the July-August 2006 war, Iran has long been its major arms supplier. Hezbollah fired Iranian-supplied rockets on Israel's northern towns during the fighting. Reported Iranian shipments to Hezbollah prior to the conflict included the "Fajr" (dawn) and Khaybar series of rockets that were fired at the Israeli city of Haifa (30 miles from the border), and over 10,000 Katyusha rockets that were fired at cities within 20 miles of the Lebanese border.[46] Iran also supplied Hezbollah with an unmanned aerial vehicle (UAV), the *Mirsad*, which Hezbollah briefly flew over the Israel-Lebanon border on November 7, 2004, and April 11, 2005; at least three were shot down by Israel during the conflict. On July 14, 2006, Hezbollah apparently hit an Israeli warship with a C-802 sea-skimming missile probably provided by Iran. Iran also purportedly provided advice during the conflict; about 50 Revolutionary Guards Qods Force personnel were in Lebanon (down from about 2,000 when Hezbollah was formed, according to a *Washington Post* report of April 13, 2005) when the conflict began; that number might have increased during the conflict to help Hezbollah operate the Iran-supplied weaponry.

Even though Hezbollah reduced its overt military presence in southern Lebanon in accordance with the conflict-related U.N. Security Council Resolution 1701 (July 31, 2006), Hezbollah was perceived as a victor in the war for holding out against Israel. Iran has since resupplied Hezbollah with at least 25,000 new rockets and [47] press reports in early 2010 said Hezbollah maintains a wide network of arms and missile caches around Lebanon. Among the post-war deliveries were 500 Iranian-made "Zelzal" (Earthquake) missiles with a range of 186 miles, enough to reach Tel Aviv from south Lebanon. In November 2009, Israel intercepted a ship that it asserted was carrying 500 tons of arms purportedly for Hezbollah. Iran also made at least $150 million available for Hezbollah to distribute to Lebanese citizens (mostly Shiite supporters of Hezbollah) whose homes were damaged in the Israeli military campaign.[48] The State Department terrorism report for 2008, released on April 30, 2009, specified Iranian aid to Hezbollah as exceeding $200 million in 2008, and said that Iran trained over 3,000 Hezbollah fighters in Iran during that year. The report for 2009 used similar figures for Iranian aid and training for Hezbollah but over an unspecified time frame.

Syria

Iran is one of Syria's few strategic allies and an investor in the Syrian economy. Some see any Israel-Syria negotiations—and Obama Administration efforts to engage Syria—as means to wean Syria away from its alliance with Iran. However, there is a widespread belief that the Iran-Syria alliance will not be severed unless and until Syria and Israel reach a peace agreement that results in the return of the Golan Heights to Syria.

Iran's relationship with Syria is key to Iran's efforts to support Hezbollah. Syria is the transit point for the Iranian weapons shipments to Hezbollah and both countries see Hezbollah as leverage against Israel to achieve their regional and territorial aims. In order to preserve its links to Syria, which is one of Iran's few real allies, Iran purportedly has acted as an intermediary with North Korea to supply Syria with various forms of WMD and missile technology. In April 2010, the Obama Administration called in Syria's ambassador to ask about reports that Syria had transferred Scud missiles to Hezbollah, although an Iranian connection to the purported transfer remains unclear. However, in late June 2010, it was reported that Iran had sent Syria a sophisticated air defense radar system that Syria could potentially use to thwart Israeli air strikes.[49] On December 13, 2009, the Syrian and Iranian defense ministers signed a defense agreement to "face common enemies and challenges."

Central Asia and the Caspian

Iran's policy in Central Asia has thus far emphasized Iran's rights to Caspian Sea resources, particularly against Azerbaijan. That country's population, like Iran's, is mostly Shiite Muslim, but its leadership is secular. In addition, Azerbaijan is ethnically Turkic, and Iran fears that Azerbaijan nationalists might stoke separatism among Iran's large Azeri Turkic population, which demonstrated some unrest in 2006. These factors could explain why Iran has generally tilted toward Armenia, which is Christian, even though it has been at odds with Azerbaijan over territory and control of ethnic Armenians. In July 2001, Iranian warships and combat aircraft threatened a British Petroleum (BP) ship on contract to Azerbaijan out of an area of the Caspian that Iran considers its own. The United States called that action provocative, and it is engaged in border security and defense cooperation with Azerbaijan directed against Iran (and Russia). The United States successfully backed construction of the Baku-Tblisi-Ceyhan oil pipeline, intended in part to provide alternatives to Iranian oil.

Along with India and Pakistan, Iran has been given observer status at the Central Asian security grouping called the Shanghai Cooperation Organization (SCO—Russia, China, Kazakhstan, Kyrgyzstan, Uzbekistan, and Tajikistan). In April 2008, Iran applied for full membership in the organization, which opposes a long-term U.S. presence in Central Asia. However, illustrating the degree to which the United States has been able to isolate Iran, in June 2010 the SCO denied Iran the opportunity to achieve full membership by adopting membership rules that bar admission to countries under U.N. Security Council sanctions.

South Asia: Afghanistan, Pakistan, and India[50]

Iran looks to its eastern neighbors in South Asia as allies and potential allies to help parry U.S. and European pressure on Iran's economy and its leaders.

Afghanistan

In Afghanistan, Iran is viewed by U.S. officials as pursuing a multi-track strategy—attempting to help develop Afghanistan and enhance its influence there, while also building leverage against the United States by arming anti-U.S. militant groups. Iran appears to be particularly interested in restoring some of its traditional sway in eastern, central, and northern Afghanistan, where Persian-speaking Afghans predominate. Iran may also want to be in position to threaten the air base at Shindand, in Herat Province, which is used by U.S. and allied forces and which Iran believes could be used for surveillance of or strikes on Iran. (The Administration has requested FY2011 military construction funds to improve that airbase.) Because Iran has some influence in Afghanistan (Karzai, with pro-government factions, and with some militant groups) some U.S. officials reportedly are arguing that the United States should develop a bilateral dialogue on Afghanistan, to be conducted by their respective ambassadors in Kabul. A similar channel was developed in Iraq, as noted above. Iran may have signaled a willingness for such engagement when it attended the October 18, 2010, meeting in Rome of the 44-nation "International Contact Group" on Afghanistan. The United States did not object to the Iranian attendance. The meeting included a briefing by Gen. David Petraeus (top U.S./NATO commander in Afghanistan), which Iran's representative (Asian affairs director Mohammad Ali Qanezadeh) attended. Iran did not attend the January 28, 2010, international meeting in Britain on Afghanistan, but it did attend a follow-up meeting in Kabul on July 20, 2010.

U.S. reports, including the April 2010 Defense Department report cited earlier, as well as the August 5, 2010, State Department terrorism report for 2009, continue to accuse the Qods Force of supplying various munitions, including 107mm rockets, to Taliban and other militants in Afghanistan; some Taliban commanders openly say they are obtaining Iranian weapons. U.S. commanders, including Gen. Petraeus, have maintained that the Iranian assistance to Afghan militants is at a relatively low level and not decisive on the battlefield, but is large enough that the Iranian government would have to have known about it. The 2009 State Department terrorism report, as it did the previous year, accused Iran of training Taliban fighters in small unit tactics, small arms use, explosives, and indirect weapons fire. In August 2010, the Treasury Department sanctioned two Iranian Qods Force officers allegedly involved in supplying funds and materiel to Afghan militants. They were sanctioned under Executive Order 13224 for supporting international terrorism.

For Afghanistan's part, President Hamid Karzai considers Iran an important neighbor and has said that he does not want proxy competition between the United States and Iran in Afghanistan (he reiterated this during his May 2010 visit to Washington). Many Afghans speak Dari, a dialect of Persian language, and have long affinity with Iran. Partly as a signal of respect for these Afghans, Karzai visited Iran for the celebration of Nowruz (Persian new year). He returned to Kabul to receive President Obama on March 28, 2010. Karzai and Ahmadinejad have met several times since, including at the summit of Persian-speaking nations in Tehran on August 5, 2010. Karzai admitted on October 26, 2010, that press reports were true that Iran has given Afghanistan direct cash payments (about $2 million per year) to support its budget and to possibly drive a wedge between Afghanistan and the United States. The funds have reportedly been passed via Karzai's chief of staff Mohammad Umar Daudzai.

Pakistan

Iran's relations with Pakistan have been partly a function of events in Afghanistan, although relations have worsened somewhat in late 2009 as Iran has accused Pakistan of supporting Sunni Muslim rebels in Iran's Baluchistan region. These Sunni guerrillas have conducted a number of attacks on Iranian regime targets in 2009, as discussed above (*Jundullah*).

Iran had a burgeoning military cooperation with Pakistan in the early 1990s, and as noted Iran's nuclear program benefitted from the A.Q. Khan network. However, Iran-Pakistan relations became strained in the 1990s when Pakistan was supporting the Taliban in Afghanistan, which committed alleged atrocities against Shiite Afghans (Hazara tribe), and which seized control of Persian-speaking areas of Afghanistan. Currently, Iran remains suspicious that Pakistan might want to again implant the Taliban in power in Afghanistan— and Iran itself is aiding the Taliban to some extent—but Iran and Pakistan now have a broad agenda that includes a potential major gas pipeline project, discussed further below.

India

Iran and India have cultivated good relations with each other in order to enable each to pursue its own interests and avoid mutual conflict. The two backed similar anti-Taliban factions in Afghanistan during 1996-2001 and have a number of mutual economic and even military-tomilitary relationships and projects. One particular source of U.S. concern has been visits to India by some Iranian naval personnel, although India has said these exchanges involve junior personnel and focus mainly on promoting interpersonal relations and not on India's provision to Iran of military expertise. India reportedly wants to expedite the development of Iran's Chabahar port, which would give India direct access to Afghanistan and Central Asia without relying on transit routes through Pakistan.

Some Indian diplomats believe that India is coming under undue U.S. pressure to reduce its ties to Iran. India has responded, to some extent, by refraining from expanding relations with Iran. A major Indian gasoline refiner, Reliance Industries Ltd, reportedly has ended gasoline sales to Iran in an effort to avoid any U.S. sanction. Another aspect of the relationship involves not the potential building of a natural gas pipeline from Iran, through Pakistan, to India. While India's participation in a trans-Pakistan pipeline remains uncertain over pricing and security issues, India and Iran reportedly are discussing a direct, undersea pipeline that would bypass Pakistan.

Al Qaeda

Iran is not a natural ally of Al Qaeda, largely because Al Qaeda is an orthodox Sunni Muslim organization. However, some experts believe that hardliners in Iran might want to use Al Qaeda activists as leverage against the United States and its allies. The 9/11 Commission report said several of the September 11 hijackers and other plotters, possibly with official help, might have transited Iran, but the report does not assert that the Iranian government cooperated with or knew about the plot. Another bin Laden ally, Abu Musab al-Zarqawi, killed by U.S. forces in Iraq on June 7, 2006, reportedly transited Iran after the September 11 attacks and took root in Iraq, becoming an insurgent leader there. Press reports in May 2010 have said that Al Qaeda figures have been regularly entering and leaving Iran.

Iran might see possibilities for tactical alliance with Al Qaeda. Three major Al Qaeda figures believed to have been in Iran include spokesman Sulayman Abu Ghaith, top operative Sayf Al Adl, and Osama bin Laden's son, Saad,[51] although some U.S. officials said in January 2009 that Saad bin Laden might have left Iran and could be in Pakistan. That information was publicized a few days after the Treasury Department (on January 16, 2009) designated four Al Qaeda operatives in Iran, including Saad bin Laden (and three lesser known figures) as terrorist entities under Executive Order 13224. Some reports in September 2010 said that Abu Ghaith may also have left Iran and gone to Pakistan. (U.S. officials blamed Saad bin Laden, Adl, and Abu Ghaith for the May 12, 2003, bombings in Riyadh, Saudi Arabia, against four expatriate housing complexes, saying they have been able to contact associates outside Iran.[52])

Iran has, to some extent, confirmed the presence of Al Qaeda militants in Iran. It asserted on July 23, 2003, that it had "in custody" senior Al Qaeda figures. On July 16, 2005, Iran's intelligence minister said that 200 Al Qaeda members are in Iranian jails.[53] U.S. officials have said since January 2002 that Iran has not prosecuted or extradited any senior Al Qaeda operatives. In December 2009, Iran's foreign minister confirmed that a teenage daughter of Osama bin Laden had sought refuge in the Saudi embassy in Tehran—the first official confirmation that members of bin Laden's family have been in Iran. She left Iran in March 2010, and one of her brothers may have left for Syria around this time. As many as 20 other family members are said to still be living in a compound in Iran since the September 11, 2001, attacks, and accusing Iran of refusing to allow them to leave for Saudi Arabia or other places. Some family members have said the young bin Ladens have never been affiliated with Al Qaeda.

Latin America

A growing concern has been Iran's developing relations with countries and leaders in Latin America considered adversaries of the United States, particularly Cuba and Venezuela's Hugo Chavez. Ahmadinejad made a high-profile visit to five Latin American countries in November 2009, including Brazil but also including, as expected, Venezuela. Of the Latin American countries, Brazil is emerging as its most noteworthy supporter, particularly because of Brazil's engagement with Iran to forge the "Tehran Declaration" on nuclear issues in June 2010.

Recent State Department terrorism reports have said that Cuba maintains "close relationships with other state sponsors of terrorism such as Iran." Iran has offered Bolivia $1 billion in aid and investment, according to an *Associated Press* report of November 23, 2008. Iran has also apparently succeeded in persuading Brazil to publicly oppose new U.N. sanctions on Iran.

Venezuela

On October 30, 2007, then Secretary of Homeland Security Michael Chertoff said that Iran's relationship with Venezuela is an emerging threat because it represents a "marriage" of

Iran's extremist ideology with "those who have anti-American views." On January 27, 2009, Secretary of Defense Gates said Iran was trying to build influence in Latin America by expanding front companies and opening offices in countries there. The April 2010 Defense Department report on Iran was the first U.S. government publication to say that Qods Force personnel are in Venezuela, where their presence has "increased" in recent years. Venezuelan President Hugo Chavez has visited Iran on several occasions, offering to engage in joint oil and gas projects.

However, many accounts say that most of the agreements between Iran and Venezuela are agreements in principle that have not been implemented in reality. Among the arrangements implemented are the establishment of direct air links through an obscure air service dedicated to this route. A firm deal for Petroleos de Venezuela to supply Iran with gasoline was signed in September 2009, apparently in a joint effort to circumvent the reduction in worldwide sales of gasoline to Iran. Petroleos reportedly has been delivering gasoline to Iran in July and August 2010, according to industry sources. About 400 Iranian engineers have reportedly been sent to Venezuela to work on infrastructure projects there.

Africa

Sensing growing isolation, Ahmadinejad appears to be reaching out to African leaders to enlist their support for Iran against U.S. pressure. Iran has cultivated Senegal as an ally, for example. In April 2010, Ahmadinejad visited Uganda and Zimbabwe, even though Zimbabwe's leader, Robert Mugabe, has himself been heavily criticized by the international community in recent years. Still, it is believed that African support for Iran is unlikely to outweigh its growing estrangement from Europe and its partial abandonment by Russia and China.

Some Members of Congress are concerned that Iran is supporting radical Islamist movements in Africa. In the 111th Congress, H.Con.Res. 16 cites Hezbollah for engaging in raising funds in Africa by trafficking in "conflict diamonds." Iran also might have supplied Islamists in Somalia with anti-aircraft and anti-tank weaponry. The possible transfer of weaponry to Hamas via Sudan was discussed above.

U.S. POLICY APPROACHES AND ADDITIONAL OPTIONS

The February 11, 1979, fall of the Shah of Iran, a key U.S. ally, opened a long and deep rift in U.S.-Iranian relations. As noted in the section on Iran's foreign policy and support of terrorism, U.S.-Iran differences significantly transcend the concerns over Iran's nuclear program. The U.S. policy focus on Iran predates the emergence of the nuclear program as a major issue, although the nuclear issue has, according to many, made a U.S. policy focus on Iran more urgent. Some experts maintain that the United States has always lacked a comprehensive and consistent strategy to limit the Islamic regime's regional influence and its weapons programs.

The Carter Administration sought a degree of engagement with the Islamic regime during 1979, but it agreed to allow in the ex-Shah for medical treatment, and Iranian officials of the new regime who engaged the United States were singled out as insufficiently loyal or revolutionary. As a result, the U.S.-Iran estrangement began in earnest on November 4, 1979, when radical pro-Khomeini "students in the line of the Imam (Khomeini)"seized the U.S. Embassy in Tehran and held its diplomats hostage until minutes after President Reagan's inauguration on January 20, 1981. The United States broke relations with Iran on April 7, 1980 (two weeks prior to the failed U.S. military attempt to rescue the hostages during April 24-25, 1980), and the two countries had only limited official contact thereafter.[54] The United States tilted toward Iraq in the 1980-1988 Iran-Iraq war, including U.S. diplomatic attempts to block conventional arms sales to Iran, providing battlefield intelligence to Iraq[55] and, during 1987-1988, direct skirmishes with Iranian naval elements in the course of U.S. efforts to protect international oil shipments in the Gulf from Iranian mines and other attacks. In one battle on April 18, 1988 ("Operation Praying Mantis"), Iran lost about one-quarter of its larger naval ships in a one-day engagement with the U.S. Navy, including one frigate sunk and another badly damaged. Iran strongly disputed the U.S. assertion that the July 3, 1988, U.S. shoot-down of Iran Air Flight 655 by the *U.S.S. Vincennes* over the Persian Gulf (bound for Dubai, UAE) was an accident.

In his January 1989 inaugural speech, President George H. W. Bush laid the groundwork for a rapprochement, saying that, in relations with Iran, "goodwill begets goodwill," implying better relations if Iran helped obtain the release of U.S. hostages held by Hezbollah in Lebanon. Iran reportedly did assist in obtaining their releases, which was completed in December 1991, but no thaw followed, possibly because Iran continued to back groups opposed to the U.S.-sponsored Middle East peace process, a major U.S. priority.

Clinton Administration Policy

Upon taking office in 1993, the Clinton Administration moved to further isolate Iran as part of a strategy of "dual containment" of Iran and Iraq. In 1995 and 1996, the Clinton Administration and Congress added sanctions on Iran in response to growing concerns about Iran's weapons of mass destruction, its support for terrorist groups, and its efforts to subvert the Arab-Israeli peace process. The election of Khatemi in May 1997 precipitated a U.S. shift toward engagement; the Clinton Administration offered Iran official dialogue, with no substantive preconditions. In January 1998, Khatemi publicly agreed to "people-to-people" U.S.-Iran exchanges as part of his push for "dialogue of civilizations, but he ruled out direct talks. In a June 1998 speech, then Secretary of State Albright called for mutual confidence building measures that could lead to a "road map" for normalization. Encouraged by the reformist victory in Iran's March 2000 *Majles* elections, Secretary Albright, in a March 17, 2000, speech, acknowledged past U.S. meddling in Iran, announcing some minor easing of the U.S. trade ban with Iran, and promised to try to resolve outstanding claims disputes. In September 2000 U.N. "Millennium Summit" meetings, Albright and President Clinton sent a positive signal to Iran by attending Khatemi's speeches.

George W. Bush Administration Policy

The George W. Bush Administration undertook multi-faceted efforts to limit Iran's strategic capabilities through international diplomacy and sanctions—both international sanctions as well as national measures outside Security Council mandate. At the same time, the Administration engaged in bilateral diplomacy with Iran on specific priority issues, such as Afghanistan and Iraq, but was hesitant to offer Iran sustained, broad engagement without preconditions. The policy framework was supported by maintenance of large U.S. conventional military capabilities in the Persian Gulf and through U.S. alliances with Iran's neighbors. On only one occasion during the Bush Administration, July 19, 2008, did a U.S. official attend the P5+1 nuclear negotiations with Iran. An amendment by then Senator Biden (adopted June 2006) to the FY2007 defense authorization bill (P.L. 109-364) supported the Administration's offer to join nuclear talks with Iran.

At times, the George W. Bush Administration considered or pursued more assertive options. Some Administration officials, reportedly led by Vice President Cheney, believed that policy should focus on using the leverage of possible military confrontation with Iran or on U.S. efforts to change Iran's regime.[56] The Bush Administration's statements that it considered Iran a great nation and respects its history could have represented efforts to win support among Iran's youth who are disaffected with the Islamic regime. Such themes were prominent in speeches by President George W. Bush such as at the Merchant Marine Academy on June 19, 2006, and his September 18, 2006, speech to the U.N. General Assembly.

As noted, Bush Administration officials engaged Iran on specific regional (Afghanistan and Iraq) and humanitarian issues, but not broadly or without some preconditions in most cases. The United States had a dialogue with Iran on Iraq and Afghanistan from late 2001 until May 2003, when the United States broke off the talks following the May 12, 2003, terrorist bombing in Riyadh. At that time, the United States and Iran publicly acknowledged that they were conducting direct talks in Geneva on those two issues,[57] the first confirmed direct dialogue between the two countries since the 1979 revolution. The United States aided victims of the December 2003 earthquake in Bam, Iran, including a reported offer—rebuffed by Iran—to send a high-level delegation to Iran including Senator Elizabeth Dole and reportedly President George W. Bush's sister, Dorothy.

"Grand Bargain Concept"

The George W. Bush Administration did not offer Iran an unconditional, direct U.S.-Iran bilateral dialogue on *all* issues of U.S. concern. Some argue that the issues that divide the United States and Iran cannot be segregated, and that the key to resolving the nuclear issue is striking a "grand bargain" on all outstanding issues. Some say the Bush Administration "missed an opportunity," saying that U.S. officials rebuffed a reported comprehensive overture from Iran just before the May 12, 2003, Riyadh bombing. The *Washington Post* reported on February 14, 2007, ("2003 Memo Says Iranian Leaders Backed Talks") that the Swiss ambassador to Iran in 2003, Tim Guldimann, had informed U.S. officials of a comprehensive Iranian proposal for talks with the United States.[58] However, State Department officials and some European diplomats based in Tehran at that time question whether that proposal represented an authoritative Iranian communication. Others argue that the offer was unrealistic because an agreement would have required Iran to abandon key tenets of its Islamic revolution.

Overview of Obama Administration Policy

President Obama's Administration came into office with an apparent belief that there was an opportunity to dissuade Iran from expanding its nuclear program, and possibly to build a new framework for relations with Iran after the decades of estrangement, suspicion, and enmity. The Administration offered to accept Iran's government as it is and to better integrate it into the world economy in return for Iranian compromises on its nuclear program. This approach influenced the course of P5+1 deliberations among its members and between the P5+1 and Iran, as discussed in the sections above on Iran's nuclear program.

Some Obama Administration officials, including Secretary of State Clinton and Secretary of Defense Gates, well before the unrest in Iran, expressed public skepticism that engagement would yield changes in Iran's policies. Others, including Dennis Ross, who was named in February 2009 as an adviser to Secretary of State Clinton for "Southwest Asia" (a formulation understood to center on Iran), and then assigned to a similar capacity in the White House in June 2009, believed that the United States and its partners need to present Iran with clear incentives and punishments if Iran continues to refuse cooperation on the nuclear issue.

Implementation of the Engagement Policy

The first major public manifestation of President Obama's approach to Iran policy came in his message to the Iranian people on the occasion of Nowruz (Persian New Year), March 21, 2009. He stated that the United States "is now committed to diplomacy that addresses the full range of issues before us, and to pursuing constructive ties among the United States, Iran, and the international community." He also referred to Iran as "The Islamic Republic of Iran," a formulation that appears to suggest that the United States fully accepts the Islamic revolution in Iran and is not seeking "regime change." (President Obama issued another Nowruz message on March 20, 2010, but it was critical of Iran's lack of acceptance of the diplomatic overtures of the past year.) In concert with that approach, Obama Administration officials did not indicate support for hardline options such as military action or regime change, although no option was explicitly "taken off the table." Prior to the June 12 election in Iran, other steps to engage Iran included:

- President Obama reportedly sent at least one letter to Iran's leadership expressing the Administration's philosophy in favor of engagement with Iran.
- The major speech to the "Muslim World" in Cairo on June 4, 2009, in which President Obama said the United States had played a role in the overthrow of Mossadeq, and said that Iran had a right to peaceful nuclear power if it complies with its responsibilities under the NPT.
- The United States publicly invited Iran to attend the March 31, 2009, conference on Afghanistan in the Netherlands, discussed above.
- The U.S. announced on April 8, 2009, that it would attend all future P5+1 meetings with Iran.

- Restrictions were loosened on U.S. diplomats to meet their Iranian counterparts at international meetings, and U.S. embassies were told they could invite Iranian diplomats to upcoming celebrations of U.S. Independence Day. (The July 4, 2009, invitations did not get issued because of the Iran unrest.)
- On the other hand, President Obama issued a formal one year extension of the U.S. ban on trade and investment with Iran on March 15, 2009 (and again on March 15, 2010).

2010: Administration Skepticism on Engagement

The election-related unrest in Iran and Iran's refusal to agree to technical terms of the October 1, 2009, nuclear agreement lessened the Administration's commitment to engagement beginning in 2010. In a statement following the June 9, 2010, passage of Resolution 1929, President Obama has described Iran as refusing, thus far, to accept the path of engagement and choosing instead to preserve all elements of its nuclear program. However, as stated repeatedly by senior U.S. officials, the United States is open to diplomacy with Iran on its nuclear program and sanctions are intended to cause Iran to bargain in good faith in those negotiations. As noted, talks were held on December 6-7, 2010, and additional talks are slated for January 2011 in Turkey.

Supreme Leader Khamene'i has not reverse the Iranian government engagement with the P5+1. However, he has ruled out bilateral talks with the United States unless the United States ceases a strategy of bringing pressure to bear on Iran through sanctions. This differs somewhat from the position of Ahmadinejad who continues to indicate willingness to talk directly to U.S. officials, including President Obama.

Military Action

Those who view a nuclear Iran as an unacceptable development believe that military action might be the only means of preventing Iran from acquiring a working nuclear device. The Obama Administration has not has not indicated an inclination toward military options against Iran's nuclear program, stressing instead the potential adverse consequences (Joint Chiefs Chairman Admiral Michael Mullen) and temporary effectiveness (Secretary Gates) of such options. Secretary Gates stressed the limited benefits during a speech in Australia on November 8, 2010, and an interview with *Wall Street Journal* editor Gerald Seib on November 16, 2010. Perhaps to maximize leverage in international dealings with Iran, Administration officials say no option is "off the table," although, on April 21, 2010, Under Secretary of Defense for Policy Michele Flournoy said that military action is "off the table *in the near term*."

However, suggesting frustration that other options have not altered Iran's nuclear program, Secretary of Defense Gates wrote a memo to the White House in January 2010 offering the view that the United States had not developed clear options to counter a nuclear Iran, if sanctions do not work.[59] Secretary Gates subsequently issued a formal statement saying his memo was mischaracterized as a "wake-up call" to develop new military options, but was rather an effort to stimulate thinking about several options, including containment in concert with the Gulf states. Still, suggesting continuing efforts to balance the risks and rewards of military options, in June and July 2010, Admiral Mullen said that it would be "incredibly dangerous" for Iran to achieve a nuclear weapons capability, while reiterating his long-standing concerns about the adverse consequences of a strike on Iran.

Proponents of U.S. air and missile strikes against suspected nuclear sites argue that military action could set back Iran's nuclear program because there are only a limited number of key targets, and these targets are known to U.S. planners and vulnerable, even those that are hardened or buried.[60] Estimates of the target set range from 400 nuclear and other WMD-related targets, to potentially a few thousand targets crucial to Iran's economy and military. Those who take an expansive view of the target set argue that the United States would need to reduce Iran's potential for retaliation by striking not only nuclear facilities but also Iran's conventional military, particularly its small ships and coastal missiles.

A U.S. ground invasion to remove Iran's regime has not, at any time, appeared to be under serious consideration in part because of the likely resistance an invasion would meet in Iran. This option has also suffered from a widespread belief that U.S. action would undercut the prospects of the Green opposition movement within Iran by rallying the public around the regime. Most U.S. allies in Europe, not to mention Russia and China, oppose military action.

Still others argue that there are military options that do not require actual combat. Some say that a naval embargo or related embargo is possible and could pressure Iran into reconsidering its stand on the nuclear issue. Others say that the imposition of a "no-fly zone" over Iran might also serve that purpose. Still others say that the United Nations could set up a special inspection mission to dismantle Iran's WMD programs, although inserting such a mission is likely to be resisted by Iran and could involve hostilities.

An Israeli Strike?

Some experts express greater concern over the potential for a strategic strike on Iran by Israel as compared to strikes by the United States. The debate over this possibility increased following the publication by the September 2010 issue of *The Atlantic* magazine of an article by Jeffrey Goldberg entitled "Point of No Return."[61] As noted in the piece, Israeli officials view a nuclear armed Iran as an existential threat and have repeatedly refused to rule out the possibility that Israel might strike Iran's nuclear infrastructure. Speculation about this possibility increased in March and April 2009 with statements by Israeli Prime Minister Benjamin Netanyahu to *The Atlantic* magazine stating that "You don't want a messianic apocalyptic cult controlling atomic bombs." This and other Israeli comments generated assessments by then CENTCOM Commander General Petraeus that Israel has become so frightened by a prospect of a nuclear Iran that it might decide to launch a strike on Iran's nuclear facilities. Adding to the prospects for this scenario, in mid-June 2008, Israeli officials confirmed reports that Israel had practiced a long-range strike such as that which would be required. Taking a position similar to that of the George W. Bush Administration, senior U.S. officials have visited Israel throughout 2010 (including Vice President Biden in March 2010) in part to express the view that the Obama Administration is committed to strict sanctions on Iran—with the implication that Israeli military action should not be undertaken. Others say that the United States, as of August 2010, is using assessments that Iran's nuclear program is not as far along as was feared to calm Israeli fears.

Although Israeli strategists say this might be a viable option, several experts doubt that Israel has the capability to make such action sufficiently effective to justify the risks. U.S. military leaders are said by observers to believe that an Israeli strike would inevitably draw the United States into a conflict with Iran but without the degree of planning that would be needed for success. Others believe Israel may also calculate that a strike would hurt the Green movement's prospects.

Iranian Retaliatory Scenarios[62]

Some officials and experts warn that a U.S. military strike on Iran could provoke conventional or, of even more concern, unconventional retaliation. As Iran sees and hears growing consideration of such possibilities, Iran's military leaders have, in mid-2010, stressed its willingness and ability to retaliate in the Gulf and cause the West economic difficulty. Iran has repeatedly stated it is capable of closing the Strait of Hormuz and would do so, if attacked. Such conflict is likely to raise world oil prices significantly out of fear of an extended supply disruption. Others say such action would cause Iran to withdraw from the NPT and refuse any IAEA inspections.

Iran has developed a strategy for unconventional warfare that partly compensates for its conventional weakness. Then CENTCOM Commander General John Abizaid said in March 2006 that the Revolutionary Guard Navy, through its basing and force structure, is designed to give Iran a capability to "internationalize" a crisis in the Strait of Hormuz. On January 30, 2007, his replacement at CENTCOM, Admiral William Fallon, said that "Based on my read of their military hardware acquisitions and development of tactics ... [the Iranians] are posturing themselves with the capability to attempt to deny us the ability to operate in [the Strait of Hormuz]." In July 2008 Iran again claimed it could close the Strait in a crisis but the then commander of U.S. naval forces in the Gulf, Admiral Kevin Cosgriff, backed by Joint Chiefs Chairman Mullen, said U.S. forces could quickly reopen the waterway. Some of these comments appear to reflect the findings of unclassified studies by the Office of Naval Intelligence that Iran has developed new capabilities and tactics, backed by new acquisitions, that could pose a threat to U.S. naval forces in the Gulf. If there were a conflict in the Gulf, some fear that Iran might try to use large numbers of boats to attack U.S. ships or to lay mines in the Strait.

Iran has tried repeatedly to demonstrate its retaliatory capacity. Iran has conducted at least five major military exercises since August 2006, including exercises simultaneous with U.S. maneuvers in the Gulf in March 2007. In February 2007, Iran seized 15 British sailors that Iran said were patrolling in Iran's waters, although Britain says they were in Iraqi waters performing coalition-related searches. They were held until April 5, 2007. On January 6, 2008, the U.S. Navy reported a confrontation in which five IRGC Navy small boats approached three U.S. Navy ships to the point where they manned battle stations. The IRGC boats veered off before any shots were fired. In October 2008, Iran announced it is building several new naval bases along the southern coast, including at Jask, indicating enhanced capability to threaten the entry and exit to the Strait of Hormuz. In late November 2009, Iran seized and held for about one week a British civilian sailing vessel and crew that Iran said had strayed into its waters.

Many experts view as potentially more significant the potential for Iran to fire missiles at Israel— and Iran's July 2008 missile tests could have been intended to demonstrate this retaliatory capability—or to direct Lebanese Hezbollah or Hamas to fire rockets at Israel. Iran could also try to direct anti-U.S. militias in Iraq and Afghanistan to attack U.S. troops. The Gulf states fear that Iran will fire coastal-based cruise missiles at their oil loading or other installations across the Gulf, as happened during the Iran-Iraq war.

Containment and the Gulf Security Dialogue

Some advocate a strategy of containment of Iran, either to dissuade Iran from pursuing a nuclear weapon or to constrain Iranian power if that capability is achieved. Stimulating support for this option may have been the intent of the Gates memo in January 2010, discussed above.

The U.S. Gulf deployments built on a containment strategy inaugurated in mid-2006 by the State Department, primarily the Bureau of Political-Military Affairs ("Pol-Mil"). It was termed the "Gulf Security Dialogue" (GSD), and represented an effort to revive some of the U.S.-Gulf state defense cooperation that had begun during the Clinton Administration but had since languished as the United States focused on the post-September 11 wars in Afghanistan and Iraq.

The Obama Administration is continuing the GSD effort. During a visit to the Middle East in March 2009, Secretary of State Clinton said, after meeting with several Arab and Israeli leaders in the region, that "there is a great deal of concern about Iran from this whole region." Iran was also the focus of her trip to the Gulf region (Qatar and Saudi Arabia) in February 2010. On this trip, she again raised the issue of a possible U.S. extension of a "security umbrella" or guarantee to regional states against Iran, as a means of preventing Gulf accommodations to Iranian demands or attempting themselves to acquire countervailing nuclear capabilities.

One goal of the GSD, kept in place by the Obama Administration, is to boost Gulf state capabilities through new arms sales to the GCC states. As noted above, the Gulf states might buy more than $120 billion worth of U.S. military equipment and services over the next several years, the core of which is a sale of $60 billion worth of aircraft, helicopters, and services for Saudi Arabia[63] that was notified to Congress in mid-October 2010. The period of congressional review has expired as of November 28, 2010. A major intent of the sales is to improve Gulf state missile defense capabilities, as well as to improve border and maritime security equipment through sales of combat littoral ships, radar systems, and communications gear. Several GSD-inspired sales include PAC-3 sales to UAE and Kuwait, and Joint Direct Attack Munitions (JDAMs) to Saudi Arabia and UAE (notified to Congress in December 2007 and January 2008). A sale to UAE of the very advanced "THAAD" (Theater High Altitude Area Defense) has also been notified, and the sale is expected to be finalized some time in 2011. In August 2010, the Administration notified to Congress a potential sale of additional Patriot missiles to Kuwait.

The containment policy may have been furthered somewhat in May 2009 when France inaugurated a small military base in UAE, its first in the region. This signaled that France is committed to helping contain Iran.

Presidential Authorities and Legislation

A decision to take military action might raise the question of presidential authorities. In the 109th Congress, H.Con.Res. 391, introduced on April 26, 2006, called on the President to not initiate military action against Iran without first obtaining authorization from Congress. A similar bill, H.Con.Res. 33, was introduced in the 110th Congress. An amendment to H.R. 1585, the National Defense Authorization Act for FY2008, requiring authorization for force against Iran, was defeated 136 to 288. A provision that sought to bar the Administration from taking military action against Iran without congressional authorization was taken out of an early draft of an FY2007 supplemental appropriation (H.R. 1591) to fund additional costs for Iraq and Afghanistan combat (vetoed on May 1, 2007). Other provisions, including requiring briefings to Congress about military contingency planning related to Iran's nuclear program, were in a House-passed FY2009 defense authorization bill (H.R. 5658). In the 111th Congress, H.Con.Res. 94 calls for the United States to negotiate an "Incidents at Sea" agreement with Iran.

Regime Change

The Obama Administration has, particularly in its first year, sought to allay Iran's long-standing suspicions that the main U.S. goal is to unseat the Islamic regime in Iran. However, the 2009 domestic unrest in Iran complicated Iran policy for President Obama, who has sought to preserve the possibility of a nuclear agreement with Iran while expressing support for human and political rights demanded by the Green movement. As 2009 progressed, the statements of President Obama and other U.S. officials became progressively more critical of the regime. On December 28, 2009, President Obama shifted further toward public support for the opposition outright by saying, in regard to the unrest in Iran, " Along with all free nations, the United States stands with those who seek their universal rights."[64] Secretary of State Clinton reiterated this position on September 19, 2010, but said the United States needs take care not to be so overtly supportive as to make the Iranian opposition appear as "stooges of the United States."

Still, some believe that a change of party control in the House of Representatives, subsequent to the November 2010 U.S. elections, might lead to increased calls in Congress to adopt an outright regime change policy toward Iran. Those who take this view might consider as insufficient the Administration's steps in 2010 to help the Green movement. The Administration has sought to help the opposition parry regime efforts to monitor or cut off its communications with itself and the international community. These steps, according to the Administration, stop short of constituting a policy of "regime change," although Iran interprets any help to the Green movement as evidence of U.S. intent to overthrow the clerical government.

Iran's suspicions are based on the widespread perception that the United States has hoped, and at times sought to promote, regime change since the 1979 Islamic revolution. The United States provided some funding to anti-regime groups, mainly pro-monarchists, during the 1980s.[65] The George W. Bush Administration's belief in this option became apparent after the September 11, 2001, attacks, when President George W. Bush described Iran as part of an "axis of evil" in his January 2002 State of the Union message. President George W. Bush's second inaugural address (January 20, 2005) and his State of the Union messages of January 31, 2006, stated that "our nation hopes one day to be the closest of friends with a free and democratic Iran."

Democracy Promotion Efforts

Clear indications of affinity for a regime change option in the George W. Bush Administration included the funding of Iranian pro-democracy activists (see below), although that Administration said that the democracy promotion programs were intended to promote political evolution in Iran and change regime behavior, not to overthrow the regime. A few accounts, such as "Preparing the Battlefield" by Seymour Hersh in the *New Yorker* (July 7 and 14, 2008) say that President George W. Bush authorized U.S. covert operations to destabilize the regime,[66] involving assistance to some of the ethnic-based armed groups discussed above. CRS has no way to confirm assertions in the Hersh article that up to $400 million was appropriated and/or used to aid the groups mentioned.

Binding legislation to favor democracy promotion in Iran was enacted in the 109th Congress. The Iran Freedom Support Act (P.L. 109-293), signed September 30, 2006, authorized funds (no specific dollar amount) for Iran democracy promotion.[67] Iran asserts that funding democracy promotion represents a violation of the 1981 "Algiers Accords" that settled the Iran hostage crisis and provide for non-interference in each others' internal affairs.

The State Department, the implementer of U.S. democracy promotion programs for Iran, has used funds in appropriations (see **Table 8**) to support pro-democracy programs run by at least 26 organizations based in the United States and in Europe; the Department refuses to name grantees for security reasons. The funds shown below have been obligated through DRL and the Bureau of Near Eastern Affairs in partnership with USAID. About $60 million has been allocated. Some of the funds have been appropriated for cultural exchanges, public diplomacy, and broadcasting to Iran. The Obama Administration requested funds for Near East regional democracy programs in its FY2010 and FY2011 budget requests, but no specific requests for funds for Iran were delineated. No U.S. assistance has been provided to Iranian exile-run stations.[68]

Many have consistently questioned the effectiveness of such funding. In the view of many experts, U.S. funds would make the aid recipients less attractive to most Iranians. Even before the post-election crackdown, Iran was arresting civil society activists by alleging they are accepting the U.S. democracy promotion funds, while others have refused to participate in U.S.-funded programs, fearing arrest.[69] In May 2007—Iranian-American scholar Haleh Esfandiari, of the Woodrow Wilson Center in Washington, DC, was imprisoned for several months, on the grounds that the Wilson Center was part of this effort. The center has denied being part of the democracy promotion effort in Iran.

Perhaps in response to some of these criticisms, the Obama Administration has altered Iran democracy promotion programs toward working directly with Iranians inside Iran who are organized around such apolitical issues as health care, the environment, and science.[70] Less emphasis has been placed on funding journalists and human rights activists in Iran, or on sponsoring visits by Iranians to the United States.[71] One issue arose concerning the State Department decision in late 2009 not to renew a contract to the Iran Human Rights Documentation Center (IHRDC), based at Yale University, which was cataloguing human rights abuses in Iran. Some outside experts believe that, particularly in the current context of a regime crackdown against democracy activists, the contract should have been renewed. That criticism went hand in hand with the view of some experts that the post-election unrest in Iran was evidence that such democracy promotion programs were working and should be enhanced.

Other Congressional Action to Assist the Green Movement

During 2010, increasing emphasis was placed on preventing the Iranian government's suppression of electronic communication. Among legislation that has been enacted is the "Voice (Victims of Iranian Censorship) Act" (Subtitle D of the FY2010 Defense Authorization, P.L. 111- 84), which contains provisions to potentially penalize companies that are selling Iran technology equipment that it can use to suppress or monitor the Internet usage of Iranians.[72] In February 2010, the Administration eased licensing requirements for Iranians to download free mass market U.S. software. And, the U.S. Office of Foreign Assets Control has reportedly licensed a California firm (Censorship Research Center) to export anti-filtering software to Iran.[73]

Several provisions of the Comprehensive Iran Sanctions, Accountability, and Divestment Act of 2010 (P.L. 111-195, signed July 1, 2010) are designed to prevent suppression of information : one provision excludes from the ban on U.S. exports to Iran equipment to promote Internet communication. Another provision (Section 105) prohibits U.S. contracts for any firm that exports to Iran equipment that Iran could use to monitor or restrict the free flow of information. Another provision bans travel to the United States and freezes the U.S.-based assets of any Iranian named by the Administration as an abuser of human rights. This represented the provisions of S. 3022 (Iran Human Rights Sanctions Act), which was a stand-alone bill. Acting under this section, President Obama issued Executive Order 13553 imposing these human rights-related sanctions and eight Iranian security and judicial officials were sanctioned simultaneously.

It is possible that some in the 112th Congress might argue for renewed emphasis on these efforts, or to go even further to express support for outright regime change policies. In the 111th Congress, one bill said that it should be U.S. policy to promote the overthrow of the regime (The Iran Democratic Transition Act, S. 3008). On December 9, 2010, at a forum in Washington, D.C., Senator-elect Mark Kirk proposed a dedicated U.S. funding stream to promote democracy and human rights in Iran which would benefit the Green movement and demonstrate to the opposition that it can count on support from the United States.

Broadcasting Issues

Another part of the democracy promotion effort has been the development of new U.S. broadcasting services to Iran. The broadcasting component of policy has been an extension of a trend that began in the late 1990s. Radio *Farda* ("tomorrow," in Farsi) began under Radio Free Europe/Radio Liberty (RFE/RL), in partnership with the Voice of America (VOA), in October 1998. The service was established with an initial $4 million from the FY1998 Commerce/State/Justice appropriation (P.L. 105-119). (It was to be called Radio Free Iran but was never formally given that name by RFE/RL.) Radio *Farda* now broadcasts 24 hours/day. The State Department also has begun a Persian-language website.

Persian News Network (PNN). VOA-TV's Persian News Network (PNN) began on July 3, 2003, and now is broadcasting to Iran about seven hours a day. VOA Persian services combined cost about $10 million per year. PNN is coming under increasing criticism from observers who say that PNN is losing its audience among young, educated Iranians who form the core of the Green movement and are looking for signs of U.S. official support. Some observers maintain that decisions on who to put on PNN panel discussion shows are made by a small group of Iranian exiles who do not seek the replacement of the Iranian regime and who deliberately exclude certain Green movement persons with whom they disagree. Still others say that PNN frequently airs the views of Iranian groups that are advocates of U.S. engagement of the regime or who downplay regime transgressions. Some have criticized PNN for covering long-standing exiled opposition groups, such as supporters of the son of the former Shah of Iran.[74] The altered Broadcasting Board of Governors (as of June 2010) has

Iran: U.S. Concerns and Policy Responses 227

formed a "PNN subcommittee," headed by Governor Enders Wimbush, to address the widespread criticisms of PNN.

Table 8. Iran Democracy Promotion Funding

FY2004	Foreign operations appropriation (P.L. 108-199) earmarked $1.5 million for "educational, humanitarian and non-governmental organizations and individuals inside Iran to support the advancement of democracy and human rights in Iran." The State Department Bureau of Democracy and Labor (DRL) gave $1 million to a unit of Yale University, and $500,000 to National Endowment for Democracy.
FY2005	$3 million from FY2005 foreign aid appropriation (P.L. 108-447) for democracy promotion. Priority areas: political party development, media, labor rights, civil society promotion, and human rights.
FY2006	$11.15 for democracy promotion from regular FY2006 foreign aid appropriation (P.L. 109-102). $4.15 million administered by DRL and $7 million for the Bureau of Near Eastern Affairs.
FY2006 supp.	Total of $66.1 million (of $75 million requested) from FY2006 supplemental (P.L. 109-234): $20 million for democracy promotion; $5 million for public diplomacy directed at the Iranian population; $5 million for cultural exchanges; and $36.1 million for Voice of America-TV and "Radio Farda" broadcasting. Broadcasting funds are provided through the Broadcasting Board of Governors.
FY2007	FY2007 continuing resolution provided $6.55 million for Iran (and Syria) to be administered through DRL. $3.04 million was used for Iran. No funds were requested.
FY2008	$60 million (of $75 million requested) is contained in Consolidated Appropriation (H.R. 2764, P.L. 110-161), of which, according to the conference report $21.6 million is ESF for pro-democracy programs, including non-violent efforts to oppose Iran's meddling in other countries. $7.9 million is from a "Democracy Fund" for use by DRL. The Appropriation also fully funded additional $33.6 million requested for Iran broadcasting: $20 million for VOA Persian service; and $8.1 million for Radio Farda; and $5.5 million for exchanges with Iran.
FY2009	Request was for $65 million in ESF "to support the aspirations of the Iranian people for a democratic and open society by promoting civil society, civic participation, media freedom, and freedom of information." H.R. 1105 (P.L. 111-8) provides $25 million for democracy promotion programs in the region, including in Iran.
FY2010	No specific democracy promotion request for Iran, but some funds (out of $40 million requested for Near East democracy programs) likely to fund continued human rights research and public diplomacy in Iran.
FY2011	No specific request for Iran, but $40 million requested for Near East democracy programs

Source: Information provided by State Department and reviewed by Department's Iran Office, February 1, 2010.

Enhanced Iran-Focused Regional Diplomatic Presence

In 2006, the George W. Bush Administration also began increasing the presence of Persian-speaking U.S. diplomats in U.S. diplomatic missions around Iran, in part to help identify and facilitate Iranian participate in U.S. democracy-promotion programs. The Iran unit at the U.S. consulate in Dubai has been enlarged significantly into a "regional presence" office, and "Iran-watcher" positions have been added to U.S. diplomatic facilities in Baku,

Azerbaijan; Istanbul, Turkey; Frankfurt, Germany; London; and Ashkabad, Turkmenistan, all of which have large expatriate Iranian populations and/or proximity to Iran.[75] An enlarged (eight-person) "Office of Iran Affairs" has been formed at State Department, and it is reportedly engaged in contacts with U.S.-based exile groups such as those discussed earlier.

Enhanced U.S. Interests Section

Some go further and say that the United States should staff the U.S. interests section in Tehran with U.S. personnel, who would mostly process Iranian visas and help facilitate U.S.-Iran peopleto-people contacts (the interests section is currently under the auspices of the Swiss Embassy). U.S. staffing was considered by the George W. Bush Administration in late 2008, but the decision was left to the Obama Administration. The Obama Administration appeared inclined toward U.S. staffing, but no decision was announced. Such a step was likely delayed or derailed outright by the Iranian response to the postelection protests. However, some observers say that there are State Department officials who see U.S. staffing as a way to broaden U.S. contacts with representatives of the Green movement and more accurately gauge its strength.

U.S. Sanctions

As discussed above, any number of additional U.N. or multilateral sanctions might come under consideration. The following are brief summaries of the major U.S. sanctions currently in place against Iran. These sanctions, as well as the economic effects of U.S. and other sanctions in place, are discussed in substantially more detail in CRS Report RS20871, *Iran Sanctions*, by Kenneth Katzman. That report also discusses, in detail, the alterations to many different U.S. sanctions provided for by CISADA (P.L. 111-195).

Ban on U.S. Trade With and Investment in Iran

Executive Order 12959 (May 6, 1995) bans almost all U.S. trade with and investment in Iran. Modifications in 1999 and 2000 allowed for exportation of U.S. food and medical equipment, and importation from Iran of luxury goods (carpets, caviar, dried fruits, nuts), but P.L. 111-195 restores the complete ban on imports from Iran (and regulations to that effect were issued by OFAC in August 2010). The trade ban does not apply to foreign subsidiaries of U.S. firms, because those firms are governed by the laws of the country where they are incorporated.

U.S. Sanctions Against Foreign Firms that Invest in Iran's Energy Sector

The Iran Sanctions Act (P.L. 104-172, August 5, 1996, as amended, most recently by P.L. 111- 195) authorizes the President to select three out of a menu of nine sanctions to impose against firms that the Administration has determined have invested more than $20 million to develop Iran's petroleum (oil and gas) sector, or which sell Iran more than $1 million worth of gasoline or equipment to import gasoline or refine oil into gasoline.

Targeted Financial Measures by Treasury Department

U.S. officials, particularly Under Secretary of the Treasury Stuart Levey say the United States is having substantial success in separate unilateral efforts ("targeted financial measures") to persuade European governments and companies to stop transactions with Iran. They assert to these countries and firms that doing so entails financial risk and furthers terrorism and proliferation.

Terrorism List Designation Sanctions

Iran's designation by the Secretary of State as a "state sponsor of terrorism" (January 19, 1984— commonly referred to as the "terrorism list") triggers several sanctions, including the following:

- a ban on the provision of U.S. foreign assistance to Iran under Section 620A of the Foreign Assistance Act.
- a ban on arms exports to Iran under Section 40 of the Arms Export Control Act (P.L. 95-92, as amended). However, Iran is already subject to a sweeping restriction on any U.S. trade under Executive Order 12959 mentioned above.
- under Section 6(j) of the Export Administration Act (P.L. 96-72, as amended), a significant restriction—amended by other laws to a "presumption of denial"—on U.S. exports to Iran of items that could have military applications.
- under Section 327 of the Anti-Terrorism and Effective Death Penalty Act (P.L. 104-132, April 24, 1996), a requirement that U.S. representatives to international financial institutions, such as the World Bank, vote against international loans to Iran (and other terrorism list states, by those institutions. The U.S. "no" vote does not ensure that Iran would not receive such loans, because the United States can be outvoted by other governments.

Sanctions Against Foreign Firms that Aid Iran's Weapons of Mass Destruction Programs

The Iran-Syria-North Korea Nonproliferation Act (P.L. 106-178, March 14, 2000, as amended) authorizes the Administration to impose sanctions on foreign persons or firms determined, under the act, to have provided assistance to Iran's weapons of mass destruction (WMD) programs. Sanctions to be imposed include restrictions on U.S. trade with the sanctioned entity.

Sanctions Against Foreign Firms that Sell Advanced Arms to Iran

The Iran-Iraq Arms Nonproliferation Act (P.L. 102-484, October 23, 1992, as amended) provides for U.S. sanctions against foreign firms that sell Iran "destabilizing numbers and types of conventional weapons" or WMD technology. Some experts criticized the act for the lack of a clear definition of what constitutes a "destabilizing number or type" of conventional weapon.

Ban on Transactions with Foreign Entities Determined to Be Supporting International Terrorism

Executive Order 13324 (September 23, 2001) authorizes a ban on U.S. transactions with entities determined, in accordance with the Order, to be supporting international terrorism.

The Order was not specific to Iran, coming 12 days after the September 11, 2001, attacks on the United States, but several Iranian entities have been designated as terrorism supporters. These entities include the Qods Force of the Islamic Revolutionary Guard Corps (IRGC), as well as Bank Saderat.

Ban on Transactions with Foreign Entities that Support Proliferation

Executive Order 13382 (June 28, 2005) amended previous executive orders to provide for a ban on U.S. transactions with entities determined, under the Order, to be supporting international proliferation. As is the case for Executive Order 13324, mentioned above, Executive Order 13382 was not specific to Iran. However, numerous Iranian entities, including the IRGC itself, have been designated as proliferation supporting entities under the Order.

Divestment

A growing trend not only in Congress but in several states is to require or call for or require divestment of shares of firms that have invested in Iran's energy sector (at the same levels considered sanctionable under the Iran Sanctions Act).[76] A Title in P.L. 111-195 authorizes and protects from lawsuits various investment managers who divest from shares of firms that conduct sanctionable business with Iran.

Counter-Narcotics

In February 1987, Iran was first designated as a state that failed to cooperate with U.S. anti-drug efforts or take adequate steps to control narcotics production or trafficking. U.S. and U.N. Drug Control Program (UNDCP) assessments of drug production in Iran prompted the Clinton Administration, on December 7, 1998, to remove Iran from the U.S. list of major drug producing countries. This exempts Iran from the annual certification process that kept drug-related U.S. sanctions in place on Iran. According to several governments, over the past few years Iran has augmented security on its border with Afghanistan in part to prevent the flow of narcotics from that country into Iran. Britain has sold Iran some night vision equipment and body armor for the counter-narcotics fight. The United States and Iran were in large measure in agreement during a March 8, 2010, meeting at the United Nations in Geneva on the issue of counter-narcotics, particularly those emanating from Afghanistan.

U.S.-Iran Assets Disputes

Iranian leaders continue to assert that the United States is holding Iranian assets, and that this is an impediment to improved relations. This is discussed in CRS Report RS20871, *Iran Sanctions*, by Kenneth Katzman.

Travel-Related Guidance

Use of U.S. passports for travel to Iran is permitted. Iranians entering the United States are required to be fingerprinted, and Iran has imposed reciprocal requirements. In May 2007, the State Department increased its warnings about U.S. travel to Iran, based largely on the arrests of the dual Iranian-American nationals discussed earlier.

CONCLUSION

Mistrust between the United States and Iran's Islamic regime has run deep for more than three decades. Some argue that, no matter who is in power in Tehran, the United States and Iran have a common long-term interest in stability in the Persian Gulf and South Asia regions. According to this view, major diplomatic overtures toward the regime might not only help resolve the nuclear issue but yield fruit in producing a new, constructive U.S.-Iran relationship.

Others argue that U.S. concerns stem first and foremost from the character of Iran's regime. Those who take this view see in the Green movement the potential to replace the regime and to integrate Iran into a pro-U.S. strategic architecture in the region. Many argue that a wholesale replacement of the current regime would produce major strategic benefits beyond reducing the threat from Iran's nuclear program, including an end to Iran's effort to obstruct a broad Arab-Israeli peace.

Table 9. Selected Economic Indicators

Economic Growth	1.5 % (2009 est.); 2.5% (2008); 7.8% (2007)
Per Capita Income	$13,100/yr purchasing power parity
GDP	$865 billion purchasing power parity (2009)
Proven Oil Reserves	135 billion barrels (highest after Russia and Canada)
Oil Production/Exports	4.0 million barrels per day (mbd)/ 2.4 mbd exports. Exports could shrink to zero by 2015-2020 due to accelerating domestic consumption.
Major Oil/Gas Customers	China—300,00 barrels per day (bpd); about 4% of China's oil imports; Japan—600,000 bpd, about 12% of oil imports; other Asia (mainly South Korea)—450,000 bpd; Italy— 300,000 bpd; France—210,000 bpd; Netherlands 40,000 bpd; other Europe—200,000 bpd; India—150,000 bpd (10% of its oil imports; Africa—200,000 bpd. Turkey—gas: 8.6 billion cubic meters/yr
Major Export Markets	Japan ($9.9 billion); China ($9.2 billion); Turkey ($5.1 billion); Italy ($4.45 billion); South Korea ($4 billion); Netherlands ($3.2 billion); France ($2.7 billion); South Africa ($2.7 billion); Spain ($2.3 billion); Greece ($2 billion)
Major Imports	Germany ($5.6 billion); China ($5 billion); UAE ($4 billion); S. Korea ($2.9 billion); France ($2.6 billion); Italy ($2.5 billion); Russia ($1.7 billion); India ($1.6 billion); Brazil ($1.3 billion); Japan ($1.3 billion).
Trade With U.S. (2009)	Total U.S. Exports to Iran: $280 million; Total Imports to U.S. from Iran: $65 million
Major Non-Oil Investments	Renault (France) and Mercedes (Germany)—automobile production in Karaj, Iran—valued at $370 million; Renault (France), Peugeot (France) and Volkswagen (Germany)— auto parts production; Turkey—Tehran airport, hotels; China—shipbuilding on Qeshm Island, aluminum factory in Shirvan, cement plant in Hamadan; UAE financing Esfahan Steel Company; India—steel plant, petrochemical plant; S. Korea—steel plant in Kerman Province; S. Korea and Germany—$1.7 billion to expand Esfahan refinery.
"Oil Stabilization Fund" Reserves	$12.1 billion (August 2008, IMF estimate). Mid-2009 estimates by experts say it may have now been reduced to nearly zero.
External Debt	$19 billion (2007 est.)
Development Assistance Received	2003 (latest available): $136 million grant aid. Biggest donors: Germany ($38 million); Japan ($17 million); France ($9 million).
Inflation	15% + (May 2009), according to Iranian officials.
Unemployment Rate	11%+

Sources: CIA, *The World Factbook*; various press; IMF; Iran Trade Planning Division; CRS conversations with experts and foreign diplomats.

Others argue that many Iranians are united on major national security issues and that a new regime would not necessarily align with the United States. Some believe that many Iranians fear that alignment with the United States would produce a degree of U.S. control and infuse Iran with Western culture that many Iranians find un-Islamic and objectionable.

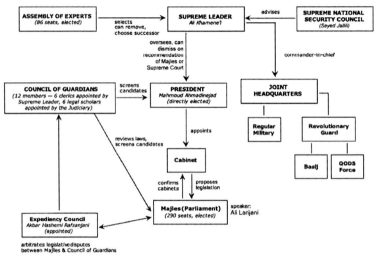

Source: CRS.

Figure 1. Structure of the Iranian Government.

Source: Map Resources. Adapted by CRS (April 2005).

Figure 2. Map of Iran.

End Notes

[1] The Assembly also has the power to amend Iran's constitution and to remove a Supreme Leader. At the time of his elevation to Supreme Leader, Khamene'i was generally referred to at the rank of Hojjat ol-Islam, one rank below Ayatollah, suggesting his religious "elevation" was political rather than through traditional mechanisms.

[2] The Council of Guardians consists of six Islamic jurists and six secular lawyers. The six Islamic jurists are appointed by the Supreme Leader. The six lawyers on the Council are selected by the judiciary but confirmed by the Majles.

[3] Kampeas, Ron. "Iran's Crown Prince Plots Nonviolent Insurrection from Suburban Washington." Associated Press, August 26, 2002.

[4] Rafsanjani was constitutionally permitted to run because a third term would not have been consecutive with his previous two terms. In the 2001 presidential election, the Council permitted 10 out of the 814 registered candidates.

[5] A paper published by Chatham House and the University of St. Andrews strongly questions how Ahmadinejad's vote could have been as large as reported by official results, in light of past voting patterns throughout A paper published by Chatham House and the University of St. Andrews strongly questions how Ahmadinejad's vote could have been as large as reported by official results, in light of past voting patterns throughout Iran. "Preliminary Analysis of the Voting Figures in Iran's 2009 Presidential Election." http://www.chathamhouse.org.uk.

[6] Takeyh, Ray. "A Green Squeeze on Iran" Washington Post, November 12, 2010.

[7] Other names by which this group is known is the Mojahedin-e-Khalq Organization (MEK or MKO) and the National Council of Resistance (NCR).

[8] The designation was made under the authority of the Anti-Terrorism and Effective Death Penalty Act of 1996 (P.L. 104-132).

[9] A March 16, 2006 "National Security Strategy" document stated that the United States "may face no greater challenge from a single country than from Iran."

[10] See http://www.whitehouse.gov/nsc/nss/2006/.

[11] For text, see http://media.washingtontimes.com/media/docs/2010/Apr/20/Iran_Military_Report.pdf. The report is required by Section 1245 of the National Defense Authorization Act for FY2010 (P.L. 111-84).

[12] For a more extensive discussion of the IRGC, see Katzman, Kenneth. "The Warriors of Islam: Iran's Revolutionary Guard," *Westview Press*, 1993.

[13] Gertz, Bill. "CIA Says Iran Has Capability to Produce Nuke Weapons." *Washington Times*, March 30, 2010.

[14] For text of the May 31, 2010, IAEA report, see http://isis-online.org/uploads/isis-reports/documents/IAEA_Report_Iran_31May2010.pdf.

[15] http://www.isis-online.org/uploads/isis-reports/documents/Iran_report-nov23.pdf

[16] Entous, Adam. "U.S. Officials See Iran Nuclear Bomb Probable in 3-5 Years." Reuters, April 13, 2010.

[17] In November 2006, the IAEA, at U.S. urging, declined to provide technical assistance to the Arak facility on the grounds that it was likely for proliferation purposes.

[18] Lancaster, John and Kamran Khan. "Pakistanis Say Nuclear Scientists Aided Iran." *Washington Post*, January 24, 2004.

[19] The text of the report is at: http://www.isis-online.org/uploads/isis-reports/documents/Iran_report-nov23.pdf

[20] For Iran's arguments about its program, see Iranian paid advertisement "An Unnecessary Crisis—Setting the Record Straight About Iran's Nuclear Program," in the *New York Times*, November 18, 2005. P. A11.

[21] Stern, Roger. "The Iranian Petroleum Crisis and United States National Security," *Proceedings of the National Academy of Sciences of the United States of America*. December 26, 2006.

[22] For text of the agreement, see http://www.iaea.org/NewsCenter/Focus/IaeaIran/eu_iran14112004.shtml. EU-3-Iran negotiations on a permanent nuclear pact began on December 13, 2004, and related talks on a trade and cooperation accord (TCA) began in January 2005.

[23] In November 2006, the IAEA, at U.S. urging, declined to provide technical assistance to the Arak facility.

[24] Voting in favor: United States, Australia, Britain, France, Germany, Canada, Argentina, Belgium, Ghana, Ecuador, Hungary, Italy, Netherlands, Poland, Portugal, Sweden, Slovakia, Japan, Peru, Singapore, South Korea, India. Against: Venezuela. Abstaining: Pakistan, Algeria, Yemen, Brazil, China, Mexico, Nigeria, Russia, South Africa, Sri Lanka, Tunisia, and Vietnam.

[25] Voting no: Cuba, Syria, Venezuela. Abstaining: Algeria, Belarus, Indonesia, Libya, South Africa.

[26] See http://daccessdds.un.org/doc/UNDOC/GEN/N06/290/88/PDF/N0629088.pdf?OpenElement.

[27] One source purports to have obtained the contents of the package from ABC News: http://www.basicint.org/pubs/ Notes/BN060609.htm.

[28] Dempsey, Judy. "U.S. Urged to Talk With Iran." *International Herald Tribune*, February 5, 2009.

[29] CRS conversations with European diplomats in July 2009.

[30] "Cooperation for Peace, Justice, and Progress." Text of Iranian proposals. http://enduringamerica. com/2009/09/11/ irans-nukes-full-text-of-irans-proposal-to-51-powers/.

[31] Text of the pact is at http://www.cfr.org/publication/22140/.

[32] Mackenzie, Kate. "Oil At the Heart of Latest Iranian Sanctions Efforts." *Financial Times*, March 8, 2010.

[33] Text of the resolution is at http://www.isis-online.org/uploads/isis-reports/documents/ Draft_resolution_on_ Iran_annexes.pdf.

[34] The text of President Obama's statement is at http://www.whitehouse.gov/the-press-office/remarks-president-unitednations-security-council-resolution-iran-sanctions.

[35] Pomfret, John. "Chinese Firms Bypass Sanctions on Iran, U.S. Says." *Washington Post*, October 18, 2010.

[36] The sanctions issue, particularly U.S. sanctions, is discussed in far greater detail in CRS Report RS20871, *Iran Sanctions*, by Kenneth Katzman.

[37] Annual Threat Assessment of the Intelligence for the Senate Select Committee on Intelligence, Dennis C. Blair, Director of National Intelligence, February 2, 2010.

[38] Broad, William and David Sanger. "Relying On Computer, U.S. Seeks to Prove Iran's Nuclear Aims." *New York Times*, November 13, 2005.

[39] Walsh, Elsa. "Annals of Politics: Louis Freeh's Last Case." *The New Yorker*, May 14, 2001. The June 21, 2001, federal grand jury indictments of 14 suspects (13 Saudis and a Lebanese citizen) in the Khobar bombing indicate that Iranian agents may have been involved, but no indictments of any Iranians were announced. In June 2002, Saudi Arabia reportedly sentenced some of the eleven Saudi suspects held there. The 9/11 Commission final report asserts that Al Qaeda might have had some as yet undetermined involvement in the Khobar Towers attacks.

[40] This issue is covered in greater depth in CRS Report RS22323, *Iran-Iraq Relations*, by Kenneth Katzman.

[41] CNN "Late Edition" interview with Hamas co-founder Mahmoud Zahar, January 29, 2006.

[42] Hamas Leader Praises Iran's Help in Gaza 'Victory.' CNN.com. February 1, 2009.

[43] Slackman, Michael. "Egypt Accuses Hezbollah of Plotting Attacks in Sinai and Arms Smuggling to Gaza." *New York Times*, April 14, 2009

[44] For detail on Hezbollah, see CRS Report R41446, *Hezbollah: Background and Issues for Congress*, by Casey L. Addis and Christopher M. Blanchard

[45] Hezbollah is believed responsible for the October 1983 bombing of the U.S. Marine barracks in Beirut, as well as attacks on U.S. Embassy Beirut facilities in April 1983 and September 1984, and for the hijacking of TWA Flight 847 in June 1985 in which Navy diver Robert Stetham was killed. Hezbollah is also believed to have committed the March 17, 1992, bombing of Israel's embassy in that city, which killed 29 people. Its last known terrorist attack outside Lebanon was the July 18, 1994, bombing of a Jewish community center in Buenos Aires, which killed 85. On October 31, 2006, Argentine prosecutors asked a federal judge to seek the arrest of Rafsanjani, former Intelligence Minister Ali Fallahian, former Foreign Minister Ali Akbar Velayati, and four other Iranian officials for this attack.

[46] "Israel's Peres Says Iran Arming Hizbollah." Reuters, February 4, 2002.

[47] Rotella, Sebastian. "In Lebanon, Hezbollah Arms Stockpile Bigger, Deadlier." *Los Angeles Times*, May 4, 2008.

[48] Shadid, Anthony. "Armed With Iran's Millions, Fighters Turn to Rebuilding." *Washington Post*, August 16, 2006.

[49] Levinson, Charles. "Iran Arms Syria With Radar." *Wall Street Journal*, June 30, 2010.

[50] Substantially more detail on Iran's activities in Afghanistan is contained in: CRS Report RL30588, *Afghanistan: Post-Taliban Governance, Security, and U.S. Policy*, by Kenneth Katzman.

[51] Gertz, Bill. "Al Qaeda Terrorists Being Held by Iran." *Washington Times*, July 24, 2003.

[52] Gertz, Bill. "CIA Points to Continuing Iran Tie to Al Qaeda." *Washington Times*, July 23, 2004.

[53] "Tehran Pledges to Crack Down on Militants." Associated Press, July 18, 2005.

[54] An exception was the abortive 1985-1986 clandestine arms supply relationship with Iran in exchange for some American hostages held by Hezbollah in Lebanon (the so-called "Iran-Contra Affair"). Iran has an interest section in Washington, DC, under the auspices of the Embassy of Pakistan; it is staffed by Iranian-Americans. The U.S. interest section in Tehran has no American personnel; it is under the Embassy of Switzerland.

[55] Sciolino, Elaine. *The Outlaw State: Saddam Hussein's Quest for Power and the Gulf Crisis*. New York: John Wiley and Sons, 1991. p. 168.

[56] Cooper, Helene and David Sanger. "Strategy on Iran Stirs New Debate at White House." *New York Times*, June 16, 2007.

[57] Wright, Robin. "U.S. In 'Useful' Talks With Iran." *Los Angeles Times*, May 13, 2003.

[58] http://www.armscontrol.org/pdf/2003_Spring_Iran_Proposal.pdf

[59] Sanger, David and Thom Shanker. "Gates Says U.S. Lacks Policy to Curb Iran's Nuclear Drive." *New York Times*, April 18, 2010.

[60] For an extended discussion of U.S. air strike options on Iran, see Rogers, Paul. *Iran: Consequences Of a War*. Oxford Research Group, February 2006.

[61] The text is at: http://www.theatlantic.com/magazine/archive/2010/09/the-point-of-no-return/8186/

[62] See also, Washington Institute for Near East Policy. "The Last Resort: Consequences of Preventive Military Action Against Iran," by Patrick Clawson and Michael Eisenstadt. June 2008.

[63] Khalaf, Roula and James Drummond. "Gulf in \$123 Bn Arms Spree." *Financial Times*, September 21, 2010.

[64] White House, Office of the Press Secretary. "Statement by the President on the Attempted Attack on Christmas Day and Recent Violence in Iran." December 28, 2009.

[65] CRS conversations with U.S. officials responsible for Iran policy. 1980-1990. After a period of suspension of such assistance, in 1995, the Clinton Administration accepted a House-Senate conference agreement to include \$18-\$20 million in funding authority for covert operations against Iran in the FY1996 Intelligence Authorization Act (H.R. 1655, P.L. 104-93), according to a *Washington Post* report of December 22, 1995. The Clinton Administration reportedly focused the covert aid on changing the regime's behavior, rather than its overthrow.

[66] Ross, Brian and Richard Esposito. Bush Authorizes New Covert Action Against Iran. http://blogs.abcnews.com/theblotter/2007/05/bush_authorizes.html.

[67] This legislation was a modification of H.R. 282, which passed the House on April 26, 2006, by a vote of 397-21, and S. 333, which was introduced in the Senate.

[68] The conference report on the FY2006 regular foreign aid appropriations, P.L. 109-102, stated the sense of Congress that such support should be considered.

[69] Three other Iranian Americans were arrested and accused by the Intelligence Ministry of actions contrary to national security in May 2007: U.S. funded broadcast (Radio Farda) journalist Parnaz Azima (who was not in jail but was not allowed to leave Iran); Kian Tajbacksh of the Open Society Institute funded by George Soros; and businessman and peace activist Ali Shakeri. Several congressional resolutions called on Iran to release Esfandiari (S.Res. 214 agreed to by the Senate on May 24; H.Res. 430, passed by the House on June 5; and S.Res. 199). All were released by October 2007. Tajbacksh was rearrested in September 2009 and remains incarcerated.

[70] CRS conversation with U.S. officials of the "Iran Office" of the U.S. Consulate in Dubai. October 2009.

[71] Solomon, Jay. "U.S. Shifts Its Strategy Toward Iran's Dissidents." *Wall Street Journal*, June 11, 2010.

[72] For more discussion of such legislation, see CRS Report RS20871, *Iran Sanctions*.

[73] Ibid.

[74] CRS conversations with Iranian members of the Green movement. December 2009-August 2010.

[75] Stockman, Farah. "'Long Struggle' With Iran Seen Ahead." *Boston Globe*, March 9, 2006.

[76] For information on the steps taken by individual states, see National Conference of State Legislatures. State Divestment Legislation.

In: The Middle East in Turmoil, Volume 3
Editor: Angela N. Castillo

ISBN: 978-1-61324-241-4
© 2011 Nova Science Publishers, Inc.

Chapter 8

UNITED NATIONS ASSISTANCE MISSION IN AFGHANISTAN: BACKGROUND AND POLICY ISSUES[*]

Rhoda Margesson

SUMMARY

The United Nations (UN) has had an active presence in Afghanistan since 1988, and it is highly regarded by many Afghans for playing a brokering role in ending the Soviet occupation of Afghanistan. As a result of the Bonn Agreement of December 2001, coordinating international donor activity and assistance have been tasked to a United Nations Assistance Mission in Afghanistan (UNAMA). However, there are other coordinating institutions tied to the Afghan government, and UNAMA has struggled to exercise its full mandate. The international recovery and reconstruction effort in Afghanistan is immense and complicated and, in coordination with the Afghan government, involves U.N. agencies, bilateral donors, international organizations, and local and international non-governmental organizations (NGOs). The coordinated aid programs of the United States and its European allies focus on a wide range of activities, from strengthening the central and local governments of Afghanistan and its security forces to promoting civilian reconstruction, reducing corruption, and assisting with elections.

Some of the major issues UNAMA is wrestling with include the following:

- Most observers agree that continued, substantial, long-term development is key, as is the need for international support, but questions have been raised about corruption, aid effectiveness (funds required, priorities established, impact received), and the coordination necessary to achieve sufficient improvement throughout the country.
- The international community and the Afghan government have sought to establish coordinating institutions and a common set of goals in order to use donor funds effectively. The international donor community has also sought to encourage Afghan

---

[*] This is an edited, reformatted and augmented version of a Congressional Research Services publication, dated December 27, 2010.

"ownership"-meaning leadership and control-of reconstruction and development efforts by the country itself.

- Although the Afghan government is taking on an increasingly central role in development planning and the management of aid funds, the international community remains extensively involved in Afghan stabilization, not only in diplomacy and development assistance, but also in combating insurgents and addressing broader security issues.

In December 2009, the Obama Administration laid out its strategy for Afghanistan in response to a battlefield assessment, reemphasized an earlier commitment to civilian efforts in cooperation with the United Nations, and further highlighted Afghanistan as a top national security priority. In 2010, a number of events and meetings took place that taken together provide a snapshot of ways that the Afghan government and international community are engaged in Afghanistan. These include the London Conference (January), the Peace Jirga (June), the Kabul Conference (July), and the NATO Summit in Lisbon (November). In addition, on September 18, 2010 Afghanistan held its second parliamentary election, the results of which were certified by electoral commissions in November. In its Afghanistan strategy review in December, the Obama Administration cautiously stated that while progress is being made on security matters, it remains fragile and requires sustained involvement by the United States and its allies.

This report examines the role of UNAMA in Afghanistan and discusses the obstacles the organization faces in coordinating international efforts and explores related policy issues and considerations for the 112th Congress. This report will be updated as events warrant.

INTRODUCTION

The United States and the international community continue to rely on the central role of the United Nations Assistance Mission in Afghanistan (UNAMA) as coordinator of international donor activity and assistance. Within a broader, ongoing debate focused on U.S. and other assessments of efforts to stabilize Afghanistan, UNAMA's role has been emphasized in different contexts, particularly in the past several years. For example, U.N. Security Council Resolution 1806 (2008) significantly expanded UNAMA's authority. The Declaration of the International Conference in Support of Afghanistan, which took place in Paris in June 2008, also underlined UNAMA's role in leading all aspects of civilian coordination.

In unveiling a new strategy for Afghanistan and Pakistan in March 2009, the Obama Administration highlighted the need for coordination and burdensharing among donors in building Afghan capacity and providing the necessary civilian expertise. It also emphasized the importance of a leadership role for UNAMA on these issues and as part of its coordination role. The Chairman's statement of the International Conference on Afghanistan (The Hague, March 31, 2009) emphasized UNAMA's coordination role and urged its expansion into as many provinces as possible. On December 1, 2009, the Obama Administration laid out a strategy for Afghanistan in response to a battlefield assessment from General McChrystal and reestablished previous commitments to civilian efforts in cooperation with the United Nations. In 2010, UNAMA was a central actor at a number of events and meetings that demonstrated ways in which the international community and Afghan government are engaged in Afghanistan. For example, the continued support of UNAMA was emphasized at a major international conference on Afghanistan in London in January 2010. The government of Afghanistan hosted the Kabul Conference in July 2010 and co-chaired the proceedings with the United Nations. UNAMA also provided advice to Afghan electoral institutions in support of the Afghan-led parliamentary elections held in September 2010.

Some observers contend that progress has been achieved so far in Afghanistan. U.S. embassy officials in Kabul have noted progress on reconstruction, governance, and security in many areas of Afghanistan, although violence is higher than previous levels and accelerating in certain areas. Experts argue that recent progress on civilian reconstruction and development in Afghanistan needs to be understood in the context out of which Afghanistan has emerged since 2001 following more than two decades of conflict that resulted in significant political, economic, and social decline. Reconstruction efforts must cope with the destructive impact of war and with the distortions in the Afghan economy, in which the war and drugs compete with agriculture and other economic activities. Despite the deteriorating security situation, some progress in Afghanistan's reconstruction continues to be made, and when considered over time, is not insignificant.

Other assessments are more pessimistic. Critics say that slow reconstruction, corruption, and the failure to extend in a sustainable way Afghan government authority into rural areas and provinces, particularly in the south and east, have contributed to continuing instability and a Taliban resurgence. Some experts raise concerns about increased insecurity in previously stable areas such as the northern part of the country and the challenges this creates in providing humanitarian and development assistance. Narcotics trafficking persists, despite countermeasures, and independent militias remain a problem throughout the country, although many have been disarmed.[1]

UNAMA has been given a lead role in the civilian reconstruction effort. Some contend that UNAMA's role in the flawed August 2009 elections and aftermath may have undermined its credibility and created disappointment among international donors. Others argue that with the passage of time and the fraud investigation process improved for the September 2010 parliamentary elections, some confidence in UNAMA has been restored. Still, many experts agree that the international effort in Afghanistan is at a critical period. The international community's expectations of UNAMA may in part reflect the impact UNAMA might have on the success or failure of international efforts in Afghanistan. This report provides an analysis of UNAMA's role in Afghanistan and the key policy issues it faces on civilian reconstruction.

SETTING THE CONTEXT

The United States, other countries, and international relief organizations have long been active in providing assistance to the Afghan people. Afghanistan was admitted as a member of the United Nations on November 19, 1946, and has had a relationship with the United Nations that goes back more than 60 years. During the 1980s, the United States, along with other countries, funded the mujahedin forces fighting against the Soviet Union, as well as provided humanitarian aid to Afghans who fled to refugee camps in Pakistan. In 1988, the Geneva Peace Accords, brokered in part by Diego Cordovez, a Special Representative of then U.N. Secretary General Javier Perez de-Cuellar, were signed, which led to the Soviet withdrawal nearly a decade after its invasion.[2]

With the peace accord in place, the United Nations established an active presence in Afghanistan. It generally maintains separate offices for (1) political and peace processes (Pillar I) and (2) humanitarian and reconstruction operations (Pillar II).[3] During the violent civil war that lasted through the 1990s, the United Nations continued to seek a peace agreement that would allow for sustained reconstruction. However, with the failure of several peace agreements, the international donor community focused primarily on humanitarian aid because the conditions were not stable for long-term development.[4] Donors also did not want to provide assistance to the Taliban, an Islamic fundamentalist movement that ruled Afghanistan between 1996 and 2001, when it was ousted by U.S.-backed Afghan factions.[5]

Afghanistan was one of the least developed countries in the world even prior to the outbreak of war in 1978.[6] The assistance situation changed dramatically once the Taliban was removed from power following the U.S.-led military intervention in 2001. The implementation of humanitarian assistance and the development of reconstruction plans quickly took shape when Afghans met under U.N. auspices to decide on a governance plan, which resulted in the Bonn Agreement, signed on December 5, 2001. On December 22, 2001, an interim government was formed with Hamid Karzai as its leader. This paved the way for a constitution, considered the most progressive in Afghan history, which was approved at a "constitutional *loya jirga*" (traditional Afghan assembly) in January 2004. Hamid Karzai was elected president in a nationwide election in October 2004, and parliamentary and provincial elections were subsequently held in September 2005. The next presidential and provincial elections were held on August 20, 2009 (details discussed later in the report), and the second post-Taliban parliamentary elections were held on September 18, 2010. The Afghan government has been working with the international donor community on reconstruction programs and plans since a major donor conference in January 2002 in Tokyo.

The Afghan government and the international community face a daunting task. Many problems remain in every sector. Strategic challenges are numerous and continue to put the institution-building effort in Afghanistan at risk. In conjunction with security, reconstruction is seen by many as the single most important factor for sustaining peace. According to many observers, successful development could stem public disillusionment with the international effort in Afghanistan, sustain Afghan participation in the reconstruction process, and help keep Afghanistan from again becoming a permanent haven for terrorists.

MANDATE, STRUCTURE, AND FUNDING

The role of UNAMA is to promote peace and stability in Afghanistan and to lead the international community in this effort. In support of the government of Afghanistan, UNAMA is tasked to coordinate efforts to rebuild the country and strengthen governance, development, and stability. However, in practice, in light of the number of donors and their own national priorities, the coordination role has been difficult for UNAMA to implement.

Mandate

On March 28, 2002, U.N. Security Council Resolution 1401 (2002) established the United Nations Assistance Mission in Afghanistan (UNAMA) as a political and "integrated" mission, directed and supported by the U.N. Department of Peacekeeping Operations, to help implement the Bonn Agreement. UNAMA aims to bring together two key elements—one with a political focus and the other dealing with humanitarian and development efforts. Lakhdar Brahimi, then Special Representative for the U.N. Secretary-General to Afghanistan, organized the Bonn Agreement and directed UNAMA until December 2004. UNAMA's mandate is renewed annually in March. U.N. Security Council Resolution 1868 (2009) extended UNAMA's mandate until March 23, 2010, and U.N. Security Council Resolution 1917 (2010) extended the mandate for another year until March 23, 2011.[7]

Significantly, U.N. Security Council Resolution 1806 (2008) expanded the mandate to include a "super envoy" concept that would represent the United Nations, the European Union, and the North Atlantic Treaty Organization (NATO) in Afghanistan. U.N. Security Council Resolution 1868 (2009) incorporates UNAMA's increased scope, which includes leading international civilian efforts to support the Afghan government, increasing cooperation with the International Security Assistance Force (ISAF), and developing greater political outreach with Afghan leaders.[8] Highlights of Security Council Resolution 1917 (2010) focus on promoting international support for the government of Afghanistan's development and governance priorities, increasing cooperation with international security forces, providing political outreach and support to the Afghan-led reconciliation and reintegration programs, and helping implement electoral reform commitments agreed at the January 2010 London Conference. Security of U.N. staff and expansion of UNAMA's presence were also emphasized.[9]

Organization

Beginning in March 2010, the head of UNAMA, and Special Representative of the U.N. Secretary-General (SRSG) for Afghanistan, is Staffan de Mistura. There are two Deputy Special Representatives of the Secretary-General (DSRSG) for Afghanistan: Martin Kobler (of Germany) covers Political Affairs. Robert Watkins (of Canada) covers Relief, Recovery, and Reconstruction (RRR). Mr. Watkins also serves as the UNDP Resident Representative, Resident Coordinator and Humanitarian Coordinator in Afghanistan. From March 2008 to March 2010, the head of UNAMA, and Special Representative of the U.N. Secretary-General (SRSG) for Afghanistan, with expanded powers over his predecessors, was Norwegian diplomat Kai Eide.[10]

UNAMA has approximately 1,500 staff, of which about 80% are Afghan nationals (see organizational chart in Appendix B.) It coordinates all activities of the U.N. system in Afghanistan, which includes the participation of 18 U.N. agencies and several other organizations considered to be part of the U.N. country team (see Appendix C).[11] UNAMA has eight regional offices and 12 provincial offices. The participants at the International Conference on Afghanistan in March 2009 and at the London Conference in January 2010 emphasized that UNAMA should expand its presence into as many provinces as possible.[12] Reports by the U.N. Secretary General have continued to underscore this point.

Budget

The total Calendar Year (CY) 2008 expenditures for UNAMA were $86.34 million, which was $10.2 million above the approved budget amount. The total CY2009 expenditures for UNAMA were $256.6 million, which was $12.6 million above the approved budget amount. The Mission's CY2010 budget is $241.9 million. These numbers reflect an increase in staff, the opening of additional provincial offices, and the strengthening of regional offices in Tehran and Islamabad. UNAMA is funded through assessed contributions to the U.N. regular budget. The U.S. assessment is 22% (the same level as for the U.N. regular budget) or approximately $53.22 million for CY2010.

FRAMEWORK FOR AFGHANISTAN'S RECONSTRUCTION STRATEGY

UNAMA was established in part to facilitate the implementation of the 2001 Bonn Agreement. In addition to this landmark document, two subsequent agreements between the Afghan government and the international community outline the overall Afghanistan reconstruction strategy: The 2006 Afghanistan Compact and the 2008 Afghanistan National Development Strategy (ANDS). The Joint Coordination and Monitoring Board (JCMB), of which UNAMA is co-chair, serves as a coordinating and monitoring mechanism for the implementation of these agreements. In addition, several international conferences have provided guidance and built international support for the way forward in Afghanistan.

Bonn Agreement—Bonn 2001

The *Agreement on Provisional Arrangements in Afghanistan Pending the Re-establishment of Permanent Government Institutions*, or Bonn Agreement, was signed in Bonn, Germany, on December 5, 2001. It was endorsed by U.N. Security Council Resolution 1385 (2001). Under U.N. auspices, Afghan participants met to outline a process for the political transition in Afghanistan. The Bonn Agreement established an Afghan Interim Authority (AIA) on December 22, 2001, which was made up of 30 members and headed by Chairman Hamid Karzai. An Emergency *"loya jirga"* (traditional Afghan assembly) held in June 2002 replaced the AIA with a Transitional Authority (TA). The TA brought together a broad transitional administration to lead the country until a full government could be elected. A constitution, considered the most progressive in Afghan history, was approved at a "constitutional *loya jirga*" in January 2004. Hamid Karzai was elected president in October 2004, and parliamentary and provincial elections were subsequently held in September 2005. The Bonn Agreement also called for the establishment of a Supreme Court of Afghanistan and a Judicial Commission. It requested the U.N. Security Council to consider authorizing the deployment of a U.N.-mandated security force, outlined the role of the United Nations during the interim period, and referred to the need for cooperation with the international community on a number of issues, including reconstruction, elections, counternarcotics, crime, and terrorism. The Bonn Agreement was fully implemented in 2005.

Afghanistan Compact—London 2006

Donor countries and the Afghan government met at the London Conference in February 2006 to adopt the Afghanistan Compact (Compact), which provided a five-year time line (2006-2011) for addressing three main areas of activity, each with identified goals and outcomes: Security, Governance (Rule of Law and Human Rights), and Economic and Social Development. It also highlighted the cross-cutting issue of narcotics. The Compact acknowledged the need for Afghanistan to become more self-reliant while affirming the responsibilities required to achieve that goal. The international community agreed to monitor implementation of the Compact and the outlined benchmarks, and to improve aid effectiveness and accountability.[13]

Afghanistan National Development Strategy (ANDS)—Paris 2008

The Afghanistan National Development Strategy (ANDS), which was signed by President Karzai in April 2008 and later presented as the "blueprint for the development of Afghanistan" at the donors conference in Paris, France, on June 12, 2008, is a policy paper created by the Afghan government. It builds on the Compact and follows a plan for establishing goals and measurable targets that is similar to the U.N. Millennium Development Goals.[14] Focusing on the three issue areas identified in the Compact (security, governance, economic growth/poverty reduction), it looks ahead to a vision for Afghanistan in the year 2020 while identifying specific goals to be achieved over five years between 2008 and 2013.[15] The ANDS envisions that most of the funding required would be provided by donors and that these funds would be distributed through the central government.

Joint Coordination and Monitoring Board (JCMB)

The Joint Coordination and Monitoring Board (JCMB) was established in 2008 and is the coordination body between the Afghan government and the international community. UNAMA is co-chair of the JCMB and has a central role in helping implement the development strategies outlined in the Compact and the monitoring activities put forward in ANDS. U.N. Security Council Resolution 1806 (2008), U.N. Security Council Resolution 1868 (2009), and U.N. Security Council Resolution 1917 (2010) direct UNAMA, in that capacity, to coordinate the work of international donors and organizations with an emphasis on aid effectiveness. The JCMB co-chairs reviewed the Compact and presented their findings at the June 2008 conference in Paris, stating that significant progress had been made in health and education, infrastructure and economic growth, and strengthening of Afghan national security forces.

INTERNATIONAL DONOR CONFERENCES AND TRUST FUNDS

The international donor communityhas established a series of institutional mechanisms for developing and coordinating reconstruction for countries emerging from conflict. Though adapted to specific situations, these mechanisms are generally similar. In November 2001, with the possibility of the fall of the Taliban and a potential opening for sustainable reconstruction work, the international donor community quickly established and implemented new initiatives. In addition to providing their own assistance to Afghanistan, international organizations and international financial institutions administered donor conferences, trust funds, and humanitarian and reconstruction programs. A brief summary of the main international donor conferences, each of which had extensive input from UNAMA and other U.N. institutions, demonstrates the ongoing challenges that remain in Afghanistan and the repeated articulation of some of the issues. At the same time, it also shows increased participation by international stakeholders, perhaps, many contend, as a barometer of the importance that has now been ascribed to Afghanistan's future.[16]

International Donor Conferences[17]

- **Bonn Conference** (December 22, 2001)—With the Bonn Agreement and interim government in place, UNDP organized a donor conference in which the interim government presented its reconstruction plans and country representatives and international NGOs made pledges in order to show international support for those plans.
- **Tokyo Conference** (January 21-22, 2002)—A ministerial conference, co-hosted by Japan, the United States, the European Union, and Saudi Arabia, was convened in Tokyo to discuss aid to Afghanistan. Donors pledged $4.5 billion.
- **Berlin Conference** (April 1, 2004)—The conference brought together 65 representatives from countries and international organizations to focus on reconstruction in Afghanistan. Pledges exceeded $8.2 billion.
- **London Conference** (February 1, 2006)—At the conference in London, the government of Afghanistan and the international community signed the Compact that outlined the principles of their cooperation over the next five years. Donors pledged $10.5 billion.
- **Paris Conference** (June 12, 2008)—The Afghan government and international community met in Paris in June of the same year to reiterate their partnership, with guidance from the Compact and the Afghan government's assigned leadership role in the implementation plan outlined in ANDS. The conferees affirmed the expanded role of UNAMA in all aspects of coordination. Key priorities identified at the conference included a wide range of activities: strengthening democracy and governance; investing in infrastructure and the private sector; improving aid effectiveness and reducing corruption; improving counter-narcotics measures; and ensuring the needs of all Afghans would be addressed through government services, greater civil society participation, and respect for human rights.

- **Hague Conference** (March 31, 2009)—More than 80 countries met in The Hague for the "International Conference on Afghanistan: A Comprehensive Strategy in a Regional Context," which was hosted by the government of the Netherlands and UNAMA. The conference reinforced the central role outlined for UNAMA as coordinator of international action and assistance.[18] It also generated consensus on several points, including the need for a more directed agenda for Afghanistan, emphasizing the civilian capacity and institution-building, with sustained priority areas: security, governance, economic growth, and regional cooperation.
- **London Conference** (January 28, 2010)—At the Commonwealth Summit in Trinidad and Tobago, on Saturday, November 28, 2009, Prime Minister Gordon Brown and U.N. Secretary General Ban Ki-moon jointly announced plans to host an international conference at the ministerial level on Afghanistan to be held in London. Along with Prime Minister Brown, German Chancellor Angela Merkel and French President Nicolas Sarkosy took the lead in proposing the conference, the purpose of which was to find ways to strengthen the Afghan government and security forces as assumed responsibilities currently carried out by the international community. President Obama linked the need for this transition to the possible withdrawal of international troops in his December 1, 2009, speech.
- **Kabul Conference** (July 20, 2010)—At the Kabul Conference, the government of Afghanistan put forward an Afghan-led plan for improving development, governance, and security. Support for sustained capacity building at the national and sub-national levels was emphasized. The "Kabul Process" is viewed by experts as a potentially important link in the transition to full Afghan leadership and builds on earlier international commitments, such as are encapsulated in the ANDS.
- **NATO Summit** (November 20, 2010)—At a November meeting of ISAF Heads of State and Government as part of the Lisbon summit, a framework under which full security responsibilities would be handed over to Afghan forces by 2014 was endorsed. The process defines the implementation of the transition province-by-province with a simultaneous drawdown of international combat forces. UNAMA will support the civilian side of this transition, particularly in areas of governance and development.

Trust Funds

At the start of the civilian reconstruction effort in Afghanistan in 2002, the international community placed great emphasis on paying the Afghan government's current expenditures, most importantly the salaries of government employees to enhance government capacity. Toward this end, several trust funds were established. Trust funds allow for rapid distribution of monies because they centralize funding and remove the administrative requirements of drawing from multiple funds. Donor countries decide to contribute to these trust funds and urge others to make contributions. The Afghan Interim Authority Fund (AIAF), for example, was created for donor contributions to the first six months during governmental operations and other related activities. On July 22, 2002, the Afghanistan Reconstruction Trust Fund (ARTF) succeeded the AIAF. In addition, the Law and Order Trust Fund for Afghanistan (LOTFA) was established to cover the rehabilitation of police facilities, salaries, training and capacity-building, and the procurement of non-lethal equipment. Following on these trust funds, the Counter-Narcotics Trust Fund was also established. There is also a NATO-run Afghan National Security Forces trust fund.

Administered by the World Bank, the ARTF continues to provide funds for the government's budget, investment activities and programs including quick-impact recovery projects, government training programs for Afghans, and support for the National Solidarity Program. ARTF has also expanded into other sectors such as education, agriculture, justice, and urban infrastructure. ARTF currently provides approximately half of the government's non-security operating costs and over a quarter of its development expenditures.[19] Recently, donors agreed to extend the ARTF until 2020. In part this reflects an ongoing commitment by donors to utilize the ARTF mechanism, and in part it is an acknowledgement of the development challenges that remain in Afghanistan. According to the World Bank, as of September 20, 2009, 30 international donors have contributed $3 billion to the ARTF since 2002.[20]

U.S. ASSISTANCE

Before 2001, U.S. aid to Afghanistan flowed mainly through U.N. agencies and NGOs, but the U.S. role increased dramatically after the start of Operation Enduring Freedom (OEF). U.S. government funding for assistance has come from three main agencies—the Department of Defense (DOD), the U.S. Agency for International Development (USAID), and the State Department.[21] Military and security assistance since 2001 represents more than half of U.S. funding for Afghanistan and has been provided through DOD, mainly through the Afghan Security Forces Fund, the Commander's Emergency Response Program (CERP), and other funds appropriated for counternarcotics and other programs. Funds provided for development and humanitarian-related activities and implemented mainly through USAID and the State Department are distributed to international organizations and non-governmental organizations, which provide services in Afghanistan, or directly to the Afghan government. Afghanistan also receives U.S. aid through multilateral institutions. The most important avenue is through the United Nations and its affiliated agencies and through international financial institutions, such as the World Bank and the International Monetary Fund (IMF). Some U.S. funding for Afghanistan comes from U.S. dues and additional voluntary donations to the United Nations through the State Department's International Organizations account or through the State Department's Migration and Refugee Assistance (MRA) account.[22]

UNAMA'S EXPANDED MANDATE FOR THE INTERNATIONAL CIVILIAN EFFORT IN AFGHANISTAN

In deciding to extend the mandate of UNAMA until March 23, 2010, the U.N. Security Council emphasized specific priorities for UNAMA and expanded its authority as a coordinating body.[23] It also asked the U.N. Secretary-General to report to the Security Council every three months on developments in Afghanistan. In addition, it requested the U.N. Secretary-General to establish benchmarks (drawing on the mandate and identified priorities) to determine progress in their implementation. The Secretary-General's June 2009 report was supposed to provide an update on the status of the benchmarks; instead, the U.N. Secretary-General requested a delay in finalizing the benchmarks, which were then outlined in the September 22, 2009, report.[24]

U.N. Security Council Resolution 1868 (2009)—UNAMA Priorities

The priorities below are outlined in U.N. Security Council resolution 1868 (2009) as key areas of UNAMA's work in Afghanistan:[25]

- promote more coherent support by the international community to the Afghan government;
- strengthen cooperation with ISAF;
- provide political outreach through a strengthened and expanded presence throughout the country;
- provide good offices in support of Afghan-led reconciliation programs;
- support efforts to improve governance and the rule of law and to combat corruption;
- play a central coordinating role to facilitate the delivery of humanitarian aid;
- monitor the human rights situation of civilians and coordinate human rights protection;
- support the electoral process through the Afghan Independent Electoral Commission;
- support regional cooperation in working for a more stable and prosperous Afghanistan.[26]

UNAMA's Benchmarks

The strategic benchmarks are outlined below.[27]

- Governance and Institution Building

Benchmark: Extension of Government authority throughout the country through the establishment of democratic, legitimate, accountable institutions, down to the local level, with the capacity to implement policies and to be increasingly capable of sustaining themselves.

- Security

Benchmark: Development of a sustainable Afghan security structure that is capable of ensuring peace and stability and protecting the people of Afghanistan.

- Economic and Social Development

Benchmark: Government policies backed by international support to promote sustainable economic growth that contributes to overall stability.

- Human Rights

Benchmark: Improved respect for the human rights of Afghans, in line with the Afghan Constitution and international law, with particular emphasis on the protection of civilians, the situation of women and girls, freedom of expression and accountability based on the rule of law.

- Counter-narcotics

Benchmark: Sustained trend in the reduction of poppy cultivation, narcotics production and drug addiction.

In his September 2009 report, the U.N. Secretary-General clarified that the benchmarks to measure progress on UNAMA's priorities would focus on broad areas in UNAMA's mandate and incorporate goals outlined in the agreed national strategies. The benchmarks would be results-based rather than tied to specific target dates, except where required under the constitution. While UNAMA has the capacity to monitor progress in some areas, the Secretary-General noted that this responsibility would also need to be shared with the Afghan government and other members of the international community. Furthermore, developing benchmarks in a comprehensive way would depend on creating an appropriate consultation process with the Afghan government and other international stakeholders.

Some experts believe that on the one hand, regular reports on benchmarks could help UNAMA execute its mandate in a more effective manner and would provide an opportunity to demonstrate the strengths and weaknesses of its strategy on a regular basis. On the other hand, others have questioned whether this is the most efficient way of measuring and tracking implementation of the mandate, whether it is possible to see progress in three-month intervals, and whether this may narrow the scope of how UNAMA's success or failure may be judged, which could have a significant impact on the perception of UNAMA's performance.

Current Report of the U.N. Secretary-General on the Situation in Afghanistan

Another key function of UNAMA and the United Nations more broadly is to provide assessments of the Afghanistan situation to U.N. institutions and member states. These reports also discuss the role of UNAMA in Afghanistan, including issue areas that UNAMA foresees an enhanced role or further activities. Some specific points from the December 10, 2010, report of the U.N. Secretary-General are highlighted below, while other key points are discussed elsewhere in this report:

Peace and Integration—as a result of the Consultative Peace Jirga in June 2010, President Karzai established a High Peace Council, at the request of the Jirga, to promote peace and national unity through confidence-building measures, including the Afghan peace and reintegration program. The Council was formally inaugurated in October and former President Burhanuddin Rabbani was approved as the Council's Chair. On October 20, the

Council called on all sides to the conflict to renounce violence and participate in talks. The Council also asked that the United Nations participate in the process and help strengthen global support for the initiative. UNAMA has since been asked to develop an internal capacity to respond to requests from the Council and has established the Salaam Support Group to meet this need. The High Peace Council has also asked the Organization of Islamic Conference (OIC) to participate.

Regional Cooperation—the Kabul Silk Road initiative had its fourth meeting in November in Kabul. The SRSG launched the initiative to facilitate informal dialogue between the government of Afghanistan, Kabul-based Ambassadors of Afghanistan's neighbors, and UNAMA.

The Kabul Process—As a follow-up to the Kabul Process (road map defined at the London and Kabul conferences that took place in 2010) the government of Afghanistan presented its first 100- day progress report on commitments undertaken at the conferences and said that more than 70% of the target benchmarks had been met. Furthermore, at the JCMB meeting the government presented a monitoring and reporting framework to track progress made in each of its 22 national priority programs aimed at delivery of services to the Afghan people. The Kabul Process is part of an overall effort to better define specific goals and achievements in discussions between the government of Afghanistan and the international community.

Aid Coherence—UNAMA is more involved in developing a coherent approach to donor assistance as part of the Afghan government's anti-corruption agenda. In addition, an increasing priority is a focus on development activities at the subnational level, in particular (1) ensuring they are consistent with national priorities; (2) promoting coordination through development activities at the provincial level, including PRTs; and (3) supporting local authorities in assuming leadership for the coordination of development activities.

POLICY ISSUES AND RECENT DEVELOPMENTS

Afghanistan remains a key priority for Congress. It is at or near the top of the Obama Administration's national security agenda, as reinforced by the summary of the Obama Administration's policy review, issued on December 16, 2010. As congressional concerns about the strategy in Afghanistan unfold, UNAMA's role as a key player in coordinating international donor activity and assistance may be of particular interest, in part because the extent to which UNAMA is successful may reduce the need for relief and reconstruction activities currently conducted by the United States and other members of the international community. Congress may also raise questions related to the budget, oversight of benchmarks and activities, and its role in overseeing aid effectiveness and election reform.

The following sections address areas where UNAMA is playing a significant role.

Deteriorating Security Situation and Limited Progress on Development

There are several issues of concern for the international community, the Afghan government, and observers. First, the increasing lack of security has threatened the progress of development. According to the U.N. Secretary-General, violence has increased in parts of the country to levels not seen since 2001.[28] In 2009, the monthly average of security incidents increased by 43%. Targeted attacks on unarmed civil servants and the aid community, including the United Nations, have also risen. Second, although progress has been made on development (see Appendix H for a list of key achievements since 2002), some observers argue that Afghans have become frustrated with what they perceive as little evidence of development. There are many possible explanations for the perceived lack of progress, including lack of security, lack of human and physical capacity to implement substantial development, inadequate funding levels, and a focus on other funding priorities.

It is well understood that both security and progress on development are necessary in order to maintain international donor interest in Afghan development, encourage private investment in Afghanistan, and maintain Afghans' hope in improvement in their country and their own lives. The deteriorating security situation continues to take center stage as the key issue in Afghanistan while international stakeholders try to find ways to enable civilian efforts to take hold and be sustained. As part of this effort, for example, UNAMA is coordinating with the Independent Directorate of Local Governance and ISAF on a pilot project to fashion local approaches to securing communities.

August 2009 Presidential and Provincial Elections

UNAMA and members of the international community placed significant emphasis on the need for credible, free, and fair presidential and provincial elections on August 20, 2009. The elections were seen as a potential benchmark in the promotion of good governance, and as an indicator of the confidence of the Afghan people in and consolidation of democracy in Afghanistan. The elections were front and center in Afghan politics and in international community circles. Of particular concern to the United Nations were questions about corruption (with some evidence that there had been some problem in the registration of candidates), finding ways to handle electoral irregularities, and ensuring the safety and security of civilians prior to and during the elections. Approximately 15.6 million voters (38% of whom are women) updated their registrations. The final list of candidates included 32 presidential candidates and 3,178 provincial council candidates, 328 of whom were women. UNAMA assisted with the registration and candidate nomination process and worked to resolve controversies such as the date of the elections and questions about the powers of the President when the Presidential term expired. UNAMA contributed technical support for the election process and worked closely with the U.N. Development Program (UNDP) on its project called Enhancing Legal and Electoral Capacity for Tomorrow (ELECT), which was the primary vehicle through which the international community supported the Afghan elections. UNAMA also provided guidance to a range of actors, including the Independent Election Commission (IEC), the Electoral Complaints Commission (ECC), the Afghanistan Independent Human Rights Commission, and members of civil society.

The Post Election Period
The August 20, 2009, presidential and parliamentary elections were the first elections run entirely under the auspices of the Afghan authorities in 30 years. Nevertheless, voting was unquestionably marred by irregularities, fraud, intimidation, and violence, all of which greatly

affected turnout and results. The IEC released vote results slowly. Final, but uncertified, results released on September 16, 2009, showed Karzai at 54.6% and Dr. Abdullah at 27.7%. Other candidates received single-digit vote counts. The ECC ordered a recount of 10% of the polling stations as part of its investigations of fraud. On October 20, 2009, the ECC determined, based on its investigations, that about 1 million Karzai votes and about 200,000 Abdullah votes were considered fraudulent and were deducted from their totals. The final, certified results of the first round were as follows: Karzai, 49.67% (according to the IEC, with a lightly lower total of about 48% according to the ECC determination); Abdullah, 30.59%; and considerably lower figures for the remainder of the field.[29] Thus, Karzai did not legitimately exceed the 50% + threshold to claim a first-round victory. On October 21, 2009, the IEC accepted the ECC finding and Karzai conceded the need for a runoff election; Dr. Abdullah initially accepted the runoff. A date was set for November 7, 2009, for the runoff election.

In an attempt to produce a clean second round, UNAMA ordered about 200 district-level election commissioners be replaced. In addition, it recommended eliminating about 400 polling stations where few votes were expected to be cast. Security procedures were to be similar to those of the first round.

The End Result

On November 1, 2009, Dr. Adullah said he would not compete in the runoff on the grounds that the conditions that enabled the fraud had not been adequately addressed. On November 2, the IEC issued a statement saying that, by consensus, the body had determined that Karzai, being the only candidate remaining in a two-person runoff, should be declared the winner and the second round should not be held. The United States, U.N. Secretary General Ban Ki-moon, and several governments congratulated Karzai on the victory. U.S. officials, including Secretary of State Clinton, praised Dr. Abdullah for his relatively moderate speech announcing his withdrawal and refusing to call for demonstrations or violence by his supporters. President Karzai was inaugurated on November 19, 2009.

U.S. and international officials publicly called on President Karzai to choose his next cabinet based on competence, merit, and dedication to curbing corruption. Some in the Afghan parliament nonetheless questioned some of his choices, and he did not achieve parliamentary of a full cabinet in two rounds of nominations during 2010; seven ministries lack permanent ministers, as of December 2010. A major U.S. and international concern remains focused on questions about the strength and legitimacy of Karzai's government and what kind of a partnership is possible.

The UNAMA Dispute

Within weeks of the August election and lead-up to the release of the initial results, a dispute ensued within UNAMA between then SRSG Kai Eide and DSRSG Peter Galbraith, which ended in the departure of Galbraith from his post at the end of September. The main issues appear to have been focused on the degree of fraud that had taken place during the election and how to deal with it. On the one hand, Eide's position was to let process run through Electoral Complaints Commission (ECC) and Independent Election Commission (IEC) to ensure adherence to the constitution and electoral laws of Afghanistan. Some also say that he was willing to encourage an Afghan compromise to avoid a second round. On the other hand, concerned with rule of law and election legitimacy, Galbraith argued that the

United Nations had the responsibility to intervene, and he questioned whether it would intervene, and to what extent if he did not speak out. This issue played out very publicly and there were allegations of support by Eide to Karzai and Galbraith to Abdullah. U.N. Secretary General Ban Ki-moon removed Galbraith from his post on the grounds that the dispute was compromising UNAMA's overall mission. Several Galbraith supporters subsequently resigned from UNAMA and at the time, morale within UNAMA was reported to be low. For Afghans, the concern was less about the fraud in the election itself (which many expected) but rather concerns over U.S. influence and unnecessary international interference in their election.

It is not clear to what degree the dispute affected UNAMA's overall standing and credibility. On December 11, 2009, SRSG Eide was reported to have said he would leave his post in March 2010 as planned when his two-year contract expires. Eide maintained that this decision was unrelated to his handling of the controversy over the August election or the deadly attack on U.N. staff in October 2009 (discussed later in this report.)[30] There had already been some calls for Eide's resignation[31] Others have suggested the need for a super envoy outside the UNAMA structure, a revival of a previous proposal that was rejected by Karzai.[32] At the time, most agreed that there was a loss of momentum and that UNAMA would have to reassert itself as a voice in the transition strategy proposed by President Obama or risk being sidelined.

Parliamentary Elections in 2010

Parliamentary elections for the Lower House of the National Assembly, the *Wolesi Jirga*, were held as planned on September 18, 2010. The final results stated that 2,506 candidates (of which 396 were women) contested 249 seats. Reportedly 5,500 polling stations opened on polling day and roughly 4.3 million Afghans voted (of approximately 12 million eligible voters.) The overall security situation did not deteriorate as it did on polling day in 2009; however, there were increased incidents of low-level violence. Some feared that the difficulties that plagued the 2009 presidential election were not adequately addressed beforehand to ensure that the parliamentary elections would be free and fair. Fraud and irregularities were seen across the country. The Independent Electoral Commission (IEC) implemented measures for auditing and recounting votes, and the Electoral Complaints Commission investigated more than 5,000 complaints. In total, 4,271,908 votes were considered valid, while 1,330,782 were invalidated. The final election results were issued at the end of November and reflected a shift in ethnic representation in the Wolesi Jirga, with the Pashtuns losing 20 seats.

The 2010 elections, which were Afghan lead under the IEC, showed technical improvement over the 2009 elections. The problems encountered raise questions about how they should be addressed and by whom. Clearly there remains a need for overall electoral reform and perhaps also a need to reassess expectations of the capacity of the electoral process in Afghanistan. Before its project comes to a close in March 2011, the U.N. Development Program Enhancing Legal and Electoral Capacity for Tomorrow (UNDP-ELECT) will review lessons learned. UNAMA is expected to continue to have a role in election reform. It is not clear how the Afghan government will view this responsibility in the evolution of its democratic process. Donors have expressed a willingness to support efforts for an Afghan-lead reform process, with political support from UNAMA and financial and technical support from the international community, notably the European Union.

UNAMA's Security

On October 28, 2009, in the lead-up to the second round, an attack on a U.N. guest house in Kabul killed five U.N. workers, most of whom were assisting election teams. UNAMA then decided to withdraw or relocate up to 600 of its 1,100 international staff temporarily for security reasons. At the time this raised several questions, including UNAMA's ability to implement its mandate, the impact on other aid groups and whether they would rethink their presence in Afghanistan, and the overall view of the United Nations in Afghanistan. The United Nations is not considered neutral because it supports the government of Afghanistan in its overall mandate. But it is also not always seen as impartial. The guest house incident appears to have been election related—perhaps meant as a deterrent for participation in the then scheduled second round or possibly a comment on UNAMA's role in the election process overall.

On October 23, 2010, the U.N. center in Herat was attacked. There were no fatalities. SRSG Staffan de Mistura, in his briefing to the Security Council on December 22, 2010, commented that luck, preparation, and support from Afghan security forces and a private security company all helped minimize the impact of the attack. In observing that efforts by Afghan and ISAF forces were showing results, he also said, " ... we are detecting from anti-Government elements attempts to show on their side some spectacular attacks in order to dilute the feeling of a change of momentum. What does this mean? It means that we should be expecting and should be ready for, I am afraid, a tense security environment over the next few months. Our assessment is that the situation may get worse before it gets better." De Mistura also said that "on reconciliation and reintegration, everyone recognizes that there is no military solution ... even the Taliban do so, even if they will not say so publicly."[33]

An agreement has been reached between UNAMA and the government of Kuwait to establish a UNAMA Support Office to ensure backup of critical data and to ensure a secure environment for technical and administrative functions. It will also serve as a relocation office should emergency conditions develop in Afghanistan.

UNAMA signed an agreement with the government of the Netherlands to transfer the Alpha compound in Kabul to the United Nations. The compound will serve as office space and residential accommodation in Kabul for up to 70 international staff and provide workspace for 80 national staff. The 2011 budget provides for the construction of security-enhanced compounds in a number of provinces.

Civilian Casualties

UNAMA also tracks progress on a major issue—the attempts of the U.S.-led coalition to limit Afghan civilian deaths caused by coalition operations. UNAMA reported that 1,013 civilian casualties occurred between January and June 2009, mostly in the south and eastern parts of the country, an increase of 24% over the same time the year before.[34] Of these casualties, 59% were caused by anti-government elements and 30.5% were attributed to international and Afghan forces (12% could not be attributed). In 2010, civilian casualties, including deaths and injuries, increased by 20% in the first 10 months by comparison with the same period in 2009, and 75% were linked to anti-government elements. Most civilian casualties resulted from targeted attacks and assassinations by the Taliban and terrorist groups. At the same time, extensive press coverage from bombing campaigns in Afghanistan reveals that there have been a number of innocent victims of erroneous bombings. While the effort to combat Taliban and other militants continues, the potential for mistaken targets remains a risk. Claims of erroneous bombing targets have highlighted the difficulty of intelligence gathering and security problems on the ground. The issue is blurred by the recognition that the end result may not be a matter of simple human error, but rather a complex combination of factors for which it is more difficult to determine responsibility. Collateral damage includes civilian losses, considered to be a by-product of war, despite efforts to minimize innocent loss of life. Concerns about civilian casualties from air strikes, particularly in populated areas, have also focused on the degree to which this affects the Afghan population's perception of the ISAF and U.S.-led forces, and whether the international forces are doing enough to protect civilians. UNAMA has been outspoken over its concerns regarding civilian casualties.[35] Afghans have raised concerns that increased troops may mean an increase in civilian casualties.

Organizational Issues

Resources and Expansion of UNAMA

The U.N. Security Council and member states have called for the expansion of UNAMA's presence to each of Afghanistan's 34 provinces, although that is considered an aspiration that would require major additional resources. UNAMA's regional and provincial offices are viewed by many as a means to help support the civilian surge, to further the work of national programs (such as the Afghan National Development Strategy), and to foster participation at the subnational level by the local government and civil society. In order to expand into each province, UNAMA would need additional resources and funding. The U.N. Secretary-General has stated that to meet the expectations outlined in its mandate and to sustain its progress so far, the mission will need to be strengthened.

Afghan Participation

Experts emphasize the need to create Afghan jobs and to build Afghan capacity. Nevertheless, very little has been said about the mechanics of doing so or discerning the differing views that exist within the Afghan community. The international donor community has put great emphasis on "ownership"—meaning leadership and control—of reconstruction efforts by the country itself. The degree to which Afghans feel a part of what is at stake in their country and to what has been achieved so far is unclear. Some argue that the people and government of Afghanistan are increasingly taking the lead and that the international community is moving toward a supporting role, while others argue just the opposite is taking place. Some are concerned that not enough aid gets directly to the people and that Afghans see little improvement in their lives. It is recognized by many that Afghans are a critical piece of the puzzle in their country's success. Finding ways to empower Afghans in Afghanistan emphasizes the importance of an integrated approach and one that builds needed capacity on multiple levels.

Donor Aid Effectiveness

In his June 2009 report, the U.N. Secretary-General commented on three "interlinked strategic shifts" in Afghanistan that point to the emergence of an "aid effectiveness framework." With UNAMA as the coordinator, these included (1) an emphasis on civilian efforts, (2) a focus on subnational governance and service delivery, and (3) signs that the international efforts are beginning to line up behind comprehensive government programs that, by agreement, serve as the basis for moving forward.[36]

International Donors

UNAMA has had to address the interests of international donors that work with UNAMA, on the one hand, and the interests of the Afghan government, which often perceives its dependence on donor funds as a loss of sovereignty. President Hamid Karzai and his ministers have repeatedly voiced complaints that international aid was decided and provided directly by international donors. Karzai has called the international development efforts a "parallel government" that was not serving the needs of Afghans. He has publicly called for a higher percentage of international aid to be channeled through the Afghan government, or at least for development priorities to be determined in partnership with the Afghan government. This Afghan sentiment was supported in the Compact and the strategy outlined in ANDS. To some extent, the Afghan government remains in a weak position to insist on greater input in setting development priorities because it is so dependent on the international community for security and development funds. In addition, the international donor community provides direct budgetary support to the Afghan government through the ARTF.

International donors, for their part, have complained about widely reported corruption, waste and abuse within the Afghan bureaucracy that have hampered implementation of projects. On the one hand, UNAMA is expected to take the lead on ensuring that donors honor their commitments and align their efforts in a transparent manner behind the financing and implementation of ANDS. To sustain international support, it needs to explain both the achievements and challenges.

Nevertheless, on the other hand, UNAMA is also keen to see the capacity of government institutions strengthened with accountability measures in place to provide donors with the confidence to commit funds to Afghanistan's central budget, and to ensure the Afghan government is able to tackle the problem of corruption. Aid effectiveness is a central part of UNAMA's mandate and an area where it places great emphasis in its work with the Afghan government and international donors. As part of the Kabul Process, the international community affirmed its commitment to the priorities and goals identified by the Afghan government, including aligning aid behind the government's initiatives.

Aid Coordination

The international community continues to struggle with establishing effective coordinating mechanisms and institutions to help move the development process forward. The institutional networks have altered over time, with UNAMA taking on the main coordinating role in March 2002 and, under its recent mandates, a renewed emphasis on expanding that role. The international community and the Afghan government have sought to establish a common set of goals in order to coordinate activities and utilize donor funds most effectively.

Some observers argue that the Afghan government, international organizations, NGOs, donor countries, and others are following their own priorities and programs, and therefore do not coordinate their efforts as effectively as possible. Some, however, have suggested that complete coordination may be both unnecessary and ineffective, especially when different organizations do not share common goals or strategies. For example, the United Nations, the United States, and others have in the past supported a specific strategy intended to bolster the Karzai government through development. For those in Afghanistan and the region who did not support this goal of Karzai empowerment or for those who were marginalized by regime change (such as former supporters of the Taliban regime), supposedly neutral, non-partisan humanitarian assistance could appear partisan. Part of the Kabul process aims to encourage all partners to align resources behind the government of Afghanistan's priorities. It remains to be seen how effectively this can be done. Coordination is a complicated matter, but some would argue that there should be coordination only among like-minded organizations, such as among humanitarian groups, separate from the coordination of political groups, and separate from the coordination of military oriented groups.[37]

Sustained Support from the United States

With the Obama Administration's latest strategy for Afghanistan, other key international stakeholders are also refocusing their efforts. Some experts argue there needs to be greater U.S., including congressional, attention to the United Nation's role in Afghanistan and the implementation of its expanded priorities. Other experts say that sustained (and increased) support from the United States in the form of public statements, reporting, transparency, and oversight is critical to UNAMA and to the importance attached to its mission. And yet some are concerned that UNAMA not become "Americanized" or controlled by the United States.[38]

Negative views about the United Nations itself could also undermine U.S. support for UNAMA. In general, Congress supports the United Nations, but it has also been critical of the organization, particularly with regard to perceived inefficiencies and insufficient accountability, duplication of efforts across agency mandates and missions, and allegations of waste, fraud, and abuse of U.N. resources. The 112th Congress may continue to focus on broad U.N. reform efforts and priorities in general, and with increased attention toward Afghanistan, could decide to conduct greater oversight of UNAMA's activities and progress.

Other questions that have raised tensions in the past, such as how much of U.S. foreign assistance to Afghanistan should be provided bilaterally and how much through multilateral organizations like the United Nations, may also prove challenging as UNAMA manages the complexities of donor relations and policy objectives in Afghanistan.

United Nations Assistance Mission in Afghanistan: Background and Policy Issues 257

APPENDIX A. MAP OF AFGHANISTAN

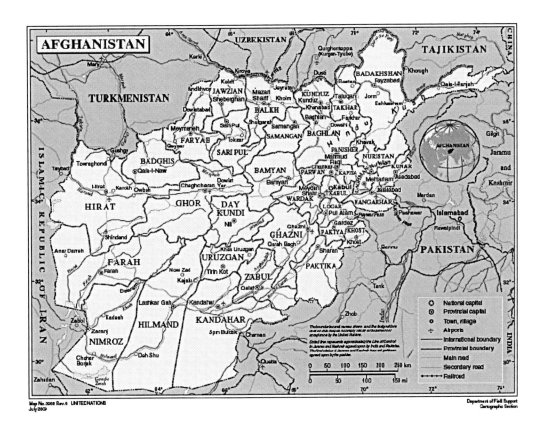

Source: UNAMA, 2009.

Figure A-1. Map of Afghanistan.

APPENDIX B. UNAMA ORGANIZATIONAL CHART

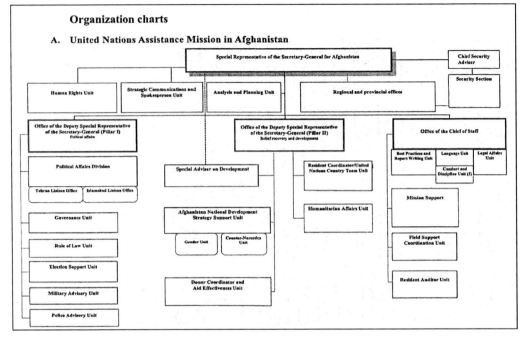

Source: UNAMA, 2008.

Figure B-1. UNAMA Organization Chart.

APPENDIX C. THE U.N. COUNTRY TEAM

The following organizations and U.N. agencies make up the county team in Afghanistan.[39]

Afghanistan's New Beginnings Programme
Asian Development Bank (ADB)
International Labor Organization (ILO)
International Organization for Migration (IOM)
Mine Action Coordination Centre for Afghanistan (MACCA)
Office of the High Commissioner for Human Rights (UNHCR)
United Nations Children's Fund (UNICEF)
United Nations Office for the Coordination of Humanitarian Affairs (OCHA)
United Nations Development Programme (UNDP)
United Nations Development Fund for Women (UNIFEM)
United Nations Educational, Scientific and Cultural Organization (UNESCO)
United Nations Environment Programme (UNEP)
United Nations Food and Agriculture Organization (FAO)
United Nations High Commissioner for Refugees (UNHCR)
United Nations Human Settlements Programme (Habitat)
United Nations Industrial Development Organization (UNIDO)

United Nations Integrated Regional Information Network (IRIN)
United Nations Population Fund (UNFPA)
United Nations Office for Project Services (UNOPS)
United Nations Office on Drugs and Crime (UNODC)
United Nations World Food Programme (WFP)
United Nations World Health Organization (WHO)
World Bank (WB)

APPENDIX D.
MAP OF U.N. PRESENCE IN AFGHANISTAN

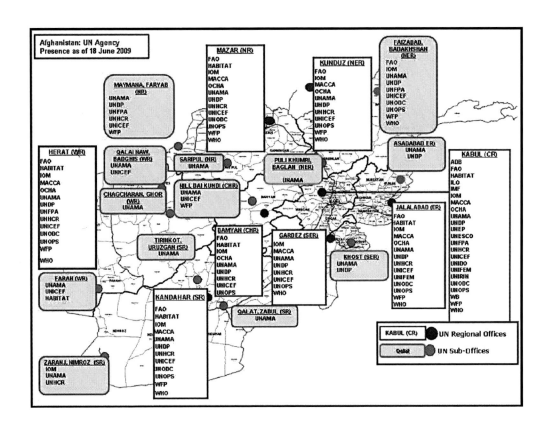

Source: UNAMA, July 2009.

Figure D-1. Map of U.N. Presence in Afghanistan.

APPENDIX E.
MAP OF UNAMA OFFICES

Source: UNAMA, 2009.

Figure E-1. Map of UNAMA Offices.

APPENDIX F. AFGHANISTAN INTERNATIONAL COMMUNITY DONORS LIST

(in $ millions)

ADB	500.00	800.00	1,300.00	2,200.00
Aga Khan	100.00		100.00	200.00
Australia	232.36		232.36	440.23
Austria				14.00
Belgium	46.80		46.80	86.80
Brazil	1.00		1.00	1.00
Canada	600.00		600.00	1,479.75
China	7.50		7.50	196.50
Croatia	28.10		28.10	28.10
Czech Republic	22.00		22.00	22.00
Denmark	430.00	0.00	430.00	683.04
EC		780.00	780.00	1,768.65
ECHO	0.00	0.00	0.00	268.20
Egypt	2.00		2.00	2.00
Estonia			0.00	.30
Finland	30.00	45.00	75.00	152.00
France	126.80	38.70	165.50	208.00
Germany	280.80	374.40	655.20	1,108.32
Global Fund				11.48
Greece	3.10		3.10	12.70
Hungary	3.00		3.00	3.00
India	450.00		450.00	1,200.00
Iran	350.00		350.00	1,164.00
Ireland	13.50		13.50	33.40
Islamic Dev Bank			0.00	70.00
Italy	234.00		234.00	637.36
Japan	550.00		550.00	1,900.00
Kazakhstan	0.00		0.00	4.00
Korea (Rep of)	30.00		30.00	86.20
Kuwait	30.00		30.00	75.00
Luxembourg	0.00		0.00	7.20
Malta	0.30		0.30	0.30
Netherlands	1,209.00		1,209.00	1,697.00

(Continued).

ADB	500.00	800.00	1,300.00	2,200.00
New Zealand	15.00		15.00	30.85
Norway	669.00	6.00	675.00	977.00
Oman	3.00		3.00	9.00
Org Islamic Conf	0.00		0.00	15.00
Pakistan	20.00		20.00	305.00
Poland	1.30		1.30	6.33
Portugal	0.00		0.00	1.20
Qatar	4.00		4.00	24.00
Russian Federation	0.00	0.00	0.00	141.00
Saudi Arabia	0.00	0.00	0.00	533.00
Slovakia	1.00		1.00	1.00
Spain	234.00		234.00	486.47
Sweden	0.00		0.00	288.60
Switzerland			0.00	134.00
Taiwan	0.00		0.00	28.60
Turkey	100.00		100.00	190.00
UAE	250.00		250.00	323.70
UK	1,200.00		1,200.00	2,897.00
UN Agencies	0.00	0.00	0.00	252.40
USA	7,095.40	3,104.60	10,200.00	31,851.86
Vietnam	0.01		0.01	0.01
World Bank	433.00	667.00	1,100.00	2,803.00
Other Donors	0.00	0.00	0.00	92.77
Total	15,305.97	5,815.70	21,121.87	57,149.62

Source: Office of the SIGAR, October 30, 2008 Report to Congress.

APPENDIX G. PRIORITIES IN UNAMA'S 2009 MANDATE

The priorities below were identified by the U.N. Security Council in resolution 1868 (2009) as key areas of UNAMA's work in Afghanistan:[40]

- promote more coherent support by the international community to the Afghan government;

Promote, as co-chair of the Joint Coordination and Monitoring Board (JCMB), more coherent support by the international community to the Afghan Government and the adherence to the principles of aid effectiveness enumerated in the Afghanistan Compact, including through mobilization of resources, coordination of the assistance provided by international donors and organizations, and direction of the contributions of United Nations agencies, funds and programmes, in particular for counter-narcotics, reconstruction, and development activities;

- strengthen cooperation with ISAF;

Strengthen the cooperation with ISAF at all levels and throughout the country, in accordance with their existing mandates, in order to improve civil-military coordination, to facilitate the timely exchange of information and to ensure coherence between the activities of national and international security forces and of civilian actors in support of an Afghan-led development and stabilization process, including through engagement with provincial reconstruction teams and engagement with non-governmental organizations;

- provide political outreach through a strengthened and expanded presence throughout the country;

Through a strengthened and expanded presence throughout the country, provide political outreach, promote at the local level the implementation of the Compact, of the ANDS and of the National Drugs Control Strategy, and facilitate inclusion in and understanding of the Government's policies;

- provide good offices in support of Afghan-led reconciliation programs;

Provide good offices to support, if requested by the Afghan Government, the implementation of Afghan-led reconciliation programmes, within the framework of the Afghan Constitution and with full respect for the implementation of measures introduced by the Security Council in its resolution 1267 (1999) and other relevant resolutions of the Council;

- support efforts to improve governance and the rule of law and to combat corruption;

Support and strengthen efforts to improve governance and the rule of law and to combat corruption at the local and national levels, and to promote development initiatives at the local level with a view to helping bring the benefits of peace and deliver services in a timely and sustainable manner;

- play a central coordinating role to facilitate the delivery of humanitarian aid;

Play a central coordinating to facilitate the delivery of humanitarian assistance in accordance with humanitarian principles and with a view to building the capacity of the Afghan government, including by providing effective support to national and local authorities in assisting and protecting internally displaced persons and to creating conditions conducive to voluntary, safe, dignified and sustainable return of refugees and internally displaced persons;

- monitor the human right situation of civilians and coordinate human rights protection;

Continue, with the support of the Office of the United Nations High Commissioner for Human Rights, to cooperate with the Afghan Independent Human Rights Commission (AIHRC), to cooperate also with relevant international and local non-governmental organizations, to monitor the situation of civilians, to coordinate efforts to ensure their protection and to assist in the full implementation of the fundamental freedoms and human rights provisions of the Afghan Constitution and international treaties to which Afghanistan is a State party; in particular those regarding the full enjoyment by women of their human rights;

- support the electoral process through the Afghan Independent Electoral Commission;

Support, at the request of the Afghan authorities, preparations for the crucial upcoming presidential elections, in particular through the IEC, by providing technical assistance, coordinating other international donors, agencies and organizations providing assistance and channeling existing and additional funds earmarked to support the process;

- support regional cooperation in working for a more stable and prosperous Afghanistan.

To work towards a stable and prosperous Afghanistan.

APPENDIX H. KEY EFFORTS IN AFGHANISTAN, 2002-2008

UNAMA has outlined the following key indicators of progress between 2002 and 2008:

- **Health**: 85% of the population has been given access to a basic package of health services.
- **Social Protection**: 2.5 million Afghans have received social support.
- **Education and Culture**: More than 6 million children are enrolled in school.
- **Agriculture and Rural Development**: 32,000 villages have benefitted from development projects.
- **Natural Resources Management**: More than 3 million have benefitted from rural water and sanitation projects.
- **Infrastructure**: 13,150 km of roads have been rehabilitated, improved, or built.
- **National Army and Police**: More than 140,000 policemen and soldiers have been recruited and trained since 2003.
- **Disarmament and Demining**: More than 7.7 million unexploded ordnances have been cleared since 2001.
- **Democracy and Governance**: 75% of voters participated in Afghanistan's first democratic elections in 2004.

- **Justice and Human Rights**: The Constitution adopted in 2004 calls for the protection of human rights.
- **Economy and Trade**: Gross Domestic Product (GDP) per capita has increased by over 70% since 2002.
- **Media and Telecoms**: 75% of Afghans have access to telecommunications, including over 5 million cell phones now in use.[41]
-

End Notes

[1] For background information, see CRS Report RL30588, *Afghanistan: Post-Taliban Governance, Security, and U.S. Policy*, by Kenneth Katzman. For a map of Afghanistan, see Appendix A. CRS interviews in Kabul, October 2009.

[2] After the Soviet Union left Afghanistan, the United States sharply reduced its aid programs to Afghanistan.

[3] Since 1988, these offices received a series of different names, but most recently until 2002, the political office was run by the United Nations Special Mission to Afghanistan (UNSMA) and the humanitarian and reconstruction office was run by the United Nations Office for Coordination of Humanitarian Affairs (UNOCHA).

[4] Usually, the international donor community is considered to be made up of international organizations and individual donor countries.

[5] From FY1994 through FY2001, the United States Agency for International Development (USAID) did not have a mission in Afghanistan, but continued to provide aid mainly through U.N. agencies and NGOs.

[6] In 2007, Afghanistan placed 174th out of 178 countries on global rankings of the Human Development Index (HDI), which fell slightly under that of 2004 and well behind its regional neighbors. See *Afghanistan Human Development Report 2007*, U.N. Development Programme and the Center for Policy and Development, Kabul University, 2007.

[7] The priorities of the Mission are outlined in detail in Appendix D, and some are discussed in the policy section of this report.

[8] ISAF is a NATO-led operation in Afghanistan authorized by the U.N. Security Council under a peace enforcement mandate (Chapter VIII of the U.N. Charter) and established to assist the Government of Afghanistan in maintaining security. See U.N. Security Council Resolutions 1386 (2001), 1413 (2002), 1444 (2002), 1510 (2003), 1563 (2004), 1623 (2005), 1707 (2006), 1776 (2007), 1817 (2008), 1833 (2008), 1890 (2009), 1917 (2010), and 1943 (2010). ISAF has been deployed in Afghanistan since the end of 2001. In 2003, NATO took over leadership of ISAF.

[9] Department of Public Information, "Security Council Extends Mandate of United Nations Assistance Mission in Afghanistan to Help Promote Government-Led Recovery Efforts," Security Council SC/9889, March 22, 2010.

[10] In January 2008, with U.S. support, U.N. Secretary-General Ban Ki-moon tentatively appointed British diplomat Paddy Ashdown to this "super envoy" position, but President Karzai rejected the appointment reportedly over concerns about the scope of authority of such an envoy, in particular its potential to dilute the U.S. role in Afghanistan. Some contend that for political purposes, Karzai might have also sought to show independence from the international community. Ashdown withdrew his name on January 28, 2008.

[11] For a map of the U.N. presence across Afghanistan, see Appendix D.

[12] Chairman's Statement of the International Conference on Afghanistan, The Hague, March 31, 2009. For a map of UNAMA offices, see Appendix E.

[13] The Afghanistan Compact, London 31 January-1 February 2006.

[14] Examples of MDGs include cutting the number of people living on less than a dollar a day by half; ensuring that all children receive primary schooling; reducing the number of people who do not have access to safe drinking water by half; and reversing the spread of diseases such as malaria and HIV, among other things. More information on MDGs is available at http://www.un.org/milleniumgoals/.

[15] See Islamic Republic of Afghanistan, Afghanistan National Development Strategy, Executive Summary, 1387 – 1391 (2008 – 2013), A Strategy for Security, Governance, Economic Growth and Poverty Reduction. ANDS also serves as Afghanistan's Poverty Reduction Strategy Paper (PRSP).

[16] Pledges represent amounts that countries have been willing to earmark for Afghanistan. See the first U.S. Special Inspector General for Afghanistan Reconstruction (SIGAR), Quarterly Report to the United States Congress, October 2008. For a list of donor country pledges 2002-2008, see Appendix F. Many inside and outside the Afghan government have criticized donors for not following through on their pledges. However, donor conferences in general exhibit problems, such as slow disbursement of funds, weak mechanisms for pledging and mobilizing assistance, inadequate devices for tracking aid flows, inappropriate forms of aid conditionality, poor articulation between relief and development efforts, and weak coordination within the donor community. Donors over-pledge, pledge already allocated funds, and slowly or never fulfill their pledges. In the case of Afghanistan, the international community has sought to avoid some of these problems through the creation of an aid database, which has made pledging, tracking, and monitoring more transparent. Whether donor conferences and trust funds are the best way to fund reconstruction has been questioned by some observers. (The latest SIGAR Quarterly Report to the United States Congress does not contain information on donor country pledges.)

[17] Several other meetings and conferences with an Afghanistan focus have taken place, including the Shanghai Cooperation Organisation March 27, 2009, in Moscow, Russia; the third Regional Economic Cooperation Conference on Afghanistan, May 13-14 in Islamabad, Pakistan; a summit with the leaders of Afghanistan and Pakistan on May 19, 2009; and a meeting between NATO heads of state and government in Strasbourg on April 3-4, 2009.

[18] Chairman's Statement of the International Conference on Afghanistan, The Hague, March 31, 2009. See also U.N. document, Report of the Secretary-General to the General Assembly and Security Council, *The Situation in Afghanistan and its Implications for International Peace and Security*, A/63/892, S/2009/323, June 23, 2009.

[19] Along with the World Bank, the Asian Development Bank, Islamic Development Bank and United Nations Development Program make up the ARTF Management Committee. The latest report on the ARTF is at http://siteresources.worldbank.org/INTAFGHANISTAN/Resources/Afghanistan-Reconstructional-Trust-Fund/ ARTF_Annual_ReportSY1387.pdf

[20] Office of the SIGAR, October 30, 2009 Report to Congress.

[21] Other funds are distributed through U.S. Department of Agriculture (USDA) and the Centers for Disease Control and Prevention (CDC).

[22] For more information on these efforts, see CRS Report R40699, *Afghanistan: U.S. Foreign Assistance*, by Curt Tarnoff.

[23] These priorities were initially set out in paragraph 4 of resolution 1806 (2008) and then restated in paragraph 4 of resolution 1868 (2009).

[24] U.N. document, Report of the Secretary-General to the General Assembly and Security Council, *The Situation in Afghanistan and its Implications for International Peace and Security*, A/64/364, S/2009/475, September 22, 2009.

[25] See Appendix G for more information on these priorities.

[26] Bullet points from UNAMA Fact Sheet, March 28, 2008.

[27] The text covering the benchmarks is drawn directly from U.N. document, Report of the Secretary-General to the General Assembly and Security Council, *The Situation in Afghanistan and its Implications for International Peace and Security*, A/64/364, S/2009/475, September 22, 2009, where information about the indicators of progress and metrics are discussed.

[28] Report of the U.N. Secretary General, *The Situation in Afghanistan and its Implications for International Peace and Security*, A/63/892, S/2009/323, June 23, 2009.

[29] See IEC website at http://www.iec.org.af/results.

[30] Mr. Eide said at the time he was not resigning and contended that he never planned to renew his contract beyond March 2010. Criticized for his handling of the flawed Afghan presidential election in August, it is unclear whether this factored into the timing of his decision to step down. See Richard A. Oppel, Jr., "U.N. Afghan Mission Chief to Resign," *New York Times*, December 12, 2009; and Ben Farmer, "U.N. Chief Kai Eide to Step Down After Criticism," Telegraph.co.uk. See Richard A. Oppel, Jr., "U.N. Afghan Mission Chief to Resign," *New York Times*, December 12, 2009; and Ben Farmer, "U.N. Chief Kai Eide to Step Down After Criticism," Telegraph.co.uk.

[31] See, for example, International Crisis Group, *Afghanistan: Elections and the Crisis of Governance*, November 25, 2009: http://www.crisisgroup.org/library/documents/asia/south_asia/ b96_afghanistan___ elections_and_the_crisis_ of_governance.pdf

[32] Ben Farmer, "U.N. Chief Kai Eide to Step Down After Criticism," Telegraph.co.uk.

[33] U.N. Security Council, *The Situation in Afghanistan*, S/PV.6464, December 22, 2010.

[34] Report of the U.N. Secretary General, *The Situation in Afghanistan and its Implications for International Peace and Security*, A/63/892, S/2009/323, June 23, 2009; UNAMA, Human Rights Unit, *Afghanistan: Mid Year Bulletin on Protection of Civilians in Armed Conflict*, 2009, July 2009.

[35] U.N. Security Council, Extending Mandate of U.N. Assistance Mission in Afghanistan, Security Council Condemns All Attacks on Civilians, Recruitment of Child Soldiers, SC/9624, March 23, 2009; Highlights of the Noon Briefing, U.N. Headquarters, New York, June 30, 2009.

[36] Report of the U.N. Secretary General, *The Situation in Afghanistan and its Implications for International Peace and Security*, A/63/892, S/2009/323, June 23, 2009.

[37] As SRSG for Afghanistan, Kai Eide, said that additional capacity-building resources were needed, and that some efforts by international donors duplicated each other or were tied to purchasing decisions by Western countries.

[38] When Peter Galbraith was appointed as DSRSG for Afghanistan, he was viewed as controversial because of fears of undue influence by the Americans.

[39] Source: UNAMA, June 2009.

[40] Text in italics is taken directly from U.N. Security Council resolution 1868 (2009). Bullet points from UNAMA Fact Sheet, March 28, 2008.

[41] U.N. Assistance Mission in Afghanistan, International Conference in Support of Afghanistan, Set of Fact Sheets, Paris, 24 May, 4 June, 12 June 2008.

In: The Middle East in Turmoil, Volume 3
Editor: Angela N. Castillo

ISBN: 978-1-61324-241-4
© 2011 Nova Science Publishers, Inc.

Chapter 9

AFGHANISTAN: POST-TALIBAN GOVERNANCE, SECURITY, AND U.S. POLICY*

Kenneth Katzman

SUMMARY

Following two high-level policy reviews on Afghanistan in 2009, and another completed in December 2010, the Obama Administration asserts that it is pursuing a well resourced and integrated military-civilian strategy intended to pave the way for a gradual transition to Afghan security leadership to begin in July 2011 and be completed by the end of 2014. The pace of that transition is to be determined by conditions on the ground. The policy is intended to ensure that Afghanistan will not again become a base for terrorist attacks against the United States. At the same time, there appears to be a debate within the Administration and between the United States and Pakistan over whether the war effort should be widened somewhat to include stepped up attacks on Afghan militants inside Pakistan. That debate raises the question of the degree to which Pakistan envisions Afghanistan as part of its strategy to avoid encirclement by or pressure from Pakistan's historic rival, India. At the same time, Afghanistan is achieving ever higher degrees of economic and political integration with its neighbors in Central Asia and the Middle East.

The December 2010 review took into account the effect of the addition of U.S. combat troops to Afghanistan in 2009 and 2010, intended to create security conditions to expand Afghan governance and economic development. A total of 51,000 additional U.S. forces were authorized by the two reviews, which has brought U.S. troop levels to about 98,000 as of September 4, 2010, with partner forces holding at about 41,000. Until October 2010, there had not been clear indications that U.S. strategy has shown success, to date. As reflected in the overview of the Administration review, released December 16, 2010, the top U.S./NATO commander in Afghanistan, Gen. David Petraeus, and his associates believe that insurgent momentum has been blunted, although gains remain "fragile and reversible." One positive sign is that insurgent commanders are exploring possible surrender terms under which they might reintegrate into society. Still, U.N. assessments and some outside experts remain pessimistic, asserting that the insurgents

---

* This is an edited, reformatted and augmented version of a Congressional Research Services publication, dated December 29, 2010.

have expanded their presence in northern Afghanistan, and that the Afghan government is too lacking in capacity or effectiveness to be able to solidify coalition security gains. Many assess that President Hamid Karzai's refusal to forcefully confront governmental corruption has caused a loss of Afghan support for his government, while others note that strong economic growth and economic development are additional causes for optimism.

In order to try to achieve a strategic breakthrough that might force key insurgent leaders to negotiate a early political settlement, Gen. Petraeus is attempting to accelerate local security solutions and experiments similar to those he pursued earlier in Iraq, and to step up the use of air strikes and Special Forces operations against Taliban commanders. In order to take advantage of an apparent new willingness by some insurgent commanders to negotiate, Karzai has named a broad-based 70-member High Peace Council to oversee negotiations. However, there are major concerns among Afghanistan's minorities and among its women that reconciliation could lead to compromises that erode the freedoms Afghans have enjoyed since 2001.

Through the end of FY2010, the United States has provided over $54.5 billion in assistance to Afghanistan since the fall of the Taliban, of which about $30 billion has been to equip and train Afghan forces. (See CRS Report RS21922, *Afghanistan: Politics, Elections, and Government Performance*, by Kenneth Katzman.)

BACKGROUND

Afghanistan has a history of a high degree of decentralization, and resistance to foreign invasion and occupation. Some have termed it the "graveyard of empires."

From Early History to the 19th Century

Alexander the Great conquered what is now Afghanistan in three years (330 B.C.E. to 327 B.C.E), although at significant cost and with significant difficulty, and requiring, among other steps, marriage to a resident of the conquered territory. From the third to the eighth century, A.D., Buddhism was the dominant religion in Afghanistan. At the end of the seventh century, Islam spread in Afghanistan when Arab invaders from the Umayyad Dynasty defeated the Persian empire of the Sassanians. In the 10th century, Muslim rulers called Samanids, from Bukhara (in what is now Uzbekistan), extended their influence into Afghanistan, and the complete conversion of Afghanistan to Islam occurred during the rule of the Gaznavids in the 11th century. They ruled over the first vast Islamic empire based in what is now Ghazni province of Afghanistan.

In 1504, Babur, a descendent of the conquerors Tamarlane and Genghis Khan, took control of Kabul and then moved onto India, establishing the Mughal Empire. (Babur is buried in the Babur Gardens complex in Kabul, which has been refurbished with the help of the Agha Khan Foundation.) Throughout the 16th and 17th centuries, Afghanistan was fought over by the Mughal Empire and the Safavid Dynasty of Persia (now Iran), with the Safavids mostly controlling Herat and western Afghanistan, and the Mughals controlling Kabul and the east. A monarchy ruled by ethnic Pashtuns was founded in 1747 by Ahmad Shah Durrani, who was a senior officer in the army of Nadir Shah, ruler of Persia, when Nadir Shah was assassinated and Persian control over Afghanistan weakened.

A strong ruler, Dost Muhammad Khan, emerged in Kabul in 1826 and created concerns among Britain that the Afghans were threatening Britain's control of India; that fear led to a British decision in 1838 to intervene in Afghanistan, setting off the first Anglo-Afghan War (1838-1842). Nearly all of the 4,500-person British force was killed in that war, which ended with a final British stand at Gandamack. The second Anglo-Afghan War took place during 1878-1880.

Early 20th Century and Cold War Era

King Amanullah Khan (1919-1929) launched attacks on British forces in Afghanistan (Third Anglo-Afghan War) shortly after taking power and won complete independence from Britain as recognized in the Treaty of Rawalpindi (August 8, 1919). He was considered a secular modernizer presiding over a government in which all ethnic minorities participated. He was succeeded by King Mohammad Nadir Shah (1929-1933), and then by King Mohammad Zahir Shah. Zahir Shah's reign (1933-1973) is remembered fondly by many older Afghans for promulgating a constitution in 1964 that established a national legislature and promoting freedoms for women, including dropping a requirement that they cover their face and hair. However, possibly believing that he could limit Soviet support for Communist factions in Afghanistan, Zahir Shah also entered into a significant political and arms purchase relationship with the Soviet Union. The Soviets began to build large infrastructure projects in Afghanistan during Zahir Shah's time, such as the north-south Salang Pass/Tunnel and Bagram airfield. He also accepted agricultural and other development aid from the United States. In part, the countryside was secured during the King's time by local tribal militias called *arbokai*.

Afghanistan's slide into instability began in the 1970s when the diametrically opposed Communist Party and Islamic movements grew in strength. While receiving medical treatment in Italy, Zahir Shah was overthrown by his cousin, Mohammad Daoud, a military leader who established a dictatorship with strong state involvement in the economy. Daoud was overthrown and killed[1] in April 1978 by People's Democratic Party of Afghanistan (PDPA, Communist party) military officers under the direction of two PDPA (Khalq faction) leaders, Hafizullah Amin and Nur Mohammad Taraki, in what is called the *Saur* (April) Revolution. Taraki became president, but he was displaced in September 1979 by Amin. Both leaders drew their strength from rural ethnic Pashtuns and tried to impose radical socialist change on a traditional society, in part by redistributing land and bringing more women into government. The attempt at rapid modernization sparked rebellion by Islamic parties opposed to such moves. The Soviet Union sent troops into Afghanistan on December 27, 1979, to prevent a seizure of power by the Islamic militias, known as the *mujahedin* (Islamic fighters). Upon their invasion, the Soviets replaced Amin with another PDPA leader perceived as pliable, Babrak Karmal (Parcham faction of the PDPA), who was part of the 1978 PDPA takeover but was exiled by Taraki and Amin.

Soviet occupation forces, which numbered about 120,000, were never able to pacify the outlying areas of the country. The *mujahedin* benefited from U.S. weapons and assistance, provided through the Central Intelligence Agency (CIA) in cooperation with Pakistan's Inter-Service Intelligence directorate (ISI). The mujahedin were also relatively well organized and coordinated by seven major parties that in early 1989 formed a Peshawar-based "Afghan

Interim Government" (AIG). The seven party leaders were Mohammad Nabi Mohammadi; Sibghatullah Mojaddedi; Gulbuddin Hikmatyar; Burhanuddin Rabbani; Yunus Khalis; Abd-i-Rab Rasul Sayyaf; and Pir Gaylani. Mohammadi and Khalis have died in recent years of natural causes, but the others are still active in Afghan politics and governance or, in the case of Hikmatyar, fighting the Afghan government.

The *mujahedin* weaponry included U.S.-supplied portable shoulder-fired anti-aircraft systems called "Stingers," which proved highly effective against Soviet aircraft. The United States decided in 1985 to provide these weapons to the mujahedin after substantial debate within the Reagan Administration and some in Congress over whether they could be used effectively and whether doing so would harm broader U.S.-Soviet relations. The *mujahedin* also hid and stored weaponry in a large network of natural and manmade tunnels and caves throughout Afghanistan. Partly because of the effectiveness of the Stinger in shooting down Soviet helicopters and fixed wing aircraft, the Soviet Union's losses mounted—about 13,400 Soviet soldiers were killed in the war, according to Soviet figures—turning Soviet domestic opinion against the war. In 1986, after the reformist Mikhail Gorbachev became leader, the Soviets replaced Karmal with the director of Afghan intelligence, Najibullah Ahmedzai (known by his first name). Najibullah was a Ghilzai Pashtun, and was from the Parcham faction of the PDPA. Some Afghans say that some aspects of his governing style were admirable, particularly his appointment of a prime minister (Sultan Ali Keshtmand and others) to handle administrative duties and distribute power.

Geneva Accords (1988) and Soviet Withdrawal

On April 14, 1988, Gorbachev agreed to a U.N.-brokered accord (the Geneva Accords) requiring it to withdraw. The withdrawal was completed by February 15, 1989, leaving in place the weak Najibullah government. A warming of relations moved the United States and Soviet Union to try for a political settlement to the Afghan conflict, a trend accelerated by the 1991 collapse of the Soviet Union, which reduced Moscow's capacity for supporting communist regimes in the Third World. On September 13, 1991, Moscow and Washington agreed to a joint cutoff of military aid to the Afghan combatants.

The State Department has said that a total of about $3 billion in economic and covert military assistance was provided by the U.S. to the Afghan *mujahedin* from 1980 until the end of the Soviet occupation in 1989. Press reports say the covert aid program grew from about $20 million per year in FY1980 to about $300 million per year during FY1986-FY1990.[2] The Soviet pullout decreased the perceived strategic value of Afghanistan, causing a reduction in subsequent covert funding. As indicated below in **Table 9**, U.S. assistance to Afghanistan remained at relatively low levels from the time of the Soviet withdrawal, validating the views of many that the United States largely considered its role in Afghanistan "completed" when Soviets troops left, and there was little support for a major U.S. effort to rebuild the country. The United States closed its embassy in Kabul in January 1989, as the Soviet Union was completing its pullout, and it remained so until the fall of the Taliban in 2001.

With Soviet backing withdrawn, Najibullah rallied the PDPA Army and the party-dominated paramilitary organization called the *Sarandoy*, and successfully beat back the first post-Soviet withdrawal *mujahedin* offensives. Although Najibullah defied expectations that his government would immediately collapse after a Soviet withdrawal, military defections

Afghanistan: Post-Taliban Governance, Security, and U.S. Policy 273

continued and his position weakened in subsequent years. On March 18, 1992, Najibullah publicly agreed to step down once an interim government was formed. That announcement set off a wave of rebellions primarily by Uzbek and Tajik militia commanders in northern Afghanistan—particularly Abdul Rashid Dostam, who joined prominent *mujahedin* commander Ahmad Shah Masud of the Islamic Society, a largely Tajik party headed by Burhannudin Rabbani. Masud had earned a reputation as a brilliant strategist by preventing the Soviets from occupying his power base in the Panjshir Valley of northeastern Afghanistan. Najibullah fell, and the *mujahedin* regime began April 18, 1992.[3] Each year, a public parade is held to mark that day. (Some major *mujahedin* figures did not attend the 2010 celebration because of a perception that they are under Afghan public and international criticism of their immunity from alleged human rights abuses during the anti-Soviet war.)

Table 1. Afghanistan Social and Economic Statistics

Population	28 million +. Kabul population is 3 million, up from 500,000 in Taliban era.
Ethnicities/Religions	Pashtun 42%; Tajik 27%; Uzbek 9%; Hazara 9%; Aimak 4%; Turkmen 3%; Baluch 2%.
Size of Religious Minorities	Religions: Sunni (Hanafi school) 80%; Shiite (Hazaras, Qizilbash, and Isma'ilis) 19%; other 1%Christians-estimated 500-8,000 persons; Sikh and Hindu-3,000 persons; Bahai's-400 (declared blasphemous in May 2007); Jews-1 person; Buddhist- small numbers, mostly foreigners. No Christian or Jewish schools. One church.
Literacy Rate	28% of population over 15 years of age. 43% of males; 12.6% of females.
Total and Per Capita GDP/Growth Rates	$23.3 billion purchasing power parity. 114th in the world. Per capita: $800 purchasing power parity. 219th in the world. Growth: 14%, about the same 12% in 2007.
Unemployment Rate	40%
Children in School/Schools Built	5.7 million, of which 35% are girls. Up from 900,000 in school during Taliban era. 8,000 schools built; 140,000 teachers hired since Taliban era. 17 universities, up from 2 in 2002. 75,000 Afghans in universities in Afghanistan; 5,000 when Taliban was in power. 35% of university students in Afghanistan are female.
Afghans With Access to Health Coverage	65% with basic health services access-compared to 8% during Taliban era. Infant mortality down 18% since Taliban to 135 per 1,000 live births. 680 clinics built .
Roads Built	About 2,500 miles paved post-Taliban, including repaving of "Ring Road" (78% complete) that circles the country. Kabul-Qandahar drive reduced to 6 hours.
Judges/Courts	About 1,000 judges trained since fall of Taliban; some removed for corruption
Banks Operating	17, including branches in some rural areas, but still about 90% of the population use hawalas, or informal money transfer services. Zero banks existed during Taliban era. Some limited credit card use. Some Afghan police now paid by cell phone (E-Paisa).
Access to Electricity	15%-20% of the population.

Table 1. (Continued).

Gov't Revenues (excl. donor funds)	About $1.4 billion in 2010; nearly double the $720 million 2007. Total Afghan budget is about $3 billion, with shortfall covered by foreign donors, including through World Bank-run Afghanistan Reconstruction Trust Fund.
Financial Reserves	About $4.4 billion, up from $180 million in 2002. Includes amounts due Central Bank.
External Debt	$8 billion bilateral, plus $500 million multilateral. U.S. forgave $108 million in debt in 2004, and $1.6 billion forgiven by other creditors in March 2010.
Foreign/Private Investment	About $500 million to $1 billion per year. Four Afghan airlines: Ariana (national) plus three privately owned: Safi, Kam, and Pamir.
Mining/Minerals	Vast untapped minerals affirmed by U.S. experts (June 2010). Chinese firm mining copper in Lowgar Province; December 2010 - contracts let to produce oil in Sar-I-Pol Province (north) and for private investers to mine gold in Baghlan Province.
Agriculture/Major Legal Exports	80% of the population is involved in agriculture. Self-sufficiency in wheat production as of May 2009 (first time in 30 years). Products for export include fruits, raisins, melons, pomegranate juice (Anar), nuts, carpets, lapis lazuli gems, marble tile, timber products (Kunar, Nuristan provinces). July 2010 Afghanistan-Pakistan trade agreement may increase these exports. Some raisins being exported to Britain.
Oil Proven Reserves	3.6 billion barrels of oil, 36.5 trillion cubic feet of gas. Current oil production negligible, but USAID funding project to revive oil and gas facilities in the north.
Import Partners/Imports	Pakistan 38.6%; U.S. 9.5%; Germany 5.5%; India 5.2%.. Main imports are food, petroleum, capital goods, textiles, autos
Cellphones/Tourism	About 12 million cellphones, up from several hundred used by Taliban government officials. Tourism: National park opened in Bamiyan June 2009. Increasing tourist visits.

Sources: CIA, *The World Factbook*; various press and U.S. government official testimony.

The *Mujahedin* Government and Rise of the Taliban

The fall of Najibullah exposed the differences among the *mujahedin* parties. The leader of one of the smaller parties (Afghan National Liberation Front), Islamic scholar Sibghatullah Mojadeddi, was president during April-May 1992. Under an agreement among the major parties, Rabbani became President in June 1992 with agreement that he would serve until December 1994. He refused to step down at that time, saying that political authority would disintegrate without a clear successor. Kabul was subsequently shelled by other *mujahedin* factions, particularly that of nominal "Prime Minister" Gulbuddin Hikmatyar, a Pashtun, who accused Rabbani of monopolizing power. Hikmatyar, who never formally assumed a working prime ministerial role in Kabul because of suspicions of Rabbani, was purportedly backed by Pakistan. Hikmatyar's radical faction of the Islamist Hizb-e-Islami (Islamic Party) had received a large proportion of the U.S. aid during the anti-Soviet war. (Yunus Khalis led a more moderate faction of Hizb-e-Islami during that war.)

In 1993-1994, Afghan Islamic clerics and students, mostly of rural, Pashtun origin, formed the Taliban movement. Many were former *mujahedin* who had become disillusioned with conflict among *mujahedin* parties and had moved into Pakistan to study in Islamic seminaries ("madrassas") mainly of the "Deobandi" school of Islam.[4]Some say this Islam is similar to the "Wahhabism" that is practiced in Saudi Arabia. Taliban practices were also consonant with conservative Pashtun tribal traditions.

The Taliban viewed the Rabbani government as corrupt and anti-Pashtun, and the four years of civil war (1992-1996) created popular support for the Taliban as able to deliver stability. With the help of defections, the Taliban peacefully took control of the southern city of Qandahar in November 1994. By February 1995, it was approaching Kabul, after which an 18-month stalemate ensued. In September 1995, the Taliban captured Herat province, bordering Iran, and imprisoned its governor, Ismail Khan, ally of Rabbani and Masud, who later escaped and took refuge in Iran. In September 1996, new Taliban victories near Kabul led to the withdrawal of Rabbani and Masud to the Panjshir Valley north of Kabul with most of their heavy weapons; the Taliban took control of Kabul on September 27, 1996. Taliban gunmen subsequently entered a U.N. facility in Kabul to seize Najibullah, his brother, and aides, and then hanged them.

Taliban Rule (September 1996-November 2001)

The Taliban regime was led by Mullah Muhammad Umar, who lost an eye in the anti-Soviet war while fighting as part of the Hizb-e-Islami *mujahedin* party of Yunis Khalis. Umar held the title of Head of State and "Commander of the Faithful," remaining in the Taliban power base in Qandahar and almost never appearing in public, although he did occasionally receive high-level foreign officials. Umar forged a political and personal bond with bin Laden and refused U.S. demands to extradite him. Like Umar, most of the senior figures in the Taliban regime were Ghilzai Pashtuns, which predominate in eastern Afghanistan. They are rivals of the Durrani Pashtuns, who are predominant in the south.

The Taliban progressively lost international and domestic support as it imposed strict adherence to Islamic customs in areas it controlled and employed harsh punishments, including executions. The Taliban authorized its "Ministry for the Promotion of Virtue and the Suppression of Vice" to use physical punishments to enforce strict Islamic practices, including bans on television, Western music, and dancing. It prohibited women from attending school or working outside the home, except in health care, and it publicly executed some women for adultery. In what many consider its most extreme action, and which some say was urged by bin Laden, in March 2001 the Taliban blew up two large Buddha statues carved into hills above Bamiyan city, considering them idols.

The Clinton Administration held talks with the Taliban before and after it took power, but was unable to moderate its policies. The United States withheld recognition of Taliban as the legitimate government of Afghanistan, formally recognizing no faction as the government. The United Nations continued to seat representatives of the Rabbani government, not the Taliban. The State Department ordered the Afghan embassy in Washington, DC, closed in August 1997. U.N. Security Council Resolution 1193 (August 28, 1998) and 1214 (December 8, 1998) urged the Taliban to end discrimination against women. Women's rights groups urged the Clinton Administration not to recognize the Taliban government. In May 1999, the

Senate-passed S.Res. 68 called on the President not to recognize an Afghan government that oppresses women.

The Taliban's hosting of Al Qaeda's leadership gradually became the Clinton Administration's overriding agenda item with Afghanistan. In April 1998, then U.S. Ambassador to the United Nations Bill Richardson (along with Assistant Secretary of State Karl Indurfurth and NSC senior official Bruce Riedel) visited Afghanistan, but the Taliban refused to hand over bin Laden. They did not meet Mullah Umar. After the August 7, 1998, Al Qaeda bombings of U.S. embassies in Kenya and Tanzania, the Clinton Administration progressively pressured the Taliban, imposing U.S. sanctions and achieving adoption of some U.N. sanctions as well. On August 20, 1998, the United States fired cruise missiles at alleged Al Qaeda training camps in eastern Afghanistan, but bin Laden was not hit.[5] Some observers assert that the Administration missed several clearer opportunities to strike him, including a purported sighting of him by an unarmed Predator drone at the Tarnak Farm camp in Afghanistan in the fall of 2000.[6] Clinton Administration officials said that domestic and international support for ousting the Taliban militarily was lacking.

The "Northern Alliance" Congeals

The Taliban's policies caused different Afghan factions to ally with the ousted President Rabbani and Masud and their ally in the Herat area, Ismail Khan—the Tajik core of the anti-Taliban opposition—into a broader "Northern Alliance." In the Alliance were Uzbek, Hazara Shiite, and even some Pashtun Islamist factions discussed in **Table 3**. Virtually all the figures mentioned remain key players in politics in Afghanistan, sometimes allied with and at other times feuding with President Hamid Karzai:

- **Uzbeks/General Dostam**. One major faction was the Uzbek militia (the Junbush-Melli, or National Islamic Movement of Afghanistan) of General Abdul Rashid Dostam. Frequently referred to by some Afghans as one of the "warlords" who gained power during the anti-Soviet war, Dostam first joined those seeking to oust Rabbani during his 1992-1996 presidency, but later joined Rabbani's Northern Alliance against the Taliban. (For more information on Dostam, see CRS Report RS21922, *Afghanistan: Politics, Elections, and Government Performance*, by Kenneth Katzman.)

- **Hazara Shiites**. Members of Hazara tribes, mostly Shiite Muslims, are prominent in Bamiyan, Dai Kundi, and Ghazni provinces (central Afghanistan) and are always wary of repression by Pashtuns and other larger ethnic factions. The Hazaras have tended to serve in working class and domestic household jobs, although more recently they have been prominent in technology jobs in Kabul, raising their economic status. They are also increasingly cohesive politically, leading to gains in the September 2010 parliamentary elections. During the various Afghan wars, the main Hazara Shiite militia was Hizb-e-Wahdat (Unity Party, composed of eight different groups). Hizb-e-Wahdat suffered a major setback in 1995 when the Taliban captured and killed its leader Abdul Ali Mazari. One of Karzai's vice president's Karim Khalili, is a Hazara. Another prominent Hazara faction leader is Mohammad Mohaqeq.

- **Pashtun Islamists/Sayyaf**. Abd-I-Rab Rasul Sayyaf, later a post-Taliban parliamentary committee chairman, headed a Pashtun-dominated hardline Islamist *mujahedin* faction called the Islamic Union for the Liberation of Afghanistan during the anti-Soviet war. Even though he is an Islamic conservative, Sayyaf viewed the Taliban as selling out Afghanistan to Al Qaeda and he joined the Northern Alliance to try to oust the Taliban. He is said to eye the speakership of the lower house of parliament.

Policy Pre-September 11, 2001

Throughout 2001, but prior to the September 11 attacks, Bush Administration policy differed little from Clinton Administration policy—applying economic and political pressure while retaining dialogue with the Taliban, and refraining from militarily assisting the Northern Alliance. The September 11 Commission report said that, in the months prior to the September 11 attacks, Administration officials leaned toward such a step and that some officials also wanted to assist ethnic Pashtuns who were opposed to the Taliban. Other covert options were reportedly under consideration as well.[7] In a departure from Clinton Administration policy, the Bush Administration stepped up engagement with Pakistan to try to reduce its support for the Taliban. At that time, there were allegations that Pakistani advisers were helping the Taliban in their fight against the Northern Alliance. In accordance with U.N. Security Council Resolution 1333, in February 2001 the State Department ordered the Taliban representative office in New York closed, although Taliban representative Abdul Hakim Mujahid continued to operate informally. (Mujahid has reconciled with the current Afghan government, and serves on a Council to oversee broader reconciliation.) In March 2001, Administration officials received a Taliban envoy to discuss bilateral issues.

Even though the Northern Alliance was supplied with Iranian, Russian, and Indian financial and military support—all of whom had different motives for that support—the Northern Alliance nonetheless continued to lose ground to the Taliban after it lost Kabul in 1996. By the time of the September 11 attacks, the Taliban controlled at least 75% of the country, including almost all provincial capitals. The Alliance suffered a major setback on September 9, 2001, two days before the September 11 attacks, when Ahmad Shah Masud was assassinated by Arab journalists who allegedly were Al Qaeda operatives. He was succeeded by his intelligence chief, Muhammad Fahim,[8] a veteran figure but one who lacked Masud's undisputed authority.

September 11 Attacks and Operation Enduring Freedom

After the September 11 attacks, the Bush Administration decided to militarily overthrow the Taliban when it refused to extradite bin Laden, judging that a friendly regime in Kabul was needed to enable U.S forces to search for Al Qaeda activists there. United Nations Security Council Resolution 1368 of September 12, 2001, said that the Security Council

> expresses its readiness to take all necessary steps to respond (implying force) to the September 11 attacks.

This is widely interpreted as a U.N. authorization for military action in response to the attacks, but it did not explicitly authorize Operation Enduring Freedom to oust the Taliban.

Nor did the Resolution specifically reference Chapter VII of the U.N. Charter, which allows for responses to threats to international peace and security.

In Congress, S.J.Res. 23 (passed 98-0 in the Senate and with no objections in the House, P.L. 107-40), was somewhat more explicit than the U.N. Resolution, authorizing[9]

> all necessary and appropriate force against those nations, organizations, or persons he determines planned, authorized, committed, or aided the terrorist attacks that occurred on September 11, 2001 *or harbored such organizations or persons.*

Major combat in Afghanistan (Operation Enduring Freedom, OEF) began on October 7, 2001. It consisted primarily of U.S. air-strikes on Taliban and Al Qaeda forces, facilitated by the cooperation between small numbers (about 1,000) of U.S. special operations forces and CIA operatives. The purpose of these operations was to help the Northern Alliance and Pashtun antiTaliban forces by providing information to direct U.S. air strikes against Taliban positions. In part, the U.S. forces and operatives worked with such Northern Alliance contacts as Fahim and Amrollah Saleh, who during November 2001–June 2010 served as Afghanistan's intelligence director, to weaken Taliban defenses on the Shomali plain north of Kabul (and just south of Bagram Airfield, which marked the forward position of the Northern Alliance during Taliban rule). Some U.S. combat units (about 1,300 Marines) moved into Afghanistan to pressure the Taliban around Qandahar at the height of the fighting (October-December 2001), but there were few pitched battles between U.S. and Taliban soldiers. Some critics believe that U.S. dependence on local Afghan militia forces in the war subsequently set back post-war democracy building.

The Taliban regime unraveled rapidly after it lost Mazar-e-Sharif on November 9, 2001, to forces led by Dostam.[10] Other, mainly Tajik, Northern Alliance forces—the commanders of which had initially promised U.S. officials they would not enter Kabul—entered the capital on November 12, 2001, to popular jubilation. The Taliban subsequently lost the south and east to U.S.- supported Pashtun leaders, including Hamid Karzai. The end of the Taliban regime is generally dated as December 9, 2001, when the Taliban surrendered Qandahar and Mullah Umar fled the city, leaving it under tribal law administered by Pashtun leaders such as the Noorzai clan.

Subsequently, U.S. and Afghan forces conducted "Operation Anaconda" in the Shah-i-Kot Valley south of Gardez (Paktia Province) during March 2-19, 2002, against 800 Al Qaeda and Taliban fighters. In March 2003, about 1,000 U.S. troops raided suspected Taliban or Al Qaeda fighters in villages around Qandahar (Operation Valiant Strike). On May 1, 2003, Secretary of Defense Rumsfeld announced an end to "major combat."

POST-TALIBAN NATION-BUILDING EFFORTS[11]

With Afghanistan devastated after more than 20 years of warfare, the 2001 fall of the Taliban regime raised questions about the extent of a U.S. and international commitment to Afghanistan. Taking the view that leaving the Afghanistan-Pakistan theater after the 1989 Soviet pullout had led Afghanistan degenerate into chaos, the decision was made by the Bush Administration to try to rebuild try to build a relatively strong central government and to

Afghanistan: Post-Taliban Governance, Security, and U.S. Policy   279

assist Afghanistan's economy, in order to prevent a return of the Taliban, Al Qaeda, and other militants to Afghanistan.

The effort, which many outside experts described as "nation-building," was supported by major international institutions and U.S. partners in several post-Taliban international meetings. The task has proved slower and more difficult than anticipated, in part because of the devastation that years of war wrought on governing institutions, on the education system, and on the already limited infrastructure. Some observers believe the international community had unrealistic expectations of what could be achieved in a relatively short time frame—particularly in establishing competent, non-corrupt governance and a vibrant democracy.

The Obama Administration's two "Afghanistan strategy reviews" in 2009 the results of which were announced on March 27, 2009, and on December 1, 2009, narrowed official U.S. goals to preventing terrorism safe haven in Afghanistan and Pakistan. However, the elements of Obama Administration strategy in many ways enhance the nation-building strategy put in place by the Bush Administration. A strategy review, the summary of results of which were released December 16, 2010, did not alter U.S. goals or strategy set in the December 1, 2009, statement.[12] Reforming Afghan governance has been a consistent theme, and was emphasized both at the two major international conferences on Afghanistan – the January 28, 2010, "London Conference" and the July 20, 2010, "Kabul Conference."[13] Although the issue of governance is inseparable from that of securing Afghanistan, the sections below briefly outline Afghan-generated and international community-led efforts to build Afghanistan's governing capacity. These governance issues are discussed in greater detail in CRS Report RS21922, *Afghanistan: Politics, Elections, and Government Performance*, by Kenneth Katzman.

Post-Taliban Political Transition

The 2001 ouster of the Taliban government paved the way for the success of a long-stalled U.N. effort to form a broad-based Afghan government and for the international community to help Afghanistan build legitimate governing institutions. In the formation of the first post-Taliban transition government, the United Nations was viewed as a credible mediator by all sides largely because of its role in ending the Soviet occupation. During the 1990s, a succession of U.N. mediators adopted many of former King Zahir Shah's proposals for a government to be selected by a traditional assembly, or *loya jirga*. However, U.N.-mediated cease-fires between warring factions did not hold. Non-U.N. initiatives made little progress, particularly the "Six Plus Two" multilateral contact group, which began meeting in 1997 (the United States, Russia, and the six states bordering Afghanistan: Iran, China, Pakistan, Turkmenistan, Uzbekistan, and Tajikistan). Other failed efforts included a "Geneva group" (Italy, Germany, Iran, and the United States) formed in 2000; an Organization of Islamic Conference (OIC) contact group; and prominent Afghan exile efforts, including discussion groups launched by Hamid Karzai and his clan, former *mujahedin* commander Abd al-Haq, and Zahir Shah ("Rome process").

Bonn Agreement

Immediately after the September 11 attacks, former U.N. mediator Lakhdar Brahimi was brought back (he had resigned in frustration in October 1999). U.N. Security Council

Resolution 1378 (November 14, 2001) called for a "central" role for the United Nations in establishing a transitional administration and inviting member states to send peacekeeping forces to promote stability and aid delivery. After the fall of Kabul in November 2001, the United Nations invited major Afghan factions, most prominently the Northern Alliance and that of the former King—but not the Taliban—to an international conference in Bonn, Germany.

On December 5, 2001, the factions signed the "Bonn Agreement."[14] It was endorsed by U.N. Security Council Resolution 1385 (December 6, 2001). The agreement was reportedly forged with substantial Iranian diplomatic help because Iran had supported the military efforts of the Northern Alliance faction and had leverage to persuade temporary caretaker Rabbani and the Northern Alliance to cede the top leadership to Hamid Karzai as leader of an interim administration. Other provisions of the agreement:

- authorized an international peace keeping force to maintain security in Kabul, and Northern Alliance forces were directed to withdraw from the capital. Security Council Resolution 1386 (December 20, 2001, and renewed yearly thereafter) gave formal Security Council authorization for the international peacekeeping force (International Security Assistance Force, ISAF);
- referred to the need to cooperate with the international community on counter narcotics, crime, and terrorism; and
- applied the constitution of 1964 until a permanent constitution could be drafted.[15]

Permanent Constitution

A June 2002 "emergency" *loya jirga* put a representative imprimatur on the transition; it was attended by 1,550 delegates (including about 200 women). Subsequently, a 35-member constitutional commission drafted the constitution, unveiling it in November 2003. It was debated by 502 delegates, selected in U.N-run caucuses, at a *"constitutional loya jirga* (CLJ)" during December 13, 2003–January 4, 2004. The CLJ, chaired by Sibghatullah Mojadeddi (mentioned above) ended with approval of the constitution with only minor changes. It set up a presidential system, with an elected president and a separately elected National Assembly (parliament). The Northern Alliance failed in its effort to set up a prime ministership (in which the elected parliament would select a prime minister and a cabinet) , but the faction did achieve some limitation to presidential powers by assigning major authorities to the parliament, such as the power to veto senior official nominees. The constitution made former King Zahir Shah honorary "Father of the Nation," a title that is not heritable. Zahir Shah died on July 23, 2007.[16]

First Post-Taliban Elections in 2004

Security conditions precluded the holding of the first post-Taliban elections simultaneously. The first election, for president, was held on October 9, 2004, missing a June constitutional deadline. Turnout was about 80%. On November 3, 2004, Karzai was declared winner (55.4% of the vote) over his 17 challengers on the first round, avoiding a runoff. Parliamentary and provincial council elections were intended for April-May 2005 but were delayed until September 18, 2005. Because of the difficulty in confirming voter registration rolls and determining district boundaries, elections for the 364 district councils, each of which

Afghanistan: Post-Taliban Governance, Security, and U.S. Policy

will likely have contentious boundaries because they will inevitably separate tribes and clans, have not been held to date.

Formation of an Elected National Assembly (Parliament)

The National Assembly (parliament), particularly the elected lower house, has emerged as a relatively vibrant body that creates accountability and has often asserted itself politically. The most notable example has been the 2009-2010 confirmation process for Karzai's cabinet choices, in which many of Karzai's nominees were voted down. The Assembly's assertiveness – expected to continue when a newly elected parliament is seated on January 20, 2011 – shows, in part, that the better educated "independents" are emerging as pivotal members of parliament. Substantial detail on the factions in the Afghan parliament is provided in CRS Report RS21922, *Afghanistan: Politics, Elections, and Government Performance*, by Kenneth Katzman.

Hamid Karzai, President of the Islamic Republic of Afghanistan

Hamid Karzai, born December 24, 1957, was selected to lead Afghanistan at the Bonn Conference because he was a prominent Pashtun leader who had been involved in Taliban-era political talks among exiled Afghans and was viewed as a compromiser rather than a "strongman." However, some observers consider his compromises as Afghanistan's leader a sign of weakness, and criticize him for indulging members of his clan and other allies with appointments.

Others view him as overly suspicious of the intentions of the United States and other outside powers, believing they are intent on replacing him or favoring certain groups of Afghans over others. He has consistently denied allegations by unnamed U.S. and other officials that he is taking mood altering medications – asserted to be a possible explanation for his occasional sharp criticisms of some aspects of U.S. Afghanistan policy.

From Karz village in Qandahar Province, Hamid Karzai has led the powerful Popolzai tribe of Durrani Pashtuns since 1999, when his father was assassinated, allegedly by Taliban agents, in Quetta, Pakistan. Karzai's grandfather was head of the consultative National Council during King Zahir Shah's reign. He attended university in India and supported the *mujahdin* party of Sibghatullah Mojadeddi (still a very close ally) during the ant-Soviet war. He was deputy foreign minister in the *mujahidin* government of Rabbani during 1992-1995, but he left the government and supported the Taliban as a Pashtun alternative to Rabbani. He broke with the Taliban as its excesses unfolded and forged alliances with other anti-Taliban factions, including the Northern Alliance. Karzai entered Afghanistan after the September 11 attacks to organize Pashtun resistance to the Taliban, supported by U.S. Special Forces. He became central to U.S. efforts after Pashtun commander Abdul Haq entered Afghanistan in October 2001 without U.S. support and was captured and hung by the Taliban. Karzai was slightly injured by an errant U.S. bomb during major combat of Operation Enduring Freedom (late 2001).

Karzai also relies heavily for advice from tribal and faction leaders from southern Afghanistan, including Sher Mohammad Akhunzadeh, the former governor of Helmand (until 2005), as well as from well-educated professionals such as his current Foreign Minister Zalmay Rasool, his brother-in-law and key Afghanistan National Security Council official Ibrahim Spinzada, and the former foreign minister, now National Security Adviser, Rangeen Spanta.

With heavy protection, Karzai has survived several assassination attempts since taking office, including rocket fire or gunfire at or near his appearances. His wife, Dr. Zenat Karzai, is a gynecologist by profession. They have been married about 11 years and have a son, Mirwais, born in 2008. In December 2009, he spoke publicly about personal turmoil among relatives in Karz village that resulted in the death of an 18-year-old relative in October 2009.

His half brother, Ahmad Wali Karzai, is the most powerful political figure in that province, He is key to Karzai's maintenance of support and the cornerstone of his information network in Qandahar but Ahmad Wali has been widely accused of involvement in or tolerating narcotics trafficking. A *New York Times* article on October 28, 2009, said Ahmad Wali is also a paid informant for the CIA and some of his property has been used by U.S. Special Forces. Ahmad Wali was the apparent target of at least two bombings in Qandahar in 2009. Others of Karzai's several brothers have lived in the United States, including Qayyum Karzai. Qayyum Karzai won a parliament seat in the September 2005 election but resigned his seat in October 2008 due to health reasons. Qayyum subsequently represented the government in inconclusive talks, held in several Persian Gulf states, to reconcile with Taliban figures close to Mullah Umar. Another brother, Mahmoud Karzai, is a businessman reportedly under U.S. Justice Department investigation of his business interests in Qandahar and Kabul, including auto dealerships, apartment houses, and a stake in Kabul Bank, which nearly collapsed in September 2010. Other Karzai relatives and associates have formed security companies and other contracting firms that have profited extensively from international reconstruction, transportation, and protection funds, including a $2.2 billion U.S. "Host Nation Trucking" contract. The United States banned contracts to one such firm, Watan Risk Management, as of January 6, 2011; the firm is co-owned by two Karzai cousins Ahmad and Rashid Popal.

2009 Presidential and Provincial Elections

The 2009 presidential and provincial elections were expected to further Afghanistan's democratic development. However, because of the widespread fraud identified by Afghanistan's U.N.- appointed "Elections Complaints Commission" (ECC) in the August 20, 2009, first round of the elections, the process did not produce that result. The election fraud difficulty may have contributed to the substantial parliamentary opposition to many of Karzai's nominees for his postelection cabinet. In each of three rounds of cabinet nominations in 2009 and 2010, many, if not most, of Karzai's nominees were voted down by the National Assembly. The latest round of nominations occurred in late June 2010, after Karzai forced Interior Minister Mohammad Hanif Atmar to resign, ostensibly for failing to prevent insurgent attacks in Kabul itself. Atmar was close to and well respected by U.S. officials. Also resigning on June 6 was National Directorate of Security (NDS, Afghan intelligence) chief Amrollah Saleh, a Tajik and an ally of the United Front leaders. Both were believed to oppose Karzai's efforts to reconcile with senior insurgent leaders. See also: CRS Report RS21922, *Afghanistan: Politics, Elections, and Government Performance*, by Kenneth Katzman.

September 18, 2010, Parliamentary Elections

A key test of Karzai's repeated commitment to reforms were the September 18, 2010, National Assembly elections. That election was held amid significant violence but not sufficient to derail the voting. Final results were expected October 30, 2010 but widespread fraud complaints delayed finalization of the results until November 24, 2010. The election is covered in CRS Report RS21922, *Afghanistan: Politics, Elections, and Government Performance*, cited earlier.

Some of the election results remain in dispute, and some worry that the disputes are widening ethnic differences because a substantial number of Pashtuns lost seats they expected to retain. Karzai's allies apparently did not win enough seats (a majority) to ensure that Pashtun conservative Sayyaf, mentioned above, would replace Yunus Qanooni, an Abdullah supporter, as lower house speaker. The Assembly convenes on January 20, 2011. Perhaps in an effort to overturn some of the results and achieve a parliament more supportive, the Karzai government has asked Afghanistan's Supreme Court to become involved in adjudicating the results, and the Court, on December 28, 2010, set up a special tribunal to review candidate complaints. It is not clear whether the tribunal will have the authority or will to try to change any results.

Other Major Governance Issues

Obama Administration policy, as articulated on March 27, 2009, and December 1, 2009, emphasizes expanding and improving Afghan governance as a long-term means of stabilizing Afghanistan. The latter Obama statement specified that there would be "no blank check" for the Afghan government if it does not reduce corruption and deliver services. This emphasis is expressed extensively in the State Department January 2010 document outlining its policy priorities, entitled *Afghanistan and Pakistan Regional Stabilization Strategy*.[17] The December 16, 2010 summary of the Administration policy review on Afghanistan did not emphasize governance issues, but did specify that "[The United States is] also supporting Afghanistan's efforts to better improve national and sub-national governance, and to build institutions with increased transparency and accountability to reduce corruption – key steps in sustaining the Afghan government. Several of the various aspects of U.S. efforts to build the capacity of the central and local government institutions are discussed in greater detail in CRS Report RS21922, *Afghanistan: Politics, Elections, and Government Performance*.

U.S. policy has been to expand governance throughout the country, a policy that is receiving increased U.S. financial and advisory resources under the Obama Administration. A key to governance strategy, particularly during 2002-2006, was to strengthen the central government by helping Karzai curb key regional strongmen and local militias—whom some refer to as "warlords." These actors controlled much of Afghanistan after the Taliban regime disintegrated in late 2001, but there was a decision by the international community to build up an accountable central government rather than leave Afghanistan in the hands of local militias. These forces often arbitrarily administer justice and use their positions to enrich themselves and their supporters.

Karzai has marginalized some of the largest regional leaders, but he is criticized by some human rights groups and international donors for continuing to tolerate or rely on others to keep order in some areas, particularly in non-Pashtun inhabited parts of Afghanistan (the north and west). Karzai's view is that maintaining ties to ethnic and regional faction leaders has prevented the emergence of ethnic conflict that would detract from the overall effort against the Taliban. Several of these faction leaders are discussed in CRS Report RS21922, *Afghanistan: Politics, Elections, and Government Performance*, by Kenneth Katzman.

Anti-Corruption Efforts

An accelerating trend in U.S. policy—and emphasized in both major Obama Administration strategy reviews as well as by many in Congress—is to press Karzai to weed out official corruption. U.S. officials believe that rife corruption in the Afghan government is undermining U.S. domestic support for the U.S. mission in Afghanistan, and causing the Afghan population to sour on the Karzai government. U.S. anti-corruption and rule of law efforts are discussed extensively in the "Afghanistan and Pakistan Regional Stabilization Strategy" issued by the office of the late Ambassador Holbrooke in January 2010, referenced above. The Obama Administration reportedly has decided to mute its public criticism of Karzai on the grounds that public criticism causes Karzai to become suspicious of U.S. intent and to ally with undemocratic elements in Afghanistan. The corruption issue—its sources, U.S. and Afghan efforts to curb corruption, and progress—is discussed in CRS Report R41484, *Afghanistan: U.S. Rule of Law and Justice Sector Assistance*, by Liana Sun Wyler and Kenneth Katzman and in CRS Report RS21922, *Afghanistan: Politics, Elections, and Government Performance*, by Kenneth Katzman.

Enhancing Local Governance

In part because building the central government has gone slowly and because official corruption is widespread, there has been a U.S. shift, predating the Obama Administration, away from reliance toward promoting local governance. Some argue that, in addition to offering the advantage of bypassing an often corrupt central government, doing so is more compatible with Afghan traditions of local autonomy.

As emphasized in the January 2010 SRAP strategy document cited earlier, there has been a major U.S. and Afghan push to build up local governing structures, reflecting a shift in emphasis from the 2001-2007 approach of focusing on building up central authority. However, building local governance has suffered from a deficit of trained and respected local government administrators ready or willing to serve, particularly where hostilities are ongoing. This deficiency has hindered U.S. counter-insurgency efforts in southern Afghanistan, as discussed further below, and accounts for many of the uncertainties clouding the prospects for transition to Afghan security leadership by the end of 2014.

U.S. policy has sought to use local governance promotion efforts to support U.S. security strategy for Afghanistan. Several districts have received special attention to become "models" of district security and governance are Nawa, in Helmand Province, and Baraki-Barak, in Lowgar Province, both cleared of Taliban militants in 2009. With substantial infusions of U.S. development funds that put sometime insurgents to work on projects (offering $5 per day to perform such tasks as cleaning irrigation canals), these districts are, by several accounts, far more stable and secure than they were in 2009. As part of "Operation Moshtarek" (Operation Together), launched February 13, 2010, to clear the city of Marjah of militants, a district governor (Hajji Zahir) and district administration were selected in advance. Zahir tried to build up his administration after the town was wrested from Taliban control, but governance there was slow to expand. Zahir was replaced in early July 2010. Still, the British civilian representative in Marjah said in October 2010 that central government ministry representation in Marjah is now in place and operating consistently.

(Marjah is currently part of Nad Ali district, and is eventually to become its own district, according to Afghan observers.)

Human Rights and Democracy

The Administration and Afghan government claim progress in building a democratic Afghanistan that adheres to international standards of human rights practices. The State Department report on human rights practices for 2009 (released March 11, 2010)[18] said that Afghanistan's human rights record remained "poor," noting in particular that the government or its agents commit arbitrary or unlawful killings. Still, virtually all observers agree that Afghans are freer than they were under the Taliban. The tables at the end of this report contain information on U.S. funding for democracy, governance, rule of law and human rights, and elections support since the fall of the Taliban. Numerous aspects of Afghan performance on human rights are covered in CRS Report RS21922, *Afghanistan: Politics, Elections, and Government Performance.*

Narcotics Trafficking/Insurgent Financing[19]

Narcotics trafficking is regarded by some as a core impediment to the U.S. mission in Afghanistan by undermining rule of law and providing funds to the insurgency. However, it is also an area on which there has been progress in recent years. The trafficking is said to generate an estimated $70 million–$100 million per year for the Taliban.

U.S. officials hope that recent progress will be sustained. A UNODC report of September 2010, continued a relatively positive trend in reporting on this issue, noting that all of the 20 provinces (out of 34 provinces in Afghanistan) in the "poppy free" category remain that way. Total production in 2010 is estimated at 3,600 metric tons, a 48% decrease from 2009, although this was due to a crop disease, for the most part. [20]

Obama Administration policy is focusing on promoting legitimate agricultural alternatives to poppy growing and, in conjunction, the late Ambassador Holbrooke announced in July 2009 that the United States would end its prior focus on eradication of poppy fields. In this view, eradication was driving Afghans into the arms of the Taliban as protectors of their ability to earn a living, even if doing so is from narcotics cultivation. Encouraging alternative livelihoods has always been the preferred emphasis of the Afghan government. The de-emphasis on eradication also put aside the long-standing differences over whether to conduct spraying of fields, particularly by air. That concept was strenuously opposed by Karzai and not implemented. Congress sided with Karzai's view; the FY2008 Consolidated Appropriation (P.L. 110-161) prohibited U.S. counter-narcotics funding from being used for aerial spraying on Afghanistan poppy fields without Afghan concurrence. That provision was reiterated in the FY2010 consolidated appropriation (P.L. 111-117). Other policies promote incentives; Helmand, for example, received about $10 million in Good Performance funding in 2009 for a 33% cut in poppy cultivation that year.

How consistently to use U.S. and NATO forces to combat narcotics has been under almost constant debate. Some NATO contributors, such as Britain, have focused on interdicting traffickers and raiding drug labs. The U.S. military, in support of the effort after initial reluctance, is flying Afghan and U.S. counter-narcotics agents (Drug Enforcement Agency, DEA) on missions and identifying targets; it also evacuates casualties from counter-drug operations. The Department of Defense is also playing the major role in training and equipping specialized Afghan counter-narcotics police, in developing an Afghan intelligence fusion cell, and training Afghan border police, as well as assisting an Afghan helicopter squadron to move Afghan counter-narcotics forces around the country. To help break up narcotics trafficking networks, the DEA presence in Afghanistan is has expanded from 13 agents in 2008 to over 80 in 2010, with additional agents in Pakistan.

The late Ambassador Holbrooke also placed additional focus on the other sources of Taliban funding, including continued donations from wealthy residents of the Persian Gulf. He has established a multinational task force to combat Taliban financing generally, not limited to narcotics, and U.S. officials are emphasizing with Persian Gulf counterparts the need for cooperation.

Narcotics trafficking control was perhaps the one issue on which the Taliban regime satisfied much of the international community. The Taliban enforced a July 2000 ban on poppy cultivation.[21]

Narcotics-Related Aid Conditionality

The Bush Administration repeatedly named Afghanistan as a major illicit drug producer and drug transit country, but did not include Afghanistan on a smaller list of countries that have "failed demonstrably to make substantial efforts" to adhere to international counter-narcotics agreements and take certain counter-narcotics measures set forth in U.S. law.[22] The Bush Administration exercised waiver provisions to a required certification of full Afghan cooperation that was needed to provide more than congressionally stipulated amounts of U.S. economic assistance to Afghanistan. A similar certification requirement (to provide amounts over $300 million) was contained in the FY2008 appropriation (P.L. 110-161); in the FY2009 regular appropriation, P.L. 111-8 ($200 million ceiling); and the FY2010 appropriation, P.L. 111-117, ($200 million ceiling). The FY2009 supplemental (P.L. 111-32) withheld 10% of State Department narcotics funding (International Narcotics Control and Law Enforcement, INCLE) pending a report that Afghanistan is removing officials involved in narcotics trafficking or gross human rights violations. No funds for Afghanistan have been held up.

Civilian U.S. and International Policy Implementation

Building the capacity of the Afghan government, and helping it develop economically, is primarily, although not exclusively, the purview of U.S. and international civilian officials and institutions. In line with the prioritization of Afghanistan policy, in February 2009, the Administration appointed Ambassador Richard Holbrooke as "Special Representative for Afghanistan and Pakistan" (SRAP), reporting to Secretary of State Clinton. Holbrooke died on December 13, 2010, but his team at the State Department, now led by his deputy, Frank Ruggiero in an acting capacity, remains intact. It consists mainly of members detailed from several different agencies; several have long-term experience on Afghanistan and Pakistan affairs. Karl Eikenberry, who served as commander of U.S. forces in Afghanistan during 2004-2005, is U.S. Ambassador. While the main focus of the civilian side of U.S. and international policy is on building governance and promoting economic development, President Obama has said he expects the civilian team to work closely with the U.S. and NATO military structure, and a U.S. civilian-military "joint campaign plan" was developed and released in mid-August 2009.[23]

On February 7, 2010, in an effort to improve civilian coordination between the United States, its foreign partners, and the Afghan government, a NATO "Senior Civilian Representative" in Afghanistan, UK Ambassador Mark Sedwill, took office. Ambassador Sedwill works not only with U.S. military officials but with representatives of the embassies of partner countries and with a special U.N. Assistance Mission–Afghanistan (UNAMA, see **Table 2**).

At U.S. Embassy Kabul, there is a "deputy Ambassador"—senior official Francis Ricciardone. Another Ambassador rank official (William Todd) manages U.S. economic assistance issues. Another Ambassador-rank official, Joseph Mussomeli, handles Embassy management. Ambassador Timothy Carney oversaw U.S. policy for the 2009 elections. Another official of Ambassador rank, Hans Klemm, (as of June 2010) coordinates U.S. rule of law programs

The U.S. Embassy has progressively expanded its personnel and facilities and will expand its facilities further to accommodate some of the additional civilian hires and Foreign Service officers who have been posted to Afghanistan as mentors and advisers to the Afghan government. U.S. officials say there are more than 1,100 U.S. civilian officials in Afghanistan, as of December 2010, up from only about 400 in early 2009. Most of the newly posted officials are being deployed outside Kabul. The tables at the end of this report include U.S. funding for State Department and USAID operations, including Embassy construction and running the "Embassy air wing," a fleet of twin-engine turboprops that ferry U.S. officials and contractors around Afghanistan. In a significant development attempting to signal normalization of certain areas of Afghanistan, in early 2010 the United States formally inaugurated U.S. consulates in Herat and Mazar-e-Sharif. In November 2010, contracts were announced for expansion of the U.S. Embassy ($511 million) and to construct the two consulates ($20 million for each facility).

The Afghan Ambassador to the United States, Sayed Tayib Jawad, served as Ambassador from 2004 until his recall in August 2010. He was recalled because of complaints in Kabul about Western-style parties that were being held at the Afghan embassy in the United States. No replacement has been named, to date. There is some discussion on the Afghan side of appointing a special envoy, possibly Ashraf Ghani, to interact on a global basis with the Afghanistan donor community.

Table 2. U.N. Assistance Mission in Afghanistan (UNAMA)

The United Nations is extensively involved in Afghan governance and national building, primarily in factional conflict resolution and coordination of development assistance. The coordinator of U.N. efforts is the U.N. Assistance Mission in Afghanistan (UNAMA), headed as of March 22, 2010, by Swedish diplomat Staffan de-Mistura, replacing Norwegian diplomat Kai Eide. Mistura formerly played a similar role in Iraq. U.N. Security Council Resolution 1806 of March 20, 2008, expanded UNAMA's authority to coordinating the work of international donors and strengthening cooperation between the international peacekeeping force (ISAF, see below) and the Afghan government. In concert with the Obama Administration's emphasis on Afghan policy, UNAMA is to open offices in as many of Afghanistan's 34 provinces as financially and logistically permissible. (The mandate of UNAMA, reviewed at one-year intervals, ran until March 23, 2010, as provided for by Resolution 1869 of March 23, 2009, and was renewed for another year on March 22,

2010 (Resolution 1917)). Resolution 1917 largely restated UNAMA's expanded mandate and coordinating role with other high-level representatives in Afghanistan, and election support role.

In keeping with its expanding role, in 2008 U.S. Ambassador Peter Galbraith was appointed as Eide's deputy, although he left Afghanistan in early September 2009 in a reported dispute with Eide over how vigorously to insist on investigating fraud in the August 20 Afghan election. Galbraith reportedly pressed Afghan and independent election bodies to be as vigorous as possible in the interests of rule of law and election legitimacy; Eide purportedly was willing to encourage an Afghan compromise to avoid a second round run-off. The split led U.N. Secretary General Ban Ki Moon to remove Galbraith from his post at UNAMA in late September 2009 on the grounds that the disharmony was compromising the UNAMA mission. Several Galbraith supporters subsequently resigned from UNAMA and Galbraith has appealed his firing amid reports he was proposing a plan to replace Karzai had an election runoff been postponed until 2010. The turmoil may have caused Eide to leave his post when his contract with the U.N. expired in March 2010.

UNAMA is co-chair of the joint Afghan-international community coordination body called the Joint Coordination and Monitoring Board (JCMB), and is helping implement the five-year development strategy outlined in a "London Compact," (now called the Afghanistan Compact) adopted at the January 31–February 1, 2006, London conference on Afghanistan. The priorities developed in that document comport with Afghanistan's own "National Strategy for Development," presented on June 12, 2008, in Paris. During his term, Eide urged the furnishing of additional capacity-building resources, and he complained that some efforts by international donors are redundant or tied to purchases by Western countries. In statements and press conferences, Eide continued to note security deterioration but also progress in governance and in reduction of drug cultivation, and he publicly supported negotiations with Taliban figures to end the war. His final speech before leaving criticized the U.S.-led coalition for focusing too much on military success and not enough on governance.

UNAMA also often has been involved in local dispute resolution among factions, and it helps organize elections. Under a March 2010 compromise with Karzai, it nominates two international members of the five person Electoral Complaints Commission (ECC), one fewer than the three it selected under the prior election law. UNAMA was a co-convener of the January 28, 2010, and July 20, 2010, London and Kabul Conferences, respectively.

The difficulties in coordinating U.N. with U.S. and NATO efforts were evident in a 2007 proposal to create a new position of "super envoy" that would represent the United Nations, the European Union, and NATO in Afghanistan. The concept advanced and in January 2008, with U.S. support, U.N. Secretary General Ban Ki Moon tentatively appointed British diplomat Paddy Ashdown as the "super envoy." However, Karzai rejected the appointment reportedly over concerns about the scope of authority of such an envoy. Karzai might have also sought to show independence from the international community. Ashdown withdrew his name on January 28, 2008. However, the concept reportedly was floated again in late 2009, but was again suppressed by Karzai and others who say it contradicts U.S. and other efforts to promote Afghan leadership. The NATO senior civilian representative post, held by Amb. Mark Sedwill (UK), appears to represent a step in the direction of improved donor coordination in Afghanistan and streamlining of the foreign representative structure there.

For more information on UNAMA, see CRS Report R40747, *United Nations Assistance Mission in Afghanistan: Background and Policy Issues*, by Rhoda Margesson.

SECURITY POLICY AND FORCE CAPACITY BUILDING[24]

The U.S. definition of "success" of the stabilization mission in Afghanistan, articulated since the ouster of the Taliban in late 2001, is to help build up an Afghan government and security force that can defend itself, expand governance, and develop economically. The Obama Administration's policy reviews in 2009 formally narrowed U.S. goals to preventing Al Qaeda from reestablishing a base in Afghanistan. However, the policy and military tools employed by the Obama Administration in most ways continue and even expand a nation-building goal. The December 1, 2009, speech by President Obama stated U.S. goals as: (1) denying Al Qaeda a safe haven [in Afghanistan]; and (2) reversing the Taliban's momentum and denying it the ability to overthrow the government. The statement generally backed the August 30, 2009, recommendations of then-top commander in Afghanistan Gen. Stanley McChrystal's to undertake a fully resourced counter-insurgency mission. The focus of the mission is on 121 districts (out of 364 total districts in Afghanistan) deemed restive and in which support for the Afghan government is lowest. Of those, 80 districts are of the most intense focus, according to Defense Department reports and officials. The Administration review, the summary of results of which were released December 16, 2010 (cited earlier) did not announce any major changes to U.S. goals or strategy.

The Obama Administration has not significantly changed the basic pillars of U.S. and NATO security strategy that have been in place since 2001, although the blend of these components often shifts as outcomes and prospects of various initiatives are evaluated. The main elements include (1) combat operations and patrols by U.S. forces and a NATO-led International Security Assistance Force (ISAF) to "provide space" for the expansion of Afghan governance, security leadership, and infrastructure and economic development; (2) U.S. and NATO operation of "provincial reconstruction teams"(PRTs) to serve as enclaves to facilitate the strategy; and (3) the equipping, training, and expansion of Afghanistan National Security Forces (ANSF). Some strategy elements that have emerged since 2008, and which are taking precedence as Western public support for the war effort erodes, include establishing local protection forces and backing efforts to reconcile with Taliban leaders who might want to end armed struggle. Another strategy element apparently under debate is whether to expand the conflict area to include additional U.S., allied, and Afghan ground action against militants over the border in Pakistan.

Who are U.S. /NATO Forces Fighting? Taliban, Al Qaeda, and Related Insurgents and Their Strength

As noted in General McChrystal's August 2009 initial assessment and the Defense Department November 2010 report, security is being challenged by a confluence of related armed groups who are increasingly well equipped and sophisticated in their tactics and operations, particularly by using roadside bombs.[25] There has not been agreement about the relative strength of insurgents in all of the areas where they operate, or their degree of cooperation with each other, although press reports in December 2010, quoting U.S. military officers in Afghanistan, say there has been increasing operational cooperation among the various Afghan insurgent groups. Afghan and U.S. assessments are that there are more than 20,000 total insurgents operating in Afghanistan, up from a few thousand in 2003.

Prior to U.S.-led offensives launched since mid-2009, the Karzai government was estimated by to control about 30% of the country, while insurgents controlled 4% (13 out of 364 districts). Insurgents "influenced" or "operated in" another 30% (Afghan Interior Ministry estimates in August 2009). Tribes and local groups with varying degrees of loyalty to the central government control the remainder. Outside groups, such as aid groups that released their own findings in September 2010, sometimes report higher percentages of insurgent control or influence.[26] U.S. military officers in Kabul told CRS in October 2009 that the Taliban had named "shadow governors" in 33 out of 34 of Afghanistan's provinces, although many provinces in northern Afghanistan were assessed as having minimal Taliban presence.

As far as tactics, U.S. commanders increasingly worry about growing insurgent use of improvised explosive devices (IEDs), including roadside bombs. IED's are the leading cause of U.S. combat deaths, and IED attacks nearly doubled again in frequency in the first four months of 2010, according to a U.N. Secretary General report of June 16, 2010. In January 2010, President Karzai issued a decree banning importation of fertilizer chemicals (ammonium nitrate) commonly used for the roadside bombs, but there reportedly is informal circumvention of the ban for certain civilian uses, and the material reportedly still comes into Afghanistan from Pakistan . U.S. commanders have said they have verified insurgent use of surface-to-air missiles.[27]

There were about 310 U.S. soldiers killed in 2009, nearly double the previous year, and U.S. deaths in 2010 appear to have reached a new high for the Afghan conflict of about 500. There were about 210 soldiers from partner countries killed during 2010. According to a UNAMA report issued in December 2010, covering the fall of 2010, there was a 66% increase in security incidents as compared to the same period in 2009. However, over 80% of those deaths are purportedly caused by insurgent attacks.

Groups: The Taliban ("Quetta Shura Taliban")

The core of the insurgency remains the Taliban movement centered around Mullah Umar, who led the Taliban regime during 1996-2001. Mullah Umar and many of his top advisers remain at large and are reportedly running their insurgency from their safe haven in Pakistan. They are believed to be primarily in and around the city of Quetta, according to Afghan officials, thus accounting for the term usually applied to Umar and his aides: "Quetta Shura Taliban" (QST).

Some believe that Umar and his inner circle blame their past association with Al Qaeda for their loss of power and want to distance themselves from Al Qaeda. Other experts see continuing close association that is likely to continue were the Taliban movement to return to power.

Some believe that the U.S. "surge" in Afghanistan may be causing Umar, or some around him, to mull the concept of a political settlement. Umar's top deputy, Mullah Bradar, was arrested in a reported joint U.S.-Pakistani operation near the city of Karachi in February 2010—Karzai considered his capture set back Afghan government-Taliban reconciliation talks, which Bradar reportedly supports. It was also reported in March 2010 that Pakistan had briefly detained another member of the Quetta Shura, Mullah Kabir, and arrested Agha Jhan Motasim, a son-in-law of Umar.[28] In recent years, other top Taliban figures, including Mullah

Dadullah, his son Mansoor, and Mullah Usmani have been killed or captured. Some observers say that informal settlement ideas floated between the Taliban and the Karzai government may envision Umar being granted exile in Saudi Arabia.

To address losses, Umar reportedly replaced Bradar with a young leader, Mullah Abdul Qayyum Zakir, a U.S. detainee in Guantanamo Bay, Cuba, until 2007.[29] Some reports assert that other aides (most notably Mullah Ghul Agha Akhund) may not recognize Zakir and might themselves be seeking the number two spot in the organization. Two members of the Quetta Shura, Mullah Hassan Rahmani, former Taliban governor of Qandahar, and Mullah Afghan Tayib, another spokesman, are said to have come under some Pakistani pressure to refrain from militant activities. The Taliban has several official spokespersons still at large, including Qari Yusuf Ahmadi and Zabiullah Mujahid, and it operates a clandestine radio station, "Voice of Shariat" and publishes videos.

Al Qaeda/Bin Laden Whereabouts

The summary of the Administration policy review, released December 16, 2010, says that "there has been significant progress in disrupting and dismantling the Pakistan-based leadership and cadre of Al Qaeda over the past year." U.S. commanders say that Al Qaeda militants are more facilitators of militant incursions into Afghanistan rather than active fighters in the Afghan insurgency. Director of Central Intelligence Leon Panetta said on June 27, 2010, that Al Qaeda fighters in Afghanistan itself might number 50-100.[30] Small numbers of Al Qaeda members— including Arabs, Uzbeks, and Chechens—have been captured or killed in battles in Afghanistan itself, according to U.S. commanders. Some of these fighters apparently belong to Al Qaeda affiliates such as the Islamic Movement of Uzbekistan (IMU). Some NATO/ISAF officials said in October 2010, however, that some Al Qaeda cells may be moving back into remote areas of Kunar and Nuristan provinces.[31]

Despite the reports of progress against Al Qaeda in Afghanistan and Pakistan, Al Qaeda's top leadership has consistently eluded U.S. efforts. In December 2001, in the course of the post-September 11 major combat effort, U.S. Special Operations Forces and CIA operatives reportedly narrowed Osama bin Laden's location to the Tora Bora mountains in Nangarhar Province (30 miles west of the Khyber Pass), but the Afghan militia fighters who were the bulk of the fighting force did not prevent his escape. Some U.S. military and intelligence officers (such as Gary Berntsen and Dalton Fury, who have written books on the battle) have questioned the U.S. decision to rely mainly on Afghan forces in this engagement.

Bin Laden and his close ally Ayman al-Zawahiri have long been presumed to be on the Pakistani side of the border. CNN reported October 18, 2010, that assessments from the U.S.-led coalition now say the two are likely in a settled area near the border with Afghanistan, and not living in a very remote uninhabited area. A U.S. strike reportedly missed Zawahiri by a few hours in the village of Damadola, Pakistan, in January 2006, suggesting that there was intelligence on his movements.[32] On the ninth anniversary of the September 11 attacks, some U.S. observers said it was still significant to try to capture bin Laden if for no other reason than for symbolic value.

Among other bin Laden aides, press reports in September 2010 said that Al Qaeda's former spokesman, Kuwait-born Sulayman Abu Ghaith, may have been released from house arrest by Iran and allowed to proceed to Pakistan. Other reports in November 2010 said that another Al Qaeda senior operative, Sayf al Adl, who was believed to be in Iran during 2002-

2010, may have left Iran and gone to Pakistan, and reportedly may have been elevated by bin Laden to top Al Qaeda operational commander.

As a consequence of other U.S. efforts, a January 2008 strike near Damadola killed Abu Laith alLibi, a reported senior Al Qaeda figure who purportedly masterminded, among other operations, the bombing at Bagram Air Base in February 2007 when Vice President Cheney was visiting. In August 2008, an airstrike was confirmed to have killed Al Qaeda chemical weapons expert Abu Khabab al-Masri, and two senior operatives allegedly involved in the 1998 embassy bombings in Africa reportedly were killed by an unmanned aerial vehicle (Predator) strike in January 2009. Such aerial-based strikes have become more frequent under President Obama, indicating that the Administration sees the tactic as effective in preventing attacks. Unmanned vehicle strikes are also increasingly used on the Afghanistan battlefield itself and against Al Qaeda affiliated militants in such countries as Yemen.

Hikmatyar Faction

Another "high value target" identified by U.S. commanders is the faction of former *mujahedin* party leader Gulbuddin Hikmatyar (Hizb-e-Islami Gulbuddin, HIG) allied with Al Qaeda and Taliban insurgents. As noted above, Hikmatyar was one of the main U.S.-backed *mujahedin* leaders during the Soviet occupation era. Hikmatyar's faction received extensive U.S. support against the Soviet Union, but is now active against U.S. and Afghan forces in Kunar, Nuristan, Kapisa, and Nangarhar provinces, north and east of Kabul. On February 19, 2003, the U.S. government formally designated Hikmatyar as a "Specially Designated Global Terrorist," under the authority of Executive Order 13224, subjecting it to financial and other U.S. sanctions. It is *not* designated as a "Foreign Terrorist Organization" (FTO). **Table 5** contains estimated numbers of HIG.

While U.S. commanders continue to battle Hikmatyar's militia, on March 22, 2010, both the Afghan government and Hikmatyar representatives confirmed they were in talks in Kabul, including meetings with Karzai. Hikmatyar has expressed a willingness to discuss a cease-fire with the Karzai government since 2007, and several Karzai's key allies in the National Assembly are former members of Hikmatyar's party. In January 2010, Hikmatyar outlined specific conditions for a possible reconciliation with Karzai, including elections under a neutral caretaker government following a U.S. withdrawal. These conditions are unlikely to be acceptable to Karzai or the international community, although many of them might be modified or dropped. Some close to Hikmatyar apparently attended the consultative peace *loya jirga* on June 2-4, 2010, which discussed the reconciliation issue, as analyzed further below.

Haqqani Faction

Another militant faction, cited repeatedly as a major threat, is the "Haqqani Network" led by Jalaludin Haqqani and his eldest son, Siraj (or Sirajjudin). Jalaludin Haqqani, who served as Minister of Tribal Affairs in the Taliban regime of 1996-2001, is believed closer to Al Qaeda than to the ousted Taliban leadership in part because one of his wives is purportedly Arab. The group is active around its key objective, Khost city, capital of Khost Province. The Haqqani network has claimed responsibility for attacks on India's embassy in Kabul and other India-related targets.

U.S. officials say they are continuing to pressure the Haqqani network with military action in Afghanistan and air strikes on the Pakistani side of the border. Haqqani property inside Pakistan has been repeatedly targeted since September 2008 by U.S. aerial drone strikes. Siraj's brother, Mohammad, was reportedly killed by a U.S. unmanned vehicle strike in late February 2010, although Mohammad was not thought to be a key militant commander. Pakistan reportedly arrested a minor family member (Nasruddin Haqqani) in December 2010 – a possible indication that Pakistan senses U.S. pressure for increased action against the network. However, some doubt has been cast that an arrest took place. The Haqqani network is said to be a major driver of the reported debate within the Obama Administration over whether to authorize additional Special Operations raids across the border into Pakistan, and presumably against the Haqqani network.[33]

Among other steps, in July 2010, it was reported that Gen. Petraeus, as part of his adjustments to policy as top commander in Afghanistan, wants the Haqqani network to be named as an FTO under the Immigration and Naturalization Act. Secretary of State Clinton said on July 19, 2010, during a visit to Pakistan, that U.S. policy is moving in that direction. Such a move would be intended to signal to Pakistan that it should not see the Haqqani network, as a whole, as part of a reconciled political structure in Afghanistan that would protect Pakistan's interests and work to limit the influence of India. This view was emphasized in a *New York Times* story of June 25, 2010.[34] The Haqqani faction has been thought not amenable to a political settlement, but some reports in November 2010 have said that members of the faction may have participated in exploratory reconciliation meetings with government representatives. **Table 5** contains estimated numbers of Haqqani fighters.

Pakistani Groups

The Taliban of Afghanistan are increasingly linked politically and operationally to Pakistani Taliban militants. The Pakistani groups might see a Taliban recapture of Afghanistan's government as helpful to the prospects for these groups inside Pakistan or in their Kashmir struggle. A major Pakistani group, the Pakistani Taliban (Tehrik-e-Taliban Pakistan, TTP), is primarily seeking to challenge the government of Pakistan, but they facilitate the transiting into Afghanistan of Afghan Taliban and support the Afghan Taliban goals of recapturing Afghanistan. The TTP may also be seeking to target the United States, based on a failed bombing in New York in May 2010. The State Department designated the TTP as a Foreign Terrorist Organization (FTO) under the Immigration and Naturalization Act on September 2, 2010, allegedly for having close connections to Al Qaeda.

Another Pakistani group said to be increasingly active inside Afghanistan is Laskhar-e-Tayyiba (LET, or Army of the Righteous). LET is an Islamist militant group that has previously been focused on operations against Indian control of Kashmir.

The U.S. Military Effort

The vast majority of U.S. troops in Afghanistan are under NATO/ISAF command. The remainder are part of the post-September 11 anti-terrorism mission Operation Enduring Freedom (OEF). There are also Special Operations Forces in Afghanistan under a separate command. Serving under General Petraeus is Maj. Gen. David Rodriguez, who heads a NATO-approved "Intermediate Joint Command" focused primarily on day-to-day operations and located in a facility adjoining Kabul International Airport. He has been in this position since mid-2009. The ISAF/U.S. Forces-Afghanistan commander reports not only to NATO but, through U.S. channels, to U.S. Central Command (CENTCOM).

Whether under NATO or OEF, many U.S. forces in Afghanistan are in eastern Afghanistan and lead Regional Command East of the NATO/ISAF operation. These U.S. forces belong to Combined Joint Task Force 101 (as of June 2010), which is commanded by Maj. Gen. John Campbell. As of November 2010, the most restive provinces in RC-E are Paktia, Paktika, Khost, Kunar, Nangarhar, and Nuristan.

Helmand, Qandahar, Uruzgan, Zabol, Nimruz, and Dai Kundi provinces constitute "Regional Command South (RC-S)," a command formally transferred to NATO/ISAF responsibility on July 31, 2006. U.S. forces have not led RC-S; the command was rotated among Britain, the Netherlands, and Canada. However, with the Dutch pullout in July 2010 and the growing U.S. troop strength in RC-S prompted a May 23, 2010, NATO decision to bifurcate RC-S, with the United States leading a "southwest" subdivision focused on Helmand and Nimruz. This is an evolution of the growing U.S. involvement in RC-S since 2008.

Perception of "Victory" in the First Five Post-Taliban Years

During 2001-mid-2006, U.S. forces and Afghan troops fought relatively low levels of insurgent violence. The United States and Afghanistan conducted "Operation Mountain Viper" (August 2003); "Operation Avalanche" (December 2003); "Operation Mountain Storm" (March-July 2004) against Taliban remnants in and around Uruzgan province, home province of Mullah Umar; "Operation Lightning Freedom" (December 2004–February 2005); and "Operation Pil" (Elephant) in Kunar Province in the east (October 2005). By late 2005, U.S. and partner commanders appeared to believe that the combat, coupled with overall political and economic reconstruction, had virtually ended any insurgency. Anticipating further stabilization, NATO/ISAF assumed lead responsibility for security in all of Afghanistan during 2005-2006.

Contrary to U.S. expectations, violence increased significantly in mid-2006, particularly in the east and the south, where ethnic Pashtuns predominate. Reasons for the deterioration include some of those discussed above in the sections on governance: Afghan government corruption; the absence of governance or security forces in many rural areas. Other factors included the safe haven enjoyed by militants in Pakistan; the reticence of some NATO contributors to actively combat insurgents; a popular backlash against civilian casualties caused by NATO and U.S. military operations; and the slow pace of economic development. Many Afghans are said to have turned to the Taliban as a source of impartial and rapid justice, in contrast to the slow and corrupt processes instituted by the central government.

Perception of Deterioration and Growing Force Levels in 2007 and 2008

Since 2006, and particularly during 2009 and 2010, the key theater of implementation of U.S. strategy has been eastern and southern Afghanistan, especially Helmand and Qandahar provinces. NATO counter-offensives during 2006-2008 – such as Operation Mountain Lion, Operation Mountain Thrust, and Operation Medusa (August-September 2006, in Panjwai district of Qandahar Province) – cleared key districts but did not prevent subsequent reinfiltration. In late 2006, British forces—who believe in negotiated local solutions—entered into an agreement with tribal elders in the Musa Qala district of Helmand Province, under which they would secure the main town of the district themselves. That strategy failed when the Taliban took over Musa Qala town in February 2007. A NATO offensive in December 2007 retook it.

As a further response, NATO and OEF forces tried to apply a more integrated strategy involving preemptive combat, increased development work, and a more streamlined command structure. Major combat operations in 2007 included U.S. and NATO attempted preemption of an anticipated Taliban "spring offensive" ("Operation Achilles," March 2007) in the Sangin district of Helmand Province, around the Kajaki dam, and Operation Silicon (May 2007), also in Helmand. (In September 2010, Britain turned over security leadership in Sangin to U.S. forces in the near future; combat in the district has accounted for nearly half of Britain's entire casualties in Afghanistan to date. U.S. strategy for the district is said to try to push out the boundaries of secure area of the district; British efforts focused on better securing the district major city.)

Despite the additional resources put into Afghanistan, throughout 2008, growing concern took hold within the Bush Administration. Pessimism was reflected in such statements as one in September 2008 by Joint Chiefs of Staff chairman Admiral Mike Mullen that "I'm not sure we're winning" in Afghanistan. Several major incidents supported that assessment, including (1) expanding Taliban operations in provinces where it had not previously been active, particularly Lowgar, Wardak, and Kapisa, close to Kabul; (2) high-profile attacks in Kabul against well-defended targets, such as the January 14, 2008, attack on the Serena Hotel in Kabul and the July 7, 2008, suicide bombing at the Indian Embassy in Kabul, killing more than 50; (3) the April 27, 2008, assassination attempt on Karzai during a military parade celebrating the ouster of the Soviet Union; and (4) a June 12, 2008, Sarposa prison break in Qandahar (several hundred Taliban captives were freed, as part of an emptying of the 1,200 inmates there).

To try to arrest deterioration, the United States and its partners decided to increase force levels. The added forces partly fulfilled a mid-2008 request by Gen. McKiernan for 30,000 additional U.S. troops (beyond the approximately 35,000 there at the time of the request). However, as the November 2008 U.S. presidential election approached, the decision whether to fulfill the entire request was deferred to the next Administration. U.S. troop levels started 2006 at 30,000; climbed slightly to 32,000 by December 2008; and reached 39,000 by April 2009. Partner forces were increased significantly as well, by about 6,000 during this time, to a total of 39,000 at the end of 2009 (rough parity between U.S. and non-U.S. forces). Many of the U.S. forces deployed in 2008 and 2009 were Marines that deployed to Helmand, large parts of which had fallen out of coalition/Afghan control.

Obama Administration Strategy Reviews and Further Buildup

In September 2008, the U.S. military and NATO each began strategy reviews. The primary U.S. review was headed by Lt. Gen. Douglas Lute, the Bush Administration's senior adviser on Iraq and Afghanistan (still in the Obama Administration with responsibility for Afghanistan). Other U.S. reviews were conducted by the Department of Defense, by CENTCOM, and by the State Department. These reviews were briefed to the incoming Obama Administration. The Obama Administration, which maintained that Afghanistan needed to be given a higher priority than it was during the Bush Administration, integrated the reviews into an overarching 60-day interagency "strategy review." It was chaired by

South Asia expert Bruce Riedel and co-chaired by Ambassador Holbrooke and Under Secretary of Defense for Policy Michele Flournoy.

March 27, 2009, Policy Announcement and Troop Increase, First Command Change, and McChrystal Assessment

President Obama announced a "comprehensive" strategy on March 27, 2009.[35] In conjunction, he announced the deployment of an additional 21,000 U.S. forces, of which about 4,000 would be trainers. Shortly after the announcement, the Administration decided that U.S. military leadership in Afghanistan was insufficiently innovative. On May 11, 2009, Secretary of Defense Gates and Joint Chiefs of Staff Chairman Michael Mullen announced that Gen. McKiernan would be replaced by Gen. Stanley McChrystal, considered an innovative commander as head of U.S. special operations from 2003 to 2008. He assumed command on June 15, 2009.

Gen. McChrystal, after assuming command, assessed the security situation and suggested a strategy in a report of August 30, 2009, and presented to NATO on August 31, 2009.[36] The main elements are:

- That the goal of the U.S. military should be to protect the population—and to help the Afghan government take steps to earn the trust of the population—rather than to search out and combat Taliban concentrations. Indicators of success such as ease of road travel and normal life for families are more important than are counts of numbers of enemy fighters killed.
- That there is potential for "mission failure" unless a fully resourced, comprehensive counter-insurgency strategy is pursued and reverses Taliban momentum within 12-18 months.
- About 44,000 additional U.S. combat troops (including trainers) would be needed to have the greatest chance for his strategy's success—beyond those approved by the Obama Administration strategy review in March 2009.

Second High-Level Review and Further Force Increase

The McChrystal assessment set off debate within the Administration. In September 2009, the Administration began a second high-level review of U.S. strategy, taking into account the McChrystal recommendations and the marred August 20, 2009, presidential election. Some senior U.S. officials, such as Secretary of Defense Gates, were concerned that adding many more U.S. forces could create among the Afghan people a sense of "occupation" that could prove counterproductive. Some Members of Congress, including Senate Armed Services Committee Chairman Carl Levin, said that the U.S. focus should be on expanding Afghan security forces capabilities before sending additional U.S. forces.

The high-level review included at least nine high-level meetings, chaired by President Obama, and reportedly concluded on November 19, 2009. The President announced his decisions in a speech at West Point military academy on December 1, 2009.[37] The major features of the December 1 statement included the following:

- That 30,000 additional U.S. forces (plus an unspecified number of additional "enablers") would be sent to "reverse the Taliban's momentum" and strengthen the capacity of Afghanistan's security forces and government in order to pave the way

Afghanistan: Post-Taliban Governance, Security, and U.S. Policy 297

for a transition, beginning in July 2011, to Afghan leadership of the stabilization effort. U.S. force levels did reach their current level of about 98,000 on/about September 4, 2010.

- The July 2011 deadline is the policy element that has caused significant controversy, as discussed below.

McChrystal Replaced by Petraeus

On June 23, 2010, President Obama accepted the resignation of Gen. McChrystal after summoning him to Washington, DC, to discuss the comments by him and his staff to a reporter for *Rolling Stone* (article cited earlier) that disparaged virtually all the civilian figures involved in Afghanistan policy. He named Gen. Petraeus as Gen. McChrystal's successor, a move that appeared to reassure President Karzai. In a June 23, 2010, statement, President Obama attributed the change purely to the disrespect of civilian authority contained in the *Rolling Stone* comments, and stated that Afghanistan policy would not change. Gen. Petraeus was confirmed by the Senate on June 30, 2010, and assumed command on July 4, 2010.

Summary of Current U.S. Strategy as Implemented by Gen. Petraeus

The major outlines of Obama Administration strategy have taken shape as outlined below, and the Administration review the summary of which was released on December 16, 2010, cited earlier, reaffirmed that U.S. strategy is "working well." The major tenets are:

- *Key Goals*: (1) disrupt terrorist networks in Afghanistan and Pakistan to degrade their ability to launch international terrorist attacks; (2) promote a more capable, accountable, and effective government in Afghanistan; (3) develop self-reliant Afghan security forces; and (4) involve the international community to actively assist in addressing these objectives. These relatively targeted goals are in line with comments by President Obama that he wants to "finish the job" in Afghanistan during his presidency.
- *Strategy Definition*: The overall counter-insurgency strategy is intended to "clear, hold, build, and transition"—to protect the population and allow time for Afghan governance and security forces to take leadership and for infrastructure and economic development to take root.
- *Limiting Civilian Casualties*. Part of the strategy is to win support of Afghans by sharply limiting air strikes and some types of raids and combat that cause Afghan civilian casualties and resentment[38] Some refer to the rules as the "Karzai 12," referring to the number of points of these rules of engagement. The NATO International Security Assistance Force (ISAF) and the Karzai government want to prevent any recurrence of incident such as the one that occurred near Herat on August 22, 2008, in which a NATO bomb killed up to 90 civilians, as well as the incident in September 2009 in Konduz in which Germany's contingent called in an airstrike on Taliban fighters who captured two fuel trucks; killing several civilians as well as Taliban fighters. Still, ISAF-caused civilian casualties continue, mainly due to misunderstandings at ISAF checkpoints, and in November 2010 President Karzai publicly called for a reduction of some of the night raids that are causing popular backlash.

- *July 2011 Deadline.* The Obama Administration emphasis on transition to Afghan security leadership beginning in July 2011 has been interpreted by some Administration officials—and by some Afghan and regional leaders—as laying the groundwork for winding down U.S. involvement in coming years.[39] The time frame stimulated considerable debate and may have been somewhat overtaken by NATO decisions in Lisbon in November, 2010, as discussed further below.
- *Resources and Troops*: The Administration and foreign partners assert that resource "inputs" are, as of October 2010, aligned with mission requirements.
- *Pressing the Afghan Government:* The Administration asserts that the Karzai government is being held to account for its performance, although, as noted, no specific penalties have been imposed on the Afghan government for shortfalls.
- *Civilian "Uplift":* A key strategy component is to develop Afghan institutions, particularly at the provincial and local levels. To be effective, the number of U.S. civilian advisors in Afghanistan reached about 1,000 in early 2010 and is over 1,100 as of the end of 2010. Of these at least 400 serve outside Kabul as part of initiatives such as the 32 "District Support Teams" and the "District Working Groups." That is up from 67 outside Kabul in early 2009.
- *Civilian-Military Integration*: There is a commitment to civilian-military integration, as outlined in a DOD-State Department joint campaign plan and the late Ambassador Holbrooke's January 2010 strategy document, referenced earlier. High-level "Senior Civilian Representatives" have been appointed to help the military formulate strategy for the regional commands where they serve. This is part of a new "Interagency Provincial Affairs" initiative that is less military-focused.
- *Reintegration and Reconciliation*: As discussed later, the Administration supports Afghan efforts to provide financial and social incentives to persuade insurgents to lay down their arms and accept the Afghan constitution. The United States was at first skeptical but is now increasingly supporting Karzai's policy of negotiating with senior insurgent leaders.
- *Pakistan*: Engagement with Pakistan and enlisting its increased cooperation is pivotal to U.S. policy. More information is in the section on Pakistan, below, and in CRS Report RL33498, *Pakistan-U.S. Relations*, by K. Alan Kronstadt.
- *International Dimension*: New international diplomatic mechanisms have been formed to better coordinate all "stakeholders" in the Afghanistan issue (NATO, Afghanistan's neighbors, other countries in Afghanistan's region, the United Nations, and other donors). Meetings such as the January 28, 2010, meeting in London and the July 20, 2010, Kabul Conference are part of that effort. To date, at least 25 nations have appointed direct counterparts to the SRAP, including the UAE, Saudi Arabia, and Turkey, which meet periodically as part of a 44-nation (and growing) "International Contact Group" for Afghanistan. It has met nine times, most recently in Rome on October 18, 2010. (Iran attended it for the first time.)
- *Partner Contributions*: Increased partner contributions of funding and troops were sought and offered. Currently, there is U.S. effort to encourage partner forces to remain in Afghanistan at least until a planned transition to Afghan leadership by 2014.
- *Metrics:* The Administration will continue to measure progress along clear metrics. Many in Congress, pressing for clear metrics to assess progress, inserted into P.L.

111-32 (FY2009 supplemental appropriation) a requirement that the President submit to Congress, 90 days after enactment (by September 23, 2009), metrics by which to assess progress, and a report on that progress every 180 days thereafter. The Administration's approximately 50 metrics were reported at the website of *Foreign Policy*[40] and were submitted. However, the difficulty in formulating useful and clear metrics that would enable Members and officials to assess progress in the war effort was demonstrated by comments by Ambassador Holbrooke on August 12, 2009, saying that on defining success in Afghanistan and Pakistan: "We will know it when we see it."[41] In its September 22, 2009, report on the situation in Afghanistan (A/64/364-S/2009/475), the United Nations developed its own "benchmarks" for progress in Afghan governance and security.

July 2011 "Drawdown" Giving Way to 2014 "Transition"

The Obama Administration emphasis on transition to Afghan security leadership beginning in July 2011 has been perhaps the most widely discussed and debated aspect of policy. Debate over whether to announce such a timeframe is covered extensively in the book "Obama's Wars," by Bob Woodward. The 2011 "deadline" was interpreted by some Administration critics—and by some Afghan and regional leaders—as laying the groundwork for winding down U.S. involvement in coming years.[42] The Administration has said it set the time frame to demonstrate to a war-weary public that U.S. military involvement in Afghanistan is not open-ended. Perhaps to address perceived criticism of such a deadline in the upper ranks of the U.S. military, in an August 31, 2010 statement, the President asserted that the pace and scope of any drawdown in 2011 would be subject to conditions on the ground. These comments appeared to modify the July 18, 2010, Vice President Biden amended earlier remarks by saying that only a few thousand U.S. forces might come out at that time as part of a process of transitioning some Afghan provinces to Afghan lead.

The debate over the July 2011 drawdwon appears to have abated somewhat with an agreement between the United States and NATO partner forces to focus on a longer time frame for transition to Afghan leadership. With European publics tiring of involvement in Afghanistan, a July 2010 agreement reportedly was reached on a joint Afghan-NATO board to decide on locations that might be selected for transition to Afghan lead. These locations, reportedly whole provinces and districts to transition to Afghan leadership beginning in 2011 – and running through the end of 2014 – were ratified at the November 19-20, 2010, NATO summit in Lisbon. The 2014 date is one that Karzai articulated in 2009 as a time frame when Afghan forces would be able to secure Afghanistan on their own. According to some U.S. commanders, some provinces in the U.S.-led eastern sector, such as Panjshir or Bamiyan, could be turned over in 2011, with Nangarhar considered a candidate for turnover thereafter. President Obama and other senior U.S. officials say that 2014 is not a date certain for a complete international pullout, but rather for a transition to Afghan lead, with some international forces remaining after 2014 to train and mentor the Afghans.

There are no firm estimates on how many U.S. forces might be withdrawn from Afghanistan in July 2011. However, observers appear to agree that the numbers will be relatively small, perhaps a few thousand, drawn from districts where U.S. forces have been "thinned out" as Afghan forces expand their responsibilities.

Implementation of Strategy, Early Results, and Doubts

As discussed, the December 16, 2010, summary of the Administration review says that U.S. strategy is showing results, particularly in the provinces of focus (Helmand, Qandahar) although such gains are "fragile and reversible." The possible signs of momentum appear to reflect the beginnings of a possible turnaround from a September 30, 2010, White House assessments of the situation and press reports about less optimistic assessments of the U.S. intelligence community or the United Nations. Several U.S. commanders say they are receiving overtures from local insurgent leaders who have lost morale and seek to discuss possible terms for their surrender and reintegration. Other reports say that insurgent factions are running low on supplies and ammunition. The less optimistic views are based on observations that the insurgency continues to make gains in previously quiet provinces, including Baghlan, Konduz, and Faryab provinces. Still others say that Afghan governance is lagging to the point where the Afghans will not be able to hold U.S./NATO gains on their own and insurgents will be able to regroup as soon as international forces thin out.

According to Gen. Petraeus, operations in 2010 have ended Taliban control in large parts of Helmand and produced major progress in Qandahar province, as discussed below. The progress is creating a contiguous secure corridor for commerce between Helmand and Qandahar. Markets and other signs of normal life have proliferated in Helmand, according to several U.S. commanders in October 2010. In August 2010, he took *NBC News* correspondents to Wardak province as a showcase of stability in a province that, in 2008, was considered largely under Taliban influence. The first of the operations in 2009 that produced some of the relatively positive assessments was Operation Khanjar—intended to expel the Taliban and reestablish Afghan governance in parts of the province. The offensive reportedly ended Taliban control of several districts in Helmand, including Nawa, Now Zad, and Musa Qala.

Some commanders attribute the signs of progress not only to the increase in numbers of U.S. forces, but to Gen. Petraeus' tactics, including nearly tripling Special Operations Force operations in Afghanistan and greatly increased UAV (unmanned aerial vehicle) strikes on concentrations across the border in Pakistan to try to drive insurgents to reconcile with the Karzai government and cease fighting. Some attribute progress to increased operations by U.S. Special Forces and CIA-trained Afghan special forces and militias, including Afghan "Counterterrorism Pursuit Teams." In November 2010, Gen.Petraeus reportedly approved the deployment of about 16 M1A1 tanks for use by the Marines in southern Afghanistan in order to put further pressure on militants. A report, cited earlier but denied by NATO officials, say the U.S. military might be seeking U.S. presidential authority to increase ground raids against militant safehavens in Pakistan. Such a move could be perceived as expanding the U.S.-led war effort and there are no firm indications that President Obama's approval for such operations is imminent.

Operation Moshtarek in Marjah/Nad Ali

The reports of progress in Helmand represent a turnaround from earlier pessimism about the outcome of "Operation Moshtarek" (Operation Together). It consisted of about 15,000 U.S., foreign partner, and Afghan forces (about 8,000 of the total) that, beginning on February 13, 2010, sought to clear Taliban militants from Marjah city (85,000 population) in Helmand. An Afghan governing structure was identified in advance (so-called "government in a box"), the population had substantial warning, and there were meetings with regional elders just

Afghanistan: Post-Taliban Governance, Security, and U.S. Policy

before the offensive began—all of which were an apparent effort to cause militants to flee and to limit civilian losses.[43] The city, for the most part, was declared cleared of militants as of February 26, 2010, but some militants continue to fight in and on the outskirts of Marjah and to assassinate and intimidate Afghans cooperating with U.S. and Afghan forces. Some Afghan officials, such as ministry representatives, are now beginning to serve regularly in the city itself, although town governor Hajji Zahir was fired in July 2010.

As part of the U.S. effort, U.S. forces, primarily Marines, disburse Commanders Emergency Response Program (CERP-funds controlled by U.S. officers) funds to clear rubble from schools, clean canals, repair markets, rebuild bridges, and compensate families who lost members due to the combat. Afghans who work on these projects in Marjah and in the previously cleared Nawa district are reportedly being paid about $5 per day as part of an effort to provide livelihoods to Afghans who might previously have supported the Taliban for purely financial reasons.[44] Some fear that many of these workers might rejoin insurgent activities when U.S. funding for these "cash for work" programs decline.

Qandahar Effort

The Administration assessment of progress in December 2010 was based largely on views of success in Qandahar Province. In early 2010, U.S. commanders had emphasized that the Qandahar effort would focus less on combat and more on conducting consultations and *shuras* with tribal leaders and other notables to enlist their cooperation against Taliban infiltrators. U.S. commanders described the operation as more of a "process," or a slow push into restive districts by setting up Afghan checkpoints to secure the city and districts around it (particularly Arghandab, Zhari, and Panjwai)—and not a classic military offensive. Qandahar's population is far larger (about 2 million in the province), and Qandahar province and city have functioning governments, which Marjah did not. The city hosts numerous businesses and has always remained vibrant, despite some Taliban clandestine activity.

A sense of doubt about the prospects for the operation built in April-August 2010 as Afghan tribal and other residential resistance—expressed at local *shuras*—to any combat to secure Qandahar. However, Gen. Petraeus has increased operations by U.S. Special Operations Forces against key militants near the city that began in April 2010.[45] Subsequently, as U.S. forces have expanded their presence in the province in partnership with Afghan forces since September 2010, Taliban control has ended in many neighborhoods and Afghan checkpoints have been established. Further *shuras* have been held to promote Afghan governance. As part of the effort to stabilize Qandahar U.S. officials are also reportedly trying to strengthen Governor Tooryalai Wesa and balance the flow of U.S. and international funds to the various tribes and clans in the province. An unstated objective is also to weaken the influence of Karzai's brother, Ahmad Wali Karzai, chair of the provincial council, who is discussed above.[46]

Security Innovations under Way

Despite the assessments of progress, Gen. Petraeus and others are said to believe that a clear end to the conflict on U.S./NATO/Afghan government terms requires new approaches that convince insurgent leaders that further conflict is futile. Discussed below are some additional or alternative approaches that are increasing feature of U.S. policy.

"Reintegration" and "Reconciliation" With Insurgents

The issue of reintegration fighters and reconciling with insurgent leaders is an Afghan-led process but one in which the United States and the international community is increasingly involved. The issue has made some in the international community, and within Afghanistan, concerned for the potential to involve compromises with insurgents and perhaps some backsliding on human rights. Most insurgents are highly conservative Islamists who agreed with the limitations in women's rights that characterized Taliban rule. Many leaders of ethnic minorities are also skeptical of the effort because they fear that it might further Pashtun political strength within Afghanistan, and enhance the influence of Pakistan in Afghan politics. Gen. Petraeus has said that the way conflicts like the one in Afghanistan end is through a political settlement. The United States and the Karzai government agree that any settlement must involve fighters and insurgent leaders: (1) cease fighting, (2) accept the Afghan constitution, and (3) sever any ties to Al Qaeda or other terrorist groups.

Reintegration/"Peace Jirga"

A January 28, 2010, London conference of international donors backed devoting more emphasis to reintegration of fighters amenable to surrendering. Some of the incentives to surrendering insurgents that the international community deemed likely to fund are jobs, amnesty, and protection, and possibly making them part of the security architecture for their communities. These are elements included in a reintegration plan drafted by the Afghan government and presented to the peace *loya jirga* during June 2-4, 2010.[47] In its final declaration, the *peace jirga* backed the plan, but also called for limits in NATO-led raids and further efforts to limit civilian casualties. It also called for the release of some detained insurgents where allegations against them are weak. The day after the *jirga* concluded, Karzai sought to implement that recommendation by calling for a review of the cases of all insurgent detentions. In late June 2010, President Karzai issued a decree to implement the plan, which involves outreach by Afghan local leaders to tribes and others who are in a position to convince insurgents to lay down their arms. The international community gave its support to the effort in the communiqué of the July 20, 2010, Kabul Conference. Britain, Japan, and several other countries have announced a total of about $160 million in donations to a new fund to support the reintegration process.[48] The United States is to contribute an additional $100 million.

Although it reached some substantive conclusions, the **peace** *jirga* itself received mixed reviews for its inclusiveness or lack thereof. Karzai tried to bring other minority communities along in backing the peace *jirga* and the reintegration process, and to do so he appointed former leader Rabbani to chair the *jirga*. However, "opposition leader" Dr. Abdullah Abdullah, Karzai's rival in the 2009 presidential election, boycotted the *jirga*.

However, despite the international funding for the effort, the Afghan-led reintegration process has moved forward only slowly. Only $200,000 of the donated funds have been spent, as of early September 2010, and only about 800 fighters have indicated willingness to reintegrate, according to a U.N. report of December 10, 2010. However, press reports in September 2010, citing briefings by Gen. Petraeus for senior U.S. officials, say he anticipates many more surrenders of insurgent fighters as the success of U.S. and NATO strategy becomes clear. In addition, press reports say that some Taliban fighters sought information on the September 18, 2010, parliamentary election as a possible prelude to joining the political process.

The Obama Administration and its partners have been separately expanding their own efforts to lure lower-level insurgents off the battlefield with job opportunities and infrastructure construction incentives. Another component of the program has been meetings with tribal elders to persuade Taliban and other insurgents in their areas to give up their fight. Some U.S. commanders are reporting some successes with this effort, using Commanders Emergency Response Program (CERP) funds. The National Defense Authorization Act for FY2010 (P.L. 111- 84) authorized the use of CERP funds to win local support, to "reintegrate" Taliban fighters who renounce violence. FY2011 budget language requested by the Administration would authorize U.S. funds to be contributed to the reintegration fund mentioned above. To help the process along from the international perspective, in November 2009, ISAF set up a "force reintegration cell," headed by Britain's Maj. Gen. Richard Barrons, to develop additional programs and policies to accelerate the effort to cause insurgents to change sides. These strategies are similar to what was employed successfully in Anbar Province in Iraq in 2006 and 2007.

Karzai has consistently advocated talks with Taliban militants who want to consider ending their fight. Noted above is the "Program for Strengthening Peace and Reconciliation" (referred to in Afghanistan by its Pashto acronym "PTS") headed by *Meshrano Jirga* speaker Sibghatullah Mojadeddi and former Vice President Karim Khalili, and overseen by Karzai's National Security Council. The program is credited with persuading 9,000 Taliban figures and commanders to renounce violence and join the political process.

Reconciliation with Taliban/Insurgent Leaders

A separate Karzai initiative—far more widely debated than reintegration—is to conduct negotiations with senior insurgent leaders. Many in the international community, and within the Obama Administration, had feared that reconciliation has the potential to result in insurgent leaders obtaining senior positions or control over some Afghan territory, and that these figures will retain ties to Al Qaeda and commit abuses similar to those under the Taliban regime. The July 20, 2010, Kabul Conference did not issue unqualified support for high-level reconciliation talks, instead endorsing establishment of an Afghan High Peace Council to build Afghan consensus on the issue. That Council was established on September 5, 2010, and its 70 members met for the first time under the leadership of Tajik leader Rabbani on October 10, 2010. Yet, the direct role of the Council in negotiations is unclear; rather, it might be asked to review and endorse any settlement that is reached.

In an apparent shift, as stated by President Obama on December 16, 2010, in announcing the results of the U.S. policy review, the United States now fully backs the concept of reconciliation with insurgent leaders who meet the conditions stated above. Earlier, in March 2009, President Obama publicly ruled out negotiations with Mullah Umar and his top aides because of their alignment with Al Qaeda. Others still differ on the willingness of senior insurgents to bargain in earnest. CIA director Panetta, in a June 27, 2010 interview cited earlier, and reflecting the reported view of several U.S. intelligence agencies as of late 2010, said he saw no indications that insurgent leaders are contemplating settling with the government.

Senior U.S. commanders have grown more optimistic about reconciliation as contacts between Taliban representatives and the Karzai government appear to have broadened. However, observers say the discussions to date are about modalities and an agenda for further talks. Several sets of talks were reported in October 2010, and some press accounts said that NATO/ISAF forces were in fact facilitation the movement of insurgent representatives to these talks. Representatives of the Quetta Shura Taliban were purported to be involved, although this was placed in doubt in late November 2010 when it was revealed that one of the purported senior Taliban interlocutors was an imposter. Still, Mullah Bradar, who is close to Mullah Umar, was said by the Afghan side to have been engaged in talks with the Afghan government prior to his arrest by Pakistan in February 2010. Karzai reportedly believes that Pakistan arrested Bradar in order to be able to influence the course of any Afghan government-Taliban settlement. The Taliban as a movement was not invited to the June 2-4, 2010, consultative peace *jirga*, but some Taliban sympathizers reportedly were there. The Taliban continues to demand that (1) all foreign troops leave Afghanistan; (2) a new "Islamic" constitution be adopted; and (3) Islamic law is imposed. However, those are viewed as opening positions; the Afghan government, for its part, may have softened its position on disallowing any changes to the Afghan constitution as part of a settlement.

In advance of the peace *jirga*, the Karzai government and representatives of Hikmatyar confirmed peace talks on March 21, 2010, in which Karzai, his brother, Ahmad Wali, and several Northern Alliance figures met with the Hikmatyar representatives. The representatives reportedly presented a 15-point peace plan to Karzai that does not necessarily demand his government step down immediately. Other accounts say that even the Haqqani faction, often viewed as least amenable to settlement, has been represented at some exploratory meetings with Karzai government representatives.

Other talks have taken place over the past few years, although with less apparent momentum than is the case in 2010. Press reports said that Afghan officials (led by Karzai's brother Qayyum) and Taliban members had met each other in Ramadan-related gatherings in Saudi Arabia in September 2008. Another round of talks was held in January 2009 in Saudi Arabia, and there were reports of ongoing contacts in Dubai, UAE. Some of these talks apparently involved Arsala Rahmani, a former Taliban official now in parliament, and the former Taliban Ambassador to Pakistan, Abdul Salam Zaeef, who purportedly is in touch with Umar's inner circle. These same Taliban representatives may have been involved in talks in the mid-late 2010 as well.

The consultative peace *jirga*, in its final declaration, supported Karzai's call for the removal of the names of some Taliban figures from U.N. lists of terrorists, lists established pursuant to Resolution 1267 and Resolution 1333 (October 15, 1999, and December 19, 2000, both pre-September 11 sanctions against the Taliban and Al Qaeda) and Resolution 1390 (January 16, 2002). Press reports before the July 20 Kabul Conference said the Afghan government has submitted a list of 50 Taliban figures it wants taken off this list as a confidence-building measure. The Conference called on Afghanistan to engage with the U.N. Security Council to provide evidence to justify such de-listings, and U.N., U.S., and other international officials said they would support considering de-listings on a case-by-case basis. On January 26, 2010, Russia, previously a hold-out against such a process, dropped opposition to removing five Taliban-era figures from these sanctions lists, including Taliban-era foreign minister Wakil Mutawwakil, who ran in 2005 parliamentary elections. Also removed was Abdul Hakim Monib, who has served Karzai as governor of Uruzgan, Abdul Hakim Mujahid, who was Taliban representative in the United States, and three others. Mujahid now is one of three deputy chairs of the High Peace Council. "Mullah Rocketi," not on the sanctions list, is a former Taliban commander who ran for president in the August 2009 elections.

Local Security Experiments: Afghan Provincial Protection Program (APPP) and Local Defense Initiative

Until mid-2008, U.S. military commanders opposed assisting local militias anywhere in Afghanistan for fear of creating new rivals to the central government who would arbitrarily administer justice. The urgent security needs in Afghanistan caused reconsideration and Gen Petraeus is seeking to expand these type of local security experiments, based on his similar and successful experiences in Iraq. Press reports in July 2010 say he succeeded, after several of his first meetings with Karzai, in overcoming Karzai's reticence to them. Gen. Petraeus reportedly has guaranteed that any local security organs would be under the administration of the Ministry of Interior.

The newest initiative is the Afghan "Local Police Initiative," in which local security organs would be formed from local recruits who want to defend their communities. It was planned that up to 10,000 volunteers will serve in the initiative, but on October 19, 2010, the Defense Department said it would be expanded to at least 20,000, if possible. The ultimate target level might be 50,000, according to press reports. The Defense Department notified Congress in September 2010 that it will reprogram about $35 million in Afghan security forces funding to support the initiative.

The Local Police Initiative follows on another program begun in 2008, termed the "Afghan Provincial Protection Program" (APPP, commonly called "AP3") and is funded with DOD (CERP) funds. The APPP got under way in Wardak Province (Jalrez district) in early 2009 and 100 local security personnel "graduated" in May 2009. It has been expanded to 1,200 personnel, in a province with a population of about 500,000. (These personnel are expected to be integrated into the local police initiative). U.S. commanders say that no U.S. weapons are supplied to the militias, but this is an Afghan-led program and the Afghan government is providing weapons (Kalashnikov rifles) to the local groups, possibly using U.S. funds. Participants in the program are given $200 per month.

Before the program was placed on hold, it was to be expanded to Ghazni, Lowgar, and Kapisa provinces and eventually include as many as 8,000 Afghans. Gen. Petraeus showcased Wardak in August 2010 as an example of the success of the APPP and similar efforts. As an indication of divisions among Afghan leaders about the concept, the upper house of the Afghan parliament (*Meshrano Jirga*) passed a resolution in November 2008 opposing the concept. The National Defense Authorization Act (P.L. 111-84) calls for a report within 120 days of enactment (October 28, 2009) on the results of the program.

Another program, the Local Defense Initiative, began in February 2010 in Arghandab district of Qandahar Province. U.S. Special Forces organized about 25 villagers into a neighborhood watch group, which is armed. The program has been credited by U.S. commanders as bringing normal life back to the district. A different militia was allowed to operate in Konduz to help secure the northern approaches to that city. Problems arose when the militia began arbitrarily administering justice, fueling concerns of Karzai and Ambassador Eikenberry about these local security approaches.

The local security experiments to date are not *arbokai*, which are private tribal militias. Still, some believe that the arbokai concept should be revived as a means of securing

Afghanistan, as the arbokai did during the reign of Zahir Shah and in prior pre-Communist eras.

Reversal of Previous Efforts: DDR and DIAG programs

As noted, the local security programs appear to reverse the 2002-2007 efforts to disarm local sources of armed force. The main program, run by UNAMA, was called the "DDR" program— Disarmament, Demobilization, and Reintegration—and it formally concluded on June 30, 2006. The program got off to a slow start because the Afghan Defense Ministry did not reduce the percentage of Tajiks in senior positions by a July 1, 2003, target date, dampening Pashtun recruitment. In September 2003, Karzai replaced 22 senior Tajiks in the Defense Ministry officials with Pashtuns, Uzbeks, and Hazaras, enabling DDR to proceed. The major donor for the program was Japan, which contributed about $140 million. Figures for collected weapons are contained in **Table 5** and U.S. spending on the program are in the U.S. aid tables at the end of this report.

The DDR program was initially expected to demobilize 100,000 fighters, although that figure was later reduced. (Figures for accomplishment of the DDR and DIAG programs are contained in **Table 5** below.) Of those demobilized, 55,800 former fighters have exercised reintegration options provided by the program: starting small businesses, farming, and other options. U.N. officials say at least 25% of these found long-term, sustainable jobs. Some studies criticized the DDR program for failing to prevent a certain amount of rearmament of militiamen or stockpiling of weapons and for the rehiring of some militiamen.[49] Part of the DDR program was the collection and cantonment of militia weapons, but generally only poor-quality weapons were collected. As one example, Fahim, still the main military leader of the Northern Alliance faction, continues to turn heavy weapons over to U.N. and Afghan forces (including four Scud missiles), although the U.N. Assistance Mission in Afghanistan (UNAMA) says that large quantities of weapons remain in the Panjshir Valley.

Despite the earlier demobilization, which affected many of the northern minorities, there are indications that some faction leaders may be seeking to revive disbanded militias. The minorities may fear increased Taliban influence as a result of the Karzai reconciliation efforts, and the minorities want to be sure they could combat any Taliban abuses that might result if the Taliban achieves a share of power.

DIAG

Since June 11, 2005, the disarmament effort has emphasized another program called "DIAG"— Disbandment of Illegal Armed Groups. It is run by the Afghan Disarmament and Reintegration Commission, headed by Vice President Khalili. Under the DIAG, no payments are available to fighters, and the program depends on persuasion rather than use of force against the illegal groups. DIAG has not been as well funded as was DDR: it has received $11 million in operating funds. As an incentive for compliance, Japan and other donors have made available $35 million for development projects where illegal groups have disbanded. These incentives were intended to accomplish the disarmament of a pool of as many as 150,000 members of 1,800 different "illegal armed groups": militiamen that were not part of recognized local forces (Afghan Military Forces, AMF) and were never on the rolls of the Defense Ministry. These goals were not met by the December 2007 target date in part because armed groups in the south say they need to remain armed against the Taliban, but UNAMA reports that some progress continues to be achieved.

Afghanistan: Post-Taliban Governance, Security, and U.S. Policy 307

Several U.S.-backed local security programs implemented since 2008, discussed below, appear to reverse the intent and implementation of the DIAG process.

POSSIBLE FUTURE LIMITS ON U.S. OPERATIONS/STATUS OF FORCES AGREEMENT

The issue of a larger Afghan government role in approving NATO-led operations has surfaced repeatedly. Such sentiments arose in 2008, when the Afghan cabinet reacted to some high-profile instances of accidental civilian deaths by demanding negotiation of a formal "Status of Forces Agreement" (SOFA). A SOFA would spell out the combat authorities of non-Afghan forces, and might limit the United States to airstrikes, detentions, and house raids.[50] As noted earlier, differences between Karzai and the U.S. command in Afghanistan erupted again in November 2010 with Karzai calling for a decrease in the number of night raids and other operations that cause civilian unrest.

A draft SOFA—or technical agreement clarifying U.S./coalition authorities in Afghanistan— reportedly has been under discussion between the United States and Afghanistan since 2007. U.S. forces currently operate in Afghanistan under a "diplomatic note" between the United States and the interim government of Afghanistan that was exchanged in November 2002; the agreement gives the United States legal jurisdiction over U.S. personnel serving in Afghanistan and states the Afghan government's acknowledgment that U.S.-led military operations were "ongoing."

Long-Term Security Commitment

As noted, some Afghan leaders perceived the Obama Administration's 2011 deadline to "begin" a transition to Afghan security leadership as a sign the Administration might want to wind down U.S. involvement in Afghanistan. In part to reassure the Afghan government, President Obama, at a May 12, 2010, press conference with visiting President Karzai, stated that the United States and Afghanistan would renew a five-year-old strategic partnership. The target for renewing the partnership is early in 2011. However, some advocate forging a security agreement with Afghanistan similar to that agreed with Iraq – that one stipulated an end date for U.S. military involvement in Iraq.

The strategic partnership was first established on May 23, 2005, when Karzai and President Bush issued a "joint declaration"[51] providing for U.S. forces to have access to Afghan military facilities, in order to prosecute "the war against international terror and the struggle against violent extremism." The joint statement did not give Karzai enhanced control over facilities used by U.S. forces, over U.S. operations, or over prisoners taken during operations. Some of the bases, both in and near Afghanistan, that support combat in Afghanistan, include those in Table 6. Karzai's signing of the partnership had been blessed by Afghan representatives on May 8, 2005, when he summoned about 1,000 delegates to a consultative *jirga* in Kabul on whether to host permanent U.S. bases. That *jirga* supported an indefinite presence of international forces to maintain security but urged Karzai to delay a decision. A FY2009 supplemental appropriation (P.L. 111-32) and the FY2010 and FY2011

National Defense Authorization Acts (P.L. 111-84 and H.R. 6523, respectively) prohibit the U.S. establishment of permanent bases in Afghanistan.

ALLIANCE ISSUES: THE NATO-LED INTERNATIONAL SECURITY ASSISTANCE FORCE (ISAF) AND OPERATION ENDURING FREEDOM[52]

Almost all U.S. troops in Afghanistan remain under the umbrella of the NATO-led "International Security Assistance Force" (ISAF)—consisting of all 26 NATO members states plus partner countries – a total of 50 countries including the United States. President Obama's December 1, 2009, policy speech on Afghanistan was explicit in seeking new partner troop commitments, and pledges met or exceeded what some U.S. officials expected. However, several key contingents have ended their combat missions (the Netherlands), will end those missions (Canada, by the summer of 2011), or are setting notional time frames for departure before the 2014 time frame agreed in the NATO summit in Lisbon (November 19-20, 2010) to complete the transition to Afghan leadership. Britain has steadily increased its troop commitment in Afghanistan—mainly in high combat Helmand Province—to about 9,500 (plus 500 Special Forces).

Table 3. Background on NATO/ISAF Formation and U.N. Mandate

The International Security Assistance Force (ISAF) was created by the Bonn Agreement and U.N. Security Council Resolution 1386 (December 20, 2001, a Chapter 7 resolution),[53] initially limited to Kabul. In October 2003, after Germany agreed to contribute 450 military personnel to expand ISAF into the city of Konduz, ISAF contributors endorsed expanding its presence to several other cities, contingent on formal U.N. approval—which came on October 14, 2003 in U.N. Security Council Resolution 1510. In August 2003, NATO took over command of ISAF— previously the ISAF command rotated among donor forces including Turkey and Britain.

NATO/ISAF's responsibilities broadened significantly in 2004 with NATO/ISAF's assumption of security responsibility for northern and western Afghanistan (Stage 1, Regional Command North, in 2004 and Stage 2, Regional Command West, in 2005, respectively). The transition process continued on July 31, 2006, with the formal handover of the security mission in southern Afghanistan to NATO/ISAF control. As part of this "Stage 3," a British/Canadian/Dutchled "Regional Command South" (RC-S) was formed. Britain is the lead force in Helmand; Canada is lead in Qandahar, and the Netherlands was lead in Uruzgan until its departure in July 2010; the three rotated the command of RC-S. "Stage 4," the assumption of NATO/ISAF command of peacekeeping in 14 provinces of eastern Afghanistan (and thus all of Afghanistan), was completed on October 5, 2006. As part of the completion of the NATO/ISAF takeover, the United States put about half the U.S. troops then operating in Afghanistan under NATO/ISAF in "Regional Command East" (RC-E).

The ISAF mission was renewed (until October 13, 2011) by U.N. Security Council Resolution 1943 (October 13, 2010), which reiterated previous resolutions' support for the Operation Enduring Freedom mission. Tables at the end of this report list contributing forces, areas of operations, and their Provincial Reconstruction Teams.

Afghanistan: Post-Taliban Governance, Security, and U.S. Policy 309

In line with other contributors, British official comments have indicated that Britain might want to end its mission before 2014. Britain has lost over 300 soldiers in Afghanistan. Italy, Poland, and Germany have also indicated an intent to try to wind down their involvement in Afghanistan before the end of 2014. As noted above, some of the provinces considered good candidates to transition to Afghan leadership are in the German sector in the north. Partner forces that continue to bear the brunt of combat in Afghanistan include Britain, Canada, Poland, France, Denmark, Romania, and Australia.

Virtually all the European governments are under pressure from their publics and parliaments to end or reduce the military involvement in Afghanistan. This pressure led Britain, France, and Germany to ask the United Nations to organize the international conference that took place in London on January 28, 2010. That conference, as these countries sought, endorsed the concept of transition to Afghan leadership on security and improvement of its governance, while also encouraging more regional assistance from India, China, and Russia.

Recent Major Contingent Developments

Following the Obama Administration's March 27, 2009, policy announcement, some additional pledges came through at the April 3-4, 2009, NATO summit. Major new force pledges were issued after the December 1 policy statement, and in conjunction with the January 28, 2010, conference in London. However, some of these forces were intended to compensate for the pullouts by the Netherlands and Canada 2010 and 2011, respectively. The major recent pledges are the following:

- April 2009: Deployment of 3,000 non-U.S. troops to secure the Afghan elections and 2,000 trainers for the Afghan security forces. Contributing forces for the election period include Spain (400), Germany (600), Poland (600), and Britain (about 900). Other pledges (from Bulgaria, Estonia, Italy, Greece, Portugal, Turkey, and Slovakia) were for trainers to fill out 61 existing Operational Mentor and Liaison Teams (OMLTs), each of which has about 30 trainers.
- April 2009: NATO agreed to new training missions for the ANSF. A NATO Training Mission—Afghanistan (NTM-A) has been established. Also that month, $500 million in additional Afghan civilian aid was pledged by several donors.
- November 10, 2009: Ahead of President Obama's visit to Asia, Japan announced a pledge of $5 billion over the next five years for Afghanistan civilian development, although it suspended its naval refueling mission.
- July 2009: South Korea announced it would increase its aid contribution to Afghanistan by about $20 million, in part to expand the hospital capabilities at Bagram Air Base. In November 2009, it announced a return of about 150 engineers to Afghanistan for development missions, protected by 300 South Korean forces. The forces deployed to Parwan Province in July 2010. (Until December 2007, 200 South Korean forces at Bagram Air Base, mainly combat engineers, were part of Operation Enduring Freedom (OEF); they left in December 2007 in fulfillment of a decision by the South Korean government the previous year. However, many observers believe South Korea did not further extend its mission beyond that, possibly as part of an

agreement in August 2007 under which Taliban militants released 21 kidnapped South Korean church group visitors.[54])

- December 2009-January 2010 (London conference): A total of about 9,000 forces were pledged (including retaining 2,000 sent for the August 2009 election who were due to rotate out). The pledges included Britain (500), Poland (600), Romania (600, plus about 30 trainers), Italy (1,000), Georgia (900+), Spain (500), Colombia (240, first time contributor of forces), Slovakia (60), Sweden (125), Portugal (120), and Germany (500 plus 350 on reserve, but still only in the north, not heavy combat zones). France pledged 80 trainers but no new combat forces. Several countries pledged police trainers.
- Other Major Civilian Aid Pledges in Context of London Conference:[55] France ($45 million); Saudi Arabia ($150 million over three years); Australia ($40 million); China ($75 million). Japan agreed to pay ANP salaries for another six months (until the end of 2010), a cost of about $125 million in a six month period, to come out of its $5 billion contribution mentioned above. Japan reiterated that commitment during Karzai's June 17, 2010, visit to Tokyo. Other pledges were made for Taliban reintegration, as noted above.
- In July 2010, Malaysia became a new contributor to the Afghanistan effort, furnishing 40 military medics.
- Later in 2010, partner countries have pledged to help fill a gap of about 750 trainers for the Afghan National Security Forces.

Equipment Issues

Some of the pledges address NATO's chronic equipment shortages—particularly helicopters, both for transport and attack—for the Afghanistan mission. In 2007, to try to compensate for the shortage, NATO chartered about 20 commercial helicopters for extra routine supply flights to the south, freeing up Chinooks and Black Hawks for other missions. Some of the Polish troops deployed in 2008 operate and maintain eight helicopters. Germany provides six Tornado combat aircraft to assist with strikes in combat situations in the south. NATO/ISAF also assists the Afghan Ministry of Civil Aviation and Tourism in the operation of Kabul International Airport (where Dutch combat aircraft also are located). In 2009, Belgium sent two more F-16 fighters.

National "Caveats" on Combat Operations

One of the most thorny issues has been the U.S. effort to persuade other NATO countries to adopt flexible rules of engagement that allow all contributing forces to perform combat missions. NATO and other partner forces have not, as they pledged at the NATO summit in April 2008, removed the so-called "national caveats" on their troops' operations that Lt. Gen. McChrystal says limits operational flexibility. For example, some nations refuse to conduct night-time combat. Others have refused to carry Afghan personnel on their helicopters. Others do not fight after snowfall. These caveats were troubling to those NATO countries with forces in heavy combat zones, such as Canada, which feel they are bearing the brunt of the fighting.

Afghanistan: Post-Taliban Governance, Security, and U.S. Policy

Table 4. Operation Enduring Freedom Partner Forces

Operation Enduring Freedom continues as a separate combat track, led by the United States but joined by a few partners. The caveat issue is less of a factor with OEF, since OEF is known as a combat-intensive mission conducted in large part by Special Forces contingents of contributing nations. The overwhelming majority of non-U.S. forces are under the NATO/ISAF mission. Prior to NATO assumption of command in October 2006, 19 coalition countries— primarily Britain, France, Canada, and Italy contributing approximately 4,000 combat troops to OEF-Afghanistan. Now, that figure is lower as most have been re-badged to ISAF. However, several foreign contingents, composed mainly of special operations forces, including a 200 person unit from the UAE, are still part of OEF-Afghanistan. This includes about 500 British special forces, some German special forces, and other special forces units. In early 2010, U.S. Special Forces operating in Afghanistan were brought under direct command of the top U.S. command in Afghanistan, now Gen. Petraeus.

Under OEF, Japan provided naval refueling capabilities in the Arabian sea, but the mission was suspended in October 2007 following a parliamentary change of majority there in July 2007. The mission was revived in January 2008 when the new government forced through parliament a bill to allow the mission to resume. It was renewed again, over substantial parliamentary opposition, in December 2008, but the opposition party won September 2009 elections in Japan and reportedly has decided on an alternative to continuing the refueling mission—by increasing its financial contributions to economic development in Afghanistan. That led to an October 2009 pledge by Japan—already the third largest individual country donor to Afghanistan, providing about $1.9 billion in civilian reconstruction aid since the fall of the Taliban—to provide another $5 billion over five years.

It has been requested to be a major financial donor of an Afghan army expansion, and, in March 2009, it pledged to pay the costs of the Afghan National Police for six months.

As part of OEF outside Afghanistan, the United States leads a multi-national naval anti-terrorist, anti-smuggling, anti-proliferation interdiction mission in the Persian Gulf/Arabian Sea, headquartered in Bahrain. That mission was expanded after the fall of Saddam Hussein to include protecting Iraqi oil platforms in the Gulf.

PROVINCIAL RECONSTRUCTION TEAMS (PRTS)

U.S. and partner officials have generally praised the effectiveness of "Provincial Reconstruction Teams" (PRTs)—enclaves of U.S. or partner forces and civilian officials that provide safe havens for international aid workers to help with reconstruction and to extend the writ of the Kabul government—in accelerating reconstruction and assisting stabilization efforts. The PRTs, announced in December 2002, perform activities ranging from resolving local disputes to coordinating local reconstruction projects, although most U.S.-run PRTs and most PRTs in combat-heavy areas focus mostly on counter-insurgency. Many of the additional U.S. civilian officials deployed to Afghanistan during 2009 and 2010 are based at PRTs, which have facilities, vehicles, and security.

There are 27 PRTs in operation; the list of PRTs, including lead country, is shown in **Table 22**. Virtually all the PRTs are now under the ISAF mission. Each PRT operated by the United States has U.S. forces (50-100 U.S. military personnel); Defense Department civil affairs officers; representatives of USAID, State Department, and other agencies; and Afghan government (Interior Ministry) personnel. Most PRTs, including those run by partner forces, have personnel to train Afghan security forces. USAID officers assigned to the PRTs administer PRT reconstruction projects, although USAID observers say there is little Afghan input, either into project decisionmaking or as contractors for facility and other construction. USAID spending on PRT projects is in the table on USAID spending in Afghanistan at the end of this report, and there is a database on development projects sponsored by each PRT available to CRS, information from which can be provided on request.

In the south, most PRTs are heavily focused on security. In August 2005, in preparation for the establishment of Regional Command South (RC-S), Canada took over the key U.S.-led PRT in Qandahar. In May 2006, Britain took over the PRT at Lashkar Gah, capital of Helmand Province. At the same time, the Netherlands took over the PRT at Tarin Kowt, capital of Uruzgan Province. However, the Tarin Kowt PRT has been led by Australia and the United States since the September 2010 Dutch departure.

Some aid agencies say they have felt more secure since the PRT program began, fostering reconstruction,[56] and many of the new civilian advisers arriving in Afghanistan under the new Obama Administration strategy work out of the PRTs. On the other hand, some relief groups do not want to associate with military forces because doing so might taint their perceived neutrality. Others, such as Oxfam International, argue that the PRTs are delaying the time when the Afghan government has the skills and resources to secure and develop Afghanistan on its own.

Evolving Civil-Military Concepts at the PRTs

Representing evolution of the PRT concept, some donor countries—as well as the United States—are trying to enhance the civilian component of the PRTs and change their image from mainly military institutions. There has been long been consideration to turn over the lead in the U.S.-run PRTs to civilians rather than military personnel, presumably State Department or USAID officials. That was first attempted in 2006 with the establishment of a civilian-led U.S.- run PRT in the Panjshir Valley. As noted, in March 2009, the Netherlands converted its PRT to civilian lead, although that alteration has not continued with the assumption of U.S. and Australian PRT command as of July 2010. Turkey opened a PRT, in Wardak Province, on November 25, 2006, to focus on providing health care, education, police training, and agricultural alternatives in that region.

As of November 2009, the "civilianization" of the PRT concept has evolved further with the decision to refer to PRTs as Interagency Provincial Affairs (IPA) offices or branches. In this new concept—a local paralled to the Senior Civilian Representatives now assigned to each regional command—State Department officers enjoy enhanced decision-making status at each PRT.

AFGHAN NATIONAL SECURITY FORCES

The U.S. "exit strategy" from Afghanistan relies heavily on increasing the capability of the Afghan National Security Forces (ANSF)—the Afghan National Army (ANA) and

Afghan National Policy (ANP)—to the point where they can assume the security mission from the international coalition. Obama Administration strategy emphasizes expanding the ANSF and improving it through partnering and more intense mentoring and training – about 70% of Afghan units are now partnered with international forces.

On January 21, 2010, the joint U.N.-Afghan "Joint Coordination and Monitoring Board" (JCMB) agreed that, by the end of 2011, the ANA would expand to 171,600 and the ANP to about 134,000. As of August 11, 2010, both forces reached their interim size of 134,000 and 109,000 respectively (two months earlier than planned). As of December 2010, the forces total about 145,000 ANA and 115,000 ANP.

U.S. forces along with partner countries and contractors, train the ANSF. In February 2010, the U.S.-run "Combined Security Transition Command-Afghanistan" (CSTC-A) that ran the training was subordinated to the broader NATO Training Mission—Afghanistan (NTM-A). NTM-A is commanded by U.S. Maj. Gen. William Caldwell. CSTC-A's mission was reoriented to building the capacity of the Afghan Defense and Interior Ministries, and to provide resources to the ANSF. The total number of required trainers (U.S. and partner) for these institutions is 4,800. There has been an unfilled gap of trainers totaling about 750, although, as of late 2010, partner countries have pledged those amounts. A separate France-led 300-person European Gendarmerie Force (EGF) has been established to train Afghan forces out in the provinces. The European Union is providing a 190-member "EUPOL" training effort, and 60 other experts to help train the ANP. These efforts are subsumed under NTM-A.

The U.S. police training effort was first led by State Department/INL, but the Defense Department took over the lead in police training in April 2005. Much of the training is still conducted through contracts with DynCorp. In addition to the U.S. effort, which includes 600 civilian U.S. police trainers (mostly still Dyncorp contractors) in addition to the U.S. military personnel (see **Table 5**)

Afghan National Army

The Afghan National Army has been built "from scratch" since 2002—it is not a direct continuation of the national army that existed from the 1880s until the Taliban era. That national army all but disintegrated during the 1992-1996 *mujahedin* civil war and the 1996-2001 Taliban period. However, some Afghan military officers who served prior to the Taliban have joined the new military.

U.S. and allied officers say that the ANA is becoming a major force in stabilizing the country and a national symbol. It now has at least some presence in most of Afghanistan's 34 provinces, working with the PRTs, and it deployed outside Afghanistan to assist relief efforts for victims of the October 2005 Pakistan earthquake. According to the Department of Defense, the ANA is able to lead a growing percentage of all combat operations, but there is substantial skepticism within the U.S. defense establishment that it can assume full security responsibility by 2014, which is the target time frame announced by Karzai. Among examples of the ANA taking overall responsibility, in August 2008, the ANA took over security of Kabul city from Italy, and it took formal control of Kabul Province in early 2009. The commando forces of the ANA, trained by U.S. Special Operations Forces, and numbering about 5,300, are considered well-trained and are taking the lead in some operations against high-value targets, particularly against HIG elements in Nuristan province.

However, some U.S. military assessments say the force remains poorly led. It still suffers from at least a 20% desertion rate. Many officers are illiterate or poorly motivated.[57] Some accounts say that a typical ANA unit is only at about 50% of its authorized strength at any given time, and there are significant shortages in about 40% of equipment items. The high desertion rate complicates U.S.-led efforts to steadily grow the force. Some recruits take long trips to their home towns to remit funds to their families, and often then return to the ANA after a long absence. Others, according to U.S. observers, often refuse to serve far from their home towns. The FY2005 foreign aid appropriation (P.L. 108-447) required that ANA recruits be vetted for terrorism, human rights violations, and drug trafficking.

ANA battalions, or "Kandaks," are the main unit of the Afghan force. There are over 120 Kandaks. The Kandaks are stiffened by the presence of U.S. and partner embeds, called "Operational Mentor and Liaison Teams" (OMLTs). Each OMLT—of which there are about 61— has about 12-19 personnel, and U.S. commanders say that the ANA will continue to need embeds for the short term, because embeds give the units confidence they will be resupplied, reinforced, and evacuated in the event of wounding.

As noted, the Obama Administration strategy is to also partner the ANA with U.S. and other foreign units to enhance effectiveness. Gen. Petraeus and others have attributed the previous lack of progress in the ANSF to the non-systematic use of the partnering concept. Among the other countries contributing training OMLTs (all or in part) are Canada, Croatia, Czech Republic, France, Germany, Italy, the Netherlands, Norway, Poland, Slovenia, Spain, Sweden, Britain, and the United States.

The United States has built five ANA bases: Herat (Corps 207), Gardez (Corps 203), Qandahar (Corps 205), Mazar-e-Sharif (Corps 209), and Kabul (Division HQ, Corps 201, Air Corps). Coalition officers conduct heavy weapons training for a heavy brigade as part of the "Kabul Corps," based in Pol-e-Charki, east of Kabul.

Ethnic and Factional Considerations

At the time the United States first began establishing the ANA, Northern Alliance figures who were then in key security positions weighted recruitment for the national army toward its Tajik ethnic base. Many Pashtuns, in reaction, refused recruitment or left the ANA program. The naming of a Pashtun, Abdul Rahim Wardak, as Defense Minister in December 2004 reduced desertions among Pashtuns (he remains in that position). U.S. officials in Afghanistan say this problem was further alleviated with better pay and more close involvement by U.S. forces, and that the force is ethnically integrated in each unit and representative. With about 41% Pashtuns, 34% Tajiks, 12% Hazaras, and 8% Uzbeks, the force is roughly in line with the broad demographics of the country, according to the April 2010 DOD report. However, U.S. commanders say that those Pashtuns who are in the force are disproportionately eastern Pashtuns (from the Ghilzai tribal confederations) rather than southern Pashtuns (mostly Durrani tribal confederations). The chief of staff was Gen. Bismillah Khan, a Tajik who was a Northern Alliance commander, although as of June 2010 he is Interior Minister.

Afghan Air Force

Equipment, maintenance, and logistical difficulties continue to plague the Afghan National Army Air Corps (Afghan Air Force). The force is a carryover from the Afghan Air Force that existed prior to the Soviet invasion, and is expanding gradually after its equipment was virtually eliminated in the 2001-2002 U.S. combat against the Taliban regime. It now has about over 3,000 personnel, including 400 pilots, as well as a total of about 46 aircraft. Afghan pilots are based at Bagram air base.

The Afghan goal is to have 61 aircraft by 2011, but it remains mostly a support force for ground operations rather than a combat-oriented Air Force. However, the Afghan Air Force has been able to make ANA units nearly self-sufficient in airlift. Afghanistan is seeking the return of 26 aircraft, including some MiG-2s that were flown to safety in Pakistan and Uzbekistan during the past conflicts in Afghanistan. U.S. plans do not include supply of fixed-wing combat aircraft such as F-16s, which Afghanistan wants, according to U.S. military officials. In 2010, Russia and Germany supplied MI-8 helicopters to the Afghan Air Force.

Afghan National Police (ANP)

U.S. and Afghan officials believe that building up a credible and capable national police force is at least as important to combating the insurgency as building the ANA. The April 2010 and November 2010 DOD reports on Afghanistan stability reinforce a widespread consensus that the ANP substantially lags the ANA in its development. Outside assessments are widely disparaging, asserting that there is rampant corruption to the point where citizens mistrust and fear the ANP. Among other criticisms are a desertion rate far higher than that of the ANA; substantial illiteracy; involvement in local factional or ethnic disputes because the ANP works in the communities its personnel come from; and widespread use of drugs. It is this view that has led to consideration of stepped up efforts to promote local security solutions such as those discussed above.

Some U.S. commanders are more positive, saying that it is increasingly successful in repelling Taliban assaults on villages and that is experiencing fewer casualties from attacks than it was previously. Afghan police in Kabul won praise from the U.S. commanders for putting down, largely on their own and without major civilian casualties, the insurgent attack on Kabul locations near the presidential palace on January 18, 2010, and a similar attack on February 26, 2010. Bismillah Khan, the new Interior Minister, was highly respected as ANA chief of staff and has taken new steps to try to improve the police force, including through unannounced visits to ANP bases and stations around the country. Still, some Pashtuns might resent him for his Tajik ethnicity.

Other U.S. commanders credit a November 2009 raise in police salaries (nearly doubled to about $240 per month for service in high combat areas)—and the streamlining and improvement of the payments system for the ANP—with reducing the solicitation of bribes by the ANP. The raise also stimulated an eightfold increase in the number of Afghans seeking to be recruited. Others note the success, thus far, of efforts to pay police directly (and avoid skimming by commanders) through cellphone-based banking relationships (E-Paisa, run by Roshan cell network).

Retraining and Other Initiatives

Some U.S. officials believe that the United States and its partners still have not centered on a clearly effective police training strategy. The latest training reorganization implemented since 2007 is called *"focused district development,"* which attempts to retrain individual police forces in districts, which is the basic geographic area of ANP activity. (There are about 10 "districts" in each of Afghanistan's 34 provinces.) In this program, a district force is taken out and retrained, its duties temporarily performed by more highly trained police (Afghan National Civil Order Police, or ANCOP, which number about 5,800 nationwide), and then reinserted after the training is complete. As of late 2010, police in at least 100 districts have undergone this process, although program success has been hampered by continuing governance and other problems in those districts. There has also been some criticism of the ANCOP performance in Marjah, even though the unit is supposed to be elite and well trained. The ANCOP officers are being used to staff the new checkpoints being set up to better secure Qandahar.

Police training now includes instruction in human rights principles and democratic policing concepts, and the State Department human rights report on Afghanistan, referenced above, says the government and outside observers are increasingly monitoring the police force to prevent abuses. In March 2010, then-Interior Minister Atmar signed a "strategic guidance" document for the ANP, which prioritizes eliminating corruption within the ANP and winning public confidence. About 1,000 ANP are women, demonstrating some commitment to gender integration of the force.

There have been few quick fixes for the chronic shortage of equipment in the ANP. Most police are under-equipped, lacking ammunition and vehicles. In some cases, equipment requisitioned by their commanders is being sold and the funds pocketed by the police officers. These activities contributed to the failure of a 2006 "auxiliary police" effort that attempted to rapidly field large numbers of new ANP officers.

Rule of Law/Criminal Justice Sector

Many experts believe that an effective justice sector is vital to Afghan governance. Some of the criticisms and allegations of corruption at all levels of the Afghan bureaucracy have been discussed throughout this report. U.S. justice sector programs generally focus on promoting rule of law and building capacity of the judicial system, including police training and court construction. The rule of law issue is covered in greater detail in CRS Report R41484, *Afghanistan: U.S. Rule of Law and Justice Sector Assistance*, by Liana Sun Wyler and Kenneth Katzman.

U.S. Security Forces Funding/"CERP"

Because the Afghan government has so few resources, the Afghan security sector is funded almost entirely through international donations. In December 2009, Karzai asserted that the Afghan government could not likely fund its own security forces until 2024. More than half of all U.S. assistance to Afghanistan since 2002 has gone toward building the ANSF. U.S. funds are used to cover ANA salaries as well as to equip and train them. Recent

Afghanistan: Post-Taliban Governance, Security, and U.S. Policy   317

appropriations for the ANA and ANP are contained in the tables at the end of this report, which also contain breakdowns for Commanders Emergency Response Program funds, or CERP, which is used for projects that build goodwill and presumably reduce the threat to use forces. The tables at the end also list breakdowns for requested ANSF funding for FY2011 and supplemental FY2010 funding. As noted in the table, as of FY2005, the security forces funding has been DOD funds, not State Department funds.

Table 5. Major Security-Related Indicators

Force	Current Level
Total Foreign Forces in Afghanistan	About 140.000: About 98,000 U.S. and 41,000 non-U.S. partner forces. (U.S. total was: 25,000 in 2005; 16,000 in 2003; 5,000 in 2002. ISAF totals were: 12,000 in 2005; and 6,000 in 2003.) US. forces deployed at 88 bases in Afghanistan, and include 1 air wing (40 aircraft) and 1 combat aviation brigade (100 aircraft).
U.S. Casualties in Afghanistan	1,337 killed, of which 1,101 by hostile action. Additional 94 U.S. deaths in other OEF theaters, including the Philippines and parts of Africa. Over 315 U.S. killed in 2009-highest yet. 150 U.S. killed from October 2001-January 2003. 45 killed in each of July and August 2009,and 50-55 in each of September and October 2009. At least 25 U.S. killed per month in 2010, with over 60 in each of June and July. Over 300 UK forces killed in Afghanistan to date.
NATO Sectors (Regional Commands-South, east, north, west, and central/Kabul)	RC-S- 35,000 (U.K. lead). RC-Southwest - 27,000 (U.S. lead); RC-E- 32,000 (U.S. lead); RC-N- 11,000 (German lead); RC-W- 6,000 (Italy lead) RC-Kabul-5,000 (Turkey, Afghan lead).
Afghan National Army (ANA)	145,000, more than the interim goal for October 2010. End goal is 171,600 by late 2011. There are 120+ battalions ranging from 300-1,000 soldiers each. About 2,000 trained per month. 5,300 are commando forces, trained by U.S. Special Forces. ANA private paid about $200 per month; generals receive about $750 per month. ANA being outfitted with U.S. M16 rifles and 4,000 up-armored Humvees.
Afghan National Police (ANP)	115,000+, exceeding the interim goal of 109,000 by October 2010. End goal is 134,000 by late 2011. Of the force, 14,000 are border police; 3,800+ counter-narcotics police; 5,300 civil order police.. 1,000+ are female, some serving in very conservative south. Most ANP salaries raised to $240 per month in November 2009, from $120, to counter corruption. Some police paid by E-Paisa system of Roshan cell phone network.
U.S. and Partner Trainers	About 4,000, with target of 4,800.
Legally Armed Fighters disarmed by DDR	63,380; all of the pool identified for the program
Number of Al Qaeda	50-100, according to CIA Director Panetta in June 2010. Also, small numbers of Lashkar-e-Tayyiba, Islamic Movement of Uzbekistan, Pakistan Taliban, others.
Number of Taliban fighters	Over 20,000 (U.S. military and Afghan estimates). Some estimates higher. Plus about 2,500 Haqqani faction and 1,000 Hikmatyar (HIG).
Attacks per day (average)	1,500+ per month in 2010; compared to 800 per month in 2007; 400 in 2005.
Afghan casualties	For extended discussion, see CRS Report R41084, *Afghanistan Casualties: Military Forces and Civilians*, by Susan G. Chesser.

Sources: CRS; testimony and public statements by DOD officials.

International Trust Fund for the ANSF

In 2007, ISAF set up a trust fund for donor contributions to fund the transportation of equipment donated to and the training of the ANSF. U.S. funding for the ANSF is provided separately, not through this fund. The fund is estimated to require $2 billion per year. However, the fund totals only about $145 million coming from several donors, according to the DoD report of November 2010.

However, the fund does not represent the extent of funding for the Afghan forces. Japan, as noted, separately pledged to pay the expenses of the Afghan police for six months (about $125 million).

Law and Order Trust Fund

There is also a separate "Law and Order" Trust Fund for Afghanistan, run by the U.N. Development Program. The fund is used to pay the salaries of the ANP and other police-related functions. Its budget for the two years September 2008 – August 2010 is about $540 million, funded by donors such as Japan (as discussed above). From 2002-2010, donors contributed $1.56 billion to the Fund, of which the United States contributed about $500 million, according to the November 2010 DoD report (p.19).

POLICY ALTERNATIVES/SUPPORT FOR REDUCED U.S. MILITARY INVOLVEMENT

Although the Administration review summarized on December 16, 2010, points to clear positive results, there is growing discussion of alternatives to address the apparent growth of support for efforts to wind down U.S. involvement in Afghanistan. Those who support policy alternatives generally believe that the current Afghanistan effort is unwinnable at acceptable cost, and that it is distracting from other priorities on foreign or domestic policy.[58] Others believe that pursuing the suggested alternatives could lead to a collapse of the Afghan government, and would produce an unraveling of the economic, political, and social gains made through the international military involvement in Afghanistan since 2001.

"Counter-Terrorism" Strategy

During the late 2009 strategy review, some, purportedly including Vice President Joseph Biden, favored a more limited mission for Afghanistan designed solely to disrupt Al Qaeda in Afghanistan and Pakistan. This approach envisioned only a small increase in U.S. or other international forces present in Afghanistan. Advocates of this approach asserted that the government of Afghanistan is not a fully legitimate partner, primarily because of widespread governmental corruption. This strategy was not adopted, in favor of the U.S. "surge" that was authorized. However, as noted above, U.S. commanders say that some of the most effective U.S. operations consist of Special Operations forces tracking and killing selected key mid-level insurgent commanders, even though such operations were not intended to be the centerpiece of U.S. strategy that was decided in 2009. Some of these operations reportedly involve Afghan commandos trained by U.S. Special Forces and the CIA, bearing such names as the "Counterterrorism Pursuit Teams" and the "Paktika Defense Force." Some believe that there could be a decision to pursue this counter-terrorism strategy more directly, and to include raids across the border into Pakistan, as 2011 progresses.

Critics of the limited counter-terrorism strategy express the view that the Afghan government might collapse and Al Qaeda would have safe haven again in Afghanistan if there are insufficient numbers of U.S. forces there to protect the government.[59] Others believed it would be difficult for President Obama to choose a strategy that could jeopardize the stability of the Afghan government, after having defined Afghan security and stability as a key national interest. Still others say that it would be difficult to identify targets to strike with unmanned or manned aircraft unless there were sufficient forces on the ground to identify targets.

Legislative Initiatives: Drawdown Plans

In Congress, some have expressed support for efforts, or planning, to wind down the U.S. involvement in Afghanistan. H.Con.Res. 248, a resolution introduced by Representative Kucinich to require removal of U.S. forces from Afghanistan not later than December 31, 2010, was defeated in the House by a vote of 65 to 356 on March 10, 2010.) Other Members have introduced legislation to require the Administration to develop, by January 1, 2011, plans to wind down the U.S. military presence in Afghanistan. This provision was voted on in consideration of a FY2010 supplemental appropriation (H.R. 4899), where it failed in the Senate (May 27, 2010) by a vote of 18-80. On July 1, 2010, the House voted 162-260 to reject a plan in that bill to require the Administration to submit, by April 4, 2011, a plan and timetable to redeploy from Afghanistan. Earlier, in House consideration of a FY2010 National Defense Authorization Act (H.R. 2647), a similar provision failed on June 25, 2009, by a vote of 138-278.

Concede Parts of Afghanistan to the Taliban

Some experts believe that the Afghanistan conflict is unwinnable and that a preferable strategy would be to work with Pakistan and other regional actors to reach a political settlement relatively favorable to the Taliban. These plans might involve allowing the Taliban to control large parts of the south and east, where the insurgency is most active, and to work with the Northern Alliance to keep other parts of Afghanistan relatively peaceful. Others believe these plans amount to little more than a managed U.S. defeat and that Al Qaeda and other militants would likely take root in Taliban-controlled areas.

REGIONAL DIMENSION

Most of Afghanistan's neighbors believed that the fall of the Taliban would stabilize the region, but Islamist militants have not only continued to challenge the Afghan government but have also battled the government of Pakistan and have conducted acts of terrorism in

India and elsewhere in the region. The Obama Administration announcement of a beginning of a "transition" to Afghan leadership in July 2011 has led some regional powers to plan for what they believe might be a post-U.S. presence scramble for influence in Afghanistan—or at least for the ability to deny their rivals influence there. Iran, which shares with India a fear of any return of radical Taliban extremism in Afghanistan, has begun discussing the future of Afghanistan with other regional countries and, to a lesser extent ,with other international actors in Afghanistan. These maneuverings, to some extent, cast doubt on the commitment of Afghanistan's six neighbors to a non-interference pledge (Kabul Declaration) on December 23, 2002. U.S. officials have sought to enlist both regional and greater international support for Afghanistan through a still expanding 44-nation "International Contact Group."

At the same time, Afghanistan has been re-integrating into regional security and economic organizations that reflect an effort to conduct relatively normal commerce and diplomatic relationships. In November 2005, Afghanistan joined the South Asian Association for Regional Cooperation (SAARC), and Afghanistan has observer status in the Shanghai Cooperation Organization, which is discussed below. Several regional summit meeting series have been established involving Afghanistan, including summit meetings between Afghanistan, Pakistan, and Turkey; and between Iran, Afghanistan, and Pakistan. The fifth of the Turkey-led meetings occurred on December 24, 2010, and resulted in a decision for joint military exercises in March 2011 between Turkey, Afghanistan, and Pakistan, and support from Karzai for the Taliban to set up an office in Istanbul for the purpose of conducting reconciliation talks with his government. Russia has put together two "quadrilateral summits," the latest of which was on August 18, 2010, among Pakistan, Russia, Afghanistan, and Tajikistan, and focused on counter-narcotics and anti-smuggling.

Other regional collaborations include the Regional Economic Cooperation Conference on Afghanistan, which was launched in 2005. Another is a UNAMA-led "Kabul Silk Road" initiative, to promote regional cooperation on Afghanistan. As shown in the table below, cooperation from several of the regional countries are crucial to U.S. and ISAF operations and resupply in Afghanistan.

Pakistan/Pakistan-Afghanistan Border[60]

Pakistan's apparent determination to retain influence over Afghanistan is heavily colored by fears of historic rival India. Pakistan viewed the Taliban regime as providing Pakistan strategic depth against rival India, and Pakistan apparently remains wary that the current Afghan government may come under the sway of India. Numerous militant groups, such as LET (Laskhar-e-Tayyiba, or Army of the Righteous) were formed in Pakistan to challenge India's control of part of the disputed territories of Jammu and Kashmir. Some observers believe Pakistan wants to retain the ability to stoke these militants against India, even though these militants may be aiding Islamist groups challenging Pakistan's stability. Pakistan says India is using its Embassy and four consulates in Afghanistan (Pakistan says India has nine such consulates) to train and recruit anti-Pakistan insurgents, and is using its reconstruction funds to build influence there.

Afghanistan: Post-Taliban Governance, Security, and U.S. Policy

Table 6. Afghan and Regional Facilities Used for Operations in and Supply Lines to Afghanistan

Facility	Use
Bagram Air Base	50 miles north of Kabul, the operational hub of U.S. forces in Afghanistan, and base for CJTF-82. At least 2000 U.S. military personnel are based there. Handles many of the 150+ U.S. aircraft (including helicopters) in country. Hospital constructed, one of the first permanent structures there. FY2005 supplemental (P.L. 109-13) provided about $52 million for various projects to upgrade facilities at Bagram, including a control tower and an operations center, and the FY2006 supplemental appropriation (P.L. 109-234) provided $20 million for military construction there. NATO also using the base and sharing operational costs. Bagram can be accessed directly by U.S. military flights following April 2010 agreement by Kazakhstan to allow overflights of U.S. lethal equipment.
Qandahar Air Field	Just outside Qandahar, the hub of military operations in the south. Turned over from U.S. to NATO/ISAF control in late 2006 in conjunction with NATO assumption of peacekeeping responsibilities. Enhanced (along with other facilities in the south) at cost of $1.3 billion to accommodate influx of U.S combat forces in the south.
Shindand Air Base	In Farah province, about 20 miles from Iran border. Used by U.S. forces and combat aircraft since October 2004, after the dismissal of Herat governor Ismail Khan, who controlled it.
Peter Ganci Base: Manas, Kyrgyzstan	Used by 1,200 U.S. military personnel as well as refueling and cargo aircraft for shipments into Afghanistan. Leadership of Kyrgyzstan changed in April 2005 in an uprising against President Askar Akayev and again in April 2010 against Kurmanbek Bakiyev. Previous Kyrgyz governments demanded the U.S. vacate the base but in both cases, (July 2006 and July 2009) agreement to use the base was extended in exchange for large increase in U.S. payments for its use (to $60 million per year in the latter case). Interim government formed in April 2010 first threatened then retracted eviction of U.S. from the base, but the issue remains subject to decisionmaking by a new government elected in Kyrgyzstan on October 11, 2010. Some questions have arisen in Congress over alleged corruption involving fuel suppliers of U.S. aircraft at the base.
Incirlik Air Base, Turkey	About 2,100 U.S. military personnel there; U.S. aircraft supply U.S. forces in Iraq and Afghanistan. U.S. use repeatedly extended for one year intervals by Turkey.
Al Dhafra, UAE	Air base used by about 1,800 U.S. military personnel, to supply U.S. forces and related transport into Iraq and Afghanistan. Could see increasing use if Manas closes.
Al Udeid Air Base, Qatar	Largest air facility used by U.S. in region. About 5,000 U.S. personnel in Qatar. Houses central air operations coordination center for U.S. missions in Iraq and Afghanistan; also houses CENTCOM forward headquarters. Could see increased use if Manas closes.
Naval Support Facility, Bahrain	U.S. naval command headquarters for OEF anti-smuggling, anti-terrorism, and anti-proliferation naval search missions, and Iraq-related naval operations (oil platform protection) in the Persian Gulf and Arabian Sea. About 5,100 U.S. military personnel there.
Karsi-Khanabad Air Base, Uzbekistan	Not used by U.S. since September 2005 following U.S.-Uzbek dispute over May 2005 Uzbek crackdown on unrest in Andijon. Once housed about 1,750 U.S. military personnel (900 Air Force, 400 Army, and 450 civilian) supplying Afghanistan. Uzbekistan allowed German use of the base temporarily in March 2008, indicating possible healing of the rift. U.S. relations with Uzbekistan improved in 2009, but U.S. officials said in 2010 that the use of the air base is still not under active discussion. Some shipments beginning in February 2009 through Navoi airfield in central Uzbekistan, and U.S. signed agreement with Uzbekistan on April 4, 2009, allowing nonlethal supplies for the Afghanistan war. Goods are shipped to Latvia and Georgia, some transits Russia by rail, then to Uzbekistan.
Tajikistan	Some use of air bases and other facilities by coalition partners, including France, and emergency use by U.S. India also uses bases under separate agreement. New supply lines to Afghanistan established in February 2009 ("northern route") make some use of Tajikistan.
Pakistan	As discussed below, most U.S. supplies flow through Pakistan. Heavy equipment docks in Karachi and is escorted by security contractors to the Khyber Pass crossing.

The Obama Administration strategy reviews in 2009 and 2010 all emphasized the linkage between militants present in Pakistan and the difficulty stabilizing Afghanistan. The December 2010 U.S. policy review says that greater cooperation with Pakistan is necessary to address militant safehavens there, but that denial of safehavens also requires effective development strategies inside Pakistan. Since the late 2009 review, in which the concept of a start of a U.S. drawdown beginning in July 2011 was stated, Pakistan appears to have tried to position a political deal between the Afghan government and the insurgency. It has done so by purportedly protecting certain Afghan militant factions, such as the Haqqani network, that might play a role in a post-settlement Afghanistan. As part of its efforts to engage Karzai on the shape of any conflict-ending settlement, during 2010 there has been a growing pattern of meetings between Karzai and Pakistan's army chief of staff Gen. Ashfaq Kiyani and with the head of Pakistan's Inter Services Intelligence Directorate (ISI), Gen. Ahmad Shuja Pasha. Through meetings such as these, Pakistan has sought to rebut allegations that its Inter Service Intelligence (ISI) directorate is supporting the Haqqani faction and others.[61] It is not certain how Pakistan would react to any U.S. effort to stage ground raids into Pakistan against the Haqqani network or other militants, if there is a U.S. decision to emphasize such operations.

Pakistan has also sought to control Afghanistan's trade, particularly with India, leading to U.S. efforts to persuade Pakistan to forge a "transit trade" agreement with Afghanistan. That effort bore success with the signature of a trade agreement between the two on July 18, 2010, allowing for an easier flow of Afghan products, which are mostly agricultural products that depend on rapid transit. The two are estimated to do about $2 billion in trade per year. The agreement could also represent a success for the Canada-sponsored "Dubai Process" of talks between Afghanistan and Pakistan on modernizing border crossings, new roads, and a comprehensive border management strategy to meet IMF benchmarks. The trade agreement comes after earlier signs of growing cooperation, including Afghan agreement to send more Afghan graduate students to study in Pakistan, and a June 2010 Afghan agreement to send small numbers of ANA officers to undergo training in Pakistan.[62]

Cooperation Against Al Qaeda

During 2001-2006, the Bush Administration praised then President Pervez Musharraf for Pakistani accomplishments against Al Qaeda, including the arrest of over 700 Al Qaeda figures since the September 11 attacks.[63] After the attacks, Pakistan provided the United States with access to Pakistani airspace, some ports, and some airfields for OEF. Others say Musharraf acted against Al Qaeda only when it threatened him directly; for example, after the December 2003 assassination attempts against him. Musharraf resigned in August 2008, and the civilian government is led by the party of the late Pakistani secular leader Benazir Bhutto. Her widower, Asif Ali Zardari, is President.

U.S. criticism of Pakistan's approach increased following a *New York Times* report (February 19, 2007) that Al Qaeda had reestablished some small terrorist training camps in Pakistan, near the Afghan border. This possibly was an outgrowth of a September 5, 2006, compromise between Pakistan and tribal elders in this region. That, and subsequent compromises were criticized, including a 2008 "understanding" with members of the Mehsud tribe, among which is Tehrik-eTaliban (TTP, Pakistan Taliban) leader Baitullah Mehsud (killed in a U.S. strike in August 2009). As noted, the TTP was named a Foreign Terrorist Organization on September 2, and some of its leaders (Hakimullah Mehsud) were named as terrorism supporting entities that day.

Increased Direct U.S. Action[64]

The Obama Administration has tried to combat Afghanistan-focused militants in Pakistan without directly violating Pakistan's restrictions on the U.S. ability to operate "on the ground" in Pakistan. The Obama Administration has significantly increased the use of Predator and Reaper unmanned aircraft to strike militant targets in Pakistan as compared to the Bush Administration. Such a strike reportedly was responsible for the death of Beitullah Mehsud, and some militant websites say the strikes are taking a major toll on their operations and networks. The *New York Times* reported on February 23, 2009, that there are about 70 U.S. military advisers on the ground in Pakistan but they are there to help train Pakistani forces to battle Al Qaeda and Taliban militants. However, a U.S. raid over the border, which killed two Pakistani Frontier Corps soldiers in early October 2010, caused Pakistan to close off for several days the northern border crossing through with much of NATO/ISAF's supplies flow.

Recent History of Pakistan-Afghanistan Relations

The fluctuating nature of Afghanistan-Pakistan relations is not a new feature, and is based on Pakistan's past involvements in Afghanistan's struggles. Afghans fondly remember Pakistan's role as the hub for U.S. backing of the mujahedin that forced the Soviet withdrawal in 1988-89. However, some Afghan leaders resent Pakistan as the most public defender of the Taliban movement when it was in power (Pakistan was one of only three countries to formally recognize it as the legitimate government; Saudi Arabia and the United Arab Emirates are the others).

Since 2008, the end of the Musharraf era, there has been a dramatic improvement in Afghanistan-Pakistan relations. Karzai attended the September 9, 2008, inauguration of Zardari. A "peace *jirga*" process—a series of meetings of notables on each side of the border—was launched at a September 28, 2006, dinner hosted by President Bush for Karzai and Musharraf, and meetings of 700 Pakistani and Afghan tribal elders were held in August 2007 and again in October, 2008. The latter, led on the Afghan side by Dr. Abdullah, and resulted in a declaration to endorse efforts to try to engage militants in both Afghanistan and Pakistan to bring them into the political process. Zardari visited Kabul and met with Karzai on January 9, 2009, where the two signed a joint declaration against terrorism that affects both countries. (A September 2010 meeting between them appeared to be a rededication of this declaration.) Additional progress was made during the visit of Afghan and Pakistani ministers to Washington, DC, during February 23-27, 2009, to participate in the Obama Administration strategic review. As noted above, Karzai and Zardari visit Washington, DC, in May 2009 to continue the strategic dialogue.

In April 2008, in an extension of the Tripartite Commission's work, the three countries agreed to set up five "border coordination centers"—which will include networks of radar nodes to give liaison officers a common view of the border area. These centers build on an agreement in May 2007 to share intelligence on extremists' movements. Three have been established to date, including one near the Torkham Gate at the Khyber Pass, one at Nawa, and one at Liwara. In June 2008, Pakistan ended a six-month suspension in attendance at meetings of the Tripartite Commission under which NATO, Afghan, and Pakistani military leaders meet regularly on both sides of the border.

Regarding the long-term relationship, Pakistan wants the government of Afghanistan to pledge to abide by the "Durand Line," a border agreement reached between Britain (signed by Sir Henry Mortimer Durand) and then Afghan leader Amir Abdul Rahman Khan in 1893, separating Afghanistan from what was then British-controlled India (later Pakistan after the 1947 partition). The border is recognized by the United Nations, but Afghanistan continues to indicate that the border was drawn unfairly to separate Pashtun tribes and should be renegotiated. As of October 2002, about 1.75 million Afghan refugees have returned from Pakistan since the Taliban fell, but as many as 3 million might still remain in Pakistan, and Pakistan says it plans to expel them back into Afghanistan in the near future.

Iran

The Obama Administration initially saw Iran as potentially helpful to its strategy for Afghanistan. Ambassador Holbrooke had advocated a "regional" component of the strategy, which focuses primarily on Pakistan but also envisioned cooperation with Iran on Afghanistan issues. However, as Iran-U.S. relations worsened in 2010 over Iran's nuclear program, the Obama Administration became more critical of Iran's activities in Afghanistan. Still, press reports in September 2010 indicated that the view within the Administration that Iran is key to helping stabilizing Afghanistan may be returning to the forefront. The Administration reported to be considering a U.S.-Iran dialogue in Kabul on Afghan issues.[65] Iran's attendance of the October 18, 2010, International Contact Group" meeting in Rome, including a briefing by Gen. Petraeus, might be an indication of more engagement between Iran and the United States on the Afghanistan issue.

Early in the Administration, Secretary of State Clinton made a point of announcing that Iran would be invited to the U.N.-led meeting on Afghanistan at the Hague on March 31, 2009. At the meeting, Special Representative Holbrooke briefly met the Iranian leader of his delegation to the meeting, and handed him a letter on several outstanding human rights cases involving Iranian-Americans. At the meeting, Iran pledged cooperation on combating Afghan narcotics and in helping economic development in Afghanistan—both policies Iran is already pursuing to a large degree. The United States and Iran took similar positions at a U.N. meeting in Geneva in February 2010 that discussed drug trafficking across the Afghan border. Iran did not attend the January 28, 2010, international meeting in London, but it did attend the July 28, 2010, international meeting in Kabul (both discussed above).

Iranian Material Support to Militants in Afghanistan
A U.S.-Iran dialogue on Afghanistan would presumably be intended to address the U.S. concerns about Iran's support for groups that operate against U.S. forces. Iran may be arming groups in Afghanistan to try to pressure U.S. forces that use Afghanistan's Shindand air base,[66] which Iran fears the United States might use to attack or conduct surveillance against Iran. Or, Iran's policy might be to gain broader leverage against the United States by demonstrating that Iran is in position to cause U.S. combat deaths in Afghanistan. Yet, the Iranian aid is not at a level that would make Iran a major player in the insurgency in Afghanistan. U.S. officials, including Gen. Petraeus in his August 2010 press meetings, has called Iranian influence in Afghanistan, including its support for armed groups, "modest." Others are puzzled by Iran's support of Taliban fighters who are Pashtun, because Iran has traditionally supported Persian-speaking non-Pashtun factions in Afghanistan.

The State Department report on international terrorism for 2009, released August 5, 2010, said the Qods Force of the Revolutionary Guard of Iran continues to provide training to the

Taliban on small unit tactics, small arms, explosives, and indirect weapons fire, as well as ships arms to "selected Taliban members" in Afghanistan. Weapons provided, according to the State Department report, as well as an April 2010 Defense Department report on Iran's military capabilities, include mortars, 107mm rockets, rocket-propelled grenades, and plastic explosives. Some reports, however, say Iran is actively paying Afghan militants to specifically target U.S. forces. On August 3, 2010, the Treasury Department, acting under Executive Order 13224, named two Qods Force officers as terrorism supporting entities (freezing assets in the United States, if any). They are: Hossein Musavi, Commander of the Qods Force Ansar Corps, which is the key Qods unit involved in Afghanistan, and Hasan Mortezavi, who is a Qods officer responsible for providing funds and materiel to the Taliban, according to the Treasury Department. [67]

Bilateral Afghan-Iranian Relations

Iran, like President Karzai, is concerned about how any reduction in U.S. involvement in Afghanistan might improve the prospects for a Taliban return to power. Iran's interest in a broad relationship with Karzai has not, to date, been affected by Iran's continued support for Taliban and other militants in Afghanistan. Aside from its always tense relations with the United States, Iran perceives its key national interests in Afghanistan as exerting its traditional influence over western Afghanistan, which Iran borders and was once part of the Persian empire, and to protect Afghanistan's Shiite and other Persian-speaking minorities. Karzai has, at times, called Iran a "friend" of Afghanistan, and in March 2010 he met with Iranian President Mahmoud Ahmadinejad on two occasions, possibly to signal to the United States that he might realign with regional actors if the United States continues to criticize his leadership. One of the meetings was just after the departure of visiting Defense Secretary Gates. Previously, Karzai received Ahmadinejad in Kabul in August 2007, and he visited Tehran at the end of May 2009 as part of the tripartite diplomatic process between Iran, Pakistan, and Afghanistan. During his visit to the United States in May 2009, Karzai said he had told both the United States and Iran that Afghanistan must not become an arena for the broader competition and disputes between the United States and Iran.[68]

Iran's pledged assistance to Afghanistan has totaled about $1.164 billion since the fall of the Taliban, mainly to build roads, schools, and electricity lines in Herat Province, near the Iranian border.[69] Iranian funds have also been used to construct mosques in the province, as well as pro-Iranian theological seminaries in Shiite districts of Kabul. Iran also offers scholarships to Afghans to study in Iranian universities, and there are consistent allegations that Iran has funded Afghan provincial council and parliamentary candidates who are perceived as pro-Tehran.[70] A controversy arose in late October 2010 when Karzai acknowledged accepting about $2 million per year in cash payments from Iran, via his chief of Staff Mohammad Daudzai. On the other hand, in December 2010, Iran suddenly ceased shipping fuel into Afghanistan, causing some spot dislocations in Afghanistan. The move could have been related to reported shortages of gasoline inside Iran, which are a result of U.S. sanctions imposed on sales of gasoline to Iran in July 2010.

Many Afghans look fondly on Iran for helping them try to oust the Taliban regime when it was in power. Iran saw the Taliban regime, which ruled during 1996-2001, as a threat to its interests in Afghanistan, especially after Taliban forces captured Herat in September 1995. Iran subsequently drew even closer to the ethnic minority-dominated Northern Alliance than previously, providing its groups with fuel, funds, and ammunition.[71] In September 1998,

Iranian and Taliban forces nearly came into direct conflict when Iran discovered that nine of its diplomats were killed in the course of the Taliban's offensive in northern Afghanistan. Iran massed forces at the border and threatened military action, but the crisis cooled without a major clash, possibly out of fear that Pakistan would intervene on behalf of the Taliban. Iran offered search and rescue assistance in Afghanistan during the U.S.-led war to topple the Taliban, and it also allowed U.S. humanitarian aid to the Afghan people to transit Iran. Iran helped construct Afghanistan's first post-Taliban government, in cooperation with the United States—at the December 2001 "Bonn Conference." In February 2002, Iran expelled Karzai-opponent Gulbuddin Hikmatyar, but it did not arrest him. At other times, Afghanistan and Iran have had disputes over Iran's efforts to expel Afghan refugees. About 1.2 million remain, mostly integrated into Iranian society, and a crisis erupted in May 2007 when Iran expelled about 50,000 into Afghanistan. About 300,000 Afghan refugees have returned from Iran since the Taliban fell.

India

The interests and activities of India in Afghanistan are almost the exact reverse of those of Pakistan. India's goal is to deny Pakistan "strategic depth" in Afghanistan, and to deny Pakistan the ability to block India from trade and other connections to Central Asia and beyond. Some believe India is increasingly concerned that any negotiated settlement of the Afghanistan conflict will give Pakistan preponderant influence in Afghanistan, and India, which supported the Northern Alliance against the Taliban in the mid-1990s, is said to be stepping up its contacts with those factions to discuss possible contingencies in the event of an Afghan settlement deal.

Many of the families of Afghan leaders have lived in India at one time or another and, as noted above, Karzai studied there. India saw the Taliban's hosting of Al Qaeda as a major threat to India itself because of Al Qaeda's association with radical Islamic organizations in Pakistan dedicated to ending Indian control of parts of Jammu and Kashmir. Some of these groups have committed major acts of terrorism in India, and there might be connections to the militants who carried out the terrorist attacks in Mumbai in November 2008.

Pakistan accuses India of using its four consulates in Afghanistan (Pakistan says there are nine such consulates) to spread Indian influence in Afghanistan. However, many U.S. observers believe India's role in Afghanistan is constructive, and some would support an Indian decision to deploy more security forces in Afghanistan to protect its construction workers, diplomats, and installations. India reportedly decided in August 2008 to improve security for its officials and workers in Afghanistan, but not to send actual troops there. Yet, Tajikistan, which also supported the mostly Tajik Northern Alliance against the Taliban when it was in power, allows India to use one of its air bases.

India is the fifth-largest single country donor to Afghan reconstruction, funding projects worth over $1.2 billion. Indian officials assert that all their projects are focused on civilian, not military, development and are in line with the development priorities set by the Afghan government. India, along with the Asian Development Bank, financed a $300 million project, mentioned above, to bring electricity from Central Asia to Afghanistan. It has also renovated the well-known Habibia High School in Kabul and committed to a $25 million renovation of Darulaman Palace as the permanent house for Afghanistan's parliament. India financed the construction of a road to the Iranian border in remote Nimruz province, and it is currently constructing the 42 megawatt hydroelectric Selwa Dam in Herat Province at a cost of about $80 million. This will increase electricity availability in the province. India is also helping the IDLG with its efforts to build local governance organizations, and it provides 1,000 scholarships per year for Afghans to undergo higher education in India. Some Afghans want to enlist even more Indian assistance in training Afghan bureaucrats in accounting, forensic accounting, oversight, and other disciplines that will promote transparency in Afghan governance.

Russia, Central Asian States, and China

Some neighboring and nearby states take an active interest not only in Afghan stability, but in the U.S. military posture that supports U.S. operations in Afghanistan. The region to the north of Afghanistan is a growing factor in U.S. efforts to secure new supply lines to Afghanistan. Some of these alternative lines have begun to open, at least to non-lethal supplies.

Russia

Russia wants to reemerge as a great power and to contain U.S. power in Central Asia, including Afghanistan. Its hosting of the "quadrilateral summits"mentioned above, the first in July 2009 and the latest on August 18, 2010, could represent stepped up efforts by Russia to exert influence on the Afghanistan issue. Still, Russia supports U.S. efforts to combat militants in the region who have sometimes posed a threat to Russia itself. Previously, Russia had kept a low profile in the country because it still feels humiliated by its withdrawal in 1989 and senses some Afghan resentment of the Soviet occupation. In November 2010, in its most significant intervention in Afghanistan since its occupation, Russian officers reportedly joined U.S. and Afghan forces attempting to interdict narcotics trafficking in Afghanistan; the move reportedly prompted a complaint by President Karzai because he was not consulted about the inclusion of the Russians. In June 2010, Russia said more economic and social assistance is needed for Afghanistan. Russia reportedly is considering investing $1 billion in Afghanistan to develop its electricity capacity and build out other infrastructure. Since 2002, Russia has been providing some humanitarian aid to Afghanistan.

Russian cooperation is crucial to the U.S. effort in Afghanistan. In February 2009, Russia resumed allowing the United States to ship non-lethal equipment into Afghanistan through Russia (following a suspension in 2008 caused by differences over the Russia-Georgia conflict). In July 2009, following President Obama's visit to Russia, it announced it would allow the transit to Afghanistan of lethal supplies as well. Russia reportedly is being urged by NATO (as evidenced in a visit by NATO Secretary General Anders Fogh Rasmussen to Russia in December 2009) to provide helicopters and spare parts to the Afghan forces (which still make heavy use of Russian-made Hind helicopters) as well as fuel.

During the 1990s, Russia supported the Northern Alliance against the Taliban with some military equipment and technical assistance in order to blunt Islamic militancy emanating from Afghanistan.[72] Although Russia supported the U.S. effort against the Taliban and Al Qaeda in Afghanistan out of fear of Islamic (mainly Chechen) radicals, Russia continues to seek to reduce the U.S. military presence in Central Asia. Russian fears of Islamic activism emanating from Afghanistan may have ebbed since 2002 when Russia killed a Chechen of Arab origin known as "Hattab" (full name is Ibn al-Khattab), who led a militant pro-Al Qaeda Chechen faction. The Taliban government was the only one in the world to recognize Chechnya's independence, and some Chechen fighters fighting alongside Taliban/Al Qaeda forces have been captured or killed.

Central Asian States

These states are becoming increasingly crucial to U.S. strategy in Afghanistan. As discussed in the chart, Uzbekistan, Turkmenistan, Tajikistan and Kazakhstan are pivotal actors in U.S. efforts to secure supply routes into Afghanistan that avoid Pakistan.

During Taliban rule, Russian and Central Asian leaders grew increasingly alarmed that radical Islamic movements were receiving safe haven in Afghanistan. Uzbekistan, in particular, has long asserted that the group Islamic Movement of Uzbekistan (IMU), allegedly responsible for four simultaneous February 1999 bombings in Tashkent that nearly killed President Islam Karimov, is linked to Al Qaeda.[73] One of its leaders, Juma Namangani, reportedly was killed while commanding Taliban/Al Qaeda forces in Konduz in November 2001. Kazakhstan and Kyrgyzstan do not directly border Afghanistan, but IMU guerrillas transited Kyrgyzstan during incursions into Uzbekistan in the late 1990s.

During Taliban rule, Uzbekistan supported Uzbek leader Abdul Rashid Dostam, who was part of that Alliance. It allowed use of Karshi-Khanabad air base by OEF forces from October 2001 until a rift emerged in May 2005 over Uzbekistan's crackdown against riots in Andijon, and U.S.- Uzbek relations remained largely frozen. Uzbekistan's March 2008 agreement with Germany for it to use Karshi-Khanabad air base temporarily, for the first time since the rift in U.S.-Uzbek relations developed in 2005, suggests that U.S.-Uzbek cooperation on Afghanistan and other issues might be rebuilt. Ambassador Holbrooke visited in February 2010, indicating further warming. Renewed U.S. discussions with Uzbekistan apparently bore some fruit with the Uzbek decision in February 2009 to allow the use of Navoi airfield for shipment of U.S./NATO goods into Afghanistan.

Central Asian Activities During Taliban Rule

In 1996, several of the Central Asian states banded together with Russia and China into a regional grouping called the Shanghai Cooperation Organization to discuss the Taliban threat. It includes China, Russia, Uzbekistan, Tajikistan, Kazakhstan, and Kyrgyzstan. Reflecting Russian and Chinese efforts to limit U.S. influence in the region, the group has issued statements, most recently in August 2007, that security should be handled by the countries in the Central Asia region. Despite the Shanghai Cooperation Organization statements, Tajikistan allows access primarily to French combat aircraft, and Kazakhstan allows use of facilities in case of emergency. In April 2010, it also agreed to allow U.S. overflights of lethal military equipment to Afghanistan, allowing the United States to use polar routes to fly materiel directly from the United States to Bagram Airfield. A meeting of the Shanghai Cooperation Organization to discuss Afghanistan was held in Moscow on March 25, 2009, and was observed by a U.S. official, as well as by Iran.

Of the Central Asian states that border Afghanistan, only Turkmenistan chose to seek close relations with the Taliban leadership when it was in power, possibly viewing engagement as a more effective means of preventing spillover of radical Islamic activity from Afghanistan. It saw Taliban control as facilitating construction of a natural gas pipeline from

Turkmenistan through Afghanistan (see below). The September 11 events stoked Turkmenistan's fears of the Taliban and its Al Qaeda guests and the country publicly supported the U.S.-led war. No U.S. forces have been based in Turkmenistan.

China[74]

China's involvement in Afghanistan policy appears to be growing. China reportedly is considering contributing some People's Liberation Army (PLA) forces, possibly in a non-combat role, to helping secure Afghanistan. A communiqué from the Obama visit to China in November 2009 implied a possible larger role for China to help stabilize Afghanistan. In late 2009, China allocated an additional $75 billion in economic aid to Afghanistan, bringing its total to close to $1 billion since 2002. On March 20, 2010, ahead of a visit to China by Karzai, China called for more international support for Afghanistan. During the visit, China stressed that its investments in Afghanistan would continue.

Chinese delegations continue to assess the potential for new investments in such sectors as mining and energy,[75] and a $3.4 billion deal was signed in November 2007 for China Metallurgical Group to develop the Aynak copper mine south of Kabul, and build related infrastructure. The deal represents the largest investment in Afghanistan in history. However, U.S. Embassy officials told CRS in October 2009 that actual work at the mine has been stalled for some time. U.S. forces do not directly protect the project, but U.S. forces are operating in Lowgar province, where the project is located, and provide general stability there. China is also a major contender to develop the Hajji Gak iron ore mine near Kabul.

A major organizer of the Shanghai Cooperation Organization, China has a small border with a sliver of Afghanistan known as the "Wakhan corridor." As noted in the U.N. report on Afghanistan of December 10, 2010, Afghanistan is increasingly involved in Shanghai Cooperation Organization affairs. China had become increasingly concerned about the potential for Al Qaeda to promote Islamic fundamentalism among Muslims in China. In December 2000, sensing China's increasing concern about Taliban policies, a Chinese official delegation met with Mullah Umar. China did not enthusiastically support U.S. military action against the Taliban, possibly because China was wary of a U.S. military buildup nearby. In addition, China has been allied to Pakistan in part to pressure India, a rival of China.

Persian Gulf States: Saudi Arabia and UAE

The Gulf states are, according to Ambassador Holbrooke, a key part of the effort to stabilize Afghanistan. As noted, Ambassador Holbrooke has focused increasing U.S. attention—and has formed a multilateral task force—to try to curb continuing Gulf resident donations to the Taliban in Afghanistan. Holbrooke has said these donations might be a larger source of Taliban funding than is the narcotics trade.

Saudi Arabia has a role to play in Afghanistan in part because, during the Soviet occupation, Saudi Arabia channeled hundreds of millions of dollars to the Afghan resistance, primarily Hikmatyar and Sayyaf. Drawing on its reputed intelligence ties to Afghanistan during that era, Saudi Arabia worked with Taliban leaders to persuade them to suppress anti-Saudi activities by Al Qaeda. Some press reports indicate that, in late 1998, Saudi and Taliban leaders discussed, but did not agree on, a plan for a panel of Saudi and Afghan Islamic scholars to decide bin Laden's fate. A majority of Saudi citizens practice the strict Wahhabi brand of Islam similar to that of the Taliban, and Saudi Arabia was one of three countries to formally recognize the Taliban government. The Taliban initially served Saudi Arabia as a potential counter to Iran, but Iranian-Saudi relations improved after 1997 and balancing Iranian power ebbed as a factor in Saudi policy toward Afghanistan.

Saudi Arabia has played a role as a go-between for negotiations between the Karzai government and "moderate" Taliban figures. This role was recognized at the London conference on January 28, 2010, in which President Karzai stated in his opening speech that he sees a role for Saudi Arabia in helping stabilize Afghanistan. As noted, some reports say that a political settlement might involve Mullah Umar going into exile in Saudi Arabia.

According to U.S. officials, Saudi Arabia cooperated extensively, if not publicly, with OEF. It broke diplomatic relations with the Taliban in late September 2001 and quietly permitted the United States to use a Saudi base for command of U.S. air operations over Afghanistan, but it did not permit U.S. airstrikes from it.

The United Arab Emirates, the third country that recognized the Taliban regime, is emerging as another major donor to Afghanistan. Its troop contribution was discussed under OEF, above. At a donors conference for Afghanistan in June 2008, UAE pledged an additional $250 million for Afghan development, double the $118 million pledged by Saudi Arabia. That brought the UAE contribution to Afghanistan to over $400 million since the fall of the Taliban. Projects funded include housing in Qandahar, roads in Kabul, a hospital in Zabol province, and a university in Khost. There are several daily flights between Kabul and Dubai emirate.

U.S. AND INTERNATIONAL AID TO AFGHANISTAN AND DEVELOPMENT ISSUES

Many experts have long believed that accelerating economic development would do more to improve the security situation—and to eliminate narcotics trafficking—than intensified antiTaliban combat. This belief appears to constitute a major element of Obama Administration strategy. Afghanistan's economy and society are still fragile after decades of warfare that left about 2 million dead, 700,000 widows and orphans, and about 1 million Afghan children who were born and raised in refugee camps outside Afghanistan. More than 3.5 million Afghan refugees have since returned, although a comparable number remain outside Afghanistan. The U.N. High Commission for Refugees (UNHCR) supervises Afghan repatriation and Afghan refugee camps in Pakistan. The literacy rate is very low and Afghanistan lacks a large pool of skilled labor.

U.S. Assistance to Afghanistan

During the 1990s, the United States became the largest single provider of assistance to the Afghan people. During Taliban rule, no U.S. aid went directly to that government; monies were provided through relief organizations. Between 1985 and 1994, the United States had a cross-border aid program for Afghanistan, implemented by USAID personnel based in Pakistan. Citing the difficulty of administering this program, there was no USAID mission for

Afghanistan from the end of FY1994 until the reopening of the U.S. Embassy in Afghanistan in late 2001.

For all of FY2002-FY2009, the United States has provided about $40 billion in assistance, including military "train and equip" for the ANA and ANP (which is about $21 billion of these funds). The Obama Administration request for FY2010 (regular and supplemental) and for FY2011 are in separate tables below. The figures in the tables do not include costs for U.S. combat operations. Including those costs, the United States spent about $105 billion for FY2010 and expects to spend about $120 billion for FY2011. For further information on combat costs, see CRS Report RL33110, *The Cost of Iraq, Afghanistan, and Other Global War on Terror Operations Since 9/11*, by Amy Belasco.

There is also a debate over how aid is distributed. Some of the more stable provinces, such as Bamiyan and Balkh, are complaining that U.S. and international aid is flowing mostly to the restive provinces in an effort to quiet them, and ignoring the needs of poor Afghans in peaceful areas. Later in this report are tables showing U.S. appropriations of assistance to Afghanistan, and **Table 20** lists U.S. spending on all sectors for FY2002-FY2009.

Direct Aid and Budget Support to the Afghan Government

Although the Afghan government has been increasing its revenue (about $1.4 billion for 2010) and is covering about one quarter of its overall budget, USAID provides funding to help the Afghan government meet gaps in its operating budget—both directly and through a U.N.-run multi-donor Afghan Reconstruction Trust Fund (ARTF) account, run by the World Bank. The Obama Administration has requested about $200 million in FY2011 funds to provide direct budget support to Afghan ministries that meet reform benchmarks. Those figures are provided in the U.S. aid tables at the end.

Currently, only about 20% of all donated aid funds disbursed are channeled through the Afghan government. The United States views only four ministries as sufficiently transparent to handle donor funds. However, the Kabul Conference (July 20, 2010) communiqué endorsed a goal of increasing that to about 50%.

Aid Oversight

Still heavily dependent on donors, Karzai has sought to reassure the international donor community by establishing a transparent budget and planning process. Some in Congress want to increase independent oversight of U.S. aid to Afghanistan; the conference report on the FY2008 defense authorization bill (P.L. 110-181) established a "special inspector general" for Afghanistan reconstruction, (SIGAR) modeled on a similar outside auditor for Iraq ("Special Inspector General for Iraq Reconstruction," SIGIR). Funds provided for the SIGAR are in the tables below. On May 30, 2008, Maj. Gen. Arnold Fields (Marine, ret.) was named to the position. He has filed several reports on Afghan reconstruction, which include discussions of SIGAR staffing levels and activities, as well as several specific project audits. However, he acknowledged that criticisms in a July 2010 "peer review" of SIGAR operations by the Inspectors General of several U.S. agencies were valid, attributing many of the shortcomings to slow pace of fully funding his office.[76] One recent SIGAR report noted deficiencies in the ability of the Afghan government's Central Audits Office to monitor how funds are used. Some Members of Congress have criticized the SIGAR for ineffective oversight and have called for his replacement.

Aid Authorization: Afghanistan Freedom Support Act

A key post-Taliban aid authorization bill, S. 2712, the Afghanistan Freedom Support Act (AFSA) of 2002 (P.L. 107-327, December 4, 2002), as amended, authorized about $3.7 billion in U.S. civilian aid for FY2003-FY2006. The law, whose authority has now expired, was intended to create a central source for allocating funds; that aid strategy was not implemented. However, some of the humanitarian, counter-narcotics, and governance assistance targets authorized by the act were met or exceeded by appropriations. No Enterprise Funds authorized by the act have been appropriated. The act authorized the following:

- $60 million in total counter-narcotics assistance ($15 million per year for FY2003-FY2006);
- $30 million in assistance for political development, including national, regional, and local elections ($10 million per year for FY2003-FY2005);
- $80 million total to benefit women and for Afghan human rights oversight ($15 million per year for FY2003-FY2006 for the Afghan Ministry of Women's Affairs, and $5 million per year for FY2003-FY2006 to the Human Rights Commission of Afghanistan);
- $1.7 billion in humanitarian and development aid ($425 million per year for FY2003-FY2006);
- $300 million for an Enterprise Fund;
- $550 million in drawdowns of defense articles and services for Afghanistan and regional militaries. (The original law provided for $300 million in drawdowns. That was increased by subsequent appropriations laws.)

A subsequent law (P.L. 108-458, December 17, 2004), implementing the recommendations of the 9/11 Commission, contained "The Afghanistan Freedom Support Act Amendments of 2004." The subtitle mandated the appointment of a U.S. coordinator of policy on Afghanistan and requires additional Administration reports to Congress.

Afghan Freedom Support Act Reauthorization

In the 110th Congress, H.R. 2446, passed by the House on June 6, 2007 (406-10), would have reauthorized AFSA through FY2010. A version (S. 3531), with fewer provisions than the House bill, was not taken up by the full Senate. AFSA reauthorization was not reintroduced in the 111th Congress. H.R. 2446 would have authorized about $1.7 billion in U.S. economic aid and $320 in military aid (including drawdowns of equipment) per fiscal year. It also would have authorized a pilot program of crop substitution to encourage legitimate alternatives to poppy cultivation; and a cut off of U.S. aid to any Afghan province in which the Administration reports that the leadership of the province is complicit in narcotics trafficking.

Table 7. Major Reporting Requirements

Several provisions require Administration reports on numerous aspects of U.S. strategy, assistance, and related issues:

- P.L. 108-458, The Afghanistan Freedom Support Act Amendments required, through the end of FY2010, an overarching annual report on U.S. strategy in Afghanistan. Other reporting requirements expired, including required reports: (1) on long-term U.S. strategy and progress of reconstruction; (2) on how U.S. assistance is being used; (3) on U.S. efforts to persuade other countries to participate in Afghan peacekeeping; and (4) a joint State and Defense Department report on U.S. counter-narcotics efforts in Afghanistan.
- P.L. 110-181 (Section 1230), FY2008 Defense Authorization Act requires a quarterly DOD report on the security situation in Afghanistan; the first was submitted in June 2008. It is required by that law through FY2011. Section 1231 requires a report on the Afghan National Security Forces through the end of FY2010.
- Section 1229 of the same law requires the quarterly report of the Special Inspector General for Afghanistan Reconstruction (SIGAR).
- P.L. 111-8 (Omnibus Appropriation, explanatory statement) required a State Department report on the use of funds to address the needs of Afghan women and girls (submitted by September 30, 2009).
- P.L. 111-32, FY2009 Supplemental Appropriation (Section 1116), required a White House report, by the time of the FY2011 budget submission, on whether Afghanistan and Pakistan are cooperating with U.S. policy sufficiently to warrant a continuation of Administration policy toward both countries, as well as efforts by these governments to curb corruption, their efforts to develop a counter-insurgency strategy, the level of political consensus in the two countries to confront security challenges, and U.S. government efforts to achieve these objectives. The report was released with a date of September 30, 2010.
- The same law (Section 1117) required a report, by September 23, 2009, on metrics to be used to assess progress on Afghanistan and Pakistan strategy. A progress report measured against those metrics is to be submitted by March 30, 2010, and every six months thereafter, until the end of FY2011.
- Section 1228 of the FY2010 National Defense Authorization Act (P.L. 111-84) required a report, within 120 days, on the Afghan Provincial Protection Program and other local security initiatives. Section 1235 authorized a DOD-funded study of U.S. force levels needed for eastern and southern Afghanistan, and Section 1226 required a Comptroller General report on the U.S. "campaign plan" for the Afghanistan (and Iraq) effort.
- The FY2011 National Defense Authorization Act (H.R. 6523, cleared for the White House) provides for:: (Section 1231) a one year extension – through FY2012 - on the security situation in Afghanistan that was begun in P.L. 11-181: a two year extension (Section 1232) in the reporting requirement – through FY 2012 - on the Afghan National Security Forces; (Section 1535) a report within six months of enactment on U.S. economic strategy for Afghanistan and a plan, to be submitted concurrent with the FY2012 budget submission, to transition the duties of the Task Force for Business and Stability Operations in Afghanistan to the Department of State; and a report by State, DoD, and USAID on the use of contractors in Afghanistan.

International Reconstruction Pledges/National Development Strategy

International (non-U.S.) donors have pledged over $30 billion since the fall of the Taliban. When combined with U.S. aid, this by far exceeds the $27.5 billion for reconstruction identified as required for 2002-2010. The major donors, and their aggregate pledges to date, are listed in Table 8, below. These amounts were pledged, in part, at the following donor conferences: (Tokyo), Berlin (April 2004), Kabul (April 2005), the London conference (February 2006), and the June 12, 2008, conference in Paris, discussed below. The January 28, 2010, London conference resulted in further pledges, as noted above. The Afghanistan Compact leaned toward the view of Afghan leaders that a higher proportion of the aid be channeled through the Afghan government, a policy adopted by the United States.

Among multilateral lending institutions, in May 2002, the World Bank reopened its office in Afghanistan after 20 years. Its projects have been concentrated in the telecommunications and road and sewage sectors. The Asian Development Bank (ADB) has also been playing a major role in Afghanistan. One of its projects in Afghanistan was funding the paving of a road from Qandahar to the border with Pakistan, and as noted above, it is contributing to a project to bring electricity from Central Asia to Afghanistan. On the eve of the London conference on January 28, 2010, the IMF and World Bank announced $1.6 billion in Afghanistan debt relief.

National Solidarity Program

The United States and the Afghan government are also trying to promote local decision making on development. The "National Solidarity Program" (NSD) largely funded by U.S. and other international donors—but implemented by Afghanistan's Ministry of Rural Rehabilitation and Development—seeks to create and empower local governing councils to prioritize local reconstruction projects. It is widely hailed as a highly successful, Afghan-run program. The assistance, channeled through donors, provides block grants of about $60,000 per project to the councils to implement agreed projects, most of which are water projects. The U.S. aid to the program is part of the World Bank-run Afghanistan Reconstruction Trust Fund (ARTF) account.

A FY2009 supplemental request asked about $85 million for the ARTF account, of which much of those funds would be used to fill a $140 million shortfall in the NSP program. P.L. 111-32, the FY2009 supplemental discussed above, earmarks $70 million to defray the shortfall. The FY2010 consolidated appropriation (P.L. 111-117) earmarked another $175 million in ESF for the program. The FY2010 National Defense Authorization Act (P.L. 111-84) authorizes the use of some CERP funds, controlled by the U.S. military, to supplement the funding for the NSP. However, this authorization, if implemented, is likely to incur opposition from some international NGOs who are opposed to combining military action with development work.

Results of U.S. and International Aid in Key Sectors

Efforts to build the legitimate economy are showing some results, by accounts of senior U.S. officials, including expansion of roads and education and health facilities constructed. The following are some key sectors and what has been accomplished with U.S. and international donor funds:

- **Roads.** Road building is considered a U.S. priority and has been USAID's largest project category there, taking up about 25% of USAID spending since the fall of the Taliban. Roads are considered key to enabling Afghan farmers to bring legitimate produce to market in a timely fashion, and former commander of U.S. forces in Afghanistan Gen. Eikenberry (now Ambassador) said "where the roads end, the Taliban begin." The major road, the Ring Road, is nearly all repaved. Among other major projects completed are a road from Qandahar to Tarin Kowt, (Uruzgan province) built by U.S. military personnel, inaugurated in 2005; and a road linking the Panjshir Valley to Kabul. In several provinces, U.S. funds (sometimes CERP funds) are being used to build roads that link up farming communities to the market for their products. Another key priority is building a Khost-Gardez road, under way currently.
- **Bridges.** Afghan officials are said to be optimistic about increased trade with Central Asia now that a new bridge has opened (October 2007) over the Panj River, connecting Afghanistan and Tajikistan. The bridge was built with $33 million in (FY2005) U.S. assistance. The bridge is helping what press reports say is robust reconstruction and economic development in the relatively peaceful and ethnically homogenous province of Panjshir, the political base of the Northern Alliance.
- **Education.** Despite the success in enrolling Afghan children in school since the Taliban era (see statistics above), setbacks have occurred because of Taliban attacks on schools, causing some to close.
- **Health.** The health care sector, as noted by Afghan observers, has made considerable gains in reducing infant mortality and giving about 65% of the population at least some access to health professionals. In addition to U.S. assistance to develop the health sector's capacity, Egypt operates a 65-person field hospital at Bagram Air Base that instructs Afghan physicians. Jordan operates a similar facility in Mazar-e-Sharif.
- **Railways.** Afghanistan does not currently have any functioning railway. However, a railway from Mazar-i-Sharif to the border with Uzbekistan, is now under construction with $165 million from the Asian Development Bank. The rail will eventually link up with Herat and will integrate Afghanistan to the former Soviet railway system in Central Asia, increasing Afghanistan's economic integration in the region.

Electricity Sector

At least 10% of USAID funds for Afghanistan have been spent on power projects, although that percentage is rising in 2010 and 2011. The Afghanistan Compact states that the goal is for electricity to reach 65% of households in urban areas and 25% in rural areas by 2010, a goal that has not been met. However, severe power shortages in Kabul, caused in part by the swelling of Kabul's population to about 3 million, up from half a million when the Taliban was in power, are fewer now than two years ago. Power to the capital has grown due to the Afghan government's agreements with several Central Asian neighbors to import electricity, as well as construction of new substations. Many shops in Kabul are now lit up at night, as observed by CRS in October 2009. Afghanistan has no hydrocarbons energy export industry and a small refining sector that provides some of Afghanistan's needs for gasoline or other fuels. Russia, Kazakhstan, and Uzbekistan are its main fuel suppliers. A major USAID and DOD focus is on power projects in southern Afghanistan. The key longterm project is to expand the capacity of the Kajaki Dam, located in unstable Helmand Province. USAID has allocated about $500 million to restore and expand the capacity of the dam. As of October 2009, two turbines were operating—one was always working, and the second was repaired by USAID contractors. This has doubled electricity production in the south and caused small factories and other businesses to come to flourish. USAID plans to further expand capacity of the dam by installing a third turbine (which there is a berth for but which never had a turbine installed.) In an operation involving 4,000 NATO troops (Operation Ogap Tsuka), components of the third turbine were successfully delivered to the dam in September 2008. It was expected to be operational in mid-late 2009 but technical and security problems, such as inability to secure and build roads leading to the dam, have delayed the project and there is no public estimate as to when the third turbine will be completed. In the interim, the U.S. military and USAID have agreed on a plan to focus on smaller substations and generator projects that can bring more electricity to Qandahar and other places in the south quickly. For this and other power projects, the Administration is requesting legislative authority for an "Infrastructure Fund" to be funded by DOD ($400 million - $600 million in FY2011) but controlled jointly by DOD and USAID.

Solar Power

There is also an apparent increasing emphasis on providing electricity to individual homes and villages through small solar power installations. A contractor to USAID, IRG, is providing small solar powered-electricity generators to homes in several districts of Afghanistan, alleviating the need to connect such homes to the national power grid. However, there are technical drawbacks, including weather-related inconsistency of power supply and the difficulty of powering appliances that require substantial power. The U.S. broadcasting service to Afghanistan, Radio Azadi, run by Radio Free Europe/Radio Liberty, has given out 20,000 solar-powered radios throughout Afghanistan, according to RFE/RL in December 2010.

Agriculture Sector

With about 80% of Afghans living in rural areas, the agriculture sector has always been key to Afghanistan's economy and stability. Ambassador Holbrooke, including in his January 2010 strategy document, has outlined U.S. policy to boost Afghanistan's agriculture sector not only to reduce drug production but also as an engine of economic growth. Prior to the turmoil that engulfed Afghanistan in the late 1970s, Afghanistan was a major exporter of agricultural products.

USAID has spent about 15% of its Afghanistan funds on agriculture (and "alternative livelihoods" to poppy cultivation), and this has helped Afghanistan double its legitimate agricultural output over the past five years. One emerging "success story" is growing Afghan exports of high-quality pomegranate juice called Anar. Other countries are promoting not only pomegranates but also saffron rice and other crops that draw buyers outside Afghanistan. Another emerging success story is Afghanistan's November 2010 start of exports of raisins to Britain.[77] Wheat production was robust in 2009 because of healthy prices for that crop, and Afghanistan is again self-sufficient in wheat production. According to the SRAP January 2010 strategy document reference earlier, 89 U.S. agricultural experts (64 from U.S.

Department of Agriculture and 25 from USAID) are in Afghanistan. Their efforts include providing new funds to buy seeds and agricultural equipment, and to encourage agri-business.

U.S. strategy has addressed not only crop choice but also trying to construct the entirety of the infrastructure needed for a healthy legitimate agriculture sector, including road building, security of the routes to agriculture markets, refrigeration, storage, transit through Pakistan and other transportation of produce, building legitimate sources of financing, and other aspects of the industry. U.S. officials in Kabul say that Pakistan's restrictions on trade between Afghanistan and India have, to date, prevented a rapid expansion of Afghan pomegranate exports to that market. Dubai is another customer for Afghan pomegranate exports. A key breakthrough on this issue was reached with the July 18, 2010, signing of a transit trade agreement between Afghanistan and Pakistan, reportedly brokered by the United States. It will allow for more rapid transit of Afghan and Pakistani trucks through each others' territories, ending a requirement that goods be offloaded at border crossings.

To help Afghanistan develop the agriculture sector, the National Guard from several states (Texas, for example) is deploying "Agribusiness Development Teams" in several provinces to help Afghan farmers with water management, soil enhancement, crop cultivation, and improving the development and marketing of their goods. The timber industry in the northwest is said to be vibrant as well.

Private Sector-Led Development

Some sectors are being developed primarily with private investment funding. There has been substantial new construction, particularly in Kabul, such as the Serena luxury hotel (opened in November 2005); a $25 million Coca Cola bottling factory (opened in September 2006); and numerous apartment complexes, marriage halls, office buildings, and other structures. The bottling factory is located near the Bagrami office park (another private initiative), which includes several other factories. The Serena was built by the Agha Khan foundation, a major investor in Afghanistan; the Agha Khan is a leader of the Isma'ili community, which is prevalent in northern Afghanistan. The foundation has also funded the successful Roshan cellphone company. An arm of the Defense Department, called the Task Force for Business and Stability Operations, headed by deputy undersecretary Paul Brinkley, is attempting to facilitate the investment. Some say that private investment could be healthier if not for the influence exercised over it by various faction leaders and Karzai relatives.

- **Telecommunications and Transportation.** Several Afghan telecommunications firms have been formed, including Afghan Wireless (another cell phone service, which competes with Roshan) and Tolo Television. The 52-year-old national airline, Ariana, is said to be in significant financial trouble due to corruption that has affected its safety ratings and left it unable to service a heavy debt load, but there are new privately run airlines, such as Pamir Air, Safi Air (run by the Safi Group, which has built a modern mall in Kabul), and Kam Air. Major new buildings include several marriage halls in Kabul city, as observed by CRS in October 2009.
- **Mining and Gems**. Afghanistan's mining sector has been largely dormant since the Soviet invasion. Some Afghan leaders complain that not enough has been done to revive such potentially lucrative industries as minerals mining, such as of copper and

lapis lazuli (a stone used in jewelry). The issue became more urgent in June 2010 when a Defense Department development team announced, based on surveys, that Afghanistan may have untapped minerals worth over $1 trillion.[78] Gen. Petraeus, in an interview with NBC News on August 15, 2010, said the amount could be in the "trillion*s*." Among the most valuable are significant reserves of such minerals as lithium in western Afghanistan; lithium is crucial to the new batteries being used to power electric automobiles.

Still, in November 2007, the Afghan government signed a deal with China Metallurgical Group for the company to invest $3.4 billion to develop Afghanistan's Aynak copper field in Lowgar Province. The agreement, viewed as generous to the point where it might not be commercially profitable for China Metallurgical Group, includes construction of two coal-fired electric power plant (one of which will supply more electricity to Kabul city); a freight railway (in conjunction with the Asian Development Bank project above); and a road from the project to Kabul. However, work on the mine reportedly has been slowed by the need to clear mines in the area. On December 14, 2010, with involvement of the DoD Task Force for Business and Stability Operations, 10 outside investors announced $50 million in investment in a gold mine in Baghlan Province. There is another gold mine operating in neighboring Takhar Province. Bids are being accepted for another large mining project, the Haji Gak iron ore mine (which may contain 60 billion tons of iron ore) near Kabul. China Metallurgy, as well as companies from India, are said to be finalists for the project.

- **Hydrocarbons and Pipelines.** As noted, Afghanistan has had virtually no operational hydrocarbon energy sector. However, Afghanistan's prospects in this sector appeared to brighten by the announcement in March 2006 of an estimated 3.6 billion barrels of oil and 36.5 trillion cubic feet of gas reserves. Experts believe these amounts, if proved, could make Afghanistan relatively self-sufficient in energy and able to export energy to its neighbors. In a major development, on December 15, 2010, the Afghan government let a six-month contract to a local firm, Ghazanfar Neft Gas, to collect and market crude oil from the Angot field in northern Afghanistan (part of a field that may contain 80 million barrels of oil), initially producing at the low rate of 800 barrels per day.

However, the sector is expected to expand to more fields in the Amu Darya basin (northern Afghanistan), and a tender will be offered to develop a larger oil field in Balkh Province, estimated to hold 1.8 billion barrels of oil. Separately, USAID is funding a test project to develop gas resources in northern Afghanistan.

TAPI (Turkmenistan-Afghanistan-Pakistan-India) Pipeline Project . Another major energy project remains under consideration. During 1996-1998, the Clinton Administration supported proposed natural gas and oil pipelines through western Afghanistan as an incentive for the warring factions to cooperate. A consortium led by Los Angeles-based Unocal Corporation proposed a $7.5 billion Central Asia Gas Pipeline that would originate in southern Turkmenistan and pass through Afghanistan to Pakistan, with possible extensions into India.[79]

The deterioration in U.S.-Taliban relations after 1998 largely ended hopes for the pipeline projects, but prospects for the project improved in the post-Taliban period. In a summit meeting in late May 2002 between the leaders of Turkmenistan, Afghanistan, and Pakistan, the three countries agreed to revive the project. Sponsors held an inaugural meeting on July 9, 2002, in Turkmenistan, signing a series of preliminary agreements. Turkmenistan's leadership (President Gurbanguly Berdimukhamedov, succeeding the late Saparmurad Niyazov) favors the project as well. Yet another agreement in principle to implement the project was signed among Karzai and other regional leaders on December 12, 2010, in the Turkmenistan capital Ashkabad. Although implementation may still be years away, some U.S. officials view this project as a superior alternative to a proposed gas pipeline from Iran to India, transiting Pakistan. However, no U.S. commitment to help finance the project has been announced.

Trade Initiatives/Reconstruction Opportunity Zones

The United States is trying to build on Afghanistan's post-war economic rebound with trade initiatives. In September 2004, the United States and Afghanistan signed a bilateral trade and investment framework agreement (TIFA). These agreements are generally seen as a prelude to a broader and more complex bilateral free trade agreement, but negotiations on an FTA have not yet begun. On December 13, 2004, the 148 countries of the World Trade Organization voted to start membership talks with Afghanistan. Another initiative supported by the United States is the establishment of joint Afghan-Pakistani "Reconstruction Opportunity Zones" (ROZ's) which would be modeled after "Qualified Industrial Zones" run by Israel and Jordan in which goods produced in the zones receive duty free treatment for import into the United States. For FY2008, $5 million in supplemental funding was requested to support the zones, but P.L. 110-252 did not specifically mention the zones.

Table 8. Major International (Non-U.S.) Pledges to Afghanistan Since January 2002 (as of March 2010; $ in millions)

Japan	6,900
Britain	2,897
World Bank	2,803
Asia Development Bank	2,200
European Commission (EC)	1,768
Netherlands	1,697
Canada	1,479
India	1,200
Iran	1,164
Germany	1,108
Norway	977
Denmark	683
Italy	637
Saudi Arabia	533
Spain	486
Australia	440
Total Non-U.S. Pledges (including donors not listed)	**30,800**

Sources: Special Inspector General for Afghanistan Reconstruction. October 2008 report, p. 140; various press announcements. Figures include funds pledged at April 2009 NATO summit and Japan's October 2009 pledge of $5 billion over the next five years.

Note: This table lists donors pledging over $400 million total.

Bills in the 110th Congress, S. 2776 and H.R. 6387, would have authorized the President to proclaim duty-free treatment for imports from ROZ's to be designated by the President. In the 111th Congress, a version of these bills was introduced (S. 496 and H.R. 1318). President Obama specifically endorsed passage of these bills in his March 2009 strategy announcement. H.R. 1318 was incorporated into H.R. 1886, a Pakistan aid appropriation that is a component of the new U.S. strategy for the region, and the bill was passed by the House on June 11, 2009, and then appended to H.R. 2410. However, another version of the Pakistan aid bill, S. 1707, did not authorize ROZ's; it was passed and became law (P.L. 111-73).

Table 9. U.S. Assistance to Afghanistan, FY1978-FY1998 ($ in millions)

Fiscal Year	Devel. Assist.	Econ. Supp. (ESF)	P.L. 480 (Title I and II)	Military	Other (Incl. Regional Refugee Aid)	Total
1978	4.989	—	5.742	0.269	0.789	11.789
1979	3.074	—	7.195	—	0.347	10.616
1980	—	(Soviet invasion-December 1979)			—	—
1981	—	—	—	—	—	—
1982	—	—	—	—	—	—
1983	—	—	—	—	—	—
1984	—	—	—	—	—	—
1985	3.369	—	—	—	—	3.369
1986	—	—	8.9	—	—	8.9
1987	17.8	12.1	2.6	—	—	32.5
1988	22.5	22.5	29.9	—	—	74.9
1989	22.5	22.5	32.6	—	—	77.6
1990	35.0	35.0	18.1	—	—	88.1
1991	30.0	30.0	20.1	—	—	80.1
1992	25.0	25.0	31.4	—	—	81.4
1993	10.0	10.0	18.0	—	30.2	68.2
1994	3.4	2.0	9.0	—	27.9	42.3
1995	1.8	—	12.4	—	31.6	45.8
1996	—	—	16.1	—	26.4	42.5
1997	—	—	18.0	—	31.9a	49.9
1998	—	—	3.6	—	49.14b	52.74

Source: Department of State.

a Includes $3 million for demining and $1.2 million for counternarcotics.

b Includes $3.3 million in projects targeted for Afghan women and girls, $7 million in earthquake relief aid, 100,000 tons of 416B wheat worth about $15 million, $2 million for demining, and $1.54 for counternarcotics.

Table 10. U.S. Assistance to Afghanistan, FY1999-FY2002
($ in millions)

	FY1999	FY2000	FY2001	FY2002 (Final)
U.S. Department of Agriculture (DOA) and USAID Food For Peace (FFP), via World Food Program(WFP)	42.0 worth of wheat (100,000 metric tons under "416(b)" program.)	68.875 for 165,000 metric tons. (60,000 tons for May 2000 drought relief)	131.1 (300,000 metric tons under P.L. 480, Title II, and 416(b))	198.12 (for food commodities)
State/Bureau of Population, Refugees and Migration (PRM) via UNHCR and ICRC	16.95 for Afghan refugees in Pakistan and Iran, and to assist their repatriation	14.03 for the same purposes	22.03 for similar purposes	136.54 (to U.N. agencies)
State Department/Office of Foreign Disaster Assistance (OFDA)	7.0 to various NGOs to aid Afghans inside Afghanistan	6.68 for drought relief and health, water, and sanitation programs	18.934 for similar programs	113.36 (to various U.N. agencies and NGOs)
State Department/HDP (Humanitarian Demining Program)	2.615	3.0	2.8	7.0 to Halo Trust/other demining
Aid to Afghan Refugees in Pakistan (through various NGOs)	5.44 (2.789 for health, training—Afghan females in Pakistan)	6.169, of which $3.82 went to similar purposes	5.31 for similar purposes	
Counter-Narcotics			1.50	63.0
USAID/Office of Transition Initiatives			0.45 (Afghan women in Pakistan)	24.35 for broadcasting/me dia
Dept. of Defense				50.9 (2.4 million rations)
Foreign Military Financing				57.0 (for Afghan national army)
Anti-Terrorism				36.4
Economic Support Funds (E.S.F)				105.2
Peacekeeping				24.0
Totals	**76.6**	**113.2**	**182.6**	**815.9**

Source: CRS.

Table 11. U.S. Assistance to Afghanistan, FY2003
($ in millions, same acronyms as Table 10)

FY2003 Foreign Aid Appropriations (P.L. 108-7)	
Development/Health	90
P.L. 108-480 Title II (Food Aid)	47
Peacekeeping	10
Disaster Relief	94
ESF	50
Non-Proliferation, De-mining, Anti-Terrorism (NADR)	5
Refugee Relief	55
Afghan National Army (ANA) train and equip (FMF)	21
Total from this law:	372
FY2003 Supplemental (P.L. 108-11)	
Road Construction (ESF, Kabul-Qandahar road)	100
Provincial Reconstruction Teams (ESF)	10
Afghan government support (ESF)	57
ANA train and equip (FMF)	170
Anti-terrorism/de-mining (NADR, some for Karzai protection)	28
Total from this law:	365
Total for FY2003	737

Source: CRS.

Note: Earmarks for programs benefitting women and girls totaled: $65 million. Of that amount, $60 million was earmarked in the supplemental and $5 million in the regular appropriation.

Table 12. U.S. Assistance to Afghanistan, FY2004
($ in millions, same acronyms as previous tables)

Afghan National Police (FMF)	160
Counter-Narcotics	125.52
Afghan National Army (FMF)	719.38
Presidential Protection (NADR)	52.14
DDR Program (disarming militias)	15.42
MANPAD destruction	1.5
Terrorist Interdiction Program	0.41
Border Control (WMD)	0.23
Good Governance Program	113.57
(Elections)	
Rule of Law and Human Rights	29.4
Roads	348.68
Education/Schools	104.11
Health/Clinics	76.85
Power	85.13
PRTs	57.4
CERP (DOD funds to build good will)	39.71
Private Sector Development/Economic Growth	63.46
Water Projects	28.9
Agriculture	50.5
Refugee/IDPs	82.6
Food Assistance	88.25
De-Mining	12.61
State/USAID Program Support	203.02
Total Aid for FY2004	**2,483.2**

Laws Derived: FY2004 supplemental (P.L. 108-106); FY2004 regular appropriation (P.L. 108- 199). Regular appropriation earmarked $5 million for programs benefitting women and girls.

Table 13. U.S. Assistance to Afghanistan, FY2005 ($ in millions)

Afghan National Police (State Dept. funds, FMF, and DOD funds, transition to DOD funds to Afghan security forces	624.46
Counter-Narcotics	775.31
Afghan National Army (State Dept. funds, FMF, and DOD funds)	1,633.24
Presidential (Karzai) Protection (NADR funds)	23.10
DDR	5.0
Detainee Operations	16.9
MANPAD Destruction	0.75
Small Arms Control	3.0
Terrorist Interdiction Program	0.1
Border Control (WMD)	0.85
Good Governance	137.49
Political Competition/Consensus-Building/Election Support	15.75
Rule of Law and Human Rights	20.98
Roads	334.1
Afghan-Tajik (Nizhny Panj) Bridge	33.1
Education/Schools	89.63
Health/Clinics	107.4
Power	222.5
PRTs	97.0
CERP	136.0
Civil Aviation (Kabul International Airport)	25.0
Private Sector Development/Economic Growth	77.43
Water Projects	43.2
Agriculture	74.49
Refugee/IDP Assistance	54.6
Food Assistance (P.L. 480, Title II)	108.6
Demining	23.7
State/USAID Program Support	142.84
Total Aid for FY2005	**4,826.52**

Laws Derived: FY2005 Regular Appropriations (P.L. 108-447); Second FY2005 Supplemental (P.L. 109-13). The regular appropriation earmarked $50 million to be used for programs to benefit women and girls.

Source: CRS.

Note: In FY2005, funds to equip and train the Afghan national security forces was altered from State Department funds (Foreign Military Financing, FMF) to DOD funds.

Table 14. U.S. Assistance to Afghanistan, FY2006 ($ in millions)

Afghan National Police (DOD funds)	1,217.5
Counter-narcotics	419.26
Afghan National Army (DOD funds)	735.98
Presidential (Karzai) protection (NADR funds)	18.17
Detainee Operations	14.13
Small Arms Control	2.84
Terrorist Interdiction	.10
Counter-terrorism Finance	.28
Border Control (WMD)	.40
Bilateral Debt Relief	11.0
Budgetary Support to the Government of Afghanistan	1.69
Good Governance	10.55
Afghanistan Reconstruction Trust Fund	47.5
Political Competition/Consensus Building/Elections	1.35
Civil Society	7.77
Rule of Law and Human Rights	29.95
Roads	235.95
Education/Schools	49.48
Health/Clinics	51.46
Power	61.14
PRTs	20.0
CERP Funds (DOD)	215.0
Private Sector Development/Economic Growth	45.51
Water Projects	.89
Agriculture	26.92
Food Assistance	109.6
De-mining	14.32
Refugee/IDP aid	36.0
State/USAID program support	142.42
Total	**3,527.16**

Laws Derived: FY2006 Regular Foreign Aid Appropriations (P.L. 109-102); FY06 supplemental (P.L. 109-234). The regular appropriation earmarked $50 million for programs to benefit women and girls.

Source: CRS.

Table 15. U.S. Assistance to Afghanistan, FY2007
($ in millions)

Afghan National Police (DOD funds)	2,523.30
Afghan National Army (DOD funds)	4,871.59
Counter-Narcotics	737.15
Presidential (Karzai) Protection (NADR)	19.9
Detainee Operations	12.7
Small Arms Control	1.75
Terrorist Interdiction Program	0.5
Counter-Terrorism Finance	0.4
Border Control (WMD)	0.5
Budget Support to Afghan Government	31.24
Good Governance	107.25
Afghanistan Reconstruction Trust Fund (incl. National Solidarity Program)	63
Political Competition/Election support (ESF)	29.9
Civil Society (ESF)	8.1
Rule of Law/Human Rights (ESF)	65.05
Roads (ESF)	303.1
Education/Schools (ESF)	62.75
Health/Clinics	112.77
Power (ESF)	194.8
PRTs (ESF)	126.1
CERP (DOD funds)	206
Private Sector Development/Economic Growth	70.56
Water Projects (ESF)	2.3
Agriculture (ESF)	67.03
Refugee/IDP Assistance	72.61
Food Assistance	150.9
Demining	27.82
State/USAID Program Support	88.7
Total	**9,984.98**

Laws Derived: Regular Appropriation P.L. 110-5; DOD Appropriation P.L. 109-289; and FY2007 Supplemental Appropriation P.L. 110-28. The regular appropriation earmarked $50 million for programs to benefit women/ girls. Providing ESF in excess of $300 million subject to certification of Afghan cooperation on counter-narcotics.

Sources: CRS; Special Inspector General for Afghanistan Reconstruction, October 2008 report.

Table 16. U.S. Assistance to Afghanistan, FY2008
(appropriated, $ in millions)

Afghan National Army (DOD funds)	1,724.68
Afghan National Police (DOD funds)	1,017.38
Counter-Narcotics (INCLE and DOD funds)	619.47
NADR (Karzai protection)	6.29
Radio Free Afghanistan	3.98
Detainee operations	9.6
Small Arms Control	3.0
Terrorist Interdiction Program	.99
Counter-Terrorism Finance	.60
Border Control (WMD)	.75
Direct Support to Afghan Government	49.61
Good Governance	245.08
Afghanistan Reconstruction Trust Fund (incl. National Solidarity program)	45.0
Election Support	90.0
Civil Society Building	4.01
Rule of Law and Human Rights	125.28
Special Inspector General for Afghanistan Reconstruction (SIGAR)	2.0
Roads	324.18
Education/Schools	99.09
Health/Clinics	114.04
Power (incl. Kajaki Dam rehabilitation work)	236.81
PRT programs	75.06
Economic Growth/Private Sector Development	63.06
Water Projects	16.4q
Agriculture	34.44
Refugee/IDP Assistance	42.1
Food Aid	101.83
De-Mining	15.0
State/USAID Program Support	317.4
Total	**5,656.53**

Appropriations Laws Derived: Regular FY2008 (P.L. 110-161); FY2008 Supplemental (P.L. 110-252). The regular appropriation earmarked $75 million for programs to benefit woman and girls. ESF over $300 million subject to narcotics cooperation certification.

Sources: Special Inspector General Afghanistan Reconstruction, October 2008 report; CRS.

Table 17. U.S. Assistance to Afghanistan, FY2009
($ in millions)

	Regular Appropriation (P.L. 111-8)	Bridge Supplemental (P.L. 110-252)	FY2009 Supplemental (P.L. 111-32)	Total
ANSF Funding		2,000	3,607	5,607
CERP (DOD funds)		683		683
Detainee ops (DOD)		4		4
Counternarcotics (C-N) (DOD)	24	150	57	232
C-N (DEA)	19			19
C-N--Alternative. Livelihoods (INCLE)	100	70	87	257
C-N--Eradication, Interdiction (INCLE)	178	14	17	209
IMET	1.4			1.4
ARTF (Incl. National Solidarity Program)	45	20	85	150
Governance building	100	68	115	283
Civil Society promotion	8	4		12
Election Support	93	56	25	174
Strategic Program Development			50	50
Rule of Law Programs (USAID)	8	15	20	43
Rule of Law (INCLE)	34	55	80	169
Roads (ESF)	74	65		139
Power (ESF)	73	61		134
Agriculture (ESF and DA)	25		85	110
PRTs/Local Governance (ESF)	74	55	159	288
Education	88	6		94
Health	61	27		88
Econ Growth/"Cash for Work"	49	37	220	306
Water, Environment, Victims Comp.	31	3		34
Karzai Protection (NADR)	32		12	44
Food Aid (P.L. 480, Food for Peace)	14	44		58
Migration, Refugee Aid		50	7	57
State Ops/Embassy Construction	308	131	450	889
USAID Programs and Ops	18	2	165	185
State/USAID IG/SIGAR	3	11	7	20
Cultural Exchanges, International Orgs	6	10		16
Totals	**1,463**	**3,640**	**5,248**	**10,352**

Notes: P.L. 111-32 (FY2009 supplemental): provides requested funds, earmarks $70 million for National Solidarity Program; $150 million for women and girls (all of FY2009); ESF over $200 million subject to narcotics certification; 10% of supplemental INCLE subject to certification of Afghan government moves to curb human rights abuses, drug involvement.

Afghanistan: Post-Taliban Governance, Security, and U.S. Policy

Table 18. FY2010 Assistance (Includes Supplemental) ($ in millions)

Afghan Security Forces Funding (DOD funds)	9,162 (6,563 appropriated plus 2,600 supplemental request)
CERP (DOD funds)	1,000
Counternarcotics (DOD)	361
INCLE: all functions: interdiction, rule of law, alternative livelihoods	620 (420 regular approp. plus 200 supplemental request)
IMET	1.5
Global Health/Child Survival	92.3
Afghanistan Reconstruction Trust Fund (Incl. National Solidarity Program) (ESF)	200
Governance building (ESF)	191
Civil Society promotion (ESF)	10
Election Support (ESF)	90
Strategic Program Development (ESF)	100
USAID Rule of Law Programs (ESF)	50
Roads (ESF)	230
Power (ESF)	230
Agriculture (ESF)	230
PRT programs/Local governance (ESF)	251
Education (ESF)	95
Health (ESF)	102
Econ Growth/"Cash for Work" (ESF)	274
Water, Environment, Victim Comp. (ESF)	15
Karzai Protection (NADR)	58
Food Aid (P.L. 480, Food for Peace)	16
Refugees and Migration	11
State Ops/Embassy Construction	697 (486 regular plus 211 supplemental)
Cultural Exchanges	6
SIGAR	37 (23 regular plus 14 supp request)
FY2010 supplemental ESF request (for ESF programs above)	1,576
Total Appropriated (Incl. Supplemental)	15,700
Laws derived: FY2010 foreign aid appropriation in Consolidated Appropriation (P.L. 111-117), which earmarks: $175 million (ESF and INCLE) for programs for women and girls, and $175 million (ESF) for the National Solidarity Program. The FY2010 Defense Appropriation (P.L. 111-118), which cut $900 million from the requested amount for the ANSF (regular defense appropriation). FY2010 supplemental funds appropriated by H.R. 4899 (P.L. 111-212)	

Source: CRS.

Table 19. FY2011 Regular Request ($ in millions)

Program/Area	Request
Afghan National Security Forces (DOD funds)	11,600
CERP	1,100
Economic Support Funds (ESF)	3,316.3
Global Health/ Child Survival	71.1
INCLE	450
Karzai Protection (NADR funds)	69.3
IMET	1.5
State Dept. Operations (not incl. security)	754
SIGAR	35.3
Total	17,398

In FY2011 legislation, on June 30, 2010, the State and Foreign Operations Subcommittee of House Appropriations Committee marked up an aid bill, deferring consideration of much of the Administration request for Afghanistan pending a Committee investigation of allegations of governmental corruption in Afghanistan and of possible diversion of U.S. aid funds by Afghan officials and other elites. The Administration has requested legislation to authorize an "Afghanistan Infrastructure Fund," to contain mostly DOD funds, beginning with $400 million in FY2011, possibly supplemented by an additional $200 million later in the fiscal year. The fund will be used mostly for electricity projects, including an ongoing major electricity project for Qandahar, but could be used for other infrastructure projects later on, such as roads. That was authorized in H.R 6523, the National Defense Authorization Act for FY2011, cleared for the White House.

Table 20. Total Obligations for Major Programs: FY2001-FY2009 ($ millions)

Security Related Programs (mostly DOD funds)	
Afghan National Security Forces	21,297
Counter-Narcotics	3,436
Karzai Protection (NADR funds)	226
DDR (Disarmament, Demobilization, Reintegration of militias)	20.42
Detainee Operations	57.33
MANPAD Destruction (Stingers left over from anti-Soviet war)	2.25
Small Arms Control	10.59
Commander Emergency Response Program (CERP)	1,976
De-Mining Operations (Halo Trust, other contractors)	98.53
International Military Education and Training Funds (IMET)	3
Security Related Programs (mostly DOD funds)	
Humanitarian-Related Programs	
Food Aid (P.L. 480, other aid)	958
Refugee/IDP aid	743
Debt Relief for Afghan government	11
Democracy and Governance Programs (mostly ESF)	
Support for Operations of Afghan Government	80.86
Good Governance (incentives for anti-corruption, anti-narcotics)	1,044
Afghanistan Reconstruction Trust Fund (funds National Solidarity Program)	305.5
Civil Society (programs to improve political awareness and activity)	31.88
Elections Support	600
Rule of Law and Human Rights (USAID and INCLE funds)	552.66
Economic Sector-Related Programs (mostly ESF)	
Roads	1,908
PRT-funded projects (includes local governance as well as economic programs)	698.11
Education (building schools, teacher training)	535.93
Health (clinic-building, medicines)	620.59
Power	934.38
Water (category also includes some funds to compensate Afghan victims/Leahy)	128.02
Agriculture (focused on sustainable crops, not temporary alternatives to poppy)	441
Private Sector Development/Economic Growth (communications, IT, but includes some cash-for-work anti-narcotics programs)	627.52
State Dept. operations/Embassy construction/USAID operations/educational and cultural exchanges/SIGAR operations	2,445
Total (including minor amounts not included in table)	39,730

Table 21. NATO/ISAF Contributing Nations
(As of December 14, 2010; http://www.isaf.nato.int/images/stories/File/Placemats/ 15%20NOV.Placemat%20page1-3.pdf)

NATO Countries		Non-NATO Partners	
Belgium	519	Albania	258
Bulgaria	589	Armenia	40
Canada	2,913	Austria	3
Czech Republic	472	Australia	1,550
NATO Countries		Non-NATO Partners	
Denmark	750	Azerbaijan	94
Estonia	139	Bosnia-Herzegovina	45
France	3,850	Croatia	311
Germany	4,877	Finland	165
Greece	134	Georgia	924
Hungary	522	Ireland	7
Iceland	4	Jordan	0
Italy	3,770	Macedonia	163
Latvia	190	Malaysia	30
Lithuania	179	Mongolia	49
Luxemburg	9	Montenegro	31
Netherlands	190	New Zealand	234
Norway	352	Singapore	38
Poland	2,448	South Korea	246
Portugal	95	Sweden	491
Romania	1,664	Ukraine	17
Slovakia	293	United Arab Emirates	35
Slovenia	80	Tonga	0
Spain	1,505		
Turkey	1,815		
United Kingdom	9,500		
United States	90,000		
Total Listed ISAF: 131,730			

Note: As noted elsewhere in this report, U.S. force totals in Afghanistan are approximately 98,000. Non-U.S. forces in the table total 41,700. In addition, the NATO/ISAF site states that troop numbers in this table are based on broad contribution and do not necessarily reflect the exact numbers on the ground at any one time.

Afghanistan: Post-Taliban Governance, Security, and U.S. Policy

Table 22. Provincial Reconstruction Teams

Location (City)	Province/Command
U.S.-Lead (all under ISAF banner)	
1. Gardez	Paktia Province (RC-East, E)
2. Ghazni	Ghazni (RC-E). with Poland.
3. Jalalabad	Nangarhar (RC-E)
4. Khost	Khost (RC-E)
5. Qalat	Zabol (RC-South, S). with Romania.
6. Asadabad	Kunar (RC-E)
7. Sharana	Paktika (RC-E). with Poland.
8. Mehtarlam	Laghman (RC-E)
9. Jabal o-Saraj	Panjshir Province (RC-E), State Department lead
10. Qala Gush	Nuristan (RC-E)
11. Farah	Farah (RC-SW)
Partner Lead (most under ISAF banner)	
PRT Location Province	Lead Force/Other forces
12. Qandahar Qandahar (RC-S)	Canada (seat of RC-S)
13. Lashkar Gah Helmand (RC-S)	Britain. with Denmark and Estonia
14. Tarin Kowt Uruzgan (RC-S)	Australia (and U.S.) (Replaced Netherlands in August 2010)
15. Herat Herat (RC-W)	Italy (seat of RC-W)
16. Qalah-ye Now Badghis (RC-W)	Spain
17. Mazar-e-Sharif Balkh (RC-N)	Sweden
18. Konduz Konduz (RC-N)	Germany (seat of RC-N)
29. Faizabad Badakhshan (RC-N)	Germany. with Denmark, Czech Rep.
20. Meymaneh Faryab (RC-N)	Norway. with Sweden.
21. Chaghcharan Ghowr (RC-W)	Lithuania. with Denmark, U.S., Iceland
22. Pol-e-Khomri Baghlan (RC-N)	Hungary
23. Bamiyan Bamiyan (RC-E)	New Zealand (not NATO/ISAF).
24. Maidan Shahr Wardak (RC-C)	Turkey
25. Pul-i-Alam Lowgar (RC-E)	Czech Republic
26. Shebergan Jowzjan (RC-N)	Turkey
27. Charikar Parwan (RC-E)	South Korea (Bagram, in Parwan Province, is the base of RC-E)

Note: RC = Regional Command.

Table 23. Major Factions/Leaders in Afghanistan

Party/Leader	Leader	Ideology/ Ethnicity	Regional Base	
Taliban	Mullah (Islamic cleric) Muhammad Umar (still at large possibly in Afghanistan. Umar, born in Tarin Kowt, Uruzgan province, is about 65 years old.	Ultra-orthodox Islamic, Pashtun	Insurgent groups, mostly in the south and east.	
Haqqani Network	Jalaludin and Siraj Haqqani. Allied with Taliban and Al Qaeda. Said to be heavily influenced by elements within Pakistani military intelligence.	Same as above	Paktia, Paktika, Khost, Kabul	
Islamic Society (leader of "Northern Alliance")	Burhannudin Rabbani/ Yunus Qanooni (speaker of lower house)/Muhammad Fahim/Dr. Abdullah Abdullah (Foreign Minister 2001-2006). Ismail Khan, a so-called "warlord," heads faction of the grouping in Herat area. Khan, now Minister of Energy and Water, visited United States in March 2008 to sign USAID grant for energy projects.	Moderate Islamic, mostly Tajik	Much of northern and western Afghanistan, including Kabul	
National Islamic Movement of Afghanistan	Abdul Rashid Dostam. During OEF, impressed U.S. commanders with horse-mounted assaults on Taliban positions at Shulgara Dam, south of Mazar-e-Sharif, leading to the fall of that city and the Taliban's subsequent collapse. Was Karzai rival in October 2004 presidential election, then his top "security adviser."	Secular, Uzbek	Jowzjan, Balkh, Faryab, Sar-i-Pol, and Samangan provinces.	
Hizb-e-Wahdat	Composed of Shiite Hazara tribes from central Afghanistan. Karim Khalili is Vice President, but Mohammad Mohaqiq is Karzai rival in 2004 presidential election and parliament. Generally pro-Iranian. Was part of Rabbani 1992-1996 government, and fought unsuccessfully with Taliban over Bamiyan city. Still revered by Hazara Shiites is the former leader of the group, Abdul Ali Mazari, who was captured and killed by the Taliban in March 1995.	Shiite, Hazara tribes	Bamiyan, Ghazni, Dai Kundi province	
Pashtun Leaders	Various regional governors and local leaders in the east and south; central government led by Hamid Karzai.	Moderate Islamic, Pashtun	Dominant in the south and east	

Table 23. (Continued).

Party/Leader	Leader	Ideology/ Ethnicity	Regional Base	
Hizb-e-Islam Gulbuddin (HIG)	Mujahedin party leader Gulbuddin Hikmatyar. Was part of Soviet-era U.S.-backed "Afghan Interim Government" based in Peshawar, Pakistan. Was nominal "prime minister" in 1992-1996 mujahedin government but never actually took office. Lost power base around Jalalabad to the Taliban in 1994, and fled to Iran before being expelled in 2002. Still allied with Taliban and Al Qaeda in operations east of Kabul, but open to ending militant activity. Leader of a rival Hizb-e-Islam faction, Yunus Khalis, the mentor of Mullah Umar, died July 2006.	Orthodox Islamic, Pashtun	Small groups in Nangarhar, Nuristan, and Kunar provinces	
Islamic Union	Abd-I-Rab Rasul Sayyaf. Islamic conservative, leads a pro-Karzai faction in parliament. Lived many years in and politically close to Saudi Arabia, which shares his "Wahhabi" ideology. During anti-Soviet war, Sayyaf's faction, with Hikmatyar, was a principal recipient of U.S. weaponry. Criticized the U.S.-led war against Saddam Hussein after Iraq's invasion of Kuwait.	orthodox Islamic, Pashtun	Paghman (west of Kabul)	

RESIDUAL ISSUES FROM PAST CONFLICTS

A few issues remain unresolved from Afghanistan's many years of conflict, such as Stinger retrieval and mine eradication.

Stinger Retrieval

Beginning in late 1985 following internal debate, the Reagan Administration provided about 2,000 man-portable "Stinger" anti-aircraft missiles to the *mujahedin* for use against Soviet aircraft. Prior to the U.S.-led ouster of the Taliban, common estimates suggested that 200-300 Stingers remained at large, although more recent estimates put the number below 100.[80] The Stinger issue resurfaced in conjunction with 2001 U.S. war effort, when U.S. pilots reported that the Taliban fired some Stingers at U.S. aircraft during the war. No hits were reported. Any Stingers that survived the anti-Taliban war are likely controlled by Afghans now allied to the United States and presumably pose less of a threat, in part because of the deterioration of the weapons' batteries and other internal components.

In 1992, after the fall of the Russian-backed government of Najibullah, the United States reportedly spent about $10 million to buy the Stingers back, at a premium, from individual *mujahedin* commanders. The *New York Times* reported on July 24, 1993, that the buy back effort failed because the United States was competing with other buyers, including Iran and North Korea, and that the CIA would spend about $55 million in FY1994 in a renewed buy-back effort.

On March 7, 1994, the *Washington Post* reported that the CIA had recovered only a fraction (maybe 50 or 100) of the at-large Stingers. In February 2002, the Afghan government found and returned to the United States "dozens" of Stingers.[81] In late January 2005, Afghan intelligence began a push to buy remaining Stingers back, at a reported cost of $150,000 each.[82]

The danger of these weapons has become apparent on several occasions, although U.S. commanders have not reported any recent active firings of these devices. Iran bought 16 of the missiles in 1987 and fired one against U.S. helicopters; some reportedly were transferred to Lebanese Hizballah. India claimed that it was a Stinger, supplied to Islamic rebels in Kashmir probably by sympathizers in Afghanistan, that shot down an Indian helicopter over Kashmir in May 1999.[83] It was a Soviet-made SA-7 "Strella" man-portable launchers that were fired, allegedly by Al Qaeda, against a U.S. military aircraft in Saudi Arabia in June 2002 and against an Israeli passenger aircraft in Kenya on November 30, 2002. Both missed their targets. SA-7s were discovered in Afghanistan by U.S. forces in December 2002.

Mine Eradication

Land mines laid during the Soviet occupation constitute one of the principal dangers to the Afghan people. The United Nations estimates that 5 million to 7 million mines remain scattered throughout the country, although some estimates are lower. U.N. teams have destroyed one million mines and are now focusing on de-mining priority-use, residential and commercial property, including lands around Kabul. As shown in the U.S. aid table for FY1999-FY2002 (**Table 10**), the U.S. de-mining program was providing about $3 million per year for Afghanistan, and the amount increased to about $7 million in the post-Taliban period. Most of the funds have gone to HALO Trust, a British organization, and the U.N. Mine Action Program for Afghanistan. The Afghanistan Compact adopted in London in February 2006 states that by 2010, the goal should be to reduce the land area of Afghanistan contaminated by mines by 70%.

APPENDIX. U.S. AND INTERNATIONAL SANCTIONS LIFTED

Virtually all U.S. and international sanctions on Afghanistan, some imposed during the Soviet occupation era and others on the Taliban regime, have now been lifted.

- P.L. 108-458 (December 17, 2004, referencing the 9/11 Commission recommendations) repealed bans on aid to Afghanistan outright. On October 7, 1992, President George H.W. Bush had issued Presidential Determination 93-3 that

Afghanistan is no longer a Marxist-Leninist country, but the determination was not implemented before he left office. Had it been implemented, the prohibition on Afghanistan's receiving Export-Import Bank guarantees, insurance, or credits for purchases under Section 8 of the 1986 Export-Import Bank Act, would have been lifted. In addition, Afghanistan would have been able to receive U.S. assistance because the requirement would have been waived that Afghanistan apologize for the 1979 killing in Kabul of U.S. Ambassador to Afghanistan Adolph "Spike" Dubs. (Dubs was kidnapped in Kabul in 1979 and killed when Afghan police stormed the hideout where he was held.)

- U.N. sanctions on the Taliban imposed by Resolution 1267 (October 15, 1999), Resolution 1333 (December 19, 2000), and Resolution 1363 (July 30, 2001) have now been narrowed to penalize only Al Qaeda (by Resolution 1390, January 17, 2002). Resolution 1267 banned flights outside Afghanistan by Ariana, and directed U.N. member states to freeze Taliban assets. Resolution 1333 prohibited the provision of arms or military advice to the Taliban (directed against Pakistan); ordered a reduction of Taliban diplomatic representation abroad; and banned foreign travel by senior Taliban officials. Resolution 1363 provided for monitors in Pakistan to ensure that no weapons or military advice was provided to the Taliban.

- On January 10, 2003, President Bush signed a proclamation making Afghanistan a beneficiary of the Generalized System of Preferences (GSP), eliminating U.S. tariffs on 5,700 Afghan products. Afghanistan had been denied GSP on May 2, 1980, under Executive Order 12204 (45 F.R. 20740).

- On April 24, 1981, controls on U.S. exports to Afghanistan of agricultural products and phosphates were terminated. Such controls were imposed on June 3, 1980, as part of the sanctions against the Soviet Union for the invasion of Afghanistan, under the authority of Sections 5 and 6 of the Export Administration Act of 1979 [P.L. 96-72; 50 U.S.C. app. 2404, app. 2405].

- In mid-1992, the George H.W. Bush Administration determined that Afghanistan no longer had a "Soviet-controlled government." This opened Afghanistan to the use of U.S. funds made available for the U.S. share of U.N. organizations that provide assistance to Afghanistan.

- On March 31, 1993, after the fall of Najibullah in 1992, President Clinton, on national interest grounds, waived restrictions provided for in Section 481 (h) of the Foreign Assistance Act of 1961 mandating sanctions on Afghanistan, including bilateral aid cuts and suspensions, including denial of Ex-Im Bank credits; the casting of negative U.S. votes for multilateral development bank loans; and a non-allocation of a U.S. sugar quota. Discretionary sanctions included denial of GSP; additional duties on exports to the United States; and curtailment of air transportation with the United States. Waivers were also granted in 1994 and, after the fall of the Taliban, by President Bush.

- On May 3, 2002, President Bush restored normal trade treatment to the products of Afghanistan, reversing the February 18, 1986, proclamation by President Reagan (Presidential Proclamation 5437) that suspended most-favored nation (MFN) tariff status for Afghanistan (51 F.R. 4287). The Foreign Assistance Appropriations for FY1986 [Section 552, P.L. 99-190] had authorized the denial of U.S. credits or most-favored-nation (MFN) status for Afghanistan.

- On July 2, 2002, the State Department amended U.S. regulations (22 C.F.R. Part 126) to allow arms sales to the new Afghan government, reversing the June 14, 1996, addition of Afghanistan to the list of countries prohibited from importing U.S. defense articles and services. Arms sales to Afghanistan had also been prohibited during 1997-2002 because Afghanistan had been designated under the Antiterrorism and Effective Death Penalty Act of 1996 (P.L. 104-132) as a state that is not cooperating with U.S. anti-terrorism efforts.
- On July 2, 2002, President Bush formally revoked the July 4, 1999, declaration by President Clinton of a national emergency with respect to Taliban because of its hosting of bin Laden. The Clinton determination and related Executive Order 13129 had blocked Taliban assets and property in the United States, banned U.S. trade with Taliban-controlled areas of Afghanistan, and applied these sanctions to Ariana Afghan Airlines, triggering a blocking of Ariana assets (about $500,000) in the United States and a ban on U.S. citizens' flying on the airline. (The ban on trade with Taliban-controlled territory had essentially ended on January 29, 2002, when the State Department determination that the Taliban controls no territory within Afghanistan.).

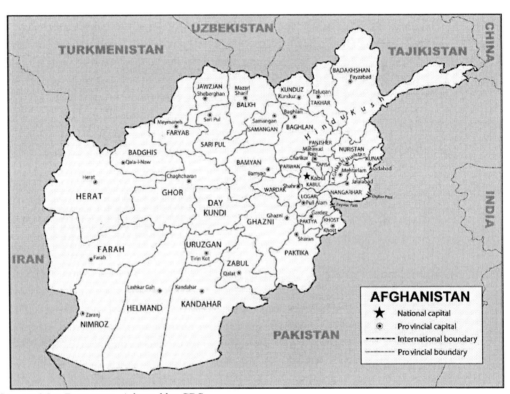

Source: Map Resources. Adapted by CRS.

Figure A-1. Map of Afghanistan.

Afghanistan: Post-Taliban Governance, Security, and U.S. Policy

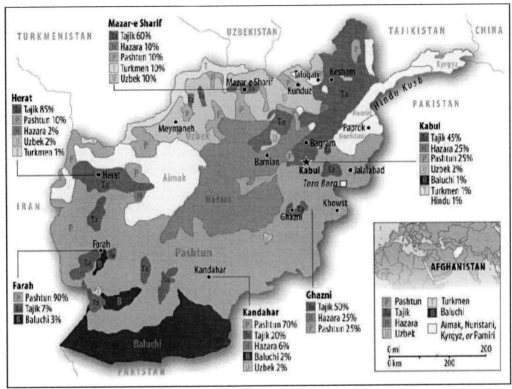

Source: 2003 National Geographic Society. http://www.afghan-network.net/maps/Afghanistan-Map.pdf. Adapted by Amber Wilhelm, CRS Graphics.

Notes: This map is intended to be illustrative of the approximate demographic distribution by region of Afghanistan. CRS has no way to confirm exact population distributions.

Figure A-2. Map of Afghan Ethnicities.

End Notes

[1] Daoud's grave was discovered outside Kabul in early 2008. He was reburied in an official ceremony in Kabul in March 2009.

[2] For FY1991, Congress reportedly cut covert aid appropriations to the *mujahedin* from $300 million the previous year to $250 million, with half the aid withheld until the second half of the fiscal year. See "Country Fact Sheet: Afghanistan," in *U.S. Department of State Dispatch,* vol. 5, no. 23 (June 6, 1994), p. 377.

[3] After failing to flee, Najibullah, his brother, and aides remained at a U.N. facility in Kabul until the Taliban movement seized control in 1996 and hanged them.

[4] The Deobandi school began in 1867 in a seminary in Uttar Pradesh, in British-controlled India, that was set up to train Islamic clerics and to counter the British educational model.

[5] A pharmaceutical plant in Sudan (Al Shifa) believe to be producing chemical weapons for Al Qaeda also was struck that day, although U.S. reviews later corroborated Sudan's assertions that the plant was strictly civilian in nature.

[6] http://www.msnbc.msn.com/id/4540958.

[7] Drogin, Bob. "U.S. Had Plan for Covert Afghan Options Before 9/11." *Los Angeles Times*, May 18, 2002.

[8] Some Afghan sources refer to him by the name "Fahim Khan," or "Marshal Fahim."

[9] Another law (P.L. 107-148) established a "Radio Free Afghanistan" under RFE/RL, providing $17 million in funding for it for FY2002.

[10] In the process, Dostam captured Taliban fighters and imprisoned them in freight containers, causing many to suffocate. They were buried in a mass grave at *Dasht-e-Laili.* This issue is covered in CRS Report RS21922, *Afghanistan: Politics, Elections, and Government Performance*, by Kenneth Katzman.

[11] See also CRS Report RS21922, *Afghanistan: Politics, Elections, and Government Performance*, by Kenneth Katzman.

[12] Text of the released summary is at http://documents.nytimes.com/the-obama-administrations-overview-on-afghanistan-and-pakistan.

[13] A draft of the final communiqué of the Kabul Conference is at http://news.yahoo.com/s/ap/20100720.ap_on_re_as/ as_afghanistan/print.

[14] Text of Bonn agreement at http://www.ag-afghanistan.de/files/petersberg.htm.

[15] The last pre-Karzai *loya jirga* that was widely recognized as legitimate was held in 1964 to ratify a constitution. Najibullah convened a *loya jirga* in 1987 to approve pro-Moscow policies, but that gathering was widely viewed by Afghans as illegitimate.

[16] Text of constitution: http://arabic.cnn.com/afghanistan/ConstitutionAfghanistan.pdf.

[17] Released by the Office of the Special Representative for Afghanistan and Pakistan, January 2010. http://www.state.gov/documents/organization/135728.pdf.

[18] For text, see http://www.state.gov/g/drl/rls/hrrpt/2009/sca/136084.htm.

[19] For a detailed discussion and U.S. funding on the issue, see CRS Report RL32686, *Afghanistan: Narcotics and U.S. Policy*, by Christopher M. Blanchard.

[20] UNDOC. Opium Survey 2010. http://www.unodc.org/documents/crop-monitoring/Afghanistan/Afg_opium_survey_2010_exsum_web.pdf

[21] Crossette, Barbara. "Taliban Seem to Be Making Good on Opium Ban, U.N. Says." *New York Times*, February 7, 2001.

[22] Afghanistan had been so designated every year during 1987-2002.

[23] For a copy of the joint campaign plan, see http://info.publicintelligence.net/0908eikenberryandmcchrystal.pdf.

[24] Some of the information in this section is taken from: Department of Defense. "Report on Progress Toward Security and Stability in Afghanistan." November 2010.

[25] http://www.defense.gov/pubs/November_1230_Report_FINAL.pdf.

[26] http://www.nytimes.com/2010/09/12/world/asia/12afghan.html?_r=1

[27] Maj. Gen. John Campbell, commander of RC-E, July 28, 2010, press briefing.

[28] Filkins, Dexter and Pir Zubair Shah. "After Arrests, Taliban Promote a Fighter." *New York Times*, March 25, 2010.

[29] Ibid.

[30] Text of the Panetta interview with ABC News is at http://abcnews.go.com/print?id=11025299.

[31] Dreazen, Yochi. "Al Qaida Returning to Afghanistan for New Attacks." Nationaljournal.com. October 18, 2010.

[32] Gall, Carlotta and Ismail Khan. "U.S. Drone Attack Missed Zawahiri by Hours." *New York Times*, November 10, 2006.

[33] Mazzzetti, Mark and Dexter Filkins. "U.S. Commanders Push to Expand Raids in Pakistan." *New York Times*, December 21, 2010.

[34] Jane Perlez, Eric Schmitt, and Carlotta Gall, "Pakistan Is Said to Pursue Foothold in Afghanistan," *The New York Times*, June 24, 2010.

[35] "White Paper": http://www.whitehouse.gov/assets/documents/Afghanistan-Pakistan_White_Paper.pdf.

[36] Commander NATO International Security Assistance Force, Afghanistan, and U.S. Forces, Afghanistan. "Commander's Initial Assessment." August 30, 2009, available at http://media.washingtonpost.com/wp-srv/politics/ documents/Assessment_Redacted_092109.pdf?

[37] President Obama speech, op. cit. Testimony of Secretary Gates, Secretary Clinton, and Admiral Mullen before the Senate Armed Services Committee and the House Foreign Affairs Committee. December 2, 2009.

[38] See CRS Report R41084, *Afghanistan Casualties: Military Forces and Civilians*, by Susan G. Chesser.

[39] Commander NATO International Security Assistance Force, Afghanistan, and U.S. Forces, Afghanistan. "Commander's Initial Assessment." August 30, 2009, available at http://media.washingtonpost.com/wp-srv/politics/ documents/Assessment_Redacted_092109.pdf. White House. Remarks by the President In Address to the Nation on the Way Forward in Afghanistan and Pakistan. December 1, 2009; Chandrasekaran, Rajiv. "Differing Views of New Afghanistan Strategy." *Washington Post*, December 26, 2009.

[40] http://www.foreignpolicy.com/articles/2009/09/16/evaluating_progress_in_afghanistan_pakistan.

Afghanistan: Post-Taliban Governance, Security, and U.S. Policy   361

[41] Schmitt, Eric. "White House Is Struggling to Measure Success in Afghanistan". *New York Times*, August 7, 2009. Comments by Ambassador Holbrooke at seminar hosted by the Center for American Progress. August 12, 2009.

[42] Commander NATO International Security Assistance Force, Afghanistan, and U.S. Forces, Afghanistan. "Commander's Initial Assessment." August 30, 2009, available at http://media.washingtonpost.com/wp-srv/politics/ documents/Assessment_Redacted_092109.pdf. White House. Remarks by the President In Address to the Nation on the Way Forward in Afghanistan and Pakistan. December 1, 2009; Chandrasekaran, Rajiv. "Differing Views of New Afghanistan Strategy." *Washington Post*, December 26, 2009.

[43] Holbrooke interview on CNN, March 14, 2010, op. cit.

[44] Nissenbaum, Dion. "Marine Forward Operating Base Marjah Takes Root." McClatchy Newspapers, March 16, 2010.

[45] "U.S. Elite Units Step Up Effort in Afghan City." *New York Times*, April 26, 2010.

[46] Partlow, Joshua. "U.S. Seeks to Bolster Kandahar Governor, Upend Power Balance." *Washington Post*, April 29, 2010.

[47] Afghanistan National Security Council. "Afghanistan Peace and Reintegration Program." April 2010.

[48] See http://afghanistan.hmg.gov.uk/en/conference/contributions/.

[49] For an analysis of the DDR program, see Christian Dennys. *Disarmament, Demobilization and Rearmament?*, June 6, 2005, http://www.jca.apc.org/~jann/Documents/Disarmament%20demobilization%20rearmament.pdf.

[50] Gall, Carlotta. Two Afghans Lose Posts Over Attack. *New York Times*, August 25, 2008.

[51] See http://merln.ndu.edu/archivepdf/afghanistan/WH/20050523-2.pdf.

[52] Twelve other countries provide forces to both OEF and ISAF.

[53] Its mandate was extended until October 13, 2006, by U.N. Security Council Resolution 1623 (September 13, 2005); and until October 13, 2007, by Resolution 1707 (September 12, 2006).

[54] Two were killed during their captivity. The Taliban kidnappers did not get the demanded release of 23 Taliban prisoners held by the Afghan government.

[55] For more information, see http://afghanistan.hmg.gov.uk/en/conference/contributions/.

[56] Kraul, Chris. "U.S. Aid Effort Wins Over Skeptics in Afghanistan." *Los Angeles Times*, April 11, 2003.

[57] Report by Richard Engel. NBC Nightly News. December 29, 2009.

[58] This argument is presented by State Dept. director of Policy Planning during the Bush Administration, now President of the Council on Foreign Relations Richard Haass in July 2010. http://www.newsweek.com/2010/07/18/we-re-notwinning-it-s-not-worth-it.html.

[59] Ibid.

[60] For extensive analysis of U.S. policy toward Pakistan, and U.S. assistance to Pakistan in conjunction with its activities against Al Qaeda and the Taliban, see CRS Report RL33498, *Pakistan-U.S. Relations,* by K. Alan Kronstadt.

[61] Mazzetti, Mark and Eric Schmitt. "CIA Outlines Pakistan Links With Militants." *New York Times*, July 30, 2008.

[62] Partlow, Joshua. "Afghans Build Up Ties With Pakistan." *Washington Post*, July 21, 2010.

[63] Among those captured by Pakistan are top bin Laden aide Abu Zubaydah (captured April 2002); alleged September 11 plotter Ramzi bin Al Shibh (September 11, 2002); top Al Qaeda planner Khalid Shaikh Mohammed (March 2003); and a top planner, Abu Faraj al-Libbi (May 2005).

[64] CRS Report RL34763, *Islamist Militancy in the Pakistan-Afghanistan Border Region and U.S. Policy*, by K. Alan Kronstadt and Kenneth Katzman.

[65] Ignatius, David. "A Chance to Engage Iran?" *Washington Post*, September 17, 2010.

[66] Rashid, Ahmed. "Afghan Neighbors Show Signs of Aiding in Nation's Stability." *Wall Street Journal*, October 18, 2004.

[67] Treasury Department. Fact Sheet: U.S. Treasury Department Targets Iran's Support for Terrorism. August 3, 2010.

[68] Comments by President Karzai at the Brookings Institution. May 5, 2009.

[69] Iranian economic and political influence efforts in Herat were discussed in a CRS visit to Herat in October 2009.

[70] King, Laura. "In Western Afghan City, Iran Makes Itself Felt." *Los Angeles Times*, November 14, 2010.

[71] Steele, Jonathon, "America Includes Iran in Talks on Ending War in Afghanistan." *Washington Times*, December 15, 1997.

[72] Risen, James. "Russians Are Back in Afghanistan, Aiding Rebels." *New York Times*, July 27, 1998.

[73] The IMU was named a foreign terrorist organization by the State Department in September 2000.

[74] For more information, see CRS Report RL33001, *U.S.-China Counterterrorism Cooperation: Issues for U.S. Policy*, by Shirley A. Kan.

[75] CRS conversations with Chinese officials in Beijing. August 2007.

[76] http://www.sigar.mil/pdf/peer_review/Section5.pdf.

[77] Lemmon, Gayle Tzemach. "New Hope for Afghan Raisin Farmers." New York Times, October 9, 2010.

[78] Risen, James. "U.S. Identifies Mineral Riches in Afghanistan." *New York Times*, June 14, 2010.

[79] Other participants in the Unocal consortium include Delta of Saudi Arabia, Hyundai of South Korea, Crescent Steel of Pakistan, Itochu Corporation and INPEX of Japan, and the government of Turkmenistan. Some accounts say Russia's Gazprom would probably receive a stake in the project. *Nezavisimaya Gazeta* (Moscow), October 30, 1997, p. 3.

[80] Saleem, Farrukh. "Where Are the Missing Stinger Missiles? Pakistan," *Friday Times*. August 17-23, 2001.

[81] Fullerton, John. "Afghan Authorities Hand in Stinger Missiles to U.S." Reuters, February 4, 2002.

[82] "Afghanistan Report," Radio Free Europe/Radio Liberty. February 4, 2005.

[83] "U.S.-Made Stinger Missiles—Mobile and Lethal." Reuters, May 28, 1999.

In: The Middle East in Turmoil, Volume 3
Editor: Angela N. Castillo

ISBN: 978-1-61324-241-4
© 2011 Nova Science Publishers, Inc.

Chapter 10

AFGHANISTAN: POLITICS, ELECTIONS, AND GOVERNMENT PERFORMANCE*

Kenneth Katzman

SUMMARY

The limited capacity and widespread corruption of all levels of Afghan governance are growing factors in debate over the effectiveness of U.S. strategy in Afghanistan, as expressed in an Administration assessment of policy released December 16, 2010. A competent, respected, and effective Afghan government is considered a major prerequisite for a transition to Afghan lead that is to take place by 2014, a timeframe agreed by the United States, its international partners, and the Afghan government. Afghan governing capacity has increased significantly since the Taliban regime fell in late 2001, but there is a broad view the Afghan government is ineffective, with many positions unfilled or filled by weak leaders, and that President Hamid Karzai has not moved decisively to reduce corruption. Karzai has agreed to cooperate with U.S.-led efforts to build the capacity of several emerging anti-corruption institutions, but these same institutions have sometimes caused a Karzai backlash when they have targeted his allies or relatives. Some of the effects of corruption burst into public view in August 2010 when major losses were announced by the large Kabul Bank, in part due to large loans to major shareholders, many of whom are close to Karzai. Some in Congress have sought to link further U.S. aid to clearer progress on the corruption issue.

Purportedly suspicious that U.S. and other donors are trying to undermine his leadership, Karzai has strengthened his bonds to ethnic and political faction leaders who undermine rule of law and are often involved in illicit economic activity. These alliances, although a consistent feature of Afghan politics long predating the thirty year period of instability there, compound continuing international concerns about Afghan democracy and political transparency. In the August 20, 2009, presidential election, there were widespread charges of fraud, many substantiated by an Electoral Complaints Commission (ECC). The ECC invalidated nearly one-third of President Karzai's votes, although Karzai's main challenger dropped out of a runoff and Karzai was declared the winner. He subsequently faced opposition to many of his cabinet nominees by the elected lower

---

* This is an edited, reformatted and augmented version of a Congressional Research Services publication, dated December 16, 2010.

house of parliament, and seven permanent ministerial posts remain unfilled. Many of the flaws that plagued the 2009 election recurred in the parliamentary elections held September 18, 2010. The alleged fraud is purportedly being addressed more openly and transparently by Afghan election bodies, but Karzai and his allies appear to be trying to use their institutional powers to alter the results in their favor, provoking a degree of political crisis.

Electoral competition aside, there is growing ethnic and political fragmentation over the terms of a potential settlement to the conflict in Afghanistan. Some leaders of minority communities boycotted a June 2-4, 2010, "consultative peace *jirga* (assembly)" in Kabul that endorsed Karzai's plan to reintegrate into society insurgents willing to end their fight against the government. However, Karzai has named a senior Tajik leader as chair of the 68-member High Peace Council that is to approve any settlement, if one is reached. Women, who have made substantial gains (including appointment to cabinet posts and governorships and election to parliament) fear their rights may be eroded under any "deal" that might erode legal protections for women. For more information, see CRS Report RL30588, *Afghanistan: Post-Taliban Governance, Security, and U.S. Policy*, by Kenneth Katzman; CRS Report R40747, *United Nations Assistance Mission in Afghanistan: Background and Policy Issues*, by Rhoda Margesson; and CRS Report R41484, *Afghanistan: U.S. Rule of Law and Justice Sector Assistance*, by Liana Sun Wyler and Kenneth Katzman.

POST-TALIBAN TRANSITION AND POLITICAL LANDSCAPE

In implementing policy to stabilize Afghanistan, a U.S. policy priority has been to increase the capabilities of and extend the authority of Afghanistan's government. The policy was predicated on the observation that weak governance was causing some Afghans to acquiesce to, or even support, Taliban insurgents as providers of security and traditional justice. Since 2007, in line with those Afghan public perceptions, the U.S. and Afghan focus has been on reforming and reducing corruption within the central government, and on expanding local governance. Then-head of the U.N. Assistance Mission Afghanistan (UNAMA) Kai Eide said in a departing news conference on March 4, 2010, that improving governance and political processes are "indispensable" for resolving the conflict in Afghanistan, and that U.S. and partner efforts have focused too much on military approaches. Eide was succeeded by Staffan de Mistura in March 2010; his substantive position on the issue is similar. Governance issues are discussed in a December 16, 2010, summary of an Administration policy review in the context of U.S. strategy to secure Afghanistan, for which promoting an effective Afghan government is considered key.[1]

Overview of Afghan Politics and Governance

Through differing regimes of widely varying ideologies, Afghanistan's governing structure has historically consisted of weak central government unwilling or unable to enforce significant financial or administrative mandates on the 80% of Afghans who live in rural areas. The tribal, clan, village, and district political structures that provided governance and security until the late 1970s were weakened by decades of subsequent war and Taliban rule. Some traditional local authority figures fled or were killed; others were displaced by *mujahedin* commanders, militia leaders, Taliban militants, and others. These local power brokers, some of whom remain in authority informally, are widely accused of selectively applying Afghan law and have resisted ceding any influence. In other cases, traditional tribal councils have remained intact, and continue to exercise their writ rather than accept the authority of local government. Still other community authorities prefer to accommodate local insurgent commanders (whom they see as wayward but not irreconcilable members of the community) rather than help the government secure their areas.

At the national level, Afghanistan had few, if any, Western-style democratic institutions prior to the international intervention that took place after the September 11, 2001, attacks on the United States. Karzai is the first directly elected president in Afghan history. There were parliamentary elections during the reign of King Zahir Shah (the last were in 1969, before his reign was ended in a 1973 military coup), but the parliament during that era was not the check on presidential power that the post-Taliban National Assembly has. The elected institutions and the 2004 adoption of a constitution were part of a post-Taliban transition roadmap established by a United Nations-sponsored agreement of major Afghan factions signed in Bonn, Germany, on December 5, 2001, ("Bonn Agreement"),[2] after the Taliban had fallen. The political transition process is depicted in Table 1.

Some believe that the elements of Western-style democracy introduced since 2001 are supported by traditional Afghan patterns of decision making that have some democratic and representative elements. On the other hand, some see the traditional patterns as competing mechanisms that resist change and modernization, generally minimize the role of women, and do not meet international standards of democratic governance. At the national level, the convening of a *loya jirga*, or traditional Afghan assembly consisting of about 1,500 delegates from all over Afghanistan, has been used on several occasions. In the post-Taliban period, *loya jirgas* have been convened to endorse Karzai's leadership, to adopt a constitution, and to back long-term defense relations with the United States. A major *peace jirga* was held on June 2-4, 2010, to review government plans to offer incentives for insurgent fighters to end their armed struggle and rejoin society. At the local level, *shuras*, or *jirgas* (consultative councils)[3] composed of local notables, are key mechanisms for making authoritative community decisions or dispensing justice. Some of these mechanisms are practiced by Taliban members in areas under their control.

Affiliations Based on Ethnicity, Tribal, and Personal Relations

Patterns of political affiliation by family, clan, tribe, village, ethnicity, region, and other relationships remain. These patterns were evident in the August 20, 2009, presidential campaign in Afghanistan. Many presidential candidates, Karzai included, pursued campaign strategies designed primarily to assemble blocs of ethnic and geographic votes, rather than advance specific new ideas. These patterns were more pronounced in campaigns for the provincial councils, which were elected concurrently, and appear to have been evident again in the September 18, 2010, parliamentary election. In these cases, electorates (the eligible voters of a specific province) are small and candidates can easily appeal to clan and familial relationships.

While Afghans continue to follow traditional patterns of affiliation, there has been a sense among Afghans that their country now welcomes members of all political and ethnic groups and factions. There have been very few incidents of ethnic-based violence since the fall of the Taliban, but jealousies over relative economic and political positions of the different ethnic communities have sporadically manifested as clashes or political disputes.

Ethnic Pashtuns (sometimes referred to as Pathans—pronounced pah-TAHNS), as the largest single ethnicity, have historically asserted a right to rule. Pashtuns are about 42% of the population and, with few exceptions, have governed Afghanistan. The sentiment of the "right to lead" is particularly strong among Pashtuns of the Durrani tribal confederation, which predominates in the south and is a rival to the Ghilzai confederation, which predominates in the east. One recent exception was the 1992-1996 presidency of the *mujahedin* government of Burhanuddin Rabbani, a Tajik. Karzai is a Durrani Pashtun, and his cabinet and inner advisory circle has come to be progressively dominated by Pashtuns and to exclude members of the other communities. The Taliban government was and its insurgency is composed almost completely of Pashtuns, although there have been non-Pashtun rebel factions with given names such as "Tajik Taliban" to denote that they are working against the Karzai government. A table on major Pashtun clans is provided below (see Table 2), as is a map showing the distribution of Afghanistan's various ethnicities (see Figure 1).

The Ethnic Politics of the Security Sector/Security Issues

Although they largely concede Pashtun rule, non-Pashtuns want to be and are represented at high levels of the central government. Non-Pashtuns also have achieved a large measure of control over how government programs are implemented in their geographic regions. The security organs are considered an arena where Pashtuns and Tajiks have worked together relatively well. The National Directorate for Security (NDS, the intelligence directorate) was headed by a nonPashtun (Amrollah Saleh, a Tajik) during 2006-2010, although he was dismissed on June 6, 2010, by Karzai for disagreements over whether and how to engage insurgent leaders in political settlement negotiations. He was replaced by a Pashtun, Rehmat Nabil, who has no previous intelligence experience but is perceived as more consultative than was Saleh. Still, he inherited a service dominated by Tajiks (although some left when Saleh was ousted) and by a mix of personnel that served during the Soviet occupation era (the service was then called Khad), and in the *mujahedin* government of 1992-1996, as well as more recent recruits. During 2002-2007, the Central Intelligence Agency reportedly paid for all of the NDS budget.[4]

Perhaps to restore the tradition of ethnic balance in the security sector of government, the chief of staff of the Afghan National Army, Bismillah Khan (a Tajik), was named interior minister on June 26, 2010. He replaced Mohammad Hanif Atmar, a Pashtun, who was fired the same day and on roughly the same grounds as Saleh. By all accounts, Khan is widely respected, even among Pashtuns. The security ministries tend to have key deputies who are of a different ethnicity than the minister or top official.

There is a National Security Council that is located in the palace complex and advises Karzai. As of February 2010, it has been headed by former Foreign Minister Rangin Spanta, a Pashtun who was in the government during the Soviet occupation era and is said to retain leftwing views. The NSC is dominated by Pashtuns; two high officials trusted by Karzai there are Ibrahim Spinzadeh, first deputy NSC adviser, and Shaida Mohammad Abdali, the second deputy NSC adviser (both are Pashtuns).

Karzai's chief of staff is Mohammad Umar Daudzai, who is considered an Islamic conservative. During the anti-Soviet war, he fought in the Pashtun Islamist faction of Gulbuddin Hikmatyar. Daudzai is said to be a skeptic of Western/U.S. influence over Afghan decision making. On October 23, 2010, the *New York Times* asserted that he has been the presidential office's liaison with Iran for accepting the approximately $2 million per year in Iranian assistance that is provided as cash. Karzai acknowledged this financial arrangement.

Some observers take a different view, asserting that Tajiks continue to control many of the command ranks of the Afghan security institutions, giving Pashtuns only a veneer of control of these organizations. U.S. commanders in Afghanistan say the composition of the national security forces—primarily the Afghan National Army and Afghan National Police—has recently been brought more into line with the population, although Pashtuns from the south (Durranis) remain underrepresented.

Others believe that ethnic differences may be on the verge of erupting over a key security issue— Karzai's plan to try to induce both low-level and leading insurgent figures to end their fight and rejoin society (reintegration and reconciliation), perhaps even in prominent posts. Tajik leaders, in particular, as the most prominent group after the Pashtuns, fear that Karzai's plans will increase the Pashtun predominance in government and lead to marginalization of the Tajiks and other nonPashtun minorities. They also assert—and ousted NDS chief Saleh has reportedly been giving speeches in Afghanistan and the West making this point extensively—that Karzai is willing to accept undue influence from Pakistan. In part to mollify this ethnic unrest on this issue, in September 2010 Karzai appointed a 68-member broad based High Peace Council that would oversee any negotiations with Taliban leaders. Former President Burhanuddin Rabbani, the most senior Tajik faction leader, was appointed Council chairman on October 10, 2010.

Pakistan supports Afghanistan's Pashtun community, and purportedly wants some insurgent factions to come into a post-settlement government. The growing rift over the reconciliation issue has alarmed Pakistan's rival India and, to a lesser extent, Iran, who traditionally support the Tajik, Uzbek, and Hazara communities and see Afghanistan's Pashtuns as surrogates of Pakistan. (For more information on the topic of reconciliation talks with insurgent leaders, see CRS Report RL30588, *Afghanistan: Post-Taliban Governance, Security, and U.S. Policy*, by Kenneth Katzman.)

Lack of Affiliation by Party
The major factions in Afghanistan identify only loosely with Afghanistan's 110 registered political parties. There is a popular aversion to formal "parties" as historically tools of neighboring powers—a perception stemming from the war against the Soviet Union when seven *mujahedin* parties were funded by and considered tools of outside parties. Partly because parties are viewed with suspicion, Karzai has not formed his own party, but many of his supporters in the National Assembly belong to a moderate faction of Hezb-i-Islam that is committed to working within the political system. This grouping was reduced somewhat in the September 2010 parliamentary elections. The putative leader of this group is Minister of Economy Abdul Hadi Arghandiwal. Other large parties that do exist, for example the Junbush Melli of Abdul Rashid Dostam, tend to be identified with specific ethnic (in his case, Uzbeks) or sectarian factions, rather than overarching themes.

Some believe that Afghan political parties are weak because the Single, Non-Transferable Vote (SNTV) system—in which each voter casts a ballot for only one candidate—favors candidates running as independents rather than as members of parties. Moreover, Western-style parties are generally identified by specific ideologies, ideas, or ideals, while most Afghans, as discussed above, retain their traditional affiliations.

Politics: Karzai, His Allies, and His Opponents

In post-Taliban Afghanistan, the National Assembly (parliament)—particularly the 249-seat elected lower house (*Wolesi Jirga,* House of the People)—has been the key institution for non-Pashtuns and political independents to exert influence on Karzai. The process of confirming Karzai's second-term cabinet—in which many of Karzai's nominees were voted down in several nomination rounds—demonstrates that the Assembly is an increasingly strong institution that is pressing for honest, competent governance. These principles are advocated most stridently, although not exclusively, by the younger, more technocratic independent bloc in the lower house. These independents were key to the lower house vote on March 31, 2010, to reject an election decree that structured the September 18, 2010, National Assembly elections.

This institutional development has come despite the fact that at least one-third of the seats in the lower house, including the newly elected lower house (according to official results released November 24, 2010), are held by personalities and factions prominent in Afghanistan's recent wars. Karzai and his allies were hoping that the September 18, 2010, parliamentary elections would produce an increase in pro-Karzai members. Both houses of parliament, whose budgets are controlled by the Ministry of Finance, are staffed by about 275 Afghans, reporting to a "secretariat." There are 18 oversight committees, a research unit, and a library.

Pro-Karzai Factions in the Parliament

Karzai's core supporters in the outgoing *Wolesi Jirga*, which he and his aides hoped to increase in the September 18, 2010, elections, have been about 50 former members of the conservative Pashtun-based Hizb-e-Islam party (the same party as that headed by insurgent leader Gulbuddin Hikmatyar); and supporters of Abd-i-Rab Rasul Sayyaf—a prominent Islamic conservative *mujahedin* era party leader.[5] Karzai's allies reportedly hope that they would win enough additional seats in the September 18 election to enable Sayyaf to become lower house Speaker, displacing Yunus Qanooni (Tajik); see below. However, it appears, according to November 24, 2010, final results, that pro-Karzai deputies are fewer than in the previous Assembly.

A major base of Karzai's support has been from Qandahar, Karzai's home province, and from Helmand provinces. These have included several Karzai clan members, most of whom were not returned to parliament by the September 18 elections (final results of November 24). One proKarzai Pashtuns in the last parliament was former militia and Taliban leaders, including Hazrat Ali (Nangarhar Province), who led the Afghan component of the failed assault on Osama bin Laden's purported redoubt at Tora Bora in December 2001. Others were Pacha Khan Zadran (Paktia) who, by some accounts, helped Osama bin Laden escape Tora Bora. A key Karzai brother, discussed further below, is Ahmad Wali Karzai, who purportedly worked to try to ensure that pro-Karzai Assembly candidates were elected in Qandahar Province, but it is not clear that this effort succeeded.

The Opposition: Dr. Abdullah and His Lower House Supporters

Although the political opposition to Karzai is fluid and often joins him on some issues, those who can be considered opposition (putting aside Taliban and other insurgents) are mainly ethnic minorities (Tajik, Uzbek, and Hazara) who were in an anti-Taliban grouping called the "Northern Alliance." Leaders of these groups, and particularly Tajiks, view as a betrayal Karzai's firing of many of the non-Pashtuns from the cabinet and, as noted, are increasingly concerned about Karzai's outreach to Taliban figures and to Pakistan (including his meetings with Pakistan's military leader and the director of its intelligence service).

The overall "leader of the opposition" is former Foreign Minister Dr. Abdullah Abdullah, who is about 50 years old and whose mother is Tajik and father is Pashtun. His identity as a key aide to the slain Tajik *mujahedin* commander Ahmad Shah Masoud causes him to be identified politically as a Tajik. He was dismissed from that post by Karzai in March 2006 and now heads a private foundation named after Masoud. He emerged as Afghanistan's opposition leader after his unsuccessful challenge against Karzai for president in the August 2009 election in which widespread fraud was demonstrated. He visited Washington, DC, one week after Karzai's May 10-14, 2010, visit, criticizing Karzai's governance at various think tanks and in a meeting with the State Department. Dr. Abdullah subsequently declined to attend the June 2-4, 2010, peace *jirga* in Kabul on the grounds that the 1,600 delegates were not representative of all Afghans, implying that it would be overwhelmingly run and dominated by Pashtuns.

Dr. Abdullah's main base of support within the National Assembly is called the United Front (UF), although some accounts refer to it as the "National Front" or "United National Front." It was formed in April 2007 by *Wolesi Jirga* Speaker Yunus Qanooni (Karzai's main challenger in the 2004 presidential election) and former Afghan President Burhanuddin Rabbani (both also prominent ethnic Tajik Northern Alliance figures and former associates of the legendary *mujahedin* commander Ahmad Shah Masood. Rabbani remains titular head of the mujahedin party to which Masoud belonged—*Jamiat Islami*, or Islamic Society). In late May 2010, Abdullah created a formal, national democratic opposition organization called the "Hope and Change Movement." Running in the September 18, 2010, elections under that name, Abdullah supporters sought to nearly double their numbers in the new Assembly from about 50 in the outgoing one. The bloc seeks to hold a commanding position that would enable it to block Karzai initiatives and possibly even obtain passage of its own alternative proposals. However, the November 24, 2010, results suggest this objective was achieved, although Abdullah supporters may now have numbers in the lower house closer to Karzai's 80-90 supporters than was the case in the last Assembly.

Although not aimed at mass appeal as is Dr. Abdullah's Hope and Change Movement, the United Front is nonetheless broader than the "Northern Alliance" in that the Front includes some Pashtuns. Examples include Soviet-occupation era security figures Sayed Muhammad Gulabzoi and Nur ul-Haq Ulumi, who has chaired the defense committee. Even before the debate over the terms of any settlement with the Taliban escalated in 2010, the UF advocated amending the constitution to give more power to parliament and to empower the elected provincial councils (instead of the president) to select governors and mayors. Such steps would ensure maximum autonomy from Kabul for non-Pashtun areas, and serve as a check and balance on Pashtun dominance of the central government.

Even before the formation of the UF, the opposition in the *Wolesi Jirga* first showed its strength in March 2006, following the December 19, 2005, inauguration of parliament, by requiring Karzai's cabinet to be approved individually, rather than *en bloc*, increasing opposition leverage. However, Karzai rallied his support and all but 5 of the 25 nominees were confirmed. In May 2006, the opposition compelled Karzai to change the nine-member Supreme Court, the highest judicial body, including ousting 74-year-old Islamic conservative

Fazl Hadi Shinwari as chief justice. The proximate justification for the ouster was Shinwari's age, which was beyond the official retirement age of 65. (Shinwari later went on to head the Ulema Council, Afghanistan's highest religious body.) Parliament approved Karzai's new court choices in July 2006, all of whom are trained in modern jurisprudence.

Lower House Independents

Karzai and Abdullah compete for the support of the "independents" in the lower house. Among them are several outspoken women, intellectuals, and business leaders. One, the 43-year-old Malalai Joya (Farah Province), was a leading critic of war-era faction leaders. In May 2007 the lower house voted to suspend her for this criticism for the duration of her term. She was not returned to the Assembly following the September 18 elections. Others in this independent camp include Ms. Fauzia Gailani (Herat Province, not returned to parliament); Ms. Shukria Barekzai, editor of *Woman Mirror* magazine and possible presidential candidate in 2014; and Mr. Ramazan Bashardost, a former Karzai minister who champions parliamentary powers and has established a "complaints tent" near the parliament building to highlight and combat official corruption. (He ran for president in the 2009 elections on an anti-corruption platform and drew an unexpectedly large amount of votes.) U.S.-based International Republican Institute (IRI) has helped train the independents; the National Democratic Institute (NDI) has assisted the more established factions.

The Upper House

Karzai has relatively fewer critics in the 102-seat *Meshrano Jirga* (House of Elder, upper house*),* partly because of his bloc of 34 appointments (one-third of that body). He engineered the appointment of an ally as speaker: Sibghatullah Mojadeddi, a noted Islamic scholar and former *mujahedin* party leader (Afghanistan National Liberation Front, ANLF), who headed the post-Communist *mujahedin* government for one month (May 1992). However, because it is composed of more elderly, established, notable Afghans who are traditionalist in their political outlook, the upper house has tended to be more Islamist conservative than the lower house, advocating a legal system that accords with Islamic law, and restrictions on press and Westernized media broadcasts. As an example of the upper house's greater support for Karzai, it voted on April 3, 2010, not to act on the election decree that the lower house had rejected on March 31, 2010, meaning that the decree applied to the September 18 parliamentary election.

Karzai also has used his bloc of appointments to the upper house to co-opt potential antagonists or reward his friends. He appointed Northern Alliance military leader Muhammad Fahim to the upper body, perhaps to compensate for his removal as defense minister, although he resigned after a few months and later joined the UF. (He was Karzai's primary running mate in the 2009 elections and is now a vice president.) Karzai named a key ally, former Helmand governor Sher Mohammad Akhunzadeh, to the body. There is one Hindu, and 23 women; 17 are Karzai appointees and six were selected in their own right.

A new upper house will be named prior to the January 21, 2010, seating of the new parliament, now that the results of the lower house elections are finalized. Karzai will appoint 34 members, and the provincial councils that were elected in 2009 will appoint a total of 68 members (two per province).

Afghanistan: Politics, Elections, and Government Performance

Traditional Influences on Karzai: Regional Leaders/"Warlords"

A significant U.S. and international concern is Karzai's willingness to sometimes ally with unelected or well-armed faction leaders. Most of these leaders are from the north and west, where non-Pashtun minorities predominate, but there are some major Pashtun faction leaders that Karzai has become dependent upon as well. The Obama Administration's March 27, 2009, and December 1, 2009, strategy statements did not outline new measures to sideline these strongmen, who are sometimes referred to by experts and others as "warlords." General McChrystal's August 2009 "initial assessment," cited below, indicated that some of these faction leaders—most of whom the United States and its partners regularly deal with and have good working relations with—cause resentment among some sectors of the population and complicate U.S. stabilization strategy. A number of them are alleged to own or have equity in security or other Afghan firms that have won business from various U.S. and other donor agencies and fuel allegations of nepotism and other forms of corruption. On the other hand, some Afghans and outside experts believe that the international community's strategy of dismantling local power structures, particularly in northern Afghanistan, and instead to empower the central government, has caused the security deterioration noted since 2006.

Some assert that the Obama Administration's criticism of Karzai has caused him to become ever more reliant on these factional power brokers. Karzai's position is that confronting faction leaders outright would likely cause their followers—who usually belong to ethnic or regional minorities—to go into armed rebellion. Even before the Obama Administration came into office, Karzai argued that keeping the faction leaders on the government side is needed in order to keep the focus on fighting "unrepentant" Taliban insurgents (who are almost all ethnic Pashtuns).

In February 2007, both houses passed a law giving amnesty to faction leaders and others who committed abuses during Afghanistan's past wars. Karzai altered the draft to give victims the right to seek justice for any abuses; Karzai did not sign a modified version in May 2007, leaving the status unclear. However, in November 2009, the Afghan government published the law in the official gazette (a process known as "gazetting"), giving it the force of law.

The following sections analyze some of the main faction leaders who often attract criticism and commentary from U.S. and international partners in Afghanistan.

Vice President Muhammad Fahim

Karzai's choice of Muhammad Fahim, a Tajik from the Panjshir Valley region who is military chief of the Northern Alliance/UF faction, as his first vice presidential running mate in the August 2009 elections might have been a manifestation of Karzai's growing reliance on faction leaders. Dividing the United Front/ Northern Alliance might have been another. The Fahim choice was criticized by human rights and other groups because of Fahim's long identity as a *mujahedin* commander/militia faction leader. A *New York Times* story of August 27, 2009, said that the Bush Administration continued to deal with Fahim when he was defense minister (2001-2004) despite reports that he was involved in facilitating narcotics trafficking in northern Afghanistan. Other allegations suggest he has engineered property confiscations and other benefits to feed his and his faction's business interests. During 2002-2007, he also reportedly withheld turning over some heavy weapons to U.N. disarmament officials who have been trying to reduce the influence of local strongmen such as Fahim. Obama Administration officials have not announced any limitations on dealings with Fahim now that he is vice president. In August 2010, NDS director Nabil appointed a Fahim relative to a senior NDS position. As of August 2010, Fahim has been undergoing treatment in Germany for a heart ailment. His ailment coincides with the accusations that his brother was a beneficiary of concessionary loans from Kabul Bank, a major bank that has faced major losses due to its lending practices and may need to be recapitalized (see below).

Abdurrashid Dostam: Uzbeks of Northern Afghanistan—Jowzjan, Faryab, Sar-iPol, and Balkh Provinces

Some observers have cited Karzai's handling of prominent Uzbek leader Abdurrashid Dostam as evidence of political weakness. Dostam commands numerous partisans in his redoubt in northern Afghanistan (Jowzjan, Faryab, Balkh, and Sar-I-Pol provinces), where he was, during the Soviet and Taliban years, widely accused of human rights abuses of political opponents. To try to separate him from his armed followers, in 2005 Karzai appointed him to the post of chief of staff of the armed forces. On February 4, 2008, Afghan police surrounded Dostam's villa in Kabul in response to reports that he attacked an ethnic Turkmen rival, but Karzai did not order his arrest for fear of stirring unrest among Dostam's followers. To try to resolve the issue without stirring unrest, in December 2008 Karzai purportedly reached an agreement with Dostam under which he resigned as chief of staff and went into exile in Turkey in exchange for the dropping of any case against him.[6]

Dostam returned to Afghanistan on August 16, 2009, and subsequently held a large pro-Karzai election rally in his home city of Shebergan. Part of his intent in supporting Karzai has been to potentially oust a strong rival figure in the north, Balkh Province governor Atta Mohammad, see below. Mohammad is a Tajik but, under a 2005 compromise with Karzai, is in control of a province that is inhabited by many Uzbeks—a source of irritation for Dostam and other Uzbeks. Dostam's support apparently helped Karzai carry several provinces in the north, including Jowzjan, Sar-i-Pol, and Faryab, although Dr. Abdullah won Balkh and Samangan. Dostam was not nominated to the post-election cabinet, but two members of his "Junbush Melli" (National Front) party were—although they were voted down by the National Assembly because the Assembly insisted on competent officials rather than party loyalists in the new cabinet. Dostam returned to Afghanistan in January 2010 and was restored to his previous, primarily honorary, position of chief of staff of the armed forces.

Dostam's reputation is further clouded by his actions during the U.S.-backed war against the Taliban. On July 11, 2009, the *New York Times* reported that allegations that Dostam had caused the death of several hundred Taliban prisoners during the major combat phase of OEF (late 2001) were not investigated by the Bush Administration. In responding to assertions that there was no investigation of the *"Dasht-e-Laili"* massacre because Dostam was a U.S. ally,[7] President Obama said any allegations of violations of laws of war need to be investigated. Dostam responded to Radio Free Europe/Radio Liberty (which carried the story) that only 200 Taliban prisoners died and primarily because of combat and disease, not intentional actions of his forces.

Atta Mohammad Noor: Balkh Province

Atta Mohammad Noor, who is about 47 years old, has been the governor of Balkh Province, whose capital is the vibrant city of Mazar-e-Sharif, since 2005. He is an ethnic Tajik and former *mujahedin* commander who openly endorsed Dr. Abdullah in the 2009 presidential election. However, Karzai has kept Noor in place because he has kept the

Afghanistan: Politics, Elections, and Government Performance 373

province secure, allowing Mazar-e-Sharif to become a major trading hub, and because displacing him could cause ethnic unrest. Observers say that Noor exemplifies the local potentate, brokering local security and business arrangements that enrich Noor and his allies while ensuring stability and prosperity.[8]

Isma'il Khan: Western Afghanistan/Herat

Another strongman that Karzai has sought to simultaneously engage and weaken is prominent Tajik political leader and former Herat governor Ismail Khan. In 2006, Karzai appointed him minister of energy and water, taking him away from his political base in the west. However, Khan remains influential there, and maintaining ties to Khan has won Karzai election support. Khan apparently was able to deliver potentially decisive Tajik votes in Herat Province that might otherwise have gone to Dr. Abdullah. Certified results showed Karzai winning that province, indicating that the deal with Khan was helpful to Karzai.

Still, Khan is said to have several opponents in Herat, and a bombing there on September 26, 2009, narrowly missed his car. U.S. officials purportedly preferred that Khan not be in the cabinet because of his record as a local potentate, although some U.S. officials credit him with cooperating with the privatization of the power sector of Afghanistan. Karzai renominated Khan in his ministry post on December 19, 2009, causing purported disappointment by parliamentarians and western donor countries who want Khan and other faction leaders weakened. His renomination was voted down by the National Assembly and no new nominee for that post was presented on January 9, 2010. Khan remains as head of the ministry but in an acting capacity. Khan is on the High Peace Council that is to oversee negotiations with insurgent leaders. However, new questions about Khan were raised in November 2010 when Afghan television broadcast audio files purporting to contain Khan insisting that election officials alter the results of the September 18, 2010, parliamentary elections.[9]

Sher Mohammad Akhundzadeh and "Koka:" Southern Afghanistan/ Helmand Province

Karzai's relationship with another Pashtun strongman, Sher Mohammad Akhundzadeh, demonstrates the dilemmas facing Karzai in governing Afghanistan. Akhunzadeh was a close associate of Karzai when they were in exile in Quetta, Pakistan, during Taliban rule. Karzai appointed him governor of Helmand after the fall of the Taliban, but in 2005, Britain demanded he be removed for his abuses and reputed facilitation of drug trafficking, as a condition of Britain taking security control of Helmand. Karzai reportedly wants to reappoint Akhundzadeh, who Karzai believes was more successful against militants in Helmand using his local militiamen than Britain has been with its more than 9,500 troops there. Akhunzadeh said in a November 2009 interview that many of his followers joined the Taliban insurgency after Britain insisted on his ouster. However, Britain and the United States have strongly urged Karzai to keep the existing governor, Ghulab Mangal, who is winning wide praise for his successes establishing effective governance in Helmand (discussed further under "Expanding Local Governance," below) and for reducing poppy cultivation there. Akhunzadeh attempted to deliver large numbers of votes for Karzai in Helmand, although turnout in that province was very light partly due to Taliban intimidation of voters.

An Akhunzadeh ally, Abdul Wali Khan (nicknamed "Koka"), was similarly removed by British pressure in 2006 as police chief of Musa Qala district of Helmand. However, Koka was reinstated in 2008 when that district was retaken from Taliban control. The Afghan government insisted on his reinstatement and his militia followers subsequently became the core of the 220-person police force in the district. Koka is mentioned in a congressional report as accepting payments from security contractors who are working under the Defense Department's "Host National Trucking" contract that secures U.S. equipment convoys. Koka allegedly agrees to secure the convoys in exchange for the payments.[10]

Ahmad Wali Karzai: Southern Afghanistan/Qandahar Province

Governing Qandahar, a province of about 2 million, of whom about half live in Qandahar city, is a sensitive issue in Kabul because of President Karzai's active political interest in his home province. Qandahar governance is particularly crucial to an ongoing 2010 U.S. military-led operation to increase security in surrounding districts. In Qandahar, Ahmad Wali Karzai, Karzai's elder brother, is chair of the provincial council. He has always been more powerful than any appointed governor of Qandahar, and President Karzai has frequently rotated the governors of Qandahar to ensure that none of them will impinge on Ahmad Wali's authority. Perceiving him as the key power broker in the province, many constituents and interest groups meet him each day, requesting his interventions on their behalf. Numerous press stories have asserted that he has protected narcotics trafficking in the province, and some press stories say he is also a paid informant and helper for CIA and Special Forces operations in the province.[11] Some Afghans explain Ahmad Wali Karzai's activities as an effort to ensure that his constituents in Qandahar have financial means to sustain themselves, even if through narcotics trade, before there are viable alternative sources of livelihood. On October 11, 2010, President Karzai said (Larry King interview) Ahmad Wali's attorney had shown President Karzai a letter from the U.S. Department of Justice to the effect that no investigation of him was under way. Observers report that President Karzai has repeatedly rebuffed U.S. and other suggestions to try to convince his brother to step down as provincial council chairman for Qandahar, and U.S. officials reportedly had ceased making those suggestions as of August 2010.

Still, U.S. officials say that policy is to try to bolster the clout in Qandahar of the appointed governor, Tooryalai Wesa. The U.S. intent to is empower Wesa to the point where petitioners seek his help on their problems, not that of Ahmad Wali. Karzai appointed Wesa—a Canadian-Afghan academic—in December 2008, perhaps hoping that his ties to Canada would convince Canada to continue its mission in Qandahar beyond 2011. The United States and its partners are trying to assist Wesa with his efforts to equitably distribute development funds and build local governing structures out of the tribal councils he has been holding. U.S. officials reportedly have sought to keep Ahmad Wali from interfering in Wesa's efforts.[12]

Ghul Agha Shirzai: Eastern Afghanistan/Nangarhar

A key gubernatorial appointment has been Ghul Agha Shirzai as governor of Nangarhar. He is a Pashtun from Qandahar, and is generally viewed in Nangarhar as an implant from the south. However, much as has Noor in Balkh, Shirzai has exercised effective leadership, particularly in curbing poppy cultivation there. At the same time, Shirzai is also widely accused of arbitrary action against political or other opponents, and he reportedly does not remit all the customs duties collected at the Khyber Pass/Torkham crossing to the central government. He purportedly uses the funds for the benefit of the province, not trusting that funds remitted to Kabul would be spent in the province. Shirzai had considered running against Karzai in 2009 but then opted not to run as part of a reported "deal" with Karzai that yielded unspecified political and other benefits for Shirzai.

AFGHAN GOVERNANCE, CAPACITY, AND PERFORMANCE[13]

Since 2001, U.S. policy has been to help expand the capacity of Afghan institutions, which were nearly non-existent during Taliban rule. At the time of the fall of the Taliban in late 2001, Afghan government offices were minimally staffed, and virtually none had computer or other modern equipment, according to observers in Kabul. Since 2007, but with particular focus during the Obama Administration, U.S. policy has been to not only try to expand Afghan governing capacity—at the central and local levels—but to push for its reform and oversight. In two major Afghanistan policy addresses—March 27, 2009, and December 1, 2009—President Obama stressed that more needed to be done to promote the legitimacy and effectiveness of the Afghan government at both the Kabul and local levels. In the latter statement, he said: "The days of providing a blank check [to the Afghan government] are over." The December 16, 2010, summary of an Administration review of Afghanistan policy says that the United States is supporting Afghan efforts to "better improve national and sub-national governance, and to build institutions with increased transparency and accountability to reduce corruption—key steps in sustaining the Afghan government."

U.S.-Karzai Relations

U.S. relations with President Hamid Karzai, and U.S. assessments of his performance, are key to U.S. efforts to implement its stabilization strategy. During 2010, Obama Administration criticism of the shortcomings of the Karzai government, particularly its corruption, have caused substantial frictions in U.S.-Karzai relations. Continuing U.S. concerns prompted President Obama to make anti-corruption efforts a particular focus of his talks with President Karzai in Kabul on March 28, 2010. Karzai's frustrations at what he sees as U.S. and international pressure on him to reform emerged in his comments throughout the year, with his comments on April 1, 2010, and April 4, 2010, exposing key differences. In those and subsequent comments, Karzai expressed frustration with what he claims was international meddling in the August 20, 2009, presidential election and, more generally, what he sees as his subordination to the decisions of Afghanistan's international partners. The April 4, 2010, comments were more specifically critical of the United States and suggested that Western meddling in Afghanistan was fueling support for the Taliban as a legitimate resistance to foreign occupation[14]—these comments nearly derailed the May 10-14, 2010, Karzai visit to Washington, DC. That visit did go forward and was widely considered productive, including a decision to review, renew, and expand a 2005 "strategic partnership" that would reflect a long-term U.S. commitment to Afghanistan.[15] Karzai also has taken exception to U.S. press reports that he is on mood-altering or other medication designed to treat psychological ailments; he denies the reports categorically.

At each downturn in the relationship, top Obama Administration officials, including Secretary of Defense Gates, Secretary of State Clinton, and General David Petraeus, have tended to issue comments apparently designed to restore the relationship.[16] Administration officials praised Karzai for holding the June 2-4, 2010, *loya jirga* on reintegration of insurgents and for recommitting to specific reform steps at the international conference in Kabul on July 20, 2010. During a December 2010 visit to Afghanistan, Secretary of Defense Gates praised Karzai at a joint news conference as a "statesman" for not complaining about reported derogatory U.S. comments about him.

Still, press reports assert that differences remain within the Administration over whether to confront Karzai more forcefully to implement reform pledges. A perception has persisted that Karzai's closest U.S. interlocutors are the top U.S. military representatives in Afghanistan (then-top commander in Afghanistan, General Stanley McChrystal, and now, General David Petraeus). Karzai reiterated that he has had very good relations with these two top U.S. and NATO commanders in an interview with Larry King on October 11, 2010. Karzai's relations with the late Special Representative for Afghanistan and the Pakistan (SRAP) Richard Holbrooke,[17] and with Ambassador Eikenberry, have been widely assessed as severely strained, although Holbrooke denied this in an October 22, 2010, State Department briefing. The perception has been fed by numerous reports and comments by observers that said that Holbrooke and Eikenberry, reportedly backed by Vice President Biden and, to a certain extent, President Obama, believed in the efficacy of public U.S. pressure on Karzai. In public statements, General Petraeus has stressed that Karzai is president of a sovereign country and his support and partnership is required in order to successfully implement U.S. strategy.

Building Central Government Capacity

The international community has attempted to shift authority from traditional leaders and relationships, such as those discussed above, to transparent and effective state institutions. That process is proceeding, although far more slowly and less completely than was expected when the Taliban regime fell.

In the nearly nine years of extensive international involvement in Afghanistan, Afghan ministries based in Kabul have been slowly but steadily increasing their staffs and technological capabilities (many ministry offices now have modern computers and communications, for example), although the government still faces a relatively small recruitment pool of workers with sufficient skills.

Afghan-led governmental reform and institution-building programs under way, all with U.S. and other donor assistance, include training additional civil servants, instituting merit-based performance criteria, basing hiring on qualifications rather than kinship and ethnicity, and weeding out widespread governmental corruption. Corruption is fed, in part, by the fact that government workers receive very low salaries (about $200 per month, as compared to the pay of typical contractors in Afghanistan that might pay as much as $6,500 per month).

Some observers assert that the Afghan government requires not only more staff and transparency, but also improved focus and organization, most notably in the presidential office. One idea that surfaced in 2009, and which some Afghans are again raising to help overcome administrative bottlenecks in the palace, was to prod Karzai to create a new position akin to a "chief administration officer." Several potential officials reportedly negotiated with Karzai about playing that role, including one of Karzai's 2009 election challengers, Ashaf Ghani. Ghani has not been given this role but he is advising Karzai on government reform and institution building after reconciling with him in November 2009 (after the election was settled). Ghani was part of Karzai's advisory team during the January 28, 2010, London conference and the July 20, 2010, Kabul conference. Some observers say Ghani might be in line for a "special envoy" role abroad.

The Obama Administration has developed about 45 different metrics to assess progress in building Afghan governance and security, as it was required to do (by September 23, 2009) under P.L. 111-32, an FY2009 supplemental appropriation.[18] To date, and under separate authorities such as provisions of supplemental appropriations and foreign aid appropriations, only small amounts of U.S. aid have been made conditional on Afghanistan's performance on such metrics, and no U.S. aid has been permanently withheld.

The Afghan Civil Service

The low level of Afghan bureaucratic capacity is being addressed in a number of ways, although slowly. There are about 500,000 Afghan government employees, although the majority of them are in the security forces. A large proportion work in the education sector.

The United States and its partners do not have in place a broad program to themselves train Afghan government officials, but instead fund Afghan institutions to conduct such training. Issues of standardizing job descriptions, salaries, bonuses, benefits and the like are being addressed by Afghanistan's Civil Service Commission. According to the April 2010 version of a mandated Defense Department report on Afghanistan,[19] the commission has thus far redefined more than 80,000 civil servant job descriptions.

Under a program called the Civilian Technical Assistance Plan, the United States is providing technical assistance to Afghan ministries and to the commission. From January 2010 until January 2011, the United States is giving $85 million to programs run by the commission to support the training and development of Afghan civil servants. One of the commission's subordinate organizations is the Afghan Civil Service Institute, which envisions training over 16,000 additional bureaucrats by the end of 2010, according to USAID.

Many Afghan civil service personnel undergo training in India, building on growing relations between Afghanistan and India. Japan and Singapore also are training Afghan civil servants on good governance, anti-corruption, and civil aviation. Singapore and Germany will, in 2011, jointly provide technical assistance in the field of civil aviation. Some of these programs are conducted in partnership with the German Federal Foreign Office and the Asia Foundation. In order to address the problem of international donors luring away Afghan talent with higher salaries, the July 20, 2010, Kabul conference included a pledge by the Afghan government to reach an understanding with donors, within six months, on a harmonized salary scale for donor-funded salaries of Afghan government personnel.

The Afghan Budget Process

The international efforts to build up the central government are reflected in the Afghan budget process. The Afghan government controls its own funds as well as those of directly supplied donor funds. Donor funds cover 100% of the development budget as well as 35% of the Afghan government operating budget. The budget year follows the solar year, which begins on March 21 of each year, which also corresponds to the Persian New Year ("*Nowruz*").

According to observers, the Afghan budget is a "unitary" system—the budget is allocated to central government ministries and other central government entities. Elected provincial councils, appointed provincial governors, and district governors do not control their own budgets, although they approve the disbursement of funds by the central entities. There are accounting offices, called *mustofiats*, in each of Afghanistan's 34 provinces, that carry out those disbursements. All revenue is collected by central government entities which, according to experts, contributes to the widespread observation that local officials sometimes seek to retain or divert locally collected revenues.

Curbing Government Corruption and Promoting Rule of Law[20]

As noted throughout, there is a consensus within the Administration—not disputed by Karzai—on the wide scope of the corruption in Afghan governance. The Administration has wrestled throughout 2010 with the degree to which to press an anti-corruption agenda with the Karzai government, but press accounts in October 2010 suggest the Administration has decided to focus on reducing low-level corruption, and less so on investigations of high-level allies of Karzai. The anti-corruption effort has sometimes come into conflict with other U.S. objectives—not only obtaining Afghan government cooperation on the security mission but also in cultivating allies within the Afghan government who can help stabilize areas of the country. Some of these Afghans are said to be paid by the CIA for information and other support, and the National Security Council reportedly has issued guidance to U.S. agencies to review which Afghans are receiving any direct U.S. funding.[21]

Yet, U.S. officials believe that an anti-corruption effort must be pursued because corruption is contributing to a souring of Western publics on the mission as well as causing some Afghans to embrace Taliban insurgents. Official corruption was identified as a key problem in the August 30, 2009, assessment by General Stanley McChrystal, then overall commander of U.S. and international forces there. His successor in the post, General Petraeus, the top U.S. and NATO commander in Afghanistan, has said he is making anti-corruption a top priority to support his counter-insurgency strategy. A key deputy, Gen. H.R. McMaster, is said to focus on anticorruption from a U.S. military/counter-insurgency perspective. In September 2010, Gen. Petraeus issued guidance throughout the theater for subordinate commanders to review their contracting strategies so as to enhance Afghan capacity and reduce the potential for corruption.

The Obama Administration's March 2009 and December 2009 strategy announcements highlighted the issue but did not specifically make U.S. forces or assistance contingent on progress on this issue. However, the December 2009 stipulation of July 2011 as the beginning of a "transition" process to Afghan leadership implied that U.S. support is not open-ended or unconditional. In the December 1, 2009, statement, the President said "We expect those [Afghan officials] who are ineffective or corrupt to be held accountable." As noted, pressing Karzai on corruption reportedly was a key component of President Obama's brief visit to Afghanistan on March 28, 2010. Attorney General Eric Holder visited Afghanistan during June 2010 to discuss anti-corruption efforts with his Afghan counterparts, including Afghan Attorney General Mohammad Ishaq Aloko.

Scope of the Problem

Partly because many Afghans view the central government as "predatory," many Afghans and international donors have lost faith in Karzai's leadership. A U.N. Office of Drugs and Crime report released in January 2010 said 59% of Afghans consider corruption as a bigger concern than the security situation and unemployment. NATO estimates that about $2.5 billion in total bribes are paid by Afghans each year. Transparency International, a German organization that assesses governmental corruption worldwide, ranked Afghanistan in 2008 as 176th out of 180 countries ranked in terms of government corruption.

At the upper levels of government, some observers have asserted that Karzai deliberately tolerates officials who are allegedly involved in the narcotics trade and other illicit activity, and supports their receipt of lucrative contracts from donor countries, in exchange for their support. Another of Karzai's brother, Mahmoud Karzai, has apparently grown wealthy through real estate and auto sales ventures in Qandahar and Kabul, purportedly by fostering the impression he can influence his brother. Mahmoud Karzai held a press conference in Washington, DC, on April 16, 2009, denying allegations of corruption and, in mid-2010, he hired attorney Gerald Posner to counter corruption allegations against him by U.S. press articles. However, in October 2010 it was reported that a Justice Department investigation of Mahmoud Karzai's dealings (he holds dual U.S.-Afghan citizenship) had begun. Mahmoud Karzai subsequently announced that he has determined that he does owe back taxes to the United States and would clear up the arrearage.

Several other high officials, despite very low official government salaries, have acquired ornate properties in west Kabul since 2002, according to Afghan observers. This raises the further question of the inadequacy of and possible corruption within Afghanistan's land titling system. Other observers who have served in Afghanistan say that Karzai has appointed some provincial governors to "reward them" and that these appointments have gone on to "prey" economically on the populations of that province.

Kabul Bank Difficulties

The near collapse of Kabul Bank is another example of how well-connected Afghans can avoid regulations and other restrictions in order to garner personal profit. Mahmoud Karzai is a major (7+%) shareholder in the large Kabul Bank, which is used to pay Afghan civil servants and police, and he reportedly received large loans from the bank to buy his position in it. Another big shareholder is the brother of First Vice President Fahim. The insider relationships were exposed in August and September 2010 when Kabul Bank reported large losses from shareholder investments in Dubai properties, prompting President Karzai to appoint a Central Bank official to run the Kabul Bank. However, the moves did not prevent large numbers of depositors from moving their money out of it. U.S. officials have asserted that no U.S. funds will be used to recapitalize the bank, if that is needed. The Afghan government said on November 27, 2010, that it has injected "far less" than $500 million into the Bank to keep it solvent and it is still operating, but doubts remain whether it can survive long term. The United States has offered to finance and audit of Afghan banks, but the Finance Ministry instead said on November 27, 2010, it would hire its own auditor—a move that suggested to some that high Afghan officials seek to avoid international scrutiny of how Afghan banks operate.

Lower-Level Corruption

Aside from the issue of high-level nepotism, observers who follow the issue say that most of the governmental corruption takes place in the course of performing mundane governmental functions, such as government processing of official documents (ex. passports, drivers' licenses), in which processing services routinely require bribes in exchange for action.[22] Other forms of corruption include Afghan security officials' selling U.S./ internationally provided vehicles, fuel, and equipment to supplement their salaries. In other cases, local police or border officials may siphon off customs revenues or demand extra payments to help guard the U.S. or other militaries' equipment shipments. Other examples security commanders' placing "ghost employees" on official payrolls in order to pocket their salaries. As noted, it is this low-level corruption that the Obama Administration reportedly has decided to focus on.

Because of corruption, only about 20% of U.S. aid is channeled through the Afghan government, although a target figure of 50% of total donor funds to be channeled through the government was endorsed at the July 20, 2010, Kabul conference. Currently, the Ministry of Public Health, the Ministry of Communications, the Ministry of Finance, and the World Bank-run Afghan Reconstruction Trust Fund (which the U.S. contributes to for Afghan budget support) qualify to have U.S. funds channeled through them.

The FY2011 Obama Administration aid request expressed the goal that six ministries would qualify for direct funding by the end of 2010. Among those potentially ready, according to criteria laid out by the late SRAP Holbrooke and USAID Director Shah on July 28, 2010, three others are nearly ready to receive direct funding: the Ministry of Education; the Ministry of Agriculture, Irrigation and Livestock, run by the widely praised Minister Asif Rahimi; and the Ministry of Rural Rehabilitation and Development (MRRD), which runs the widely praised National Solidarity Program. That program awards local development grants for specific projects. The MRRD has developed a capability, widely praised by Britain and other observers, to account for large percentages of donated funds to ensure they are not siphoned off by corruption.

Karzai Responses

Karzai has taken note of the growing U.S. criticism, and Obama Administration officials have credited him with taking several steps, tempered by congressional and some Administration criticism of slow implementation and allegations that he continues to shield his closest allies from investigation or prosecution. At the January 28, 2010, London conference, the Afghan government committed to 32 different steps to curb corruption; many of them were pledged again at the July 20, 2010, Kabul conference. Only a few of the pledges have been completed outright, others have had their deadlines extended or been modified. The following are measures pledged and the status of implementation, if any:

- *Assets Declarations and Verifications.* During December 15-17, 2009, Karzai held a conference in Kabul to combat corruption. It debated, among other ideas, requiring deputy ministers and others to declare their assets, not just those at the ministerial level. That requirement was imposed. Karzai himself earlier declared his assets on March 27, 2009. On June 26, 2010, Karzai urged anti-corruption officials to monitor the incomes of government officials and their families, including his, to ensure their monies are earned legally. The July 20, 2010, Kabul conference communiqué[23]

Afghanistan: Politics, Elections, and Government Performance 381

included an Afghan pledge to verify and publish these declarations annually, beginning in 2010. This will presumably be accomplished by a Joint Monitoring and Evaluation Committee, which, according to the Kabul conference communiqué, is to be established within three months of the conference.

- *Establishment of High Office of Oversight.* In August 2008 Karzai, with reported Bush Administration prodding, set up the "High Office of Oversight for the Implementation of Anti-Corruption Strategy" (commonly referred to as the High Office of Oversight, HOO) with the power to identify and refer corruption cases to state prosecutors, and to catalogue the overseas assets of Afghan officials. On March 18, 2010, Karzai, as promised during the January 28, 2010, international meeting on Afghanistan in London, issued a decree giving the High Office direct power to investigate corruption cases rather than just refer them to other offices. The United States gave the High Office about $1 million in assistance during FY2009 and its performance was audited by the Special Inspector General for Afghanistan Reconstruction (SIGAR), in an audit released in December 2009.[24] USAID will provide the HOO $30 million during FY2011-FY2013 to build capacity at the central and provincial level, according to USAID officials. USAID pays for salaries of 6 HOO senior staff and provides some information technology systems as well.

- *Establishment of Additional Investigative Bodies: Major Crimes Task Force and Sensitive Investigations Unit.* Since 2008, several additional investigative bodies have been established under Ministry of Interior authority. The most prominent is the "Major Crimes Task Force," tasked with investigating public corruption, organized crime, and kidnapping. A headquarters for the MCTF was inaugurated on February 25, 2010. According to the FBI press release that day, the MTCF is Afghan led, but it is funded and mentored by the FBI, the DEA, the U.S. Marshal Service, Britain's Serious Crimes Organized Crime Agency, the Australian Federal Police, EUPOL (European police training unit in Afghanistan), and the U.S.-led training mission for Afghan forces. The MCTF currently has 169 investigators working on 36 cases, according to the late SRAP's July 28, 2010, testimony.

  A related body is the Sensitive Investigations Unit (SIU), run by several dozen Afghan police officers, vetted and trained by the DEA.[25] This body led the arrest in August 2010 of a Karzai NSC aide, Mohammad Zia Salehi, on charges of soliciting a bribe from the large New Ansari money trading firm in exchange for ending a money-laundering investigation of the firm. The middle-of-the-night arrest prompted Karzai, by his own acknowledgment on August 22, 2010, to obtain Salehi's release and to say he would establish a commission to place the MCTF and SIU under more thorough Afghan government control. Following U.S. criticism that Karzai is protecting his aides (Salehi reportedly has been involved in bringing Taliban figures to Afghanistan for conflict settlement talks), Karzai pledged to visiting Senate Foreign Relations Committee Chairman John Kerry on August 20, 2010, that the MCTF and SIU would be allowed to perform their work without political interference. In November 2010, the Attorney General's office said it had ended the prosecution of Salehi.

- *Anti-Corruption Unit," and an "Anti-Corruption Tribunal."* These investigative and prosecutory bodies have been established by decree. Eleven judges have been appointed to the tribunal. The tribunal, under the jurisdiction of the Supreme Court, tries cases referred by an Anti-Corruption Unit of the Afghan Attorney General's office. According to testimony before the House Appropriations Committee (State and Foreign Operations Subcommittee) by Ambassador Richard Holbrooke on July 28, 2010, the Anti-Corruption Tribunal has received 79 cases from the Anti-Corruption Unit and is achieving a conviction rate of 90%. President Obama said on September 10, 2010, that 86 Afghan judges have been indicted in 2010 for corruption, up from 11 four years ago. (The July 20, 2010, Kabul conference included a pledge by the Afghan government to establish a statutory basis for the Anti-Corruption Tribunal and the Major Crimes Task Force with laws to be passed by parliament and signed by July 20, 2011.)

- *Implementation: Prosecutions and Investigations of High-Level Officials.* According to the Afghanistan Attorney General's office on November 9, 2010, there are ongoing investigations of at least 20 senior officials, including two sitting members of the cabinet. The two are believed to be Minister of Mining Sharani, and his father, who is a cabinet-rank adviser to Karzai on religious affairs. Two former ministers under investigation currently are former Commerce Minister Amin Farhang for allegedly submitting inflated invoices for reimbursement, and former Transportation Minister Hamidullah Qadri. There have also been investigations of former Minister of Mines Mohammad Ibrahim Adel, who reportedly accepted a $30 million bribe to award a key mining project in Lowgar Province (Aynak Copper Mine) to China;[26] and former Minister of the Hajj Mohammad Siddiq Chakari, under investigation for accepting bribes to steer Hajj-related travel business to certain foreign tourist agencies. Chakari was able to flee Afghanistan to Britain. Karzai publicly criticized the December 2009 embezzlement conviction of then Kabul Mayor Abdul Ahad Sahibi. On December 13, 2009, the deputy Kabul mayor (Wahibuddin Sadat) was arrested at Kabul airport for alleged misuse of authority.
- *Salary Levels.* The government has tried to raise salaries of security forces in order to reduce their inclination to solicit bribes. In November 2009, the Afghan government also has announced an increase in police salaries (from $180 per month to $240 per month).
- *Bulk Cash Transfers.* At the July 2010 Kabul conference, the government pledged to adopt regulations and implement within one year policies to govern the bulk transfers of cash outside the country. This is intended to grapple with issues raised by reports, discussed below, of officials taking large amounts of cash out of Afghanistan (an estimated $1 billion per year taken out). U.S. officials say that large movements of cash are inevitable in Afghanistan because only about 5% of the population use banks and 90% use informal cash transfers ("hawala" system). Ambassador Holbrooke testified on July 28, 2010 (cited earlier), that the Afghan Central Bank has begun trying to control hawala transfers; 475 hawalas have been licensed, to date. None were licensed as recently as three years ago. In June 2010, U.S. and Afghan officials announced establishment of a joint task force to monitor the flow of money out of Afghanistan, including monitoring the flow of cash out of Kabul International Airport. On August 21, 2010, it was reported that Afghan and U.S. authorities would implement a plan to install U.S.-made currency counters at Kabul airport to track how officials had obtained their cash (and ensure it did not come from donor aid funds).[27]

- *Auditing Capabilities*. The U.S. Special Inspector General for Afghanistan Reconstruction (SIGAR) has assessed that the mandate of Afghanistan's Control and Audit Office is too narrow and lacks the independence needed to serve as an effective watch over the use of Afghan government funds.[28] At the Kabul conference, the government pledged to submit to parliament an Audit Law within six months, to strengthen the independence of the Control and Audit Office, and to authorize more auditing by the Ministry of Finance.
- *Legal Review*. The Kabul conference communiqué commits the government to establish a legal review committee, within six months, to review Afghan laws for compliance with the U.N. Convention Against Corruption. Afghanistan ratified the convention in August 2008.
- *Local Anti-Corruption Bodies*. Some Afghans have taken it upon themselves to oppose corruption at the local level. Volunteer local inspectors, sponsored originally by Integrity Watch Afghanistan, are reported to monitor and report on the quality of donor-funded, contractor implemented construction projects. However, these local "watchdog" groups do not have an official mandate, and therefore their authority and ability to rectify inadequacies are limited.

Moves to Penalize Lack of Progress on Corruption

Several of the required U.S. "metrics" of progress, cited above, involve Afghan progress against corruption. A FY2009 supplemental appropriation (P.L. 111-32) mandated the withholding of 10% of about $90 million in State Department counter-narcotics funding subject to a certification that the Afghan government is acting against officials who are corrupt or committing gross human rights violations. No U.S. funding for Afghanistan has been withheld because of this or any other legislative certification requirement. In FY2011 legislation, in June 2010, the Foreign Operations Subcommittee of the House Appropriations Committee deferred consideration of some of the nearly $4 billion in civilian aid to Afghanistan requested for FY2011, pending the outcome of a committee investigation of the issue. The subcommittee's action came amid reports that Afghan leaders are impeding investigations by the Afghan justice system of some politically well-connected Afghans, and following reports that as much as $3 billion in funds have been allegedly embezzled by Afghan officials over the past several years.[29] The Senate Appropriations Committee's FY2011 omnibus appropriation require Administration certifications of progress against corruption as a condition of providing aid to Afghanistan.

Rule of Law Efforts

U.S. efforts to curb corruption go hand-in-hand with efforts to promote rule of law. As of July 2010, the U.S. Embassy has an Ambassador rank official, Hans Klemm, as a rule of law coordinator. U.S. funding supports training and mentoring for Afghan justice officials, direct assistance to the Afghan government to expand efforts on judicial security, legal aid and public defense, gender justice and awareness, and expansion of justice in the provinces. At the July 20, 2010, Kabul conference, the Afghan government committed to:

- Enact its draft Criminal Procedure Code into law within six months.
- Improve legal aid services within the next 12 months.
- Strengthen judicial capabilities to facilitate the return of illegally seized lands.

- Align strategy toward the informal justice sector (discussed below) with the National Justice Sector Strategy.
- Separate from the Kabul conference issues, USAID has provided $56 million during FY2005-2009 to facilitate property registration. An additional $140 million is being provided from FY2010-2014 to inform citizens of land processes and procedures, and to establish a legal and regulatory framework for land administration.

One concern is how deeply the international community should become involved in the informal justice sector. Afghans turn often to local, informal mechanisms (*shuras, jirgas*) to adjudicate disputes, particularly those involving local property, familial or local disputes, or personal status issues, rather than use the national court system. Some estimates say that 80% of cases are decided in the informal justice system. In the informal sector, Afghans can usually expect traditional practices of dispute resolution to prevail, including those practiced by Pashtuns. Some of these customs, including traditional forms of apology ("*nanawati*" and "*shamana*") and compensation for wrongs done, are discussed at http://www.khyber.org/ articles/2004/ JirgaRestorativeJustice.shtml.

However, the informal justice system is dominated almost exclusively by males. Some informal justice *shuras* take place in Taliban-controlled territory, and some Afghans may prefer Talibanrun *shuras* when doing so means they will be judged by members of their own tribe or tribal confederation. The rule of law issue is discussed in substantially greater depth in: CRS Report R41484, *Afghanistan: U.S. Rule of Law and Justice Sector Assistance*, by Liana Sun Wyler and Kenneth Katzman

Expanding Local Governance

As U.S. concerns about corruption in the central government increased after 2007, U.S. policy has increasingly emphasized building local governance. The U.S. shift in emphasis complements those of the Afghan government, which asserts that it has itself long sought to promote local governance as the next stage in Afghanistan's political and economic development. A key indicator of the Afghan intent came in August 2007 when Karzai placed the selection process for local leaders (provincial governors and down) in a new Independent Directorate for Local Governance (IDLG)—and out of the Interior Ministry. As noted above, the IDLG is headed by Jelani Popal, a member of Karzai's Popolzai tribe and a close Karzai ally. Some international officials say that Popal packed local agencies with Karzai supporters, where they were able to fraudulently produce votes for Karzai in the August 2009 presidential elections.

Provincial Governors and Provincial Councils

Many believe that the key to effective local governance is the appointment of competent governors in all 34 Afghan provinces. U.N., U.S., and other international studies and reports all point to the beneficial effects (reduction in narcotics trafficking, economic growth, lower violence) of some of the strong Afghan civilian appointments at the provincial level. However, many of the governors are considered weak, ineffective, or corrupt. Others, such as Ghul Agha Shirzai and Atta Mohammad Noor, discussed above in the section on faction leaders, are considered effective, but also relatively independent of central authority.

One of the most widely praised gubernatorial appointments has been the March 2008 replacement of a weak and ineffective governor of Helmand with Gulab Mangal, who is from Laghman Province. The U.N. Office of Drugs and Crime (UNODC) praised Mangal in its September 2009 report for taking effective action to convince farmers to grow crops other than poppy. The UNODC report said his efforts account for the 33% reduction of cultivation in Helmand in 2009, as compared with 2008. Mangal has played a key role in convening tribal *shuras* and educating local leaders on the benefits of the U.S.-led offensive to remove Taliban insurgents from Marjah town and install new authorities there. A key Mangal ally, who has reportedly helped bring substantial stability to the Nawa district, is Abdul Manaf.

Still, there are widespread concerns about governing capacity at the local level. For example, out of over 200 job slots available for the Qandahar provincial and Qandahar city government, only about 30% are filled. In four key districts around Qandahar city, there are 44 significant jobs, including district governors, but only about 12 officials are routinely present for work.[30] As noted above, only a few dozen of the 150 local representative positions of the various ministry positions of the central government in Qandahar are filled. Similar percentages are reported in neighboring Helmand Province, the scene of substantial U.S.-led combat during 2010.

As far as the relationship between local representatives of the central government ministries and district governments, some difficulties have been noted. As noted above, the provincial governors and district governors do not control Afghan government funds; all budgeting and budget administration is done through the central government, either at ministry headquarters or through provincial offices of those ministries. Local officials sometimes disagree on priorities or on implementation mechanisms.

Provincial Councils

One problem noted by governance experts is that the role of the elected provincial councils is unclear. The elections for the provincial councils in all 34 provinces were held on August 20, 2009, concurrent with the presidential elections. The previous provincial council elections were held concurrent with the parliamentary elections in September 2005. The 2009 election results for the provincial councils were certified on December 29, 2009. In most provinces, the provincial councils do not act as true legislatures, and they are considered weak compared to the power and influence of the provincial governors.

Still, the provincial councils will play a major role in choosing the upper house of the National Assembly (*Meshrano Jirga)*. The next selection process is to occur in late December 2010, after certification of results of the lower house elections. In the absence of district councils (no elections held or scheduled), the provincial councils elected in 2009 will choose two-thirds (68 seats) of the 102-seat *Meshrano Jirga*.

District-Level Governance

District governors are appointed by the president, at the recommendation of the IDLG. Only about half of all district governors (there are 364 districts) have any staff or vehicles. Efforts to expand village local governance have been hampered by corruption and limited availability of skilled Afghans. In some districts of Helmand that had fallen under virtual Taliban control until the July 2009 U.S.-led offensives in the province, there were no district governors in place at all. Some of the district governors, including in Nawa (mentioned above) and Now Zad district, returned after the U.S.-led expulsion of Taliban militants.

The ISAF campaign plan to retake the Marjah area of Helmand (Operation Moshtarak), which ended Taliban control of the town, included recruiting, in advance, civilian Afghan officials who would govern the district once military forces had expelled Taliban fighters from it. Haji Zahir, a businessman who was in exile in Germany during Taliban rule, took up his position to become the chief executive in Marjah (which is to become its own district). He held meetings with Marjah residents, one of which included hosting a visit to Marjah by President Karzai (March 7, 2010). He had planned to expand his staff to facilitate the "build phase" of the ISAF counter-insurgency plan for the area. However, the expansion of that staff—and the building of governance in Marjah more generally—has been slow and some officials assigned to the city refused to serve in it for fear of Taliban assassination. As an example of the difficulties in building up local governance, Zahir was replaced in early July 2010, apparently because of his inability to obtain cooperation from Marjah tribal leaders. However, British civilian representatives in Marjah reported in October 2010 that many central government ministries now have personnel in place in Marjah and they live there and are showing up daily. Still, as noted, many slots are unfilled.

District Councils and Municipal and Village Level Authority

No elections for district councils have been held due to boundary and logistical difficulties. However, in his November 19, 2009, inaugural speech, Karzai said the goal of the government is to hold these elections along with the 2010 parliamentary elections. However, subsequently, Afghan officials have said that there will not be district elections in September 2010 when the parliamentary elections were to be held.

As are district governors, mayors of large municipalities are appointed. There are about 42 mayors nationwide, many with deputy mayors. Karzai pledged in his November 2009 inaugural that "mayoral" elections would be held "for the purpose of better city management." However, no municipal elections have been held and none is scheduled.

The IDLG, with advice from India and other donors, is also in the process of empowering localities to decide on development priorities by forming Community Development Councils (CDC's). Thus far, there are about 30,000 CDC's established, and they are eventually to all be elected.

U.S. Local Governance Advisory Capacity

As a consequence of the March 2009 Obama Administration review, to help build local governing capacity, the Administration recruited about 500 U.S. civilian personnel from the State Department, USAID, the Department of Agriculture, and several other agencies—and many additional civilians from partner countries will join them—to advise Afghan ministries, and provincial and district administrations. That effort raised the number of U.S. civilians in Afghanistan to about 975 by early 2010. Of these, nearly 350 are serving outside Kabul, up from 67 in early 2009. USAID Director Rajiv Shah testified on July 28, 2010, that 55% of USAID's 420 personnel in Afghanistan are serving outside Kabul. A strategy document released by the office of the late Ambassador Holbrook in January 2010 said that the number of U.S. civilians is slated to grow by another 30% (to about 1,300) in 2010.[31] Those numbers are purported to have been achieved.

Although many U.S. civilian officials now work outside Kabul, there are about 1,100 employees at the U.S. Embassy in Kabul, rising to about 1,200 by the end of 2010. To accommodate the swelling ranks, in early November 2010 a $511 million contract was let to

Caddell Construction to expand it, and two contracts of $20 million each were let to construct U.S. consulates in Herat and Mazar-e-Sharif.

Senior Civilian Representative Program

The Administration also has instituted appointments of "Senior Civilian Representatives" (SCR),[32] who are counterparts to the military commanders of each NATO/ISAF regional command (there are currently five of them). Each Senior Civilian Representative is to have 10-30 personnel on their team. For example, Ambassador Frank Ruggiero, who is serving in Qandahar as the SCR for Regional Command South, is based at Qandahar airfield and interacts closely with the military command of the southern sector. He testified before the Senate Foreign Relations Committee on May 6, 2010. USAID official Dawn Liberi is SCR for Regional Command East (RC-E), which is U.S.-run. She was mentioned specifically by President Obama in his address to U.S. forces at Bagram Airfield (headquarters of RC-E) on March 28, 2010.

Promoting Human Rights

None of the Obama Administration strategy reviews in 2009 specifically changed U.S. policy on Afghanistan's human rights practices. U.S. policy has been to build capacity in human rights institutions in Afghanistan and to promote civil society and political participation. On human rights issues, the overall State Department judgment is that the country's human rights record remains poor, according to the department's report for 2009 (issued March 11, 2010).[33] The latest State Department report was similar in tone and substance to that of previous years, citing Afghan security forces and local faction leaders for abuses, including torture and abuse of detainees.

One of the institutional human rights developments since the fall of the Taliban has been the establishment of the Afghanistan Independent Human Rights Commission (AIHRC). It is headed by a woman, Sima Simar, a Hazara Shiite from Ghazni Province. It acts as an oversight body but has what some consider to be too cozy relations with Karzai's office and is not as aggressive as some had hoped. The July 20, 2010, Kabul conference communiqué contained a pledge by the Afghan government to begin discussions with the AIHRC, within six months, to stabilize its budgetary status. USAID has given the AIHRC about $10 million per year since the fall of the Taliban.

Media and Freedom of Expression/Social Freedoms

Afghanistan's conservative traditions have caused some backsliding in recent years on media freedoms, which were hailed during 2002-2008 as a major benefit of the U.S. effort in Afghanistan. A press law was passed in September 2008 that gives some independence to the official media outlet, but also contains a number of content restrictions, and requires that new newspapers and electronic media be licensed by the government. Backed by Islamic conservatives in parliament, such as Sayyaf (referenced above), and Shiite clerics such as Ayatollah Asif Mohseni, Afghanistan's conservative Council of Ulema (Islamic scholars) has been ascendant. With the council's backing, in April 2008 the Ministry of Information and Culture banned five Indian-produced soap operas on the grounds that they are too risque, although the programs were restored in August 2008 under a compromise that also brought in some Islamic-oriented programs from Turkey. At the same time, according to the State Department there has been a growing number of arrests or intimidation of journalists who criticize the central government or local leaders.

Ulema Council

Press reports in September 2010 note that the Ulema Council, a network of 3,000 clerics throughout Afghanistan, has increasingly taken conservative positions more generally. Each cleric in the council is paid about $100 per month and, in return, is expected to promote the government line. However, in August 2010, 350 members of the Council voted to demand that Islamic law (Sharia) be implemented. If the government were inclined to adopt that recommendation, either on its own or as part of a peace agreement with major Taliban leaders, it is likely that doing so would require amending the Afghan constitution, which does not implement Sharia. Some believe the Ulema Council is drifting out of government control in part because of the incapacity of its chairman, former Supreme Court Chief Justice Fazl Hadi Shinwari, who has been in a coma in India for several months. No replacement for him has been named by the government.

In September 2010, some Ulema Council figures organized protests against plans by a Florida pastor to burn Qurans on the anniversary of the September 11 attacks (plans which were abandoned). As another example of the growing power of harder line Islamists, alcohol is increasingly difficult to obtain in restaurants and stores, although it is not banned for sale to non-Muslims. There were reports in April 2010 that Afghan police had raided some restaurants and prevented them from selling alcoholic beverages at all.

Harsh Punishments

In October 2007, Afghanistan resumed enforcing the death penalty after a four-year moratorium, executing 15 criminals. In August 2010, the issue of stoning to death as a punishment arose when Taliban insurgents ordered a young couple who had eloped stoned to death in a Taliban-controlled area of Konduz Province. Although the punishment was not meted out by the government, it was reported that many residents of the couple's village supported the punishment. The stoning also followed one week after the national Council of Ulema issued a statement (August 10, 2010), following a meeting with government religious officials, calling for more application of Shariah punishments (including such punishments as stoning, amputations, and lashings) in order to better prevent crime.

Religious Freedom

The 2010 International Religious Freedom report (released November 17, 2010)[34] says that respect for religious freedom deteriorated throughout the reporting period, particularly for Christian groups and individuals. Members of minority religions, including Christians, Sikhs, Hindus, and Baha'i's, often face discrimination; the Supreme Court declared the Baha'i faith to be a form of blasphemy in May 2007. Northeastern provinces have a substantial population of Islmailis, a Shiite Muslim sect often called "Seveners" (believers in the Seventh Imam as the true Imam). Many Ismailis follow the Agha Khan IV (Prince Qarim al-Husseini), who chairs the large Agha Khan Foundation that has invested heavily in Afghanistan.

One major case that drew international criticism was a January 2008 death sentence, imposed in a quick trial, against 23-year-old journalist Sayed Kambaksh for allegedly distributing material critical of Islam. On October 21, 2008, a Kabul appeals court changed his sentence to 20 years in prison, a judgment upheld by another court in March 2009. He was pardoned by Karzai and released on September 7, 2009.

A positive development is that Afghanistan's Shiite minority, mostly from the Hazara tribes of central Afghanistan (Bamiyan and Dai Kundi provinces) can celebrate their holidays openly, a development unknown before the fall of the Taliban. Some Afghan Shiites follow Iran's clerical leaders politically, but Afghan Shiites tend to be less religious and more socially open than their co-religionists in Iran. The Hazaras are also advancing themselves socially and politically through education in such fields as information technology.[35] The former Minister of Justice, Sarwar Danesh, is a Hazara Shiite, the first of that community to hold that post. He studied in Qom, Iran, a center of Shiite theology. (Danesh was voted down by the parliament for reappointment on January 2, 2010, and again on June 28 when nominated for Minister of Higher Education.) The justice minister who was approved on January 16, 2010, Habibullah Ghalib, is part of Dr. Abdullah's faction, but not a Shiite Muslim. Ghaleb previously (2006) was not approved by the *Wolesi Jirga* for a spot on the Supreme Court. There was unrest among some Shiite leaders in late May 2009 when they learned that the Afghan government had dumped 2,000 Iranian-supplied religious texts into a river when an Afghan official complained that the books insulted the Sunni majority.

Several religious freedom cases have earned international attention. An Afghan man, Abd alRahman, who had converted to Christianity 16 years ago while working for a Christian aid group in Pakistan, was imprisoned and faced a potential death penalty trial for apostasy—his refusal to convert back to Islam. Facing international pressure, Karzai prevailed on Kabul court authorities to release him (March 29, 2006). His release came the same day the House passed H.Res. 736 calling on protections for Afghan converts. In May 2010, the Afghan government suspended the operations of two Christian-affiliated international relief groups claiming the groups were attempting to promote Christianity among Afghans—an assertion denied by the groups (Church World Service and Norwegian Church Aid). Another case arose in May 2010, when an amputee, Said Musa, was imprisoned for converting to Christianity from Islam. The arrest came days after the local Noorin TV station broadcast a show on Afghan Christians engaging in their rituals.

Human Trafficking

Afghanistan was placed in Tier 2: Watch List in the State Department report on human trafficking issued on June 14, 2010 (Trafficking in Persons Report for 2010). The placement was a downgrade from the Tier 2 placement of the 2009 report. The Afghan government is assessed in the report as not complying with minimum standards for eliminating trafficking, but making significant efforts to do so. However, the downgrade was attributed to the fact that the government did not prosecute any human traffickers under a 2008 law. The State Department report says that women from China, some countries in Africa, Iran, and some countries in Central Asia are being trafficked into Afghanistan for sexual exploitation. Other reports say some are brought to work in night clubs purportedly frequented by members of many international NGOs. In an effort to also increase protections for Afghan women, in August 2008 the Interior Ministry announced a crackdown on sexual assault—an effort to publicly air a taboo subject. The United States has spent about $500,000 to eliminate human trafficking in Afghanistan since FY2001.

Advancement of Women

Freedoms for women have greatly expanded since the fall of the Taliban with their elections to the parliament and their service at many levels of government. According to the State Department human rights report for 2009, numerous abuses, such as denial of educational and employment opportunities, continue primarily because of Afghanistan's conservative traditions. Other institutions, such as Human Rights Watch, report backsliding due in part to the lack of security.[36] Many Afghan women are concerned that the efforts by Karzai and the international community to persuade insurgents to end their fight and rejoin the political process ("reintegration and reconciliation" process) could result in backsliding on women's rights. Most insurgents are highly conservative Islamists who oppose the advancement of women that has occurred. They are perceived as likely to demand some reversals of that trend if they are allowed, as part of any deal, to control territory, assume high-level government positions, or achieve changes to the Afghan constitution. Karzai has said that these concessions are not envisioned, but skepticism remains, and some Afghan officials close to Karzai do not rule out the possibility of amending the constitution to accommodate some Taliban demands. Women have been a target of attacks by Taliban supporters, including attacks on girls' schools and athletic facilities.

A major development in post-Taliban Afghanistan was the formation of a Ministry of Women's Affairs dedicated to improving women's rights, although numerous accounts say the ministry's influence is limited. It promotes the involvement of women in business ventures, and it plays a key role in trying to protect women from domestic abuse by running a growing number of women's shelters across Afghanistan. Husn Banu Ghazanfar remains minister in an acting capacity, having been voted down by the lower house for reappointment.

The Afghan government tried to accommodate Shiite leaders' demands in 2009 by enacting (passage by the National Assembly and signature by Karzai in March 2009) a "Shiite Personal Status Law," at the request of Shiite leaders. The law was intended to provide a legal framework for members of the Shiite minority in family law issues. However, the issue turned controversial when international human rights groups and governments—and Afghan women in a demonstration in Kabul—complained about provisions that would appear to sanction marital rape and which would allow males to control the ability of females in their family to go outside the home. President Obama publicly called these provisions "abhorrent." In early April 2009, taking into account the outcry, Karzai sent the law back to the Justice Ministry for review, saying it would be altered if it were found to conflict with the Afghan constitution. The offending clauses were substantially revised by the Justice Ministry in July 2009, requiring that wives "perform housework," but also apparently giving the husband the right to deny a wife food if she refuses sex. The revised law was passed by the National Assembly in late July 2009, signed by Karzai, and published in the official gazette on July 27, 2009, although it remains unsatisfactory to many human rights and women's rights groups.

On August 6, 2009, perhaps in an effort to address some of the criticisms of the Shiite law, Karzai issued, as a decree, the "Elimination of Violence Against Women" law. Minister of Women's Affairs Ghazanfar told CRS in October 2009 that the bill was long contemplated and not related to the Shiite status law.[37] However, it is subject to review and passage by the National Assembly, where some Islamic conservatives, such as Sayyaf (cited above) have been blocking final approval. Sayyaf and others reportedly object to the provisions of the law criminalizing child marriages.

Women in Key Positions

Despite conservative attitudes, women have moved into prominent positions in all areas of Afghan governance, although with periodic setbacks. Three female ministers were in the 2004- 2006 cabinet: former presidential candidate Masooda Jalal (Ministry of Women's Affairs), Sediqa Balkhi (Ministry for Martyrs and the Disabled), and Amina Afzali (Ministry of Youth). Karzai nominated Soraya Sobhrang as minister of women's affairs in the 2006 cabinet, but she was voted down by Islamist conservatives in parliament. He eventually appointed another female, Husn Banu Ghazanfar, as minister. Ghazanfar, who is a Russian-speaking Uzbek from northern Afghanistan, has been the only woman in the cabinet for several years. She was renominated on December 19, 2009, was voted down on January 2, 2010, but remains in an acting capacity. Karzai subsequently named three women in new selections presented on January 9, 2010, including Afzali (to Labor and Social Affairs). Of the three, however, only Afzali was confirmed on January 16, 2009; the other two were opposed by Islamic conservatives. In March 2005, Karzai appointed a former minister of women's affairs, Habiba Sohrabi, as governor of Bamiyan province, inhabited mostly by Hazaras. (She hosted then First Lady Laura Bush in Bamiyan in June 2008.)

The constitution reserves for women at least 17 of the 102 seats in the upper house and about one quarter of the 249 seats in the lower house of parliament. There are 23 serving in the outgoing upper house, 6 more than Karzai's mandated bloc of 17 female appointees. There are 68 women in the outgoing lower house (when the quota was 62), meaning 6 were elected without the quota. About the same number will be in the incoming lower house, after certification of the results on November 24, 2010. (For the September 18, 2010, parliamentary elections, about 400 women ran—about 16% of all candidates.) The target ratio is ensured by reserving an average of two seats per province (34 provinces) for women—the top two female vote getters per province. (Kabul province reserves 9 female seats.) Two women ran for president for the August 20, 2009, election, as discussed below, although each received less than one-half of 1%. Some NGOs and other groups believe that the women elected by the quota system are not viewed as equally legitimate parliamentarians.

About 350 women were delegates to the 1,600-person "*peace jirga*" that was held during June 2- 4, 2010, which endorsed an Afghan plan to reintegrate insurgents who want to end their fight. The High Peace Council to oversee the reconciliation process, which met for the first time on October 10, 2010, has eight women out of 68 members.

More generally, women are performing jobs that were rarely held by women even before the Taliban came to power in 1996, including in the new police force. There are over 200 female judges and 447 female journalists working nationwide. The most senior Afghan woman in the police force was assassinated in Qandahar in September 2008. Press reports say Afghan women are increasingly learning how to drive. Under the new government, the wearing of the full body covering called the *burqa* is no longer obligatory, and fewer women are wearing it than was the case a few years ago.

U.S. and International Posture on Women's Rights

U.S. officials have had some influence in persuading the government to codify women's rights. After the Karzai government took office, the United States and the new Afghan government set up a U.S.-Afghan Women's Council to coordinate the allocation of resources to Afghan women. Some believe that, in recent years, the U.S. government has dropped women's issues as a priority for Afghanistan. Some criticized President Obama's speech on

December 1, 2009, for its absence of virtually any mention of women's rights. Promoting women's rights was discussed at the January 28, 2010, London conference but primarily in the context of the reintegration issue.

Specific earmarks for use of U.S. funds for women's and girls' programs in Afghanistan are contained in recent annual appropriations, and these earmarks have grown steadily. The United States provided $153 million to programs for Afghan women in FY2009, and expects to provide $175 million for FY2010, in line with these earmarks.[38] A Senate Appropriations Committee version of FY2011 omnibus appropriations contains several provisions intended to guarantee protections for women and direct continued provisions of aid to programs for women.

According to State Department reports on U.S. aid to women and girls, covering FY2001-2008, and then FY2008-2009, the United States has numerous, multi-faceted projects directly in support of Afghan women, including women's empowerment, maternal and child health and nutrition, funding the Ministry of Women's Affairs, and micro-finance projects. Some programs focus on training female police officers.[39] Some donors, particularly those of Canada, have financed specific projects for Afghan women farmers.

The Afghanistan Freedom Support Act of 2002 (AFSA, P.L. 107-327) authorized $15 million per year (FY2003-FY2006) for the Ministry of Women's Affairs. Those monies are donated to the Ministry from Economic Support Funds (ESF) accounts controlled by USAID. S. 229, the Afghan Women Empowerment Act of 2009, introduced in the 111th Congress, would authorize $45 million per year in FY2010-FY2012 for grants to Afghan women, for the ministry of Women's Affairs ($5 million), and for the AIHRC ($10 million).

Democracy, Governance, and Elections Funding Issues

U.S. funding for democracy, governance, and rule of law programs has grown, in line with the Obama Administration strategy for Afghanistan. During FY2002-FY2008, a total of $1.8 billion was spent on democracy, governance, rule of law and human rights, and elections support. Of these, by far the largest category was "good governance," which, in large part, are grant awards to provinces that make progress against narcotics.

The following was spent in FY2010 (regular appropriation and FY2010 supplemental request): $1.7 billion for all democracy and governance, including

- $1.15 billion for "good governance";
- $411 million for rule of law and human rights (ESF funds controlled by USAID and INCLE funds);
- $113 million for "civil society" building programs; and
- $25 million for political competition and consensus building (elections).

Key Components of FY2011 request:

- $1.388 billion for all democracy and governance funds, including:
    - $1.01 billion for "good governance." This program is used to build the financial and management oversight capability of the central government.
    - $248 million for rule of law and human rights;

Afghanistan: Politics, Elections, and Government Performance 393

- $80 million for civil society building; and
- $50 million for political competition and consensus building.

For comprehensive tables on U.S. aid to Afghanistan, by fiscal year and by category and type of aid, see CRS Report RL30588, *Afghanistan: Post-Taliban Governance, Security, and U.S. Policy*, by Kenneth Katzman.

ELECTIONS IN 2009 AND 2010

As noted throughout, the 2009 presidential and provincial elections were anticipated to be a major step in Afghanistan's political development. They were the first post-Taliban elections run by the Afghan government itself in the form of the Afghanistan Independent Electoral Commission. Donors, including the United States, invested almost $500 million in 2009 to improve the capacity of the Afghan government to conduct the elections.[40]

Nonetheless, there were assertions of a lack of credibility of the IEC, because most of its commissioners, including then-Chairman Azizullah Ludin, were selected by and politically close to Karzai. As a check and balance to ensure electoral credibility, there was also a U.N.-appointed Elections Complaints Commission (ECC) that reviews fraud complaints. Under the 2005 election law, there were three seats for foreign nationals, appointed by the Special Representative of the U.N. Secretary General/head of U.N. Assistance Mission–Afghanistan, UNAMA. The two Afghans on the ECC governing council[41] were appointed by the Supreme Court and Afghanistan Independent Human Rights Commission, respectively.

2009 Presidential Election

The late Special Representative Holbrooke said at a public forum on August 12, 2009, that the August 20, 2009, presidential elections were key to legitimizing the Afghan government, no matter who won. Yet, because of the widespread fraud identified by Afghanistan's U.N.-appointed Elections Complaints Commission (ECC) in the first round of the elections, the process did not produce full legitimacy. The marred elections process was a major factor in a September-November 2009 high-level U.S. strategy reevaluation because of the centrality of a credible, legitimate partner Afghan government to U.S. strategy.[42]

Problems with the election began in late 2008 with a dispute over the election date. On February 3, 2009, Afghanistan's Independent Election Commission (IEC) set August 20, 2009, as the election date (a change from a date mandated by Article 61 of the Constitution as April 21, 2009, in order to allow at least 30 days before Karzai's term expired on May 22, 2009). The IEC decision on the latter date cited Article 33 of the Constitution as mandating universal accessibility to the voting—and saying that the April 21 date was precluded by difficulties in registering voters, printing ballots, training staff, advertising the elections, and the dependence on international donor funding, in addition to the security questions.[43]

In response to UF insistence that Karzai's presidency ended May 22, and that a caretaker government should run Afghanistan until elections, Karzai issued a February 28, 2009, decree directing the IEC to set the elections in accordance with all provisions of the constitution. The IEC reaffirmed on March 4, 2009, that the election would be held on August 20, 2009. Karzai argued against his stepping down, saying that the Constitution does not provide for any transfer of power other than in case of election or death of a President. The Afghan Supreme Court backed that decision on March 28, 2009, and the Obama Administration publicly backed these rulings.

Election Modalities and Processes

Despite the political dispute between Karzai and his opponents, enthusiasm among the public appeared high in the run-up to the election. Registration, which updated 2005 voter rolls, began in October 2008 and was completed as of the beginning of March 2009. About 4.5 million new voters registered, and about 17 million total Afghans were registered. However, there were widespread reports of registration fraud (possibly half of all new registrants), with some voters registering on behalf of women who do not, by custom, show up at registration sites. U.S. and other election observers found instances of fraudulent registration cards and evidence that cards had been offered for sale. U.S./NATO military operations in some areas, including in Helmand in January 2009, were conducted to secure registration centers; however, some election observers noted that there was insufficient international assistance to the IEC, which ran the election, to ensure an untainted registration process.

Candidates filed to run during April 24-May 8, 2009. A total of 44 registered to run for president, of which three were disqualified for various reasons, leaving a field of 41 (later reduced to 32 after several dropped out).

In the provincial elections, 3,200 persons competed for 420 seats nationwide. Those elections were conducted on the "Single Non-Transferable Vote" (SNTV) system, in which each voter votes for one candidate in a multi-member constituency. That system encourages many candidacies and is considered to discourage the participation of political parties. Although about 80% of the provincial council candidates ran as independents, some of Afghanistan's parties, including Hezb-i-Islam, fielded multiple candidates in several different provinces.

The provincial elections component of the election received little attention, in part because the role of these councils is unclear. Of the seats up for election, about 200 women competed for the 124 seats reserved for women (29%) on the provincial councils, although in two provinces (Qandahar and Uruzgan) there were fewer women candidates than reserved seats. In Kabul Province, 524 candidates competed for the 29 seats of the council.

The European Union, supported by the Organization for Security and Cooperation in Europe (OSCE) sent a few hundred observers, and the International Republican Institute and National Democratic Institute sent observers as well. About 8,000 Afghans assisted the observation missions, according to the U.N. Nations Development Program. Because much of Afghanistan is inaccessible by road, ballots were distributed (and were brought for counting) by animals in addition to vehicles and fixed and rotary aircraft.

Security was a major issue for all the international actors supporting the Afghan elections process, amid open Taliban threats against Afghans who vote. In the first round, about 7,000 polling centers were to be established (with each center having multiple polling places, totaling about 29,000), but, of those, about 800 were deemed too unsafe to open, most of them in restive Helmand and Qandahar provinces. A total of about 6,200 polling centers opened on election day.

The total cost of the Afghan elections in 2009 were about $300 million. Other international donors contributing funds to close the gap left by the U.S. contribution of about $175 million.

The Political Contest and Campaign

The presidential competition took shape in May 2009. In the election-related political dealmaking,[44] Karzai obtained an agreement from Fahim to run as his first vice presidential running mate. Karzai, Fahim, and incumbent second Vice President Karim Khalili (a Hazara) registered their ticket on May 4, 2009, just before Karzai left to visit the United States for the latest round of three-way strategic talks (U.S.-Pakistan-Afghanistan).

Karzai convinced several prominent Pashtuns not to run. Ghul Agha Shirzai, a member of the powerful Barakzai clan, reportedly reached an arrangement with Karzai the week of the registration period that headed off his candidacy. Anwar al-Haq Ahady, the former finance minister and Central Bank governor, did not run. (He did receive a cabinet nomination in the December 19 ministry list but was voted down by the parliament.)

Anti-Karzai Pashtuns did not coalesce around one challenger. Former Interior Minister Ali Jalali (who resigned in 2005 over Karzai's compromises with faction leaders), and former Finance Minister (2002-2004) and Karzai critic Ashraf Ghani did not reach agreement to forge a single ticket. In the end, Ghani, the 56-year-old former World Bank official, registered his candidacy, but without Jalali or prominent representation from other ethnicities in his vice presidential slots.

The UF had difficulty forging a united challenge to Karzai. Dr. Abdullah registered to run with UF backing. His running mates were Dr. Cheragh Ali Cheragh, a Hazara who did poorly in the 2004 election, and a little known Pashtun, Homayoun Wasefi. However, the presence of a key Tajik, Fahim, on Karzai's ticket showed the UF to be split.

The Campaign

Karzai went into the election as a clear favorite, but the key question was whether he would win in the first round (more than 50% of the vote). IRI and other pre-election polls showed him with about 45% support. Dr. Abdullah polled about 25% and emerged as the main challenger. The conventional wisdom has always been that the two-round format favors a Pashtun candidate.

Although Karzai's public support was harmed by perceptions of ineffectiveness and corruption, many Afghan voters apparently see many of Afghanistan's problems as beyond Karzai's control. He used some U.S. policy setbacks to bolster his electoral prospects, for example by railing against civilian casualties resulting from U.S./NATO operations, and by proposing new curbs on international military operations in Afghanistan. Karzai said he would hold a *loya jirga*, if elected, including Taliban figures, to try to reach a settlement with the insurgency. He restated that intent in his November 19, 2009, inaugural speech and has moved on that front, as noted.

Karzai was criticized for a campaign that relied on personal ties to ethnic faction leaders rather than a retail campaign based on public appearances. Karzai agreed to public debates with rivals, although he backed out of a scheduled July 23 debate with Abdullah and Ghani (on the private Tolo Television network) on the grounds that the event was scheduled on short notice and was limited to only those three. Abdullah and Ghani debated without Karzai, generating additional criticism of Karzai. Karzai did attend the next debate (on state-run

Radio-Television Afghanistan) on August 16, debating Ghani and Bashardost, but without Abdullah. Karzai was said to benefit from his ready access to media attention, which focuses on his daily schedule as president.

Dr. Abdullah stressed his background of mixed ethnicity (one parent is Pashtun and one is Tajik) to appeal to Pashtuns, but his experience and background has been with other Tajik leaders and he campaigned extensively in the north and west, which are populated mainly by Tajiks. However, he also campaigned in Qandahar, in Pashtun heartland. Both Karzai and Abdullah held large rallies in Kabul and elsewhere.

Ghani polled at about 6% just before the election, according to surveys. Ghani appeared frequently in U.S. and Afghan media broadcasts criticizing Karzai for failing to establish democratic and effective institutions, but he has previously spent much time in the United States and Europe and many average Afghans viewed him as out of touch with day-to-day problems in Afghanistan. Ghani made extensive use of the Internet for advertising and fundraising, and he hired political consultant James Carville to advise his campaign.[45]

Another candidate who polled unexpectedly well was 54-year-old anti-corruption parliamentarian Ramazan Bashardost, an ethnic Hazara. He was polling close to 10% just before the election. He ran a low-budget campaign with low-paid personnel and volunteers, but attracted a lot of media. This suggests that, despite most Hazara ethnic leaders, such as Mohammad Mohaqiq, endorsing Karzai, Bashardost would do well among Hazaras, particularly those who are the most educated. Some believe the Shiite personal status law, discussed above, was an effort by Karzai to win Hazara Shiite votes. According to the preliminary results, Bashardost carried several Hazara provinces, including Ghazni and Dai Kondi, but Mohaqiq's backing apparently helped Karzai carry the Hazara heartland of Bamiyan province. Other significant candidates are shown below.

The Election Results

Taliban intimidation and voter apathy appears to have suppressed the total turnout to about 5.8 million votes cast, or about a 35% turnout, far lower than expected. Twenty-seven Afghans, mostly security forces personnel, were killed in election-day violence. Turnout was said by observers and U.S. and other military personnel based there to have been very low in Helmand Province, despite the fact that Helmand was the focus of a U.S. military-led offensive.

Some observers said that turnout among women nationwide was primarily because there were not sufficient numbers of female poll workers recruited by the IEC to make women feel comfortable enough to vote. In general, however, election observers reported that poll workers were generally attentive and well trained, and the voting process appeared orderly.

In normally secure Kabul, turnout was said to be far lighter than in the 2004 presidential election. Turnout might have been dampened by a suicide bombing on August 15, 2009, outside NATO/ISAF military headquarters and intended to intimidate voters not to participate. In addition, several dozen provincial council candidates, and some workers on the presidential campaigns, were killed in election-related violence. A convoy carrying Fahim (Karzai vice presidential running mate, see below) was bombed, although Fahim was unharmed.

Afghanistan: Politics, Elections, and Government Performance

> ## Other Candidates
>
> Abd al-Salam Rocketi ("Mullah Rocketi"). A Pashtun, reconciled Taliban figure, member of the lower house of parliament. Was expected to do well if Taliban sympathizers participated, but received less than 1% (preliminary totals), putting him in 9th place out of 32.
>
> Hedayat Amin Arsala. A Pashtun, was a vice president during 2001-2004. He was Foreign Minister in the 1992-96 Rabbani-led *mujahedin* government. He is a prominent economist and perceived as close to the former royal family. Finished 30th out of 32.
>
> Abd al Jabbar Sabit. A Pashtun, was fired by Karzai in 2007 for considering a run against Karzai in the election. Finished in 19th place.
>
> Shahnawaz Tanai. A Pashtun. Served as defense minister in the Communist government of Najibullah (which was left in place after the Soviets withdrew in 1989) but led a failed coup against Najibullah in April 1990. Finished an unexpectedly strong sixth place and did well in several Pashtun provinces.
>
> Mirwais Yasini. Another strong Pashtun candidate, was viewed as a dark horse possible winner. 48-year-old deputy speaker of the lower house of parliament, but also without well-known non-Pashtun running mates. Finished fifth.
>
> Frozan Fana and Shahla Ata. The two women candidates in the race. Fana is the wife of the first post-Taliban aviation minister, who was killed during an altercation at Kabul airport in 2002. These two candidates are widely given almost no chance of winning, but attracted substantial media attention as trail-blazers. Fana finished seventh but Ata finished in 14th place.

Clouding the election substantially were the widespread fraud allegations coming from all sides. Dr. Abdullah held several news conferences after the election, purporting to show evidence of systematic election fraud by the Karzai camp. Karzai's camp made similar allegations against Abdullah as applied to his presumed strongholds in northern Afghanistan. The ECC, in statements, stated its belief that there was substantial fraud likely committed, and mostly by Karzai supporters. However, the low turnout in the presumed Karzai strongholds in southern Afghanistan led Karzai and many Pashtuns to question the election's fairness as well, on the grounds that Pashtuns were intimidated from voting in greater proportions than were others.

The IEC released vote results slowly. Preliminary results were to be announced by September 3. However, the final, uncertified total was released on September 16, 2009. It showed Karzai at 54.6% and Dr. Abdullah at 27.7%. Bashardost and Ghani received single-digit vote counts (9% and 3% respectively), with trace amounts for the remainder of the field.

Vote Certified/Runoff Mandated

The constitution required that a second-round runoff, if needed, be held two weeks after the results of the first round are certified. Following the release of the vote count, the complaints evaluation period began which, upon completed, would yield a "certified" vote result. On September 8, 2009, the ECC ordered a recount of 10% of polling stations (accounting for as many as 25% total votes) as part of its investigations of fraud. Polling stations were considered "suspect" if: the total number of votes exceeded 600, which was the maximum number allotted to each polling station; or where any candidate received 95% or more of the total valid votes cast at that station (assuming more than 100 votes were cast there). Perhaps reflecting political sensitivities, the recount consisted of a sampling of actual votes.[46] Throughout the investigation period (September 16-October 20), the ECC said it was not "in a rush" to finish.

On October 20, 2009, the ECC determined, based on its investigation, that about 1 million Karzai votes, and about 200,000 Abdullah votes, were considered fraudulent and were deducted from their totals. The final, certified, results of the first round were as follows: Karzai—49.67% (according to the IEC; with a slightly lower total of about 48% according to the ECC determination); Abdullah—30.59%; Bashardost—10.46%; Ghani—2.94%, Yasini—1.03%, and lower figures for the remaining field.[47]

During October 16-20, 2009, U.S. and international officials, including visiting Senator John Kerry, met repeatedly with Karzai to attempt to persuade him to acknowledge that his vote total did not legitimately exceed the 50%+ threshold to claim a first-round victory. On October 21, 2009, the IEC accepted the ECC findings and Karzai conceded the need for a runoff election. A date was set as November 7, 2009. Abdullah initially accepted.

In an attempt to produce a fair second round, UNAMA, which provided advice and assistance to the IEC, requested that about 200 district-level election commissioners be replaced. In addition, it recommended there be fewer polling stations—about 5,800, compared to 6,200 previously—to eliminate polling stations where very few votes are expected to be cast. Still, there were concerns that some voters may be disenfranchised because snow had set in some locations. Insurgents were expected to resume their campaign to intimidate voters from casting ballots.

After a runoff was declared, no major faction leader switched support of either candidate, making it difficult to envision an Abdullah victory. Prior to the ECC vote certification, Dr. Abdullah told CRS at a meeting in Kabul on October 15, 2009, that he might be willing to negotiate with Karzai on a "Joint Program" of reforms—such as direct election of governors and reduced presidential powers—to avoid a runoff. Abdullah told CRS he himself would not be willing to enter the cabinet, although presumably such a deal would involve his allies doing so. However, some said the constitution does not provide for a negotiated settlement and that the runoff must proceed. Others said that a deal between the two, in which Abdullah dropped his candidacy, could have led the third-place finisher, Bashardost, to assert that he must face Karzai in a runoff. Still others say the issue could have necessitated resolution by Afghanistan's Supreme Court.

Election Conclusion

The various pre-runoff scenarios were mooted on November 1, 2009, when Dr. Abdullah refused to participate in the runoff on the grounds that the problems that plagued the first round were likely to recur. He asserted that Karzai, in negotiations during October 2009, was refusing to replace the IEC head, Azizullah Ludin, to fire several cabinet ministers purportedly campaigning for Karzai, or to address several other election-related complaints. The IEC refused to follow a UNAMA recommendation to reduce the number of polling stations. Some believe Abdullah pulled out because of his belief that he would not prevail in the second round.

On November 2, 2009, the IEC issued a statement saying that, by consensus, the body had determined that Karzai, being the only candidate remaining in a two-person runoff, should be declared the winner and the second round not held. The Obama Administration accepted the outcome as "within Afghanistan's constitution," on the grounds that the fraud had been investigated. On that basis, the United States, as well as U.N. Secretary General Ban

Ki Moon (visiting Kabul), and several governments, congratulated Karzai on the victory. U.S. officials, including Secretary of State Clinton, praised Dr. Abdullah for his relatively moderate speech announcing his pullout, in particular his refusal to call for demonstrations or violence. Dr. Abdullah denied that his pullout was part of any "deal" with Karzai for a role for his supporters in the next government. Amid U.S. and international calls for Karzai to choose his next cabinet based on competence, merit, and dedication to curbing corruption, Karzai was inaugurated on November 19, 2009, with Secretary of State Clinton in attendance.

As noted above, the election for the provincial council members were not certified until December 29, 2009. The council members have taken office.

Fallout for UNAMA

The political fallout for UNAMA was significant. During the complaint period, a dispute between UNAMA head Kai Eide and the American deputy, Ambassador Peter Galbraith, broke out over how vigorously to press for investigation of the fraud. This led to the September 29, 2009, dismissal by Secretary General Ban Ki Moon of Galbraith, who had openly accused UNAMA head Kai Eide of soft-pedaling on the fraud charges and siding with Karzai. Galbraith appealed his dismissal, amid press reports that he had discussed a plan with some U.S. officials to replace Karzai with an interim government, if the second round could not be held until after the winter. In December 2009, Eide announced he would not seek to renew his two year agreement to serve as UNAMA chief. The replacement named at the January 28, 2010, London conference was Staffan de Mistura, who previously played a similar U.N. role in Iraq. He arrived in Kabul in mid-March 2010.

Post-Election Cabinet

U.S. officials stated they would scrutinize the post-election cabinet for indications that Karzai would professionalize his government and eliminate corruption. Complicating Karzai's efforts to obtain confirmation of a full cabinet was the need to present his choices as technically competent while also maintaining a customary and expected balance of ethnic and political factions. In the parliamentary confirmation process that has unfolded, National Assembly members, particularly the well-educated independents, objected to many of his nominees as "unknowns," as having minimal qualifications, or as loyal to faction leaders who backed Karzai in the 2009 election. Karzai's original list of 24 ministerial nominees (presented December 19) was generally praised by the United States for retaining the highly praised economic team (and most of that team was confirmed). However, overall, only 7 of the first 24 nominees were confirmed (January 2, 2010), and only 7 of the 17 replacement nominees were confirmed (January 16, 2010), after which the Assembly went into winter recess. Another five (out of seven nominees) were confirmed on June 28, 2010, although one was a replacement for the ousted Interior Minister Atmar.

Although then UNAMA head Kai Eide called the vetoing of many nominees a "setback" to Afghan governance, Pentagon Press Secretary Geoff Morrell said on January 6, 2010, that the vetoing by parliament reflected a "healthy give and take" among Afghanistan's branches of government. Outside experts have said the confirmation process—and the later parliamentary review of a 2010 election decree, discussed below—reflects the growing institutional strength of the parliament and the functioning of checks and balances in the Afghan government. Of the major specific developments in the cabinet selection process to date (and with seven ministries remaining unfilled by permanent appointees, as of September 2010):

The main security ministers—Defense Minister Abdal Rahim Wardak and Interior Minister Mohammad Hanif Atmar—were renominated by Karzai and confirmed on January 2, 2010. They work closely with the U.S. military to expand and improve the Afghan national security forces. (Atmar was later dismissed, as discussed below.)

- Three key economic/civilian sector officials who work very closely with USAID and U.S. Embassy Kabul—Finance Minister Omar Zakhiwal, Agriculture Minister Mohammad Rahimi, and Education Minister Ghulam Faruq Wardak— were renominated and also were confirmed on January 2. The highly praised Minister of Rural Rehabilitation and Development (Ehsan Zia), who runs the widely touted and effective National Solidarity Program, was not renominated, to the chagrin of U.S. officials. His named replacement (Wais Barmak, a Fahim and Dr. Abdullah ally) was voted down. The second replacement, Jarullah Mansoori, was confirmed on January 16.
- The U.S.-praised Commerce Minister Wahidollah Sharani was selected to move over to take control of the Mines Ministry from the former minister, who is under investigation for corruption. Sharani was confirmed on January 2, 2010. However, as noted, Sharani is reportedly under investigation for corruption as of November 2010. Also confirmed that day was Minister of Culture Seyyed Makhdum Raheen. He had been serving as Ambassador to India.
- The clan of former moderate *mujahedin* party leader Pir Gaylani rose to prominence in the December 19 list. Gaylani son-in-law Anwar al Haq Al Ahady (see above) was named as economy minister and Hamid Gaylani (Pir Gaylani's son) was named as minister of border and tribal affairs. However, neither was confirmed and neither was renominated.
- Ismail Khan was renominated as minister of energy and water on December 19, disappointing U.S. officials and many Afghans who see him as a faction leader (Tajik leader/*mujahedin* era commander, Herat Province) with no technical expertise. He was voted down but remains in an acting capacity.
- Karzai initially did not nominate a permanent foreign minister, leaving Spanta in place as a caretaker. However, in the second nomination round, Karzai selected his close ally Zalmay Rassoul, who has been national security adviser since 2004, to the post. Rassoul was confirmed on January 16. Spanta is head of the National Security Council.
- Minister of Women's Affairs Ghazanfar was renominated to remain the only female minister, but was voted down (January 2). In the cabinet renominations, Karzai named three women—Suraiya Dalil to Public Health, Pelwasha Hassan to Women's Affairs, and Amina Afzali (minister of youth in an earlier Karzai cabinet) to Labor and Social Affairs. Of those, only Afzali was confirmed on January 16. Ghazanfar and Dalil are heading those ministries in an acting capacity. In the December 16, 2009, list, Karzai proposed a woman to head a new Ministry of Literacy, but parliament did not vote on this nomination because it had not yet acted to approve formation of the ministry
- Of the other nominees confirmed on January 16, 2010, at least one has previously served in high positions. The Assembly confirmed that day: Zarar Moqbel (who previously

was interior minister) as Counternarcotics Miinister; Economy Minister Abdul Hadi Arghandiwal, who belongs to the party linked with proTaliban insurgent leader Gulbuddin Hikmatyar (although the faction in the government has broken with Hikmatyar and rejects violence); Yousaf Niazi, minister of Hajj and Waqf (religious endowments) affairs; and Habibullah Ghalib, Minister of Justice.

- The following 10 were voted down on January 16: (1) Palwasha Hassan, nominated to head the Ministry of Women's Affairs; (2) Dalil, Public Health, now acting minister, mentioned above; (3) Muhammad Zubair Waheed, minister of commerce; (4) Muhammad Elahi, minister of higher education; (5) Muhammad Laali, Public Works; (6) Abdul Rahim, who was telecommunications minister in the first Karzai cabinet, as minister of refugee affairs (acting); (7) Arsala Jamal, formerly the governor of Khost Province who was widely praised in that role by Secretary Gates, as minister of border and tribal affairs (and now is acting minister); (8) Abdul Qadus Hamidi, minister of communications; (9) Abdur Rahim Oraz, minister of transport and aviation; and (10) Sultan Hussein Hesari, minister of urban development (acting).

- On June 28, 2010, Karzai obtained parliamentary approval for five positions out of seven nominees. Approved were Bismillah Khan as interior minister (replacing Atmar, who was fired on June 6); Al Ahady as commerce minister; former Qandahar governor Asadullah Khalid as minister of border and tribal affairs; Hamidi (see above) as minister of public works; and Jamahir Anwari as minister of refugees and repatriation. Voted down were two Hazara Shiites: Sarwar Danesh as minister of higher education, and former IEC chief Daud Ali Najafi as minister of transportation. Their rejection caused Hazara members in the Assembly to demonstrate their disapproval of the vote, and Karzai called for Hazaras to be approved in the future to ensure all-ethnic participation in government.

SEPTEMBER 18, 2010, PARLIAMENTARY ELECTIONS

Some, including the referenced report by the SIGAR, feared that the difficulties that plagued the 2009 presidential election were not adequately addressed to ensure that the September 18, 2010, parliamentary elections were fully free and fair. Many of these fears apparently were realized. A dispute over a new election decree that governed the election, which weakened the international voice on the ECC, is discussed below. The July 20, 2010, Kabul conference final communiqué included an Afghan government pledge to initiate, within six months, a strategy for long-term electoral reform.

Election Timing

On January 2, 2010, the IEC had initially set National Assembly elections for May 22, 2010. The IEC view was that this date was in line with a constitutional requirement for a new election to be held well prior to the expiry of the current Assembly's term. However, U.S., ECC, UNAMA, and officials of donor countries argued that Afghanistan's flawed institutions would not be able to hold free and fair elections under this timetable. Among the difficulties noted were that the IEC lacks sufficient staff, given that some were fired after the 2009 election; that the IEC lacks funds to hold the election under that timetable; that the U.S.

military buildup will be consumed with securing still restive areas at election time; and that the ECC's term expired at the end of January 2010. A functioning ECC was needed to evaluate complaints against registered parliamentary candidates because there are provisions in the election law to invalidate the candidacies of those who have previously violated Afghan law or committed human rights abuses.

The international community pressed for a delay of all of these elections until August 2010 or, according to some donors, mid-2011.[48] Bowing to funding and the wide range of other considerations mentioned, on January 24, 2010, the IEC announced that the parliamentary elections would be postponed until September 18, 2010. Other experts said that the security issues, and the lack of faith in Afghanistan's election institutions, necessitated further postponement.[49]

About $120 million was budgeted by the IEC for the parliamentary elections, of which at least $50 million came from donor countries, giving donors leverage over when the election might take place. The remaining $70 million was funds left over from the 2009 elections. Donors had held back the needed funds, possibly in an effort to pressure the IEC to demonstrate that it is correcting the flaws identified in the various "after-action" reports on the 2009 election. With the compromises and Karzai announcements below, those funds were released as of April 2010.

Election Decree/Reform

With the dispute between the Karzai government and international donors continuing over how to ensure a free and fair election, the Afghan government drafted an election decree that would supersede the 2005 election law and govern the 2010 parliamentary election.[50] Karzai signed the decree in February 2010. The Afghan government argues that the decree supersedes the constitutional clause that any new election law not be adopted less than one year prior to the election to which that law will apply.

Substantively, some of the provisions of the election decree—particularly the proposal to make the ECC an all-Afghan body—caused alarm in the international community. Another controversial element was the registration requirements of a financial deposit (equivalent of about $650), and that candidates obtain signatures of at least 1,000 voters. On March 14, 2010, after discussions with outgoing UNAMA head Kai Eide, Karzai reportedly agreed to cede to UNAMA two "international seats" on the ECC, rather than to insist that all five ECC members be Afghans. Still, the majority of the ECC seats were Afghans.

The election decree became an issue for Karzai opponents and others in the National Assembly who seek to assert parliamentary authority. On March 31, the *Wolesi Jirga* voted to reject the election decree. However, on April 3, 2010, the *Meshrano Jirga* decided not to act on the election decree, meaning that it was not rejected by the Assembly as a whole and will likely stand to govern the September 18, 2010, National Assembly elections. Karzai upheld his pledge to implement the March 2010 compromise with then UNAMA head Eide by allowing UNAMA to appoint two ECC members and for decisions to require that at least one non-Afghan ECC member concur.

Among other steps to correct the mistakes of the 2009 election, the Afghan Interior Ministry planned instituted a national identity card system to curb voter registration fraud. However, observers say that registration fraud still occurred. On April 17, 2010, Karzai appointed a new IEC head, Fazel Ahmed Manawi, who drew praise from many factions

Afghanistan: Politics, Elections, and Government Performance

(including "opposition leader" Dr. Abdullah) for impartiality. The IEC also barred 6,000 poll workers who served in the 2009 election from working the 2010 election.

Preparations and the Vote

Preparations for the September 18 election proceeded without major disruption, according to the IEC. Candidates registered during April 20-May 6, 2010. A list of candidates was circulated on May 13, 2010, including 2,477 candidates for the 249 seats.[51] These figures included 226 candidates who registered but whose documentation was not totally in order; and appeal restored about 180 of them. On May 30, 2010, in a preliminary ruling, 85 candidates others were disqualified as members of illegal armed groups. However, appeals and negotiations restored all but 36 in this latter category. A final list of candidates, after all appeals and decisions on the various disqualifications, was issued June 22. The final list included 2,577 candidates, including 406 women. Since then, 62 candidates were invalidated by the ECC, mostly because they did not resign their government positions, as required.

Voter registration was conducted June 12-August 12. According to the IEC, over 375,000 new voters were registered, and the number of eligible voters was about 11.3 million. Campaigning began June 23. Many candidates, particularly those who are women, said that security difficulties have prevented them from conducting active campaigning. At least three candidates and 13 candidate supporters were killed by insurgent violence.

On August 24, 2010, the IEC announced that the Afghan security forces say they would only be able to secure 5,897 of the planned 6,835 polling centers. To prevent so-called "ghost polling stations" (stations open but where no voters can go, thus allowing for ballot-stuffing), the 938 stations considered not secure were not opened. The IEC announcement stated that further security evaluation could lead to the closing of still more stations and, on election day, a total of 5,355 centers opened, 304 of those slated to open did not, and for 157 centers there was no information available. In part to compensate, the IEC opened extra polling stations in centers in secure areas near to those that were closed.

On election day, about 5.6 million votes were cast out of about 11.3 million eligible voters. Turnout was therefore about 50%. A major issue was security. At first, it appeared as though election-day violence was lower than in the 2009 presidential election. However, on September 24, NATO/ISAF announced that there were about 380 total attacks, about 100 more than in 2009. However, voting was generally reported as orderly and the attacks did not derail the election.

Outcomes

Preliminary results were announced on October 20, 2010, and final, certified results were to be announced by October 30, 2010, but were delayed until November 24, 2010, due to investigation of fraud complaints. While the information below illustrates that there was substantial fraud, the IEC and ECC have been widely praised by the international community for their handling of the fraud allegations. Among the key outcomes, both in terms of process and results, are:

- Of the 5.6 million votes cast, the ECC invalidated 1.3 million (about 25%) after investigations of fraud complaints. The ECC prioritized complaints filed as follows: 2,142 as possibly affecting the election, 1,056 as unable to affect the result, and 600 where there will be no investigation. Causes for invalidation most often included ballot boxes in which all votes were for one candidate.

- About 1,100 election workers have been questioned, and 413 candidates have been referred by the ECC to the Attorney General for having allegedly committed election fraud.
- There have been at least three demonstrations against the fraud by about 300 candidates who felt deprived of victory, under a banner called the "Union of Afghan Wolesi Jirga Candidates 2010."

Political Results

The results, as certified by the Afghan election bodies, have resulted in substantial controversy within Afghanistan and have led to a political crisis. According to the certified results:

- The incoming lower house, to be seated on/about January 21, 2011, will have approximately 50% new membership, meaning that many incumbents apparently have lost their seats.
- The camps of both Karzai as well as those of Dr. Abdullah and the opposition appear to have failed to meet their political objectives, according to observers and press reports. Each camp sought to hold commanding blocs of about 100 seats in the next lower house. However, Karzai will likely have about 80-90 supporters (out of the 249 in the body) and Abdullah might have about 60. This apparent result also complicates any effort to pin blame for fraud clearly on one camp or another. It also makes in unlikely that Karzai's allies will be able to install Sayyaf as next lower house speaker, replacing Abdullah ally Qanooni.
- Karzai's allies fared worse than expected because several pro-Karzai candidates losing in Qandahar Province, and because many Pashtuns did not vote, due to security reasons, in mixed Ghazni Province. The poor Pashtun turnout in Ghazni has led Hazara candidates to have won all 11 seats from the province, instead of 6 Pashtuns and 5 Hazaras in the outgoing lower house.
- If the election results hold and declared winners are seated, it is likely that the next lower house will be more diverse politically than the outgoing one, and less predictable in its votes. The Hazara strength, which has prompted a Pashtun political backlash, has no clear impact because many Hazaras support Karzai while many also oppose him as a representative of the political strength of the Pashtuns (who have a reputation of repressing or discriminating against the Hazaras).
- Because of the widespread fraud allegations, it is possible that the results might not hold. Some outcomes include invalidating the entire election, or invalidating the results from Ghazni, in particular. Seeking to address Pashtun grievances, the Karzai government has arrested 4 IEC officials, ostensibly for violations in the 2009 elections, and the deputy Attorney General, in December 2010, urged election results to be voided and the Afghan Supreme Court to order a recount. The IEC and EC, largely backed by the international community, have insisted that the certified results stand, asserting they are the only bodies under Afghan electoral law that have legitimate jurisdiction over election results.

Afghanistan: Politics, Elections, and Government Performance

- Some believe that President Karzai seeks to appear to support his Pashtun allies but might ultimately drop the government's objections to the result. Others believe his government might pursue the issue in the hopes of obtaining an altered result that increases the numbers of Pashtuns in the incoming lower house.

Table 1. Afghanistan Political Transition Process

Interim Administration	Formed by Bonn Agreement. Headed by Hamid Karzai, an ethnic Pashtun, but key security positions dominated by mostly minority "Northern Alliance." Karzai reaffirmed as leader by June 2002 "emergency loya jirga." (A jirga is a traditional Afghan assembly).
Constitution	Approved by January 2004 "Constitutional Loya Jirga" (CLJ). Set up strong presidency, a rebuke to Northern Alliance that wanted prime ministership to balance presidential power, but gave parliament significant powers to compensate. Gives men and women equal rights under the law, allows for political parties as long as they are not "un-Islamic"; allows for court rulings according to Hanafi (Sunni) Islam (Chapter 7, Article 15). Set out electoral roadmap for simultaneous (if possible) presidential, provincial, and district elections by June 2004. Named ex-King Zahir Shah to non-hereditary position of "Father of the Nation;" he died July 23, 2007.
Presidential Election	Elections for President and two vice presidents, for 5-year term, held Oct. 9, 2004. Turnout was 80% of 10.5 million registered. Karzai and running mates (Ahmad Zia Masud, a Tajik and brother of legendary mujahedin commander Ahmad Shah Masud, who was assassinated by Al Qaeda two days before the Sept. 11 attacks, and Karim Khalili, a Hazara) elected with 55% against 16 opponents. Second highest vote getter, Northern Alliance figure (and Education Minister) Yunus Qanooni (16%). One female ran, got about 1%. Hazara leader Mohammad Mohaqiq got 11.7%; and Dostam won 10%. Funded with $90 million in international aid, including $40 million from U.S. (FY2004 supplemental, P.L. 108-106).
First Parliamentary Elections	Elections held Sept. 18, 2005, on "Single Non-Transferable Vote" System; candidates stood as individuals, not part of party list. Parliament consists of a 249 elected lower house (Wolesi Jirga, House of the People) and a selected 102 seat upper house (Meshrano Jirga, House of Elders). Voting was for one candidate only, although number of representatives varied by province, ranging from 2 (Panjshir Province) to 33 (Kabul Province). Herat has 17; Nangahar, 14; Qandahar, Balkh, and Ghazni, 11 seats each. The body is 28% female (68 persons), in line with the legal minimum of 68 women—two per each of the 34 provinces. Upper house appointed by Karzai (34 seats, half of which are to be women), by the provincial councils (34 seats), and district councils (remaining 34 seats). There are 23 women in it, above the 17 required by the constitution. Because district elections (400 district councils) were not held, provincial councils selected 68 on interim basis. 2,815 candidates for Wolesi Jirga, including 347 women. Turnout was 57% (6.8 million voters) of 12.5 million registered. Funded by $160 million in international aid, including $45 million from U.S. (FY2005 supplemental appropriation, P.L. 109-13).
First Provincial Elections/ District Elections	Provincial elections held Sept. 18, 2005, simultaneous with parliamentary elections. Exact powers vague, but now taking lead in deciding local reconstruction Provincial council sizes range from 9 to the 29 seats on the Kabul provincial council. Total seats are 420, of which 121 held by women. 13,185 candidates, including 279 women. Some criticize the provincial election system as disproportionately weighted toward large districts within each province. District elections not held due to complexity and potential tensions of drawing district boundaries.
Second Presidential and Provincial Elections	Presidential and provincial elections were held Aug. 20, 2009, but required a runoff because no candidate received over 50% in certified results issued October 20. Second round not held because challenger, Dr. Abdullah, pulled out of a second-round runoff vote. Election costs about $300 million.
Parliamentary Elections	Originally set for May 22, 2010; held September 18, 2010. Results disputed; Karzai government seeks to overturn some or all results.

Implications for the United States of the Afghan Elections

U.S. officials express clear U.S. neutrality in all Afghan elections. However, in the 2009 presidential election, Karzai reportedly believed the United States was hoping strong candidates might emerge to replace him. This perception was a function of the strained relations between Karzai and some Obama Administration officials, particularly Ambassadors Holbrooke and Eikenberry. Ambassador Timothy Carney was appointed to head the 2009 U.S. election support effort at U.S. Embassy Kabul, tasked to ensure that the United States was even-handed.

The legitimacy of the Afghan partner continues to be a consideration for U.S. policy, as made clear yet again in the December 16, 2010, summary of a U.S. strategy assessment. The reviiew summary did not specifically discuss the political crisis triggered by the September 18, 2010, parliamentary elections, but many U.S. officials believe that a continued crisis would complicate U.S. planning to begin a transition to Afghan security leadership starting in early 2011. That transition is to include a drawdown of some U.S. forces in July 2011.

Table 2. Major Pashtun Tribal Confederations

Clan/Tribal Confederations	Location	Example
Durrani	Mainly southern Afghanistan: Qandahar, Helmand, Zabol, Uruzgan,Nimruz	
Popalzai (Zirak branch of Durrani Pashtun)	Qandahar	Hamid Karzai, President of Afghanistan; Jelani Popal, head of the Independent Directorate of Local Governance; Mullah Bradar, the top aide to Mullah Umar, captured in Pakistan in Feb. 2010. Two-thirds of Qandahar's provincial government posts held by Zirak Durrani Pashtuns
Alikozai	Qandahar	Mullah Naqibullah (deceased, former anti-Taliban faction leader in Qandahar)
Clan/Tribal Confederations	Location	Example
Barakzai	Qandahar, Helmand	Ghul Agha Shirzai (Governor, Nangarhar Province)
Achakzai	Qandahar, Helmand	Abdul Razziq, Chief of Staff, Border Police, Qandahar Province
Alozai	Helmand (Musa Qala district)	Sher Mohammad Akhunzadeh (former Helmand governor); Hajji Zahir, former governor of Marjah
Noorzai	Qandahar	Noorzai brothers, briefly in charge of Qandahar after the fall of the Taliban in November 2001
Ghilzai	Eastern Afghanistan: Paktia, Paktika, Khost, Nangarhar, Kunar	
Ahmadzai		Mohammed Najibullah (pres. 1986-1992); Ashraf Ghani, Karzai adviser, Finance Minister 2002-2004

Afghanistan: Politics, Elections, and Government Performance

Table 2. (Continued).

Clan/Tribal Confederations	Location	Example
Hotak		Mullah Umar, but hails from Uruzgan, which is dominated by Durranis
Taraki		Nur Mohammed Taraki (leader 1978-1979)
Kharoti		Hafizullah Amin (leader September-December1979); Gulbuddin Hekmatyar, founder of Hezb-e-Islami (Gulbuddin), former mujahedin party leader now anti-Karzai insurgent.
Zadran	Paktia, Khost	Pacha Khan Zadran; Insurgent leader Jalaluddin Haqqani
Kodai		
Mangal	Paktia, Khost	Ghulab Mangal (Governor of Helmand Province)
Orkazai		
Shinwari	Nangarhar province	Fasl Ahmed Shinwari, former Supreme Court Chief Justice
Mandezai		
Sangu Khel		
Sipah		
Wardak (Pashtu-speaking non-Pashtun)	Wardak Province	Abdul Rahim Wardak (Defense Minister)
Afridis	Tirah, Khyber Pass, Kohat	
Zaka khel		
Jawaki		
Adam khel		
Malikdin, etc		
Yusufzais	Khursan, Swat, Kabul	
Akozais		
Malizais		
Loezais		
Khattaks	Kohat, Peshawar, Bangash	
Akorai		
Terai		
Mohmands	Near Khazan, Peshawar	
Baizai		
Alimzai		
Uthmanzais		
Khawazais		
Wazirs	Mainly in Waziristan	
Darwesh khel		
Bannu		

Source: This table was prepared by Hussein Hassan, Information Research Specialist, CRS. Note: N/A indicates no example is available.

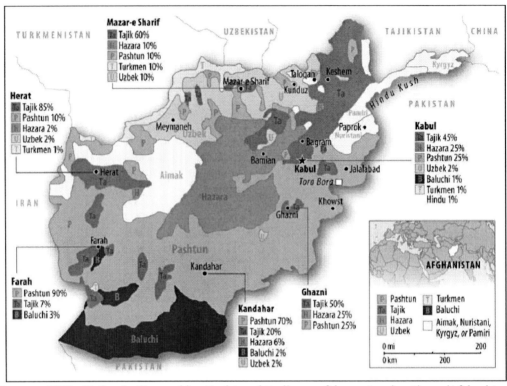

Source: 2003 National Geographic Society, http://www.afghan-network.net/maps/Afghanistan-Map.pdf. Adapted by Amber Wilhelm, CRS

Notes: This map is intended to be illustrative of the approximate demographic distribution by region of Afghanistan. CRS has no way to confirm exact population distributions.

Figure 1. Map of Afghan Ethnicities.

ACKNOWLEDGMENTS

The table of major Pashtun tribes was prepared by Hussein Hassan, Information Research Specialist, CRS.

End Notes

[1] http://documents.nytimes.com/the-obama-administrations-overview-on-afghanistan-and-pakistan

[2] For text, see http://www.un.org/News/dh/latest/afghan/afghan-agree.htm.

[3] *Shura* is the term used by non-Pashtuns to characterize the traditional assembly concept. *Jirga* is the Pashtun term.

[4] Filkins, Dexter, and Mark Mazzetti. "Key Karzai Aide in Graft Inquiry is Linked to C.I.A." *New York Times*, August 26, 2010.

[5] Sayyaf led the *Ittihad Islami* (Islamic Union) *mujahedin* party during the war against the Soviet occupation.

[6] CRS e-mail conversation with a then National Security aide to President Karzai, December 2008.

[7] This is the name of the area where the Taliban prisoners purportedly died and were buried in a mass grave.

[8] Gall, Carlotta. "In Afghanistan's North, Ex-Warlord Offers Security." *New York Times*, May 17, 2010.

[9] Partlow, Joshua. "Audio Files Raise New Questions About Afghan Elections." *Washington Post*, November 11, 2010.

Afghanistan: Politics, Elections, and Government Performance 409

[10] House of Representatives. Subcommittee on National Security and Foreign Affairs, Committee on Oversight and Government Reform. "Warlord, Inc.: Extortion and Corruption Along the U.S. Supply Chain in Afghanistan." Report of the Majority Staff, June 2010.

[11] Filkins, Dexter, Mark Mazetti and James Risen, "Brother of Afghan Leader Is Said to be on C.I.A. Payroll," *New York Times*, October 28, 2009.

[12] Partlow, Joshua, "U.S. Seeks to Bolster Kandahar Governor, Upend Power Balance," *Washington Post*, April 29, 2010.

[13] Some information in this section is from the State Department reports on human rights in Afghanistan for 2009, March 11, 2010; for text, see http://www.state.gov/g/drl/rls/hrrpt/2009/sca/136084.htm and the International Religious Freedom Report, released October 26, 2009, http://www.state.gov/g/drl/rls/irf/2009/127362.htm.

[14] An exact English translation of his April 4 comments, in which he purportedly said that even he might consider joining the Taliban if U.S. pressure on him continues, is not available.

[15] Interview with Admiral Mike Mullen, Chairman of the Joint Chiefs of Staff. CNN, May 30 2010.

[16] Dreazen, Yochi, and Sarah Lynch. "U.S. Seeks to Repair Karzai Tie." *Wall Street Journal*, April 12, 2010.

[17] Ambassador Frank Ruggiero is acting SRAP following the December 13, 2010, death of Holbrooke.

[18] "Evaluating Progress in Afghanistan-Pakistan" Foreign Policy website, http://www.foreignpolicy.com/articles/2009/09/16/evaluating_progress_in_afghanistan_pakistan.

[19] Department of Defense. "Report on Progress Toward Security and Stability in Afghanistan." April 2010. http://www.defense.gov/pubs/pdfs/report_final_secdef_04_26_10.pdf.

[20] For more information, particularly on Rule of Law programs, see: CRS Report R41484, *Afghanistan: U.S. Rule of Law and Justice Sector Assistance*, by Liana Sun Wyler and Kenneth Katzman.

[21] Chandrasekaran, Rajiv. "A Subtler Takc to Fight Afghan Corruption." Washington Post, September 13, 2010.

[22] Filkins, Dexter, "Bribes Corrode Afghan's Trust in Government," *New York Times*, January 2, 2009.

[23] Communique text at http://www.nytimes.com/2010/07/21/world/asia/21kabultext.html.

[24] http://www.sigar.mil/reports/pdf/audits/SIGAR20Audit-10-2.pdf.

[25] Nordland, Ron and Mark Mazzetti. "Graft Dispute in Afghanistan Is Test for U.S." *New York Times*, August 24, 2010.

[27] Miller, Greg and Joshua Partlow. "Afghans, U.S. Aim to Plug Cash Drain." *Washington Post*, August 21, 2010.

[28] Madhani, Aamer. "U.S. Reviews Afghan Watchdog Authority." *USA Today*, May 12, 2010.

[29] Rosenberg, Matthew. "Corruption Suspected in Airlift of Billions in Cash From Kabul." Wall Street Journal, June 28, 2010.

[30] Partlow, Joshua and Karen DeYoung. "Afghan Government Falters in Kandahar." Washington Post, November 3, 2010.

[31] For text, see http://www.state.gov/documents/organization/135728.pdf.

[32] For more information, see the Defense Department report on Afghanistan stability, April 2010, cited earlier. pp. 19-20.

[33] Department of State. 2009 Human Rights Report: Afghanistan, March 11, 2010.

[34] http://www.state.gov/g/drl/rls/irf/2010/148786.htm.

[35] Oppel, Richard Jr. and Abdul Waheed Wafa, "Hazara Minority Hustles to Head of the Class in Afghanistan," *New York Times*, January 4, 2010.

[36] "We Have the Promises of the World:Women's Rights in Afghanistan," Human Rights Watch, December 2009, http://www.wluml.org/sites/wluml.org/files/hrw_report_2009.pdf.

[37] CRS meeting with the Minister of Women's Affairs, October 13, 2009.

[38] For prior years, see CRS Report RL30588, *Afghanistan: Post-Taliban Governance, Security, and U.S. Policy*, by Kenneth Katzman, in the section on aid to Afghanistan, year by year.

[39] Department of State and U.S. Agency for International Development, "Report on U.S. Government Activities 2008- 2009 For Women and Girls in Afghanistan," October 20, 2009.

[40] Report by the Special Inspector General for Afghanistan Reconstruction (SIGAR). September 9, 2010.

[41] ECC website, http://www.ecc.org.af/en/.

[42] Fidler, Stephen and John W. Miller, "U.S. Allies Await Afghan Review," *Wall Street Journal*, September 25, 2009.

[43] Statement of the Independent Election Commission Secretariat, February 3, 2009, provided to CRS by a Karzai national security aide.

[44] Some of the information in this section obtained in CRS interviews with a Karzai national security aide, December 2008.

[45] Mulrine, Anna, "Afghan Presidential Candidate Takes a Page From Obama's Playbook," *U.S. News and World Report*, June 25, 2009.

[46] "Afghan Panel to Use Sampling in Recount," *USA Today*, September 22, 2009.

[47] See IEC website for final certified tallies, http://www.iec.org.af/results.

[48] Trofimov, Yaroslav, "West Urges Afghanistan to Delay Election," *Wall Street Journal*, December 11, 2009.

[49] Rondeaux, Candace. "Why Afghanistan's September Elections Ought to Be Postponed." *Washington Post*, July 11, 2010.

[50] Partlow, Joshua, "Afghanistan's Government Seeks More Control Over Elections," *Washington Post*, February 15, 2010.

[51] The seat allocation per province is the same as it was in the 2005 parliamentary election—33 seats up for election in Kabul; 17 in Herat province; 14 in Nangarhar, 11 each in Qandahar, Balkh, and Ghazni; 9 in Badakhshan, Konduz, and Faryab, 8 in Helmand, and 2 to 6 in the remaining provinces. Ten are reserved for Kuchis (nomads).

INDEX

#

20th century, 168
9/11, 113, 214, 234, 331, 332, 356, 359
9/11 Commission, 113, 214, 234, 332, 356

A

abolition, 187
Abraham, 43, 50
abuse, 255, 256, 387, 390
access, 14, 15, 27, 29, 47, 73, 86, 102, 107, 121, 124, 127, 132, 194, 214, 264, 265, 273, 307, 322, 328, 335, 396
accommodation, 64, 253
accommodations, 223
accountability, 25, 55, 57, 243, 248, 255, 256, 281, 283, 375
accounting, 290, 327, 378, 397
acquisitions, 222
activism, 42, 123, 183, 327
Activists, 176
administrators, 284
adults, 22
advancement, 227, 390
advisory body, 138
aerospace, 135
affirming, 243
Afghan insurgency, 291
Africa, 206, 216, 231, 292, 317, 389
age, 142, 188, 273, 370
agencies, 9, 24, 97, 99, 237, 241, 246, 258, 263, 264, 265, 286, 303, 311, 312, 331, 341, 371, 378, 382, 384, 386
aggression, 23, 64, 82
agriculture, 101, 196, 239, 246, 274, 336, 337

Air Force, 78, 82, 126, 164, 172, 191, 315, 321
Al Qaeda, 11, 18, 19, 44, 51, 79, 127, 144, 147, 149, 156, 157, 214, 215, 234, 276, 277, 278, 279, 289, 290, 291, 292, 293, 302, 303, 304, 317, 318, 319, 322, 323, 326, 327, 328, 329, 354, 355, 356, 357, 359, 361, 405
Al Qaeda cells, 291
Albania, 352
Algeria, 111, 233
ambassadors, 40, 213
AMF, 306
ammonium, 290
Andijon, 321, 328
anger, 40, 170
annual rate, 98
Anti-Defamation League, 32, 67
apathy, 396
appointees, 370, 391, 400
appointments, 154, 155, 163, 176, 178, 179, 281, 370, 379, 384, 385, 387
appropriations, 35, 65, 126, 156, 225, 235, 317, 331, 332, 359, 377, 392
Appropriations Act, 55, 60, 126
Arab countries, 53, 131
Arab world, 14, 40, 46, 47, 75
architect, 74, 145, 173
Argentina, 233
armed conflict, 92
armed forces, 82, 122, 151, 170, 190, 372
armed groups, 8, 167, 185, 225, 289, 306, 324, 403
Armenia, 212, 352
Armenians, 212
arms control, 200
arms sales, 96, 168, 206, 217, 223, 358

arrest, 43, 52, 119, 134, 155, 171, 174, 175, 186, 187, 225, 234, 291, 293, 295, 304, 322, 326, 372, 381, 389

arrests, 32, 35, 44, 53, 78, 79, 172, 182, 186, 189, 230, 388

arson, 65

articulation, 244, 266

Asia, 9, 69, 79, 112, 173, 212, 219, 231, 296, 309, 328, 339, 377

aspiration, 34, 254

assassination, 38, 45, 50, 52, 53, 55, 71, 119, 128, 132, 171, 181, 206, 281, 295, 322, 386

assault, 22, 78, 368, 389

assertiveness, 281

assessment, 9, 78, 141, 182, 190, 193, 201, 238, 242, 253, 289, 295, 296, 301, 363, 371, 378, 406

assets, 31, 36, 44, 81, 86, 105, 125, 127, 128, 129, 179, 193, 196, 197, 202, 203, 207, 226, 230, 325, 357, 358, 360, 380, 381

asylum, 189

atmosphere, 116, 188

atrocities, 214

audit, 252, 379, 381, 383

audits, 56, 331, 409

Austria, 133, 199, 261, 352

authoritarianism, 48

authorities, 13, 53, 89, 96, 105, 107, 109, 122, 163, 164, 175, 201, 223, 250, 264, 280, 307, 365, 377, 382, 385, 389

authority, 25, 64, 86, 96, 108, 121, 125, 128, 129, 133, 135, 138, 139, 170, 171, 192, 199, 203, 233, 235, 238, 239, 246, 247, 265, 274, 277, 283, 284, 287, 292, 297, 332, 357, 364, 374, 376, 381, 382, 383, 384, 402

automobiles, 338

autonomy, 28, 284, 369

aversion, 367

awareness, 63, 351, 383

Ayman al Zawahiri, 18

Azerbaijan, 190, 212, 228, 352

B

background information, 7, 11, 96, 265

backlash, 9, 68, 131, 294, 297, 363, 404

Bahrain, 38, 100, 168, 206, 207, 208, 311, 321

bail, 189

ballistic missiles, 96, 113, 204, 205

Baluchistan, 168, 185, 214

ban, 69, 124, 125, 126, 127, 189, 196, 198, 200, 202, 203, 217, 220, 226, 228, 229, 230, 286, 290, 358

banking, 27, 31, 36, 78, 113, 199, 203, 207, 208, 315

banking sector, 208

banks, 79, 83, 86, 105, 130, 193, 200, 202, 203, 208, 273, 379, 382

bargaining, 150, 200, 201

barriers, 15

base, 9, 11, 14, 19, 29, 45, 69, 82, 96, 122, 153, 176, 179, 193, 204, 213, 223, 269, 273, 275, 289, 314, 315, 321, 324, 328, 330, 335, 353, 355, 368, 369, 373

basic needs, 33

basic services, 35

batteries, 338, 355

Beijing, 87, 362

Belarus, 190, 233

Belgium, 91, 233, 261, 310, 352

benchmarks, 7, 140, 141, 243, 246, 247, 248, 249, 266, 299, 322, 331

beneficial effect, 384

benefits, 26, 28, 109, 132, 134, 209, 220, 231, 263, 371, 375, 377, 385

beverages, 388

bilateral aid, 357

bilateral relationship, 109, 134

biological weapons, 204

births, 273

blame, 143, 144, 156, 207, 290, 404

blasphemy, 388

blockades, 32

blogger, 187

blogs, 65, 187, 235

blood, 204

blueprint, 243

Bolivia, 215

bomb attack, 116

bonds, 203, 363

bonuses, 377

border control, 79

border crossing, 41, 51, 322, 323, 337

border security, 79, 87, 101, 212

borrowers, 180

Bosnia, 352

Bosnia-Herzegovina, 352

Brazil, 189, 199, 200, 201, 215, 231, 233, 261

breakdown, 38, 57

bribes, 315, 379, 380, 382

Britain, 74, 153, 168, 171, 195, 196, 213, 222, 230, 233, 271, 274, 285, 294, 295, 302, 303, 308, 309,

310, 311, 312, 314, 323, 336, 339, 353, 373, 380, 381, 382
brothers, 215, 281, 406
Buddhism, 270
building code, 155
Bulgaria, 309, 352
bureaucracy, 79, 131, 255, 316
burn, 388
business partners, 108
businesses, 127, 130, 180, 187, 193, 301, 336
buyers, 336, 356

C

Cabinet, 113, 176, 399
cables, 206
Cairo, 40, 219
Camp David, 50
campaign strategies, 365
campaigns, 76, 254, 365
canals, 284, 301
candidates, 47, 53, 77, 142, 145, 146, 148, 150, 151, 170, 177, 208, 233, 250, 251, 252, 309, 325, 365, 367, 368, 391, 394, 396, 397, 402, 403, 404, 405, 406
capacity building, 245
capital goods, 274
capital projects, 164
Capitol Hill, 114
cargoes, 202
cash, 29, 36, 65, 67, 83, 180, 213, 301, 325, 351, 367, 382
Caspian Sea, 212
casting, 357, 398
category a, 351, 393
Caucasus, 168
caucuses, 280
CDC, 266, 386
ceasefire, 184
cell phones, 265
Central Asia, 9, 112, 114, 134, 192, 212, 214, 269, 326, 327, 328, 334, 335, 338, 389
certification, 110, 125, 151, 178, 230, 286, 346, 347, 348, 383, 385, 391, 398
chain of command, 55
challenges, 12, 19, 22, 40, 41, 64, 164, 190, 212, 239, 240, 244, 246, 255, 333
chaos, 278
charitable organizations, 31, 32
charities, 30, 31, 35, 37, 44, 45

Chechens, 291
checks and balances, 169, 399
cheese, 28
chemical, 112, 129, 204, 292, 359
chemicals, 290
Chief Justice, 388, 407
Chief of Staff, 406
children, 22, 24, 79, 83, 185, 189, 264, 265, 330, 335
China, 16, 83, 124, 131, 136, 196, 199, 203, 206, 207, 212, 216, 221, 231, 233, 261, 279, 309, 310, 327, 328, 329, 338, 361, 382, 389
Chinese firms, 201
Chinese government, 201
Christianity, 389
Christians, 18, 24, 156, 160, 187, 188, 273, 388, 389
CIA, 44, 67, 70, 75, 169, 231, 233, 234, 271, 274, 278, 281, 291, 300, 303, 317, 318, 356, 361, 374, 378
CIS, 175
cities, 16, 34, 45, 63, 70, 122, 138, 144, 164, 173, 180, 182, 211, 308
citizens, 14, 20, 32, 36, 59, 75, 77, 123, 126, 127, 138, 211, 315, 329, 384
citizenship, 379
City, 64, 84, 86, 144, 353, 361
civil law, 139
civil servants, 250, 376, 377, 379
civil service, 27, 47, 377
civil society, 77, 123, 225, 227, 244, 250, 254, 387, 392, 393
civil war, 144, 240, 275, 313
classes, 174, 180, 181
cleaning, 284
clients, 40, 175
climate, 74, 122
Clinton Administration, 44, 120, 217, 223, 230, 235, 275, 276, 277, 338
close relationships, 215
closure, 12, 14, 16, 32, 34, 35, 37, 38, 41, 42, 48, 51, 52, 63
clothing, 75, 173, 187
C-N, 348
CNN, 89, 91, 234, 291, 361, 409
coal, 99, 338
coffee, 32
coherence, 263
Cold War, 271
collaboration, 34, 50
Colombia, 310
coma, 388

commander-in-chief, 151, 170

commerce, 300, 320, 401

commercial, 65, 74, 96, 98, 107, 109, 112, 134, 135, 196, 207, 310, 356

commercial bank, 65

commercial ties, 109

communication, 182, 218, 225, 226

Communist Party, 271

communities, 8, 16, 63, 137, 138, 146, 157, 188, 250, 302, 305, 315, 335, 364, 366, 367

community, 14, 21, 23, 24, 30, 35, 40, 46, 48, 59, 76, 83, 122, 123, 131, 133, 138, 148, 150, 156, 171, 173, 176, 178, 188, 193, 201, 208, 216, 219, 224, 234, 237, 238, 239, 240, 242, 243, 244, 245, 247, 248, 249, 250, 253, 254, 255, 256, 262, 265, 266, 279, 280, 283, 286, 287, 292, 297, 300, 302, 303, 331, 337, 365, 367, 371, 376, 384, 389, 390, 402, 403, 404

community support, 250

compensation, 100, 384

competition, 8, 85, 132, 137, 144, 158, 209, 213, 325, 364, 392, 393, 395

competitors, 109, 143

compilation, 90

complexity, 405

compliance, 77, 126, 164, 195, 196, 197, 204, 210, 306, 383

composition, 367

compounds, 253

computer, 194, 205, 375

conference, 83, 113, 181, 183, 219, 227, 235, 239, 240, 243, 244, 245, 280, 287, 302, 307, 309, 310, 330, 331, 334, 361, 364, 376, 377, 379, 380, 382, 383, 384, 387, 392, 399, 401

configuration, 85

conflict, 12, 18, 28, 34, 40, 41, 51, 63, 64, 68, 96, 120, 123, 143, 150, 157, 178, 206, 210, 211, 214, 216, 221, 222, 239, 244, 249, 272, 275, 283, 287, 289, 290, 301, 319, 322, 326, 327, 355, 364, 378, 381, 390

conflict resolution, 287

confrontation, 171, 190, 208, 218, 222

Congress, 5, 7, 8, 9, 11, 12, 13, 20, 32, 34, 36, 38, 47, 48, 57, 58, 64, 69, 73, 81, 84, 85, 86, 90, 93, 95, 96, 97, 101, 102, 103, 104, 105, 107, 110, 113, 114, 115, 117, 124, 125, 128, 132, 135, 145, 161, 216, 217, 223, 224, 225, 226, 230, 234, 235, 238, 249, 256, 262, 266, 272, 278, 284, 285, 296, 298, 305, 319, 321, 331, 332, 340, 359, 363, 392

consensus, 21, 22, 73, 122, 158, 162, 173, 195, 198, 245, 251, 303, 315, 333, 378, 392, 393, 398

consent, 56, 57, 58, 60, 103, 112, 177

Consolidated Appropriations Act, 55, 65, 126, 156

consolidation, 250

conspiracy, 113

constituents, 29, 374

Constitution, 135, 139, 152, 159, 248, 263, 264, 265, 280, 393, 394, 405

construction, 16, 37, 53, 79, 97, 99, 109, 121, 130, 193, 212, 213, 253, 287, 303, 312, 316, 321, 326, 327, 328, 335, 337, 338, 351, 383

consulting, 48, 100

consumer protection, 155

consumption, 66, 87, 231

Container Security Initiative, 80, 106

containers, 80, 360

contingency, 224

controversial, 181, 267, 390, 402

controversies, 250

convention, 96, 142, 383

conversations, 87, 231, 234, 235, 362

conviction, 382

cooking, 32

cooperation, 7, 8, 36, 38, 44, 68, 73, 80, 82, 83, 95, 96, 100, 101, 102, 103, 104, 105, 106, 107, 108, 109, 110, 111, 112, 113, 120, 134, 198, 212, 214, 219, 223, 233, 238, 241, 242, 244, 247, 263, 271, 278, 286, 287, 289, 298, 301, 320, 322, 324, 326, 327, 328, 346, 347, 378, 386

coordination, 9, 38, 96, 105, 237, 238, 240, 243, 244, 249, 256, 263, 266, 287, 323

copper, 274, 329, 337, 338

corruption, 9, 48, 66, 123, 129, 131, 155, 171, 177, 237, 239, 244, 247, 249, 250, 251, 255, 263, 270, 273, 283, 284, 294, 315, 316, 317, 318, 321, 333, 337, 350, 351, 363, 364, 370, 371, 375, 376, 377, 378, 379, 380, 381, 382, 383, 384, 385, 395, 396, 399, 400

cost, 98, 134, 180, 193, 226, 270, 310, 318, 321, 327, 356, 395

Council of Ministers, 96

Council of the European Union, 51

counterterrorism, 44, 45, 80, 96

Court of Appeals, 184

covering, 64, 146, 226, 266, 290, 331, 391, 392

credentials, 18, 189

creditors, 274

crimes, 113

criminals, 388

crises, 15

critical period, 239

criticism, 18, 34, 41, 65, 76, 81, 86, 168, 171, 174, 179, 180, 181, 184, 186, 189, 210, 225, 226, 273, 284, 299, 316, 322, 370, 371, 375, 380, 381, 388, 395

Croatia, 261, 314, 352

crop, 285, 332, 336, 337, 360

crops, 336, 351, 385

crown, 65, 74, 75

CRS report, 12

crude oil, 75, 98, 136, 338

cruise missiles, 121, 204, 205, 222, 276

CSS, 205

Cuba, 7, 89, 90, 126, 215, 233, 291

cues, 43

cultivation, 248, 285, 286, 287, 332, 336, 337, 373, 374, 385

cultural practices, 38

culture, 172, 189, 232

currency, 83, 125, 203, 207, 382

Customs and Border Protection, 80

Cyprus, 210

Czech Republic, 91, 204, 261, 314, 352, 353

D

danger, 356

Darfur, 67

database, 266, 312

death penalty, 388, 389

deaths, 15, 89, 90, 92, 182, 186, 189, 253, 290, 307, 317, 324

debts, 180

decentralization, 270

defence, 91

deficiencies, 331

deficiency, 284

deficit, 284

degenerate, 278

delegates, 280, 307, 365, 369, 391

Delta, 362

democracy, 12, 42, 46, 47, 59, 64, 77, 132, 138, 158, 175, 176, 202, 224, 225, 226, 227, 244, 250, 278, 279, 285, 363, 365, 392

democratic elections, 46, 264

Democratic Party, 271

democratization, 77

demonstrations, 77, 85, 169, 174, 182, 183, 207, 251, 399, 404

denial, 134, 155, 229, 322, 357, 390

Denmark, 68, 91, 261, 309, 339, 352, 353

Department of Agriculture, 266, 337, 341, 386

Department of Commerce, 130, 134

Department of Defense, 89, 90, 91, 92, 246, 285, 295, 313, 360, 409

Department of Energy, 106, 112, 136

Department of Justice, 67, 113, 374

deployments, 223

deposits, 139

deprivation, 122

depth, 40, 180, 234, 320, 326, 384

destruction, 22, 58, 64, 343

detainees, 24, 122, 163, 185, 387

detection, 107

detention, 185, 186

deterrence, 18

developed countries, 240

development assistance, 34, 47, 134, 238, 239, 287

diamonds, 75, 216

diplomacy, 41, 85, 167, 195, 209, 218, 219, 220, 225, 227, 238

diplomatic efforts, 85

diplomatic engagement, 38

directives, 115, 124, 135

directors, 193

disappointment, 24, 239, 373

disbursement, 266, 378

discrimination, 176, 188, 189, 275, 388

discussion groups, 279

diseases, 265

dismantlement, 211

dispersion, 25

displaced persons, 263

dissatisfaction, 7, 73, 169

dissidents, 174, 175, 206, 207, 208

distortions, 239

distribution, 77, 162, 245, 359, 366, 408

Doha, 50, 52, 207

domestic policy, 171, 318

dominance, 369

donations, 15, 26, 31, 62, 246, 286, 302, 316, 329

donors, 9, 84, 210, 231, 237, 238, 239, 240, 243, 246, 255, 263, 264, 266, 267, 274, 283, 287, 298, 302, 306, 309, 318, 330, 331, 334, 339, 363, 377, 379, 386, 392, 395, 402

draft, 99, 139, 142, 150, 155, 193, 199, 200, 224, 307, 360, 371, 383

drawing, 30, 245, 246, 405

dream, 43

drinking water, 265
drought, 131, 341
drug addict, 248
drug addiction, 248
drug trafficking, 314, 324, 373
drugs, 78, 239, 315
dual-use items, 41, 52, 105, 107, 113, 134
due process, 122
durability, 141
duty free, 339
duty-free treatment, 340

E

early warning, 28, 99
economic activity, 98, 363
economic assistance, 286, 287
economic damage, 173
economic development, 13, 269, 286, 289, 294, 297, 311, 324, 330, 335, 384
economic downturn, 78, 86, 87
economic growth, 243, 245, 270, 336, 384
economic integration, 335
economic resources, 138
economic status, 276
economics, 7
Ecuador, 233
education, 27, 35, 139, 192, 243, 246, 279, 312, 334, 377, 389
educational materials, 56
Egypt, 12, 14, 16, 20, 26, 32, 37, 38, 39, 41, 42, 43, 46, 49, 51, 52, 55, 63, 68, 85, 102, 103, 110, 111, 112, 114, 117, 131, 133, 136, 205, 210, 234, 261, 335
elders, 173, 294, 300, 303, 322, 323
election fraud, 282, 397, 404
electricity, 16, 27, 97, 98, 99, 136, 138, 155, 194, 325, 326, 327, 334, 335, 336, 338, 350
e-mail, 93, 408
embargo, 175, 221
embassy, 131, 182, 215, 234, 239, 272, 275, 287, 292
emergency, 128, 135, 253, 280, 321, 328, 405
employees, 27, 108, 245, 377, 380, 386
employers, 79
employment, 57, 150, 390
employment opportunities, 390
empowerment, 140, 256, 392
endowments, 401
end-users, 135

enemies, 212
energy, 80, 87, 95, 97, 98, 99, 100, 101, 108, 110, 111, 118, 130, 132, 139, 154, 155, 193, 194, 195, 196, 198, 200, 201, 203, 230, 329, 335, 338, 354, 373, 400
energy consumption, 87, 97
enforcement, 30, 70, 79, 80, 85, 96, 105, 106, 135, 164, 202, 207, 265
engineering, 16, 99, 109, 200
environment, 15, 45, 101, 155, 225, 253
equipment, 18, 33, 35, 68, 80, 82, 84, 99, 101, 102, 107, 110, 125, 126, 128, 130, 164, 197, 201, 203, 223, 226, 228, 230, 246, 310, 314, 315, 316, 318, 321, 327, 328, 332, 337, 374, 375, 380
equity, 371
Eritrea, 7, 89, 90
espionage, 188, 189
EST, 90
Estonia, 91, 261, 309, 352, 353
estrangement, 216, 217, 219
ethnic groups, 141, 365
ethnic minority, 325
ethnicity, 315, 365, 366, 376, 396
EU, 40, 69, 184, 185, 195, 196, 197, 198, 199, 201, 203, 233
Europe, 29, 31, 37, 45, 130, 173, 175, 184, 192, 205, 206, 210, 216, 221, 225, 226, 231, 336, 362, 372, 394, 396
European Commission, 38, 339
European Union, 11, 12, 34, 35, 44, 47, 48, 51, 58, 69, 71, 132, 167, 184, 201, 241, 244, 253, 287, 313, 394
evidence, 17, 20, 28, 44, 70, 180, 184, 194, 201, 209, 224, 225, 250, 304, 372, 394, 397
evil, 24, 168, 224
evolution, 224, 252, 294, 312
exclusion, 39, 145
execution, 133, 182, 189
executive branch, 30, 69, 87, 170
Executive Order, 30, 44, 45, 70, 105, 124, 127, 128, 129, 135, 186, 187, 193, 208, 213, 215, 226, 228, 229, 230, 292, 325, 357, 358
executive orders, 36, 230
exercise, 9, 58, 90, 96, 146, 155, 237, 365
exile, 11, 14, 15, 29, 43, 53, 70, 123, 146, 147, 171, 176, 183, 225, 228, 279, 291, 330, 372, 373, 386
expenditures, 126, 178, 242, 245, 246
expertise, 214, 238, 400
exploitation, 188, 389
explosives, 116, 213, 325

export control, 79, 80, 87, 96, 100, 101, 105, 106, 110, 113
export market, 75, 97
exporter, 87, 336
exporters, 83
exports, 38, 80, 86, 96, 97, 98, 102, 105, 125, 127, 128, 130, 131, 134, 194, 200, 207, 208, 210, 226, 229, 231, 274, 336, 337, 357
expulsion, 185, 207, 385
extremists, 147, 163, 323

F

Facebook, 182
facilitators, 291
factories, 336, 337
fairness, 397
faith, 64, 109, 123, 156, 220, 379, 388, 402
families, 28, 31, 73, 79, 84, 108, 123, 139, 156, 296, 301, 314, 326, 380
family members, 85, 139, 171, 215
farmers, 180, 335, 337, 385, 392
FBI, 189, 381
FDI, 135
fear, 15, 37, 48, 82, 116, 123, 148, 188, 203, 210, 222, 232, 271, 301, 302, 305, 306, 315, 320, 326, 327, 364, 367, 372, 386
fears, 15, 26, 83, 109, 141, 142, 146, 153, 171, 185, 194, 207, 208, 212, 221, 267, 320, 324, 327, 329, 401
Federal Bureau of Investigation, 43
federal government, 74, 76, 86
Federal Register, 87, 113, 126, 135
feelings, 109
feminism, 183
financial, 7, 11, 12, 13, 25, 29, 30, 31, 32, 35, 36, 46, 47, 53, 56, 70, 73, 74, 77, 79, 84, 86, 99, 105, 118, 125, 126, 127, 128, 129, 130, 131, 196, 197, 198, 202, 229, 253, 277, 283, 292, 298, 301, 311, 337, 364, 367, 374, 392, 402
financial crisis, 74
financial institutions, 30, 56, 79, 125, 127, 128, 130
financial resources, 86
financial sector, 118, 131
financial system, 127
Finland, 91, 112, 183, 261, 352
fires, 21, 279
flaws, 364, 402
flexibility, 26, 185, 201, 310
flight, 53, 128, 203

flights, 82, 202, 310, 321, 330, 357
fluid, 368
food, 35, 41, 67, 127, 134, 146, 185, 228, 274, 341, 390
force, 7, 12, 14, 23, 32, 41, 42, 45, 73, 75, 81, 82, 84, 90, 95, 100, 101, 102, 104, 110, 114, 124, 129, 135, 144, 149, 157, 168, 174, 180, 182, 185, 191, 222, 223, 242, 270, 271, 277, 278, 280, 286, 287, 289, 291, 295, 297, 303, 306, 308, 309, 313, 314, 315, 316, 317, 329, 333, 352, 371, 374, 382, 391
Ford, 124
forecasting, 70
foreign affairs, 154, 201
foreign aid, 7, 11, 13, 32, 85, 227, 235, 314, 349, 377
foreign assistance, 124, 126, 134, 229, 256
foreign companies, 130
foreign direct investment, 135
foreign exchange, 125
foreign firms, 167, 229
foreign intelligence, 52
foreign investment, 131, 138, 155
foreign nationals, 134, 393
foreign person, 229
foreign policy, 117, 125, 132, 135, 138, 171, 192, 201, 204, 216
formation, 43, 44, 118, 138, 139, 141, 155, 157, 279, 369, 390, 400
formula, 140, 153
foundations, 180, 192
France, 38, 57, 68, 69, 82, 85, 91, 99, 103, 109, 118, 131, 133, 135, 169, 184, 195, 196, 199, 201, 206, 223, 231, 233, 243, 261, 309, 310, 311, 313, 314, 321, 352
fraud, 151, 177, 182, 239, 250, 251, 256, 282, 283, 287, 363, 369, 393, 394, 397, 398, 399, 402, 403, 404
free market economy, 86
free trade, 86, 97, 339
freedom, 15, 19, 23, 73, 77, 78, 123, 188, 189, 209, 227, 248, 388, 389
Freedom Support Act, 225, 332, 333, 392
freezing, 36, 128, 325
friction, 143, 150
fruits, 44, 228, 274
funding, 25, 30, 31, 32, 33, 36, 47, 48, 57, 59, 62, 66, 158, 210, 224, 225, 226, 235, 243, 245, 246, 250, 254, 272, 274, 285, 286, 287, 298, 301, 302, 305, 317, 318, 326, 329, 331, 334, 337, 338, 339, 359, 360, 378, 380, 383, 392, 393, 402
fundraising, 43, 62, 150, 396

funds, 30, 31, 32, 56, 83, 85, 86, 125, 126, 175, 189, 213, 214, 216, 225, 227, 237, 238, 243, 245, 246, 255, 256, 263, 264, 266, 274, 281, 284, 285, 286, 301, 302, 303, 305, 306, 314, 316, 320, 325, 331, 332, 333, 334, 335, 336, 339, 343, 344, 345, 346, 347, 348, 349, 350, 351, 356, 357, 374, 377, 378, 379, 380, 382, 383, 392, 395, 401, 402

fusion, 286

G

GAO, 141, 162

Gaza Strip, 11, 12, 13, 14, 20, 22, 28, 29, 33, 42, 48, 49, 51, 53, 62, 63, 65, 70, 86, 210

GDP, 191, 231, 265, 273

gender inequality, 187

Generalized System of Preferences, 357

Geneva Convention, 185

genocide, 181

George Mitchell, 39, 134

Georgia, 91, 198, 310, 321, 327, 352

Germany, 68, 83, 91, 168, 195, 196, 198, 228, 231, 233, 241, 242, 261, 274, 279, 280, 297, 308, 309, 310, 314, 315, 328, 339, 352, 353, 365, 372, 377, 386

gestures, 124

globalization, 78

God, 181

google, 67

governance, 7, 9, 25, 39, 63, 132, 239, 240, 241, 243, 244, 245, 247, 250, 255, 263, 266, 269, 272, 279, 283, 284, 285, 286, 287, 289, 294, 297, 299, 300, 301, 309, 316, 327, 332, 349, 351, 363, 364, 365, 368, 369, 373, 374, 375, 377, 378, 384, 385, 386, 391, 392, 399

government funds, 79, 383, 385

government policy, 98

governments, 9, 37, 40, 41, 49, 52, 95, 97, 100, 101, 108, 111, 120, 122, 126, 133, 154, 163, 176, 184, 185, 207, 210, 229, 230, 251, 301, 309, 321, 333, 385, 390, 399

governor, 141, 142, 149, 150, 160, 181, 275, 281, 284, 291, 301, 304, 321, 370, 372, 373, 374, 385, 391, 395, 401, 406

graduate students, 322

grand jury, 234

grants, 197, 334, 380, 392

grassroots, 25, 32

gravity, 143

Greece, 231, 261, 309, 352

Gross Domestic Product, 75, 265

grouping, 175, 197, 212, 328, 354, 367, 368

growth, 146, 318

Guantanamo, 7, 89, 90, 291

guardian, 67

guidance, 79, 172, 209, 242, 244, 250, 316, 378

guidelines, 74

guiding principles, 97

guilty, 31, 70

gynecologist, 281

H

hair, 271

Hamas, 5, 7, 8, 11, 12, 13, 14, 15, 16, 17, 18, 19, 20, 21, 22, 23, 24, 25, 26, 27, 28, 29, 30, 31, 32, 33, 34, 35, 36, 37, 38, 39, 40, 41, 42, 43, 44, 45, 46, 47, 48, 49, 50, 51, 52, 53, 54, 55, 56, 57, 58, 60, 61, 62, 63, 64, 65, 66, 67, 68, 69, 70, 71, 85, 117, 120, 132, 167, 206, 210, 216, 222, 234

hardliners, 168, 173, 174, 176, 181, 182, 192, 214

healing, 321

health, 27, 35, 134, 189, 225, 243, 264, 273, 275, 281, 312, 334, 335, 341, 392

health care, 35, 225, 275, 312, 335

health care sector, 335

health problems, 189

health services, 264, 273

hegemony, 14, 171

height, 8, 141, 143, 156, 157, 163, 164, 167, 183, 278

Hezbollah, 8, 11, 12, 19, 20, 29, 36, 38, 42, 51, 57, 58, 60, 64, 66, 70, 115, 116, 117, 118, 119, 120, 121, 123, 129, 132, 133, 134, 160, 167, 192, 197, 206, 207, 208, 210, 211, 212, 216, 217, 222, 234

higher education, 327, 401

hiring, 376

history, 8, 167, 189, 218, 240, 242, 270, 329, 365

HIV, 265

holding company, 129

homes, 28, 155, 211, 336

homosexuality, 78

host, 85, 112, 124, 245, 307

hostilities, 40, 221, 284

hostility, 42

hotel, 52, 75, 337

hotels, 231

House, 38, 41, 56, 57, 58, 59, 60, 65, 68, 69, 80, 87, 103, 104, 106, 108, 110, 112, 114, 125, 126, 181,

185, 187, 224, 233, 235, 252, 278, 319, 332, 340, 350, 360, 368, 370, 382, 383, 389, 405, 409

House of Representatives, 38, 41, 69, 125, 224, 409

housing, 86, 207, 215, 330

hub, 43, 74, 96, 105, 321, 323, 373

human, 7, 34, 41, 43, 50, 54, 68, 70, 73, 77, 78, 93, 99, 101, 108, 114, 122, 132, 155, 156, 168, 175, 184, 186, 189, 224, 225, 226, 227, 244, 247, 248, 250, 254, 264, 265, 273, 283, 285, 286, 302, 314, 316, 324, 332, 348, 371, 372, 383, 387, 389, 390, 392, 402, 409

Human Development Index, 265

Human Development Report, 265

human resources, 99

human right, 7, 34, 43, 50, 68, 70, 77, 78, 108, 114, 122, 132, 155, 156, 168, 175, 184, 186, 189, 225, 226, 227, 244, 247, 248, 264, 265, 273, 283, 285, 286, 302, 314, 316, 324, 332, 348, 371, 372, 383, 387, 390, 392, 402, 409

human rights, 7, 34, 43, 50, 68, 70, 77, 78, 108, 114, 122, 132, 155, 156, 168, 175, 184, 186, 189, 225, 226, 227, 244, 247, 248, 264, 265, 273, 283, 285, 286, 302, 314, 316, 324, 332, 348, 371, 372, 383, 387, 390, 392, 402, 409

humanitarian aid, 33, 38, 239, 240, 247, 263, 326, 327

Hungary, 91, 233, 261, 352, 353

Hurricane Katrina, 85

husband, 189, 390

hybrid, 24

hydrocarbons, 139, 335

Hyundai, 362

I

Iceland, 352, 353

ideal, 18, 194

ideals, 192, 367

identity, 19, 149, 369, 371

ideology, 7, 11, 21, 54, 194, 204, 216, 355

illiteracy, 315

image, 15, 29, 42, 46, 144, 181, 206, 312

images, 120, 352

IMF, 231, 246, 322, 334

immunity, 273

impeachment, 178

imports, 83, 87, 98, 228, 231, 274, 340

improvements, 33

inauguration, 182, 209, 217, 323, 369

income, 125

incumbents, 142, 177, 404

independence, 49, 77, 78, 83, 116, 123, 134, 145, 187, 208, 265, 271, 287, 328, 383, 387

Independence, 220

India, 9, 136, 190, 212, 214, 231, 233, 261, 269, 270, 271, 274, 281, 292, 293, 309, 320, 321, 322, 324, 326, 329, 337, 338, 339, 356, 359, 367, 377, 386, 388, 400

individuals, 19, 30, 32, 42, 45, 63, 92, 106, 122, 123, 126, 127, 128, 129, 132, 148, 198, 227, 388, 405

Indonesia, 197, 233

industrial sectors, 118

industries, 337

industry, 100, 101, 109, 131, 169, 173, 180, 216, 335, 337

ineffectiveness, 37, 395

inertia, 34

infant mortality, 335

inflation, 180

informal sector, 384

information technology, 130, 381, 389

infrastructure, 14, 28, 37, 45, 59, 60, 101, 204, 216, 221, 243, 244, 246, 271, 279, 289, 297, 303, 327, 329, 337, 350

ingredients, 16

injuries, 92, 254

injury, 55

inmates, 295

insecurity, 239

inspections, 80, 195, 197, 200, 222

inspectors, 121, 194, 383

institution building, 377

institutions, 7, 8, 9, 20, 24, 27, 34, 45, 46, 59, 123, 129, 137, 192, 196, 229, 237, 239, 244, 246, 247, 248, 255, 256, 279, 283, 286, 298, 312, 313, 334, 363, 365, 367, 375, 376, 377, 387, 390, 396, 401, 402

insurgency, 140, 147, 284, 285, 289, 290, 294, 296, 297, 300, 311, 315, 319, 322, 324, 333, 366, 373, 378, 386, 395

integration, 8, 9, 39, 167, 269, 298, 316

intellectual property, 134, 155

intellectual property rights, 155

intelligence, 15, 18, 25, 28, 30, 34, 38, 44, 64, 80, 106, 123, 128, 129, 133, 154, 176, 181, 187, 192, 193, 205, 215, 217, 254, 272, 277, 278, 282, 285, 291, 300, 303, 323, 329, 354, 356, 366, 369

intelligence gathering, 254

interest groups, 374

interest rates, 180

interference, 155, 163, 190, 194, 209, 225, 252, 320, 381

internally displaced, 263

International Atomic Energy Agency, 111, 116, 121, 122, 193, 194

International Covenant on Civil and Political Rights, 188

international diplomacy, 218

international financial institutions, 197, 229, 244, 246

International Financial Institutions, 203

international investment, 200

international law, 41, 185, 248

international meetings, 220, 279

International Monetary Fund, 246

International Narcotics Control, 286

international standards, 285, 365

international terrorism, 60, 67, 115, 124, 125, 134, 183, 206, 213, 229, 324

international trade, 77

internationalization, 203

internship, 62

interpersonal relations, 214

intervention, 8, 74, 137, 153, 163, 178, 179, 181, 240, 327, 365

intifada, 15, 24, 42, 43, 44, 45, 48, 49, 50, 53, 63, 70

intimidation, 156, 180, 250, 373, 388, 396

investment, 74, 81, 86, 118, 131, 194, 200, 201, 203, 215, 220, 228, 230, 246, 329, 337, 338, 339

investments, 118, 130, 329, 379

investors, 74, 86, 129, 338

Iran Sanctions Act, 56, 203, 228, 230

Iraq, 5, 7, 8, 40, 46, 50, 52, 80, 81, 82, 83, 84, 96, 116, 118, 123, 127, 129, 132, 133, 135, 137, 138, 139, 140, 141, 142, 143, 144, 145, 146, 147, 148, 149, 150, 151, 152, 153, 155, 156, 157, 158, 159, 160, 161, 162, 163, 164, 165, 167, 168, 169, 173, 177, 184, 185, 186, 189, 190, 192, 197, 206, 207, 209, 213, 215, 217, 218, 222, 223, 224, 229, 234, 270, 287, 295, 303, 305, 307, 321, 331, 333, 355, 399

Ireland, 261, 352

Irish Republican Army, 39

iron, 329, 338

irradiation, 102

irrigation, 134, 284

Islam, 18, 19, 22, 24, 31, 43, 61, 64, 65, 78, 123, 133, 139, 168, 171, 176, 181, 182, 193, 233, 270, 275, 328, 330, 355, 367, 368, 389, 394, 405

Islamabad, 242, 266

Islamic law, 139, 170, 187, 304, 370, 388

Islamic movements, 47, 271, 328

Islamic society, 24

Islamic state, 22, 24, 29, 172

Islamism, 183

islands, 83, 207, 208

isolation, 48, 172, 174, 216

isotope, 112

Israel, 8, 11, 12, 13, 14, 15, 16, 18, 19, 21, 22, 23, 24, 25, 26, 28, 29, 30, 32, 33, 34, 35, 36, 37, 38, 39, 40, 41, 42, 43, 44, 45, 46, 47, 48, 49, 50, 51, 52, 53, 54, 55, 57, 58, 59, 60, 62, 63, 64, 65, 66, 67, 68, 69, 70, 71, 85, 96, 97, 115, 116, 117, 118, 119, 120, 121, 122, 124, 126, 133, 169, 171, 173, 181, 188, 201, 205, 209, 210, 211, 212, 221, 222, 234, 339

issues, 7, 8, 11, 13, 25, 29, 33, 35, 37, 40, 77, 79, 85, 105, 106, 107, 109, 115, 122, 124, 139, 146, 152, 167, 171, 173, 176, 178, 179, 186, 189, 201, 209, 214, 215, 218, 219, 225, 232, 238, 242, 244, 249, 251, 277, 279, 283, 287, 310, 324, 328, 333, 355, 364, 368, 382, 384, 387, 390, 391, 402

Italy, 68, 91, 131, 231, 233, 261, 271, 279, 309, 310, 311, 313, 314, 317, 339, 352, 353

J

Japan, 98, 99, 103, 109, 112, 167, 183, 201, 231, 233, 244, 261, 302, 306, 309, 310, 311, 318, 339, 362, 377

Jews, 18, 19, 22, 24, 64, 188, 273

jihadist, 19, 64

Jirga, 238, 248, 252, 302, 303, 305, 368, 369, 370, 385, 389, 402, 404, 405, 408

Jordan, 8, 16, 35, 39, 42, 49, 50, 52, 53, 55, 65, 69, 85, 89, 90, 100, 108, 111, 114, 117, 131, 157, 205, 210, 335, 339, 352

journalists, 78, 225, 277, 388, 391

judiciary, 170, 172, 186, 189, 233

jurisdiction, 28, 102, 105, 125, 307, 381, 404

justification, 82, 370

K

Kazakhstan, 212, 261, 321, 328, 335

Kenya, 8, 89, 90, 276, 356

kidnapping, 78, 156, 381

kill, 18

kinship, 376

Korea, 95, 97, 99, 109, 114, 121, 126, 205, 231, 261, 309

Kurd, 159, 161

Kurds, 123, 139, 140, 141, 142, 143, 146, 149, 152, 153, 158, 159, 160, 162, 186, 187, 188

Kuwait, 26, 42, 43, 49, 50, 52, 53, 69, 82, 133, 206, 207, 209, 223, 253, 261, 291, 355

Kyrgyzstan, 8, 89, 90, 212, 321, 328

L

landscape, 150

Latin America, 206, 215, 216

Latvia, 91, 321, 352

law enforcement, 38, 80, 106, 155

laws, 24, 38, 79, 100, 125, 135, 138, 141, 155, 162, 163, 228, 229, 251, 332, 372, 382, 383

lawyers, 233

layoffs, 74, 86

lead, 9, 29, 40, 41, 69, 75, 122, 138, 158, 185, 201, 208, 217, 224, 239, 240, 242, 245, 251, 252, 253, 254, 255, 270, 281, 294, 299, 308, 311, 312, 313, 317, 318, 353, 363, 366, 367, 403, 405

leadership, 7, 9, 11, 14, 15, 18, 21, 23, 25, 26, 28, 29, 31, 35, 39, 45, 46, 48, 49, 50, 52, 53, 54, 59, 62, 64, 65, 71, 73, 74, 75, 77, 119, 138, 150, 151, 152, 170, 172, 173, 192, 210, 212, 219, 238, 244, 245, 249, 254, 265, 269, 276, 280, 284, 287, 289, 291, 292, 295, 296, 297, 298, 299, 303, 307, 308, 309, 320, 325, 328, 332, 339, 363, 365, 374, 378, 379, 406

leadership development, 192

Leahy, 351

leakage, 7, 73, 79, 81, 82, 201

learning, 391

Lebanon, 19, 20, 25, 29, 35, 43, 45, 46, 49, 50, 51, 53, 54, 66, 67, 70, 86, 115, 116, 118, 119, 120, 123, 127, 128, 129, 131, 132, 133, 134, 135, 150, 192, 200, 206, 211, 217, 234

legal protection, 364

legality, 20

legislation, 35, 36, 38, 65, 69, 74, 77, 96, 106, 110, 111, 124, 126, 127, 134, 138, 139, 141, 155, 159, 163, 167, 168, 170, 201, 225, 235, 319, 350, 383

legislative authority, 336

legislative proposals, 96

legs, 78

lending, 197, 202, 203, 334, 372

liberation, 22, 23, 206

light, 43, 95, 98, 101, 104, 107, 116, 194, 196, 199, 200, 201, 202, 210, 233, 240, 373

Lion, 294

literacy, 330

lithium, 338

Lithuania, 91, 352, 353

livestock, 131

loans, 9, 56, 86, 126, 197, 229, 357, 363, 372, 379

local authorities, 249, 263

local government, 9, 237, 254, 283, 284, 365

locus, 45

loyalty, 29, 179, 192, 290

Luxemburg, 352

M

Macedonia, 352

machinery, 75

major issues, 74, 162, 209, 237

majority, 20, 21, 23, 31, 46, 47, 51, 58, 120, 123, 137, 139, 140, 142, 143, 144, 151, 152, 153, 154, 283, 293, 311, 329, 377, 389, 402

malaise, 28

malaria, 265

Malaysia, 105, 118, 310, 352

man, 54, 68, 181, 355, 356, 389

management, 7, 73, 99, 238, 287, 322, 337, 386, 392

manipulation, 168

manpower, 18

manufacturing, 118, 132

marginalization, 367

maritime security, 83, 223

market economy, 131

marketing, 337

marriage, 118, 215, 270, 337

martial law, 45

mass, 27, 35, 53, 226, 360, 369, 408

materials, 75, 106, 114, 124, 128

matter, 23, 64, 106, 114, 158, 164, 204, 231, 254, 256, 393

media, 22, 24, 25, 29, 38, 40, 43, 46, 54, 57, 59, 65, 66, 68, 69, 77, 78, 119, 163, 175, 183, 192, 227, 233, 341, 360, 361, 370, 387, 396, 397

medical, 32, 35, 41, 54, 83, 84, 112, 185, 194, 199, 216, 228, 271

medical care, 35

medication, 375

medicine, 101, 127, 196

Mediterranean, 69, 116, 133, 136

MEK, 233

membership, 14, 25, 74, 134, 212, 339, 404
mentor, 29, 172, 299, 355
mentoring, 313, 383
mentorship, 70
messages, 25, 176, 224
Mexico, 233
Microsoft, 134
middle class, 180
Middle East, 1, 2, iii, 7, 8, 9, 11, 17, 18, 20, 39, 43, 44, 47, 50, 54, 57, 63, 64, 65, 66, 68, 69, 70, 73, 78, 85, 97, 100, 102, 108, 111, 112, 114, 115, 117, 131, 133, 134, 136, 188, 196, 205, 217, 223, 269
militancy, 11, 18, 54, 327
militarization, 42
military aid, 272, 332
military exercises, 222, 320
military-to-military, 190
militia, 63, 139, 140, 149, 150, 157, 163, 164, 177, 190, 209, 273, 276, 278, 291, 292, 305, 306, 365, 368, 371, 374
militias, 19, 44, 143, 150, 163, 164, 197, 209, 222, 239, 271, 283, 300, 305, 306, 343, 351
Ministry of Education, 380
minorities, 123, 156, 165, 169, 185, 270, 271, 302, 306, 325, 367, 368, 371
minority groups, 187
mission, 41, 84, 138, 140, 149, 152, 157, 176, 181, 221, 241, 252, 254, 256, 265, 284, 285, 287, 289, 293, 296, 298, 308, 309, 310, 311, 313, 318, 330, 374, 378, 381
missions, 96, 133, 227, 256, 285, 308, 309, 310, 321, 394
misuse, 382
mobile phone, 129
models, 42, 284
moderates, 210
modernization, 74, 271, 365
momentum, 43, 141, 170, 182, 252, 253, 269, 289, 296, 300, 304
money laundering, 32, 37, 56, 79, 127, 130
Mongolia, 352
Montenegro, 352
Moon, 159, 287, 399
morale, 42, 252, 300
moratorium, 388
Morocco, 208
mortality, 273
Moscow, 116, 266, 272, 328, 360, 362
multimedia, 65, 69
murder, 116, 119, 123, 189

museums, 75
music, 275
Muslim states, 188
Muslims, 25, 26, 64, 78, 123, 185, 187, 188, 207, 209, 210, 276, 329, 388

N

naming, 53, 150, 314
narcotics, 230, 243, 244, 248, 263, 280, 281, 285, 286, 317, 320, 324, 327, 329, 330, 332, 333, 345, 346, 347, 348, 351, 371, 374, 379, 383, 384, 392
national borders, 19
National Defense Authorization Act, 223, 233, 303, 305, 308, 319, 333, 334, 350
national emergency, 125, 128, 135, 358
national identity, 402
National Intelligence Estimate, 193
national interests, 204, 325
national security, 8, 103, 104, 125, 128, 135, 154, 167, 170, 190, 232, 235, 238, 243, 249, 344, 367, 400, 409
National Security Council, 40, 170, 172, 281, 303, 361, 366, 378, 400
nationalism, 21, 46, 143
nationalists, 169, 212
nation-building, 279, 289
NATO, 16, 38, 68, 83, 89, 90, 204, 213, 238, 241, 245, 246, 265, 266, 269, 285, 286, 287, 289, 291, 293, 294, 295, 296, 297, 298, 299, 300, 301, 302, 304, 307, 308, 309, 310, 311, 313, 317, 321, 323, 327, 328, 336, 339, 352, 353, 360, 361, 376, 378, 379, 387, 394, 395, 396, 403
natural gas, 87, 98, 112, 118, 136, 208, 214, 328, 338
NDI, 370
negative outcomes, 34
negotiating, 14, 40, 86, 97, 167, 198, 298
nerve, 52, 204
Netherlands, 68, 91, 189, 219, 231, 233, 245, 253, 261, 294, 308, 309, 312, 314, 339, 352, 353
neutral, 145, 253, 256, 292
new media, 78
New Zealand, 91, 262, 352, 353
next generation, 129
NGOs, 9, 237, 244, 246, 256, 265, 334, 341, 389, 391
Nigeria, 233
Niyazov, 339
Nobel Prize, 175
nodes, 323

nominee, 373
non-citizens, 78
North Africa, 68
North America, 37, 62
North Atlantic Treaty Organization, 16, 241
North Korea, 80, 113, 114, 118, 119, 121, 126, 133, 134, 168, 190, 200, 205, 212, 229, 356
Northern Ireland, 39
Norway, 68, 91, 103, 262, 314, 339, 352, 353
NPT, 99, 102, 107, 111, 114, 133, 195, 219, 222
nuclear program, 7, 8, 96, 97, 98, 99, 100, 102, 107, 112, 121, 167, 168, 183, 188, 193, 194, 195, 196, 200, 207, 208, 214, 216, 219, 220, 221, 224, 231, 324
nuclear talks, 196, 218
nuclear weapons, 96, 97, 99, 104, 107, 111, 112, 121, 193, 194, 201, 221
nutrition, 392

O

obstacles, 15, 238
occupied territories, 14, 18, 120
offenders, 79
oil, 16, 32, 74, 81, 83, 86, 87, 96, 97, 112, 131, 139, 150, 154, 162, 169, 175, 193, 194, 196, 200, 201, 203, 207, 208, 212, 216, 217, 222, 228, 231, 274, 311, 321, 338
oil production, 131, 274
oil revenues, 81, 139
open economy, 79
operating costs, 246
Operation Enduring Freedom, 7, 82, 89, 90, 246, 277, 278, 281, 293, 308, 309, 311
Operation Iraqi Freedom, 82, 184
operations, 15, 20, 25, 28, 29, 32, 35, 41, 45, 49, 63, 66, 68, 75, 81, 82, 96, 105, 128, 129, 159, 225, 227, 235, 240, 245, 253, 270, 278, 285, 287, 289, 292, 293, 294, 295, 296, 300, 301, 307, 308, 310, 311, 313, 315, 318, 320, 321, 322, 323, 327, 330, 331, 347, 351, 355, 374, 389, 394, 395
opinion polls, 54
opportunities, 73, 100, 118, 176, 276, 303
opportunity costs, 99
opposition movement, 170, 184, 221
oppression, 24, 174
optimism, 141, 270
organize, 123, 139, 171, 182, 210, 281, 287, 309
organs, 25, 39, 63, 65, 78, 141, 171, 305, 366
OSCE, 394

outreach, 46, 150, 241, 247, 263, 302, 369
oversight, 7, 11, 32, 36, 39, 56, 73, 153, 170, 249, 256, 327, 331, 332, 368, 375, 387, 392
ownership, 238, 254

P

Pacific, 112
Pakistan, 7, 9, 79, 80, 84, 89, 90, 113, 185, 194, 212, 213, 214, 215, 233, 234, 238, 239, 262, 266, 269, 271, 274, 275, 277, 278, 279, 281, 283, 284, 286, 289, 290, 291, 293, 294, 297, 298, 299, 300, 302, 304, 313, 315, 317, 318, 319, 320, 321, 322, 323, 324, 325, 326, 328, 329, 330, 333, 334, 337, 338, 340, 341, 355, 357, 360, 361, 362, 367, 369, 373, 376, 389, 395, 406, 409
Palestinian Authority, 12, 13, 14, 16, 27, 28, 43, 44, 45, 50, 55, 58, 59, 60, 65, 67, 68
Palestinian Islamic Jihad, 43, 49, 50, 51, 62, 63, 120, 210
parallel, 38, 95, 104, 255
parity, 20, 273, 295
Parliament, 281, 368, 370, 405
participants, 149, 241, 242, 362
partition, 324
Pashtun, 272, 273, 274, 275, 276, 278, 281, 283, 302, 306, 314, 324, 354, 355, 366, 367, 368, 369, 371, 373, 374, 395, 396, 397, 404, 405, 406, 407, 408
Patriot Act, 130
payroll, 131
peace, 8, 11, 12, 13, 19, 21, 29, 39, 40, 42, 43, 44, 45, 46, 49, 50, 52, 57, 59, 64, 69, 70, 85, 115, 116, 117, 120, 123, 132, 134, 209, 210, 212, 217, 231, 235, 240, 247, 248, 263, 265, 278, 280, 287, 292, 302, 304, 308, 321, 323, 333, 364, 365, 369, 388, 391
peace accord, 240
peace plan, 304
peace process, 8, 11, 12, 29, 39, 40, 44, 45, 46, 50, 57, 85, 115, 117, 123, 210, 217, 240
peacekeeping, 280, 287, 308, 321, 333
peacekeeping forces, 280
peer review, 331
penalties, 67, 78, 80, 127, 298
Pentagon, 205, 399
permit, 52, 135, 194, 196, 197, 330
perpetrators, 60

Persian Gulf, 31, 62, 77, 82, 83, 86, 169, 192, 194, 196, 206, 207, 210, 217, 218, 231, 281, 286, 311, 321, 329
persuasion, 306
Peru, 233
pessimism, 300
petroleum, 118, 194, 228, 274
Petroleum, 130, 212, 233
pharmaceutical, 359
Philippines, 8, 89, 90, 317
phosphates, 357
photographs, 121
physicians, 335
plants, 8, 95, 97, 98, 99, 111
platform, 38, 321, 370
playing, 9, 32, 129, 192, 237, 249, 285, 334, 377
plutonium, 102, 103, 106, 107, 112, 121, 194
PMOI, 183, 184, 194
Poland, 91, 204, 233, 262, 309, 310, 314, 352, 353
polar, 328
police, 18, 24, 44, 83, 90, 116, 134, 164, 172, 182, 185, 245, 273, 285, 305, 310, 312, 313, 315, 316, 317, 318, 357, 372, 373, 379, 380, 381, 382, 388, 391, 392
policy, 7, 9, 11, 12, 13, 25, 26, 27, 32, 34, 39, 64, 65, 74, 89, 97, 100, 103, 107, 109, 111, 130, 132, 133, 134, 135, 153, 168, 176, 180, 194, 204, 212, 216, 218, 219, 223, 224, 226, 235, 238, 239, 243, 249, 256, 265, 269, 277, 281, 283, 285, 286, 287, 289, 291, 293, 297, 298, 299, 308, 309, 318, 324, 329, 330, 332, 333, 334, 363, 364, 374, 375, 387
policy choice, 194
policy initiative, 12
policy issues, 238, 239
policy responses, 7
policymakers, 8, 26
political crisis, 148, 364, 404, 406
political instability, 97
political leaders, 11, 14, 31, 53
political legitimacy, 43, 133
political opposition, 123, 368
political participation, 77, 387
political parties, 76, 118, 142, 367, 394, 405
political party, 58, 227
political pluralism, 175
political power, 8, 137, 157
political system, 8, 46, 129, 137, 192, 367
politics, 7, 18, 19, 26, 32, 34, 37, 41, 46, 67, 129, 142, 143, 152, 154, 172, 250, 272, 276, 302, 360, 361, 363

polling, 142, 161, 177, 182, 251, 252, 394, 396, 397, 398, 403
Popular Front, 62, 66, 120, 210
popular support, 14, 275
population, 19, 30, 41, 63, 84, 123, 133, 139, 146, 156, 157, 178, 187, 189, 199, 203, 210, 212, 227, 254, 264, 273, 274, 284, 296, 297, 300, 301, 305, 335, 359, 366, 367, 371, 382, 388, 408
portfolio, 78, 154
Portugal, 91, 233, 262, 309, 310, 352
poverty, 243
poverty reduction, 243
power generation, 98, 118, 136
power plants, 8, 95, 97, 99, 111, 130
pragmatism, 21, 25
prayer, 79, 182
precedent, 108, 149
precedents, 40
precipitation, 15
preparation, 253, 312
preparedness, 99
presidency, 146, 149, 151, 152, 176, 196, 207, 210, 276, 297, 366, 393, 405
president, 14, 52, 73, 74, 75, 78, 96, 122, 129, 138, 139, 140, 145, 151, 152, 153, 155, 170, 171, 173, 177, 181, 199, 207, 210, 211, 234, 240, 242, 271, 274, 276, 280, 305, 365, 369, 370, 372, 376, 385, 391, 394, 396, 397
President Clinton, 126, 217, 357, 358
President Obama, 34, 40, 96, 102, 103, 108, 124, 135, 144, 153, 171, 187, 193, 198, 200, 213, 219, 220, 224, 226, 234, 245, 252, 286, 289, 292, 296, 297, 299, 300, 303, 307, 308, 309, 319, 327, 340, 360, 372, 375, 376, 378, 382, 387, 390, 391
presidential authority, 300
presidential campaign, 174, 365, 396
presidential campaigns, 396
press conferences, 287
prestige, 171
primacy, 51, 123
primary school, 265
principles, 21, 22, 35, 36, 39, 40, 42, 47, 55, 66, 181, 244, 262, 263, 316, 368
prisoners, 27, 122, 307, 361, 372, 408
private investment, 250, 337
privatization, 373
probe, 122, 205
production technology, 97
professionalism, 34
professionalization, 27

professionals, 281, 335
profit, 26, 379
programming, 22, 38, 39, 57, 69, 87
project, 37, 46, 68, 86, 87, 97, 99, 116, 129, 190,
    214, 250, 252, 274, 312, 326, 329, 331, 334, 335,
    336, 338, 350, 362, 382
proliferation, 80, 95, 97, 101, 102, 103, 104, 105,
    106, 107, 108, 109, 111, 112, 113, 124, 127, 133,
    193, 197, 201, 208, 229, 230, 233, 311, 321
propaganda, 62
proposition, 152
prosperity, 33, 373
protection, 101, 102, 155, 164, 183, 247, 248, 264,
    265, 281, 289, 302, 321, 342, 345, 347
provincial councils, 139, 141, 142, 365, 369, 370,
    378, 385, 394, 405
public affairs, 54
public awareness, 187
public opinion, 26, 28, 123
public sector, 27
public service, 26, 46
public support, 168, 210, 224, 289, 395
punishment, 388
purchasing power, 75, 231, 273
purchasing power parity, 75, 231, 273
purity, 26

Q

qualifications, 376, 399
query, 112
questioning, 81, 181

R

Rab, 272, 276, 355, 368
race, 173, 177, 397
racing, 79
radar, 118, 212, 223, 323
radiation, 101
Radiation, 84
radicals, 169, 327
radio, 24, 176, 291
radioactive waste, 101
Ramadan, 152, 201, 304
rape, 390
ratification, 96
raw materials, 16
real estate, 74, 86, 129, 379

reality, 40, 216
recall, 287
recession, 74, 86
recognition, 29, 35, 55, 59, 111, 254, 275
recommendations, 69, 77, 159, 202, 289, 296, 332,
    356
reconciliation, 24, 140, 141, 156, 158, 174, 241, 247,
    253, 263, 270, 277, 290, 292, 293, 303, 306, 320,
    367, 390, 391
reconstruction, 9, 83, 164, 237, 238, 239, 240, 242,
    244, 245, 249, 254, 263, 265, 266, 281, 289, 294,
    311, 312, 320, 326, 331, 333, 334, 335, 405
recovery, 9, 237, 246
recruiting, 43, 157, 386
recurrence, 297
reelection, 150, 209
reform, 7, 33, 67, 76, 77, 78, 96, 173, 174, 175, 177,
    187, 241, 249, 252, 256, 331, 375, 376, 377, 401
Reform, 19, 46, 67, 68, 76, 145, 160, 402, 409
reformers, 123
reforms, 131, 282, 398
refugee camps, 239, 330
refugees, 23, 29, 33, 35, 42, 43, 263, 324, 326, 330,
    341, 401
regional cooperation, 245, 247, 264, 320
regional policy, 84, 210
Registry, 200
regulations, 96, 100, 105, 111, 126, 134, 135, 228,
    358, 379, 382
regulatory bodies, 97
regulatory framework, 384
rehabilitation, 245, 347
reinsurance, 203
rejection, 11, 12, 45, 141, 159, 401
relatives, 9, 281, 337, 363
relaxation, 175
relief, 13, 76, 239, 249, 266, 312, 313, 330, 334, 340,
    341, 389
religion, 78, 181, 187, 188, 270
remittances, 131
repair, 301
repatriate, 43
reporters, 105
repression, 170, 175, 182, 183, 188, 276
reprocessing, 95, 97, 99, 102, 103, 104, 106, 107,
    108, 109, 111, 112, 197
reputation, 15, 29, 45, 70, 145, 273, 372, 404
requirements, 23, 101, 104, 105, 110, 114, 196, 226,
    230, 245, 298, 333, 402
resentment, 149, 327, 371

reserves, 74, 86, 338, 391

residential neighborhood, 41

resistance, 11, 12, 14, 15, 18, 23, 24, 26, 42, 43, 46, 48, 49, 54, 62, 120, 124, 175, 185, 221, 270, 281, 301, 329, 375

resolution, 12, 81, 83, 104, 106, 110, 113, 114, 141, 158, 169, 175, 186, 197, 198, 199, 200, 201, 203, 210, 227, 234, 247, 262, 263, 266, 267, 287, 305, 308, 319, 384, 398

resources, 14, 27, 30, 37, 101, 150, 162, 192, 194, 212, 254, 256, 263, 267, 283, 287, 295, 312, 313, 316, 338, 391

response, 14, 41, 43, 50, 93, 99, 107, 118, 121, 151, 189, 192, 195, 196, 202, 217, 225, 228, 238, 277, 295, 372, 393

restaurants, 388

restoration, 48

restrictions, 14, 15, 35, 36, 37, 38, 41, 55, 77, 80, 83, 125, 127, 132, 134, 173, 229, 323, 337, 357, 370, 379, 387

retail, 395

retaliation, 53, 221, 222

retirement, 370

retirement age, 370

revenue, 26, 99, 162, 331, 378

Revolutionary Guard, 66, 113, 148, 170, 171, 172, 174, 177, 178, 179, 180, 181, 185, 190, 191, 192, 193, 197, 200, 202, 206, 211, 222, 230, 233, 324

rewards, 220

rhetoric, 22, 29, 188

rights, 7, 24, 64, 76, 77, 78, 112, 122, 123, 155, 175, 186, 187, 188, 212, 224, 225, 226, 227, 247, 264, 275, 285, 302, 316, 364, 387, 390, 391, 405

risk, 20, 103, 105, 107, 111, 126, 229, 240, 252, 254

risks, 12, 42, 47, 96, 97, 104, 220, 221

Romania, 91, 204, 309, 310, 352, 353

root, 215, 297, 319

roots, 30

routes, 214, 328, 337

rule of law, 34, 77, 155, 247, 248, 251, 263, 284, 285, 287, 316, 349, 363, 383, 384, 392

rules, 140, 146, 175, 212, 297, 310

runoff, 177, 251, 280, 287, 363, 397, 398, 405

rural areas, 182, 239, 273, 294, 335, 336, 364

Russia, 35, 40, 47, 53, 118, 121, 131, 133, 136, 168, 190, 195, 196, 197, 198, 199, 201, 203, 204, 206, 212, 216, 221, 231, 233, 266, 279, 304, 309, 315, 320, 321, 327, 328, 335, 362

S

Saddam Hussein, 50, 82, 83, 118, 132, 133, 135, 138, 143, 156, 184, 209, 234, 311, 355

safe haven, 29, 55, 62, 164, 279, 289, 290, 294, 311, 319, 328

safe havens, 311

safety, 24, 96, 97, 99, 100, 104, 108, 128, 135, 156, 250, 315, 337

Salafiyya, 64

sanctions, 7, 8, 11, 13, 32, 37, 41, 55, 56, 68, 82, 96, 106, 115, 121, 124, 125, 126, 127, 130, 131, 132, 133, 134, 135, 167, 168, 171, 180, 181, 188, 189, 193, 194, 196, 197, 198, 199, 200, 201, 202, 203, 204, 206, 207, 208, 212, 215, 217, 218, 220, 221, 226, 228, 229, 230, 234, 276, 292, 304, 325, 356, 357, 358

Saudi Arabia, 30, 31, 39, 45, 48, 63, 69, 79, 84, 85, 86, 97, 100, 111, 116, 118, 119, 131, 137, 138, 157, 200, 205, 206, 207, 210, 215, 223, 234, 244, 262, 275, 291, 298, 304, 310, 323, 329, 330, 339, 355, 356, 362

scaling, 35

scarcity, 32

school, 24, 41, 172, 264, 273, 275, 301, 325, 335, 351, 359, 390

science, 225

SCO, 212

scope, 102, 103, 109, 110, 111, 121, 126, 241, 248, 265, 287, 299, 378

Secretary of Commerce, 125, 135

Secretary of Defense, 180, 209, 216, 219, 220, 278, 296, 376

Secretary of Homeland Security, 215

Secretary of the Treasury, 128, 229

sectarianism, 145, 155

security assistance, 33, 34, 246

security forces, 9, 18, 20, 24, 26, 27, 33, 34, 44, 47, 48, 54, 63, 68, 76, 122, 139, 141, 170, 175, 179, 180, 186, 207, 237, 241, 245, 253, 263, 294, 296, 297, 305, 309, 312, 316, 326, 344, 377, 382, 387, 396, 403

security services, 122

seizure, 106, 169, 182, 271

self-sufficiency, 68

seminars, 101

Senate, 34, 38, 40, 56, 57, 58, 59, 60, 69, 103, 104, 110, 112, 114, 124, 125, 134, 177, 181, 234, 235, 276, 278, 296, 297, 319, 332, 360, 381, 383, 387, 392

Senate Foreign Relations Committee, 34, 38, 57, 58, 60, 104, 110, 134, 381, 387
senses, 293, 327
sensing, 329
sensitivity, 37
sentencing, 174
separatism, 212
services, 32, 69, 80, 90, 97, 100, 101, 106, 113, 123, 126, 163, 182, 223, 226, 244, 246, 249, 263, 273, 283, 332, 358, 380, 383
SES, 135
settlements, 15, 28, 63, 120
sewage, 334
sex, 79, 390
Seychelles, 8, 89, 90
Shanghai Cooperation Organization, 212, 320, 328, 329
shape, 25, 143, 146, 240, 297, 322, 395
shareholders, 9, 363
Sharia, 66, 388
shelter, 35
Shiite factions, 138, 144, 152
Shiites, 19, 79, 132, 138, 139, 140, 143, 148, 163, 276, 354, 389, 401
shock, 45
shoot, 217
shortage, 310, 316
shortfall, 274, 334
showing, 46, 51, 137, 143, 145, 176, 205, 253, 300, 331, 334, 366, 386
signs, 183, 226, 255, 300, 322
Sinai, 16, 29, 31, 37, 49, 55, 234
Singapore, 233, 352, 377
siphon, 380
skimming, 211, 315
Slovakia, 233, 262, 309, 310, 352
small businesses, 306
smuggling, 12, 16, 26, 29, 31, 36, 37, 38, 48, 49, 55, 63, 68, 131, 208, 311, 320, 321
Smuggling, 15, 16, 36, 37, 68, 234
soccer, 202
social behavior, 175
social ills, 7, 73
social organization, 44
social problems, 79
social services, 15, 42
social support, 264
social welfare, 25, 30, 32, 180
socialization, 192

society, 7, 24, 39, 41, 66, 73, 77, 131, 170, 180, 192, 227, 269, 271, 326, 330, 364, 365, 367
software, 128, 226
solidarity, 59, 60, 145
solution, 12, 22, 23, 28, 39, 42, 82, 98, 253
Somalia, 216
South Africa, 41, 231, 233
South Asia, 69, 75, 213, 231, 296, 320
South Asian Association for Regional Cooperation, 320
South Korea, 91, 95, 97, 99, 109, 167, 201, 231, 233, 309, 352, 353, 362
sovereignty, 23, 83, 120, 129, 134, 135, 138, 169, 185, 208, 255
Soviet Union, 79, 133, 239, 265, 271, 272, 292, 295, 357, 367
soybeans, 131
Spain, 91, 231, 262, 309, 310, 314, 339, 352, 353
specter, 37
speculation, 64, 149, 159
speech, 40, 77, 123, 134, 155, 176, 181, 209, 217, 218, 219, 220, 245, 251, 287, 289, 296, 308, 330, 360, 386, 391, 395, 399
spending, 164, 306, 312, 331, 335
spin, 194
Spring, 235
Sri Lanka, 233
stability, 24, 35, 83, 116, 119, 123, 134, 138, 141, 157, 172, 173, 231, 240, 247, 275, 280, 300, 315, 319, 320, 327, 329, 336, 373, 385, 409
stabilization, 238, 263, 289, 294, 297, 311, 371, 375
staffing, 228, 331
stakeholders, 244, 248, 250, 256, 298
state, 12, 15, 20, 22, 23, 28, 29, 32, 34, 35, 40, 42, 55, 56, 58, 62, 64, 66, 68, 89, 102, 107, 109, 111, 114, 120, 123, 125, 129, 131, 132, 134, 135, 138, 154, 155, 157, 165, 171, 172, 173, 174, 175, 180, 181, 183, 184, 187, 189, 200, 204, 206, 207, 208, 215, 223, 229, 230, 266, 271, 358, 360, 376, 381, 395, 409
state authorities, 42
state control, 171, 173, 175
state intervention, 174
state of emergency, 123
statehood, 42
states, 15, 21, 27, 30, 31, 32, 38, 39, 41, 47, 59, 67, 68, 73, 76, 83, 84, 85, 86, 95, 97, 99, 100, 102, 103, 107, 108, 110, 113, 114, 126, 129, 135, 153, 168, 192, 197, 206, 207, 208, 220, 222, 223, 229,

230, 235, 248, 254, 279, 280, 281, 307, 308, 327, 328, 329, 335, 337, 352, 356, 357

statistics, 7, 89, 335

steel, 37, 231

stereotypes, 22

stock exchange, 131, 132

stockpiling, 306

storage, 99, 102, 103, 184, 337

Strait of Hormuz, 192, 222

stress, 153

structure, 55, 60, 138, 140, 147, 192, 204, 222, 247, 252, 286, 287, 293, 295, 300, 364

style, 16, 55, 63, 64, 74, 272, 287, 365, 367

subsidy, 180

substitution, 332

succession, 279

Sudan, 8, 25, 38, 89, 90, 210, 216, 359

suicide, 14, 15, 32, 43, 44, 45, 50, 51, 59, 92, 128, 135, 157, 295, 396

suicide attacks, 92

suicide bombers, 32, 135

Sun, 284, 316, 364, 384, 409

Sunnis, 19, 138, 139, 140, 141, 143, 145, 146, 147, 148, 157, 163, 185, 187, 188

supplier, 121, 131, 133, 211

suppliers, 65, 81, 109, 111, 118, 321, 335

supply disruption, 222

suppression, 182, 225, 226

Supreme Council, 73, 74, 96, 99, 139, 140, 161

Supreme Court, 151, 242, 283, 369, 381, 388, 389, 393, 394, 398, 404, 407

surplus, 26

surrogates, 118, 367

surveillance, 213, 324

survival, 18, 25, 37, 49

suspensions, 357

sustainable economic growth, 247

Sweden, 91, 112, 233, 262, 310, 314, 352, 353

swelling, 335, 386

Switzerland, 103, 112, 234, 262

Syria, 5, 7, 8, 11, 12, 13, 14, 15, 19, 20, 29, 35, 37, 39, 42, 51, 52, 55, 62, 68, 80, 115, 116, 117, 118, 119, 120, 121, 122, 123, 124, 125, 126, 127, 128, 129, 130, 131, 132, 133, 134, 135, 136, 157, 206, 212, 215, 227, 229, 233, 234

T

tactics, 39, 54, 115, 119, 123, 213, 222, 289, 290, 300, 325

Taiwan, 262

Tajikistan, 8, 89, 90, 206, 212, 279, 320, 321, 326, 328, 335

takeover, 20, 26, 27, 29, 48, 53, 63, 81, 168, 179, 182, 183, 210, 271, 308

talent, 377

tanks, 85, 300, 369

Tanzania, 276

target, 15, 36, 38, 68, 156, 181, 194, 199, 210, 221, 248, 249, 281, 292, 293, 305, 306, 307, 313, 317, 325, 380, 390, 391

tariff, 357

tax evasion, 131

tax increase, 173, 180

taxes, 26, 180, 379

teacher training, 351

teachers, 187, 188, 273

teams, 253, 263, 289, 356

technical assistance, 8, 95, 101, 109, 233, 264, 327, 377

technical support, 250, 253

technologies, 7, 73, 106, 109, 202

technology, 18, 79, 80, 81, 82, 96, 97, 100, 102, 104, 105, 107, 109, 110, 113, 125, 128, 192, 194, 195, 196, 197, 200, 202, 205, 207, 212, 226, 229, 276

technology transfer, 81

telecommunications, 128, 265, 334, 337, 401

television stations, 176

tension, 25, 209

tensions, 12, 40, 42, 47, 83, 132, 207, 256, 405

terminals, 109

territorial, 14, 20, 21, 28, 149, 152, 169, 212

territorial control, 14, 28

territory, 11, 13, 14, 16, 28, 49, 102, 120, 121, 128, 204, 211, 212, 270, 303, 358, 384, 390

terrorism, 30, 33, 36, 44, 56, 59, 60, 64, 67, 69, 79, 80, 120, 125, 126, 176, 184, 186, 190, 193, 206, 209, 210, 211, 213, 215, 216, 229, 230, 242, 279, 280, 293, 314, 319, 321, 322, 323, 325, 326, 342, 345, 358

terrorist activities, 11, 18, 60, 184

terrorist acts, 126, 184

terrorist groups, 7, 11, 59, 60, 63, 66, 79, 116, 120, 127, 217, 254, 302

terrorist organization, 11, 12, 34, 39, 44, 51, 56, 57, 58, 59, 129, 135, 183, 184, 210, 361

terrorists, 30, 32, 36, 50, 57, 58, 60, 66, 105, 121, 163, 240, 304

textiles, 274

Third World, 272

threats, 7, 11, 12, 42, 44, 45, 64, 80, 85, 155, 168, 190, 208, 210, 278, 394

time frame, 77, 146, 195, 205, 212, 279, 298, 299, 308, 313

time periods, 90, 103

Title I, 124, 340, 341, 342, 344

Title II, 124, 341, 342, 344

Tonga, 352

torture, 27, 77, 107, 155, 186, 387

tourism, 86

toxin, 52

tracks, 253

trade, 12, 16, 32, 36, 38, 42, 78, 80, 81, 85, 86, 96, 97, 115, 118, 124, 125, 131, 132, 195, 196, 200, 202, 203, 207, 217, 220, 228, 229, 233, 274, 322, 326, 329, 335, 337, 339, 357, 358, 374, 379

trade agreement, 196, 274, 322, 337

Trade and Development Act of 2000, 125

trade-off, 12, 42

trading partners, 131

traditional practices, 384

traditions, 275, 284, 387, 390

trafficking, 7, 73, 77, 79, 155, 188, 189, 216, 230, 239, 281, 285, 286, 327, 330, 332, 371, 374, 384, 389

trafficking in persons, 79, 188, 189

training, 11, 12, 29, 33, 34, 48, 60, 62, 66, 79, 101, 144, 149, 157, 173, 190, 192, 209, 210, 212, 213, 245, 246, 276, 285, 289, 309, 312, 313, 314, 316, 318, 322, 324, 327, 341, 376, 377, 381, 383, 392, 393

training programs, 34, 79, 246

transactions, 29, 44, 56, 79, 125, 126, 127, 128, 129, 193, 196, 198, 229, 230

transformation, 24, 43

translation, 65, 160, 409

transmission, 98

transparency, 57, 121, 131, 256, 283, 327, 363, 375, 376

transport, 65, 85, 128, 200, 310, 321, 401

transportation, 118, 281, 318, 337, 357, 401

transshipment, 105, 106

Treasury, 30, 31, 38, 52, 53, 66, 67, 70, 105, 113, 126, 127, 128, 129, 130, 135, 193, 208, 213, 215, 229, 325, 361

treaties, 264

treatment, 27, 41, 63, 73, 83, 185, 188, 201, 216, 271, 339, 357, 372

trial, 108, 119, 188, 189, 388, 389

triggers, 229

Trinidad, 245

Trinidad and Tobago, 245

trust fund, 244, 245, 266, 318

Trust Fund, 244, 245, 274, 318, 331, 334, 345, 346, 347, 349, 351, 380

tumor, 209

tunneling, 16

Turkey, 8, 21, 39, 41, 53, 89, 90, 91, 111, 120, 123, 124, 131, 136, 157, 161, 167, 190, 199, 200, 201, 205, 206, 220, 228, 231, 262, 298, 308, 309, 312, 317, 320, 321, 352, 353, 372, 388

Turkmenistan, 168, 190, 228, 279, 328, 338, 362

turnout, 148, 151, 177, 251, 373, 396, 397, 404

turnover, 299

U

U.N. Security Council, 21, 83, 106, 114, 167, 172, 181, 196, 197, 211, 212, 238, 241, 242, 243, 246, 247, 254, 262, 265, 267, 275, 277, 279, 280, 287, 304, 308, 361

U.S. assistance, 34, 35, 44, 87, 158, 225, 272, 316, 333, 335, 357, 361

U.S. Department of Commerce, 105, 130, 131, 134, 135, 136

U.S. policy, 7, 8, 11, 12, 15, 32, 36, 38, 39, 41, 42, 49, 57, 69, 85, 115, 118, 120, 132, 153, 168, 176, 198, 216, 226, 283, 284, 287, 293, 298, 301, 303, 322, 333, 336, 361, 364, 375, 384, 387, 395, 406

U.S. Secretary of Commerce, 106, 114

U.S. Treasury, 30, 66, 67, 70, 118, 128, 129, 361

UK, 61, 62, 66, 67, 70, 262, 287, 317

Ukraine, 131, 190, 352

UN, 9, 237, 262

UNESCO, 258

UNHCR, 258, 330, 341

uniform, 35

unions, 187

United Kingdom, 68, 91, 99, 103, 109, 130, 352

United Nations, 5, 7, 9, 35, 41, 47, 57, 62, 68, 89, 92, 93, 106, 116, 133, 134, 138, 149, 159, 176, 197, 221, 230, 237, 238, 239, 240, 241, 242, 246, 248, 249, 250, 252, 253, 256, 258, 259, 263, 264, 265, 266, 275, 276, 277, 279, 280, 287, 298, 299, 300, 309, 324, 356, 364, 365

United Nations Development Programme, 258

United Nations High Commissioner for Refugees, 258

United Nations Industrial Development Organization, 258

universal access, 393

universities, 273, 325

UNRWA, 24, 26, 33, 35, 47, 56, 57, 65, 68

uranium, 95, 97, 99, 101, 102, 104, 106, 107, 108, 111, 112, 121, 122, 193, 194, 195, 196, 197, 198, 199, 200, 201, 202

urban, 118, 147, 173, 175, 178, 182, 246, 335, 401

urban areas, 335

urban youth, 175

USA PATRIOT Act, 127, 130

USDA, 266

Uzbekistan, 7, 89, 90, 212, 270, 279, 291, 315, 317, 321, 328, 335

V

vacancies, 141

vacuum, 138, 150, 157

variables, 33

vehicles, 26, 67, 157, 182, 311, 316, 380, 385, 394

Venezuela, 118, 215, 216, 233

ventilation, 16

vessels, 96

veto, 35, 77, 139, 142, 146, 152, 165, 280

Vice President, 148, 153, 218, 221, 292, 299, 303, 306, 318, 354, 371, 376, 379, 395

victims, 84, 85, 218, 254, 313, 351, 371

videos, 291

Vietnam, 233, 262

violence, 14, 21, 23, 24, 34, 35, 38, 39, 40, 47, 57, 59, 70, 84, 116, 138, 140, 141, 142, 143, 145, 147, 149, 155, 156, 157, 158, 164, 183, 184, 185, 186, 209, 210, 239, 249, 250, 251, 252, 282, 294, 303, 365, 384, 396, 399, 401, 403

violent extremist, 64

vision, 59, 192, 204, 230, 243

volatility, 28, 83

Volkswagen, 231

vote, 38, 41, 47, 56, 58, 60, 69, 124, 140, 141, 142, 143, 146, 148, 149, 150, 151, 152, 153, 154, 158, 159, 161, 164, 173, 177, 186, 187, 197, 200, 229, 233, 235, 251, 280, 319, 368, 391, 394, 395, 396, 397, 398, 400, 401, 404, 405

voters, 139, 140, 142, 143, 146, 147, 151, 161, 177, 250, 252, 264, 365, 373, 393, 394, 395, 396, 398, 402, 403, 405

voting, 41, 140, 142, 146, 151, 153, 196, 233, 250, 283, 393, 396, 397, 403

vulnerability, 194

W

wages, 79, 180

Wahhabism, 64, 275

waiver, 108, 126, 128, 141, 286

war, 9, 18, 21, 35, 49, 59, 71, 85, 91, 118, 120, 125, 173, 177, 181, 190, 192, 209, 210, 211, 217, 222, 239, 240, 254, 269, 271, 272, 273, 274, 275, 276, 277, 278, 279, 281, 287, 289, 299, 300, 307, 321, 326, 329, 339, 351, 355, 364, 366, 367, 370, 372, 408

War on Terror, 331

warlords, 276, 283, 371

Washington, 25, 31, 46, 60, 61, 64, 66, 67, 70, 87, 102, 103, 112, 114, 121, 133, 134, 135, 149, 165, 173, 176, 205, 211, 213, 218, 225, 226, 233, 234, 235, 272, 275, 297, 323, 356, 360, 361, 369, 375, 379, 408, 409, 410

waste, 23, 99, 255, 256

waste management, 99

water, 27, 83, 95, 101, 107, 134, 194, 195, 196, 197, 202, 264, 334, 337, 341, 373, 400

Waziristan, 407

weakness, 222, 281, 372

wealth, 26, 86, 208

weapons, 16, 19, 29, 37, 38, 41, 43, 60, 62, 63, 65, 66, 68, 80, 105, 107, 110, 112, 115, 119, 121, 127, 129, 132, 134, 135, 190, 192, 193, 194, 203, 204, 206, 210, 212, 213, 216, 217, 229, 271, 272, 275, 292, 305, 306, 314, 325, 355, 356, 357, 359, 371

weapons of mass destruction, 80, 115, 127, 132, 135, 190, 217, 229

wear, 187

web, 31, 360

websites, 65, 187, 323

well-being, 33

wells, 84

West Bank, 11, 12, 14, 15, 16, 19, 20, 22, 25, 26, 27, 28, 29, 31, 33, 34, 35, 36, 42, 43, 44, 45, 47, 48, 49, 50, 52, 53, 61, 66, 68, 70, 71, 192

Western countries, 267, 287

Western Europe, 62, 123

White House, 135, 201, 219, 220, 235, 300, 333, 350, 360, 361

wholesale, 231

withdrawal, 120, 144, 157, 211, 239, 245, 251, 272, 275, 292, 323, 327

witnesses, 119

WMD, 80, 87, 105, 121, 127, 190, 192, 194, 196, 197, 200, 202, 207, 212, 221, 229, 343, 344, 345, 346, 347
workers, 27, 74, 79, 86, 142, 174, 187, 253, 301, 311, 326, 376, 396, 403, 404
working class, 276
working conditions, 77, 79
working groups, 85
World Bank, 197, 229, 246, 259, 262, 266, 274, 331, 334, 339, 380, 395
World Health Organization, 259
World Health Organization (WHO), 86, 195, 196, 259, 339
World War I, 168, 181
worldwide, 113, 192, 202, 210, 216, 379

worry, 283, 290
wrestling, 237
WTO, 86, 196

Y

Yale University, 61, 225, 227
Yemen, 8, 67, 89, 90, 233, 292
yield, 210, 219, 231, 397

Z

Zimbabwe, 216